중학영어듣기 만점 솔루션

듣기는 실전이다

중학 3

24회

디딤돌

듣기는 실전이다 중학3 24회

저자 강보배, 김대성, 서성용, 소원석, 육상태, 윤진섭, 이수윤, 장정근, 전광훈

펴낸날 [초판 4쇄] 2021년 1월 30일

펴낸이 이기열

펴낸곳 (주)디딤돌 교육

주소 (03972) 서울특별시 마포구 월드컵북로 122 청원선와이즈타워

대표전화 02-3142-9000

구입문의 02-322-8451

내용문의 02-325-3224

팩시밀리 02-335-6038

홈페이지 www.didimdol.co.kr

등록번호 제10-718호

출간 이후 발견되는 오류는 "디딤돌 홈페이지 ⇨ 영어 ⇨ 정오표"를 통해
알려드리고 있습니다.

중학영어듣기 만점 솔루션

듣기는 실전이다

중학 3

24 회

딤돌

듣기만점 실전공부법

1 단계
나를 진단한다!

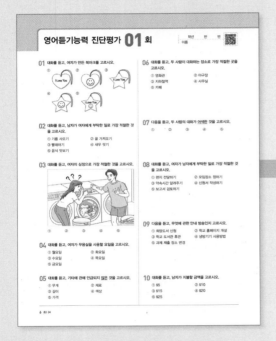

최근 3개년 기출 문제로
나만의 듣기실력 진단!

2 단계
듣기는 실전이다!

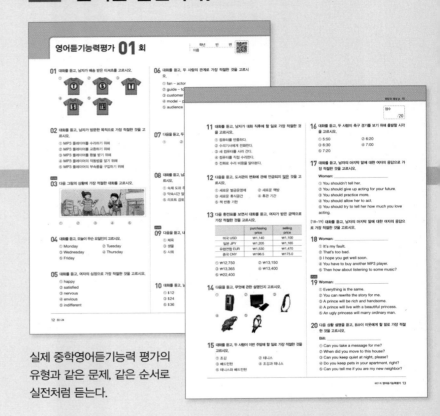

실제 중학영어듣기능력 평가의
유형과 같은 문제, 같은 순서로
실전처럼 듣는다.

만점 듣기전략

교육과정 성취 기준에 맞춰 듣기능력평가 출제 유형을 제시, 각각의 유형을 잘 드러내는
기출문제로 유형별 실전 솔루션을 익힌다.

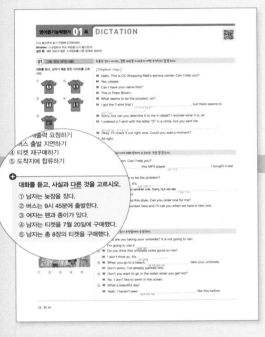

3 단계
만점 듣기 PLUS BOOK

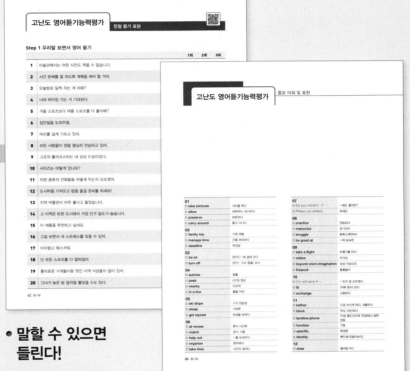

듣기 만점으로 가는
DICTATION과 실전 PLUS!

DICTATION 스크립트의 주요 부분을 다시
들으면서!

실전 Plus 세부 정보가 많은 스크립트를
다른 문제로 샅샅이!

말할 수 있으면
들린다!

회별 주요 표현을
우리말을 보면서
영어로 듣고 또 듣고
영어를 보면서 듣고
따라 말하고

주요 어휘 및 표현

회별, 문항별 주요 어휘와 표현을
시간 날 때마다 반복, 또 반복! 사진처럼 저장한다.

꼼꼼한 해설로 듣기 만점에 도전!

유형 안내부터 스크립트, 해석, 만점 솔루션, 어휘와 표현으로 이어지는 꼼꼼 해설로 듣기 만점에
도전하세요!

듣기는 실전이다

CONTENTS

중학영어듣기 진단평가

- 01회 06
- 02회 08
- 03회 10

중학영어듣기능력 평가

계획을 세워 매일 정해진 양을 공부하고,
공부가 끝나면 공부한 날과 맞힌 문항 수를 체크해 보세요.

	찾아가기	공부한 날		맞힌 개수
01회	12	월	일	/
02회	22	월	일	/
03회	30	월	일	/
04회	40	월	일	/
05회	48	월	일	/
06회	58	월	일	/
07회	66	월	일	/
08회	76	월	일	/
09회	84	월	일	/
10회	94	월	일	/
11회	102	월	일	/
12회	112	월	일	/
13회	120	월	일	/
14회	130	월	일	/
15회	140	월	일	/
16회	148	월	일	/
17회	158	월	일	/
18회	166	월	일	/
19회	176	월	일	/
20회	184	월	일	/
고난도	194	월	일	/

만점 듣기전략

01 어색한 대화 찾기 ··· 20

02 장소 · 관계 · 직업 · 심정 파악 ······························· 38

03 적절한 응답/상황에 적절한 말 ······························· 56

04 숫자 정보 파악 ··· 74

05 언급 유무 파악 ··· 92

06 말의 내용/소재 파악 ··· 110

07 위치 · 도표 파악 ··· 120

08 그림 정보 파악 / 그림 상황에 적절한 대화 찾기 ··· 138

09 특정 정보 파악 ··· 156

10 목적 · 의도 파악 ··· 174

11 할 일 · 부탁한 일 파악 ··· 192

학년　　　반　　　번
이름

01 대화를 듣고, 여자가 만든 북마크를 고르시오.

02 대화를 듣고, 남자가 여자에게 부탁한 일로 가장 적절한 것을 고르시오.

① 기름 사오기　　　② 꿀 가져오기
③ 빨래하기　　　　④ 새우 씻기
⑤ 음식 맛보기

03 다음 그림의 상황에 가장 적절한 대화를 고르시오.

① 　② 　③ 　④ 　⑤

04 대화를 듣고, 여자가 무용실을 사용할 요일을 고르시오.

① 월요일　　　　② 화요일
③ 수요일　　　　④ 목요일
⑤ 금요일

05 대화를 듣고, 기타에 관해 언급되지 <u>않은</u> 것을 고르시오.

① 무게　　　　　② 재료
③ 길이　　　　　④ 색상
⑤ 가격

06 대화를 듣고, 두 사람이 대화하는 장소로 가장 적절한 곳을 고르시오.

① 영화관　　　　② 야구장
③ 지하철역　　　④ 사무실
⑤ 카페

07 다음을 듣고, 두 사람의 대화가 <u>어색한</u> 것을 고르시오.

① 　② 　③ 　④ 　⑤

08 대화를 듣고, 여자가 남자에게 부탁한 일로 가장 적절한 것을 고르시오.

① 편지 전달하기　　② 모임장소 정하기
③ 약속시간 알려주기　④ 신청서 작성하기
⑤ 보고서 검토하기

09 다음을 듣고, 무엇에 관한 안내 방송인지 고르시오.

① 희망도서 신청　　② 학교 홈페이지 개설
③ 학교 도서관 휴관　④ 냉방기기 사용방법
⑤ 과제 제출 장소 변경

10 대화를 듣고, 남자가 지불할 금액을 고르시오.

① $5　　　　　② $10
③ $15　　　　④ $20
⑤ $25

점수
/20

11 대화를 듣고, 여자가 할 일로 가장 적절한 것을 고르시오.

① 병문안 가기　　　② 음료수 가져오기
③ 과일 사기　　　　④ 치킨 주문하기
⑤ 돗자리 챙기기

12 다음을 듣고, *Career Event*에 관해 언급되지 않은 것을 고르시오.

① 날짜　　　　　　② 초대 강사
③ 강연 주제　　　　④ 등록 방법
⑤ 참가비

13 대화를 듣고, 두 사람이 사용할 회의실을 고르시오.

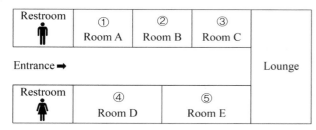

14 다음을 듣고, 무엇에 관한 설명인지 고르시오.

① 스키　　　　　　② 축구
③ 핸드볼　　　　　④ 야구
⑤ 아이스하키

15 대화를 듣고, 남자가 대화 직후에 할 일로 가장 적절한 것을 고르시오.

① 날씨 확인하기　　② 우산 가져오기
③ 차 태워주기　　　④ 도서 대출하기
⑤ 외투 수선하기

16 대화를 듣고, 여자가 냉장고를 받기로 한 날짜를 고르시오.

① May 7th　　　　② May 8th
③ May 9th　　　　④ May 10th
⑤ May 11th

17 대화를 듣고, 남자의 마지막 말에 대한 여자의 응답으로 가장 적절한 것을 고르시오.

Woman: _____

① I left my wallet in the shop.
② I can't lend you my computer.
③ This coffee machine doesn't work.
④ I can't move because my back hurts.
⑤ The papers don't come out of the printer.

18 대화를 듣고, 여자의 마지막 말에 대한 남자의 응답으로 가장 적절한 것을 고르시오.

Woman: _____

① Your handwriting needs more help.
② Let me tell you the website address.
③ I'm not good at solving math questions.
④ I enjoy listening to music on the Internet.
⑤ My teacher shows us how to make a blog.

19 대화를 듣고, 남자의 마지막 말에 대한 여자의 응답으로 가장 적절한 것을 고르시오.

Woman: _____

① Sorry. I'm busy this Saturday.
② No problem. I'll walk when I go home.
③ Okay. I won't forget to see you after school.
④ Sure. You can visit my new house this weekend.
⑤ Right. I need to set the alarm for an earlier time.

20 다음 상황 설명을 듣고, Jiho가 Mr. Jung에게 할 말로 가장 적절한 것을 고르시오.

Jiho: Mr. Jung, _____

① when does the music concert begin?
② where should I put my new textbooks?
③ can I practice my violin in the living room?
④ could you tell me where the music room is?
⑤ how can I make a photocopy of this timetable?

01 대화를 듣고, 여자가 구입할 시계를 고르시오.

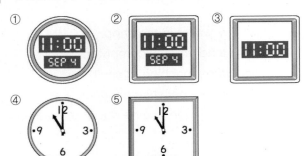

02 대화를 듣고, 여자가 남자에게 전화한 목적으로 가장 적절한 것을 고르시오.

① 주문을 취소하려고　　② 배송 지연을 알리려고
③ 환불 방법을 알리려고　　④ 제품 이상을 문의하려고
⑤ 배송 위치를 확인하려고

03 다음 그림의 상황에 가장 적절한 대화를 고르시오.

①　　　　②　　　　③　　　　④　　　　⑤

04 대화를 듣고, 남자가 테니스 코트를 사용할 수 없는 요일을 고르시오.

① 월요일　　　　　② 수요일
③ 목요일　　　　　④ 금요일
⑤ 토요일

05 다음을 듣고, Evergreen Community Center에 관해 언급되지 않은 것을 고르시오.

① 운영 프로그램　　② 식당 메뉴
③ 셔틀 버스 운행　　④ 운영 시간
⑤ 휴관일

06 대화를 듣고, 두 사람의 관계로 가장 적절한 것을 고르시오.

① 수의사 - 애견 주인　　② 서점 직원 - 고객
③ 미용사 - 손님　　　　④ 진행자 - 작가
⑤ 사육사 - 관객

07 다음을 듣고, 두 사람의 대화가 어색한 것을 고르시오.

①　　　　②　　　　③　　　　④　　　　⑤

08 대화를 듣고, 여자가 남자에게 부탁한 일로 가장 적절한 것을 고르시오.

① 도서 반납하기　　② 숙제 도와주기
③ 우편물 보내기　　④ 연체료 내주기
⑤ 도서관에 태워다주기

09 대화를 듣고, 남자의 마지막 말에 담긴 의도로 가장 적절한 것을 고르시오.

① 위로　　　　　　② 감사
③ 거절　　　　　　④ 칭찬
⑤ 제안

10 대화를 듣고, 남자가 지불할 금액을 고르시오.

① $10　　　　　　② $ 20
③ $30　　　　　　④ $ 40
⑤ $50

점수

/20

11 대화를 듣고, 여자가 할 일로 가장 적절한 것을 고르시오.

① CD 빌려주기   ② 전화 번호 알려주기

③ 음악 숙제 도와주기   ④ 콘서트 티켓 예매하기

⑤ 좋아하는 가수 물어보기

12 다음을 듣고, Oakwood Flea Market에 관해 언급되지 않은 것을 고르시오.

① 개최 날짜   ② 취급 품목

③ 판매자 참가비   ④ 접수 장소

⑤ 신청 기한

13 다음 표를 보면서 대화를 듣고, 여자가 선택할 강좌를 고르시오.

	Model	Printing Color	Printing Type	Price
①	A	Wednesday	Kelly	$50
②	B	Wednesday	Michelle	$70
③	C	Thursday	Kelly	$50
④	D	Thursday	Serena	$60
⑤	E	Thursday	Michelle	$70

14 다음을 듣고, 무엇에 관한 설명인지 고르시오.

① 주사기   ② 청진기

③ 체온계   ④ 혈압계

⑤ 습도계

15 대화를 듣고, 남자가 할 일로 가장 적절한 것을 고르시오.

① 지하철 갈아타기   ② 극장 위치 확인하기

③ 지하철 시간 확인하기   ④ 연극표 구매하기

⑤ 분실물 찾기

16 대화를 듣고, 남자가 구입할 물건을 고르시오.

① gloves   ② helmet

③ bicycle   ④ backpack

⑤ soccer shoes

17 대화를 듣고, 여자의 마지막 말에 대한 남자의 응답으로 가장 적절한 것을 고르시오.

Man: _____

① Yes, I hope you find it soon.

② No, I'd love to play with you.

③ Thank you. That would be great.

④ Sorry. I already had lunch.

⑤ Really? Isn't it scary?

18 대화를 듣고, 남자의 마지막 말에 대한 여자의 응답으로 가장 것을 고르시오.

Woman: _____

① Don't worry. We can be a great team.

② Congratulations! I knew you'd win.

③ No, I'm not interested in singing at all.

④ I've never considered joining the contest.

⑤ Thanks for helping me.

19 대화를 듣고, 여자의 마지막 말에 대한 남자의 응답으로 가장 적절한 것을 고르시오.

Man: _____

① Okay. I'll send them to you by email.

② All right. You can fix my laptop now.

③ Well, the sports day will be cancelled.

④ Great. I'm glad you finished it by yourself.

⑤ I'm sorry. I can't take part in sports event.

20 다음 상황 설명을 듣고, Jihoon이 점원에게 할 말로 가장 적절한 것을 고르시오.

Jihoon: _____

① Then, can you make these pants shorter?

② I'm sorry, but I want to get a refund.

③ When will you get the bigger size?

④ I like this style so much.

⑤ Long pants are not my style.

01 대화를 듣고, 두 사람이 구입할 풍선을 고르시오.

①
②
③

④
⑤

02 대화를 듣고, 여자가 남자에게 전화한 목적으로 가장 적절한 것을 고르시오.

① 귀가가 늦을 것을 알리려고
② 차를 태워달라고 부탁하려고
③ 회의 시간 변경을 요청하려고
④ 자동차 이상 유무를 확인하려고
⑤ 수리 기사 연락처를 물어보려고

03 다음 그림의 상황에 가장 적절한 대화를 고르시오.

①　　　　②　　　　③　　　　④　　　　⑤

04 대화를 듣고, 두 사람이 만나기로 한 요일을 고르시오.

① 월요일
② 화요일
③ 수요일
④ 목요일
⑤ 금요일

05 다음을 듣고, Drone-X에 관해 언급되지 않은 것을 고르시오.

① 크기
② 조종 범위
③ 작동 시간
④ 촬영 기능
⑤ 가격

06 대화를 듣고, 두 사람의 관계로 가장 적절한 것을 고르시오.

① 경찰관-목격자
② 버스 기사-승객
③ 우체국 직원-고객
④ 아파트 경비원-주민
⑤ 교사- 학생

07 다음을 듣고, 두 사람의 대화가 <u>어색한</u> 것을 고르시오.

①　　　　②　　　　③　　　　④　　　　⑤

08 대화를 듣고, 여자가 남자에게 부탁한 일로 가장 적절한 것을 고르시오.

① 대본 작성하기
② 연기 평가하기
③ 소품 제작하기
④ 연극 주제 정하기
⑤ 연극 의상 고르기

09 대화를 듣고, 남자의 마지막 말에 담긴 의도로 가장 적절한 것을 고르시오.

① 충고
② 감사
③ 거절
④ 요청
⑤ 위로

10 대화를 듣고, 여자가 지불할 금액을 고르시오.

① $2
② $5
③ $7
④ $9
⑤ $11

점수 /20

11 대화를 듣고, 남자가 할 일로 가장 적절한 것을 고르시오.

① 영화 시간 확인   ② 저녁 식사 준비
③ 파티 물품 구입   ④ 영화평 작성
⑤ 시험 준비

12 다음을 듣고, Parkway School Marathon Day에 관해 언급되지 <u>않은</u> 것을 고르시오.

① 운영 책임자   ② 개최 날짜
③ 참가 대상   ④ 참가비
⑤ 접수 장소

13 다음 표를 보면서 대화를 듣고, 여자가 구입할 프린터를 고르시오.

	Model	Printing Color	Printing Type	Price
①	A	Black and white	Laser	$70
②	B	Black and white	Ink jet	$90
③	C	Color	Laser	$120
④	D	Color	Ink jet	$150
⑤	E	Color	Ink jet	$200

14 다음을 듣고, 무엇에 관한 설명인지 고르시오.

① 자전거   ② 기차
③ 배   ④ 비행기
⑤ 버스

15 대화를 듣고, 남자가 할 일로 가장 적절한 것을 고르시오.

① 교실 방문   ② 콘서트 관람
③ 팸플릿 제작   ④ 공연 일정 조정
⑤ 미술 준비물 구입

16 대화를 듣고, 어머니가 아들을 깨울 시각을 고르시오.

① 6 a.m.   ② 7 a.m.
③ 8 a.m.   ④ 9 a.m.
⑤ 10 a.m.

17 대화를 듣고, 남자의 마지막 말에 대한 여자의 응답으로 가장 적절한 것을 고르시오.

Woman: _____

① I failed the science test, too.
② I'll catch up with classes soon.
③ Sorry. I can't open some of your files.
④ Right. I hope this cold weather ends soon.
⑤ Sure. I'll get you my notebook this afternoon.

18 대화를 듣고, 여자의 마지막 말에 대한 남자의 응답으로 가장 적절한 것을 고르시오.

Man: _____

① Sorry, I don't remember.
② That's too bad. Cheer up.
③ Why not? Let's go together.
④ Thank you. It's because of you.
⑤ Congratulations. You deserve it.

19 대화를 듣고, 남자의 마지막 말에 대한 여자의 응답으로 가장 적절한 것을 고르시오.

Woman: _____

① I wish you could come to the show with me.
② I really enjoyed watching that movie.
③ I'm glad you can come with me.
④ I'm sorry you couldn't go on a family trip.
⑤ I'm disappointed that the show is canceled.

20 다음 상황 설명을 듣고, Susie가 남자에게 할 말로 가장 적절한 것을 고르시오.

Susie: Excuse me, _____

① are you a stranger here?
② I'm the owner of this wallet.
③ are you looking for the wallet?
④ we have to wait for a bus here.
⑤ do you know where the bus stop is?

01 대화를 듣고, 남자가 배송 받은 티셔츠를 고르시오.

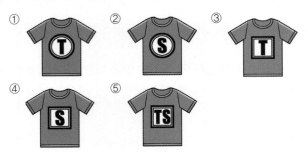

02 대화를 듣고, 남자가 방문한 목적으로 가장 적절한 것을 고르시오.

① MP3 플레이어를 수리하기 위해
② MP3 플레이어를 교환하기 위해
③ MP3 플레이어를 환불 받기 위해
④ MP3 플레이어의 작동법을 알기 위해
⑤ MP3 플레이어의 부속품을 구입하기 위해

고난도
03 다음 그림의 상황에 가장 적절한 대화를 고르시오.

① ② ③ ④ ⑤

04 대화를 듣고, 오늘이 무슨 요일인지 고르시오.

① Monday   ② Tuesday
③ Wednesday   ④ Thursday
⑤ Friday

05 대화를 듣고, 여자의 심정으로 가장 적절한 것을 고르시오.

① happy
② satisfied
③ nervous
④ envious
⑤ indifferent

06 대화를 듣고, 두 사람의 관계로 가장 적절한 것을 고르시오.

① fan – actor
② guide – tourist
③ customer – mechanic
④ model – photographer
⑤ audience – announcer

07 다음을 듣고, 두 사람의 대화가 <u>어색한</u> 것을 고르시오.

① ② ③ ④ ⑤

08 대화를 듣고, 남자가 여자에게 부탁한 일로 가장 적절한 것을 고르시오.

① 숙제 도와 주기   ② 모임장소 정하기
③ 약속시간 알려주기   ④ 음식 사다 주기
⑤ 리포트 검토하기

고난도
09 다음을 듣고, 내용과 가장 관련이 있는 과목을 고르시오.

① 체육   ② 역사
③ 생물   ④ 도덕
⑤ 사회

10 대화를 듣고, 남자가 지불할 금액을 고르시오.

① $12   ② $15
③ $24   ④ $30
⑤ $36

점수
/20

11 대화를 듣고, 남자가 대화 직후에 할 일로 가장 적절한 것을 고르시오.

① 컴퓨터를 반품하다.
② 수리기사에게 전화한다.
③ 새 컴퓨터를 사러 간다.
④ 컴퓨터를 직접 수리한다.
⑤ 전화로 수리 비용을 알아본다.

12 다음을 듣고, 도서관의 변화에 관해 언급되지 <u>않은</u> 것을 고르시오.

① 새로운 벌금운영제　　② 새로운 책방
③ 새로운 휴식공간　　④ 휴관 기간
⑤ 책 반환 기한

13 다음 환전표를 보면서 대화를 듣고, 여자가 받은 금액으로 가장 적절한 것을 고르시오.

	purchasing price	selling price
미국 USD	₩1,140	₩1,100
일본 JPY	₩1,205	₩1,165
유럽연합 EUR	₩1,530	₩1,470
중국 CNY	₩196.5	₩175.0

① ₩12,750　　② ₩13,150
③ ₩13,365　　④ ₩13,400
⑤ ₩22,400

14 다음을 듣고, 무엇에 관한 설명인지 고르시오.

① ② ③

④ ⑤

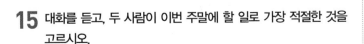

15 대화를 듣고, 두 사람이 이번 주말에 할 일로 가장 적절한 것을 고르시오.

① 조깅　　② 테니스
③ 배드민턴　　④ 조깅과 테니스
⑤ 테니스와 배드민턴

16 대화를 듣고, 두 사람이 축구 경기를 보기 위해 출발할 시각을 고르시오.

① 5:50　　② 6:20
③ 6:30　　④ 7:00
⑤ 7:20

[17~19] 대화를 듣고, 남자의 마지막 말에 대한 여자의 응답으로 가장 적절한 것을 고르시오.

17 Woman: _____

① You shouldn't tell her.
② You should give up acting for your future.
③ You should practice more.
④ You should allow her to act.
⑤ You should try to tell her how much you love acting.

18 Woman: _____

① It's my fault.
② That's too bad.
③ I hope you get well soon.
④ You have to buy another MP3 player.
⑤ Then how about listening to some music?

고난도
19 Woman: _____

① Everything is the same.
② You can rewrite the story for me.
③ A prince will be rich and handsome.
④ A prince will live with a beautiful princess.
⑤ An ugly princess will marry ordinary man.

20 다음 상황 설명을 듣고, Bill이 이웃에게 할 말로 가장 적절한 것을 고르시오.

Bill: _____

① Can you take a message for me?
② When did you move to this house?
③ Can you keep quiet at night, please?
④ Do you keep pets in your apartment, right?
⑤ Can you tell me if you are my new neighbor?

다시 들으면서 듣기 만점에 도전하세요!
Dictation: 스크립트의 주요 부분을 다시 들으면서!
실전 ⊕: 세부 정보가 많은 스크립트를 다른 문제로 샅샅이!

---

01 그림 정보 파악(사물)

대화를 들고, 남자가 배송 받은 티셔츠를 고르시오.

① ② ③ ④ ⑤

주문한 것이 아니라, 잘못 배송된 티셔츠가 어떤 모양인지 잘 듣는다.

[Telephone rings.]

W Hello. This is DC Shopping Mall's service center. Can I help you?

M Yes, please.

W Can I have your name first?

M This is Peter Brown.

W What seems to be the problem, sir?

M I got the T-shirt that I _____ _____ _____, but there seems to
(인터넷으로 주문했다)
_____ _____ _____.
(착오가 있다)

W Sorry, but can you describe it to me in detail? I wonder what it is, sir.

M I ordered a T-shirt with the letter "S" in a circle, but you sent me
_____ _____ _____ _____ _____ _____.
(정사각형 안에 'T'자가 있는 것)

W Okay. I'll check it out right now. Could you wait a moment?

M All right.

---

02 목적 파악(방문)

대화를 들고, 남자가 방문한 목적으로 가장 적절한 것을 고르시오.

① MP3 플레이어를 수리하기 위해
② MP3 플레이어를 교환하기 위해
③ MP3 플레이어를 환불 받기 위해
④ MP3 플레이어의 작동법을 알기 위해
⑤ MP3 플레이어의 부속품을 구입하기 위해

고장 난 MP3 플레이어에 대해 남자가 요구하는 것을 잘 듣는다.

W Good afternoon. Can I help you?

M I'd like _____ _____ this MP3 player _____ _____ _____. I bought it last
(교환하기)   (다른 것으로)
Saturday.

W Okay. What seems to be the problem?

M Look at this button. It's _____.
(벌써 고장이 난)

W Let me see if we have another one. Sorry, but we are _____ _____ _____.
(그 종류가 없는)
How about this one?

M Sorry, but I really like this style. Can you order one for me?

W Sure. Leave your number here and I'll call you when we have a new one.

M Thank you.

W You're welcome.

고난도

03 상황에 적절한 대화(그림)

다음 그림의 상황에 가장 적절한 대화를 고르시오.

① ② ③ ④ ⑤

그림에서 우산의 용도가 무엇일까에 주목한다.

① W Why are you taking your umbrella? It is not going to rain.
   M I'm going to use it _____ _____.
   (그늘을 위해)

② W Do you think this umbrella looks good on me?
   M I don't think so. It's _____ _____.
   (너무 어두운)

③ W When you go to a beach, _____ _____ _____ take your umbrella.
   (~할 것을 잊지 마라)
   M Don't worry. I've already packed one.

④ W Don't you want to go in the water when you get hot?
   M No. I don't like to swim in the ocean.

⑤ W What a beautiful day!
   M Yeah. I haven't seen _____ _____ _____ like this before.
   (그렇게 파란 하늘)

시험이 있는 요일에서 남은 날 수를 빼면 오늘이 무슨 요일인지 알 수 있다.

대화를 듣고, 오늘이 무슨 요일인지 고르시오.

① Monday　　② Tuesday
③ Wednesday　④ Thursday
⑤ Friday

Thanks for giving me a rain check. (다음 기회를 줘서 고마워.) : rain check은 비가 올 때 환불 대신에 다음 경기 입장표를 준 데서 유래한 표현으로 '다음 기회'라는 의미이다.

[Telephone rings.]

W Hello? Can I speak to Issac? This is Christine.

M Hi, Christine. It's me. What's up?

W Well, are you free this evening? If so, why don't we go to a movie?

M Sorry, but I can't go.

W Why not?

M I ＿＿＿＿ ＿＿＿＿ ＿＿＿＿ ＿＿＿＿ , and I only ＿＿＿＿
이번 금요일에 영어 시험이 있다
＿＿＿＿ ＿＿＿＿ ＿＿＿＿ before the test.
오늘을 포함해서 이틀 남다

W Only two days left? Then, let's go together some other time.

M Okay. Thanks for ＿＿＿＿ ＿＿＿＿ ＿＿＿＿ ＿＿＿＿ , Christine.
나에게 다음 기회 주기

내일 있을 시험공부를 위해 과학책이 필요한데 몇 가지 사유로 친구로부터 책을 돌려받지 못한 상황이다.

대화를 듣고, 여자의 심정으로 가장 적절한 것을 고르시오.

① happy 행복한
② satisfied 만족한
③ nervous 긴장되는
④ envious 부러워하는
⑤ indifferent 무관심한

W Hi, Gilbert. Did you see Smith in class today?

M Smith? No, I didn't see him. What's the matter?

W I ＿＿＿＿ ＿＿＿＿ ＿＿＿＿ ＿＿＿＿ last Friday, and he promised to return
그에게 과학책을 빌려줬다
it to me Monday.

M He ＿＿＿＿ ＿＿＿＿ about it.
잊어버렸을지도 모른다

W I guess so, but I need it for tomorrow's test. He was absent from school yesterday, too.

M Well, I heard ＿＿＿＿ ＿＿＿＿ ＿＿＿＿ ＿＿＿＿ these days.
독감이 유행하고 있다

W I know. By the way, do you know his Cellphone number?

M I'm afraid not. He has ＿＿＿＿ ＿＿＿＿ his Cellphone.
최근에 바꾸다

W Oh, what am I supposed to do now?

사인을 받고 함께 사진을 찍고 싶은 사람이 누구인지 생각해 본다.

대화를 듣고, 두 사람의 관계로 가장 적절한 것을 고르시오.

① fan – actor 팬 – 배우
② guide – tourist 안내원 – 관광객
③ customer – mechanic 고객 – 기술자
④ model – photographer 모델 – 사진 작가
⑤ audience – announcer 청중 – 아나운서

W Excuse me, but you're Mr. Gerard Butler, right?

M Yes, I am.

W Wow! This is incredible! I'm so pleased to see you in this museum.

M You seem to know me well, right?

W Sure. I've seen ＿＿＿＿ ＿＿＿＿ ＿＿＿＿ ＿＿＿＿ . *Legends of the Fall* is one of my favorites.

M Oh, really? Thank you.

W I'm sorry to bother you, but could I have ＿＿＿＿ ＿＿＿＿ ?
당신의 사인

M Of course.

W Oh, just one more thing. Can I ＿＿＿＿ ＿＿＿＿ ＿＿＿＿ you?
~와 사진을 찍다

M No problem.

음식 권유를 받았을 때 어떤 말을 할 수 있는지 생각해 본다.

다음을 듣고, 두 사람의 대화가 <u>어색한</u> 것을 고르시오.

①　②　③　④　⑤

① **W** ＿＿＿＿ ＿＿＿＿ ＿＿＿＿ ＿＿＿＿ the concert?
~에 대해 어떻게 생각하니?
　M I think she is a nice singer. Her songs are so powerful.

② **W** I ＿＿＿＿ ＿＿＿＿ you can give me a ride home.
~인지 아닌지 궁금하다
　M No problem. Get in.

③ **W** Would you like some more cake?
　M Sure. ＿＿＿＿ ＿＿＿＿ ＿＿＿＿ this cake.
~을 마음껏 먹다

④ **W** We ＿＿＿＿ ＿＿＿＿ ＿＿＿＿ milk and bread.
~이 떨어지다
　M Then, let's go grocery shopping this afternoon.

⑤ **W** I want to start exercising. What sports would you recommend?
　M How about swimming or cycling?

부탁을 할 때 쓰이는 표현을 집중해서 듣는다.

대화를 듣고, 남자가 여자에게 부탁한 일로 가장 적절한 것을 고르시오.

① 숙제 도와 주기
② 모임장소 정하기
③ 약속시간 알려주기
④ 음식 사다 주기
⑤ 리포트 검토하기

W Did you hear that? What was that noise?

M That was my stomach. I didn't have time for breakfast this morning.

W James, you have to eat! It's not healthy to skip breakfast.

M I know, but I have to finish reading this book and then write a book report. The deadline is tomorrow!

W Is there anything I can do to help?

M Well, _____ _____ _____ picking up some food for me?
~해주겠니?

W Not at all. What would you like to have?

M Umm… I suddenly _____ very _____. A small pizza and an orange soda, please.
배고 고프다

고난도

09 말의 내용(담화)

식물과 동물의 생태계 설명과 가장 가까운 과목을 선택한다.

다음을 듣고, 내용과 가장 관련이 있는 과목을 고르시오.

① 체육   ② 역사
③ 생물   ④ 도덕
⑤ 사회

W An ecosystem is a community of plants and animals. They interact with each other and their environment. An ecosystem _____ _____ when the number of plants and
균형 잡힌
animals stay pretty much the same. Do you know why? Well, if there are too many plant-eating animals, they will _____ _____ _____ by eating the
식물군을 파괴하다
plants faster than the plants can grow back. So they will _____ _____ _____.
굶어 죽다

10 숫자 정보 파악(금액)

주중에 구매하는 티켓의 가격과 주말에 구매하는 티켓의 가격을 파악한다.

대화를 듣고, 남자가 지불할 금액을 고르시오.

① $12   ② $15
③ $24   ④ $30
⑤ $36

M Jenny, I heard that we can get a student discount on concert tickets.

W Yes, we can. But the student discount only applies to tickets for weekday concerts.

M Really? How much are they?

W On the weekend, the tickets are $15 each. But if we go during the week, they're $12.

M Well, I _____ _____ paying the extra money to go on the weekend.
괜찮아

W Same here. Let's just go _____ _____ _____.
주말에

M Okay. I'll buy two tickets for the concert on Saturday.

➕

대화를 듣고, 남자가 할 일로 가장 적절한 것을 고르시오.

① 콘서트 리뷰쓰기
② 학생 할인 받기
③ 주말 티켓 구매하기
④ 평일 티켓 구매하기
⑤ 티켓 판매하기

11 할 일 파악

대화를 듣고, 남자가 대화 직후에 할 일로 가장 적절한 것을 고르시오.

① 컴퓨터를 반품하다.
② 수리기사에게 전화한다.
③ 새 컴퓨터를 사러 간다.
④ 컴퓨터를 직접 수리한다.
⑤ 전화로 수리 비용을 알아본다.

M What's up? You look upset.

W Well, I think there's a problem with the computer. It isn't working.

M Oh, dear! Didn't we _____ _____ and get the computer fixed several
수리기사에게 전화하다
weeks ago?

W We did. What should we do now?

M I'll _____ _____ _____ last time and ask him what
그것을 고쳤던 사람에 전화하다
the problem is.

W Don't you think we should just _____ _____ _____ _____?
새것을 사다

M I _____ _____ yet. I think we can use it for at least two more years.
그렇게 생각하지 않는다

W I see.

다음을 듣고, 도서관의 변화에 관해 언급되지 않은 것을 고르시오.

① 새로운 벌금운영제
② 새로운 책방
③ 새로운 휴식공간
④ 휴관 기간
⑤ 책 반환 기한

W Attention, library users. The library will be undergoing many changes. We are going to _____ _____ _____ with new shelves for more books. We will also be
_{새로운 방을 추가한다}
adding a new cafeteria, where you can enjoy drinks and snacks. All _____ _____
_____ the cafeteria will be used to buy more books. Because of these changes, the
_{~로 번 돈}
library will be closed from April 20 until May 4. Any books due during that time can be
returned on May 4 without penalty. Thank you for your attention.

환전할 화폐의 종류와, 구매하는 것인지 판매하는 것인지를 잘 파악한다.

다음 환전표를 보면서 대화를 듣고, 여자가 받은 금액으로 가장 적절한 것을 고르시오.

	purchasing price	selling price
미국 USD	₩1,140	₩1,100
일본 JPY	₩1,205	₩1,165
유럽연합 EUR	₩1,530	₩1,470
중국 CNY	₩196.5	₩175.0

① ₩12,750
② ₩13,150
③ ₩13,365
④ ₩13,400
⑤ ₩22,400

W Excuse me, I'd like _____ _____ _____ _____ Korean
_{이 외국 돈을 ~으로 교환하다}
currency.
M Let's see... you are selling ten American dollars, right?
W Yes. I also want to exchange these Chinese bills.
M Just a minute, please. You have ten Chinese yuan, too.
W Yes, I'd like to _____ _____ into Korean currency.
_{~으로 모두 바꾸다}
M Here you are. You might want to check the exchange rates on the wall and make sure
that you have the correct amount.
W I had ten American dollars and ten Chinese yuan, so yes, that's all right. Thank you very
much.
M My pleasure.

다음을 듣고, 무엇에 관한 설명인지 고르시오.

①
②
③
④
⑤

M This is _____ _____ _____ _____. This _____
_{기계가 아니라 동물} _{날 수 있다}
_____, but it cannot swim. This _____ _____ _____
_{몇 개의 단어들도 말할 수 있다}
_____. So you can understand what this is saying. Teaching this how to speak is
easy and simple. You just say some words again and again to this. After a while this will
_____ _____ soon. But this doesn't really understand the meaning of
_{당신을 따라 말하다}
words. Of course, there are some of these animals which can't learn to say a word. Can
you guess what this is?

15 할 일 파악

이번 주말에 할 운동과 다음 주말에 할 운동을 구별해서 듣는다.

대화를 듣고, 두 사람이 이번 주말에 할 일로 가장 적절한 것을 고르시오.

① 조깅　　　　② 테니스
③ 배드민턴　　④ 조깅과 테니스
⑤ 테니스와 배드민턴

W Hey, Nadal, do you want to _____ this weekend?
　　　　　　　　　　　　　　　　배드민턴을 치다
M Sorry, but I can't play badminton well.

W Are you joking? I heard you can play badminton well. And everybody can play it.

M Well, I can't. But I can _____ well.
　　　　　　　　　　　테니스를 치다
W Really? I can play tennis, too. But not very well.

M Then I have an idea. Why don't we _____ _____ _____ and then
　　　　　　　　　　　　　　　　　　　이번 주말에 테니스를 치다
_____ _____ ?
다음 주말에 배드민턴을 치다
W Okay. That's a good idea.

M I don't play badminton and you don't play tennis well. So we both can practice sports we're not good at.

16 특정 정보 파악(시간)

현재 시각을 메모한 후 얼마 후에 출발하는지 잘 듣고 간단한 계산을 해 본다.

대화를 듣고, 두 사람이 축구 경기를 보기 위해 출발할 시각을 고르시오.

① 5:50 five fifty　　② 6:20 six twenty
③ 6:30 six thirty　　④ 7:00 seven
⑤ 7:20 seven twenty

W Sorry for being late, Donald.

M That's all right. I just got here a few minutes ago.

W How much time do we have before the soccer game? Do we have to hurry up?

M No, we don't have to. _____ _____ _____ .
　　　　　　　　　　　이제 겨우 5시 50분이다
W Then, when does the game start?

M It starts at seven. I guess _____ _____ _____ to get to the
　　　　　　　　　　　　　　　단지 20분 걸린다
stadium. So let's leave in thirty minutes.

W In thirty minutes? Sorry, but what time is it now again?

M I told you it's five fifty.

W Okay. Let's get started _____ _____ _____ .
　　　　　　　　　　　30분 후에

17 적절한 응답

뮤지컬 배우를 반대하는 엄마에게 할 수 있는 말을 생각해 본다.

[17~19] 대화를 듣고, 남자의 마지막 말에 대한 여자의 응답으로 가장 적절한 것을 고르시오.

Woman: _____

① You shouldn't tell her.
② You should give up acting for your future.
③ You should practice more.
④ You should allow her to act.
⑤ You should try to tell her how much you love acting.

＋
대화를 듣고 여자의 마지막 말에 담긴 의도로 가장 적절한 것을 고르시오.

① 거절　　　② 감사
③ 충고　　　④ 비판
⑤ 위로

M Hi, Karen. Can I talk to you for a minute?

W Hi, Rick! Sure!

M You know that I've always _____ being a musical actor, don't you?
　　　　　　　　　　　　　　~을 꿈꾸다
W Yes, I know that it's your dream.

M As a matter of fact, I auditioned for a part in a musical last week. And I _____
_____ _____ !　　　　　　　　　　　　　　　　　　　　　　　역을 맡다
W Wow, congratulations! Good for you!

M But I'm worried about what my mom will say. She doesn't want me to be a musical actor. What should I tell her?

W _____

음악을 즐기는 친구가 아빠에게 MP3 플레이어를 빼앗겼을 때해 줄 수 있는 위로의 말을 생각해 본다.

Woman: _____

① It's my fault.
② That's too bad.
③ I hope you get well soon.
④ You have to buy another MP3 player.
⑤ Then how about listening to some music?

It depends on what it is. : 어떤 부탁이냐에 달려 있다.

W Tom, can you do me a favor?
M It _____ _____ _____ .
　　　무엇인지에 달려 있다
W Can you lend me your MP3 player?
M I'm afraid I can't because I don't have it right now.
W Where is it?
M My dad _____ _____ _____ yesterday.
　　　　　그것을 빼앗았다
W How come?
M He told me to study harder _____ _____ _____ _____ . It
　　　　　　　　　　　　　　　　　음악 감상을 하는 대신에
　really _____ _____ . As you know, music helps me study hard.
　　　나를 미치게 한다
W _____

왕자가 아름다운 공주와 결혼하는 이야기가 마음에 안 든다면 여학생 입장에서 어떻게 바꿀지 생각해 본다.

Woman: _____

① Everything is the same.
② You can rewrite the story for me.
③ A prince will be rich and handsome.
④ A prince will live with a beautiful princess.
⑤ An ugly princess will marry ordinary man.

What do you think of the movie? (그 영화를 어떻게 생각하니?) : What do you think of ~?는 상대방의 의견을 물을 때 쓰는 표현이다.

W Have you seen this movie before?
M No, I haven't. Have you?
W Yes, a long time ago.
M Then, what do you _____ the movie?
　　　　　　　　　　~에 대해 생각하다
W I don't want to complain, but I _____ _____ _____ .
　　　　　　　　　　　　　　　그 이야기가 마음에 들지 않는다
M What's wrong with it?
W We know what's going to happen. It's like every other fairy tale. I mean the prince
　always _____ _____ _____ the beautiful princess.
　　　　~와 결혼하다
M Right. If you made this movie, how would you _____ _____ ?
　　　　　　　　　　　　　　　　　　　　　　　　줄거리를 바꾸다
W _____

Bill이 위층 이웃집에 간 이유를 파악한다.

다음 상황 설명을 듣고, Bill이 이웃에게 할 말로 가장 적절한 것을 고르시오.
Bill: _____

① Can you take a message for me?
② When did you move to this house?
③ Can you keep quiet at night, please?
④ Do you keep pets in your apartment, right?
⑤ Can you tell me if you are my new neighbor?

M Bill moved to a new apartment last Saturday. He was very happy at first. He thought his
　apartment was _____ _____ _____ , but it wasn't. His neighbors living
　　　　　　　　　조용한 장소
　above _____ _____ _____ _____ _____ . So he
　　　　매일 밤마다 엄청난 소음을 냈다
　_____ _____ _____ and had some trouble with them last
　그것을 더 이상 참을 수 없었다
　night. He went upstairs and knocked on the door. A man came out and asked what was
　wrong. In this situation, what would Bill say to the neighbor?

어색한 대화 찾기

무엇을 평가하는가?	일상생활이나 친숙한 일반적 주제에 관한 말이나 대화를 듣고 화자의 의도나 목적을 추론할 수 있는지를 평가한다.
어떻게 출제되는가?	• 다음을 듣고, 두 사람의 대화가 어색한 것을 고르시오.

key solution

❶ 의문사로 시작하는 의문문은 Yes/No의 답변을 취할 수 없고, 의문사가 답변의 단서가 되므로 집중하며 듣는다.

❷ 비슷한 뜻이나 발음의 어휘가 반복되어 나오는 경우 오답일 확률이 높으므로 주의한다.

[기출로 전략 확인]

다음을 듣고, 두 사람의 대화가 <u>어색한</u> 것을 고르시오. [2018 기출]

①   ②   ③   ④   ⑤

....

① M How did you like the pancake?
　 W I really enjoyed it. It was delicious.

② M I failed the singing audition again.
　 W Don't give up. You'll do better next time.

③ M How often do you go to the gym?
　 W It costs $ 60 a month. ──────────────────── ❶ 'How often~?'이라는 빈도를
　　　　　　　　　　　　　　　　　　　　　　　　묻는 질문에 'It costs~ '라는
　　　　　　　　　　　　　　　　　　　　　　　　비용을 답하는 답변을 했다.

④ M Is it possible for you to join the race?
　 W I'm not sure. My leg still hurts.

⑤ M What do you do in your free time?
　 W I usually enjoy cooking.

① 남 팬케이크 어땠어요?
　 여 진짜 좋았어요. 맛있었어요.

② 남 노래 오디션에서 또 떨어졌어.
　 여 포기하지 마. 다음에 더 잘할 거야.

③ 남 체육관에 얼마나 자주 가?
　 여 한달에 6달러야.

④ 남 너 달리기 경주에 참가하는 게 가능해?
　 여 모르겠어. 다리가 아직 아파.

⑤ 남 자유 시간에 뭐해?
　 여 보통 요리를 해.

다음을 듣고, 두 사람의 대화가 <u>어색한 것</u>을 고르시오.   [2017 기출]

①   ②   ③   ④   ⑤

만점 잡는 문장   ③ **M**   Something smells <u>strange</u> here.

                 W   I'm a <u>stranger</u> here, too.

다음을 듣고, 두 사람의 대화가 <u>어색한 것</u>을 고르시오.   [2016 기출]

①   ②   ③   ④   ⑤

만점 잡는 문장   ⑤ **W**   <u>Why</u> do you like comedy movies?

                 M   <u>Yes</u>. I like horror movies a lot.

● **질문(의문사)**

A What are you going to do during your vacation? 방학동안 뭐 할 거야?

B I'm going to visit my grandfather. 할아버지 댁에 갈 거야.

A How long will it take to get to Busan? 부산까지 가는 데 얼마나 걸리나요?

B I think it'll take about two hours by car. 차로 2시간 정도 걸릴 거 같아요.

● **질문(be동사)**

A You look so pretty! Is that a new dress? 예쁘다! 새 드레스야?

B Yes. It's a birthday gift from my mom. 응. 엄마가 준 생일선물이야.

● **질문(조동사)**

A Can I borrow your pen? 펜 좀 빌릴 수 있을까?

B Sure, here you are. 물론이야. 여기.

● **질문(일반동사)**

A Don't you think it's too loud? 너무 시끄럽다고 생각하지 않니?

B Sorry, I'll turn the volume down. 미안. 소리 줄일게.

● **평서문**

A I was disappointed with the film. 그 영화에 실망했어.

B You were? I felt the same way. 그랬어? 나도 그랬어.

A This jacket is too big for me. 이 재킷은 나에게 너무 커요.

B Would you like to exchange it for a smaller one? 더 작은 걸로 교환하시겠어요?

01 대화를 듣고, 남자가 가리키는 여자를 고르시오.

02 대화를 듣고, 여자가 애완동물 가게에 간 목적으로 가장 적절한 것을 고르시오.

① 애완견을 치료하려고
② 애완견을 이발하려고
③ 애완견을 목욕시키려고
④ 애완견의 체중을 알아보려고
⑤ 애완견에게 입힐 옷을 주문하려고

03 다음 그림의 상황에 가장 적절한 대화를 고르시오.

①　　　　②　　　　③　　　　④　　　　⑤

04 대화를 듣고, 두 사람이 함께 볼 영화의 제목을 고르시오.

① Shotgun
② War in Peace
③ Bed of Flowers
④ I Have Nothing to Say
⑤ Gambler

05 대화를 듣고, 남자의 심정 변화로 가장 적절한 것을 고르시오.

① worried → relaxed
② upset → amused
③ relieved → troubled
④ angry → disappointed
⑤ confused → hopeful

06 대화를 듣고, 두 사람의 관계로 가장 적절한 것을 고르시오.

① 기자 – 목격자
② 강사 – 수강생
③ 동창생 – 동창생
④ 경찰관 – 운전자
⑤ 교사 – 학생

07 다음을 듣고, 두 사람의 대화가 <u>어색한 것</u>을 고르시오.

①　　　　②　　　　③　　　　④　　　　⑤

08 대화를 듣고, 남자가 여자에게 부탁한 일로 가장 적절한 것을 고르시오.

① 티켓 전달하기　　　② 티켓 재출력 요청하기
③ 버스 출발 지연하기　④ 티켓 재구매하기
⑤ 도착지에 합류하기

09 대화를 듣고, 여자의 의견으로 가장 적절한 것을 고르시오.

① 별명 부르는 것은 재미있다.
② 외모를 가지고 놀려서는 안 된다.
③ 어려운 이웃을 도와주자.
④ 친구끼리 애칭을 부르자.
⑤ 개성 있는 외모는 친근감을 준다.

고난도
10 대화를 듣고, 여자가 지불해야 할 금액을 고르시오.

① ₩3,500　　　　② ₩4,000
③ ₩4,500　　　　④ ₩6,000
⑤ ₩6,500

점수

/20

11 대화를 듣고, 두 사람이 대화하는 장소로 가장 적절한 곳을 고르시오.

① 주차장 　　　　② 면허 시험장
③ 버스 정류장 　　④ 자동차 판매점
⑤ 자동차 정비소

12 다음을 듣고, 기부행사에 대해 언급되지 않은 것을 고르시오.

① 행사 개최 이유 　　② 행사 지원 독려
③ 행사 개최 일정 　　④ 행사 개최 장소
⑤ 행사 결과 보고

13 다음 대화를 듣고 남자가 찾아갈 장소로 알맞은 곳을 고르시오.

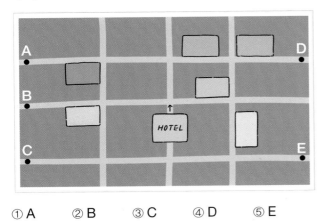

① A 　② B 　③ C 　④ D 　⑤ E

14 다음을 듣고, 무엇에 관한 내용인지 가장 적절한 것을 고르시오.

① paper 　　　　② eraser
③ pencil 　　　　④ knife
⑤ fountain pen

15 대화를 듣고, 두 사람이 대화 직후에 할 일로 가장 적절한 것을 고르시오.

① 낮잠 자기 　　　② 영화 관람
③ 탑승 수속 　　　④ 공원 산책
⑤ 예약 전화

16 대화를 듣고, 현재 시각을 고르시오.

① about 2:30 　　　② about 3:00
③ about 4:00 　　　④ about 4:30
⑤ about 5:00

[17~19] 대화를 듣고, 남자의 마지막 말에 대한 여자의 응답으로 가장 적절한 것을 고르시오.

17 Woman: _____

① I think it'd be a good idea to quit science class.
② In that case, I think you'd better walk faster.
③ Math is my favorite class.
④ Then, you should really focus on passing the exam.
⑤ Why don't you try to find someone to do the homework with?

18 Woman: _____

① That is my private business.
② I looked at the record of calls.
③ That's what people say all the time.
④ From the newspaper I read yesterday.
⑤ I know it's not right, but that's my job.

19 Woman: _____

① This is for you.
② You went too far!
③ That's what friends are for.
④ Sorry I can't recognize your voice.
⑤ What a nice surprise to see you here!

20 다음 상황 설명을 듣고, 민호가 여자에게 할 말로 가장 적절한 것을 고르시오.

Minho: _____

① My report is due today.
② I wonder if you like coffee.
③ I'm terribly sorry. Are you all right?
④ Don't worry. I'll finish the report in time.
⑤ I'll make coffee for you. How do you like it?

다시 들으면서 듣기 만점에 도전하세요!
Dictation: 스크립트의 주요 부분을 다시 들으면서!
실전 ⊕: 세부 정보가 많은 스크립트를 다른 문제로 샅샅이!

---

01 그림 정보 파악   인물의 위치나 동작을 잘 듣는다.

대화를 듣고, 남자가 가리키는 여자를 고르시오.

W Chris, I think that girl is the Olympic gold medalist in tennis.
M What girl? Is she being interviewed here?
W The girl with the book in her hands. I don't think so, it looks like she's just with a friend.
M Who are you talking about? That girl _____ _____ _____ is my friend's cousin.
　　　　　　　　　　　　　벤치에 있는
W Not her. She's not reading a book. She's just carrying one.
M Oh, I see her. You mean the girl _____ _____ with a stack of books?
　　　　　　　　　　　　　　　모자를 쓰고 있는
W No, not her either. She only has one book.
M I still don't know who you're talking about.
W She's standing _____ _____ _____ _____ and talking with another girl.
　　　　　　　　분수 옆에
M Oh, I see her now! Yes, I've seen her on TV a few times.

---

02 목적 파악   애완견 가게에서 제공하는 서비스 중 손님이 원하는 것을 찾는다.

대화를 듣고, 여자가 애완동물 가게에 간 목적으로 가장 적절한 것을 고르시오.

① 애완견을 치료하려고
② 애완견을 이발하려고
③ 애완견을 목욕시키려고
④ 애완견의 체중을 알아보려고
⑤ 애완견에게 입힐 옷을 주문하려고

W Do you _____ _____ _____ for pets?
　　　　　　이발 서비스가 있다
M Certainly. We _____ _____ cut their hair, _____ _____ bathe pets.
　　　　　　~뿐만 아니라　　　　　　　　~도 역시
W How much is the service?
M $20 per dog _____ _____ _____ .
　　　　　　그것의 사이즈와 상관없이
W Um.... that's reasonable. All right, can you do it right now?
M Sorry, there are a lot of dogs scheduled for today. So you need to _____ _____
　　　　　　　　　　　　　　　　　　　　　　　　　　　　　　　　　　예약을 하다
_____ first.
W Then, is this Friday possible?
M I think so.

고난도

03 상황에 적절한 대화(그림)

다음 그림의 상황에 가장 적절한 대화를 고르시오.

① M We will be late. Let's hurry.
　W Don't worry. We can arrive in time.
② M We'd better pull into the next gas station.
　W Are we _____ _____ _____ ?
　　　　　기름이 떨어지다
③ M Do you need a ride home?
　W No, thanks. My father will pick me up.
④ M Watch out! _____ _____ _____ !
　　　　　　　저 차가 하마터면 널 칠 뻔 했다
　W Oh, thank you! _____ _____ _____ !
　　　　　네가 내 생명을 구해 줬다
⑤ M What took you so long?
　W I got held up in traffic.

① ② ③ ④ ⑤

볼 수 없거나 보지 않을 이유를 파악하며 해당 제목을 지워나가 본다.

대화를 듣고, 두 사람이 함께 볼 영화의 제목을 고르시오.

① Shotgun
② War in Peace
③ Bed of Flowers
④ I Have Nothing to Say
⑤ Gambler

W Whew! We're finally here.

M Yeah, but 30 minutes later than we expected to arrive.

W *Shotgun* _____ _____ (이미 시작되었다), so we have to wait for two hours to see it.

M I have only two and half an hour. What else have we got here?

W We have four other movies: *War in Peace, Bed of Flowers, I Have Nothing to Say*, and *Gambler*.

M I _____ *I Have Nothing to Say* _____ _____ (봤다 / 지난주에). It's worth watching.

W What about *Bed of Flowers*?

M No. Its running time is _____ _____ (너무 긴). How about *Gambler*?

W I _____ _____ _____ _____ _____ (도박에 관한 것은 알고 싶지 않다).

M Then we have only one choice.

W Let's see that.

기차가 연착된 상황과 기차표를 예매한 요일에 착오가 있음을 참고한다.

대화를 듣고, 남자의 심정 변화로 가장 적절한 것을 고르시오.

① worried → relaxed
② upset → amused
③ relieved → troubled
④ angry → disappointed
⑤ confused → hopeful

W How can I help you?

M I'm trying to get on the three fifty train to Seoul. Am I on time?

W Not exactly. It's already three fifty-five p.m. now, but luckily that train has been delayed.

M Wow, I'm so happy about the delay.

W Okay. Can you _____ _____ _____ (저에게 당신의 승차권을 보여주다)?

M Here you are. Which platform does the train leave from?

W Platform six. However, you _____ _____ (~하지 않기로 되어 있다) get on this train.

M Of course, I am. This is my train to Seoul _____ _____ _____ (3시 50분에 떠나는).

W Yes, but today is Friday. Your ticket is for Saturday.

M What? Oh, _____ _____ _____ _____ (내가 심각한 실수를 했다).

오랜만에 만난 상황임을 파악하며 적절한 관계를 선택한다.

대화를 듣고, 두 사람의 관계로 가장 적절한 것 고르시오.

① 기자 – 목격자
② 강사 – 수강생
③ 동창생 – 동창생
④ 경찰관 – 운전자
⑤ 교사 – 학생

What do you do? (무슨 일을 하니?) : 직업을 물어볼 때 쓰는 표현이다. (=What do you do for a living?)

W Steve, is that you?

M Excuse me. _____ _____ _____ (뵌 적이 없는 것 같다) .... Ah, Alice?

W That's right. I am.

M Wow! You _____ _____ (많이 변했다).

W Yeah. I lost a lot of weight. How long has it been since we met last?

M Well, maybe ten years. We learned to swim together from Mr... I can't remember his name.

W Yes. That was the year after _____ _____ _____ _____ (우리는 같은 중학교를 졸업했다) _____ .

M You're right. By the way, what do you do?

W I am a reporter. There was a big fire downtown. I'm going back to my office.

M A reporter! Your job must be exciting.

오랜 만에 만나서 안부를 물을 때 적절한 응답을 생각해 본다.

다음을 듣고, 두 사람의 대화가 <u>어색한</u> 것을 고르시오.

① ② ③ ④ ⑤

① **W** How do you like your new school?

　M I love it! I like the teachers.

② **W** Would you pick up a hitchhiker?

　M That's a hard question. I guess it depends.

③ **W** Do you know where the nearest gas station is?

　M I'm sorry, but ＿＿＿＿＿ ＿＿＿＿ ＿＿＿＿, too.
　　　　　　　　　　나는 여기가 처음이다

④ **W** Can I try this on?

　M Sure. The fitting room is over there.

⑤ **W** Long time no see. ＿＿＿＿ ＿＿＿＿ ＿＿＿＿ ＿＿＿＿?
　　　　　　　　　　　　　　어떻게 지냈니

　M I came here ＿＿＿＿ ＿＿＿＿, not ＿＿＿＿ ＿＿＿＿.
　　　　　　　　　버스로　　　　　　　　　걸어서

대화를 듣고, 남자가 여자에게 부탁한 일로 가장 적절한 것을 고르시오.

① 티켓 전달하기
② 티켓 재출력 요청하기
③ 버스 출발 지연하기
④ 티켓 재구매하기
⑤ 도착지에 합류하기

➕ 대화를 듣고, 사실과 <u>다른</u> 것을 고르시오.

① 남자는 늦잠을 잤다.
② 버스는 9시 45분에 출발한다.
③ 여자는 펜과 종이가 있다.
④ 남자는 티켓을 7월 20일에 구매했다.
⑤ 남자는 총 8장의 티켓을 구매했다.

[Cellphone rings.]

M *[sleepily]* Um... Hello?

W Jack? Were you sleeping?

M *[surprised]* Uh-oh! What time is it?

W It's nine thirty. The bus is leaving ＿＿＿＿ ＿＿＿＿ ＿＿＿＿.
　　　　　　　　　　　　　　　　　　15분 후에

M Oh, no! My alarm didn't go off. I have the bus tickets for all of you. I ＿＿＿＿＿＿
　＿＿＿＿＿ the bus tickets yesterday.
　　　　　　　　　　　　　　　　　너에 줬어야 했다

W I know! I guess we'll have to buy new ones.

M Hmm... Wait! I have the ticket numbers. ＿＿＿＿ ＿＿＿＿ someone at the
　　　　　　　　　　　　　　　　　　　요청할 수 있니?
　ticket office to reprint the tickets?

W All right. Let me try. Give me the numbers of the tickets. I've got a pen and paper.

M Sure, I bought them on July 20, and the numbers are from AF71 to AF77.

대화를 듣고, 여자의 의견으로 가장 적절한 것을 고르시오.

① 별명 부르는 것은 재미있다.
② 외모를 가지고 놀려서는 안 된다.
③ 어려운 이웃을 도와주자.
④ 친구끼리 애칭을 부르자.
⑤ 개성 있는 외모는 친근감을 준다.

M I can't understand why Christine ＿＿＿＿ ＿＿＿＿ me.
　　　　　　　　　　　　　　　　　　～에 화가 났다

W Did you make a fool of her?

M No, I just called her by her nickname, 'Cabbage.'

W Come on. Don't you know she ＿＿＿＿ ＿＿＿＿ Cabbage?
　　　　　　　　　　　　　　　　～로 불리기를 싫어하다

M Really? I didn't know that.

W And in my opinion, you have to say sorry to her first.

M Yes, I will.

W And remember it's not polite to ＿＿＿＿ ＿＿＿＿ ＿＿＿＿ someone's appearance.
　　　　　　　　　　　　　　　　　　놀리다

M I'll keep that in mind.

10 숫자 정보 파악(금액)

대화를 듣고, 여자가 지불해야 할 금액을 고르시오.

① ₩3,500   ② ₩4,000
③ ₩4,500   ④ ₩6,000
⑤ ₩6,500

복사할 부수를 한 장당 복사비와 매수를 곱한 후에 제본 값을 더한다.

W Can you _____ _____ of this document?
   2부 복사를 하다

M Sure. How many pages does it have?

W It's 25 pages.

M Do you want them in color, or in black and white?

W Just black and white. How much will that cost?

M We _____ _____ a page for black and white.
   50원을 청구하다

W Do you do binding, too?

M Of course. There's a two thousand-won _____ _____.
   추가 비용

W Please bind the two copies. I'll be back to pick them up tomorrow.

M OK. That's 50 black and white pages plus binding the two copies.

11 대화 장소 파악

대화를 듣고, 두 사람이 대화하는 장소로 가장 적절한 곳을 고르시오.

① 주차장   ② 면허 시험장
③ 버스 정류장   ④ 자동차 판매점
⑤ 자동차 정비소

There are too many cars to count. : 차가 너무 많아서 셀 수가 없다.

차를 찾고 있는 상황임을 파악한다.

W Honey! We need to turn to the right here.

M Are you sure? It looks strange.

W I'm sure. It is _____ _____ _____. Don't worry. We're almost there.
   B101에 있는

M Oh, there are _____ _____ _____ to count.
   너무 많은 차

W I think lots of people in town are driving to this new shopping mall today.

M Yes. Wait a second. Isn't it right over there?

W Where? I don't see it.

M There. _____ _____ _____.
   저 검정색 레저용 차량 뒤에요

W Oh, you're right.

12 언급 유무 파악(담화)

다음을 듣고, 기부행사에 대해 언급되지 않은 것을 고르시오.

① 행사 개최 이유   ② 행사 지원 독려
③ 행사 개최 일정   ④ 행사 개최 장소
⑤ 행사 결과 보고

➕

다음을 듣고, 무엇에 관한 설명인지 고르시오.

① 봉사활동   ② 체육대회
③ 학생회 총회   ④ 학교 축제
⑤ 기부행사

M Most of you _____ probably _____ _____ _____ the earthquake that hit
   이미 알다
Pohang. Many people have been left homeless and _____ _____
   ~을 필요로 하다
_____ food and clothing. Our student council will be holding a charity event this
weekend to help these people. Please join us and help us organize the event. The event
will run from 9 a.m. to 5 p.m. _____ _____ _____. It'll
   주말에
_____ the lawn in front of the student union building. If you're available on Saturday
   ~에서 열리다
or Sunday, please join us. Let's work together to help the earthquake victims.

13 지도, 위치 파악(지도) – 배치도

다음 대화를 듣고 남자가 찾아갈 장소로 알맞은 곳을 고르시오.

① A   ② B   ③ C   ④ D   ⑤ E

W Good morning, sir. How may I help you?

M Can I ask how to get to Seoul Museum?

W Oh, sure. Seoul Museum isn't that _____ _____ _____. Just go out of our hotel and make a left turn. Go straight about 30 meters, and then turn right.

M So, I go out and turn left and then turn right?

W Correct. Then _____ _____ _____ you come to a flower shop. Turn left at the flower shop, and you'll see the museum.

M Great. Thanks a lot.

W No problem. You can't miss it. The museum is huge.

14 소재 파악(담화)

다음을 듣고, 무엇에 관한 내용인지 가장 적절한 것을 고르시오.

① paper 종이   ② eraser 지우개
③ pencil 연필   ④ knife 칼
⑤ fountain pen 만년필

M As a student, you can easily find this in your daily life. It is _____ _____ _____. There is a long piece of lead inside, which is _____ _____. It usually _____ _____ _____ _____ so that you can erase what you wrote. As you use it, its lead is worn down, so you need to cut some wood off regularly. You can _____ _____ _____ _____. For example, you can use it to write a letter or keep a diary.

15 할 일 파악

대화를 듣고, 두 사람이 대화 직후에 할 일로 가장 적절한 것을 고르시오.

① 낮잠 자기   ② 영화 관람
③ 탑승 수속   ④ 공원 산책
⑤ 예약 전화

Enough is enough. : 이제 됐다.. 그쯤 해둬.

M Enough is enough. You have to get up.

W What time is it, honey?

M Four o'clock in the afternoon. Wake up, sweetheart! You won't be able to sleep tonight.

W I have terrible jet lag. I can't keep my eyes open.

M I know, but I'm not going to _____ _____ _____ in the middle of the afternoon.

W But I'm really tired and sleepy.

M Get up! I have _____ _____ _____ _____ _____.

W Don't tell me you want to walk with me in the park.

M Look what I've got. _____ _____ _____ at 6 o'clock.

W All right. I'll get ready.

고난도

16 특정 정보 파악(시간)

주차 요금, 시간당 주차비, 주차하려 온 시각을 잘 듣고 계산해 본다.

대화를 듣고, 현재 시각을 고르시오.

① about 2:30
② about 3:00
③ about 4:00
④ about 4:30
⑤ about 5:00

W Ticket, please.

M Sorry, but I can't remember where I put it.

W What's the license plate number of your car?

M It's 42 G 9232.

W Hold on. _____ _____.

M Really? That much?

W Yes. We charge _____ _____ _____ _____ after parking. And you parked your car _____ _____.

M Oh, I thought it was about three.

W Look at this. You didn't park at three. It was two thirty.

M OK. I guess you're right.

17 적절한 응답

많은 수학 문제를 푸는 것에 어려움을 느끼고 있는 친구에게 할 수 있는 말을 생각한다.

[17~19] 대화를 듣고, 남자의 마지막 말에 대한 여자의 응답으로 가장 적절한 것을 고르시오.

Woman: _____

① I think it'd be a good idea to quit science class.
② In that case, I think you'd better walk faster.
③ Math is my favorite class.
④ Then, you should really focus on passing the exam.
⑤ Why don't you try to find someone to do the homework with?

W Hi, Josh. How's it going?

M Well, I've been so tired lately.

W Yeah, actually, you do _____ quite _____. I've seen you studying in the library almost every day.
<small>지쳐 보인다</small>

M Yeah, I have to study really hard _____ _____ my math class. I find that so difficult.
<small>~때문에</small>

W I understand. Besides, the math teacher gives _____ _____ _____, doesn't he?
<small>많은</small> <small>숙제</small>

M Exactly. We're assigned twenty math questions each week.

W Oh, that's just too much.

M It takes about an hour to finish just one question. I'm totally stressed out.

W _____

18 적절한 응답

Woman: _____

① That is my private business.
② I looked at the record of calls.
③ That's what people say all the time.
④ From the newspaper I read yesterday.
⑤ I know it's not right, but that's my job.

I bet it's Ronnie. (틀림없이 Ronnie이겠지.) : I bet ~.은 확신을 나타낼 때 쓰는 표현이다.

W Ralph! Where are you?

M I'm in my room, Mommy.

W Oh, Ralph. Are you _____ _____ _____?
<small>또 문자 메시지를 보내는</small>

M Yes. I have a message to convey to my friend.

W I bet it's Ronnie.

M How do you know that?

W Why do you need to _____ _____ _____?
<small>그와 그렇게 자주 연락하다</small>

M We have a lot to talk about. You know friends are supposed to share a lot.

W I know, but you need to call him more than ten times a day?

M Maybe. But _____ _____ _____ how many times I talk to him over the phone?
<small>어떻게 아세요</small>

W _____

19 적절한 응답

강도를 가장하여 깜짝 파티를 한 남자에 대해 공포감을 느낀 여자가 할 수 있는 말을 생각해 본다.

Woman: _____

① This is for you.
② You went too far!
③ That's what friends are for.
④ Sorry I can't recognize your voice.
⑤ What a nice surprise to see you here!

M Shh! Be quiet.

W Who is it?

M If you scream, you'll get hurt. Open the door.

W All right. I'll do whatever you tell me to do. _____ _____, please.
<small>다치게는 마세요</small>

M What a good girl! Turn on the light. Good. Now move to the sofa.

W Let me open my eyes. I can't see anything.

M No. Now sit down. [popping sound] Surprise!

W Tom! _____ _____ _____!
<small>무서워 죽는 줄 알았다</small>

M I'm sorry. But this is what _____ _____ is supposed to be, isn't it?
<small>깜짝 파티</small>

W _____

20 상황에 적절한 말(담화)

커피를 들고 있는 여자와 부딪혔을 때 할 수 있는 말을 생각해 본다.

다음 상황 설명을 듣고, 민호가 여자에게 할 말로 가장 적절한 것을 고르시오.

Minho: _____

① My report is due today.
② I wonder if you like coffee.
③ I'm terribly sorry. Are you all right?
④ Don't worry. I'll finish the report in time.
⑤ I'll make coffee for you. How do you like it?

M Minho sat up late last night to finish his report and he turned it in ten minutes ago. He feels tired and sleepy. So he decides to drink coffee. He walks over to the vending machine. He happens to _____ _____ _____ holding a cup of coffee. She _____ _____ _____. In this situation, what would Minho say to the woman?
<small>한 젊은 여성과 부딪친다</small>
<small>커피를 온 몸에 쏟다</small>

영어듣기능력평가 **03**회

01 대화를 듣고, 소년이 선택한 티셔츠를 고르시오.

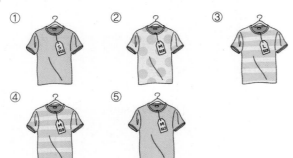

① ② ③ ④ ⑤

02 대화를 듣고, 남자가 예약한 시각을 고르시오.

① 11:00 a.m.
② 11:30 a.m.
③ 2:30 p.m.
④ 3:00 p.m.
⑤ 3:30 p.m.

03 다음 그림의 상황에 가장 적절한 대화를 고르시오.

① ② ③ ④ ⑤

고난도
04 대화를 듣고, 오늘이 무슨 요일인지 고르시오.

① Monday　　　　　② Tuesday
③ Wednesday　　　④ Thursday
⑤ Friday

05 다음을 듣고, 여자가 묘사하는 강아지를 고르시오.

06 대화를 듣고, 두 사람의 관계로 가장 적절한 것을 고르시오.

① a hunter – a camper
② a camper – a fire fighter
③ a hunter – a police officer
④ an anchor – a fire fighter
⑤ a reporter – a police officer

07 다음을 듣고, 두 사람의 대화가 어색한 것을 고르시오.

① ② ③ ④ ⑤

08 대화를 듣고, 여자가 남자에게 부탁한 일로 가장 적절한 것을 고르시오.

① 세탁물 맡기기
② 가게에서 세제 사오기
③ 세탁소 전화번호 알아오기
④ 세탁소에 전화번호 알려주기
⑤ 세탁물이 다 되었는지 확인하기

09 다음을 듣고, 무엇에 관한 안내인지 가장 적절한 것을 고르시오.

① 송년 모임 참여
② 송년 자선 행사
③ 신년 카드 발송
④ 성탄절 선물 구입
⑤ 성탄절 특별 행사

10 대화를 듣고, 남자가 지불할 금액을 고르시오.

① $5　　　　　② $50
③ $55　　　　④ $65
⑤ $70

점수
/20

11 대화를 듣고, 두 사람이 대화하는 장소로 가장 적절한 곳을 고르시오.

① in a bank
② in a taxi
③ at a hotel
④ at an information center
⑤ at the National Museum

12 다음을 듣고, 내용과 일치하지 <u>않는</u> 것을 고르시오.

① 정규 수업 시간 – 오전 8:30 ~ 오후 3:30
② 방과 후 수업 활동 내용 – 음악, 운동
③ 클럽 활동 시간 – 2시간 30분
④ 방과 후 클럽 활동 내용 – 악기 연주, 축구, 테니스 등
⑤ 저녁 일과 – 악기 및 운동 연습

13 대화를 듣고, 교무실을 고르시오.

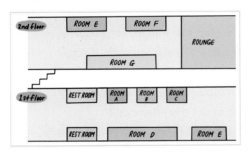

① Room B   ② Room D
③ Room G   ④ Room E
⑤ Room F

고난도
14 다음을 듣고, 무엇에 관한 설명인지 고르시오.

① 조종사   ② 낙하산
③ 비행기   ④ 비행장
⑤ 안테나

15 대화를 듣고, 여자가 대화 직후에 할 일로 가장 적절한 것을 고르시오.

① 검정색 운동화 신어보기
② 흰색 운동화 신어보기
③ 흰색 운동화 사기
④ 다른 가게로 가보기
⑤ 흰색 운동화 주문해 놓기

16 대화를 듣고, 두 사람이 이용할 교통수단으로 가장 적절한 것을 고르시오.

① bus   ② car
③ taxi   ④ subway
⑤ ship

17 대화를 듣고, 여자가 요구하는 것으로 가장 적절한 것을 고르시오.

① 환불   ② 물건 교환
③ 치마 수선   ④ 물건 배달
⑤ 사이즈 교환

[18~19] 대화를 듣고, 남자의 마지막 말에 대한 여자의 응답으로 가장 적절한 것을 고르시오.

18 Woman: _____

① That's good.
② It's not a bad idea.
③ You can use my USB.
④ Why don't you just keep quiet?
⑤ Why don't you call a repairman?

고난도
19 Woman: _____

① I don't like mice, either.
② Don't be late for the party.
③ I mean, it's not that expensive.
④ I've lent out two cat costumes.
⑤ The party was canceled a while ago.

20 다음 상황 설명을 듣고, 친구에게 할 말로 가장 적절한 것을 고르시오.

① What a pity!
② You did a good job.
③ Glad you could make it!
④ Try to get up as early as possible.
⑤ Why don't you take a bus next time?

다시 들으면서 듣기 만점에 도전하세요!
Dictation: 스크립트의 주요 부분을 다시 들으면서!
실전 ➕: 세부 정보가 많은 스크립트를 다른 문제로 샅샅이!

---

01 그림 정보 파악(사물)

묘사하는 표현(색깔, 무늬 등)을 잘 듣는다.

대화를 듣고, 소년이 선택한 티셔츠를 고르시오.

① ② ③ ④ ⑤

W May I help you?

B Yes! ＿＿＿＿＿＿＿＿ ＿＿＿＿ a nice T-shirt.
나는 ~을 찾고 있다.

W What size do you wear?

B Medium, usually.

W Ah, right over here. All these T-shirts are your size.

B Hmm. I like these yellow ones. How much are they?

W This one is twelve dollars, and the other design is eighteen dollars.

B This one ＿＿＿＿＿＿＿＿ ＿＿＿＿, but it's too simple for me. I like the one with the
적절한 가격이다.
stripes. May I try it on?

W Sure. The fitting room is right behind the jeans section

➕ 대화를 듣고, 남자가 할일로 가장 적합한
고르시오.
① 티셔츠 고르기 ② 티셔츠 구매하
③ 티셔츠 입어보기 ④ 티셔츠 선물하
⑤ 티셔츠 환불하기

---

02 전화한 목적

시간을 조정하는 말에 유의하며, 마지막에 정해지는 시각을 잘 듣는다.

대화를 듣고, 남자가 예약한 시각을 고르시오.

① 11:00 a.m. eleven a.m.
② 11:30 a.m. eleven thirty a.m.
③ 2:30 p.m. two thirty p.m.
④ 3:00 p.m. three p.m.
⑤ 3:30 p.m. three thirty p.m.

[Telephone rings.]

W Dr. Bream's office. May I help you?

M Hello. It's Tim Brown here. I'm having trouble with my left shoulder.

W I'm sorry to hear that. What day would you like to meet Dr. Bream?

M I want to see him as soon as possible. The pain is terrible.

W Let me see if I can get you in this morning. Is eleven a.m. OK?

M I have no time in the morning. How about this afternoon?

W Let's see.... There's an opening at three thirty.

M Oh, please check again. I ＿＿＿＿ ＿＿＿＿ ＿＿＿＿ ＿＿＿＿ ＿＿＿＿.
3시경에 뵙고 싶다

W ＿＿＿＿ ＿＿＿＿ ＿＿＿＿ ＿＿＿＿? There's ＿＿＿＿
30분 더 일찍은 어때요   2시 30분이 비어 있다
＿＿＿＿ ＿＿＿＿.

M That's great. Thank you.

---

03 상황에 적절한 대화(그림)

다음 그림의 상황에 가장 적절한 대화를 고르시오.

① ② ③ ④ ⑤

Can I borrow your Cellphone? (휴대 전화를 빌릴 수 있을까요?) : Can I borrow ~?는 May I use ~?와 같은 의미로 허락을 구할 때 쓰는 표현이다.

① **W** I'm ＿＿＿＿＿＿＿＿ a new Cellphone.
~을 찾고 있는
M Please come in and look around. We have ＿＿＿＿ ＿＿＿＿.
많은 선택

② **W** How can I help you, sir?
M My Cellphone ＿＿＿＿＿＿＿＿ ＿＿＿＿ this morning.
작동을 멈췄다

③ **W** Can I borrow your Cellphone for a minute?
M Sure. Here it is.

④ **W** Hello, may I help you?
M Yes, I'd like to ＿＿＿＿＿＿＿＿ ＿＿＿＿.
계좌를 개설하다

⑤ **W** You bought a new Cellphone, didn't you?
M Yes, I did. Isn't it nice?

04 특정 정보 파악(요일)

대화를 듣고, 오늘이 무슨 요일인지 고르시오.

① Monday
② Tuesday
③ Wednesday
④ Thursday
⑤ Friday

M Hi, Patricia. Are you getting ready for Saturday?

W I'm afraid not. Something's come up and I can't make it.

M What's up?

W I have to go see my grandma this afternoon. She's very sick.

M Sorry to hear that. But we still _____ _____ .

이틀 더 남다

W We _____ _____ _____, right?

화요일에 그 프로젝트를 시작했다

M Yes. And just _____ _____ _____ .

하루 지났다

W Well, I think I can get back late tonight.

M Then we _____ _____ _____ . Give me a call early tomorrow morning, OK?

목요일과 금요일이 있다

W Of course. I will.

05 그림 정보 파악

묘사하는 표현(색깔, 무늬 등)을 잘 듣는다.

다음을 듣고, 여자가 묘사하는 강아지를 고르시오.

①　②
③　④
⑤

W I have a cute puppy. It is a white dog _____ _____ all over the body. I

검은 얼룩반점이 있는
like him more because he _____ _____ some words. Look at him now.

이해하는 것 같다
If I say "sit up", he _____ _____ _____ and waits for my

두 앞다리를 들다
next word. Also if I say, "Bring me a newspaper.", he goes to the front door and
_____ _____ . He is very clever. So I call him 'Clever'.

나에게 신문을 가져오다

06 관계 파악

산불을 끈 소방관을 뉴스에 초대하여 당시 상황을 묻고 있는 상황이다.

대화를 듣고, 두 사람의 관계로 가장 적절한 것을 고르시오.

① a hunter – a camper
② a camper – a fire fighter
③ a hunter – a police officer
④ an anchor – a fire fighter
⑤ a reporter – a police officer

W Good afternoon, Mr. Park. Thank you for being on Channel 9 News.

M Thanks for having me. But just call me Peter.

W Okay, Peter. Was it hard _____ _____ _____ ?

그 화재와 맞서다

M Yes, it was very hot and the fire was moving fast! It almost reached several houses nearby.

W How long did it take _____ _____ _____ ?

그것을 진화하다

M There were 18 fire fighters and it took about two hours.

W Do you know _____ _____ ?

무엇이 그 화재를 유발시켰는지를

M Some campers might have left _____ _____ in the

모닥불을 끄지 않고
forest.

book은 '책'이라는 뜻 외에 '예약하다'는 뜻도 있음에 유의한다.

다음을 듣고, 두 사람의 대화가 <u>어색한</u> 것을 고르시오.

① ② ③ ④ ⑤

① **W** Hey, you dropped something.

M Oh, it's my Cellphone. Thanks.

② **W** Why don't we have a pizza for lunch?

M That sounds like a good idea.

③ **W** You don't look good. What's the matter?

M I just _____ _____ _____. Don't worry.
미열이 좀 있다

④ **W** _____ _____ _____ this MP3 player.
반환하고 싶다

M What seems to be the problem, ma'am?

⑤ **W** All the rooms _____ _____, sir.
예약되었다

M Oh, I want to _____ _____ _____.
이 책을 빌리다

반복되고 있는 표현인 check if my [your] coat is ready를 놓치지 <u>않는</u>다.

대화를 듣고, 여자가 남자에게 부탁한 일로 가장 적절한 것을 고르시오.

① 세탁물 맡기기
② 가게에서 세제 사오기
③ 세탁소 전화번호 알아오기
④ 세탁소에 전화번호 알려 주기
⑤ 세탁물이 다 되었는지 확인하기

Would you do me a favor? (부탁 하나 해도 될까요?) : 상대방에게 부탁할 때 자주 쓰는 표현이다. (=May(Can) I ask you a favor?)

W Where are you going?

M I'm going to the supermarket.

W Oh, would you do me a favor while you are out?

M Sure. What's that?

W There's _____ _____ _____ near the supermarket. So, I'd like you to _____
세탁소
내 코트가 다 되었는지 확
_____ _____.

M OK. Does the owner know your name?

W Well, I don't know. I left my phone number there so you just give it to her.

M All right. Check if _____ _____ _____ _____ be picked up... that's it?
당신의 코트가 준비되다

W That's it.

구매 고객에게 무료 선물(free gifts)을 준다는 내용의 안내 방송임을 파악한다.

다음을 듣고, 무엇에 관한 안내인지 가장 적절한 것을 고르시오.

① 송년 모임 참여
② 송년 자선 행사
③ 신년 카드 발송
④ 성탄절 선물 구입
⑤ 성탄절 특별 행사

W Good morning, customers. We are glad to tell you about our store's _____ _____.
특별 행사
In order to celebrate Christmas, we will _____ _____
1,000달러 상당의 공짜 선물을 주다
_____ _____ every day. When you buy things in our store, please keep your receipts. If the total amount of your receipts adds up to $100 or more, please visit our service desk and _____ _____ _____. Again we wish you a Merry
공짜 선물을 받다
Christmas!

10 숫자 정보 파악(금액)

성인과 어린이의 표 가격과 총 구입 장수를 파악한다.

대화를 듣고, 남자가 지불할 금액을 고르시오.

① $5
② $50
③ $55
④ $65
⑤ $70

➕ 다음을 듣고, 대화가 일어나는 장소로 가장 적합한 것을 고르시오.

① 공항
② 버스 터미널
③ 선착장
④ 렌터카 센터
⑤ 마트

M Hi. I need to buy a ticket for the ferry.

W No problem. The ferry ticket is $55 _____ _____.
_{차량} _{한 대당}

M All right. That is a pretty reasonable price.

W How many people are there in your car?

M Five of us: my wife, our three kids, and me.

W That _____ _____ only four people per automobile. You'll have to _____
_{가격을} _{포함한다} _{별도의 요금을 내다}
_____ $10 for the fifth person.

M All right. My youngest son is only two years old. Do you charge the same price for him?

W Oh, children under three ride for free. They don't _____ _____ the four person
_{포함되다}
maximum.

11 대화 장소 파악

대화를 나누는 두 사람의 관계를 통해 대화 장소를 추론한다.

대화를 듣고, 두 사람이 대화하는 장소로 가장 적절한 곳을 고르시오.

① in a bank
② in a taxi
③ at a hotel
④ at an information center
⑤ at the National Museum

M _____ _____, ma'am?
_{어디로 모실까요?}

W The Korea Hotel, please.

M I see. Is this your first trip to Seoul?

W Yes, it is. I'm here for two weeks _____ _____. Do you know if there is anything
_{업무상}
interesting happening in the city this weekend?

M Well, if you're interested in art, you might like _____ _____ _____
_{한국전통미술 전시회}
_____ at the National Museum.

W That sounds great. Are we almost at the hotel?

M Yes, here we are. That'll be eight thousand won, please.

W Here's ten thousand won. _____ _____ and thanks for the information.
_{거스름돈은 가지다}

12 내용 일치 파악

숫자 표현에 유의하며 듣는다.

다음을 듣고, 내용과 일치하지 <u>않는</u> 것을 고르시오.

① 정규 수업 시간 – 오전 8:30 ~ 오후 3:30
② 방과 후 수업 활동 내용 – 음악, 운동
③ 클럽 활동 시간 – 2시간 30분
④ 방과 후 클럽 활동 내용 – 악기 연주, 축구, 테니스 등
⑤ 저녁 일과 – 악기 및 운동 연습

M Welcome to my school. My name is Ian. I'm proud of my school. Our _____ _____
_{정규 수업}
start 8:30 a.m. and finish 3:30 p.m. After school, my school teaches _____
_{음악과 운동}
_____. Most students attend club activities _____ _____ _____
_{1시간 30분 동안}
_____. Some students are interested in music. They sing or practice
playing musical instruments. Others are interested in sports. They play football, tennis,
basketball, or baseball. In the evenings, they _____ _____ their instruments and
_{연습하기를 즐기다}
sports.

13 지도, 위치 파악(지도) – 배치도

대화를 듣고, 교무실을 고르시오.

```
2nd floor   ROOM E    ROOM F
                              ROUNGE
            ROOM G
1st floor  REST ROOM  ROOM  ROOM  ROOM
                       A     B     C

           REST ROOM   ROOM D    ROOM E
```

① Room B   ② Room D
③ Room G   ④ Room E
⑤ Room F

M Hi, it's my first day at this school. Would you mind letting me know where the teachers' office is?

W No trouble at all. When you enter the building _____ _____ _____, 정문을 통해 there are restrooms on both sides of you. Go down the hall. The teachers room is two doors down.

M Oh, really? I heard there are only classrooms _____ _____ _____.
일층에

W Oh, you're right. Sorry. Go upstairs. The teachers' office is _____ _____ 이층에 _____. So, after you go up to the second floor, go down the hall toward the lounge. When you're _____ _____, the second room on your left is the teachers' 대합실을 마주하다 office.

M Thanks a lot.

[고난도]

14 소재 파악(담화)

다음을 듣고, 무엇에 관한 설명인지 고르시오.

① 조종사   ② 낙하산
③ 비행기   ④ 비행장
⑤ 안테나

사람이 하늘에서 떨어질 때 사용하는 것으로, 반복되고 있는 fall, safely 등을 들을 수 있어야 한다.

W This was invented _____ _____ _____ 사람들이 하늘에서 안전하게 떨어지는 것을 돕기 위해 _____. It has some pieces of cloths and a lot of strings. Before a person jumps out of an airplane, it is packed into a backpack. As _____, it quickly _____ _____ _____. This 사람이 떨어지다   공기를 안기 위해 펼치다 slows his or her falling speed so that the person can _____ _____. The upper part of this usually _____ _____ _____, a round 안전하게 땅에 착륙하다   동처럼 생겼다 roof.

15 할 일 파악

대화를 듣고, 여자가 대화 직후에 할 일로 가장 적절한 것을 고르시오.

① 검정색 운동화 신어보기
② 흰색 운동화 신어보기
③ 흰색 운동화 사기
④ 다른 가게로 가보기
⑤ 흰색 운동화 주문해 놓기

사이즈 250인 운동화가 꽉 끼므로 더 큰 운동화를 신어보는 것이 자연스럽다.

M Hi, may I help you?

W Yes, I'm looking for running shoes in size 250.

M We have _____ _____ _____ of running shoes.
많은 선택

W Can I try these white ones?

M Sure. _____ _____ _____. They're in size 250.
그것들을 신어보다

W Are these really 250? Well, they're _____ _____ _____. Can I try a larger pair in 조금 꽉 끼는 the same color?

M Sorry, but white ones are _____ _____ _____. How about these black ones? 재고가 없는 They're 255.

W Hmm.... let me try them on.

16 특정 정보 파악(교통 수단)

대화를 듣고, 두 사람이 이용할 교통수단으로 가장 적절한 것을 고르시오.

① bus   ② car
③ taxi   ④ subway
⑤ ship

W Terry, hurry up. We're late.

M Just a few seconds, Mom. I'm almost done.

W I'm afraid we'll be a little late. Let's go.

M Then are we going to take a taxi?

W No. I know it's fast but it'll _____ _____ _____ to get there. So we 우리에게 비용이 너무 들다 _____ _____ _____ _____. 지하철을 탈 것이다

M How long will it take, then?

W Well, about 30 minutes. It will be _____ _____ _____. 버스보다 더 빠른

M OK, Mom.

17 할 일 파악 | 블라우스를 치마로 바꾸기를 원하는 상황임을 파악한다.

대화를 듣고, 여자가 요구하는 것으로 가장 적절한 것을 고르시오.

① 환불
② 물건 교환
③ 치마 수선
④ 물건 배달
⑤ 사이즈 교환

M Good afternoon. May I help you?

W Yes, please. I bought this blouse the other day. But it's too large for me.

M You can _____ _____ _____. Or if you want, you can _____ _____
(좀 더 작은 것으로 선택하다) (환불 받다)
_____ on that blouse.

W Thank you, but I'd like to _____ _____. I _____ _____ _____.
(다른 것을 고르다) (치마가 필요하다)

M The skirts are over here. What color would you like?

W Brown, please.

M How about this one?

W That looks nice. Let me check the size.... OK. I'll choose this one. Could you please wrap it?

M No problem. Wait a moment.

18 적절한 응답 | 고장 난 컴퓨터를 작동시키려 애쓰지만 안 될 경우 해야 할 일을 생각해 본다.

[18~19] 대화를 듣고, 남자의 마지막 말에 대한 여자의 응답으로 가장 적절한 것을 고르시오.

Woman: _____

① That's good.
② It's not a bad idea.
③ You can use my USB.
④ Why don't you just keep quiet?
⑤ Why don't you call a repairman?

W You don't look good. What happened?

M I have to _____ _____ but my computer _____ _____.
(내 보고서를 인쇄하다) (작동하지 않는다)

W Oh, what seems to be the problem?

M I don't know. I pressed the power button as usual, but nothing happened.

W You can use mine if you have _____ _____ on your USB.
(문서를 저장했다)

M Sorry I didn't save it on a USB memory stick.

W That's too bad. So, what will you do now?

M Well, I'll try again a couple of more times and _____ _____ _____
(만약 여전히 작동하지 않는다면)
_____ ... I don't know.

W _____

고난도

19 적절한 응답 | 가장 파티에서 쥐의 복장을 할 남자에게 조심하라고 말한 이유를 유머러스한 관점에서 생각해 본다.

Woman: _____

① I don't like mice, either.
② Don't be late for the party.
③ I mean, it's not that expensive.
④ I've lent out two cat costumes.
⑤ The party was canceled a while ago.

W Hello. Can I help you?

M I'm going to a costume party on Saturday, and I'd like to _____ _____.
(의상을 대여하다)

W What kind of costume?

M It has to be _____ _____ _____.
(동물 의상)

W Let me see. I have a mouse costume.

M It'll be a very big mouse. Okay, I'll rent it.

W Here it is. Oh, by the way, _____ _____.
(조심해라)

M Be careful? What do you mean?

W _____

20 상황에 적절한 말(담화) | had a long day에 이어지는 내용을 통해 친구가 겪은 일을 파악한다.

다음 상황 설명을 듣고, 친구에게 할 말로 가장 적절한 것을 고르시오.

① What a pity!
② You did a good job.
③ Glad you could make it!
④ Try to get up as early as possible.
⑤ Why don't you take a bus next time?

W One of my close friends _____ _____ _____. First, he had a hard time
(힘든 하루를 보냈다)
going to school. The bus didn't come for twenty minutes, so he ran to the subway
station. The subway _____ _____ a lot of people. A man stepped on his
(~로 붐볐다)
foot, but he didn't say sorry. And a lady _____ over her Cellphone loudly.
(계속해서 이야기했다)
After getting off, he ran as fast as he could. But he was ten minutes late. He had to
_____ _____ before the first class. In this situation, what would you
(팔굽혀 펴기를 30번 하다)
most likely say to your close friend?

장소·관계·직업·심정 파악

무엇을 평가하는가?	일상생활이나 친숙한 일반적 주제에 관한 말이나 대화를 듣고 상황 및 화자 간의 관계, 그리고 화자의 심정이나 태도를 추론할 수 있는지를 평가한다.
어떻게 출제되는가?	• 대화를 듣고, 두 사람이 만나기로 한 장소를 고르시오. • 대화를 듣고, 두 사람의 관계로 가장 적절한 것을 고르시오. • 대화를 듣고, 남자의 직업으로 가장 적절한 것을 고르시오. • 대화를 듣고, 여자의 심정으로 가장 적절한 것을 고르시오.

key solution

❶ 장소, 관계, 직업을 묻는 경우, 대화의 주제나 소재가 중요한 역할을 하므로 주의하며 듣는다.

❷ 심정을 묻는 경우, 화자의 어조와 전체적인 상황을 동시에 파악한다.

[기출로 전략 확인]

대화를 듣고, 두 사람의 관계로 가장 적절한 것을 고르시오. [2017 기출]

① 수의사 – 애견 주인
② 서점 직원 – 고객
③ 미용사 – 손님
④ 진행자 – 작가
⑤ 사육사 – 관객

....

M Thank you for being a guest on our show, *New Books Weekly*.

W Thank you for inviting me.

M Congratulations on your new book. How would you describe your book in one sentence?

W Well, it's about friendship between a boy and his dog.

M I see. And why do you think this book has become so popular among children?

W Well, maybe because dogs are children's best friends.

M You're right. Are you writing a new book now?

W Yes, I'm writing a book about a cat who lost her mother.

❶ 남자가 쇼를 진행하면서 게스트인 여성에게 새로 나온 책의 스토리나 책의 인기의 요인, 현재 작업중인 책에 대해 질문하는 것으로 둘의 관계를 유추할 수 있다.

남 *New Books Weekly*쇼의 게스트가 되어 주셔서 감사합니다.

여 초대해 주셔서 감사합니다.

남 새로운 책이 나온 것을 축하합니다. 당신의 책을 한 문장으로 어떻게 표현할 수 있을까요?

여 음, 한 소년과 개의 우정에 관한 책입니다.

남 그렇군요. 이 책이 아이들 사이에서 인기를 끄는 이유가 뭐라고 생각하시나요?

여 글쎄요, 아마 개들이 아이들의 가장 친한 친구이기 때문이지 않을까요.

남 맞습니다. 지금 새 책을 쓰고 계시나요?

여 네, 어미를 잃은 고양이에 관한 책을 쓰고 있습니다.

대화를 듣고, 남자의 직업으로 가장 적절한 것을 고르시오.　[2016 기출]

① engineer　　　　② photographer　　　③ cartoonist

④ travel guide　　　⑤ flight attendant

만점 잡는 문장　**W** I also need photos for my passport. <u>Do you take passport pictures as well?</u>

M Of course. <u>Please wait for a second while I set up the camera.</u>

대화를 듣고, 여자의 심정으로 가장 적절한 것을 고르시오.　[2015 기출]

① bored　　　　　② excited　　　　　③ satisfied

④ thankful　　　　⑤ frustrated

M I'm afraid that's not possible. The deadline was last Friday.

만점 잡는 문장　**W** Oh, no! <u>I can't believe that I made such a big mistake.</u>

● **장소(휴대폰 수리점)**

A I dropped my cellphone on the floor, and its screen got broken.

핸드폰을 바닥에 떨어트려서 화면이 깨졌어요.

B That's too bad. You have to replace it with a new one. It'll cost about 100 dollars.

안됐네요. 새 걸로 갈아야 하겠네요. 100달러입니다.

● **관계(호텔직원 – 투숙객)**

A Excuse me. Can you give me a wake-up call for 7 a.m.? 실례합니다. 7시에 모닝콜 좀 해주실 수 있나요?

B Sure. What's your room number? 물론이죠. 방 번호가 어떻게 되나요?

● **직업(animal doctor)**

W My dog got away from me and was hit by a car. 개가 저에게서 도망쳤다가 차에 치였어요.

M Let me see. Oh, it doesn't seem that bad, but she needs to get an X-ray.

어디 봅시다. 아, 그렇게 심하진 않네요. 그래도 엑스레이는 찍을 필요가 있네요.

● **심정**

relieved 안도한	relaxed 여유 있는	pleased 기쁜	thankful 고맙게 생각하는
peaceful 평안한	impressive 인상적인	worried 걱정하는	bored 지루해 하는
scared 무서워하는	frustrated 좌절한	annoyed 짜증 난	embarrassed 당황한

다시 들으면서 듣기 만점에 도전하세요!
Dictation: 스크립트의 주요 부분을 다시 들으면서!
실전 ⊕: 세부 정보가 많은 스크립트를 다른 문제로 샅샅이!

01 그림 정보 파악(인물)

shirt, shorts, caps에 대해 묘사하는 표현을 놓치지 않고 듣는다.

다음을 듣고, 여자가 묘사하는 아이를 고르시오.

① ② ③

④ ⑤

W Hello, shoppers. We're looking for a lost boy. His name is Marshall. He _____ _____ in the sporting goods section on the third floor about twenty minutes ago. 실종됐다 He's five years old, and he's wearing _____ _____ _____ 긴소매의 흰 셔츠 _____, _____ _____, and 검정 반바지 _____. If you find him, please take him to the information desk at the main exit. 검정 줄무늬가 있는 야구 모자 Thank you.

02 전화한 목적

대화를 듣고, 여자가 남자에게 전화한 목적으로 가장 적절한 것을 고르시오.

① 여행 인원을 변경하려고
② 여행을 취소 하려고
③ 이동 수단을 바꾸려고
④ 방문할 도시를 추가하려고
⑤ 여행 비용을 줄이려고

[Cellphone rings.]

W Hi, Jack. I'd like to _____ _____ _____ _____ for our trip to Japan. I'm 계획에 대해 말하다 happy we're planning to visit Tokyo, Kyoto and Osaka.

M But you want to change something, right?

W Yes. _____ _____ _____ one more city? I want to add Kobe to the list. I really 방문하는 거 어때? want to go there.

M Well, Sarah, that would make our trip longer and make the trip more expensive.

W I know, but I have some friends there that I'd really like to visit. We can _____ _____ _____ to save money. 그들 집에 머무르다

M All right, if that's what you really want, I'm okay with it.

고난도

03 상황에 적절한 대화(그림)

재킷 구입에 대한 대화와 혼 동하지 않도록 유의한다.

다음 그림의 상황에 가장 적절한 대화를 고르시오.

① ② ③ ④ ⑤

① W Excuse me, is there a place near here _____ _____ _____ 내가 재킷을 살 수 있는 곳 _____ _____?

　M Let me see. I think there's a shop on Spring Street.

② W This looks much larger. Have you got something smaller?

　M Sorry, but that's _____ _____ _____. 우리가 갖고 있는 마지막 하나

③ W Have you seen my jacket anywhere?

　M I saw it on the chair yesterday.

④ W Excuse me. Could you _____ _____, please? 네 재킷을 옮기다

　M Oh, sorry. I didn't know it was bothering you.

⑤ W Excuse me. Can you show me that jacket?

　M Sure, but you'll have to _____ _____. 잠깐 기다리다

04 특정 정보 파악(장소)

장소가 계속 변경될 수 있으니 마지막까지 집중해서 듣는다.

대화를 듣고, 두 사람이 만나기로 한 장소를 고르시오.

① 지하철역   ② 영화관
③ 은행   ④ 병원
⑤ 서점

➕
대화를 듣고, 여자가 처음에 만나자고 제안한 장소를 고르시오.

① 지하철역   ② 영화관
③ 은행   ④ 병원
⑤ 서점

[Cellphone rings.]

W   Hey, Sam. Are you free now? Let's go to the Grand Mall together.

M   Sounds good. Where do you want to meet?

W   At the Grand Mall subway station. I want to ＿＿＿＿ ＿＿＿＿ ＿＿＿＿ (새로운 서점에 가다) ＿＿＿＿ there.

M   Oh, is the new bookstore open?

W   Yes, it is. I heard that it's ＿＿＿＿ (아주 넓은) with many kinds of books. They also have huge sections for music and stationery.

M   Really? Then, ＿＿＿＿ (우리 ~ 하는 게 어때?) ＿＿＿＿ just meet in front of the bookstore? Please wait for me there.

W   That'll be even better. Call me when you ＿＿＿＿ (서점에 도착하다) ＿＿＿＿ ＿＿＿＿.

05 심정 파악

현재 여자가 겪고 있는 어려운 상황이 무엇인지 파악한다.

대화를 듣고, 여자의 심정으로 가장 적절한 것을 고르시오.

① calm 침착한   ② upset 화난
③ lonely 외로운   ④ scared 겁먹은
⑤ thankful 감사하는

That's nice of you! (참 친절하시군요!) : 상대방을 칭찬할 때 쓰는 표현이다. (=It's very nice of you.)

M   Oh, you're walking ＿＿＿＿ (목발을 짚고) ＿＿＿＿ ＿＿＿＿ ＿＿＿＿. Is it OK if I ＿＿＿＿ (당신이 길 건너는 것을 돕다) ＿＿＿＿ ＿＿＿＿?

W   Sure, thanks. ＿＿＿＿ (너는 정말 친절하다) ＿＿＿＿ to help me.

M   You're welcome. I'm glad to help you.

W   In fact, I've had a hard time crossing the street these days.

M   I know ＿＿＿＿ (그것이 어떤 기분인지) ＿＿＿＿. My friend used to have the same problem. He had his right leg in a cast, too.

W   Oh, did he?

M   Yes. He couldn't walk well, either. So I carried his schoolbag for him to school.

W   That's nice of you!

M   Oh, there are no cars passing by right now. Let's cross the street now.

06 특정 정보 파악

이번 시험(this quiz) 범위를 이미 치룬 두 번째 시험(the second quiz) 범위와 혼동하지 않도록 한다.

대화를 듣고, 시험 범위와 시험 시간이 바르게 짝지어진 것을 고르시오.

① 2장 ~ 3장 - 다음 수업 시간
② 3장 ~ 4장 - 다음 수업 시간
③ 3장 ~ 4장 - 다음 주
④ 4장 ~ 7장 - 다음 수업 시간
⑤ 4장 ~ 7장 - 다음 주

That's all for today. (오늘은 여기까지 입니다.) : 수업을 마칠 때 주로 쓰는 표현이다.

M   Okay, everyone. That's all for today.

W   Thank you, Mr. Jones.

M   By the way, do you remember this quiz is on ＿＿＿＿ (4장에서 7장까지) ＿＿＿＿ ＿＿＿＿ ＿＿＿＿?

W   Chapters four through seven? I thought it was on chapters three and four.

M   Nope, I'm afraid not. The second quiz was on chapters two and three.

W   Oh, yeah. I forgot.

M   Are there any other questions?

W   Is the quiz ＿＿＿＿ (다음 주) ＿＿＿＿?

M   No, ＿＿＿＿ (다음 수업 시간) ＿＿＿＿. Prepare for it well and see you then!

다음을 듣고, 두 사람의 대화가 <u>어색한</u> 것을 고르시오.

① ② ③ ④ ⑤

① M When did you arrive?

W I just arrived about 10 minutes ago.

② M I hate history class.

W Watch some movies about history. That'll help.

③ M How much do you pay for the swimming lessons?

W _____ _____ _____.
시간이 좀 걸리다

④ M Can you come to the party?

W I'm afraid I can't. I have a lot of things to do.

⑤ M What are you going to do _____ _____ _____?
휴가동안

W I'm not sure. I'll have to think about it.

대화를 듣고, 여자가 남자에게 부탁한 일로 가장 적절한 것을 고르시오.

① TV 시청하기　　② 친구 초대하기
③ 치킨 요리하기　　④ 치킨 배달하기
⑤ 치킨 사오기

부탁할 때 쓰이는 표현에 집중한다.

W Sam, how many of your friends are coming over tonight?

M There'll be five of us. They want to _____ _____ _____ on TV to cheer
축구 경기를 보다
for the Korean team.

W That sounds exciting. _____ _____ snacks would you like to have?
어떤 종류의~?

M Fried chicken and potato chips would be great.

W If I give you some money, can you go get some chicken?

M Sure, I'd be glad to.

대화를 듣고, 여자의 마지막 말의 의도로 가장 적절한 것을 고르시오.

① 칭찬　　　　② 격려
③ 사과　　　　④ 권유
⑤ 꾸중

I'll keep my fingers crossed for you. (행운을 빌게.) : 검지손가락과 중지손가락을 교차시키는 것이 행운을 바란다는 의미로 자주 쓰이는 것에서 유래한 표현으로, 기원을 말할 때 쓰는 표현이다.

시험에 대해 걱정하고 있는 상황임을 파악한다.

W What's up? You look worried.

M You know, final exams _____ _____ _____.
얼마 남지 않았다

W Are there any problems?

M Well, _____ _____ English and Korean, but I'm not so sure about
나는 ~에 자신이 있다
science.

W I thought you were good at both math and science.

M Actually, I'm not.

W What do you mean?

M I don't worry about math. But the biology part in science is really _____
나에게 어려운
_____. I hope the problems are not so hard.

W Well, I'll _____ _____ _____ for you.
행운을 빌다

10 숫자 정보 파악(금액)

커피와 머핀의 가격과 쿠폰 사용 여부를 확인한다.

대화를 듣고, 여자가 지불할 금액을 고르시오.

① $5   ② $7
③ $10   ④ $2
⑤ $4

W Hello! Can I get my usual morning coffee? And please make it two today. I'm getting one for my sister.

M All right. Would you like anything else with those?

W Hmm... Those plain muffins _____ _____.
　　　　　　맛있어 보인다.

M They were just baked.

W Okay. I'll take three of those, then.

M All right. The coffees are $2.00 each, plus the three muffins at $1.00 each.
_____ _____ $7.00.　　　　　　　　　　　(가격이) ~이다

W Great. Oh, I want to _____ today. I've got ten stamps
　　　　　　　　　　　쿠폰을 사용하다
already.

M Well, with ten stamps, you can get one free coffee.

11 대화 장소 파악

두 번 반복해서 나오는 on the grass를 놓치지 않고 듣는다.

대화를 듣고, 두 사람이 대화하는 장소로 가장 적절한 곳을 고르시오.

① 공원 매점
② 육상 경기장
③ 수건 판매점
④ 공원 잔디밭
⑤ 샌드위치 판매점

M Hey, look at those kids.

W You mean _____ _____? They are so cute.
　　　　　풀밭에서 뛰노는 아이들

M And you see their parents _____ _____?
　　　　　　　　　　　　누워서 책을 읽고 있는

W Yeah. They look so happy. Anyway, did you bring our lunch?

M Sure. You like cheese sandwiches, right?

W That's right. And where are some cold drinks?

M Gee, I totally forgot those. I'll go get some from the cafeteria.

W No. That's OK. Don't bother yourself. I have some water.

M OK then. Why don't you _____
　　　　　　　　　　잔디 위에 큰 수건을 깔다
_____ so we can sit down?

W OK.

12 언급 유무 파악(담화)

다음을 듣고, 남자가 체중 감량을 위해 권장한 방법이 아닌 것을 고르시오.

① 산책하기
② 자전거 타기
③ 계단 이용하기
④ 좋아하는 운동하기
⑤ 헬스 클럽 이용하기

M Most teenagers are very sensitive about gaining weight. That's why you go on a diet. But the best way to lose weight is 'to exercise.' It's important to remember you can
_____ . You _____
언제 어디서나 운동하다　　　　　　헬스 클럽에 갈 필요가 없다
_____ . Take a walk for 20 minutes at least three times a week.
Enjoy _____ during the weekend. Find a sport you like: soccer,
　　　자전거 타기
basketball, tennis, etc. It doesn't matter whatever you choose. And _____
　　　　　　　　　　　　　　　　　　　　　　　　　계단을 이용하라
_____ instead of the elevator. These things can help you lose weight and keep you in shape. Just go for it!

13 지도, 위치 파악(지도) – 배치도

지도를 보면서 대화를 듣고, 남자가 찾아 갈 장소를 고르시오.

① A   ② B   ③ C   ④ D   ⑤ E

M Excuse me, do you know where _____ is? I need to find an ATM.
　　　　　　　　　　　　　　　　　　　가장 가까운 은행

W Well, there isn't a bank near here. But there is an ATM in the lobby of the hospital.

M Oh, where's the hospital?

W The hospital is _____ . Go straight from here, and you'll
　　　　　　　　　식료품점 건너편의
see a big coffee shop on your right. Make a right turn there, and you'll see a grocery store.

M Okay, so I go straight and turn right.

W Yes, then _____ at the grocery store. You can't miss the entrance
　　　　　　　길을 건너다
of the hospital.

M Thanks a lot.

14 소재 파악(담화)

다음을 듣고, 무엇에 관한 내용인지 가장 적절한 것을 고르시오.

① 가벼운 자전거 개발
② 새로운 자전거 배낭
③ 안전한 자전거 타기
④ 건전한 여가 활동
⑤ 자전거 타기 적절한 시간

W Nowadays many people enjoy bike riding in the evening. However, it may be dangerous especially in the winter months, because it is dark during those hours. We _____ _____ _____ _____ to help people ride a bike safely. This backpack has little lights on it. The lights are very small, _____ _____. With this backpack, you can safely ride a bike along the road in the dark. The lights make the riders more visible to the car drivers. This can _____ _____ _____ _____ a lot.

(자전거 배낭을 개발하다 / 밝고 가벼운 / 교통사고의 위험을 감소하다)

15 할 일 파악

대화를 듣고, 여자가 할 일로 가장 적절한 것을 고르시오.

① 옷 사러가기 ② 축제 참여하기
③ 소포 배송 신청하기 ④ 공연 연습하기
⑤ 공연 응원하기

➕ 대화를 듣고, 내용과 일치하지 않은 것을 고르시오.

① 택배 배송지는 부산이다.
② 빠른 배송은 하루가 걸린다.
③ 택배의 내용물은 축제 홍보물이다
④ 택배 배송은 제시간에 되야 한다.
⑤ 택배는 신청서를 써야한다.

W I'd like to send this package to Busan, please.
M Just put it on the scale. Would you like to send it _____ _____ _____?
(속달 우편으로)
W Yes. I'd like to get it there _____ _____ _____.
(가능한 빨리)
M Then, it will cost $30, and it will reach Busan tomorrow.
W That's _____ _____. But my friend needs to wear the clothes in the package at a school festival. It has to arrive before Thursday.
(상당히 비싼)
M It will. Do you want to send it by express mail?
W Yes.
M Fill out this form, please.

16 특정 정보 파악(구하려는 직업)

여자가 전에 했던 직업과, 앞으로 하고 싶어 하는 직업을 구별한다.

대화를 듣고, 여자가 구하려는 직업을 고르시오.

① 조종사
② 간호사
③ 수학 교사
④ 육상 선수
⑤ 여행사 직원

M Karen, long time no see.
W Daniel, it's been a long time since I saw you last time.
M How's your job going?
W Not so good. You know, I had to travel a lot for my job.
M Did you? But you enjoy travelling, don't you?
W Well, traveling all the time was really hard though. So I _____ _____ _____.
(지난달에 그만두다)
M So what are you going to do now?
W I'm interested in _____ _____ _____ _____. So I'm planning to take vocational nursing courses.
(아픈 사람들 돌보기)
M That's wonderful! I know you always like to _____ _____ _____ a hospital and help others.
(~에서 자원봉사활동을 하다)
W Yes, I really enjoy it.

17 적절한 응답

자신의 컴퓨터를 함부로 사용한 남자에게 할 수 있는 말을 생각한다.

[17~19] 대화를 듣고, 남자의 마지막 말에 대한 여자의 응답으로 가장 적절한 것을 고르시오.

Woman: _____

① Please take care of yourself.
② I can't sell my computer to you.
③ You are a good brother.
④ Don't ever touch my computer again!
⑤ Where did you put my computer?

W Rob, did you use my computer today?
M Oh, yeah. About that... I know I shouldn't have used your computer, but I had to research something on the Internet. Why? Is anything wrong?
W Yeah. You _____ _____ project _____. How many times do I have to tell you not to use my computer?
(내 파일을 다 지웠다)
M I swear I didn't do anything with your files. I just _____ _____ for half an hour.
(인터넷을 검색하다)
W I don't care what you had to do. The thing is that my files are gone.
M I'm really sorry.
W _____

18 적절한 응답

남자의 마지막 말에 제시된 try on과 관련 있는 응답을 선택한다.

Woman: _____

① It looks really cool on you.
② We have it in color red, too.
③ Well, you don't have to do it today.
④ This is just what you're looking for.
⑤ Sure. The fitting room is just over there.

W Can I help you find something?
M Yes, please. I'm looking for a men's round-necked sweater _____.
　　　　　　　　　　　　　　　　　　　중간 사이즈의
W How do you like this one? This style is _____.
　　　　　　　　　　　　　　　　요즘에 유행하는
M I like the style, but do you have that in many colors?
W Yes, we do. What color do you like most?
M I prefer brown sweaters. Do you have this _____?
　　　　　　　　　　　　　　　　　　　갈색으로
W Sure. Here you are.
M Looks nice, but it might be a little tight for me. Can I _____?
　　　　　　　　　　　　　　　　　　　그것을 입어 보다
W _____

19 적절한 응답

제안(How about -ing?)에 대한 응답으로 알맞은 것을 선택한다.

Woman: _____

① Sorry, I must be going now.
② I'm planning to take a short trip.
③ That's exactly what I was thinking.
④ I wonder if you can lend me their CD.
⑤ Could you get the sign from your favorite singer?

How do you like this song? (이 노래 마음에 드니?) : How do you like ~?는 상대방의 의견이나 생각을 물어볼 때 쓰는 표현이다.

W How do you like this song? It's _____.
　　　　　　　　　　　　　　내가 가장 좋아하는 노래들 중 하나
M What a great song! I love it.
W I'm glad you like it that much.
M Do you happen to know the title of the song and the name of the musical group?
W Yes, I do. The title is 'As Long As You Love Me,' and the group is 'Backstreet Boys.'
M Is there _____ in the song?
　　　　　　어떤 특별한 내용
W They are singing about love. The message is that they don't care about anything else as long as somebody loves them.
M It's _____. How about singing this song with me in the school
　　　노래 부르기 쉬운
English pop song contest?
W _____

20 상황에 적절한 말(담화)

David는 자기가 하는 모든 것이 중요하다고 생각하고 있는 점을 반영한다.

다음 상황 설명을 듣고, David가 Scott 선생님에게 할 말로 가장 적절한 것을 고르시오.

David: _____

① Your advice is useful in many ways.
② Can you teach me how to study effectively?
③ Sorry, but I'm too tired to do homework.
④ Thank you, but I can't give up any of them.
⑤ I'll give up all of these activities sooner or later.

W _____ these days David hasn't done well in studies. He does a lot of things.
　~은 당연하다
Before going to school, he takes a tennis lesson. During lunch break he volunteers at the student cafeteria. After school, he practices basketball from four to five and then
_____ the convenience store from six to nine. After returning
~에서 아르바이트를 하다
home, of course, he's _____. His
　　　　　너무 피곤해서 그의 숙제를 할 수 없다
homeroom teacher, Mr. Scott, advises him to quit one of the activities, but David thinks
_____. In this situation, what is David most
그가 하는 모든 것이 중요하다
likely to say to Mr. Scott?

학년　　　반　　　번

이름

01 대화를 듣고, 여자의 가방을 고르시오.

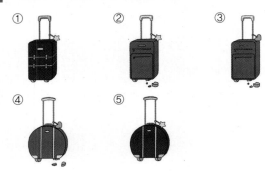

02 대화를 듣고, 여자가 남자에게 전화를 건 목적으로 가장 적절한 것을 고르시오.

① 도서를 대출하려고
② 휴대폰 수리를 요청하려고
③ 수행평가 점수를 알고 싶어서
④ 도서관 개장 시간을 알아내려고
⑤ 작문 교정을 봐 줄 것을 부탁하려고

03 다음 그림의 상황에 가장 적절한 대화를 고르시오.

① ② ③ ④ ⑤

04 대화를 듣고, 현재 시각을 고르시오.

① 9:00　　　　　② 12:00
③ 3:30　　　　　④ 4:00
⑤ 8:00

05 대화를 듣고, 여자의 심정으로 가장 적절한 것을 고르시오.

① angry　　　　② lonely
③ worried　　　④ happy
⑤ envious

06 대화를 듣고, 두 사람의 관계로 가장 적절한 것을 고르시오.

① 변호사 – 의뢰인
② 점원 – 고객
③ 경찰관 – 운전자
④ 여행사 직원 – 관광객
⑤ 배달원 – 수령인

07 다음을 듣고, 두 사람의 대화가 어색한 것을 고르시오.

① ② ③ ④ ⑤

08 대화를 듣고, 여자가 남자에게 부탁한 일로 가장 적절한 것을 고르시오.

① 음식 배달하기　　　② 욕실 청소하기
③ 애완견 산책시키기　④ 정원 정리하기
⑤ 동생 보살피기

09 대화를 듣고, 남자의 마지막 말에 담긴 감정으로 가장 적절한 것을 고르시오.

① 혼란스러움　　　② 감사함
③ 슬픔　　　　　　④ 놀라움
⑤ 고마움

10 대화를 듣고, 여자가 지불해야 할 금액을 고르시오.

① $14　　　　　② $20
③ $30　　　　　④ $42
⑤ $60

점수

/20

11 대화를 듣고, 두 사람이 대화하는 장소로 가장 적절한 곳을 고르시오.

① 사진관
② 영화 보급사
③ 컴퓨터 학원
④ 고속도로 톨게이트
⑤ 프로그램 개발회사

고난도
12 대화를 듣고, 여자가 일일교장이 되어 하고 싶은 일로 언급되지 않은 것을 고르시오.

① 등교 시간 늦추기
② 수업 시간 줄이기
③ 낮잠 시간 만들기
④ 개인 활동 시간 주기
⑤ 숙제 없는 날 선포하기

고난도
13 다음 표를 보면서 대화를 듣고, 여자가 탄 기차를 고르시오.

	Train No.	Departure	Arrival	Time (departure-arrival)
①	S1	Busan	Seoul	2:00~6:00 p.m.
②	D1	Busan	Daejeon	2:00~4:00 p.m.
③	S2	Busan	Seoul	3:00~7:00 p.m.
④	D2	Busan	Daejeon	3:00~5:00 p.m.
⑤	S3	Busan	Seoul	5:00~9:00 p.m.

고난도
14 다음을 듣고, This가 가리키는 것을 고르시오.

① 하품
② 트림
③ 방귀
④ 재채기
⑤ 딸꾹질

15 대화를 듣고, 여자가 할 일로 가장 적절한 것을 고르시오.

① 집 청소하기
② 우체국에 가기
③ 항공권 예매하기
④ 현관 자물쇠 수리하기
⑤ 고객서비스 센터에 전화하기

16 대화를 듣고, 여자가 구입할 것을 고르시오.

① fine dust
② masks
③ a drug store
④ filter-out rate
⑤ a box

[17~19] 대화를 듣고, 여자의 마지막 말에 대한 남자의 응답으로 가장 적절한 것을 고르시오.

17 Man: _____

① I'll ask the teacher.
② I don't know about the fee.
③ I can't wait!
④ I want to get a good score.
⑤ The phone is out of order.

18 Man: _____

① I can answer the questions, too.
② Oh, yes. Thanks for your advice.
③ I hope he can feel better by now.
④ I don't know how much it costs to get help.
⑤ Yes, this medicine works well on headaches.

19 Man: _____

① Thank you for visiting us.
② What is your name, please?
③ You can use the pay phone over there.
④ Certainly, ma'am. May I have your card?
⑤ Of course. There is a bank around the corner.

20 다음 상황 설명을 듣고, Tom이 Sam에게 할 말로 가장 적절한 것을 고르시오.

Tom: _____

① Hey, can I borrow a pen there?
② Excuse me. Can you say that again?
③ It doesn't work. Give me another one.
④ Don't forget to take notes. I'll copy yours.
⑤ Don't throw it away. You can use it later.

다시 들으면서 듣기 만점에 도전하세요!
Dictation : 스크립트의 주요 부분을 다시 들으면서!
실전 ⊕ : 세부 정보가 많은 스크립트를 다른 문제로 샅샅이!

---

01 그림 정보 파악(사물)

가방의 모양, 색상, 특징을 잘 듣는다.

대화를 듣고, 여자의 가방을 고르시오.

① ② ③ ④ ⑤

M May I help you?

W I've _____ _____ . I think someone took it while I was using the restroom.
  (가방을 잃어버리다)

M Oh, that's too bad. Can you tell me what it looks like?

W It is a suitcase, so of course it's rectangular. And it's brown.

M Can you describe the suitcase in detail?

W Well, _____ _____ _____ _____ was broken, so it's not easy to pull along.
  (바퀴 중 하나)
  Oh, and I attached a heart-shaped luggage tag on it.

M Okay. We'll look for it. Please fill out this form.

---

02 전화한 목적

대화를 듣고, 여자가 남자에게 전화를 건 목적으로 가장 적절한 것을 고르시오.

① 도서를 대출하려고
② 휴대폰 수리를 요청하려고
③ 수행평가 점수를 알고 싶어서
④ 도서관 개장 시간을 알아내려고
⑤ 작문 교정을 봐 줄 것을 부탁하려고

[Telephone rings.]

M Hello?

W Hello, Henry. This is Sara.

M Hi, Sara. What's up?

W Will you _____ _____ _____ ?
  (내 부탁을 들어주다)

M It _____ _____ _____ _____ .
  (그것이 무엇인가에 달려있다)

W Can you _____ _____ _____ ? It's my homework. I really need
  (내 영어 작문을 교정보다)
  _____ _____ in this class.
  (좋은 점수를 받다)

M That's no problem. By the way, what time exactly is it?

W It's ten to nine.

M Then, let's meet at 11 o'clock at the library.

W Okay. See you then.

고난도

03 상황에 적절한 대화(그림)

다음 그림의 상황에 가장 적절한 대화를 고르시오.

① ② ③ ④ ⑤

① W What's wrong? You don't look well.

  M I'm not feeling well. I _____ _____ bad _____ .
    (두통이 있다)

② W I've been waiting for his new novel to come out!

  M Same here. My friend said the novel is a great read.

③ W Jane recommended this new song.

  M Really? _____ _____ the name of the artist. I'll check it out.
    (~을 알려줘)

④ W May I help you?

  M I'd like to _____ _____ . It's too small for me.
    (이 셔츠를 환불하다)

⑤ W How about this one? It is very cute.

  M I don't like the color. It's too bright for me.

항공편 출발 시각에서 현재 남은 시간을 빼면 현재 시각을 알 수 있다.

대화를 듣고, 현재 시각을 고르시오.
① 9:00 ② 12:00
③ 3:30 ④ 4:00
⑤ 8:00

W When does the plane leave for Sydney?

M There are two planes for Sydney. Flight 351 goes via Singapore and it leaves at 3:30. Flight 488 is a nonstop flight.

W I mean the nonstop flight.

M Then, it _____ _____ _____.

4시에 떠나다

W At 4 o'clock in the afternoon?

M That's right.

W Do you think I have enough time to catch it?

M I think so. You still _____ _____ _____.

4시간이 남다

W Okay. And _____ _____ _____ _____ to get to Sydney?

시간이 얼마나 오래 걸리니

M It _____ 9 hours.

약 ~의 시간이 걸리다

대화를 듣고, 여자의 심정으로 가장 적절한 것을 고르시오.

① angry 화난 ② lonely 외로운
③ worried 걱정되는 ④ happy 행복한
⑤ envious 부러운

How beautiful! : 「How+형용사(+주어+동사)!」의 감탄문으로 '정말 아름답구나!'라는 의미이다.

M Mom, I'm home. Guess what I got?

W You _____ _____ _____, right?

A나 뭐 그런 것을 받았다

M No, it's not that. Close your eyes.

W Come on, Jake. What is it?

M Close your eyes, please.

W All right. I am closing them.

M Now, open your eyes. _____ _____ _____.

당신을 위한 것이다

W How beautiful! By the way, what's the occasion?

M Just to _____ _____ _____ you do for me.

모든 일에 대해 감사드리다

W Oh, my son!

신원을 확인한 뒤 소포를 건네주고 서명을 받는 사람의 직업을 추론해 본다.

대화를 듣고, 두 사람의 관계로 가장 적절한 것을 고르시오.

① 변호사 – 의뢰인
② 점원 – 고객
③ 경찰관 – 운전자
④ 여행사 직원 – 관광객
⑤ 배달원 – 수령인

M Are you Ms. Edward?

W Yes, I am.

M I _____ _____ _____ _____. I need your signature.

당신에게 온 소포가 있다

W Oh, thank you. Where should I sign?

M You should _____ _____ _____ _____.

여기 아래쪽에 서명하다

W Oh, I see. Here it is. Will you wait for a second? I'll get you something to drink.

M That's very kind of you, but I am in a hurry.

W All right. Thank you.

버스를 타기에 앞서 행선지를 물을 때 어떤 말을 할 수 있을지 생각해 본다.

다음을 듣고, 두 사람의 대화가 <u>어색한</u> 것을 고르시오.

①   ②   ③   ④   ⑤

① W _____ _____ _____ _____ Seoul Station?
이 버스가 ~에 가나요
    M Yes, you can _____ _____ _____.
여기서 기차를 타다

② W Will you turn off the lights?

    M Sure, no problem.

③ W Let me carry one of your bags.

    M Oh, thank you very much.

④ W Thanks for _____ _____ _____ _____.
집에까지 태워다 준 것
    M You are welcome. It was on my way.

⑤ W How long does it take to your school?

    M It takes _____ _____ _____ _____.
걸어서 5분

고난도

대화를 듣고, 여자가 남자에게 부탁한 일로 가장 적절한 것을 고르시오.

① 음식 배달하기
② 욕실 청소하기
③ 애완견 산책시키기
④ 정원 정리하기
⑤ 동생 보살피기

➕ 대화를 듣고, 남자가 일을 할 장소를 고르시오.

① 거실   ② 욕실
③ 정원   ④ 공원
⑤ 자기방

W Joe, can you _____ _____ _____? Can you mow the lawn today?
내 부탁을 들어주다
M Sure, Mom. It's been a long time since I last _____ _____ _____.
잔디를 깎다
W And we need to remove the dead flowers in the garden, too.

M *[sigh]* I know. But it's a beautiful day, Mom. I want to go out and have fun with friends.

W Come on, Joe. There are a lot of things to do around the house. You can enjoy the nice weather another day.

M OK, OK. Then, would you _____ _____ _____, please? I'll _____
호스를 틀다
_____ _____ first.
꽃에 물을 주다
W Sure. Let's get to work.

우연히 옛 학교 동창을 만났을 때 감정을 생각한다.

대화를 듣고, 남자의 마지막 말에 담긴 감정으로 가장 적절한 것을 고르시오.

① 혼란스러움   ② 감사함
③ 슬픔   ④ 놀라움
⑤ 고마움

➕ 대화를 듣고, 두 사람의 관계로 가장 적절한 것을 고르시오.

① 스승과 제자   ② 요리사와 손님
③ 학교 동창   ④ 회사 동료
⑤ 남매

M Excuse me. Would you happen to be from Jeju Island?

W Um, yes, I am from there. I _____ _____ _____ _____ and went to
제주도에서 자랐다
elementary school there, before my family moved to Seoul.

M I thought so! Your name is Rachael, right?

W Yes, that's right! And you are... ?

M Jason. We went to Jeju Elementary School together. Don't you remember?

W Jason! Is that you? Oh my! _____ _____ _____! We were in the same
정말 오랜만이다
swimming club, right?

M Yes, right. I can't believe it! It's been so long to see you.

---

10 숫자 정보 파악(금액)

정가와 할인율, 사려는 개수를 파악하여 계산해 본다.

대화를 듣고, 여자가 지불해야 할 금액을 고르시오.

① $14
② $20
③ $30
④ $42
⑤ $60

W Excuse me.

M Yes. Is there anything I can help you with?

W Yes, I need T-shirts for working out at the gym.

M Well, these shirts are nice. They don't absorb sweat. And they keep you cool when you work out.

W That's great! How much are they?

M _____ _____, but they are on sale. I can _____ _____ _____

개당 20달러   30% 할인해 주다

_____.

W How lucky! Give me _____ _____ _____.

그 셔츠 3장

11 대화 장소 파악

develop가 필름을 '현상하다'라는 의미가 있음을 참고한다.

대화를 듣고, 두 사람이 대화하는 장소로 가장 적절한 곳을 고르시오.

① 사진관
② 영화 보급사
③ 컴퓨터 학원
④ 고속도로 톨게이트
⑤ 프로그램 개발회사

M Good morning. How may I help you?

W Good morning. How long does it take to _____ _____ _____

이 필름 한 통을 현상하다

_____?

M It takes about 30 minutes.

W Wow, that's pretty quick! Last time it _____ _____ at Smith's

약 1주일 걸렸다

photo shop! How much is it for each one?

M It's 30 cents each. But I can give you our special coupon. _____ _____,

이 교환권으로

you can develop your first roll _____ _____.

공짜로

W That's really a good deal. I have two rolls of film.

M By the way, if you have a digital camera, you don't have to come here. You can

_____ _____ directly to our website.

너의 디지털 사진들을 전송하다

W Thank you.

12 언급 유무 파악

대화를 듣고, 여자가 일일교장이 되어 하고 싶은 일로 언급되지 않은 것을 고르시오.

① 등교 시간 늦추기
② 수업 시간 줄이기
③ 낮잠 시간 만들기
④ 개인 활동 시간 주기
⑤ 숙제 없는 날 선포하기

M What are you doing?

W I'm applying for the "Principal for a Day" contest. If I win the contest, I can be the principal for a day.

M What are you going to do if you become the principal for a day?

W First, I'll declare the day " _____, _____ _____ _____."

무시험, 숙제 없는 날

M I guess students will like you a lot.

W Then, I'll allow students to _____ _____ _____ _____.

한 시간 늦게 등교하다

M That's a great idea. There'll be no students who are late.

W Finally, I'll _____ _____ _____ _____ and

하루 수업을 오전으로 제한하다

_____ _____ _____ in the afternoon.

학생들이 좋아하는 일을 무엇이든 하게 하다

M Wow! It sounds like my dream school.

13 특정 정보 파악(도표)

기차를 탄 시각과 소요 시간을 파악하면 도착지를 유추할 수 있다.

다음 표를 보면서 대화를 듣고, 여자가 탄 기차를 고르시오.

	Train No	Departure	Arrival	Time (departure-arrival)
①	S1	Busan	Seoul	2:00~6:00 p.m.
②	D1	Busan	Daejeon	2:00~4:00 p.m.
③	S2	Busan	Seoul	3:00~7:00 p.m.
④	D2	Busan	Daejeon	3:00~5:00 p.m.
⑤	S3	Busan	Seoul	5:00~9:00 p.m.

고난도

[Telephone rings.]

M Hello?

W Hi, Alex. I have just gotten on the train and it has just left now.

M Linda, I thought you took the 2 o'clock train.

W I was going to catch the two o'clock train, but I missed it.

M _____ _____ _____ _____ _____ _____ , then you
3시 기차를 탄다면
will arrive one hour later than scheduled.

W Yes. _____ _____ _____ _____ _____ _____ unless there are delays.
4시간 정도 걸릴 것이다
Will you pick me up at the station?

M Of course. Have a nice trip and see you then.

---

14 소재 파악(담화)

따분하거나(bored) 피곤할(tried) 때, 졸릴(sleepy) 때한다는 말에 유의한다.

다음을 듣고, This가 가리키는 것을 고르시오.

① 하품　　② 트림
③ 방귀　　④ 재채기
⑤ 딸꾹질

고난도

W This is the coming in and out of air at the same time. We do this almost every day. We
do this _____ _____ _____ _____ _____ . However, this helps
따분하거나 피곤할 때
the brain by cooling brain cells. When we do this, most people think that we are
_____ . We tend to do this _____ _____ _____ _____ _____
졸린　　　　　　　　　　　　　옆 사람이 반복적으로 이것을 할 때
_____ _____ _____ .

---

15 할 일 파악

자물쇠 수리공이 수리를 하는 동안에 여자는 미국에 계신 부모님께 소포를 부칠 곳으로 갈 것이다.

대화를 듣고, 여자가 할 일로 가장 적절한 것을 고르시오.

① 집 청소하기
② 우체국에 가기
③ 항공권 예매하기
④ 현관 자물쇠 수리하기
⑤ 고객서비스 센터에 전화하기

[Mobile phone rings.]

M Hi, honey! What's up?

W I'm trying to get into our house, but the new doorlock seems to be _____ _____
고장 난
_____ .

M Really? Why don't you call customer service?

W I already did. They're going to _____ _____ _____ .
수리공을 보내다

M I see. How long is it going to take him to arrive?

W They said no more than thirty minutes.

M Then what are you going to do _____ _____ _____ ?
그 동안에

W Actually, I'd like to _____ _____ _____ _____ . _____ in America
내 부모님께 소포를 보내다
before the post office closes.

M No worries. Take your time. I'll be home within twenty minutes, and _____ _____
그 문제를 처리하다
_____ _____ _____ .

W Thanks, honey!

---

16 특정 정보 파악(구입할 물건)

대화를 듣고, 여자가 구입할 것을 고르시오.

① fine dust　　② masks
③ a drug store　④ filter—out rate
⑤ a box

W Jake, the fine dust levels are very high today. We're _____ _____ _____ fine
~을 다 써버린
dust masks.

M Do you want me to buy some more at the drug store?

W Well, let's order them online. *[Clicking sound]* This shop has a lot of different kinds. Let's choose one.

M I saw on the news that the filter rate should be at least 90%.

W Okay, then these three models are good options. What about the price? I don't want to
_____ _____ _____ $30 a box.
~이상 (돈을) 쓰다

M Then we have two options left. Shall we order the white ones?

W Yes. Let's _____ _____ _____ .
주문하다

17 적절한 응답

동아리의 회원이 아닌 친구가 동아리 현장 학습에 참여하고 싶을 때 할 수 있는 말을 생각한다.

[17~19] 대화를 듣고, 여자의 마지막 말에 대한 남자의 응답으로 가장 적절한 것을 고르시오.

Man: _____

① I'll ask the teacher.
② I don't know about the fee.
③ I can't wait!
④ I want to get a good score.
⑤ The phone is out of order.

[Telephone rings.]

W Hi, Sam! Do you have any special plans for this weekend?

M Yeah, I'm going on a field trip with my history club on Saturday. We're going to Gyeongju.

W Wow! Sounds great. Actually, I've never been there, but I've heard that it's one of _____ _____ _____ Korean history.
   ～에 대해 배우기 가장 좋은 장소

M Yeah, there are a lot of old temples, towers, and of course museums. But it's _____ _____ tourists.
   항상 ～로 붐비다

W Well, I know that I'm not a member of your club, but can I _____ _____?
   여행에 참여하다

M _____

18 적절한 응답

충고를 해 준 사람에게 할 수 있는 응답을 찾는다.

Man: _____

① I can answer the questions, too.
② Oh, yes. Thanks for your advice.
③ I hope he can feel better by now.
④ I don't know how much it costs to get help.
⑤ Yes, this medicine works well on headaches.

W You _____, Minwoo.
   걱정이 있는 것으로 보이다

M Yes, I am worried because of Jiho.

W What's wrong with him?

M Well, he _____ _____ and wants to talk to no one.
   친한 친구들이 없다

W Really? I hope it's not too serious.

M Me, too. But I _____ _____ about him.
   걱정하지 않을 수 없다

W Then _____ _____ email to 'Dear Wise' to get help?
   ～하는 게 어떠니

M That's a good idea! She loves to answer the questions about school life.

W Do you feel better now?

M _____

19 적절한 응답

식당에서 신용카드로 지불이 가능한지 묻고 있음에 주목한다.

Man: _____

① Thank you for visiting us.
② What is your name, please?
③ You can use the pay phone over there.
④ Certainly, ma'am. May I have your card?
⑤ Of course. There is a bank around the corner.

Do you mind if I pay by check? (수표로 지불해도 되나요?) : Do you mind if ~?는 상대방에게 허락을 구할 때 쓰는 표현이다.

M Did you enjoy your meal?

W Yes. It was nice. How much is it?

M It's $25 in total.

W Do you mind if I _____ _____?
   수표로 지불하다

M I'm sorry, ma'am. I'm afraid that isn't possible.

W But I've always paid by check in this restaurant. What's the problem?

M We used to accept checks, but _____ _____ _____ now. I'm sorry.
   정책이 바뀌었다

W Okay. Can I _____ then?
   신용카드로 지불하다

M _____

20 상황에 맞는 말 찾기

펜이 없는 상황에서 동료가 여분의 펜을 가지고 있는 것을 알았을 때 할 말을 생각해 본다.

다음 상황 설명 듣고, Tom이 Sam에게 할 말로 가장 적절한 것을 고르시오.

Tom: _____

① Hey, can I borrow a pen there?
② Excuse me. Can you say that again?
③ It doesn't work. Give me another one.
④ Don't forget to take notes. I'll copy yours.
⑤ Don't throw it away. You can use it later.

W Tom works for a company. He is in a meeting now. He _____ in order to take some notes. He finds that he forgot to bring one. Sam, his co-worker, is sitting next to Tom and he _____ in his upper pocket. Tom _____ _____ _____ from him. In this situation, what would Tom say to Sam?
   펜이 필요하다 / 여분의 펜을 가지고 있다 / 그 펜을 빌리고 싶어 한다

적절한 응답/상황에 적절한 말

무엇을 평가하는가?	일상생활이나 친숙한 일반적 주제에 관한 말이나 대화를 듣고 상황 및 대화의 흐름을 추론할 수 있는지 평가한다.
어떻게 출제되는가?	• 대화를 듣고, 남자의 마지막 말에 대한 여자의 응답으로 가장 적절한 것을 고르시오. • 대화를 듣고, 여자의 마지막 말에 대한 남자의 응답으로 가장 적절한 것을 고르시오. • 다음 상황 설명을 듣고, Sean이 엄마에게 할 말로 가장 적절한 것을 고르시오.

key solution

❶ 적절한 응답을 고르는 경우, 전반적인 내용을 이해하면서 마지막 말에 집중한다.

❷ 상황에 적절한 말을 고르는 문제의 경우, 전체적인 상황을 파악하며 듣도록 한다.

[기출로 전략 확인]

대화를 듣고, 남자의 마지막 말에 대한 여자의 응답으로 가장 적절한 것을 고르시오.

[2017 기출]

Woman: _____

① Don't worry. We can be a great team.

② Congratulations! I knew you'd win.

③ No, I'm not interested in singing at all.

④ I've never considered joining the contest.

⑤ Thanks for helping me.

. . . .

W Mike, are you going to join the singing contest?

M I'm thinking about it, but I'm scared to sing in front of people.

W Don't be. You're a good singer.

M At the last contest, I made a lot of mistakes during my song.

W Why don't we join the contest as a team? If you are in trouble, I can help you.

M I don't know. I don't want to look bad in front of everyone again. ──────▶ ❶ 남자가 실수를 걱정하며 노래 대회에 나가길 주저하고 있는 마지막 말에 집중한다.

여 Mike, 너 노래 대회에 참가할 거니?

남 생각 중이야. 하지만 사람들 앞에서 노래하는 게 두려워.

여 그러지 마. 너 노래 잘 하잖아.

남 마지막 대회에서도 노래 중에 실수를 많이 했어.

여 팀으로 대회에 참여하면 어떨까? 너가 실수하면 내가 도와줄 수 있잖아.

남 모르겠어. 모두들 앞에서 또 실수하길 원하지 않아.

대화를 듣고, 남자의 마지막 말에 대한 여자의 응답으로 가장 적절한 것을 고르시오. [2018 기출]

Woman: _____

① I left my wallet in the shop.
② I can't lend you my computer.
③ This coffee machine doesn't work.
④ I can't move because my back hurts.
⑤ The papers don't come out of the printer.

만점 잡는 문장　**W** Hi. I bought a printer from your shop last week, but there's a little problem with it.

⋮

M Thank you. Can you tell me what the problem is?

다음 상황 설명을 듣고, Jiho가 Mr. Jung에게 할 말로 가장 적절한 것을 고르시오. [2018 기출]

Jiho: Mr. Jung, _____

① when does the music concert begin?
② where should I put my new textbooks?
③ can I practice my violin in the living room?
④ could you tell me where the music room is?
⑤ how can I make a photocopy of this timetable?

만점 잡는 문장　**M** Jiho decides to ask Mr. Jung where the music room is.

● 축하/감사

Congratulations. You deserve it. 축하해. 넌 자격이 있어.

Thanks for helping me. 도와줘서 고마워.

● 거절/제안

Sorry. I'm busy this Saturday. 미안. 나 토요일에 바빠.

No, I'm not interested in singing at all. 아니. 난 노래 부르는 것에 전혀 관심이 없어.

You should make sure the website is safe first. 우선 넌 그 웹사이트가 안전한지 알아봐야 해.

● 격려/후회

Don't worry. We can be a great team. 걱정 마. 우리는 멋진 팀이 될 수 있어.

That's too bad. Cheer up. 안됐다. 힘내.

Oh, no. I should have studied harder. 이럴 수가. 내가 공부를 더 열심히 해야 했어.

학년　　반　　번
이름

01 대화를 듣고, 남자가 구입하려는 휴대 전화 고리를 고르시오.

① ② ③ ④ ⑤

02 대화를 듣고, 남자가 여자에게 전화를 건 목적으로 가장 적절한 것을 고르시오.

① 여자의 첼로를 빌리려고
② 음악 선생님의 연락처를 알아보려고
③ 음악 수업 준비물에 대해 물어보려고
④ 바이올린을 빌릴 수 있는지 알아보려고
⑤ 아파서 내일 학교에 못 간다고 알려주려고

03 다음 그림의 상황에 가장 적절한 대화를 고르시오.

① ② ③ ④ ⑤

04 대화를 듣고, 두 사람이 만나기로 한 장소를 고르시오.

① 쇼핑몰 ② 영화관
③ 해변 ④ 샌드위치 가게
⑤ 수족관

고난도
05 대화를 듣고, 두 사람의 휴가 계획으로 언급되지 않은 것을 고르시오.

① 바다에서의 수영 ② 숲에서의 산책
③ 천문대 방문 ④ 역사 박물관 관람
⑤ 호텔에서의 저녁식사

06 대화를 듣고, 두 사람의 관계로 가장 적절한 것을 고르시오.

① 공무원 – 시민
② 관광객 – 가이드
③ 택시 기사 – 승객
④ 주유소 직원 – 손님
⑤ 보험회사 직원 – 고객

07 다음을 듣고, 두 사람의 대화가 어색한 것을 고르시오.

① ② ③ ④ ⑤

08 대화를 듣고, 남자가 여자에게 부탁한 일로 가장 적절한 것을 고르시오.

① UCC 영상 리뷰하기 ② UCC 촬영 돕기
③ UCC 토픽 정하기 ④ UCC 인터뷰 주선하기
⑤ UCC 내용 구성하기

고난도
09 대화를 듣고, Crater Lake에 대한 내용과 일치하지 않는 것을 고르시오.

① 미국의 국립공원 중 하나이다.
② 여자가 어릴 때 살던 곳 근처이다.
③ 봄, 여름, 가을에는 지내기 좋다.
④ 겨울에 눈이 많이 내리는 곳이다.
⑤ 미국 서부에 위치하고 있다.

10 대화를 듣고, 여자가 지불할 금액을 고르시오.

① $36 ② $40
③ $44 ④ $72
⑤ $80

점수 /20

11 대화를 듣고, 두 사람이 대화하는 장소로 가장 적절한 곳을 고르시오.

① 노래방　　　　　② 전자 상가
③ 녹음 스튜디오　　④ 라디오 방송국
⑤ 전자기기 수리점

12 다음을 듣고, 내용과 일치하는 것을 고르시오.

① 졸업 시험 정보를 제공하고 있다.
② 장래 직업 선호도를 조사하고 있다.
③ 다음 주간 행사 일정을 안내하고 있다.
④ 선배와의 대화에 참석을 권유하고 있다.
⑤ 졸업생의 직업 만족도를 분석하고 있다.

고난도
13 다음 표를 보면서 대화를 듣고, 남자가 선택하게 될 좌석의 구역을 고르시오.

Robertson Stadium Ticket Prices

	North Stand	South Stand
Lower Row	$21	$39
Middle Row	$15	$29
Upper Row	$10	$19

① North Stand – Lower Row
② North Stand – Middle Row
③ North Stand – Upper Row
④ South Stand – Lower Row
⑤ South Stand – Middle Row

14 다음을 듣고, 무엇에 관한 설명인지 고르시오.

① school　　　　② exam
③ luck　　　　　④ happiness
⑤ communication

15 대화를 듣고, 두 사람이 대화 직후에 할 일로 가장 적절한 것을 고르시오.

① 학교에 가기
② 병원에 가기
③ 외식하러 가기
④ 집에서 휴식하기
⑤ 패스트푸드점에 가기

16 대화를 듣고, 남자가 선택할 방과 후 활동으로 가장 적절한 것을 고르시오.

① 　② 　③
④ 　⑤

17 대화를 듣고, 여자의 심정으로 가장 적절한 것을 고르시오.

① calm　　　　② excited
③ worried　　　④ happy
⑤ gloomy

[18~19] 대화를 듣고, 남자의 마지막 말에 대한 여자의 응답으로 가장 적절한 것을 고르시오.

18 Woman: _____

① How much do I owe you then?
② Are you going to buy another one?
③ I need to visit the store tomorrow.
④ I was surprised to see it was on sale.
⑤ Oh, it looks like I missed a good chance!

19 Woman: _____

① What day are you free then?
② Sorry but I don't like Italian food much.
③ Thanks but I have a meeting on Wednesday.
④ Oh, will you? That's very kind of you, Mark.
⑤ Good choice. Let's have Chinese food this time.

20 다음 상황 설명을 듣고, Susan이 남자에게 할 말로 가장 적절한 것을 고르시오.

Susan: _____

① Please help yourself.
② I'd like to order more pizzas.
③ I think you should go next door.
④ Thank you for coming to my place.
⑤ I'm sorry you have the wrong number.

다시 들으면서 듣기 만점에 도전하세요!
Dictation: 스크립트의 주요 부분을 다시 들으면서!
실전 ➕: 세부 정보가 많은 스크립트를 다른 문제로 샅샅이!

---

01 그림 정보 파악(사물)

선택지의 그림을 보면서 heart, star, jewel 등 형태를 묘사하는 표현을 예상해 본다.

대화를 듣고, 남자가 구입하려는 휴대 전화 고리를 고르시오.

① ②
③ ④
⑤

W Look at those _____ _____.
　　　　　　　　　　　휴대 전화 고리
M They are cute. I want to buy one for my daughter.
W She'll be happy to get one. I think the stars look pretty.
M Sorry. She already has lots of stars in her room.
W Oh, she _____ _____ _____ _____.
　　　　별에 싫증날 수도 있다
M Right. So I'm going to choose one from the two heart-shaped ones.
W How about the one with some jewels? It looks beautiful to me.
M Does it? But jewels _____ _____ _____.
　　　　　　　　　　쉽게 빠질 수도 있다
W Then you have only one choice.

---

02 전화한 목적

I'm calling you to ~ 다음에 나오는 내용에 귀 기울인다.

대화를 듣고, 남자가 여자에게 전화를 건 목적으로 가장 적절한 것을 고르시오.

① 여자의 첼로를 빌리려고
② 음악 선생님의 연락처를 알아보려고
③ 음악 수업 준비물에 대해 물어보려고
④ 바이올린을 빌릴 수 있는지 알아보려고
⑤ 아파서 내일 학교에 못 간다고 알려주려고

[Telephone rings.]
M Hello, Lara. This is Bill.
W Hi, Bill. What's up?
M You know, I _____ _____ _____ today.
　　　　　　　　학교에 못 갔다
W You're coming tomorrow?
M Yes. I'm calling you _____ _____ _____ _____
　　　　　　　　　　　내 악기를 갖고 가야 하는지 알아보려고
_____ for music class.
W You mean Ms. Baker's class tomorrow?
M Yes. As I remember, I _____ _____ _____ _____.
　　　　　　　　　　　내 첼로를 가져가야 한다
W You're right. Gee, I almost forgot that. We're going to _____
　　　　　　　　　　　　　　　　　　　　　　　우리 각자의 악기를 연주하다
_____. So I have to bring my violin.
M I guess I helped you. I'll see you tomorrow. Bye.

---

03 상황에 적절한 대화(그림)

자동차 고장이나 수리에 관한 대화를 추측해 본다.

다음 그림의 상황에 가장 적절한 대화를 고르시오.

① ② ③ ④ ⑤

① M You _____ here, ma'am. It's close to the bus stop.
　　　　주차하면 안 된다
　W Oh, I'm sorry. Is there a parking lot near here?
② M Did you fasten your seat belt?
　W Sure. I always do whenever I drive.
③ M What seems to be the problem, ma'am?
　W I hear _____ _____ _____ _____.
　　　　엔진에서 나는 이상한 소리
④ M Oh, you have a flat tire.
　W Thank you _____ _____ _____ _____. I'll take it to the garage.
　　　　　　　　내게 알려줘서
⑤ M Are you OK now?
　W I still _____ _____ _____.
　　　미열이 좀 있다

04 특정 정보 파악(장소)

대화를 듣고, 두 사람이 만나기로 한 장소를 고르시오.

① 쇼핑몰　　　② 영화관
③ 해변　　　　④ 샌드위치 가게
⑤ 수족관

➕

대화를 듣고, 무엇에 관한 내용인지 고르시오.

① 학교 생활　　② 봉사 활동
③ 환경 보호　　④ 방학 계획
⑤ 장래 희망

[Cellphone rings.]

W Hi, Roy. I can't believe exams are finally over!

M Same here! _____ _____ _____ _____ _____ on the first day of
〔무엇을 할 거니?〕
vacation?

W I was thinking we could go to the beach to _____ _____ _____ .
〔서핑하는 법을 배우다〕

M Well, I'd love to, but I don't want to get a sunburn on the first day of vacation. What
about visiting the aquarium or going shopping?

W Come on! Let's _____ _____ . It'll probably be more exciting.
〔새로운 무언가를 하다〕

M Okay, okay. Surfing should be at the top of our list of things to do. But first, I'm starving.
Let's talk about it over lunch.

W Good idea. We can _____ _____ over lunch.
〔우리 계획을 정하다〕

M Let's meet at the Uncle Joe's Sandwich Shop in 30 minutes.

[고난도]

05 언급 유무 파악(대화)

대화를 듣고, 두 사람의 휴가 계획으로 언급되지 않은 것을 고르시오.

① 바다에서의 수영
② 숲에서의 산책
③ 천문대 방문
④ 역사 박물관 관람
⑤ 호텔에서의 저녁식사

M What will the weather be like during our holidays?

W It's going to be fine for the first week.

M Great. There will be no problem at the beach.

W Are we going to _____ _____ _____ all day long?
〔바다에서 수영하다〕

M Of course not. I'm planning to _____ _____ _____ _____
〔근처 숲에서 산책하다〕
_____ .

W Wow, that's wonderful. I like to breathe in the fresh air of the forest, too.

M And the next day we'll _____ _____ _____ _____ .
〔역사 박물관에 가다〕

W That's good. I like history.

M And after that we'll _____ _____ _____ _____ near the museum.
〔호텔에서 저녁식사를 즐기다〕

---

06 관계 파악

주유하고 엔진 오일 및 배터리 점검을 하는 사람과 관련된 것을 고른다.

대화를 듣고, 두 사람의 관계로 가장 적절한 것을 고르시오.

① 공무원 – 시민
② 관광객 – 가이드
③ 택시 기사 – 승객
④ 주유소 직원 – 손님
⑤ 보험회사 직원 – 고객

M Can I help you, ma'am?

W _____ _____ , please.
〔기름을 가득 채워주세요〕

M Do you want me to take a look under the hood?

W Yes, please.

M You're a little low on engine oil. I'll _____ _____ _____
〔공짜로 기름을 좀 넣다〕
_____ .

W Thanks.

M I'll check the battery for you, too.

W Thank you. Ah, I _____ _____ you can do me a favor?
〔~인지 아닌지 궁금하다〕

M Sure. What is it?

W Well, I hate to say this, but _____ _____ . Do you happen to know where the City
〔난 길을 잃었다〕
Hall is?

M Oh, it's just up this road a bit. First, drive to the first intersection. Then you can see it on
your left.

W Thanks.

음식이 상하는 날씨에 대해 생각해 본다.

다음을 듣고, 두 사람의 대화가 <u>어색한</u> 것을 고르시오.

① ② ③ ④ ⑤

How much do I owe you? (제가 얼마를 드려야 하죠?) : 지불할 금액을 물어볼 때 쓰는 표현이다.

① W I don't like the color. Show me another, please.

   M How about this one? It's much brighter.

② W This meat smells strange. I'm afraid _____ _____ .

그것이 상했다

   M It's _____ _____ _____ . It will be OK soon.

추운 날씨 때문에

③ W How much do _____ _____ ?

내가 당신에게 빚지다

   M It's $30 but there is a $3 _____ _____ .

배달비

④ W I bought this last night and I'd like _____ _____ .

환불

   M What seems to be the problem, ma'am?

⑤ W Can I see your newspaper for a moment?

   M No problem. Here you are.

고난도

08 부탁한 일

대화를 듣고, 남자가 여자에게 부탁한 일로 가장 적절한 것을 고르시오.

① UCC 영상 리뷰하기
② UCC 촬영 돕기
③ UCC 토픽 정하기
④ UCC 인터뷰 주선하기
⑤ UCC 내용 구성하기

➕ 대화를 듣고, 들려주는 내용과 일치하지 <u>않</u>는 것을 고르시오.

① Jason 은 UCC 학교 과제가 있다.
② Jason 은 과제의 주제를 정했다.
③ Jason의 할아버지는 도자기를 만든다.
④ Jason 은 할아버지의 작업과정을 촬영할 계획이다.
⑤ Jason 은 영상편집을 혼자 할 계획이다.

W Jason, how's it going with your UCC assignment?

M I think it's going well.

W What are you doing it on?

M Well, the topic is about _____ _____ . So I decided to make a UCC video

내가 존경하는 누군가

   about _____ _____ _____ _____ .

가족 중 한 명

W Yeah? Who did you choose?

M My grandpa—he has _____ _____ _____ making beautiful pottery.

~에 그의 삶을 바쳤다

W Sounds wonderful!

M I'm going to film his work process to show how much effort he puts into every single piece of pottery. By the way, after I finish my UCC video, can you watch it and give me some feedback?

고난도

09 내용 일치 파악

대화를 듣고, Crater Lake에 대한 내용과 일치하지 <u>않는</u> 것을 고르시오.

① 미국의 국립공원 중 하나이다.
② 여자가 어릴 때 살던 곳 근처이다.
③ 봄, 여름, 가을에는 지내기 좋다.
④ 겨울에 눈이 많이 내리는 곳이다.
⑤ 미국 서부에 위치하고 있다.

W Where are you from?

M I am from a town near Crater Lake.

W I know Crater Lake. It's _____ _____ _____ _____

가장 아름다운 국립공원들 중 하나

_____ in America, right?

M Yeah. I _____ _____ _____ when I was young.

그 호수 근처에서 살았다

W I think you had a great time there.

M That's true only in the spring, summer and fall.

W What do you mean?

M In the winter I had to _____ _____ _____ _____ _____ every

집 주변의 눈을 치우다

day!

W Ha ha! Crater Lake is one of the snowiest places _____ _____ _____ _____ .

미국 서부에서

10 숫자 정보 파악(금액)

지불할 원래 금액과 할인되는 조건에 주의해서 듣도록 한다.

대화를 듣고, 여자가 지불할 금액을 고르시오.

① $36　　② $40
③ $44　　④ $72
⑤ $80

I'm looking for a pair of gloves. (장갑을 찾고 있다.) : I'm looking for ~.는 무언가(사람, 물건, 직업, 건물 등)를 찾을 때 쓰는 표현이다.

M Good morning. How may I help you?
W I'm looking for a pair of gloves.
M Are they for you?
W No, they're for my husband.
M OK. How about these black leather ones?
W They look good. How much are they?
M _____.
　　　　40달러예요
W Good. I'll _____. You take credit cards, don't you?
　　　　　　그것들을 사다
M Sure, ma'am. But _____ _____ _____ _____, you'll get _____
　　　　　　만약 현금으로 지불하면　　　　　　　　　　10% 할인하여
_____.
W Sorry I _____ _____ _____ now. Here's my card.
　　　충분한 현금이 없다

11 대화 장소 파악

song book, microphone 등 장소를 결정하는 표현을 놓치지 않는다.

대화를 듣고, 두 사람이 대화하는 장소로 가장 적절한 곳을 고르시오.

① 노래방　　② 전자 상가
③ 녹음 스튜디오　④ 라디오 방송국
⑤ 전자기기 수리점

W This is great! There's _____ _____ _____ _____.
　　　　　　　　　　큰 TV 화면
M And the air conditioner is also very good.
W I heard from the owner that this has just opened.
M Oh, really? Look at _____ _____ _____. It has a lot of the latest songs.
　　　　　　　이 노래책
W It sure does. Where's the microphone?
M Right here. It's _____ _____ _____ I took it for a pen or something.
　　　　　　너무 세련돼서
W How can I turn it on?
M Let's see. It isn't working.
W Come on. The _____ _____ is broken!
　　　　신형 마이크
M I'll go to the owner and ask for another one.

12 내용 일치 파악(담화)

다음을 듣고, 내용과 일치하는 것을 고르시오.

① 졸업 시험 정보를 제공하고 있다.
② 장래 직업 선호도를 조사하고 있다.
③ 다음 주간 행사 일정을 안내하고 있다.
④ 선배와의 대화에 참석을 권유하고 있다.
⑤ 졸업생의 직업 만족도를 분석하고 있다.

M Attention, please. The student council will be holding an information meeting called '_____ _____ _____' this Friday. We know that you have many
　졸업생과의 대화
questions about jobs in the future. I believe that this information meeting will help you know _____ _____ _____ _____ _____ you want. You will
　직업을 준비하는 방법
_____ _____ _____ _____ our school's graduates. Please
~로부터 유용한 정보를 좀 얻다
_____ _____ this Friday at 4:30 to learn more about jobs you
강당으로 와라
can have.

13 특정 정보 파악(도표)

햇볕에 타는 것과 금액에 맞춰 좌석을 선택하는 과정을 놓치지 않고 듣는다.

다음 표를 보면서 대화를 듣고, 남자가 선택하게 될 좌석의 구역을 고르시오.

Robertson Stadium Ticket Prices

	North Stand	South Stand
Lower Row	$21	$39
Middle Row	$15	$29
Upper Row	$10	$19

① North Stand – Lower Row
② North Stand – Middle Row
③ North Stand – Upper Row
④ South Stand – Lower Row
⑤ South Stand – Middle Row

M Let's buy tickets online.
W Sure. I see upper rows are much cheaper than lower rows.
M Right. I have only $30 for a ticket, but I really want to sit in the lower row.
W Then you have only one choice.
M Well, I _____ _____ _____ _____ _____
　　　북쪽 스탠드에서 내 피부를 태우고 싶지 않다
_____ _____. The sun is still hot in the afternoon.
W You're right. How about the middle row? All the tickets _____ _____.
　　　　　　　　　　　　　　　　　　30달러 미만이다
M That's not a bad idea. If I _____ _____ _____ _____, I can enjoy
　　　　　　　아랫줄을 포기하다
the game _____ _____ _____.
　　　　　남쪽 스탠드에서
W And you won't have to worry about sunburn.

14 소재 파악(담화)

student, semester, questions, grade, problems, studied 등을 놓치지 않는다.

다음을 듣고, 무엇에 관한 설명인지 고르시오.

① school 학교
② exam 시험
③ luck 운
④ happiness 행복
⑤ communication 의사소통

M If you are a student, you are supposed to take this several times a semester or a year. _____ _____ _____ to others or make any noise during this.
아무도 말해서는 안 된다
You will usually get a couple of sheets of paper and see a number of questions printed on them. _____ _____ _____ _____, you do your best to
좋은 점수를 받기 위해서
_____ _____ _____ _____. Though nobody likes to take this,
가능한 한 많은 문제를 풀다
people think this is a necessary thing to see how hard you studied.

15 할 일 파악 – 대화 직후

병원에 혼자 갈 수 없다고 하면서 도움 요청한 것에 상대방이 그렇게 하겠다고 한 점을 참고한다.

대화를 듣고, 두 사람이 대화 직후에 할 일로 가장 적절한 것을 고르시오.

① 학교에 가기
② 병원에 가기
③ 외식하러 가기
④ 집에서 휴식하기
⑤ 패스트푸드점에 가기

M What's the matter, Jessica? You don't look too well!

W I have _____ _____ _____ _____ _____ _____ _____
아주 심한 복통과 고열
all afternoon.

M Did you take any medicine?

W Yes, I did. But it _____ _____ _____. I feel worse.
아무 효과가 없었다

M Sorry to hear that. What did you eat for lunch?

W I just had a hamburger and French fries.

M How was the hamburger cooked?

W Rare. I always like to eat my hamburgers rare.

M Oh, Jessica, I guess you're _____ _____ after eating that. Do
식중독으로 고생을 하고 있는
you think you can go to the clinic?

W I can't go _____ _____ because I've been vomiting all afternoon. Please help me.
혼자서

M Okay, I will.

16 특정 정보 파악(방과후 활동)

대화를 듣고, 남자가 선택할 방과 후 활동으로 가장 적절한 것을 고르시오.

① ②

③ ④

⑤

W Have you _____ _____ _____, Paul?
결심하다

M You mean _____ _____?
방과 후 활동

W Yeah. I'm thinking of taking yoga. It would be fun.

M That's a good choice, Maria. As for me, I like sports.

W I know _____ _____ _____ like soccer, basketball, and baseball.
너는 구기경기를 좋아한다

M You're right. Last year I really enjoyed baseball but now _____
나는 그것이 약간 실증이 난다.
_____ _____ _____.

W What will you do this year, then?

M Well, I'd like to try indoor sports like table tennis or basketball.

W There's no table tennis this year, you know.

M Really? There's _____ _____ then.
딱 한 가지 남은

W I'm afraid so.

17 심정 파악

전화를 받지 않고 늦게 들어오는 아들에 대한 엄마의 심정을 생각해 본다.

대화를 듣고, 여자의 심정으로 가장 적절한 것을 고르시오.

① calm 차분한 ② excited 흥분된
③ worried 걱정되는 ④ happy 행복한
⑤ gloomy 우울한

W It's seven o'clock. I want to know ＿＿＿＿ ＿＿＿＿ ＿＿＿＿.

Mike에게 무슨 일이 생겼는지
M He's just a little late.
W He's never late for dinner.
M Maybe he doesn't realize the time because he's with his friends.
W When did you see him last?
M Four thirty.
W He ＿＿＿＿ ＿＿＿＿ ＿＿＿＿. This is ＿＿＿＿ ＿＿＿＿ ＿＿＿＿.

그의 전화를 받지 않는다 　　 내가 그렇게 걱정하는 이유
M He usually keeps his phone in the pocket of his jacket. Maybe he's not wearing it now.

18 적절한 응답

여자가 백화점을 먼저 나간 후 무슨 일이 있었는지에 집중하여 듣는다.

[18~19] 대화를 듣고, 남자의 마지막 말에 대한 여자의 응답으로 가장 적절한 것을 고르시오.

Woman: ＿＿＿＿＿＿＿

① How much do I owe you then?
② Are you going to buy another one?
③ I need to visit the store tomorrow.
④ I was surprised to see it was on sale.
⑤ Oh, it looks like I missed a good chance!

W That's ＿＿＿＿＿＿＿ I really want! When did you buy it?

최신 MP3 플레이어
M Yesterday, at the Sunrise Department Store.
W Are you kidding? You and I met there and we shopped together.
M Right. But you left the store earlier.
W Yeah. I had to leave earlier because I ＿＿＿＿ ＿＿＿＿ with the dentist.

약속이 있었다
M Right after you left, I ＿＿＿＿ ＿＿＿＿ ＿＿＿＿ anything was on sale.

~인지 알아보려고 위층으로 올라갔다
W You mean this ＿＿＿＿ ＿＿＿＿?

할인 판매 중이었다
M It sure was. Just for one day it was 30% off!
W ＿＿＿＿＿＿＿＿＿

19 적절한 응답

식사 대접을 하겠다는 말에 적절한 응답을 생각해 본다.

Woman: ＿＿＿＿＿＿＿

① What day are you free then?
② Sorry but I don't like Italian food much.
③ Thanks but I have a meeting on Wednesday.
④ Oh, will you? That's very kind of you, Mark.
⑤ Good choice. Let's have Chinese food this time.

I heard it serves great Italian food (거기에서 아주 좋은 이탈리아 음식을 제공한다고 들었다.) : I heard (from) ~.는 '…에서 ~을 들었다'는 의미로 정보나 들은 이야기를 전할 때 쓰는 표현이다.

M Cathy, have you heard about the new Italian restaurant near here?
W ＿＿＿＿ ＿＿＿＿ the Colosseum?

~을 의미하다
M Right. I heard it serves great Italian food.
W Really? I like Italian food.
M Why don't we go there ＿＿＿＿ ＿＿＿＿?

다음 주쯤 언젠가
W Great idea, Mark. When are you free?
M Maybe Tuesday or Wednesday. How about you?
W I have an important meeting on Tuesday, so Wednesday will be fine.
M Good. ＿＿＿＿ ＿＿＿＿ this time.

내가 당신을 대접하겠다
W ＿＿＿＿＿＿＿＿＿

20 상황에 적절한 말(담화)

옆집으로 가야 할 피자가 잘못 배달되어 온 상황임을 파악한다.

다음 상황 설명을 듣고, Susan이 남자에게 할 말로 가장 적절한 것을 고르시오.

Susan: ＿＿＿＿＿＿＿

① Please help yourself.
② I'd like to order more pizzas.
③ I think you should go next door.
④ Thank you for coming to my place.
⑤ I'm sorry you have the wrong number.

W People are having a party in Susan's house. At the start of the party, they eat cake, fruit, and other foods. Then they ＿＿＿＿ ＿＿＿＿ for over two hours. Her father orders

수다를 즐긴다
some Chinese food because they are hungry again. ＿＿＿＿ ＿＿＿＿ ＿＿＿＿ the

잠시 후에
door bell rings. When Susan opens the door she sees a man with three pizzas. She asks him which address he has for the delivery and finds out ＿＿＿＿ ＿＿＿＿ ＿＿＿＿

그녀의 이웃 사람이 그것들을 주문했다
＿＿＿＿＿＿＿. In this situation, what would Susan say to him?

학년　　반　　번

이름

01 대화를 듣고, 남자가 지금 취하고 있는 동작을 고르시오.

02 대화를 듣고, 남자가 도서관을 방문한 목적으로 가장 적절한 것을 고르시오.

① 책을 대출하기 위해
② 책을 반납하기 위해
③ 연체료를 내기 위해
④ 도서관 카드를 만들기 위해
⑤ 책 대출 기간을 연장하기 위해

03 다음 그림의 상황에 가장 적절한 대화를 고르시오.

① ② ③ ④ ⑤

고난도
04 다음 달력을 보면서 대화를 듣고, Rebecca의 생일 파티가 있었던 날짜를 고르시오.

7월						
일	월	화	수	목	금	토
				1	2	3
4	5	6	7	8	9	10
11	12	13	14	15	16	17
18	19	20	21	22	23	24
25	26	27	28	29	30	31

① 7월 13일　　　　② 7월 21일
③ 7월 24일　　　　④ 7월 27일
⑤ 7월 30일

05 대화를 듣고, 두 사람이 대화하는 장소로 가장 적절한 곳을 고르시오.

① 은행　　　　　　② 호텔
③ 대피소　　　　　④ 캠핑장
⑤ 운전면허시험장

고난도
06 대화를 듣고, 여자가 속초에 살았던 연도를 고르시오.

① 2000　　　② 2003　　　③ 2004
④ 2006　　　⑤ 2007

07 다음을 듣고, 두 사람의 대화가 <u>어색한</u> 것을 고르시오.

① ② ③ ④ ⑤

08 대화를 듣고, 여자가 남자에게 부탁한 일로 가장 적절한 것을 고르시오.

① 주문한 음식 확인해 주기
② 음식 포장용 상자 가져다 주기
③ 잘못 주문된 음식을 취소해 주기
④ 추가로 음식 주문 받기
⑤ 남은 음식 배달해 주기

09 대화를 듣고, 여자의 마지막 말에 담긴 의도로 가장 적절한 것을 고르시오.

① 위로　　　　　　② 감사
③ 거절　　　　　　④ 칭찬
⑤ 제안

10 대화를 듣고, 여자가 받을 거스름돈을 고르시오.

① $1　　　② $2　　　③ $3
④ $4　　　⑤ $5

점수

/20

11 대화를 듣고, 여자의 직업으로 가장 적절한 것을 고르시오.

① 국악인　　　② 경찰관　　　③ 아나운서
④ 운동 선수　　⑤ 관광 안내소 직원

12 다음을 듣고, 언급되지 <u>않은</u> 것을 고르시오.

① 진행자 이름　　　② 프로그램 이름
③ 프로그램 내용　　④ 초청 강사 이름
⑤ 프로그램 진행 시간

고난도

13 다음 표를 보면서 대화를 듣고, 남자가 예약할 기차표로 가장 적절한 것을 고르시오.

	도착지	출발일자	편도/왕복	출발 시각
①	서울	20일	편도	07:00
②	서울	20일	왕복	10:00
③	대전	20일	편도	11:30
④	대전	27일	왕복	14:00
⑤	대전	27일	편도	19:00

14 다음을 듣고, 무엇에 관한 설명인지 고르시오.

① 봉사활동　　　② 체육대회
③ 학생회 총회　　④ 학교 축제
⑤ 동아리 장터

15 대화를 듣고, 여자가 대화 직후에 할 일로 가장 적절한 것을 고르시오.

① 영화 관람하기　　② 점심 식사하기
③ 현금 인출하기　　④ 식당 예약하기
⑤ 친구 접대하기

16 대화를 듣고, 남자가 먹을 음식으로 가장 적절한 것을 고르시오.

① 스파게티　　　　② 라면
③ 스테이크　　　　④ 김밥
⑤ 햄버거

17 대화를 듣고, 남자의 마지막 말에 대한 여자의 응답으로 가장 적절한 것을 고르시오.

Woman: _____

① I want to read it again and again.
② I think he is the greatest writer in history.
③ I can give you a ride to the library.
④ I have to return it to him by this Tuesday.
⑤ I see. I will bring it to you tomorrow morning.

[18~19] 대화를 듣고, 여자의 마지막 말에 대한 남자의 응답으로 가장 적절한 것을 고르시오.

18 Man: _____

① She teaches me English once a week.
② I think I have to listen to your advice.
③ She sends me e-mails on Fridays, too.
④ I write to her at least four times a month.
⑤ She doesn't know how to write in English well.

19 Man: _____

① I'm a history lover, too.
② You're not interested in the past.
③ Wow, all of your answers is correct!
④ I promise I'll go to the library with you soon.
⑤ How did you know that history is my favorite?

20 다음 상황 설명을 듣고, Norah가 점원에게 할 말로 가장 적절한 것을 고르시오.

Norah: _____

① Can I leave a message?
② How do you feel about your new job?
③ Are you looking forward to seeing me?
④ Is it okay if I use the phone for a moment?
⑤ Can I try on a T-shirt before I buy it right here?

다시 들으면서 듣기 만점에 도전하세요!
Dictation: 스크립트의 주요 부분을 다시 들으면서!
실전 ⊕: 세부 정보가 많은 스크립트를 다른 문제로 샅샅이!

---

01 그림 정보 파악(동작)

지시되는 동작을 하나씩 머릿속으로 직접 따라해 본다.

대화를 듣고, 남자가 지금 취하고 있는 동작을 고르시오.

① ② ③ ④ ⑤

M I heard you're taking a yoga class every Wednesday and Saturday.
W Yes, I am. I think it's good for the mind as well as the body.
M It's very hard, isn't it?
W No, not at all. It's easy. I'll show you ＿＿＿＿＿ ＿＿＿＿.
　　　　　　　　　　　　　　　　　　　　　　한 가지 간단한 자세
M OK, I'll just give it a try.
W First, stand up straight ＿＿＿＿＿ ＿＿＿＿＿
　　　　　　　　　　　　　두 손을 옆구리에 붙인 채로
　　＿＿＿＿. Next, breathe in deeply and bend your body ＿＿＿＿ slowly
　　　　　　　　　　　　　　　　　　　　　　　　　뒤로　　　　무릎을 구부리지 않고
　　＿＿＿＿ ＿＿＿＿ ＿＿＿＿. Then stay still for a few seconds.
M Like this? Am I doing it right?
W Yes, you're doing it pretty well.

---

02 목적 파악(방문)

방문 목적을 말하고 있는 I'd like to ~ 뒤에 이어지는 말에 귀 기울인다.

대화를 듣고, 남자가 도서관을 방문한 목적으로 가장 적절한 것을 고르시오.

① 책을 대출하기 위해
② 책을 반납하기 위해
③ 연체료를 내기 위해
④ 도서관 카드를 만들기 위해
⑤ 책 대출 기간을 연장하기 위해

W Good afternoon. May I help you?
M Yes, please. I'd like to ＿＿＿＿ ＿＿＿＿ ＿＿＿＿.
　　　　　　　　　　　　　이 책들을 대출하다
W Can I have your library card, please?
M Here it is.
W Sorry, but according to our records, you ＿＿＿＿ ＿＿＿＿, *Harry Potter and*
　　　　　　　　　　　　　　　　　　　그 책을 반납했다
　　the Sorcerer's Stone, ＿＿＿＿ ＿＿＿＿ ＿＿＿＿.
　　　　　　　　　　　　하루 늦게
M I beg your pardon. What should I do?
W You must pay a late charge ＿＿＿＿ ＿＿＿＿ ＿＿＿＿ ＿＿＿＿.
　　　　　　　　　　　　　　　　이 책들을 대출하기 전에
M How much is it?
W It's two dollars.

고난도

03 상황에 적절한 대화(그림)

사무실에서 피자배달을 하는 사람과 나눌 수 있는 대화 상황을 추측해 본다.

다음 그림의 상황에 가장 적절한 대화를 고르시오.

① ② ③ ④ ⑤

You'd better see a doctor. (진찰을 받는 게 좋겠어요.) : You'd better ~.는 충고나 조언을 할 때 쓰는 표현이다.

① W What would you like ＿＿＿＿ ＿＿＿＿?
　　　　　　　　　　　　주문하기
　　M I'd like a combination pizza and a Coke.
② W This pizza looks delicious. Please tell me ＿＿＿＿ ＿＿＿＿ ＿＿＿＿.
　　　　　　　　　　　　　　　　　　　그것을 만드는 방법
　　M You can find the recipe on the Internet.
③ W Hi, I'm from Deli Pizza. Someone ＿＿＿＿ ＿＿＿＿.
　　　　　　　　　　　　　　　　이 피자를 주문했다
　　M Oh, right. Can you give it to the lady over there?
④ W I ate some pizza, and got a stomachache.
　　M That's too bad. You'd better ＿＿＿＿ ＿＿＿＿.
　　　　　　　　　　　　　　　진찰을 받다
⑤ W What do you think of the new teacher?
　　M Well, she is friendly and helpful.

04 특정 정보 파악(날짜)

Rebecca의 생일과 실제로 그녀의 생일 파티가 있었던 날을 잘 듣고 계산해 본다.

다음 달력을 보면서 대화를 듣고, Rebecca의 생일 파티가 있었던 날짜를 고르시오.

7월

일	월	화	수	목	금	토
				1	2	3
4	5	6	7	8	9	10
11	12	13	14	15	16	17
18	19	20	21	22	23	24
25	26	27	28	29	30	31

① 7월 13일 ② 7월 21일
③ 7월 24일 ④ 7월 27일
⑤ 7월 30일

M Oh, no!

W What's the matter with you?

M Rebecca, I totally ＿＿＿＿＿＿ ＿＿＿＿. I'm so sorry.
　　[네 생일을 잊었다]

W It doesn't really matter.

M Was it ＿＿＿＿＿ ＿＿＿＿＿, the 21st? ＿＿＿ ＿＿＿ ＿＿＿＿?
　　　　 [지난 수요일]　　　　　　　　[7월 21일]

W Yes, it was. But the party was ＿＿＿＿ ＿＿＿＿ ＿＿＿. It was on ＿＿＿＿.
　　　　　　　　　　　　　　　　　 [3일 후]　　　　　　　 [토요일]

M How many friends were there at your party?

W Thirteen.

M Anyway, I'm terribly sorry again.

W That's all right.

05 대화 장소 파악

valley, camper, camping experience 등과 관련된 장소를 추론한다.

대화를 듣고, 두 사람이 대화하는 장소로 가장 적절한 곳을 고르시오.

① 은행 ② 호텔
③ 대피소 ④ 캠핑장
⑤ 운전면허시험장

W Hi, there. Was everyone all right last night?

M Well, it was raining so hard that we all ＿＿＿＿ ＿＿＿＿ the van.
　　　　　　　　　　　　　　　　　 [결국 ~에서 잤다]

W I'm glad you're all okay. But I suggest you leave here ＿＿＿ ＿＿＿
　　　　　　　　　　　　　　　　　　　　　　　　 [가능한 한 빨리]
＿＿＿＿.

M What for? Is something wrong?

W The river is overflowing its banks ＿＿＿ ＿＿＿ ＿＿＿ ＿＿＿.
　　　　　　　　　　　　　　　　 [그 폭우 때문에]
Crossing the valley can be dangerous in a few hours.

M Then we'd better get going as soon as we finish packing.

W I hope you have a safe trip home. Then I must get going to warn other campers in this site.

M ＿＿＿＿ ＿＿＿ ＿＿＿ here was just amazing! Thank you for your help.
　　[우리의 야영 경험]

W My pleasure! I hope to see you here again. Drive carefully ＿＿＿ ＿＿＿.
　　　　　　　　　　　　　　　　　　　　　　　 [가파른 언덕길을 내려가다]

M I will. Have a nice day!

06 특정 정보 파악

대화를 듣고, 여자가 속초에 살았던 연도를 고르시오.

① 2000 ② 2003
③ 2004 ④ 2006
⑤ 2007

You can say that again! (맞아!) : 상대방의 의견에 강한 동의를 나타낼 때 쓰는 표현이다.

M Isn't this a picture of you in Sokcho?

W Yes. How did you know ＿＿＿ ＿＿＿ ＿＿＿?
　　　　　　　　　　 [그것이 찍힌 곳]

M I lived there ＿＿＿ ＿＿＿ ＿＿＿.
　　　　　　 [거의 4년 동안]

W Wow. Then, you must know a lot about Sokcho, right?

M Sure. Sokcho has a lot of beautiful beaches and great seafood restaurants.

W You can say that again! By the way, when did you live there?

M ＿＿＿ ＿＿＿ ＿＿＿.
　 [2002년에서 2005년까지]

W Really? I can't believe it! ＿＿＿ ＿＿＿ ＿＿＿ you were there, I was
　　　　　　　　　　　 [마지막 2년]
there, too.

07 어색한 대화 찾기

다음을 듣고, 두 사람의 대화가 <u>어색한</u> 것을 고르시오.

①   ②   ③   ④   ⑤

① **W** Our _____ _____ are tomorrow, aren't they?
    <small>기말시험</small>
  M Yes, they are. I'm so nervous.

② **W** Have you seen my MP3 player, Dad?
  M Yes. I saw it on the upper shelf of the bookcase yesterday.

③ **W** What's _____ _____ _____ _____ _____ this weekend?
    <small>날씨가 ~할 것이다</small>
  M It's supposed to be sunny.

④ **W** What kind of movie _____ _____ _____ _____ _____?
    <small>보고 싶다</small>
  M I'd like to see an adventure movie like *Indiana Jones*.

⑤ **W** If I have my laptop computer fixed, I can use it for a long time.
  M You're right. You _____ _____ _____ _____ _____ soon.
    <small>새 것을 사야만 한다</small>

08 부탁한 일 파악

<small>포장용 박스를 주문했고, 남자가 즉시 갖다 주겠다고 한 점을 참고한다.</small>

대화를 듣고, 여자가 남자에게 부탁한 일로 가장 적절한 것을 고르시오.

① 주문한 음식 확인해주기
② 음식 포장용 상자 가져다주기
③ 잘못 주문된 음식 취소해주기
④ 추가로 음식 주문 받기.
⑤ 남은 음식 배달해주기

M Here's _____ _____, ma'am.
    <small>네가 주문한 것</small>
W This is not what I ordered!
M _____ _____ _____ says that you ordered chicken combo A.
  <small>주문서</small>
W Yes, but there are too many legs here.
M Sorry, ma'am, but our chicken combo A _____ _____ _____.
                            <small>6개의 닭다리가 나오다</small>
W Really? I didn't know that. Let me check the menu. Umm... I guess you're right.
M Then would you like to _____ _____ _____, ma'am?
                      <small>주문을 바꾸다</small>
W No, it's all right. It's my fault. I will take some of them home.
M Very well. Is there anything else I can do for you, ma'am?
W Yes, would you _____ _____ _____ _____?
               <small>나에게 포장용 상자를 주다</small>
M No problem, ma'am. I'll get you one right away.

09 마지막 말 의도

대화를 듣고, 여자의 마지막 말에 담긴 의도로 가장 적절한 것을 고르시오.

① 위로   ② 감사
③ 거절   ④ 칭찬
⑤ 제안

＋

대화를 듣고 남자가 할 일을 고르시오.

① 독서하기   ② 발음 훈련하기
③ 책 구입하기   ④ 운동하기
⑤ 숙제하기

W Hi, Kevin. How are you today?
M *[Worried]* So so. The speech contest is next week. That means my performance is next week, too.
W You don't _____ _____ much _____.
      <small>자신감을 가진 것처럼 보이다</small>
M Well, I'm practicing pretty hard every day, but I still _____ _____ _____.
                                        <small>잘 할 수 없다</small>
W I'm sorry to hear that. What do you think is the problem?
M First of all, my pronunciation isn't clear enough, but I don't know how to improve it.
W Well, I think practicing while holding a pencil in your mouth could help. _____ _____ _____ try that?
                                            <small>~하는 게 어때?</small>

10 숫자 정보 파악(금액)

가격, 할인율, 지불한 돈을 잘 듣고 메모한 후 계산해 본다.

대화를 듣고, 여자가 받을 거스름을 고르시오.

① $1
② $2
③ $3
④ $4
⑤ $5

M Good afternoon. May I help you?

W Yes, please. Could you help me find an easy book to read?

M Sure. What is it for, ma'am?

W I want a book for bedtime reading.

M In that case, I'd recommend this book of poems. See if you like it.

W Looks very good and the poems are easy to understand, too. How much is it?

M _____. But all poetry books are _____
그것은 10달러이다   정가에서 20% 할인된
_____.

W I see. Here's _____ _____.
10달러 지폐

M Here's your change.

11 직업 파악

한국 문화 행사에 대한 전반적인 정보를 제공하고 있음에 유의하여 직업을 선택한다.

대화를 듣고, 여자의 직업으로 가장 적절한 것을 고르시오.

① 국악인
② 경찰관
③ 아나운서
④ 운동 선수
⑤ 관광 안내소 직원

W Good morning. May I help you?

M Oh, yes. I'm looking for a brochure on _____ _____ in Seoul.
한국 문화 행사

W Is there something in particular that you're interested in?

M Well, I'm not sure, but I wonder if I can enjoy _____ _____.
한국 전통 음악

W You mean you want to see _____, right?
한국 음악 공연들

M Yes, I'd love to go to a *Pansori* concert.

W Here's a brochure. You can find _____ _____ such concerts in it.
~에 관한 정보

M Thank you so much.

12 언급 유무 파악(담화)

다음을 듣고, 언급되지 않은 것을 고르시오.

① 진행자 이름
② 프로그램 이름
③ 프로그램 내용
④ 초청 강사 이름
⑤ 프로그램 진행 시간

M Welcome to _____ _____ from Channel 17. I am _____, Dr.
우주 쇼   여러분의 진행자
Morris, and this show will bring you _____ _____.
우주 여행에 대한 정보   오늘의 초청 강사
_____ _____, Professor James Hudson at the MIT University, is going to talk
about space travel. He is an expert on space travel, and he believes that space travel is
coming to us sooner than we think. Welcome to the show, Professor James Hudson.

고난도

13 특정 정보 파악(도표)

날짜, 편도인지 왕복인지에 유의하며 듣는다.

다음 표를 보면서 대화를 듣고, 남자가 예약할 기차표로 가장 적절한 것을 고르시오.

	도착지	출발일자	편도/왕복	출발 시각
①	서울	20일	편도	07:00
②	서울	20일	왕복	10:00
③	대전	20일	편도	11:30
④	대전	27일	왕복	14:00
⑤	대전	27일	편도	19:00

M Excuse me. I reserved the train ticket _____ for August
서울에서 대전으로
20th. But I've put off my trip _____ _____.
27일까지

W You want to change your reservation from the 20th to the 27th, right?

M Yes, correct.

W Is that one way or round trip?

M _____, please.
왕복

W What time of the day would you like to go?

M _____ _____ _____, please.
오후에

W Let me check to see if it's available in the computer first.

14 소재 파악(담화)

activity clubs, booths, information, various clubs 등 힌트를 놓치지 않는다.

다음을 듣고, 무엇에 관한 설명인지 고르시오.

① 봉사활동   ② 체육대회
③ 학생회 총회   ④ 학교 축제
⑤ 동아리 장터

W As many of you already know, next Thursday, March 18, the student council will be holding a fair for the activity clubs. All the clubs can ＿＿＿＿＿ ＿＿＿＿＿ ＿＿＿＿＿ (정보를 제공하는 부스를 설치하다) about their programs and activities. The fair will be held after school, between 5 p.m. and 8 p.m. We ＿＿＿＿＿ (강하게 권장하다) everyone—especially freshmen—to attend it and get to know about the various clubs at our school. There will be free drinks offered to ＿＿＿＿＿ ＿＿＿＿＿ ＿＿＿＿＿ (참석하는 모두). Please do not miss this great event!

15 할 일 파악 – 대화 직후

영화 및 식사를 하기 전에 해야 할 일을 말하는 부분을 놓치지 않는다.

대화를 듣고, 여자가 대화 직후에 할 일로 가장 적절한 것을 고르시오.

① 영화 관람
② 점심 식사
③ 현금 인출
④ 식당 예약
⑤ 친구 접대

I don't really want to go there right now. (당장은 정말 가고 싶지 않다.) : I don't really want to ~.는 제안을 받았지만 원하지 않을 때 쓰는 표현이다.

M Lisa, why don't we go to the movies?
W I don't really want to go there right now. You know, ＿＿＿＿＿ (난 배가 고파 죽겠다). Let's have something to eat. It's lunchtime.
M Sounds great. Where shall we ＿＿＿＿＿ ＿＿＿＿＿ (점심을 먹다)?
W How about that Italian restaurant over there?
M It looks like an expensive one.
W Yes. So I think I should ＿＿＿＿＿ ＿＿＿＿＿ (은행에서 돈을 좀 인출하다) from the bank first.
M I think I don't have enough money, either.
W Don't worry. This is on me. I mean it's ＿＿＿＿＿ ＿＿＿＿＿ (나의 대접).
M Thank you.

16 특정 정보 파악(먹을 음식)

음식 재료를 메모한 후 그것으로 만들 수 있는 음식을 선택한다.

대화를 듣고, 남자가 먹을 음식으로 가장 적절한 것을 고르시오.

① 스파게티   ② 라면
③ 스테이크   ④ 김밥
⑤ 햄버거

Help yourself. (맘껏 드세요.) : 음식을 권유하는 표현이다.

M Happy birthday, Hana.
W Thank you for coming. Come on in, Fred.
M Hana, what a pretty hat!
W My mother bought it for my birthday present. She also ＿＿＿＿＿ ＿＿＿＿＿ (이 음식을 만들었다), too.
M It looks very delicious.
W Yes, it does. It's a popular ＿＿＿＿＿ ＿＿＿＿＿ (한국식 간편 음식). Help yourself.
M I haven't tried that before. Are there noodles in it?
W Nope. It's made of ＿＿＿＿＿ ＿＿＿＿＿ (흰밥), ham, eggs, some ＿＿＿＿＿ (야채), and ＿＿＿＿＿ (여러 장의 김) ＿＿＿＿＿ ＿＿＿＿＿.
M OK. I'll try some.

17 적절한 응답

빨리 독후감을 써야하는 남자에게 책을 가지고 있는 여자가 할 말을 생각한다.

대화를 듣고, 남자의 마지막 말에 대한 여자의 응답으로 가장 적절한 것을 고르시오.

Woman: _____

① I want to read it again and again.
② I think he is the greatest writer in history.
③ I can give you a ride to the library.
④ I have to return it to him by this Tuesday.
⑤ I see. I will bring it to you tomorrow morning.

[Telephone rings.]

M Hi, Gina! Do you have the novel The Old Man and The Sea?
W Yes, I do. That's by Hemingway, one of my favorite writers. I have a collection of his books.
M Great! _____ _____ _____ ?
　　　　　　　　　그걸 빌려도 될까요?
W Sure, it's _____. When do you need it?
　　　　읽을 가치가 있는
M Well, actually, I have to write a book review of it by next Friday. I should start reading it as soon as possible.
W _____

대화를 듣고, 여자가 내일 할 일을 고르시오.

① 독서평 쓰기　　② 책 구매하기
③ 책 가져다 주기　④ 책 되돌려주기
⑤ 숙제 도와주기

18 적절한 응답

[18~19] 대화를 듣고, 여자의 마지막 말에 대한 남자의 응답으로 가장 적절한 것을 고르시오.

Man: _____

① She teaches me English once a week.
② I think I have to listen to your advice.
③ She sends me e-mails on Fridays, too.
④ I write to her at least four times a month.
⑤ She doesn't know how to write in English well.

W Are you playing computer games again, Elvis?
M No, Mom.
W Then what are you doing now?
M I'm _____ _____ in English to my Australian e-pal, Melina.
　　　이메일을 쓰고 있는
W You _____ _____ _____ _____, right?
　　지난 금요일에도 이메일을 썼다
M Yes, Mom. But I want to improve my English writing skills _____ _____
　　　　　　　　　　　　　　　　　　　　　　　　　가능한 한 빨리
_____.
W Oh, I see. Then, _____ _____ _____ _____ to your e-pal?
　　　　　　　　　　너는 얼마나 자주 쓰니
M _____

19 적절한 응답

퀴즈를 풀면서 지금까지 어떻게 풀고 있는지에 대한 응답으로 알맞은 것을 고른다.

Man: _____

① I'm a history lover, too.
② You're not interested in the past.
③ Wow, all of your answers are correct!
④ I promise I'll go to the library with you soon.
⑤ How did you know that history is my favorite?

W Look. Here's the 20th Century World History Quiz in the magazine.
M Oh, let me _____ _____ _____. You know, I'm a world history lover.
　　　　　　　그것을 한번 시도해 보다
W All right. First question: When did the Second World War take place?
M I guess it lasted from 1939 to 1945.
W The second question: How long has the United Nations been _____ _____ ?
　　　　　　　　　　　　　　　　　　　　　　　　　　　　　　　존재하는
M Uh, since 1945 when World War II ended. So the answer is 68 years.
W Hmm. Next question: How long were the Beatles together?
M Well, they started in 1960 and _____ _____ _____, so they were
　　　　　　　　　　　　　　　　　　1970년에 해체됐다
together for 10 years. How am I doing so far?
M _____

20 상황에 적절한 말(담화)

휴대 전화를 집에 두고 온 상황에서 꼭 전화를 사용할 필요가 있을 때 할 말을 생각해 본다.

다음 상황 설명을 듣고, Norah가 점원에게 할 말로 가장 적절한 것을 고르시오.

Norah: _____

① Can I leave a message?
② How do you feel about your new job?
③ Are you looking forward to seeing me?
④ Is it okay if I use the phone for a moment?
⑤ Can I try on a T-shirt before I buy it right here?

M Norah was on her way home. Then she saw a nice T-shirt in a clothing store. She thought it would look good on her brother, Harry. So Norah _____
　　　　　　　　　　　　　　　　　　　　　　　　　　　　그녀의 동생에게 전화하기를 원했다
_____ to know about his size and his favorite color. But she _____
_____ when she left home. There was _____
그녀의 휴대 전화 가져오는 것을 잊었다
_____ around. So, Norah decided to enter the store and _____
공중전화 박스가 없는
_____. In this situation, what would Norah say
점원에게 도움을 청하다
to the clerk?

숫자 정보 파악

무엇을 평가하는가?	일상생활 관련 대상이나 친숙한 일반적 주제에 관한 말이나 대화를 듣고 세부 정보를 파악할 수 있는지를 평가한다.

어떻게 출제되는가?	• 대화를 듣고, 남자가 지불할 금액을 고르시오.
	• 대화를 듣고, 여자가 지불할 금액을 고르시오.

key solution

❶ 금액을 묻는 경우, 물건의 가격(정가), 구입할 물건, 개수, 행사 혜택, 할인율 등의 정보에 주의해서 듣는다.

[기출로 전략 확인]

대화를 듣고, 남자가 지불할 금액을 고르시오.　　　　　　　　　　　　　[2018 기출]

① $ 5　　　　② $ 10　　　　③ $ 15　　　　④ $ 20　　　　⑤ $ 25

- -

W Welcome to the *Happy Gift Shop*. How may I help you?

M Hi. I'd like to buy some gifts for my parents. Can you recommend something?

W Well, our best-sellers are coffee cups and T-shirts. The cups are $ 5 each and the T-shirts are $ 10 each.

M I'd prefer the coffee cups.

W Okay. If you buy two cups, then you can get an extra one for free.

M Oh, great! I'll take two cups.

W Good choice.

❶ 물건의 정가, 구입할 물건, 행사 혜택, 개수의 정보를 들을 수 있다.

여 *Happy Gift Shop*에 어서 오세요. 무엇을 도와드릴까요?

남 안녕하세요. 부모님께 드릴 선물을 사려고 하는데요. 추천해주실 게 있나요?

여 저희 가게에서 제일 잘 나가는 건 커피 컵과 티셔츠에요. 컵은 개당 5달러고 티셔츠는 개 당 10달러에요.

남 커피 컵이 좋겠네요.

여 알겠습니다. 컵 두개를 사시면 한 개는 공짜로 얻으실 수 있어요.

남 좋네요! 컵 두 개 주세요.

여 좋은 선택이에요.

대화를 듣고, 남자가 지불할 금액을 고르시오.   [2017 기출]

① $ 10   ② $ 20   ③ $ 30
④ $ 40   ⑤ $ 50

만점 잡는 문장   ① This swimsuit is the most popular design and it's just 20 dollars.
                 ② I also need swimming goggles.
                 ③ I'll take the 10 dollar swimming goggles.

대화를 듣고, 여자가 지불할 금액을 고르시오.   [2015 기출]

① $40   ② $50   ③ $60
④ $90   ⑤ $100

만점 잡는 문장   ① A sports uniform is 50 dollars.
                 ② Running shoes are 40 dollars.
                 ③ I can't afford them both. I'll just take the sports uniform for now.

● 가격

Your total is 30 dollars. 전부해서 30달러입니다.

$20 for an adult set and $10 for a junior set.
어른 세트는 20달러이고 주니어 세트는 10달러입니다.

The prices are from 10 dollars to 30 dollars. 가격은 10달러에서 30달러 사이입니다.

● 행사 혜택/할인

If you pay two dollars more, you can get a drink and fries.
2달러를 더 내시면 음료와 감자튀김을 드립니다.

It's $30 a month, but if you sign up for three months, it's only $70.
한 달에 30달러지만 3달을 등록하시면 70달러입니다.

You get 10% off if you pay with this card.
이 카드로 계산하시면 10% 할인이 됩니다.

We can give you a one-dollar discount for each ticket.
각 표에서 1달러씩 할인 받을 수 있습니다.

학년 　 반 　 번

이름

01 다음을 듣고, 남자의 형이 취하고 있는 동작을 고르시오.

① ② ③ ④ ⑤

02 대화를 듣고, 여자가 남자에게 전화한 목적으로 가장 적절한 것을 고르시오.

① 여행 국가에 대해 물으려고
② 여행 일정을 변경하려고
③ 여행지 숙소에 대해 물으려고
④ 애완동물 관리를 부탁하려고
⑤ 집 관리를 부탁하려고

03 다음 그림의 상황에 가장 적절한 대화를 고르시오.

① ② ③ ④ ⑤

04 대화를 듣고, 두 사람이 만나기로 한 요일을 고르시오.

① 금요일 　　　　　 ② 토요일
③ 일요일 　　　　　 ④ 목요일
⑤ 화요일

05 대화를 듣고, 여자의 심정으로 가장 적절한 것을 고르시오.

① happy
② angry
③ worried
④ scared
⑤ disappointed

06 대화를 듣고, 두 사람의 관계로 가장 적절한 것을 고르시오.

① 의사 – 간호사
② 장교 – 사병
③ 영화 감독 – 기자
④ 코치 – 운동 선수
⑤ 물리치료사 – 환자

07 다음을 듣고, 두 사람의 대화가 <u>어색한</u> 것을 고르시오.

① ② ③ ④ ⑤

08 대화를 듣고, 여자가 남자에게 부탁한 일로 가장 적절한 것을 고르시오.

① 추천서 써 주기
② 편지 발송해 주기
③ 보고서 제출해 주기
④ 마감 기한 확인해 주기
⑤ 보고서 제출 여부 확인해 주기

09 다음을 듣고, 무엇에 관한 안내인지 가장 적절한 것을 고르시오.

① 놀이 공원 이용 안내　　② 안전 벨트 착용 요령
③ 정기 열차 운행 일정　　④ 놀이 기구 탑승 수칙
⑤ 미아 발생 신고 요령

10 대화를 듣고, 여자가 지불할 금액을 고르시오.

① 20,000원　　　　　② 16,000원
③ 10,000원　　　　　④ 24,000원
⑤ 15,000원

점수 /20

11 대화를 듣고, 두 사람이 대화하는 장소로 가장 적절한 곳을 고르시오.

① 미용실　　　　　② 세탁소
③ 빨래방　　　　　④ 옷 가게
⑤ 결혼식장

12 다음을 듣고, 재즈기타 그룹 세션에 관해 언급되지 않은 것을 고르시오.

① 세션 내용 소개　　② 세션 등록 방법
③ 세션 등록 기한　　④ 세션 등록 비용
⑤ 그룹 세션 장소

13 다음 쇼핑몰 지도를 보면서 대화를 듣고, 남자가 방문할 곳을 고르시오.

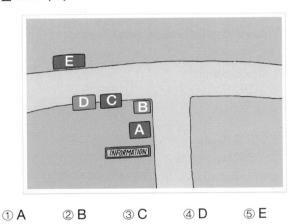

① A　　② B　　③ C　　④ D　　⑤ E

14 다음을 듣고, 무엇에 관한 설명인지 고르시오.

① 동물 권리활동　　② 취미 생활
③ 봉사 활동　　　　④ 애완동물 산책
⑤ 애완동물 미용

15 대화를 듣고, 남자가 할 일로 가장 적절한 것을 고르시오.

① 자동차 주차하기
② 음료수 사러 가기
③ 자리 지키고 있기
④ 다리 아래에 자리 잡기
⑤ 돗자리 가지러 집에 가기

16 대화를 듣고, 남자가 받은 상금을 고르시오.

① $10　　　　　　② $100
③ $500　　　　　④ $1,000
⑤ $2,000

17 대화를 듣고, 여자의 마지막 말에 대한 남자의 응답으로 가장 적절한 것을 고르시오.

Man: _____

① Then let's get there as early as possible.
② Then let's clean up the room.
③ Then I'll get my bike fixed.
④ Then I'll let everyone know about it.
⑤ Then I'll return the printer as soon as possible.

[18~19] 대화를 듣고, 남자의 마지막 말에 대한 여자의 응답으로 가장 적절한 것을 고르시오.

18 Woman: _____

① Well, my house is warm.
② Sure. I'll help you move in.
③ Yes, we are. It's next Saturday.
④ We don't need to move any more.
⑤ The party won't start until you arrive.

고난도
19 Woman: _____

① I made mistakes myself, too.
② It matters that we did our best.
③ That's okay. I can manage that.
④ Here it should be Haiti, not Eiti.
⑤ Don't be afraid of making mistakes.

20 다음 상황 설명을 듣고, Mr. Park이 할 말로 가장 적절한 것을 고르시오.

Mr. Park: _____

① How can I get to your country?
② Can we meet on Saturday or Sunday?
③ Do you like to teach my students English?
④ I'm sure you can be a nice Korean teacher, too.
⑤ Which English dictionary do you recommend for me?

다시 들으면서 듣기 만점에 도전하세요!
Dictation: 스크립트의 주요 부분을 다시 들으면세!
실전 ➕: 세부 정보가 많은 스크립트를 다른 문제로 샅샅이!

---

01 그림 정보 파악(동작)

다음을 듣고, 남자의 형이 취하고 있는 동작을 고르시오.

① ② ③ ④ ⑤

M I really envy my older brother. First, he has such a great sense of humor that people always laugh and smile when they are around him. Second, he is ＿＿＿＿＿＿＿＿, 신체적으로 튼튼한 which I envy him most. He can do many things that I can't even dream of doing. Now he is ＿＿＿＿＿ ＿＿＿＿ ＿＿＿＿. He can even ＿＿＿＿＿ 물구나무서기를 하고 있는   물구나무서기를 한 채 걷다 ＿＿＿＿. I can't do that for a second. I can't do that even when someone holds my legs.

---

02 전화한 목적

대화를 듣고, 여자가 남자에게 전화한 목적으로 가장 적절한 것을 고르시오.

① 여행 국가에 대해 물으려고
② 여행 일정을 변경하려고
③ 여행지 숙소에 대해 물으려고
④ 애완동물 관리를 부탁하려고
⑤ 집 관리를 부탁하려고

[Cellphone rings.]

W Hi, James.

M Hey, is everything ready for your trip?

W Almost. I've booked the flight tickets and guest houses. And I've almost finished packing.

M Great. How long will you stay in New Zealand?

W Ten days. Actually, James, I ＿＿＿＿＿ ＿＿＿ ＿＿＿ ＿＿＿ you. 부탁할 것이 있다

M What is it?

W The thing is, I haven't found anyone ＿＿＿＿＿ ＿＿＿ ＿＿＿ while I'm 고양이 밥을 먹일 away. Can you help me with that?

M No problem. I'll ＿＿＿ ＿＿＿＿ ＿＿＿＿ and take care of your cat every 너네 집에 들르다 day. I'll give him food and empty the litter box.

W Thank you so much!

M You're welcome. You ＿＿＿ ＿＿＿ ＿＿＿ ＿＿＿＿ while I was away 개를 돌봤다 last month.

---

03 상황에 적절한 대화(그림)

다음 그림의 상황에 가장 적절한 대화를 고르시오.

① ② ③ ④ ⑤

자전거를 처음 배우고 있는 상황에 알맞은 대화를 찾는다.

① M ＿＿＿ ＿＿＿ ＿＿＿ ＿＿＿ this bike? 너는 ~에 대한 값으로 얼마를 원하니?
   W It's $150.

② M Don't be afraid and just ＿＿＿ ＿＿＿. 계속해서 페달을 돌리다
   W Wow, this is a lot of fun. But don't let it go.

③ M Can you ＿＿＿ ＿＿＿ for me? 그것을 포장하다
   W Sure. Hold on a second.

④ M When can I pick the bike up?
   W In two or three hours.

⑤ M How long will it take from here to your school?
   W It'll ＿＿＿ ＿＿＿ ＿＿＿. 자전거로 30분이 걸리다

중간에 요일이 바뀔 수 있으니 끝까지 집중하며 듣는다.

대화를 듣고, 두 사람이 만나기로 한 요일을 고르시오.

① 금요일　　② 토요일
③ 일요일　　④ 목요일
⑤ 화요일

➕ 대화를 듣고, 여자에 대해 사실이 <u>아닌</u> 것을 고르시오.

① 친구와 영화를 보고자 한다.
② 집보다는 극장에서 영화 보는 것을 좋아한다.
③ 스릴러 영화를 보고 싶어한다.
④ 테니스 수업을 받고 있다.
⑤ 토요일에는 영화를 보고 싶지 않다.

M Tina, it's almost Friday. Do you have any ＿＿＿＿＿＿＿＿＿＿＿＿＿＿?

　　　　　　　　　　　　　　　　　　　　이번 주말을 위한 계획
W Nothing special.
M Then, let's ＿＿＿＿＿ ＿＿＿＿＿ together.

　　　　영화를 보다
W Okay! Where do you want to watch one, at your place or at the movie theater?
M It's always more fun to ＿＿＿ ＿＿＿ ＿＿＿ ＿＿＿.

　　　　　　　　　　　　　영화관에 가다
W I think so too. Let's watch a thriller.
M Sounds good. What about meeting at 5 on Saturday?
W Oh, sorry, but I have a tennis lesson at 4, and it finishes at 5. ＿＿＿ ＿＿＿

　　　　　　　　　　　　　　　　　　　　　　　　　　　　　　　6시 어때?
＿＿＿ ＿＿＿ on Saturday, or anytime on Sunday?
M Then, let's meet at 6 p.m. on Saturday. See you in front of New Line Theater.

대화를 듣고, 여자의 심정으로 가장 적절한 것을 고르시오.

① happy
② angry
③ worried
④ scared
⑤ disappointed

I'd like to, but I can't. (가고는 싶지만 갈 수가 없다.) : 상대방의 제안을 거절할 때 쓰는 표현이다. (=Sorry, but I can't.)

[Telephone rings.]
W Hello.
M Hi, Jenny. It's Torres. Guess what I have?
W Torres. You know I'm working. What is it?
M All right. I've got two tickets for Jim Tommy's first concert tomorrow. Do you want to come?
W ＿＿＿＿＿ ＿＿＿＿＿ ＿＿＿＿＿, ＿＿＿＿＿ ＿＿＿＿＿ ＿＿＿＿＿.

　　가고는 싶지만 갈 수가 없다
M Why? Isn't he your favorite singer?
W Yes, he is. But I've promised my co-worker that I'd ＿＿＿＿＿＿＿＿＿＿＿＿

　　　　　　　　　　　　　　　　　　　　　　　　　　　　　내일 밤에 그녀 대신 야근을 하다
＿＿＿＿＿ ＿＿＿＿＿.
M Can't you reschedule it?
W Yes, but if I try, she'll be disappointed in me.

수비할 때의 자세에 관해 남자가 가르쳐 주고 여자가 따라해 보는 상황임을 파악한다.

대화를 듣고, 두 사람의 관계로 가장 적절한 것을 고르시오.

① 의사 – 간호사
② 장교 – 사병
③ 영화 감독 – 기자
④ 코치 – 운동 선수
⑤ 물리치료사 – 환자

M Jessica, come over here.
W Yes, sir.
M When you're playing defense, ＿＿＿ ＿＿＿ ＿＿＿ and ＿＿＿

　　　　　　　　　　　　　　　　　　　무릎을 굽혀라　　　　　　　　　　　　몸을 낮춰라
＿＿＿ ＿＿＿.
W ＿＿＿ ＿＿＿?

　이렇게요
M That's right. That way, you can keep your balance.
W Should I stand with my legs close together or far apart?
M It is best to ＿＿＿ ＿＿＿ ＿＿＿ ＿＿＿.

　　　　　　　　　　어깨 넓이로 벌리다
W I see. I'll ＿＿＿ ＿＿＿ ＿＿＿.

　　　염두에 두다

07 어색한 대화 찾기

다음을 듣고, 두 사람의 대화가 <u>어색한</u> 것을 고르시오.

①   ②   ③   ④   ⑤

Are you ready to order? (주문하시겠습니까?) : 음식 주문을 받을 때 쓰는 표현이다. (=May I take your order?)

전화를 잘못 건 사람에게 메시지를 남기라는 응답은 어색하다.

① **M** _____ _____ _____ .
　　　　당신은 전화를 잘못 걸었다
　W Let me _____ _____ .
　　　　　　　메시지를 남기다
② **M** Can I speak to Damon?
　W I'm sorry, but _____ _____ _____ .
　　　　　　　　　　　그는 통화 중이다
③ **M** How do you come to school?
　W I go to school by bicycle.
④ **M** Excuse me. What time do you have?
　W It's a quarter to seven.
⑤ **M** Are you ready to order?
　W _____ _____ _____ .
　　　　커피 주세요

08 부탁한 일 파악

대화를 듣고, 여자가 남자에게 부탁한 일로 가장 적절한 것을 고르시오.
① 추천서 써 주기
② 편지 발송해 주기
③ 보고서 제출해 주기
④ 마감 기한 확인해 주기
⑤ 보고서 제출 여부 확인해 주기

부탁할 때 사용하는 기본적인 표현인 do ~ a favor 뒤에 이어지는 말을 잘 듣는다.

W Steve, where are you going?
M I'm going to Professor Johnson's office.
W Didn't you _____ _____ _____ yet?
　　　　　　　　네 보고서를 제출하다
M Yes, I did. It was due yesterday. I'm going to ask him to write me a letter of recommendation.
W Oh, I see. _____ _____ _____ _____ _____ ?
　　　　　　　　부탁 하나 들어줄래
M Sure. What is it?
W Can you _____ _____ _____ _____ _____ ? I mailed it
　　　　　　내 보고서가 제출되었는지 확인하다
the other day.
M No problem.

09 소재 파악(담화)

다음을 듣고, 무엇에 관한 안내인지 가장 적절한 것을 고르시오.
① 놀이 공원 이용 안내
② 안전 벨트 착용 요령
③ 정기 열차 운행 일정
④ 놀이 기구 탑승 수칙
⑤ 미아 발생 신고 요령

Make sure to hold the safety bar. (안전 막대를 반드시 잡아주세요.) : Make sure to ~.는 '꼭 ~해라'는 뜻으로 당부를 나타낼 때 쓰는 표현이다.

반복되는 rider, ride 등을 놓치지 않고 듣는다.

W _____ , _____ ! For your wonderful experience, I'd like to say a few things. First,
　　　안녕하세요, 탑승객 여러분
make sure to _____ _____ _____ in front of you. Second, _____
　　　　　　　　　　안전 막대를 잡아라
_____ _____ _____ _____ . Last, don't leave your seat until the
　　　　　　　　　　　　　　　탑승 동안 일어나서는 안 된다
train comes to a complete stop. Now, you're ready for _____ _____ .
　　　　　　　　　　　　　　　　　　　　　　　　　　　　흥미진진한 탑승
Here we go!

10 숫자 정보 파악(금액)

대화를 듣고, 여자가 지불할 금액을 고르시오.
① 20,000원　　② 16,000원
③ 10,000원　　④ 24,000원
⑤ 15,000원

➕
대화를 듣고, 두 사람이 있는 장소를 고르시오.
① 전시회장　　② 결혼식장
③ 터미널　　　④ 백화점
⑤ 공원

표 가격과 포인트 사용 여부를 확인한다.

M Good afternoon. How may I help you?
W I'd like to buy two tickets for the Dali exhibition.
M I'm sorry, but the tickets for the morning admission _____ _____ _____ . We do
　　　　　　　　　　　　　　　　　　　　　　　　　　　　매진되다
have a few tickets left for the afternoon admission.
W Okay. I'll buy two of those.
M They're 10,000 won each. Do you have our membership card?
W Here you are.
M You have a total of 4,000 points. You can use them as 4,000 won and _____
　　　　　　　　　　　　　　　　　　　　　　　　　　　　　　　　　　차액을 지불하다
_____ _____ , if you want.
W Yes, I'll do that. Here's 20,000 won.

11 대화 장소 파악

대화를 듣고, 두 사람이 대화하는 장소로 가장 적절한 곳을 고르시오.

① 미용실　　　② 세탁소
③ 빨래방　　　④ 옷 가게
⑤ 결혼식장

드라이클리닝 후 흰 드레스가 변색된 점을 참고한다.

M Hello, come on in.

W Hi. I hate to complain, but there is _____ _____ this white dress.
～에 뭔가 잘못된 것

M Really? What is it?

W Look at the dress. It _____ after dry-cleaned.
노랗게 변하다

M Oh, no. I'm sorry about that. How can I _____ the dress, ma'am?
～에 대해 보상하다

W Could you dry-clean the dress again for free?

M Of course, I will do that. Also I'll give you five 50%-off coupons.

W That would be great. Thanks.

12 언급 유무 파악(담화)

다음을 듣고, 재즈기타 그룹 세션에 관해 언급되지 <u>않은</u> 것을 고르시오.

① 세션 내용 소개
② 세션 등록 방법
③ 세션 등록 기한
④ 세션 등록 비용
⑤ 그룹 세션 장소

W Hello, everyone. I'd like to announce that there will be a jazz guitar session next Friday. We've invited the famous jazz musician Sandra Park to _____ _____ _____ of playing jazz music. While playing a popular jazz piece, she will demonstrate
요점을 알려준다
basic guitar skills. _____ _____ with Ms. Lee by next
관심있는 사람은 등록해야 한다
Wednesday. The session is free, but please _____ _____ _____. Ms.
개인 기타를 가져오다
Park will work one-on-one with each of the participants after her demonstration. Thank you.

13 지도, 위치 파악(지도) – 배치도

다음 쇼핑몰 지도를 보면서 대화를 듣고, 남자가 방문할 곳을 고르시오.

```
  E

  D  C   B
        A
     INFORMATION
```

① A　② B　③ C　④ D　⑤ E

W Welcome to the Organic Mall. How may I help you?

M I want to visit the Herbal Tea Garden. _____ _____ where it is?
알려줄 수 있나요?

W Here's a map of the mall. I'll show you where it's located. We're right here next to the Green Food Restaurant.

M Oh, great! I can _____ _____ _____ for lunch.
나중에 여기 다시 오다

W Next to the restaurant, there's a fruit stand called True Apples. They sell apples grown without using any harmful chemicals.

M Oh, sounds great.

W If you turn left, you'll see Pies & Bakery. And next to the bakery, there's a gallery showing pictures of world organic farms. And there, _____ _____
갤러리 건너편에
_____, you'll find the Herbal Tea Garden.

14 소재 파악(담화)

animal rights, animal testing, must be stopped 등의 표현에 주목한다.

다음을 듣고, 무엇에 관한 설명인지 고르시오.

① 동물 권리활동 ② 취미 생활
③ 봉사 활동   ④ 애완동물 산책
⑤ 애완동물 미용

W Miranda loves animals. She has been interested in working as an animal rights activist. She has been doing volunteer work _____ _____ _____. She takes
동물 보호소에서
care of abandoned or abused animals there. Last year, she adopted two cats from the shelter. She also keeps an online blog and _____ _____ _____
동물 권리에 대한 글을 쓴다
_____. She has been writing a _____ _____ _____. She thinks that
동물 실험에 대한 기사
all experiments on animals must be stopped.

15 할 일 파악

would you like to ~? 뒤에 이어지는 말을 집중하여 듣는다.

대화를 듣고, 남자가 할 일로 가장 적절한 것을 고르시오.

① 자동차 주차하기
② 음료수 사러 가기
③ 자리 지키고 있기
④ 다리 아래에 자리 잡기
⑤ 돗자리 가지러 집에 가기

I'll go buy some. (내가 가서 좀 사올게요.) : I'll go and buy some.에서 and를 관용적으로 생략하고 쓰는 경우가 많다.

W I think we _____ _____ _____ to come out.
올바른 결정을 했다
M Yes. At least we don't feel like being trapped in a hot cell.
W Look! There's an empty space here.
M We're lucky. Spread the mat. Wow! It's much cooler here.
W Look down the bridge. There are so many people under the bridge.
M Mary, _____ _____ _____ _____ _____ _____?
차가운 음료수를 마시고 싶어요
W Sure.
M _____ _____ _____. You just stay here and keep this place.
내가 가서 좀 사오겠다

16 특정 정보 파악(상금)

마지막 두 문제를 틀려서 1,000 달러 대신 100달러를 상금으로 받았다.

대화를 듣고, 남자가 받은 상금을 고르시오.

① $10   ② $100
③ $500   ④ $1,000
⑤ $2,000

M You know what? I have good news and bad news.
W What's the good news?
M I had an opportunity to _____ _____ _____ _____.
상금을 타는 퀴즈 대회에 참가하다
W Great! What's the bad news?
M I _____ _____ _____ _____ to the last two questions, so I just won
정답을 제시하지 못했다
$100 instead of $1,000.
W You are still lucky to win $100.
M I guess you're right, but I could have won $1,000.

17 적절한 응답

세일이 시작되는 시간에 줄이 길 것이라는 말을 듣고 할 수 있는 말을 생각한다.

대화를 듣고, 여자의 마지막 말에 대한 남자의 응답으로 가장 적절한 것을 고르시오.

Man: _____

① Then let's get there as early as possible.
② Then let's clean up the room.
③ Then I'll get my bike fixed.
④ Then I'll let everyone know about it.
⑤ Then I'll return the printer as soon as possible.

[Telephone rings.]

W Did you hear that Jenny's Big Market is closing down?
M Yeah. I'm sad to hear that _____ _____ _____ _____.
폐업하다
W Me, too. Anyway, everything in the store will be 75% off.
M Seventy-five percent? That's great. I need a new Bluetooth speaker in my room. I should look for one there. Do you plan on getting anything?
W The last time I was there, I saw _____ _____ _____ _____ I liked. I
러닝화 한 켤레
need some because I've started jogging.
M Great! Let's go together. When does the sale begin?
W Oh, at 10 a.m. on Saturday. I think there'll be _____ _____.
긴 줄
M _____

18 적절한 응답

집을 장만해 이사 간 친구에게 집들이 계획을 묻고 있는 상황임을 파악한다.

[18~19] 대화를 듣고, 남자의 마지막 말에 대한 여자의 응답으로 가장 적절한 것을 고르시오.

Woman: _____

① Well, my house is warm.
② Sure. I'll help you move in.
③ Yes, we are. It's next Saturday.
④ We don't need to move any more.
⑤ The party won't start until you arrive.

M Tara, _____?
　_{새 집으로 이사 들어갔니}
W Yes. We finally have our own place.
M So how do you feel?
W It's terrific. You know my husband and I constantly moved from one place to another. It was terrible.
M I can understand. And now are you going to _____ _____ _____?
　　　　　　　　　　　　　　　　　　　　　　　　　_{집들이 파티를 하다}
W _____

고난도

19 적절한 응답

조별 보고서에서 남자의 실수를 지적하는 상황임을 파악한다.

Woman: _____

① I made mistakes myself, too.
② It matters that we did our best.
③ That's okay. I can manage that.
④ Here it should be Haiti, not Eiti.
⑤ Don't be afraid of making mistakes.

M Did you turn in our group report?
W Yes, Jack. But you should be more careful next time.
M What do you mean?
W I've taken a look at your part, _____, _____ _____ _____.
　　　　　　　　　　　　　　　　　　　　_{몇 가지 실수를 발견해서 수정했다}
M Oh, really? Like what?
W This is a copy of yours. Look. The year should be 2010, not 2009.
M Oh, that's right! I am sorry. And _____ _____?
　　　　　　　　　　　　　　　　　　　_{또 뭐가 있지}
W _____

---

20 상황에 적절한 말(담화)

주말에 최소한 3시간 정도 만나기로 합의한 점을 참고한다.

다음 상황 설명을 듣고, Mr. Park이 할 말로 가장 적절한 것을 고르시오.

Mr. Park: _____

① How can I get to your country?
② Can we meet on Saturday or Sunday?
③ Do you like to teach my students English?
④ I'm sure you can be a nice Korean teacher, too.
⑤ Which English dictionary do you recommend me?

W Mr. Park went to an English village with his students last week. There he met a native English teacher named Grey. They _____ _____ _____ and
　　　　　　　　　　　　　　　　　　　　　　　　_{공통점이 많았다}
_____ _____ _____ a lot of issues. Mr. Park wanted to have
_{~에 대해 의견이 일치하다}
an opportunity to practice his English. Mr. Grey also wanted to learn Korean. So they
_____ _____ on weekends at least for three hours to practice English
_{만나기로 합의했다}
and Korean, and _____. In this
　　　　　　　　　　　_{각 나라의 문화에 대해 배우기 위하여}
situation, what will Mr. Park say to Mr. Grey?

01 대화를 듣고, 남자가 사려고 하는 액자를 고르시오.

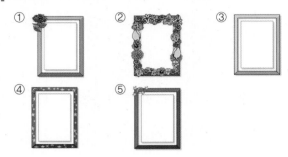

02 대화를 듣고, 남자의 정기 구독 기간과 지불할 금액이 바르게 짝지어진 것을 고르시오.

① six months, $57
② six months, $63
③ one year, $108
④ one year, $120
⑤ one year, $132

03 다음 그림의 상황에 가장 적절한 대화를 고르시오.

①　　　②　　　③　　　④　　　⑤

04 대화를 듣고, 두 사람이 만나기로 한 장소를 고르시오.

① Ted의 집　　② 치과
③ 학교 정문　　④ 집
⑤ 공원

05 다음을 듣고, 여자의 심정으로 가장 적절한 것을 고르시오.

① angry　　② sorry
③ grateful　　④ envious
⑤ confused

06 대화를 듣고, 남자가 요구하는 것을 고르시오.

① 수선　　② 교환　　③ 환불
④ 사과　　⑤ 통보

07 다음을 듣고, 두 사람의 대화가 <u>어색한</u> 것을 고르시오.

①　　②　　③　　④　　⑤

08 대화를 듣고, 여자가 남자에게 부탁한 일로 가장 적절한 것을 고르시오.

① 스케줄 변경하기
② 주제 선정하기
③ 관련 자료 모으기
④ 프레젠테이션 자료 만들기
⑤ 전체 프레젠테이션 하기

09 다음을 듣고, 남자의 주장으로 가장 적절한 것을 고르시오.

① 인터넷을 효율적으로 이용해야 한다.
② 외국 여행은 책을 통해서도 할 수 있다.
③ 외국 여행 시에는 명소 위주로 둘러봐야 한다.
④ 여행할 때는 시간을 효율적으로 써야 한다.
⑤ 외국 여행을 떠나기 전에 그 나라에 대한 공부를 해야 한다.

10 대화를 듣고, 남자가 받을 거스름돈을 고르시오.

① $2.00　　② $2.30
③ $3.00　　④ $4.00
⑤ $4.30

점수

/20

11 다음 메모를 보면서 대화를 듣고, 내용과 일치하지 <u>않는</u> 것을 고르시오.

> **Phone Memo**
>
> To   : ① Julian Russell
> Time   : 4:00 p.m.
> From   : ② Kevin Battle of Sunny Trading
> Number : ③ 2033-1232
> Message: ④ Don't come to his company tomorrow.
>   ⑤ Please call back as soon as possible.

12 다음을 듣고, 언급되지 <u>않은</u> 내용을 고르시오.

① Maria의 직업　　　② Maria의 고향
③ Bill Smith의 나이　④ Maria가 태어난 해
⑤ Maria와 Bill의 관계

13 다음 캠핑장 배치도를 보면서 대화를 듣고, 텐트가 자리한 구역을 고르시오.

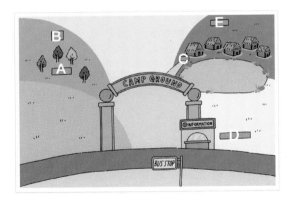

① A　　② B　　③ C　　④ D　　⑤ E

14 다음을 듣고, 무엇에 관한 설명인지 고르시오.

① 소풍　　　　　② 체육 대회
③ 야외 콘서트　　④ 영화제
⑤ 세미나

15 대화를 듣고, 남자의 마지막 말의 의도로 가장 적절한 것을 고르시오.

① 동의　　　② 변명　　　③ 용서
④ 요청　　　⑤ 꾸중

16 대화를 듣고, 여자의 장래 희망으로 가장 적절한 것을 고르시오.

① 선교사　　　　② 의사
③ 탐험가　　　　④ 여행가
⑤ 외교관

17 대화를 듣고, 남자가 게임을 할 수 <u>없는</u> 이유로 가장 적절한 것을 고르시오.

① 학교 숙제가 너무 많아서
② 컴퓨터 수리가 불가능해서
③ 컴퓨터 게임이 너무 어려워서
④ 노트북 컴퓨터 사용법을 몰라서
⑤ 엄마가 컴퓨터를 사용해야 해서

[18~19] 대화를 듣고, 남자의 마지막 말에 대한 여자의 응답으로 가장 적절한 것을 고르시오.

18 Woman: _____

① Thank you, sir.
② No, I don't think so.
③ Why is it so expensive?
④ Your total comes to $4.50.
⑤ Sorry. I don't like French fries.

19 Woman: _____

① But the traffic is heavy.
② My car broke down again.
③ OK. I'll keep that in mind.
④ Sure. You really like your car.
⑤ Why don't we go for a drive now?

20 다음 상황 설명을 듣고, Christina가 Paul에게 할 말로 가장 적절한 것을 고르시오.

Christina: _____

① I'm good at bowling.
② Can you take the class for me?
③ I'm sorry I can't put it off till tomorrow.
④ Can you put off the lesson till tomorrow?
⑤ Are you supposed to practice the piano today?

다시 들으면서 듣기 만점에 도전하세요!
Dictation: 스크립트의 주요 부분을 다시 들으면서!
실전 ➕: 세부 정보가 많은 스크립트를 다른 문제로 샅샅이!

---

01 그림 정보 파악(사물)

선택지의 그림을 보면서 moon, stars, flower 등 관련된 표현을 예상해 본다.

대화를 듣고, 남자가 사려고 하는 액자를 고르시오.

① ② ③ ④ ⑤

W Look at _____ _____. Aren't they pretty?
　　　　　　저 액자들
M Yes, they are. I want to buy one for my sister.
W Good idea. Which one would you like?
M How about _____ _____ _____ _____ _____
　　　　　　달과 별이 있는 것
　in the corner?
W I think it's too simple. I like the one with a lot of stars.
M Well, actually a lot of things on one frame don't look good.
W Then how about this? It has _____ _____ _____.
　　　　　　　　　　　　　　　　꽃 한 송이만
M Hmm.... It looks simple and cute. I'll take it.

---

02 전화한 목적

6개월 구독에 5%, 12개월 구독에 10% 할인해 주는 점을 참고한다.

대화를 듣고, 남자의 정기 구독 기간과 지불할 금액이 바르게 짝지어진 것을 고르시오.

① six months, $57
② six months, $63
③ one year, $108
④ one year, $120
⑤ one year, $132

W Hello, School Life, Customer Service. How can I help you?
M Hi, I'd like to subscribe to your magazine.
W Sure. It's _____ _____ _____. If you subscribe for six months, we'll _____
　　　　　　한 달에 10달러　　　　　　　　　　　　　　　　　　너에게 5% 할인을 해주다
　_____ _____ _____ _____ of the total cost.
M _____ _____ _____ I subscribe for one year?
　~라면 어떻게 하겠는가?
W Then, you will get a 10% discount.
M Oh, that's great. Okay, I'll _____ _____ _____ _____
　　　　　　　　　　　　　　　　　　1년 동안 당신의 잡지를 구독신청하다
　_____.
W No problem. May I have your name and address?
M My name is James Brown, and I live in 241 Paradise Apartment on Lake Street.
W That's all. Thank you very much.

고난도

03 상황에 적절한 대화(그림)

다음 그림의 상황에 가장 적절한 대화를 고르시오.

Full

① ② ③ ④ ⑤

① M Hi, Caren. Can you _____ _____ _____ _____?
　　　　　　　　　　　　나를 태워 주다
　W Sure. Which way are you going?
② M Sorry, ma'am. We _____ _____ _____ _____.
　　　　　　　　　　어떤 공간도 없다
　W Then, are there any other parking lots around here?
③ M Where did you park your car today?
　W I can't remember _____ _____ _____ _____.
　　　　　　　　　　　내 차가 있는 곳
④ M _____ _____ _____ _____ to go to your school?
　얼마나 오래 걸릴 것인가
　W Well, it'll take about 30 minutes by car.
⑤ M Ma'am. You _____ _____.
　　　　　　　　　과속했다
　W No, I wasn't. I was driving at 80km per hour.

04 특정 정보 파악(장소)

대화를 듣고, 두 사람이 만나기로 한 장소를 고르시오.

① Ted의 집   ② 치과
③ 학교 정문   ④ 집
⑤ 공원

➕

대화를 듣고, 남자가 여자에게 부탁한 일로 맞는 것을 고르시오.

① 통증 치료해 주기
② 팀 과제 제출하기
③ 선생님께 외출 허락받기
④ 치과에 데려다 주기
⑤ 점심 함께 하기

W What's wrong, Ryan?

M Well, my mouth was a bit sore yesterday. And I _____ terrible _____ this
<small>치통이 있다</small>
morning.

W Oh, dear. I think you should go to the dental clinic after school.

M Today? But I have to meet up with my team to talk about a group project at Ted's
house. It was so difficult to _____ _____ _____ when everyone was free to
<small>시간을 잡다</small>
meet.

W Then, why don't you go to the clinic during your lunch break?

M Can you _____ _____ _____ _____?
<small>태워주다</small>

W No problem. Please get permission from your teacher to leave school.

M I will. The lunch break starts at noon.

W All right. I'll wait for you _____ _____ _____ _____.
<small>정문에서</small>

05 심정 파악

<small>친구 생일파티에 참석하지 못한 점에 대해서 미안해 하고 있다.</small>

다음을 듣고, 여자의 심정으로 가장 적절한 것을 고르시오.

① angry
② sorry
③ grateful
④ envious
⑤ confused

W Hi, Michael. Did you say you had a party last Friday?

M Yeah. You didn't know about it? As you know, it was my birthday.

W No, I didn't know that. Did you invite me?

M Of course, I did. I sent you a Cellphone text message last week.

W Are you sure? I didn't get it. Oh, you know what? I didn't tell you something.

M What do you mean by that?

W I have a new Cellphone. I _____ _____ you my new phone number.
<small>말을 했어야 했는데</small>
That's my fault.

M That's okay. But I was _____ _____ that you didn't come to my party.
<small>약간 당황하다</small>

W Really? _____ _____ _____ today. I want to do something
<small>저녁식사 하러 외출하자</small>
for your birthday.

M Thanks, but you don't have to do that.

06 관계 파악

<small>하자가 있는 물건에 대한 해결책 2가지 중 마지막에 최종 선택된 것을 잘 듣는다.</small>

대화를 듣고, 남자가 요구하는 것을 고르시오.

① 수선   ② 교환
③ 환불   ④ 사과
⑤ 통보

W How may I help you?

M Yes. I bought this yesterday and I found _____ _____ this morning.
<small>이 노란색 얼룩</small>

W Oh, I'm sorry, sir. I will exchange it for you.

M I want _____ _____ _____ _____ _____ _____.
<small>같은 디자인과 색상의 다른 물건</small>

W Sorry we don't have any more now.

M That's too bad. Then can you order one for me?

W Yes. Maybe it'll take one week or so. When the new one arrives, we'll call you.

M Oh, that's too long. I _____ _____ _____.
<small>내 돈을 돌려받는 게 낫겠다</small>

W All right, sir.

07 어색한 대화 찾기

다음을 듣고, 두 사람의 대화가 <u>어색한</u> 것을 고르시오.

① ② ③ ④ ⑤

① M Are you interested in drawing?
　W Of course! I like art a lot.

② M Why don't you come skiing with us this weekend?
　W Because I had too much homework to do.

③ M We'll ＿＿＿＿ ＿＿＿＿ ＿＿＿＿ ＿＿＿＿ this Sunday.
　　　　　　소풍가다
　W I'm looking forward to it.

④ M What kind of job do you want to have ＿＿＿＿ ＿＿＿＿ ＿＿＿＿?
　　　　　　　　　　　　　　　　　　　　　　　　　미래에
　W I want to be a game developer.

⑤ M What do you usually do after school?
　W I ＿＿＿＿ ＿＿＿＿ ＿＿＿＿ at the park.
　　　자전거를 타다

08 부탁한 일

대화를 듣고, 여자가 남자에게 부탁한 일로 가장 적절한 것을 고르시오.

① 스케줄 변경하기
② 주제 선정하기
③ 관련 자료 모으기
④ 프레젠테이션 자료 만들기
⑤ 전체 프레젠테이션 하기

➕ 대화를 듣고, 여자가 할 일이 <u>아닌</u> 것을 고르시오.

① 프로젝트 주제를 정한다.
② 주제에 맞는 자료를 모은다.
③ 프레젠테이션 자료를 만든다.
④ 프레젠테이션 연습을 한다.
⑤ 프레젠테이션을 진행한다.

W I'm glad we can work together on the assignment.
M Me too, Sandy. Let's talk about the schedule.
W Sure. First, we need to ＿＿＿＿ ＿＿＿＿ ＿＿＿＿.
　　　　　　　　　　주제를 정하다
M Right. Let's choose one by Tuesday, after having a chance to think about it.
W All right.
M After we agree on the topic, we need to ＿＿＿＿ ＿＿＿＿ ＿＿＿＿
　materials. We should finish by June 1.
　　　　　　　　조사와 수집을 시작하다
W Okay. And then, let's finish our visual aids for our presentation by [pause] June 21.
　Around that time, we can start practicing for the presentation.
M Great. Well, Sandy... do you think you can ＿＿＿＿ ＿＿＿＿ whole ＿＿＿＿? You're
　　　　　　　　　　　　　　　　　　　　　발표를 하다
　much better than I am at giving presentations.
W Oh, you want me to do it? Sure, why not? Then, can you handle ＿＿＿＿
　　　　　　　　　　　　　　　　　　　　　　　　　　　　　　　시각 자료를 만드는 것
　＿＿＿＿ ＿＿＿＿ yourself?
M Definitely. I'll do a good job.

09 주장 파악(담화)

다음을 듣고, 남자의 주장으로 가장 적절한 것을 고르시오.

① 인터넷을 효율적으로 이용해야 한다.
② 외국 여행은 책을 통해서도 할 수 있다.
③ 외국 여행 시에는 명소 위주로 둘러봐야 한다.
④ 여행할 때는 시간을 효율적으로 써야 한다.
⑤ 외국 여행을 떠나기 전에 그 나라에 대한 공부를 해야 한다.

외국 여행을 계획할 때 그 나라를 이해하기 위한 준비 사항이 무엇인지 생각해 본다.

M When you ＿＿＿＿ ＿＿＿＿ ＿＿＿＿, try to be prepared before you leave. If
　　　　　　　다른 나라들을 여행하다
　you don't know a lot about the country, you might ＿＿＿＿ ＿＿＿＿
　　　　　　　　　　　　　　　　　　　　　　　　　아주 중요한 장소를 그냥 지나치다
　＿＿＿＿ ＿＿＿＿ ＿＿＿＿. So you must be prepared. You can read books or
　＿＿＿＿ ＿＿＿＿ ＿＿＿＿ in order to learn about the history, language, culture and
　인터넷을 검색하다
　historical places to visit before you leave home. Then you will have a much more
　enjoyable trip.

10 숫자 정보 파악(금액)

대화를 듣고, 남자가 받을 거스름돈을 고르시오.

① $2.00　　② $2.30
③ $3.00　　④ $4.00
⑤ $4.30

W What can I help you with, sir?
M How much will it ＿＿＿＿ ＿＿＿＿ ＿＿＿＿?
　　　　　　　　　이 보고서를 복사하는 데 비용이 들다
W It's ＿＿＿＿ ＿＿＿＿ ＿＿＿＿.
　　　한 쪽당 10센트
M There are ＿＿＿＿ ＿＿＿＿. I need ＿＿＿＿ ＿＿＿＿ ＿＿＿＿
　　　　　　40쪽　　　　　　　　　　　　　보고서 전체 2부 복사
　＿＿＿＿.
W OK, sir. They'll be ready by 2:30.
M Could you make it a little earlier? I need them by 2:00
W Well, let's see.... OK. I'll try. Please come back and pick them up then.
M Thanks. Here is $10.

11 내용 일치 파악

다음 메모를 보면서 대화를 듣고, 내용과 일치하지 <u>않는</u> 것을 고르시오.

Phone Memo	
To	: ① Julian Russell
Time	: 4:00 p.m.
From	: ② Kevin Battle of Sunny Trading
Number	: ③ 2033-1232
Message	: ④ Don't come to his company tomorrow.
	⑤ Please call back as soon as possible.

[Telephone rings.]

W Genesis Shipping. May I help you?

M Hello. I'm Kevin Battle of Sunny Trading. Can I speak to Julian Russell?

W Sorry. He's not in now. Would you like to _____ _____ _____?
_{메시지를 남기다}

M Thanks. Please tell him that he _____ _____ come to our company
_{~할 필요가 없다}
tomorrow.

W OK. Let me have him call you as soon as he gets back.

M Good. My number is 2033-1232. Hmm.... _____ _____ _____. What
_{내가 그에게 다시 전화하겠다}
time will he be back in the office?

W He will come back in an hour. Please _____ _____ _____ and you can
_{5시경에 다시 전화하다}
talk to him.

M All right. Thanks. Bye.

12 언급 유무 파악(담화)

다음을 듣고, 언급되지 <u>않은</u> 내용을 고르시오.

① Maria의 직업
② Maria의 고향
③ Bill Smith의 나이
④ Maria가 태어난 해
⑤ Maria와 Bill의 관계

M Good afternoon. Welcome to the JBS FM show and I'm your host Jerry Hoffman. Today, we have Maria Robertson in this studio. She is one of the most _____ of
_{재능 있는 가수들}
our time. She _____ and moved to
_{1995년 시카고에서 태어났다}
New York when she was ten years old. In New York she started
_____ _____ _____, Bill Smith. As you know, Bill
_{삼촌으로부터 노래와 춤 수업을 받다}
Smith was one of the world-famous entertainers during the 1990s. After six years' hard training, she became the most popular singer in the country. Please welcome Maria Robertson.

13 지도, 위치 파악(지도) – 배치도

다음 캠핑장 배치도를 보면서 대화를 듣고, 텐트가 자리한 구역을 고르시오.

① A　② B　③ C　④ D　⑤ E

[Cellphone rings.]

M Hi, Emma.

W Hi, Mike. I've just _____ _____ _____ at the campground. I'm right in
_{버스에서 내렸다}
front of the entrance. Where is your tent?

M Can you see the information center? It is _____
_{버스 정류장 건너편에}
_____.

W Yes, I can see it.

M Well, walk inside the campground, passing by the information center, and you will see a small lake on your right.

W Got it.

M When you _____ _____ _____ around the lake, there are lots of picnic
_{오두막을 지나다}
tables.

W Okay.

M You'll find a couple of tents behind them. My tent is the red one.

W Okay. I think I can find you. See you in a few minutes.

M Yup. See you!

14 소재 파악(담화)

park, lawn, musicians, concert를 보고 파악한다.

다음을 듣고, 무엇에 관한 설명인지 고르시오.

① 소풍　　　② 체육 대회
③ 야외 콘서트　④ 영화제
⑤ 세미나

W We invite all of you to the Concert in the Park! It is a perfect event for the entire family to enjoy a summer night out! It's going to be held at Central Park on Saturday from 6 to 9 p.m. Bring your own picnic blanket and chairs to ＿＿＿ ＿＿＿ ＿＿＿
느긋한 시간을 보내다
on the lawn. Food will be available at food trucks in the park, or you can bring your own food and drinks. Please visit the park website and check out ＿＿＿
콘서트에서 공연하는 음악가들
＿＿＿ ＿＿＿ ＿＿＿ ＿＿＿.

---

15 마지막 말 의도

I couldn't agree with you more.는 completely agree with you.의 의미이다.

대화를 듣고, 남자의 마지막 말의 의도로 가장 적절한 것을 고르시오.

① 동의
② 변명
③ 용서
④ 요청
⑤ 꾸중

I couldn't agree with you more.는 '더 이상 동의 할 수 없었다.'라는 의미로 부정어 not이 있으나 강한 긍정의 의미가 있는 문장이다.

M What are you reading, Susan?

W I'm reading a newspaper. Look at the pictures! I can't believe my eyes!

M What are they?

W These pictures show ＿＿＿ ＿＿＿ ＿＿＿ ＿＿＿.
수 마일에 걸쳐 바다를 덮고 있는 기름

M Again?

W Yes, it's near the western coast. The newspaper says it has ＿＿＿ ＿＿＿
많은 오염 문제
＿＿＿ ＿＿＿.

M That's true. We throw away too much and don't recycle enough.

W Yes, we're ＿＿＿ ＿＿＿ ＿＿＿ all our garbage. Don't you
~를 위한 장소들이 고갈되고 있는
think so?

M You're absolutely right. I think we should find ＿＿＿ ＿＿＿
이러한 환경 문제들 해결을 위한 방안들
＿＿＿ ＿＿＿ right away.

W I couldn't agree with you more.

---

16 특정 정보 파악(장래 희망)

반복되는 표현인 help sick people을 놓치지 않는다.

대화를 듣고, 여자의 장래 희망으로 가장 적절한 것을 고르시오.

① 선교사　　② 의사
③ 탐험가　　④ 여행가
⑤ 외교관

M What are you going to do when you grow up?

W I'd like to travel to Africa and help people there.

M Sounds like a great idea. But in what way?

W I'll stay there for a while and find out ＿＿＿ ＿＿＿
내가 아픈 사람들을 도울 수 있는 방법
＿＿＿.

M Then how about ＿＿＿ ＿＿＿?
의학을 공부하다

W Yes. That's what I am thinking now.

M Or you can help them by teaching them ＿＿＿ ＿＿＿ ＿＿＿.
더 많은 식량을 재배하는 방법

W You're right. Many people are starving there. But mostly I want to ＿＿＿
아픈 사람들을 돕다
＿＿＿.

17 적절한 응답

컴퓨터로 엄마와 아들이 하고 싶은 일을 구별하여 듣는다.

대화를 듣고, 남자가 게임을 할 수 없는 이유로 가장 적절한 것을 고르시오.

① 학교 숙제가 너무 많아서
② 컴퓨터 수리가 불가능해서
③ 컴퓨터 게임이 너무 어려워서
④ 노트북 컴퓨터 사용법을 몰라서
⑤ 엄마가 컴퓨터를 사용해야 해서

W Kyle, it's time you _____ _____ _____ _____.
　　　　　　　　　　　　　다시 너의 숙제를 하다
M Can I have 30 more minutes, Mom?
W Come on. You should finish your homework first.
M OK. But can I play games again after I finish?
W No, you can't. _____ _____ _____ _____ _____. I have
　　　　　　　　지금부터는 내가 쓸 것이다
　_____ _____ _____ _____ by tomorrow.
　해야 할 일
M What about your laptop?
W It doesn't work. I _____ _____ _____ _____ _____.
　　　　　　　　　　　　　수리점에 그것을 가져갔다
M Again? Oh, no. When is it coming back?
W I don't know. They will call me when it's ready.

18 적절한 응답

금액을 묻는 말 다음에는 구체적인 액수가 나올 것을 예측하고 집중해서 듣는다.

[18~19] 대화를 듣고, 남자의 마지막 말에 대한 여자의 응답으로 가장 적절한 것을 고르시오.

Woman: _____

① Thank you, sir.
② No, I don't think so.
③ Why is it so expensive?
④ Your total comes to $4.50.
⑤ Sorry. I don't like French fries.

I'll have a hamburger. (햄버거 주세요.) : I'll have ~.는 음식을 주문할 때 쓰는 표현이다.
(= I'd like (to have) ~.)

W _____ _____ _____ _____, sir?
　주문하시겠습니까
M I'll have a hamburger and a cup of cocoa, please.
W A hamburger and a cup of cocoa. Will that be all?
M Wait a second. How much is _____ _____ _____ French fries?
　　　　　　　　　　　　　　　　　　　　　　　~의 1인분
W It's $1.50.
M OK. I'll take that, too. _____ _____ _____ _____ now?
　　　　　　　　　　　　제가 낼 돈이 얼마인가요
W _____

19 적절한 응답

상대방의 충고를 받아들이는 응답을 생각해 본다.

Woman: _____

① But the traffic is heavy.
② My car broke down again.
③ OK. I'll keep that in mind.
④ Sure. You really like your car.
⑤ Why don't we go for a drive now?

W Quick. Get in the car. I don't want to _____ _____ _____.
　　　　　　　　　　　　　　　　　　　　　　빨간 신호등을 무시하고 달리다
M Hey, don't start driving yet.
W Why? The engine is running.
M It is. But it still needs to warm up first.
W What do you mean?
M When it's cold you have to _____ _____ _____ before driving.
　　　　　　　　　　　　　　엔진을 예열하다
W Oh, should I wait until the car is warmed up?
M Right. That's the best way _____ _____ _____ _____ in the future.
　　　　　　　　　　　　　　　엔진의 문제가 없도록 하는
W _____

20 상황에 적절한 말(담화)

wants to know if ~ 이후를 놓치지 않는다.

다음 상황 설명을 듣고, Christina가 Paul에게 할 말로 가장 적절한 것을 고르시오.

Christina: _____

① I'm good at bowling.
② Can you take the class for me?
③ I'm sorry I can't put it off till tomorrow.
④ Can you put off the lesson till tomorrow?
⑤ Are you supposed to practice the piano today?

W Paul had final exams last week. He is glad the exams _____
　　　　　　　　　　　　　　　　　　　　　　　　　　　　　이제 모두 끝나다
　_____. Christina calls Paul and tells him that she _____
　　　　　　　　　　　　　　　　　　　　　　　　　　그와 함께 볼링 치러 가고 싶어 하다
　_____ _____ _____ at 5:00. But Paul tells her he has a piano lesson this
　evening. Christina _____ _____ _____ he can cancel the lesson and
　　　　　　　　　　　　~인지 아닌지 알고 싶어 한다
　_____ _____ _____. In this situation, what would Christina most
　대신 내일 그것을 받다
　likely say to Paul?

언급 유무 파악

무엇을 평가하는가?	일상생활 관련 대상이나 친숙한 일반적 주제에 관한 말이나 대화를 듣고 세부 정보를 파악할 수 있는지를 평가한다.

어떻게 출제되는가?	• 대화를 듣고, 기타에 관해 언급되지 않은 것을 고르시오. • 다음을 듣고, Spelling Genius Contest에 관해 언급되지 않은 것을 고르시오.

❶ 선택지를 보고, 대화나 담화에서 주의해서 들어야 할 부분을 파악한다.

❷ 대화나 담화에서 언급된 선택지를 하나씩 지워가며 정답을 찾는다.

[기출로 전략 확인]

다음을 듣고, Oakwood Flea Market에 관해 언급되지 <u>않은</u> 것을 고르시오.　　　[2017 기출]

① 개최 날짜　　　② 취급 품목　　　③ 판매자 참가비

④ 접수 장소　　　⑤ 신청 기한

- - - - - - - - - - - -

M Hello, Oakwood community members. This is David Kim from City Hall. I'm happy to tell you that we'll be having the Oakwood Flea Market on October 13th, 2017. You can buy and sell toys, books, and clothing at this event. There is a five-dollar registration fee for sellers. Please register at the public service center if you plan to attend. Thank you.

❷ 개최 날짜, 취급 품목, 판매자 참가비, 접수 장소 모두 순서대로 언급되었지만 신청 기한은 언급되지 않았다.

남 안녕하세요. Oakwood 주민 여러분. 저는 시청 직원인 David Kim입니다. Oakwood 벼룩 시장이 2017년 10월 13일 열리게 될 것을 알려드리게 되어 기쁩니다. 여러분들은 이 행사에서 장난감, 책 그리고 옷 등을 사고 팔 수 있습니다. 판매자는 5달러의 등록비가 있습니다. 참여할 예정인 분들은 민원실에서 등록해주세요. 감사합니다.

대화를 듣고, 기타에 관해 언급되지 <u>않은</u> 것을 고르시오.　　　　[2018 기출]

① 무게　　　　　② 재료　　　　　③ 길이
④ 색상　　　　　⑤ 가격

만점 잡는 문장　① It's only three kilograms.
　　　　　　　② It's made of wood.
　　　　　　　③ We have black and pink. And they are $300 each.

다음을 듣고, Career Event에 관해 언급되지 <u>않은</u> 것을 고르시오.　　[2018 기출]

① 날짜　　　　　② 초대 강사　　　　③ 강연 주제
④ 등록 방법　　　⑤ 참가비

만점 잡는 문장　① The event will be held in the multimedia room on May 23rd.
　　　　　　　② This time, we have invited a famous web designer, Paul Wilson.
　　　　　　　③ He's going to talk about how to design a website.
　　　　　　　④ If you are interested, please register through our school website.

● 장소&시간 표현

The event will be held at Lake Park next Friday at 8 p.m.
행사는 다음주 화요일 8시에 Lake Park에서 열립니다.

The camp is located in Ottawa. 야영지는 오타와에 위치하고 있습니다.

● 행사 내용 표현

The firework show will be presented in the form of storytelling.
불꽃놀이 쇼는 스토리텔링 형태로 보여질 것입니다.

Our program includes English conversation and sports activities.
우리 프로그램은 영어회화와 스포츠 활동을 포함합니다.

● 자격 표현

Children aged 5 to 7 are welcome to attend. 5~7살 어린이들의 참여를 환영합니다.
Anyone interested in K-pop and Korean culture can join us.
K-pop과 한국 문화에 관심이 있는 누구나 참여할 수 있습니다.

● 행사 등록 표현

If you are interested, please register through our school website.
관심 있다면, 학교 웹사이트를 통해 등록하세요.

To sign up for this event, please go to the teachers' office.
이 행사에 참가하려면 교무실로 가세요.

학년	반	번
이름		

01 대화를 듣고, 여자가 고른 공기 청정기를 고르시오.

①   ②   ③

④   ⑤

02 대화를 듣고, 여자가 남자에게 전화를 건 목적으로 가장 적절한 것을 고르시오.

① 컴퓨터 수리를 부탁하려고
② 사진 현상 장소를 물어보려고
③ 이미지 확대 방법을 알아보려고
④ 마우스 구입 장소를 알아보려고
⑤ 이미지 저장 방법을 물어보려고

03 다음 그림의 상황에 가장 적절한 대화를 고르시오.

①   ②   ③   ④   ⑤

04 대화를 듣고, 남자가 의사를 만나기로 한 요일을 고르시오.

① Monday   ② Tuesday
③ Thursday   ④ Friday
⑤ Saturday

05 대화를 듣고, 남자의 현재 심정으로 가장 적절한 것을 고르시오.

① sorry   ② angry
③ happy   ④ excited
⑤ satisfied

06 대화를 듣고, 두 사람의 관계로 가장 적절한 것을 고르시오.

① 의사 – 환자   ② 변호사 – 증인
③ 기자 – 운동 선수   ④ 사진 작가 – 모델
⑤ 경찰관 – 운전자

고난도
07 다음을 듣고, 두 사람의 대화가 어색한 것을 고르시오.

①   ②   ③   ④   ⑤

고난도
08 대화를 듣고, 여자가 남자에게 부탁한 일로 가장 적절한 것을 고르시오.

① 저녁 요리하기
② 식재료 정리하기
③ 영수증 정리하기
④ 가게에 두고 온 식재료 찾아오기
⑤ TV 시청 시간 지키기

09 다음을 듣고, 목적지에 도착할 예정 시각을 고르시오.

① 3:10 p.m.   ② 3:40 p.m.
③ 4:10 p.m.   ④ 4:40 p.m.
⑤ 5:10 p.m.

10 대화를 듣고, 여자가 지불해야 할 금액을 고르시오.

① $20   ② $50   ③ $80
④ $100   ⑤ $200

점수
/20

11 대화를 듣고, 두 사람이 대화하는 장소로 가장 적절한 곳을 고르시오.

① at a bank   ② at a park
③ at a stadium   ④ at an airport
⑤ at a subway station

12 다음을 듣고, Jenny의 일상에 관해 언급되지 <u>않은</u> 것을 고르시오.

① Jenny의 직업   ② Jenny의 기상 시간
③ Jenny의 아침 메뉴   ④ Jenny의 산책 시간
⑤ Jenny의 작업 시간

13 다음 표를 보면서 대화를 듣고, 여자가 선택할 냉장고를 고르시오.

	Color	Number of Doors	Capacity
①	white	4	800 L
②	gold	4	1,000 L
③	white	2	1,000 L
④	silver	3	840 L
⑤	gold	3	800 L

14 다음을 듣고, this가 가리키는 것을 고르시오.

① play   ② dream
③ musical   ④ history
⑤ emotion

15 대화를 듣고, 진수가 토요일에 할 일로 가장 적절한 것을 고르시오.

16 대화를 듣고, 여자의 마지막 말의 의도로 가장 적절한 것을 고르시오.

① 경고   ② 허락   ③ 거절
④ 초대   ⑤ 예약

17 대화를 듣고, 여자의 마지막 말에 대한 남자의 응답으로 가장 적절한 것을 고르시오.

Man: _____

① Your neighbors can't solve the problem.
② You'd better talk with the management office first.
③ You'd better make a lot of noise, too.
④ I don't understand the issue.
⑤ You need to move out.

[18~19] 대화를 듣고, 남자의 마지막 말에 대한 여자의 응답으로 가장 적절한 것을 고르시오.

18 Woman: _____

① What a good idea!
② What! That's so unfair.
③ But I want to visit a zoo.
④ Yes, we must be on a diet.
⑤ No, thanks. I've had enough.

19 Woman: _____

① By credit card.
② Oh, I almost forgot.
③ Don't take it so hard.
④ Yes, my aunt lives there.
⑤ My dad and I can speak English well.

20 다음 상황 설명을 듣고, Judy가 버스기사에게 할 말로 가장 적절한 것을 고르시오.

Judy: _____

① How much is it?
② What a careless driver!
③ Excuse me, I'm looking for my wallet.
④ Could you let me know where I should get off?
⑤ I forgot my wallet. Can I put extra in next time?

다시 들으면서 듣기 만점에 도전하세요!
Dictation : 스크립트의 주요 부분을 다시 들으면서!
실전 ⊕ : 세부 정보가 많은 스크립트를 다른 문제로 살살이!

---

01 그림 정보 파악(사물)

대화를 듣고, 여자가 고른 공기 청정기를 고르시오.

① ② ③ ④ ⑤

모양을 나타내는 표현에 주목한다.

M How may I help you?
W I'm looking for an air purifier for my new house.
M These are all brand-new models.
W Oh, great. Do they _____ a lot of _____ ?
   _{소리가 난다}
M Well, they're not that noisy—about as loud as an electronic fan.
W Then, I think I like that one that has a square base and _____ _____
   _{맨 위에 원형}
   _____ _____ . How much is it?
M It's $500. If you have our shop's membership card, we can give you a 10% discount.
W Oh, great! Then, I'll take that one.

---

02 전화한 목적

대화를 듣고, 여자가 남자에게 전화를 건 목적으로 가장 적절한 것을 고르시오.

① 컴퓨터 수리를 부탁하려고
② 사진 현상 장소를 물어보려고
③ 이미지 확대 방법을 알아보려고
④ 마우스 구입 장소를 알아보려고
⑤ 이미지 저장 방법을 물어보려고

Are you following me? (내 말 알아듣고 있니?)
: 절차나 방법을 이야기할 때 상대방의 이해를 점검하는 표현이다.

반복되는 save, image(s) 등을 놓치지 않는다.

[Telephone rings.]
M Hello. Who's speaking?
W Hi, Bill. It's Cindy. Can you tell me _____ _____ _____ from the
   _{이미지들을 저장하는 방법}
   websites?
M No problem. Are you in front of your computer now?
W Yes, I'm ready.
M First click on the thumbnail image to see the full size version.
W I did. And then?
M Right-click on the mouse button, and _____ ' _____ '. And select a
   _{'다른 이름으로 저장하기'를 선택하라}
   destination on your hard drive _____ _____ _____ . Are you following
   _{그 파일을 저장하기 위해}
   me?
W Yes, I am. Now is the file available for me to use?
M Yes, it is.
W Thanks, Bill. You're always so helpful.

---

03 상황에 적절한 대화(그림)

다음 그림의 상황에 가장 적절한 대화를 고르시오.

① ② ③ ④ ⑤

① W May I help you?
   M Yes, I'd like to _____ _____ I bought here.
   _{이 셔츠를 교환하다}
② W *[sigh]* It was such a long trip.
   M You must be very tired. Let me take your suitcase for you.
③ W Excuse me. Where is Max's Kitchen?
   M I'm sorry. I'm _____ _____ _____ this neighborhood.
   _{잘 모르는}
④ W Can you help me clean up the classroom?
   M Sure. I can help you.
⑤ W How are you feeling today?
   M I have a terrible headache. And I'm coughing a lot.

04 특정 정보 파악(요일)

대화를 듣고, 남자가 의사를 만나기로 한 요일을 고르시오.

① Monday ② Tuesday
③ Thursday ④ Friday
⑤ Saturday

[Telephone rings.]

W Dr. Jones's clinic. How may I help you?

M Hi, this is Kevin Clark. I _____ _____ _____ for Wednesday, but I'd like to
_{예약을 했다}
see the doctor today if possible.

W I'm sorry, Mr. Clark. It's Monday today, and Monday _____ always _____
_{예약이 가득 차다}
_____ . It's hard to schedule an appointment on such short notice.

M I _____ _____ _____ _____ scheduled from Tuesday to Friday. I really need
_{출장을 가다}
to see him before I go.

W Hmm... Let me see if I can squeeze you in. What about at 5:00 p.m. today?

M Could I see him this morning?

W Hmm... Dr. Jones has a break from 10:30. I'll _____ _____ _____ before
_{예약을 잡다}
then. Please arrive here by 10 at the latest.

M Okay. Thank you so much.

05 심정 파악

I was too selfish.라고 생각하는 사람의 심정과 관련 있는 것을 선택한다.

대화를 듣고, 남자의 현재 심정으로 가장 적절한 것을 고르시오.

① sorry 미안한 ② angry 화난
③ happy 행복한 ④ excited 흥분한
⑤ satisfied 만족한

W Calvin, are you OK?

M Yeah, I guess. In fact, I _____ _____ _____ _____ my brother and
_{~와 싸웠다}
I feel bad.

W What did you fight about?

M I wanted to use the computer to play a game and he wanted to write a report.
I was _____ _____ .
_{너무 이기적인}

W Cheer up! He'll _____ _____ _____ soon.
_{그것을 잊다}

M Thanks. I know you're right.

W Maybe you'd better call him _____ _____ .
_{사과하기 위하여}

M Good idea! Can I use your Cellphone?

W Sure! Here it is.

06 관계 파악

목격한 일, 생김새, 이유 등을 묻고 답하는 관계로 적절한 것을 선택한다.

대화를 듣고, 두 사람의 관계로 가장 적절한 것을 고르시오.

① 의사 – 환자
② 변호사 – 증인
③ 기자 – 운동 선수
④ 사진 작가 – 모델
⑤ 경찰관 – 운전자

M OK. _____ _____ next?
_{무슨 일이 일어났다}

W The woman gave him a large box.

M A box! What did it _____ _____ ?
_{~처럼 생기다}

W It was just square and brown. Nothing special.

M What did Mr. Smith do then?

W He took the box. And he _____ _____ _____ .
_{매우 겁에 질린 것처럼 보였다}

M Why did he look frightened? What was in the box?

W I don't know. He didn't open it. He just took it and left in a hurry.

M Where did he go? And where did the woman go?

W Toward the parking lot. And the woman was still there when I heard his car
_{전속력으로 차를 몰고 사라지다}
_____ _____ _____ .

07 어색한 대화 찾기

다음을 듣고, 두 사람의 대화가 <u>어색한</u> 것을 고르시오.

① ② ③ ④ ⑤

Do you have the time? (몇 시니?) : 시간을 물어볼 때 쓰는 표현으로 Do you have time? (시간 있니?)과 혼동하지 않도록 한다.

Look on the bright side. (긍정적으로 생각해.) : 안 좋은 일이 있는 상대방을 위로할 때 쓰는 표현이다.

① M Do you have the time?

W It's _____ .
　　　7시 10분 전

② M Excuse me, but _____ _____ _____ ?
　　　　　　　　　　　이 좌석에 사람 있나요

W No, have a seat.

③ M I'm sorry we lost the final match.

W Look on the bright side. You played _____ _____ _____ .
　　　　　　　　　　　　　　　　전보다 더 잘

④ M Some teenagers need to work. It's unfair not to let teenagers work.

W I cannot agree with you. They need jobs _____ _____ _____ .
　　　　　　　　　　　　　　　　　　　　돈을 좀 벌기 위하여

⑤ M Drinking soda is unhealthy for teenagers because their teeth can rot.

W That's a good point.

08 부탁한 일

대화를 듣고, 여자가 남자에게 부탁한 일로 가장 적절한 것을 고르시오.

① 저녁 요리하기
② 식재료 정리하기
③ 영수증 정리하기
④ 가게에 두고 온 식재료 찾아오기
⑤ TV 시청 시간 지키기

➕ 다음을 듣고, 대화가 이루어지는 장소를 고르시오.

① 도서관　　　② 집안
③ 가게안　　　④ 주차장
⑤ 식당

B Mom, I brought in the groceries from the car.

W Thank you, dear. I'll make dinner for you soon.

B What are you going to make?

W I'm thinking of making a spicy pork stew and salmon salad.

B Mmm... my favorites. Can I watch TV until dinner is ready?

W Of course. Oh, wait. I can't find the pork in the shopping bag.

B Well, _____ _____ _____ in the car.
　　　남은 것이 없다

W That's strange. I remember buying it. Where did it go?

B Let me check the receipt. [pause] Here, you paid for the pork. See?

W Then, I _____ _____ _____ at the store. Can you run back and get it?
　　　그것을 두고 온 것이 분명하다

B No problem.

09 특정 정보 파악(시각)

현재 시각과 비행 시간을 메모한 후 계산해 본다.

다음을 듣고, 목적지에 도착할 예정 시각을 고르시오.

① 3:10 p.m.　　　② 3:40 p.m.
③ 4:10 p.m.　　　④ 4:40 p.m.
⑤ 5:10 p.m.

M Good afternoon, ladies and gentlemen. This is your purser Jinsu Kim. On behalf of Captain Park and the entire crew, _____ this Korean Airlines flight from
　　　　　　　　　　　　　　　　　　　　　　　　　탑승을 환영한다
Seoul to Nagoya, Japan. _____ _____ _____ . The flying time will be
　　　　　　　　　　　　현재 시각은 오후 2시 30분이다
_____ _____ _____ . To be at your service is an honor for
1시간 40분
the captain and all his crew. Please enjoy the pleasant flight with us. Thank you.

10 숫자 정보 파악(금액)

제시한 가격과 할인율을 메모하며 들은 뒤 계산해 본다.

대화를 듣고, 여자가 지불해야 할 금액을 고르시오.

① $20　　　② $50
③ $80　　　④ $100
⑤ $200

M Good afternoon. May I help you?

W Yes, please. I'm looking for a digital camera. Oh, this one looks good. How much is it?

M _____ .
　　그것은 100달러이다

W $100! I think it's a bit pricey.

M But this kind of brand-new camera usually costs $200. So, $100 is a reasonable price.

W Oh, really? But, you see, this one has some scratches on the bottom. Can I have it _____ _____ ?
　　　절반 가격에

M I can't do that. Listen, I can offer you _____ _____ _____ , but that's
　　　　　　　　　　　　　　　　　　　　　　　20% 할인
_____ _____ I can go.
　　　　　　　　　　　최저 가격

W OK. I'll take it.

11 대화 장소 파악

지하철로 공항에 가는 방법을 설명하고 있음에 주목한다.

대화를 듣고, 두 사람이 대화하는 장소로 가장 적절한 곳을 고르시오.

① at a bank 은행에서
② at a park 공원에서
③ at a stadium 경기장에서
④ at an airport 공항에서
⑤ at a subway station 지하철역에서

M I'd like to go to Incheon International Airport. _____ _____ should I take?
어느 노선

W Let me see. You should take Line Number 2, and then _____ Line Number
~로 갈아타다
5 at Dongdaemun History & Culture Park.

M Is there any easy way to find the right line?

W Line Number 2 is green, and Line Number 5 is violet on all subway maps.

M Oh, I see. How much is _____ _____ _____ _____ ?
공항까지 요금

W It's 4,500 won.

M Two tickets, please.

W Here are _____ _____ _____ _____ .
당신의 승차권과 거스름돈

12 언급 유무 파악(담화)

다음을 듣고, Jenny의 일상에 관해 언급되지 않은 것을 고르시오.

① Jenny 의 직업
② Jenny 의 기상 시간
③ Jenny 의 아침 메뉴
④ Jenny 의 산책 시간
⑤ Jenny 의 작업 시간

W Jenny is a famous writer. She writes mystery novels. Her daily routine is very different from most people's. She gets up around noon. Then, she has a late breakfast. After that, she _____ some _____ , like dusting and the laundry. At about 4 in the
집안일을 하다
afternoon, she _____ _____ around the neighborhood. She talks with
개를 산책시키다
her neighbors and buys groceries at the store. After dinner, she starts working—usually at about 9 p.m. She _____ _____ _____ _____ and focuses on writing until
밤새 깨어 있다
the next morning.

13 특정 정보 파악(도표)

색상, 문의 개수, 용량 등을 체크하며 듣는다.

다음 표를 보면서 대화를 듣고, 여자가 선택할 냉장고를 고르시오.

	Color	Number of Doors	Capacity
①	white	4	800 L
②	gold	4	1,000 L
③	white	2	1,000 L
④	silver	3	840 L
⑤	gold	3	800 L

M Look! Refrigerators are on sale.

W Oh, yeah! Let's look around. We need to get a new one.

M _____ _____ _____ better, white or silver?
어느 색상이 좋아?

W Those colors are too common. Let's get a gold one.

M I don't mind gold. What about the number of doors?

W I want _____ _____ _____ _____ .
최소 문 3개가 있는 것

M OK. More importantly, we have to _____ _____ _____ .
용량에 대해 생각하다

W Don't you think we need one with a capacity of 1,000 liters?

M I think that refrigerator is too big for our house. An 800-liter capacity fridge is big enough.

W If you think so, I'll follow your decision.

14 소재 파악(담화)

다음을 듣고, this가 가리키는 것을 고르시오.

① play 연극   ② dream 꿈
③ musical 뮤지컬   ④ history 역사
⑤ emotion 감정

W Even though we can't remember this clearly all the time, we _____ _____
자는 동안 이것을 한다
_____ . We are usually active in this. We are talking, moving, walking, or traveling as the other people are doing these things in this. We usually _____
이 안에서 이상하고 별난 것들을 한다
_____ _____ _____ like flying or falling. We often _____
이 안에서 좋지 않은 기분들을 갖는다
_____ _____ like anger, fear, sadness, and tears. Can you guess what this is?

15 할 일 파악

진수가 처음에 하고 싶어 했던 일과 토요일에 하기로 한 일을 구별하여 듣는다.

대화를 듣고, 진수가 토요일에 할 일로 가장 적절한 것을 고르시오.

① ② ③ ④ ⑤

M Mom, can I go to A Future Science & Technology Show this Saturday?

W I'm afraid not, Jinsu. We're supposed to _____ _____ (할머니 생신 파티에 참석하다) _____ _____ .

M I remember. But I'm interested in future science and technology.

W I know, but we already made plans.

M Besides, it takes too much time to go to grandma's.

W Yes, it's a long trip, but let's try to look on the bright side.

M What's the bright side _____ (할머니 댁을 방문하는 데 있어서), Mom?

W You can enjoy beautiful sights _____ _____ _____ (버스를 타는 동안에) and go fishing near grandma's house.

M I see, Mom.

16 마지막 말 의도

테니스 치는 것을 허락해 달라는 아들의 요구에 폭풍우 때문에 안 된다는 엄마의 입장을 표현하고 있다.

대화를 듣고, 여자의 마지막 말의 의도로 가장 적절한 것을 고르시오.

① 경고 ② 허락
③ 거절 ④ 초대
⑤ 예약

W Jacob, where are you off to?

M It's Saturday, so I'm going to play tennis with my friends. _____ _____ (우리는 만나기로 되어 있다) _____ at our school.

W Didn't you _____ _____ _____ (일기예보를 듣다) ?

M No, I didn't. What did it say?

W There's a heavy rainstorm coming soon. You shouldn't go outside.

M It's not raining now. I'm sure it'll be OK today.

W Can't you see _____ _____ _____ (몰려오는 저 먹구름들) ? And the wind is _____ (점점 더 거세진다) _____ _____ .

M But I've promised my friends to be there. Please _____ _____ (가게 허락하다) .

W The rainstorm will be here sooner than you expect.

17 적절한 응답

층간 소음으로 고통받는 지인에게 할 수 있는 말을 생각한다.

대화를 듣고, 여자의 마지막 말에 대한 남자의 응답으로 가장 적절한 것을 고르시오.

Man: _____

① Your neighbors can't solve the problem.
② You'd better talk with the management office first.
③ You'd better make a lot of noise, too.
④ I don't understand the issue.
⑤ You need to move out.

➕ 대화를 듣고, 남자의 심경으로 가장 적절한 것을 고르시오.

① glad ② bored
③ concerned ④ curious
⑤ confused

[Telephone rings.]

M Hi, Jenny! How are you today?

W I'm so tired. I _____ (잠을 자지 못했다) any _____ last night.

M Why not? Were you worried about the quiz today?

W No, it's because of my new upstairs neighbors.

M Oh, no. Do they make a lot of noise?

W Yes. They don't seem to sleep at night. Last night was the worst. They _____ _____ _____ (시끄러운 음악을 틀었다) until almost 3 a.m.

M That's terrible.

W I think I'll have to knock on their door and talk to them about it today.

M Jenny... It might _____ _____ (갈등이 있다) with them.

W That's what I'm worried about.

M _____

18 적절한 응답

남자와 여자의 놀이 역할이 불공평한 상황임을 파악한다.

[18~19] 대화를 듣고, 남자의 마지막 말에 대한 여자의 응답으로 가장 적절한 것을 고르시오.

Woman: _____

① What a good idea!
② What! That's so unfair.
③ But I want to visit a zoo.
④ Yes, we must be on a diet.
⑤ No, thanks. I've had enough.

M I'm so bored. Can you play with me now?

W Sure. Any interesting games to play with me?

M Yes. I know an interesting game.

W Let me know how to play the game.

M OK. Let me explain. I'll be _____ _____ _____ (아기 돼지), and you can be _____ (엄마 돼지) _____ _____ .

W Then, what am I supposed to do next?

M You have to _____ _____ _____ (아기 돼지에게 주다) a cookie, a sandwich, and a Coke.

W What are you going to do then?

M You know, I'm just a baby pig, so I'll just sit and eat the food.

W _____

19 적절한 응답

예약 여부를 묻는 질문과 직접적으로 관련 있는 응답을 선택한다.

Woman: _____

① By credit card.
② Oh, I almost forgot.
③ Don't take it so hard.
④ Yes, my aunt lives there.
⑤ My dad and I can speak English well.

M What are you going to do this winter vacation, Hana?

W I'm planning to take a trip to Sydney with my family.

M _____ (얼마나 오랫동안) are you going to stay there?

W Just one week.

M Where are you thinking of staying? _____ _____ _____ (~에 친척들이 있니) _____ Sydney?

W We have no relatives there, so we're staying _____ _____ _____ (호텔에) .

M Did you _____ _____ _____ (예약하다) , then?

W _____

20 상황에 적절한 말(담화)

지갑을 집에 두고 온 채 버스를 탔을 때 버스기사에게 할 수 있는 말을 생각해 본다.

다음 상황 설명을 듣고, Judy가 버스기사에게 할 말로 가장 적절한 것을 고르시오.

Judy: _____

① How much is it?
② What a careless driver!
③ Excuse me, I'm looking for my wallet.
④ Could you let me know where I should get off?
⑤ I forgot my wallet. Can I put extra in next time?

W The other day, Judy asked her mom for some money to buy a drawing book. She put the money in her wallet. There was _____ _____ _____ (지갑에 있는 버스 카드) _____ , too. After she had a good breakfast, she started for school. She got on the bus as usual. And she _____ _____ _____ (지갑을 찾았다) . Oh, no! She _____ _____ _____ (지갑을 두었다) on the table. It meant she _____ _____ _____ (돈이 없었다) , and no bus card. In this situation, what would Judy most likely say to the bus driver?

01 대화를 듣고, 여자가 사려는 수영복을 고르시오.

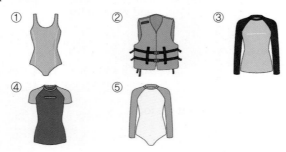

02 대화를 듣고, 남자가 여자에게 전화를 건 목적으로 가장 적절한 것을 고르시오.

① 음식 주문을 하려고
② 예약 조정을 하려고
③ 진료 예약을 하려고
④ 파티 취소를 알리려고
⑤ 식당의 위치를 알아보려고

03 다음 그림의 상황에 가장 적절한 대화를 고르시오.

①   ②   ③   ④   ⑤

04 대화를 듣고, 두 사람이 스케이트보드 수업을 수강할 요일을 고르시오.

① 월요일   ② 화요일
③ 수요일   ④ 목요일
⑤ 금요일

05 대화를 듣고, 두 사람이 대화하는 장소로 가장 적절한 곳을 고르시오.

① 법원   ② 법률 회사
③ 졸업식장   ④ 보석 가게
⑤ 결혼식장

06 대화를 듣고, 여자의 심정으로 가장 적절한 것을 고르시오.

① happy   ② sorry
③ excited   ④ upset
⑤ calm

07 다음을 듣고, 두 사람의 대화가 <u>어색한</u> 것을 고르시오.

①   ②   ③   ④   ⑤

08 대화를 듣고, 여자가 남자에게 부탁한 일로 가장 적절한 것을 고르시오.

① 항의 편지 함께 쓰기   ② 항의 집회 참석하기
③ 택배 회사 알아보기   ④ 환불 정책 리뷰하기
⑤ 보고서 검토하기

09 대화를 듣고, 여자의 마지막 말의 의도로 가장 적절한 것을 고르시오.

① 공부를 열심히 해라.
② 건강관리에 힘써라.
③ 집 청소를 자주 해라.
④ 어머니를 도와드려라.
⑤ 요리에 관심을 가져라.

10 대화를 듣고, 여자가 일주일에 받게 될 금액을 고르시오.

① $200   ② $250
③ $400   ④ $450
⑤ $925

점수

/20

11 대화를 듣고, 두 사람의 관계로 가장 적절한 것을 고르시오.

① 상주 – 문상객
② 환자 – 면회객
③ 엄마 – 아들
④ 목사 – 신도
⑤ 의사 – 환자의 보호자

12 다음을 듣고, 태풍에 대비하여 갖추어야 할 것으로 언급되지 <u>않은</u> 것을 고르시오.

① 생수
② 예비 전력
③ 통조림 식품
④ 초와 성냥
⑤ 전지용 라디오

13 다음 표를 보면서 대화를 듣고, 남자가 선택할 요금제를 고르시오.

	Free calls	Free text messages	Data Capacity	Price
①	2 hours	500	1.5 GB	50,000
②	3 hours	Unlimited	2.0 GB	70,000
③	3 hours	1,000	Unlimited	90,000
④	3 hours	500	Unlimited	70,000
⑤	3 hours	Unlimited	Unlimited	80,000

14 다음을 듣고, 무엇에 관한 설명인지 고르시오.

① 확성기
② 녹음기
③ 보청기
④ 라디오
⑤ 무전기

15 대화를 듣고, 두 사람이 토요일에 할 일로 가장 적절한 것을 고르시오.

① 독서
② 볼링
③ 도서 대여
④ 연극 관람
⑤ 남자의 여동생 방문

16 대화를 듣고, 내일 예상되는 날씨를 고르시오.

① foggy
② rainy
③ sunny
④ windy
⑤ cloudy

17 대화를 듣고, 여자의 직업으로 가장 적절한 것을 고르시오.

① 은행원
② 건물 관리인
③ 건축 설계사
④ 부동산 중개인
⑤ 체육관 트레이너

[18~19] 대화를 듣고, 여자의 마지막 말에 대한 남자의 응답으로 가장 적절한 것을 고르시오.

18 Man: _____

① I'll try, but I'm not sure I can do that.
② That's okay. I sweat when I feel nervous, too.
③ I did what you said and it worked perfectly.
④ Don't speak ill of others when they are away.
⑤ I wonder if I can give the presentation for you.

19 Man: _____

① OK. Let me show you the map.
② Yes, I learned it the hard way.
③ I don't think so. He was mean to me.
④ Right. Next time I won't drive near a school.
⑤ Yes, I should. That's why I don't like schools.

20 다음 상황 설명을 듣고, Paul이 계산원에게 할 말로 가장 적절한 것을 고르시오.

Paul: _____

① I want to get a refund.
② Can I pay for it by credit card?
③ I am afraid I was overcharged.
④ Is there another bookstore around here?
⑤ Excuse me, I want to exchange this book.

다시 들으면서 듣기 만점에 도전하세요!
Dictation: 스크립트의 주요 부분을 다시 들으면서!
실전 ➕: 세부 정보가 많은 스크립트를 다른 문제로 샅샅이!

---

01 그림 정보 파악(사물)

수영복을 묘사하는 표현에 집중하여 듣는다.

대화를 듣고, 여자가 사려는 수영복을 고르시오.

① ② ③ ④ ⑤

W Josh, let's _____ _____ the swimwear section.
둘러보다
M Do you want to buy a new swimsuit?
W I want to buy a rash guard instead of a swimsuit.
M What's a rash guard?
W It's tight-fitting swimwear. It's designed to be skin tight; so you can _____ _____ _____ _____ and not expose much of your skin.
그것을 셔츠처럼 입다
M That sounds great. So, do you want a one-piece suit?
W It won't be comfortable at the beach. I'd like to buy only a rash guard shirt—a short-sleeve one.
M That sounds great. Let's _____ _____ _____.
둘러보다

---

02 전화한 목적

목적을 말하는 We'd like to ~ 이후에 주목하여 듣는다.

대화를 듣고, 남자가 여자에게 전화를 건 목적으로 가장 적절한 것을 고르시오.

① 음식 주문을 하려고
② 예약 조정을 하려고
③ 진료 예약을 하려고
④ 파티 취소를 알리려고
⑤ 식당의 위치를 알아보려고

[Telephone rings.]

W Hello, The Maestro. How may I help you?
M Hello. We have reservations for 8 o'clock tonight but _____ _____ _____ _____ _____ _____. One of the people in our party is sick.
우리가 못 갈 것 같다
W Oh, I am so sorry. What's your name?
M Holland. _____ _____ _____ _____ _____ _____. Is it possible?
다음 주로 변경하고 싶다
W All right. What day do you like?
M Friday, if possible.
W We're booked up at eight. What about seven o'clock? Is it okay with you?
M That's okay. Thanks.

---

03 상황에 적절한 대화(그림)

다음 그림의 상황에 가장 적절한 대화를 고르시오.

① ② ③ ④ ⑤

① W Put all those books on that shelf.
   M Where? Right here?
② W You can't _____ _____ _____ _____.
   이 책들을 모두 대출하다
   M Really? How many books can I check out?
③ W Is there a bookstore nearby?
   M _____ _____ _____ _____.
   없을 것이다
④ W The door needs to be painted.
   M Is that so? I'll do that right away.
⑤ W _____ _____ _____ _____ for you.
   내가 문을 열어 주다
   M Thank you. You are very kind.

---

04 특정 정보 파악(요일)

마지막에 확정된 요일이 나올 수 있으니 끝까지 주의해서 듣는다.

대화를 듣고, 두 사람이 스케이트보드 수업을
수강할 요일을 고르시오.

① 월요일   ② 화요일
③ 수요일   ④ 목요일
⑤ 금요일

M Hey, here's the schedule at the skateboarding school I go to.

W Great! I'm thinking of starting again.

M Why don't you _____ _____ _____ _____? I'm taking the
(나와 같은 수업을 듣다)
advanced class on Tuesdays and Thursdays.

W Hmm. I don't know. I've only taken a few skateboard lessons before.

M Then, how about the intermediate class on Friday?

W I want to take a class on the same days as you.

M Then, _____ _____ _____ on Thursdays? We can
(초급반을 듣는 게 어때?)
take the bus together.

W Oh, that'd be great. Let's meet on Thursdays after school.

05 대화 장소 파악

walk down the aisle, groom, guests, celebrate the day 등을 놓치지 않고 듣는다.

대화를 듣고, 두 사람이 대화하는 장소로 가장
적절한 곳을 고르시오.

① 법원   ② 법률 회사
③ 졸업식장   ④ 보석 가게
⑤ 결혼식장

M Look! Doris is _____ _____ _____ _____
(그녀의 삼촌과 결혼식 제단 쪽으로 걸어가고 있는)
Johnny. She is so beautiful.

W Yes, she is. Look at the groom! He is coming down to greet her.

M Oh, _____ _____ _____! What is his name?
(정말 아름다운 커플이네요)

W Ted. He works for the same law firm as Doris works.

M Oh, I see. There are _____ _____ _____ _____
(이 날을 축하하러 여기에 온 아주 많은 하객)
_____.

W Yes. There are more people than we expected.

M Maybe the groom has a lot of friends or relatives.

W Look! Ted is giving Doris a ring. What a beautiful moment!

06 심정 파악

5살짜리 동생이 휴대폰을 갖고 놀다 망가졌다면 어떤 기분일까 생각해 본다.

대화를 듣고, 여자의 심정으로 가장 적절한
것을 고르시오.

① happy 행복한
② sorry 미안한
③ excited 흥분된
④ upset 화난
⑤ calm 평온한

M _____ _____ your Cellphone? You didn't answer all morning.
(~에게 무슨 일이 생기다)

W It doesn't work _____ _____. I think my brother dropped it or something.
(전혀)

M You mean your 5-year-old brother, Joe?

W Right. He loves to play with my phone when I'm not using it.

M I think you should visit the repair shop, then.

W I know, but this is the third time he broke my phone!

M Are you sure Joe did it again?

W I am. I _____ _____ _____ last night and this morning I
(침대 위에 그것을 놓았다)
found it in his toy box.

07 어색한 대화 찾기

자신의 코트를 받아서 걸어주려는 사람에게 할 말을 생각해 본다.

다음을 듣고, 두 사람의 대화가 <u>어색한</u> 것을
고르시오.

①   ②   ③   ④   ⑤

① **W** I'm sorry to _____ _____ _____.
(계속 기다리게 했다)
M That's okay. I just got here, too.

② **W** Is there anything to declare?
M No. This bag is all I have.

③ **W** I was wondering if you could do me a favor.
M Sure. What is it?

④ **W** Come in. _____ _____ _____ _____
(내가 당신 코트를 받아 주겠다)
M Sure. _____ _____ _____.
(탈의실은 저쪽에 있다)

⑤ **W** It was nice having talked to you.
M It was my pleasure.

08 부탁한 일

대화를 듣고, 여자가 남자에게 부탁한 일로 가장 적절한 것을 고르시오.

① 항의 편지 함께 쓰기
② 항의 집회 참석하기
③ 택배 회사 알아보기
④ 환불 정책 리뷰하기
⑤ 보고서 검토하기

➕ 대화를 듣고, 여자가 할 일로 가장 적절한 것을 고르시오.

① 온라인 스토어에 항의하기
② 택배사에 항의하기
③ 소비자 보호센터에 신고하기
④ 초코렛 제조 회사에 항의하기
⑤ 부모님과 상의하기

M What's up? You _____ _____.

화나 보이다
W I ordered a box of chocolate bars from an online store. But the chocolate bars had all melted when I got them.
M Oh, no. Did you complain to the online store?
W Sure, but they said that it wasn't their fault because the delivery service company was responsible for _____ _____ _____. Anyway, they said that I can't

박스를 차갑게 유지하는 것
_____ _____ _____ from the store.

환불받다
M What a joke!
W I know. It's not fair at all. So I'm going to _____ _____ _____ _____

이걸 보고하는 편지를 쓰다
_____ to a consumer rights group. Would you help me write the letter?
M Sure! I can help you with that.

09 마지막 말 의도

대화를 듣고, 여자의 마지막 말의 의도로 가장 적절한 것을 고르시오.

① 공부를 열심히 해라.
② 건강관리에 힘써라.
③ 집 청소를 자주 해라.
④ 어머니를 도와드려라.
⑤ 요리에 관심을 가져라.

W I'll see you tomorrow. Bye.
M Are you going home this early?
W Yes. My mother is not well, so I have to _____ _____ _____.

그녀와 같이 있는
M Oh, I'm sorry to hear that. Can I ask what's wrong with her?
W She _____ _____ _____ last month and is still recovering.

수술을 받았다
M So you have some cooking and washing-up to do, I presume.
W Yes. After that I'm going to _____ _____ _____ _____.

집 청소를 하다
M How nice of you. I think I should help my mom more often.
W Great idea. Then why don't you go home now and _____ _____ _____

네가 말한 것을 하다
_____?

10 숫자 정보 파악(금액)

하루 근무 시간, 주당 근무 일 수, 시간당 임금을 파악하여 계산해 본다.

대화를 듣고, 여자가 일주일에 받게 될 금액을 고르시오.

① $200　　② $250
③ $400　　④ $450
⑤ $925

M We're looking for a person who is good at computers.
W Don't worry. I'm good at computers.
M Great. You will _____ _____ _____ _____ _____

월요일부터 금요일까지 하루 8시간 근무하다
_____ _____ _____. Nine to five, five days a week. Is it okay with you?
W Sure. No problem.
M You'll _____ _____ _____ _____ _____. Payday is every Friday.

시간당 10달러를 받다
W I know that.
M When can you start?
W I can work from tomorrow.

11 관계 파악

대화를 듣고, 두 사람의 관계로 가장 적절한 것을 고르시오.

① 상주 – 문상객
② 환자 – 면회객
③ 엄마 – 아들
④ 목사 – 신도
⑤ 의사 – 환자의 보호자

Don't mention it. (천만에요.) : 고마움을 표시하는 말에 대한 대답을 나타낼 때 쓰는 표현이다.
(= You're welcome.)

pass away, mourners 등을 종합하여 관계를 파악한다.

M　Thank you for coming.

W　Don't mention it. How did it happen?

M　I have no idea. He ＿＿＿＿ 〔아픈 징후는 보이지 않았다〕 ＿＿＿＿ ＿＿＿＿ ＿＿＿＿ until last night.

W　I can't still believe that ＿＿＿＿ 〔당신의 아버님이 돌아가셨다〕 ＿＿＿＿ ＿＿＿＿ . He looked so healthy.

M　Yes, but he was quite old, 89, you know.

W　I don't know what to say. I hope he will ＿＿＿＿ 〔하늘나라로 가서 편안하다〕 ＿＿＿＿ ＿＿＿＿ ＿＿＿＿ ＿＿＿＿ .

M　I guess he will. Thanks.

W　＿＿＿＿ 〔조문객들〕 are coming in. You go and greet them.

12 언급 유무 파악(담화)

다음을 듣고, 태풍에 대비하여 갖추어야 할 것으로 언급되지 않은 것을 고르시오.

① 생수 bottled water
② 예비 전력
③ 통조림 식품 canned food
④ 초와 성냥 candles and matches
⑤ 전지용 라디오 battery-powered radio

언급된 내용을 지워나가며 듣되, 상식에 의존하지 않도록 유의한다.

M　It's hurricane season, isn't it? There are many things you need to get ready, aren't there? ＿＿＿＿ 〔충분한 생수〕 ＿＿＿＿ ＿＿＿＿ , of course. You ＿＿＿＿ 〔통조림 식품을 갖추어야 한다〕 ＿＿＿＿ ＿＿＿＿ in case the electricity goes out. For the same reason, you need ＿＿＿＿ 〔초와 성냥〕 ＿＿＿＿ ＿＿＿＿ . Finally, you need ＿＿＿＿ 〔전지용 라디오〕 ＿＿＿＿ to keep yourself informed about approaching hurricanes.

13 특정 정보 파악(도표)

다음 표를 보면서 대화를 듣고, 남자가 선택할 요금제를 고르시오.

무료 통화시간, 무료 문자건수, 데이터 용량, 가격 등을 주의해서 듣는다.

	Free calls	Free text messages	Data Capacity	Price
①	2 hours	500	1.5 GB	50,000
②	3 hours	Unlimited	2.0 GB	70,000
③	3 hours	1,000	Unlimited	90,000
④	3 hours	500	Unlimited	70,000
⑤	3 hours	Unlimited	Unlimited	80,000

➕ 다음을 듣고, 대화가 일어나는 장소를 고르시오.

① 부동산　　② 휴대폰 수리처
③ 분실센터　　④ 여행 안내처
⑤ 휴대폰 판매처

W　Okay, sir, now you have to decide ＿＿＿＿ 〔어떤 요금제를 선택할지〕 ＿＿＿＿ ＿＿＿＿ .

M　Do you have any with three hours of free calls?

W　Sure, we do. Do you make a lot of phone calls?

M　Yes. I'm a sales representative, so clients call me quite often.

W　I see. How about free text messages? You can choose 500, 1,000, or an unlimited number.

M　I think 500 text messages should be enough for me.

W　Super. Now you need to decide ＿＿＿＿ 〔데이터가 얼마나 필요한지〕 ＿＿＿＿ ＿＿＿＿ ＿＿＿＿ . We can offer from 1.5 GB to unlimited data.

M　Well, my monthly budget for my smartphone bill is 70,000 won. Can I choose unlimited data and not go over 70,000 won?

W　Yes, we can offer unlimited data for 70,000 won.

M　I'll take this payment plan then.

14 소재 파악(담화)

다음을 듣고, 무엇에 관한 설명인지 고르시오.

① 확성기   ② 녹음기
③ 보청기   ④ 라디오
⑤ 무전기

목소리를 특정 방향으로 확대하는 데 도움을 주는 것이 무엇인지 생각해 본다.

W This is a hand-held, cone-shaped device. This helps us _____

_____ _____ _____ _____. So when we speak to a large crowd in front of

우리의 목소리를 특정 방향으로 확대하다

us, we can use this so that our voice can travel the farthest. But when a listener is to the

side, it is more difficult to hear what is being said. Common uses for this are at sporting

events or generally _____ _____ _____ _____

_____ _____ in an open space.

많은 사람들에게 연설할 필요가 있을 때

---

15 할 일 파악

대화를 듣고, 두 사람이 토요일에 할 일로 가장 적절한 것을 고르시오.

① 독서   ② 볼링
③ 도서 대여   ④ 연극 관람
⑤ 남자의 여동생 방문

What are you going to do this Saturday?
(이번 주 토요일에 뭐 할 거야?) : What are you going to do ~?는 앞으로의 계획을 묻는 표현으로 What are you planning to do ~?로 말할 수도 있다.

Would you like to ~?에 이어지는 제안과 그에 대한 대답을 잘 듣고 함께 할 일을 파악한다.

M What are you going to do this Saturday?

W I'm going to go to the library and get some books to read.

M What will you do after that?

W I'll read them in the afternoon.

M Well, _____ _____ _____ _____ _____ this Saturday

너와 함께 하고 싶은 일이 있다

afternoon.

W What? I don't want to go bowling again.

M My sister _____ _____ _____ _____ to *The Moon of Seoul*. _____ _____

내게 두 장의 표를 주었다   나와 함께 가고 싶니

_____ _____ _____ _____ _____?

W Oh, that famous play? Sure, _____ _____ _____ _____.

가고 싶다

M Then, meet me at three in front of the theater.

---

16 특정 정보 파악(내일 날씨)

대화를 듣고, 내일 예상되는 날씨를 고르시오.

① foggy 안개 낀   ② rainy 비 오는
③ sunny 화창한   ④ windy 바람 부는
⑤ cloudy 흐린

What a relief! (다행이야!) : 안도를 나타낼 때 쓰는 표현이다.

오늘 날씨와 혼동하지 않도록 한다.

W I can't believe this!

M It was foggy when we arrived here four days ago.

W And since then, _____ _____ _____ _____ _____.

3일 동안 비가 내리고 있다

M It's strange. It usually doesn't rain much around here at this time of year.

W It's _____ , _____ _____ _____ _____.

대개 바람은 좀 불지만 이처럼 비가 내리지는 않는다

M Maybe this rain will ruin our vacation.

W Not from tomorrow, I guess.

M What do you mean?

W I just heard the weather report. It'll be still cloudy this evening, but _____

내일부터는 날씨가 화창할 것이다

_____ _____ _____ _____.

M Really? What a relief!

대화를 듣고, 여자의 직업으로 가장 적절한 것을 고르시오.

① 은행원
② 건물 관리인
③ 건축 설계사
④ 부동산 중개인
⑤ 체육관 트레이너

W Now, have you decided which house you'll move into?

M Not yet. It's hard to choose. I need your advice.

W Gladly. First let me ask you what the most important thing in a house is.

M Well, I want a quiet place with clean air so I can take a good rest at home.

W Really? Look at this picture. This house is exactly _____ _____. (당신이 찾고 있는 것) But it's over 20 minutes walk away from the subway station.

M That's okay to me. I love walking. By the way, is there a fitness center near this house?

W Yes. There's one _____ _____ _____ _____. (바로 길 건너편)

M Great. Can you check when the house will be available?

[18~19] 대화를 듣고, 여자의 마지막 말에 대한 남자의 응답으로 가장 적절한 것을 고르시오.

Man: _____

① I'll try, but I'm not sure I can do that.
② That's okay. I sweat when I feel nervous, too.
③ I did what you said and it worked perfectly.
④ Don't speak ill of others when they are away.
⑤ I wonder if I can give the presentation for you.

발표시 마음가짐에 대한 여자의 조언을 들은 남자가 할 수 있는 말을 생각해 본다.

W Gary, how did the presentation go?

M It was terrible.

W Really? Didn't you say it was very important?

M Yes, but when I saw those people in front of me, I was so nervous that (나는 땀이 얼굴에 범벅이 되어 버렸다) _____ _____ _____ _____ _____ _____ .

W I'm sorry to hear that. Don't be disappointed. Next time you make a presentation, (방에 아무도 없다고 상상해 봐라) _____ _____ _____ _____ _____ .

M _____

Man: _____

① OK. Let me show you the map.
② Yes, I learned it the hard way.
③ I don't think so. He was mean to me.
④ Right. Next time I won't drive near a school.
⑤ Yes, I should. That's why I don't like schools.

법규 위반을 한 사람의 태도가 어떠야 할지 추측한다.

W You _____ _____. Can you tell me what's wrong? (언짢은 표정이다)

M I was unlucky today. I got a ticket for speeding!

W Oh, _____ _____ _____. How fast did you drive anyway? (그것 참 안 됐다)

M About 50km per hour.

W 50km per hour? I don't understand. It's not too fast.

M It is when you're within the school zone.

W Now I know why the policeman _____ _____ _____. You should've (당신에게 딱지를 발부하다) been more careful near a school.

M _____

다음 상황 설명을 듣고, Paul이 계산원에게 할 말로 가장 적절한 것을 고르시오.

Paul: _____

① I want to get a refund.
② Can I pay for it by credit card?
③ I am afraid I was overcharged.
④ Is there another bookstore around here?
⑤ Excuse me, I want to exchange this book.

W Paul goes to a bookstore to buy his favorite author's new novel. He picks it up and pays for it. When he gets home, he opens the book and _____ _____ _____ _____. (일부 페이지가 빠져 있음을 발견한다) He goes back to the bookstore. He wants to let them know some pages are missing and _____ _____. (그것을 교환하다) He walks over to the cashier at the counter. In this situation, what will Paul most likely say to the cashier?

무엇을 평가하는가?	일상생활이나 친숙한 일반적 주제에 관한 말이나 대화를 듣고 주제, 요지를 파악할 수 있는지를 평가한다.
어떻게 출제되는가?	• 다음을 듣고, 무엇에 관한 설명인지 고르시오.

key
solution

❶ 한 두 문장의 특징만으로 섣부르게 답을 고르지 않도록 주의하며, 전체적인 내용을 포함하고 있는 답을 찾는다.

[기출로 전략 확인]

다음을 듣고, 무엇에 관한 설명인지 고르시오.　　　　　　　　[2018 기출]

① 스키　　　　　　② 축구　　　　　　③ 핸드볼
④ 야구　　　　　　⑤ 아이스하키

....

W This is a team sport. Players play this on ice with skates on. For safety, players should wear a helmet and special equipment to protect their bodies. In order to score, they use a long stick to hit a small round flat object, called a puck, into the opposing team's net. It's one of the popular winter sports in North America.

❶ 팀 스포츠, 스케이트, 보호 장비, 긴 막대 사용, 골대, 겨울 스포츠 등의 내용을 전체적으로 포함하고 있는 답을 찾는다.

여 이것은 팀 스포츠입니다. 선수들은 얼음 위에서 스케이트를 타고 경기를 합니다. 안전을 위해 선수들은 몸에 헬멧과 특수한 장비를 착용합니다. 점수를 따기 위해, 선수들은 긴 막대를 사용하여 '퍽'이라고 불리는 작고 동그란 납작한 물건을 상대팀 골대로 칩니다. 북아메리카에서 인기있는 겨울 스포츠 중 하나입니다.

다음을 듣고, 무엇에 관한 설명인지 고르시오. [2017 기출]

① 주사기   ② 청진기   ③ 체온계
④ 혈압계   ⑤ 습도계

만점 잡는 문장   ① It's usually used in homes, hospitals, schools, and other places.

② The tip of this device is usually inserted into the mouth or into the ear.

③ It's used to measure body temperature for medical purposes.

다음을 듣고, 무엇에 관한 설명인지 고르시오. [2016 기출]

① 계단   ② 비상구   ③ 사다리
④ 엘리베이터   ⑤ 에스컬레이터

만점 잡는 문장   ① You can use this in a building.

② It is one of the fastest ways to move to the different levels of a building.

③ You must not use this when there is a fire. You can get stuck in it.

말의 내용/소재 파악에 쓰이는 표현

● 물건

It is a machine for measuring the weight of an object. 물건의 무게를 측정하기 위한 기계이다.
It is used when people go out or travel. 사람들이 밖에 나가거나 여행할 때 사용한다.
It is designed to keep drinks either hot or cold. 뜨겁거나 차가운 것을 보관하도록 위해 만들어졌다.
It comes in many sizes and shapes. 많은 크기와 모양이 있다.

● 스포츠

This is a team sport using a ball. 공을 사용한 팀 스포츠이다.
You can play it both indoors and outdoors. 실내와 실외 모두에서 할 수 있다.
People score by throwing the ball into the net. 골대 안에 공을 던져서 점수를 얻는다.
You don't need any other equipment to play. 경기하는데 장비는 필요 없다.

● 교통수단

This is a vehicle which you ride by sitting on it. 앉아서 타는 탈 것이다.
It carries a lot of passengers at a time. 많은 승객들을 한 번에 옮긴다.
It stops at stations and people get on and get off there.
정거장에 서고 그곳에서 사람들이 타고 내린다.
It has many wheels but it can only run on rails. 많은 바퀴가 있지만 철도 위로만 달릴 수 있다.

01 대화를 듣고, 두 사람이 구입할 그림을 고르시오.

02 대화를 듣고, 여자가 학교에 다시 가는 목적으로 가장 적절한 것을 고르시오.

① 친구를 만나려고
② 영화 공부를 하려고
③ 동아리에 등록하려고
④ 영화 감독을 만나려고
⑤ 놓고 온 물건을 가져오려고

03 다음 그림의 상황에 가장 적절한 대화를 고르시오.

①   ②   ③   ④   ⑤

04 대화를 듣고, 여자의 현재 직업으로 가장 적절한 것을 고르시오.

① model
② reporter
③ school teacher
④ basketball coach
⑤ basketball player

고난도
05 대화를 듣고, 두 사람이 대화하는 장소로 가장 적절한 곳을 고르시오.

① 공원
② 병원
③ 남자의 집
④ 여자의 집
⑤ 체육관

06 대화를 듣고, 여자의 심정 변화로 가장 적절한 것을 고르시오.

① upset → relieved
② happy → upset
③ frustrated → happy
④ regretful → calm
⑤ gloomy → excited

07 다음을 듣고, 두 사람의 대화가 <u>어색한</u> 것을 고르시오.

①   ②   ③   ④   ⑤

08 대화를 듣고, 여자가 남자에게 부탁한 일로 가장 적절한 것을 고르시오.

① 피자 배달하기
② 피자가게 주소 알아보기
③ 피자 재료 쇼핑하기
④ 피자가게 함께 가기
⑤ 피자 만들어 보기

고난도
09 대화를 듣고, 남자가 여자를 서점에서 만나자고 한 이유로 가장 적절한 것을 고르시오.

① 책을 구입하기 위하여
② 여자가 즐겨 찾는 장소라서
③ 소설가 사인회에 참석하려고
④ 신간소설을 선물하기 위해서
⑤ 좋아하는 소설의 배경이 되는 장소라서

고난도
10 대화를 듣고, 여자가 지불할 총 금액을 고르시오.

① $55
② $70
③ $77
④ $100
⑤ $110

11 대화를 듣고, 여자가 할 일로 가장 적절한 것을 고르시오.

① 저녁 요리를 한다   ② 요리하는 법을 알려준다
③ 요리할 재료를 사러간다   ④ 요리학원을 등록한다
⑤ 부엌 뒷정리를 한다

12 다음을 듣고, bubble wrap에 대해 언급되지 않은 것을 고르시오.

① 개발 시기   ② 기원
③ 용도   ④ 인기
⑤ 부작용

13 다음 표를 보면서 대화를 듣고, 여자가 살 진공청소기를 고르시오.

	Model	Suction Power	Dust Bag/Bagless	Price
①	LS-200	240	Dust Bag	$220
②	TG-201	260	Bagless	$270
③	PG-230	255	Dust Bag	$245
④	LT-320	235	Bagless	$275
⑤	SG-330	270	Bagless	$310

14 다음을 듣고, 무엇에 관한 설명인지 고르시오.

① recipe   ② destiny
③ exercise   ④ medicine
⑤ weather report

15 대화를 듣고, 두 사람이 대화 직후에 할 일로 가장 적절한 것을 고르시오.

① 쇼핑몰에 간다.
② Jack의 집에 간다.
③ 영화를 보러 간다.
④ Tommy에게 전화한다.
⑤ Tommy의 선물을 사러 간다.

16 대화를 듣고, 남자가 맨 먼저 구입할 물건을 고르시오.

① laptop   ② external hard drive
③ printer   ④ digital camera
⑤ Cellphone

17 대화를 듣고, 여자가 서두르는 이유로 가장 적절한 것을 고르시오.

① 영국행 비행기를 타려고
② 분실한 책을 찾아오려고
③ 마감 시간 전에 우체국에 가려고
④ 우체국 앞에서 언니를 만나기로 해서
⑤ 서점이 닫기 전에 책을 사러 가야 해서

[18~19] 대화를 듣고, 여자의 마지막 말에 대한 남자의 응답으로 가장 적절한 것을 고르시오.

18 Man: _____

① Don't go there anymore.
② OK. I'll do it for the doctor.
③ You'd better cut down a little.
④ What about coming to my birthday?
⑤ Why don't we go shopping together?

19 Man: _____

① You'd better study harder.
② I want to work at a restaurant.
③ You should have got a part-time job.
④ How about trying to find another one?
⑤ What about taking a few days off?

20 다음 상황 설명을 듣고, Sally가 손님에게 할 말로 가장 적절한 것을 고르시오.

Sally: _____

① Would like a refund, sir?
② How much do I owe you?
③ We'll take your order now.
④ How much will you pay for this?
⑤ Would you wait until we call you?

다시 들으면서 듣기 만점에 도전하세요!
Dictation: 스크립트의 주요 부분을 다시 들으면서!
실전 ⊕: 세부 정보가 많은 스크립트를 다른 문제로 샅샅이!

---

01 그림 정보 파악(사물)

그림을 묘사하는 표현에 집중하며 듣는다.

대화를 듣고, 두 사람이 구입할 그림을 고르시오.

① ② ③ ④ ⑤

W These paintings are all impressive.

M Yes, they're all painted in a very unique style.

W Why don't you choose one _____ _____ _____ _____ _____ _____? (네 방에 걸) It'll make your room look nice. How about this one with the skyscrapers?

M I'd prefer something a bit brighter, like this painting of sunflowers in a vase.

W Maybe that abstract painting would _____ (네 방에 어울리다) _____ better—the one with circles and triangles.

M Oh, you're right. I really love it. I think it would look great hanging over my desk.

W Okay, let's get that one.

고난도

02 목적 파악

잊어버리고 안 한 일이 무엇인지에 집중해서 듣는다.

대화를 듣고, 여자가 학교에 다시 가는 목적으로 가장 적절한 것을 고르시오.

① 친구를 만나려고
② 영화 공부를 하려고
③ 동아리에 등록하려고
④ 영화 감독을 만나려고
⑤ 놓고 온 물건을 가져오려고

I'm interested in movies. (영화에 관심이 있다.) : A be interested in + (동)명사 B는 '~에 관심이 있다'는 의미로 관심이나 흥미를 나타낼 때 쓰는 표현이다.

M Hi, Mary. Where are you going?

W I'm going back to school. I _____ _____ _____. (할 일을 깜박했다)

M What is it? Anything important?

W Yeah. It's about _____ _____. (동아리에 가입하기) I _____ _____ _____ (등록해야 한다) by today.

M That's what you forgot to do. What's the club?

W It's a kind of movie making club. You know how much I like movies.

M Wow, that's great. So you're going to _____ _____ _____? (언젠가는 감독이 되다)

W Maybe. I don't know yet. I'm just interested in movies.

---

03 상황에 적절한 대화(그림)

남자가 배 멀미하는 상황이므로 그와 어울리는 seasick이라는 표현을 미리 생각해 둔다.

다음 그림의 상황에 가장 적절한 대화를 고르시오.

① ② ③ ④ ⑤

① W What's wrong with you? You look ill.
   M I think _____ _____. (배 멀미를 하다)

② W You don't look OK. What's the matter?
   M _____ _____ _____ _____ (내 등이 아파 왔다) a little since I got on board.

③ W You don't like to travel by ship, do you?
   M Yes, I do. I really like it.

④ W What do you want to be?
   M I'd like to be a sailor.

⑤ W Do you _____ _____? (멀미 나다)
   M No, I feel fine. Thanks.

04 특정 정보 파악(현재 직업)

예전에 했던 일과 현재 하는 일을 구별하여 듣도록 한다.

대화를 듣고, 여자의 현재 직업으로 가장 적절한 것을 고르시오.

① model 모델
② reporter 기자
③ school teacher 학교 교사
④ basketball coach 농구 코치
⑤ basketball player 농구 선수

M Susan, you're really good at basketball.

W Thank you. Actually I'm not ＿＿＿＿ ＿＿＿＿ ＿＿＿＿ ＿＿＿＿
　　　　　　　　　　　　　　　　　예전만큼 잘하는
＿＿＿＿.

M What do you mean?

W I was ＿＿＿＿ ＿＿＿＿ ＿＿＿＿ ＿＿＿＿ ＿＿＿＿.
　　　　　고교 스타 농구 선수

M Oh, really?

W Most people don't know about me.

M Why did you ＿＿＿＿ ＿＿＿＿ ＿＿＿＿, not a basketball player?
　　　　　　　　　모델이 되다

W In a game I ＿＿＿＿ ＿＿＿＿ ＿＿＿＿ ＿＿＿＿ ＿＿＿＿.
　　　　　　　넘어져서 내 발목을 심하게 접질렀다

M And you quit afterwards?

W Yes.

고난도

05 대화 장소 파악

Thanks for coming, go home 등을 놓치지 않고 듣는다.

대화를 듣고, 두 사람이 대화하는 장소로 가장 적절한 곳을 고르시오.

① 공원　　　　② 병원
③ 남자의 집　　④ 여자의 집
⑤ 체육관

W How are you feeling today?

M Much better than yesterday. ＿＿＿＿ ＿＿＿＿.
　　　　　　　　　　　　　　　　와 줘서 고맙다

W What happened?

M I fell down and ＿＿＿＿ ＿＿＿＿ ＿＿＿＿.
　　　　　　　　　오른쪽 팔이 부러졌다

W Oh, that's too bad. When are you supposed to ＿＿＿＿ ＿＿＿＿ anyway?
　　　　　　　　　　　　　　　　　　　　　　　　집으로 가다

M Maybe this weekend. I'll ask the doctor.

W And I also hope you ＿＿＿＿ ＿＿＿＿ ＿＿＿＿ ＿＿＿＿ soon.
　　　　　　　　　　　　깁스를 풀다

M So do I. Thanks again for coming.

---

06 심정 파악

규칙상 개를 기를 수 없다는 말에 여자가 보이는 반응에 유의한다.

대화를 듣고, 여자의 심정 변화로 가장 적절한 것을 고르시오.

① upset → relieved
② happy → upset
③ frustrated → happy
④ regretful → calm
⑤ gloomy → excited

W Good morning. I'm Cindy Brown. I'm new here.

M Oh, you ＿＿＿＿ ＿＿＿＿, right? Nice to meet you. I'm Chris, manager of
　　　　　어제 이사 들어왔다
this apartment.

W Nice to meet you, too. I'd like to ask you one thing. Is it okay to park my car in front of
this building?

M Sure. You'll ＿＿＿＿ ＿＿＿＿ there reserved for residents.
　　　　　약간의 공간을 보다

W I'm glad to hear that. And what about house pets? Is there any rules about keeping a
dog?

M Sorry, pets ＿＿＿＿ here.
　　　　　허용되지 않는다

W Oh, no. I can't live without my dog. What should I do?

M Well, as long as you live here, you should follow the rules.

W Then should I throw my dog away? That's not possible.

M I'm just telling you the rules. I don't care about your dog.

W Oh, please. Could you find a way for me to ＿＿＿＿ ＿＿＿＿ ＿＿＿＿?
　　　　　　　　　　　　　　　　　　　　　나의 개와 함께 살다

안부 인사를 전해 달라는 부탁에 대한 응답을 생각해 본다.

다음을 듣고, 두 사람의 대화가 <u>어색한</u> 것을 고르시오.

①   ②   ③   ④   ⑤

Sorry to hear that! (안됐네요.) : 유감을 나타낼 때 쓰는 표현이다. (=That's too bad.)

① W   What seems to be the problem?

   M   This phone _____ _____ _____ when I press the "call" button.
<small>계속 꺼진다</small>

② W   I'd like to rent a car, please.

   M   What size car would you like?

③ W   Please _____ _____ _____ _____ for me.
<small>당신의 부모님께 안부를 전하다</small>

   M   Sure. What time are you going to call them?

④ W   I'd like to _____ _____ _____ _____.
<small>당신에게 부탁하다</small>

   M   OK. What is it?

⑤ W   I failed the driving test again.

   M   Oh, sorry to hear that.

대화를 듣고, 여자가 남자에게 부탁한 일로 가장 적절한 것을 고르시오.

① 피자 배달하기
② 피자가게 주소 알아보기
③ 피자 재료 쇼핑하기
④ 피자가게 함께 가기
⑤ 피자 만들어 보기

W   Wow, this pizza is very tasty. Where did you get it?

M   It's called Sam's Pizza. They use very good cheese and fresh vegetables.

W   I'd love to order from them again. Can you let me know their phone number?

M   They don't deliver. It's a very small place _____ _____ _____
<small>주인이 혼자 운영하다</small>
_____ _____ _____. I can let you know the address.

W   Oh, I see. Could you _____ _____ _____ sometime?
<small>나와 함께 거기에 가다</small>

M   Sure, we can go someday after school.

W   That would be great. Thanks!

고난도

여자가 Bernard Werber의 열렬한 팬일 것을 알고서 그의 책 사인회에 같이 참여하기 위해서이다.

대화를 듣고, 남자가 여자를 서점에서 만나고 한 이유로 가장 적절한 것을 고르시오.

① 책을 구입하기 위하여
② 여자가 즐겨 찾는 장소라서
③ 소설가 사인회에 참석하려고
④ 신간소설을 선물하기 위해서
⑤ 좋아하는 소설의 배경이 되는 장소라서

M   Oh, I'm sorry for being late, Monica.

W   That's all right. _____ _____ _____ _____ at the new arrivals section.
<small>책들을 구경하고 있었다</small>

M   Did you find anything you want to buy?

W   No, I don't want to buy anything. How about you? What do you want to buy?

M   Nothing.

W   What? Then, is there _____ _____ _____ asking me to meet you here?
<small>~에 대한 특별한 이유</small>

M   Sure. I've got surprised for you. Bernard Werber will _____ _____
<small>책 사인회를 열다</small>
_____ here at three today _____ _____ _____.
<small>그의 새 소설 판매 촉진을 위해</small>

W   Really? You know, I'm a big fan of him.

M   I know. Why don't we go to his book signing together?

W   Sounds great!

10 숫자 정보 파악(금액)

세금 포함 여부와 차를 빌리는 일수에 유의하여 계산해 본다.

대화를 듣고, 여자가 지불할 총 금액을 고르시오.

① $55
② $70
③ $77
④ $100
⑤ $110

M Good morning. May I help you?

W Yes. I'd like to _____ _____ _____ here.
　　　　　　　　　　차를 빌리다

M OK. What size car do you have in mind?

W Well, any car is OK if it's not expensive.

M Good. This one is only $35 a day. But as you see, the trunk is not so spacious.

W I see. How about that one? It looks like it can carry big suitcases.

M It's $50. Would you like it?

W Yes. Does _____ _____ _____?
　　　　　가격이 세금을 포함하다

M No, _____ _____ _____ _____.
　세금은 10%이다

W OK. I'll rent it _____ _____ _____.
　　　　　　　　　이틀 동안

11 할 일 파악

대화를 듣고, 여자가 할 일로 가장 적절한 것을 고르시오.

① 저녁 요리를 한다
② 요리하는 법을 알려준다
③ 요리할 재료를 사러간다
④ 요리학원을 등록한다
⑤ 부엌 뒷정리를 한다

➕ 대화를 듣고, 남자에 대한 내용과 일치하지 않은 것을 고르시오.

① 요리를 잘한다.
② 여자에게 요리를 가르쳐 주기를 좋아한다
③ 남자의 요리 방법은 쉽고 빠르다
④ 금요일에 여자를 만날 계획이다.
⑤ 요리 재료를 직접 쇼핑할 것이다.

W Daniel, I heard you're a great cook.

M Well, thanks for saying so, but I'm not that good. Cooking is just a hobby for me.

W Why don't you teach me _____ _____ _____ _____?
　　　　　　　　　　　　너가 가장 잘 만드는 음식을 어떻게 만드는지

M I'd love to. I can show you how to make quick and tasty dishes if you'd like. All of my recipes are _____ _____ _____.
　　　　　따라하기 꽤 쉬운

W Really? That would be great! Just name the day so that I can go grocery shopping first.

M How about this Friday?

W Friday works for me. Text me _____ _____ _____.
　　　　　　　　　　　　　내가 사야 할 것

M OK, I will soon. See you Friday!

12 언급 유무 파악(담화)

다음을 듣고, bubble wrap에 대해 언급되지 않은 것을 고르시오.

① 개발 시기
② 기원
③ 용도
④ 인기
⑤ 부작용

M Bubble wrap is _____ _____ _____. Like a lot of really cool things, it
　　　　　　　　50년이 된

_____ _____ _____ _____. Now bubble wrap
비행기 착륙 장면을 보다가 우연히 만들어졌다

_____ _____ _____ _____, protecting everything from
포장 재료로 이용되다

vases to computers. Bubble wrap is also a fun toy. When you pop it, it creates a sound. When a room is full of kids and the floor is doubly covered with many pieces of bubble wrap, you don't need anything else to play with. Bubble wrap _____
　　　　　　　　　　　　　　　　　　　　　　　　거의 100만 명에 육박하는 팬들을 가지고 있다

_____ _____ on Facebook. This is Warren Robinson from the Associated Press.

13 특정 정보 파악(도표)

고르는 물건의 특징을 놓치지 않고 하나씩 제외해 가며 정답을 찾는다.

다음 표를 보면서 대화를 듣고, 여자가 살 진공청소기를 고르시오.

	Model	Suction Power	Dust Bag /Bagless	Price
①	LS–200	240	Dust Bag	$220
②	TG–201	260	Bagless	$270
③	PG–230	255	Dust Bag	$245
④	LT–320	235	Bagless	$275
⑤	SG–330	270	Bagless	$310

M Hi, Can I help you?

W Yes, please. I'd like to buy a _____ _____.
　　　　　　　　　　　　　　　진공청소기

M All right, ma'am. Do you have a specific model in mind?

W Well, as long as the suction power is over 250 air watts, it'll be OK with me.

M About the suction power, you _____ _____ _____. And what about the dust bags?
　　　　　　　　　　　　　세 가지 선택이 있다

W Let me see the brochure. It says bagless vacuums are more expensive but convenient.

M That's right. And they _____ _____.
　　　　　　　　　　전력을 덜 소비하다

W I see. Then I'd like to buy a bagless vacuum with the lowest price tag.

M Sure, I've got the one for you!

14 소재 파악(담화)

sunny, cloudy, rainy or windy 등에 대해 말해 주는 것이 무엇인지 추측해 본다.

다음을 듣고, 무엇에 관한 설명인지 고르시오.

① recipe 요리법 　 ② destiny 운명
③ exercise 운동 　 ④ medicine 약
⑤ weather report 일기예보

W We hear about this every day, especially in the morning and at night. We want to know whether today or tomorrow will be sunny, cloudy, rainy or windy. Also we want to know ＿＿＿ ＿＿＿ ＿＿＿ ＿＿＿ ＿＿＿ ＿＿＿ ＿＿＿ . Some
　　얼마나 더울지 혹은 얼마나 추울지
people are especially interested in this because their plans change if this is not good.
Mostly we ＿＿＿＿＿＿ ＿＿＿ ＿＿＿ from the news but nowadays we
　　　　　이것에 대한 정보를 얻다
can use the Internet.

15 할 일 파악 – 대화 직후

남자가 형을 만나기로 한 장소에 유의하여 듣는다.

대화를 듣고, 두 사람이 대화 직후에 할 일로 가장 적절한 것을 고르시오.

① 쇼핑몰에 간다.
② Jack의 집에 간다.
③ 영화를 보러 간다.
④ Tommy에게 전화한다.
⑤ Tommy의 선물을 사러 간다.

W Jack, what are you going to do this Friday evening?
M I'm going to watch a movie with my brother.
W Oh, you mean Tommy? Is he here now?
M Yes. He came to see me last Sunday.
W I want to see him soon.
M No problem. He's going to stay here for two weeks.
W Will you ＿＿＿＿＿＿＿＿ ＿＿＿ ＿＿＿ sometime?
　　　　　나에게 전화하라고 그에게 말해 주다
M Why don't you come with me now? We're supposed to ＿＿＿＿＿ ＿＿＿
　　　　　　　　　　　　　　　　　　　　　　　　　　　쇼핑몰에서 만나다
＿＿＿ ＿＿＿ .
W Oh, that's great. I really missed him.
M You'll be surprised to see ＿＿＿＿＿ ＿＿＿＿ ＿＿＿ .
　　　　　　　　　　　　그가 얼마나 많이 변했는지

16 특정 정보 파악(구입할 물건)

대화를 듣고, 남자가 맨 먼저 구입할 물건을 고르시오.

① laptop
② external hard drive
③ printer
④ digital camera
⑤ Cellphone

➕
대화를 듣고, 남자의 심경으로 가장 적절한 것을 고르시오.

① excited 　 ② bored
③ concerned 　 ④ curious
⑤ confused

W You need to buy a lot of things for your first year of college, right? What would you like to get first?
M As a college student, the most important thing will be a laptop. I'll need to ＿＿＿
　　　　　　　　　　　　　　　　　　　　　　　　　　　　　　　강의 중에 필기하다
＿＿＿ ＿＿＿ ＿＿＿ , write essays, and make slides for presentations.
W Right. And you'll definitely need an external hard drive so that you can ＿＿＿
　　　　　　　　　　　　　　　　　　　　　　　　　　　데이터를 저장하고 쉽게 옮기다
＿＿＿ ＿＿＿ ＿＿＿ ＿＿＿ ＿＿＿ .
M That's right. Should I also get a printer?
W I don't think so. You can print things out at the library or the student union building. Don't bother buying one.
M OK. Oh, I really want to get a digital camera, too. It's my dream ＿＿＿
　　　　　　　　　　　　　　　　　　　　　　　　　　여행하고 사진 찍는 것
＿＿＿ ＿＿＿ ＿＿＿ .
W All those gadgets are going to cost a lot.
M Right. I guess I need a laptop before everything else. The semester starts soon!

17 이유 파악

우체국에 가는 이유를 말하는 부분에 집중하여 듣는다.

대화를 듣고, 여자가 서두르는 이유로 가장 적절한 것을 고르시오.

① 영국행 비행기를 타려고
② 분실한 책을 찾아오려고
③ 마감 시간 전에 우체국에 가려고
④ 우체국 앞에서 언니를 만나기로 해서
⑤ 서점이 닫기 전에 책을 사러 가야 해서

M Hi, Cathy. Where are you going?
W To the post office. I have ___ ___ ___ to my sister.
　　　　　　　　　　　　　보낼 것
M I'm going that way, too. What is it by the way?
W It's my sister's book. She ___ ___ ___ when she
　　　　　　　　　　　　우리 집에 그것을 놓고 갔다
　visited me yesterday.
M She can get it when she visits you next time.
W You know, she is studying in the U.K. She said she needs it for a report.
M So you're going to ___ ___ ___ ___
　　　　　　　　　　마감 시간 전에 속달 우편으로 그것을 보내다
　___ ?
W Right. Let's walk faster.

18 적절한 응답

초콜릿 도넛을 사다 달라는 여자에 대한 의사 선생님의 권유가 무엇이었을지 추측해 본다.

[18~19] 대화를 듣고, 여자의 마지막 말에 대한 남자의 응답으로 가장 적절한 것을 고르시오.

Man: _____

① Don't go there anymore.
② OK. I'll do it for the doctor.
③ You'd better cut down a little.
④ What about coming to my birthday?
⑤ Why don't we go shopping together?

M I'm going to the department store. Can you come with me?
W No, I have things to do by this afternoon.
M Can I buy something for you then?
W Oh, that's kind of you. Please buy some chocolate donuts.
M Again? You ___ ___ .
　　　　　　방금 한 개를 먹었다
W Yes. You know how I like them.
M Do you remember ___ ___ ___ to you?
　　　　　　　　　　의사가 말했던 것
W Sure I do. But I ___ ___ .
　　　　　　　　어쩔 수가 없다
M _____

19 적절한 응답

Man: _____

① You'd better study harder.
② I want to work at a restaurant.
③ You should have got a part-time job.
④ How about trying to find another one?
⑤ What about taking a few days off?

M You look sleepy, Jennifer. What happened?
W I worked at a restaurant last night.
M Worked at a restaurant? You mean you ___ ___ ___ ?
　　　　　　　　　　　　　　　　　시간제 일을 가졌다
W Right. Yesterday was my first day.
M But you don't look good. Are you OK?
W Actually, I have ___ ___ .
　　　　　　　　약간의 열
M I don't think your new job suits you.
W Well, I'll ___ ___ ___ .
　　　　그것에 익숙해지다
M _____

20 상황에 적절한 말(담화)

다음 상황 설명을 듣고, Sally가 손님에게 할 말로 가장 적절한 것을 고르시오.

Sally: _____

① Would like a refund, sir?
② How much do I owe you?
③ We'll take your order now.
④ How much will you pay for this?
⑤ Would you wait until we call you?

M Sally is a salesperson in a department store. A man comes to her and shows her a cap.
　He says he found that a button ___ ___ when he got home. He
　　　　　　　　　　　　　　　　떨어져 나갔다
　says that he ___ ___ for a new one. But the same one is
　　　　　　그것을 교환하고 싶다
　not available. She asks the man if he would like to wait ___ ___
　　　　　　　　　　　　　　　　　　　　　　　　　모자가 수선될 때까지
　___ ___ ___ . But he wants a new cap. In order to solve this problem,
　Sally wants to ___ ___ ___ . In this situation, what would Sally
　　　　　　　　그의 돈을 돌려주다
　say to him?

위치·도표 파악

무엇을 평가하는가?	일상생활이나 친숙한 일반적 주제에 관한 위치 또는 도표에 관한 말이나 대화를 듣고 세부 정보를 파악할 수 있는지를 평가한다.

어떻게 출제되는가?	• 다음 배치도를 보면서 대화를 듣고, 두 사람이 앉을 좌석의 구역을 고르시오. • 다음 표를 보면서 대화를 듣고, 여자가 구입할 프린터를 고르시오.

key solution

❶ 위치를 묻는 경우, 배치도를 보고 입구, 휴게실, 화장실 등의 위치를 파악한다.

❷ 각 구역의 장단점에 대해 이야기 하다가 마지막에 위치가 결정됨으로 섣부르게 답을 체크하지 말고 대화를 끝까지 주의 깊게 듣는다.

❸ 도표의 경우, 주의해서 들어야 할 내용을 파악 한 후 선택지를 지워가며 정답을 찾는다.

[기출로 전략 확인]

대화를 듣고, 두 사람이 사용할 회의실을 고르시오. [2018 기출]

Restroom 👨	Room A	Room B	Room C	
Entrance ➡				Lounge
Restroom 👩	Room D		Room E	

❶ 배치도를 보고 입구, 화장실과 라운지의 위치를 파악한다.

M Mary, which room is good for our meeting this Thursday?

W What about Room D?

M I heard that Robert will use it on that day.

W Hmm…, how about using one of the rooms next to the lounge? They're convenient.

M But the lounge is often crowded, so those rooms may be noisy.

W You're right. Then, we have two rooms left, Room A and Room B.

M Let's not use the room next to the restroom.

W Okay. Let's use this room.

❷ 여자가 다른 구역의 장점에 대해 언급하지만 결국 마지막에 위치가 결정된다.

남 Mary, 이번주 목요일 회의 어느 룸에서 하는 게 좋을까?

여 D룸 어때?

남 Robert가 그날 사용한다고 들었어.

여 음… 라운지 옆에 있는 룸을 사용하는 거 어때? 편리하잖아.

남 하지만 라운지는 항상 붐비니까 룸이 시끄러울 수도 있어.

여 맞아. 그럼 A룸과 B룸 두 룸이 남네.

남 화장실 옆에 있는 룸은 쓰지 말자.

여 그래. 이 룸으로 하자.

다음 벼룩시장 배치도를 보면서 대화를 듣고, 두 사람이 선택한 구역의 위치를 고르 [2015 기출]
시오.

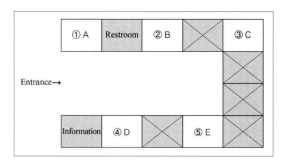

만점 잡는 문장 ① The sections next to the restroom are not good. I don't like the smell.

② Section C is too far from the entrance.

③ I think the section right next to the information booth is better because there'll be more people walking by.

다음 표를 보면서 대화를 듣고, 여자가 선택할 강좌를 고르시오. [2017 기출]

	Model	Printing Color	Printing Type	Price
①	A	Wednesday	Kelly	$50
②	B	Wednesday	Michelle	$70
③	C	Thursday	Kelly	$50
④	D	Thursday	Serena	$60
⑤	E	Thursday	Michelle	$70

만점 잡는 문장 ① I have a dance class every Wednesday, so I can't take it then.

② I'm going to choose one of Michelle and Serena classes.

③ I'll take the cheaper class.

● 위치

Let's avoid both sites directly next to the showers. 샤워실 바로 옆 장소 두 곳은 피하자.

They may be crowded in the afternoon. 그곳은 오후에 붐빌 수도 있어.

It's too far from the parking lot. 그곳은 주차장에서 너무 멀어.

I want to sit in one of the three front sections closer to the stage.
무대에서 가까운 앞에 세 구획 중 한 곳에 앉고 싶어.

The science club has already been given that section. 과학 클럽이 이미 그 구역을 갖게 되었어.

● 도표

I prefer a color printer so I can print pictures. 사진들을 뽑을 수 있는 컬러 프린터를 선호해요.

I'll take the expensive one. 비싼 걸 선택할 게요.

I'll take the cheaper class. 더 싼 강좌를 선택할 게요.

I'd like to buy a bagless vacuum with the lowest price tag.
먼지 주머니가 없는 가장 싼 진공청소기를 사고 싶어요.

영어듣기능력평가 13회

01 대화를 듣고 여자가 선택한 가방을 고르시오.

① ② ③ ④ ⑤

02 대화를 듣고, 내용에 언급되지 <u>않은</u> 것을 고르시오.

① 사고 시각
② 사고 장소
③ 여자의 이름
④ 남자의 연락처
⑤ 전화를 건 목적

03 다음 그림의 상황에 가장 적절한 대화를 고르시오.

① ② ③ ④ ⑤

04 대화를 듣고, 남자가 제주로 출발하는 요일을 고르시오.

① 일요일
② 토요일
③ 금요일
④ 목요일
⑤ 수요일

05 다음을 듣고, B의 심정으로 가장 적절한 것을 고르시오.

① calm
② nervous
③ regretful
④ bored
⑤ excited

06 대화를 듣고, 두 사람이 대화하는 장소로 가장 적절한 곳을 고르시오.

① 은행
② 옷 가게
③ 이불 가게
④ 보험 회사
⑤ 가구 판매점

07 다음을 듣고, 두 사람의 대화가 <u>어색한</u> 것을 고르시오.

① ② ③ ④ ⑤

08 대화를 듣고, 여자가 남자에게 부탁한 일로 가장 적절한 것을 고르시오.

① 알람시계 사주기
② 알람시계 꺼주기
③ 아침에 전화해 주기
④ 버스표 예약해 주기
⑤ 다음 주 월요일에 전화하기

09 대화를 듣고, 두 사람이 실망한 이유로 가장 적절한 것을 고르시오.

① 영화표가 너무 비싸서
② 영화관이 너무 시끄러워서
③ 주연 배우의 연기가 형편없어서
④ 영화의 줄거리가 너무 지루해서
⑤ 영화 감상 중 간식을 먹을 수 없어서

10 대화를 듣고, 남자가 지불할 금액을 고르시오.

① $150
② $250
③ $400
④ $360
⑤ $300

점수

/20

11 다음 표를 보면서 대화를 듣고, 오늘이 무슨 요일인지 고르시오.

Korean Art Exhibition

Day	Open	Closed
Mon.	Closed	
Tue. ~ Fri.	9:00 a.m.	6:00 p.m.
Sat.	10:00 a.m.	5:00 p.m.
Sun.	10:00 a.m.	2:00 p.m.

① 월요일 ② 목요일 ③ 금요일

④ 토요일 ⑤ 일요일

12 다음을 듣고, K-pop Dance Festival에 관해 언급되지 <u>않은</u> 것을 고르시오.

① 축제 기간 ② 축제 참석할 동문들의 수

③ 축제 참석 비용 ④ 축제 참석 요건

⑤ 축제의 하이라이트

13 다음 가정집 그림을 보면서 대화를 듣고, 여자가 패드를 찾은 곳을 고르시오.

14 다음을 듣고, 무엇에 대한 사용 설명인지 가장 적절한 것을 고르시오.

① 보청기 ② 자동 판매기

③ 온도 조절기 ④ 공기 정화기

⑤ 전자 체온기

고난도
15 대화를 듣고, 여자가 대화 직후에 할 일로 가장 적절한 것을 고르시오.

① 도자기를 산다.

② 한 블록을 걸어간다.

③ 도자기 상점을 찾는다.

④ 한국 전통 인형을 산다.

⑤ 관광 안내원에게 길을 묻는다.

16 대화를 듣고, 남자가 마지막 여행지로서 대만으로 재입국하는 날짜를 고르시오.

① 6월 4일 ② 6월 24일

③ 6월 30일 ④ 7월 7일

⑤ 7월 14일

고난도
17 대화를 듣고, Ted에 대한 내용과 일치하지 <u>않는</u> 것을 고르시오.

① 누나가 두 명 있다.

② 막내이다.

③ 누나들은 모두 결혼했다.

④ Judy와는 사촌 관계이다.

⑤ 누나 Lisa는 아직 자녀가 없다.

[18~19] 대화를 듣고, 여자의 마지막 말에 대한 남자의 응답으로 가장 적절한 것을 고르시오.

18 Man: _____

① That's just what I was thinking.

② I wonder if you could do me a favor.

③ Can I borrow your English textbook?

④ Why don't you take part in the music contest, instead?

⑤ Just cheer up! Remember, you're good at English.

19 Man: _____

① By cash.

② But I don't like the design.

③ I hope it's not too expensive.

④ Can I have this gift-wrapped?

⑤ You don't have to pay attention to it.

고난도
20 다음 상황 설명을 듣고, Harold가 Hana에게 할 말로 가장 적절한 것을 고르시오.

Harold: _____

① Hana, I'm afraid I don't have enough T-money.

② Hana, how about waiting for the next bus here?

③ Hana, we'd better take a subway to the stadium.

④ Hana, what did you think of today's baseball game?

⑤ Hana, how about going to the movies instead today?

다시 들으면서 듣기 만점에 도전하세요!
Dictation: 스크립트의 주요 부분을 다시 들으면세!
실전 ⊕: 세부 정보가 많은 스크립트를 다른 문제로 샅샅이!

---

01 그림 정보 파악(사물)

여자가 원하는 가방의 특징에 집중하며 듣는다.

대화를 듣고 여자가 선택한 가방을 고르시오.

① ② ③ ④ ⑤

다음을 듣고, 대화가 일어나는 장소를 고르시오.

① 여행사　② 공항　③ 가방 매장
④ 호텔　⑤ 거리

M May I help you?

W I'm looking for luggage for my trip.

M Are you traveling abroad?

W Yes. I'm going to South Africa.

M How about this suitcase? You can ＿＿＿ ＿＿＿ ＿＿＿ ＿＿＿ in it, (많은 것을 넣다) and it's easy to pull along.

W I'm sure it'd be easy to roll it along the street in a city, but I have to travel on lots of unpaved roads in the countryside.

M I see. Then how about ＿＿＿ ＿＿＿ ＿＿＿ ＿＿＿ ＿＿＿? (저기에 있는 배낭 중 하나)

W Those backpacks look convenient.

M Yes, they are. This backpack has a lot of pockets. It is very ＿＿＿ ＿＿＿ ＿＿＿ ＿＿＿. It's only $100. (작은 물건들을 가지고 다니기에 유용한)

W I think this one is perfect for me. I'll take it.

---

02 언급 유무 파악

전화를 통해 보험사에 알려주는 내용을 하나하나 체크해 본다.

대화를 듣고, 내용에 언급되지 <u>않은</u> 것을 고르시오.

① 사고 시각
② 사고 장소
③ 여자의 이름
④ 남자의 연락처
⑤ 전화를 건 목적

[Telephone rings.]

M Hello, this is Kangin Insurance. How may I help you?

W Hello, this is Sarah Smith. I ＿＿＿ ＿＿＿ ＿＿＿ this morning. (자동차 사고를 겪다)

M I'm sorry to hear that. Are you okay, ma'am?

W Fortunately, I'm, but my car ＿＿＿ ＿＿＿. (파손 당하다)

M Can I have your license plate number and your phone number, please?

W It's 25 Na 2039 and 010-234-8778.

M Thank you for the information. Could you tell me when, where and how the accident happened?

W Yes. It was 10 a.m. I was driving slowly ＿＿＿ (주차장을 찾기 위해서) in front of the Spring department store. Suddenly a taxi came from behind and bumped into my car.

---

03 상황에 적절한 대화(그림)

상대방의 양해를 구할 때 쓰는 공손한 표현에 주목한다.

다음 그림의 상황에 가장 적절한 대화를 고르시오.

① ② ③ ④ ⑤

Why not? (왜 안 되겠어?, 좋아.) : 상대방의 제안을 수락할 때 쓰는 표현이다. (=Of course. / Sure.)

① M ＿＿＿ ＿＿＿ ＿＿＿ ＿＿＿ I take the last piece of cake? (~해도 될까요)
  W Of course not. Help yourself.

② M Would you recommend a nice restaurant?
  W Sure. There's a great Korean restaurant ＿＿＿ ＿＿＿ the bakery. (바로 ~의 건너편에)

③ M What's your favorite Korean food?
  W *Bulgogi* is my favorite.

④ M Are you ＿＿＿ ＿＿＿ something for desert? (주문할 준비가 된)
  W I'd like a piece of cake and a coffee, please.

⑤ M I'm getting hungry. Let's ＿＿＿ ＿＿＿ ＿＿＿. (간단히 요기하다)
  W Why not?

04 특정 정보 파악(요일)

대화를 듣고, 남자가 제주로 출발하는 요일을 고르시오.

① 일요일　　　　② 토요일
③ 금요일　　　　④ 목요일
⑤ 수요일

➕ 다음을 듣고, 남자가 금요일에 출발할 수 없는 이유를 고르시오.

① 비행기편이 취소되어서
② 급한 사정이 생겨서
③ 비행기 예약이 끝나서
④ 제주도 기상악화로
⑤ 여행 일정이 변경되어서

W Airline reservation center. How may I help you?

M Can I _____ _____ to Jeju Island?
　　　　　　표를 구매하다

W Sure. What day would you like to travel?

M I'd like to fly this Friday.

W This Friday, May 12? Just a moment, please... *[pause]* I'm sorry, but _____ _____ _____ _____ _____ on May 12. All flights are fully booked. There are lots of
　　　　좌석이 없다
group tours these days.

M Oh, I see. Do you have any seats on Saturday morning?

W Let me see... It's not easy to _____ _____ _____ _____ notice
　　　　　　　　　　갑자기 좌석을 찾다
these days. Ah-ha! How about 7 p.m. on Saturday evening? Other than that, we only
have seats available on Sunday, sir.

M Okay, then. I'll take the Saturday evening flight.

05 심정 파악

최고의 선수이지만 어젯밤에 잠을 잘 못 잔 이유를 생각한다.

다음을 듣고, Bill의 심정으로 가장 적절한 것을 고르시오.

① calm 평온한
② nervous 긴장되는
③ regretful 후회되는
④ bored 지루한
⑤ excited 흥분된

M Now Bill is ready, _____ _____ his racing suit. He wants to win the auto race
　　　　　　　~를 입고 있는
today. Though everyone in his team thinks he is the best driver, he still thinks he has to
learn more. He _____ _____ _____ _____ into the
　　　　대기실을 걸어 나간다
hallway that leads to the platform. Two other drivers, Jack and Roy, are also walking
toward the platform. Bill suddenly feels his own confidence fading. There are a lot of
drivers in the race, but Jack and Roy are the ones who _____ _____
　　그를 가장 걱정하게 하다
_____. They always seem to have no fear and because of this Bill couldn't sleep well
last night.

06 대화 장소 파악

여자가 구입하려는 물건이 매트리스(mattress)인 점을 참고한다.

대화를 듣고, 두 사람이 대화하는 장소로 가장 적절한 곳을 고르시오.

① 은행　　　　② 옷 가게
③ 이불 가게　　④ 보험 회사
⑤ 가구 판매점

Can you give me a discount? (할인해 주실 수 있나요?) : 물건 구입시 할인해 달라고 말할 때 쓰는 표현이다.

M Good afternoon. May I help you?

W No, thanks. I'm just _____ _____.
　　　　　　　　　　　　둘러보고 있는

M All right. If you need any help, please let me know.

W Sure, I will. Hmm, _____ _____ looks firm.
　　　　　　　　　　이 매트리스

M You're right. It's a good brand. It comes with a lifetime warranty, so you don't need to
worry about the quality.

W Do you happen to carry _____ _____ _____ this mattress cover, too?
　　　　　　　　　　　　　~와 어울리는 담요들

M Unfortunately, we don't. But you can get a blanket at _____ _____
　　　　　　　　　　　　　　　　　　　　　　　　　　　　　　　　　　우리 가게 건너편에 있는 가게
_____ _____ _____.

W Oh, I see. By the way, can you give me a discount?

M Sure, you can get a ten percent discount.

be made of는 어떤 물건의 소재를 묻는 표현임에 유의한다.

다음을 듣고, 두 사람의 대화가 <u>어색한</u> 것을 고르시오.

①   ②   ③   ④   ⑤

How often do you watch movies? (얼마나 자주 영화를 관람하세요?) : How often ~?은 빈도를 물을 때 쓰는 표현이다.

① **M** Excuse me. Where's the subway station around here?

  W It's _____ _____, next to City Hall.
<u>모퉁이를 돌아</u>

② **M** Excuse me, would you happen to know who that lady is over there?

  W You mean, the one _____ _____ _____?
<u>빨간색 스카프를 한</u>

③ **M** How often do you watch movies?

  W About _____ _____ _____.
<u>한 달에 두 번</u>

④ **M** Can you tell me what this bag _____ _____?
<u>~으로 만들어진다</u>

  W Sure. It's made in Korea.

⑤ **M** What are you planning to do next Saturday?

  W It depends on the weather. I might play tennis unless it's too windy.

알람 시계가 울려도 끄고 바로 다시 자는 사람이 무엇을 부탁하는지 알아본다.

대화를 듣고, 여자가 남자에게 부탁한 일로 가장 적절한 것을 고르시오.

① 알람시계 사주기
② 알람시계 꺼주기
③ 아침에 전화해 주기
④ 버스표 예약해 주기
⑤ 다음 주 월요일에 전화하기

W I'm going home now. I need to _____ _____ _____ to catch a bus.
<u>내일 아침 일찍 일어나다</u>

M Are you going somewhere?

W Yes. I'm going to Gyeongju to see my grandmother. Tomorrow is her 80th birthday.

M So, you _____ _____ _____ _____ early, don't you?
<u>잠자리에 들기를 원하다</u>

W Yes, I do. I need a good night's sleep because I feel like I'm coming down with something.

M Alright then. I'll see you next Monday.

W Do me a favor. Will you _____ _____ _____ _____ _____ early
<u>전화로 나를 깨워 주다</u>
in the morning?

M Don't you have an alarm clock?

W I do, but I'm afraid I might turn off the alarm and fall back to sleep again.

영화를 보다가 몇 차례 졸기도 한 이유와 관련 있는 것을 선택한다.

대화를 듣고, 두 사람이 실망한 이유로 가장 적절한 것을 고르시오.

① 영화표가 너무 비싸서
② 영화관이 너무 시끄러워서
③ 주연 배우의 연기가 형편없어서
④ 영화의 줄거리가 너무 지루해서
⑤ 영화 감상 중 간식을 먹을 수 없어서

M How did you like the movie, Amy?

W I was _____ _____.
<u>아주 실망한</u>

M Me, too. Maybe we expected too much.

W Yeah. I _____ _____ a few times, too.
<u>잠들었다</u>

M But I think the lead character's acting wasn't that bad.

W I agree. His acting was just great, but _____ _____ _____ _____.
<u>줄거리가 너무 지루했다</u>

M You're right. I _____ what the story was about at all.
<u>이해할 수 없었다</u>

W Yeah. Me, neither.

정가와 할인율에 집중하여 듣는다.

대화를 듣고, 남자가 지불할 금액을 고르시오.

① $150   ② $250
③ $400   ④ $360
⑤ $300

W Look at these goose down jackets! I'd better get one.

M Me too! They start at $150.

W I think $150 is reasonable. I like this blue one. Oh. It's $250.

M That's quite expensive. Why do you prefer that one?

W It's made of 100% goose down, and it's _____ _____ _____ my thighs. I think it'll keep me much warmer.
<u>가릴만큼 충분히 긴</u>

M Hmm. I need to get a cheaper one. This red one will be good for me. It's $150, and that's _____ _____.
<u>예산 범위 안에</u>

W Okay! Hey! If we buy two, they'll give us a 10% discount.

M Really? Then, I'll pay for both of them. You can pay me back later.

W Sounds good.

각 요일마다 전람회장의 문을 닫는 시각이 다른 것에 유의하며 듣는다.

다음 표를 보면서 대화를 듣고, 오늘이 무슨 요일인지 고르시오.

Korean Art Exhibition

Day	Open	Closed
Mon	Closed	
Tue~Fri	9:00 a.m.	6:00 p.m.
Sat	10:00 a.m.	5:00 p.m.
Sun	10:00 a.m.	2:00 p.m.

① 월요일 　　② 목요일
③ 금요일 　　④ 토요일
⑤ 일요일

M Long time no see, Judy.

W What a nice surprise, Paul!

M By the way, where are you going?

W I'm going to the exhibition to write a report about Korean art.

M That's cool. But, Judy, it's two o'clock already. I think the exhibition is _____ _____ _____ _____ .
　　주말에는 2시에 문을 닫는

W Don't worry. I already _____ _____ _____ the Internet. It says it
　　~에서 시간을 확인했다
_____ _____ _____ today.
5시에 문을 닫는다

M Really? I didn't know that. Then, have a good time!

W Thanks.

다음을 듣고, K-pop Dance Festival에 관해 언급되지 <u>않은</u> 것을 고르시오.

① 축제 기간
② 축제 참석할 동문들의 수
③ 축제 참석 비용
④ 축제 참석 요건
⑤ 축제의 하이라이트

W Hello, students. This September, we will be celebrating the 50th anniversary of our school's foundation and the very first K-pop Dance Festival. The festival will _____ _____ _____ _____ starting on August 7. Two hundred alumni members are
　　　　　　　　　　　　3일간 열리다
expected to come and enjoy this festival. We'll _____ K-pop _____ every afternoon. Admission to the festival _____ _____ _____ _____ . The
　　　　　　　　　　춤 강의를 제공하다
highlight of the festival will be a stage dance performance on the last day. Come and
　　무료이다
enjoy! You'll have a great time!

다음 가정집 그림을 보면서 대화를 듣고, 여자가 패드를 찾은 곳을 고르시오.

W Kevin, I can't find my tablet anywhere.

M I think I _____ it _____ _____ _____ in the hall cabinet. You usually keep it there.
　　서랍 안에 넣다

W I've already checked, but it's not there. *[sigh]* Kevin, I have a very important meeting with my client. I really have to leave now.

M I'm sorry, Mom. Let me think... Did you _____ _____ _____ _____ in the living room?
　　　　　　　　　　탁자를 확인하다

W I did. But it's not there, either. There's only a pile of books on the coffee table!

M Calm down, Mom. Oh! It might be in my backpack on the couch.

W I'll check. Yes, it was in your backpack. Next time, please _____ _____
　　　　　　　　　　　　　　　　　　　　　　　그것을 다시 올바른 장소에 놓다
_____ _____ _____ _____ after using it.

M Okay. Sorry.

fever, ear, temperature 등과 관계 있는 물건을 선택한다.

다음을 듣고, 무엇에 대한 사용 설명인지 가장 적절한 것을 고르시오.

① 보청기 　　② 자동 판매기
③ 온도 조절기 　④ 공기 정화기
⑤ 전자 체온기

W If you _____ _____ _____ , you have to check yourself by using this. First, take
　　열이 난다
the cover off the tip. Second, _____ _____ _____ to turn the unit on. Third,
　　　　　　　　버튼을 눌러라
place the sensor tip well _____ _____ _____ . Fourth, keep still for about 5
　　　　　　　　당신의 귀 속으로
seconds. Fifth, when _____ _____ _____ is reached, the unit will beep.
　　　　　　최고 온도
Finally, read and record the temperature. You'd better see a doctor if you _____
　　　　　　　　　　　　　　　　　　　　　　　　　　　　　　온도가 너무 높다
_____ _____ _____ _____ .

15 할 일 파악 – 대화 직후

길 안내를 받은 뒤에 처음 취할 행동을 생각한다.

대화를 듣고, 여자가 대화 직후에 할 일로 가장 적절한 것을 고르시오.

① 도자기를 산다.
② 한 블록을 걸어간다.
③ 도자기 상점을 찾는다.
④ 한국 전통 인형을 산다.
⑤ 관광안내원에게 길을 묻는다.

M Good afternoon, ma'am. Can I help you?

W Yes, I'm looking for _____ _____ _____ traditional Korean dolls.
_{두어 개의}

M Sorry, we don't carry dolls. We sell only pottery here.

W I'm sorry. What did you say you sell?

M Korean _____ _____, you know, like bowls or plates.
_{전통 도자기}

W Oh, I see. Then where can I buy dolls near here?

M I have no idea, but you could try the tourist information center. They might be able to help you there.

W Where is it? Is it far from here?

M No, just _____ _____ _____ and it's on you right.
_{이쪽으로 한 블록}

W Oh, thank you. Bye.

16 특정 정보 파악(날짜)

대화를 듣고, 남자가 마지막 여행지로서 대만으로 재입국하는 날짜를 고르시오.

① 6월 4일　　② 6월 24일
③ 6월 30일　　④ 7월 7일
⑤ 7월 14일

W Hi, Jack! Our holiday starts next week.

M That's right.

W Are you going to travel somewhere?

M Yes, I'm going on a trip to Asia with my family.

W Oh? Where are you going?

M We're flying to Taiwan on June 24 and then taking a connecting flight to Korea. We're going to _____ _____ in Korea, until June 30.
_{일주일을 보내다}

W Wow, that's great!

M Then we're going to visit Japan for a week. On July 7, we're flying back to Taiwan again to spend a week there. We're going to _____ _____ _____ on July 14.
_{집으로 돌아가기 위해 대만을 떠나다}

W That's so exciting! I went to Taiwan last year, and I loved it. I _____
_{빨리 듣고 싶다}
_____ _____ about your trip.

17 내용 일치 파악

자신과 누나 딸의 촌수를 파악해 본다.

대화를 듣고, Ted에 대한 내용과 일치하지 않는 것을 고르시오.

① 누나가 두 명 있다.
② 막내이다.
③ 누나들은 모두 결혼했다.
④ Judy와는 사촌 관계이다.
⑤ 누나 Lisa는 아직 자녀가 없다.

W Ted, who are these people in this picture?

M Here are my parents and down here are _____ _____ _____, Eva and Lisa. I don't have any brothers.
_{내 누나들}

W Are you _____ in your family?
_{가장 나이가 어린}

M Yes, I am. Both of my sisters are older than me. And both of them are married.

W Then these are their husbands, right?

M Yes. Eva got married to Paul and this is _____, _____.
_{그들의 딸 Judy}

W What about Lisa?

M She got married, but she doesn't have any children yet.

18 적절한 응답

[18~19] 대화를 듣고, 여자의 마지막 말에 대한 남자의 응답으로 가장 적절한 것을 고르시오.

Man: _____

① That's just what I was thinking.
② I wonder if you could do me a favor.
③ Can I borrow your English textbook?
④ Why don't you take part in the music contest, instead?
⑤ Just cheer up! Remember, you're good at English.

무대 공포증이 있는 친구에게 조언해 줄 수 있는 말을 생각해 본다.

M You look down. Do you have any problems?

W Yes, I do.

M What is that _____ _____?
  (너를 괴롭히는)

W Thanks for asking, but leave me alone.

M Come on, Laura. I'm your best friend. Maybe I can help.

W Actually, I'm planning to _____ _____ _____ the English speech contest next
  (~에 참가하다)
  week.

M Wow, that sounds cool. Then, what's the problem?

W I'm _____ _____ _____ _____ _____. Any advice?
  (무대에 설 때마다 너무 긴장되는)

M _____

19 적절한 응답

Man: _____

① By cash.
② But I don't like the design.
③ I hope it's not too expensive.
④ Can I have this gift-wrapped?
⑤ You don't have to pay attention to it.

물건 값의 지불 수단을 묻는 질문에 알맞은 응답을 생각해 본다.

W How may I help you?

M I'd like to buy an electronic dictionary for my son.

W Do you _____ _____ _____ _____?
  (특별한 어떤 것을 마음에 두다)

M No, I don't.

W Then, how about this PowerDic 2000? It contains four languages: Korean, English, Japanese, and Chinese.

M Can I play MP3 files with it?

W Sure.

M That's the one I've been looking for. I'll take it.

W Your son will like it. _____ _____ _____ _____ _____
  this? (어떻게 ~의 값을 지불하기를 원하나요)

M _____

20 상황에 적절한 말(담화)

다음 상황 설명을 듣고, Harold가 Hana에게 할 말로 가장 적절한 것을 고르시오.

Harold: _____

① Hana, I'm afraid I don't have enough T-money.
② Hana, how about waiting for the next bus here?
③ Hana, we'd better take a subway to the stadium.
④ Hana, what did you think of today's baseball game?
⑤ Hana, how about going to the movies instead today?

교통 혼잡이 심한 상황에서 목적지에 빠르게 갈 수 있는 제안을 하는 것이 적절하다.

M Harold and his sister Hana are going to watch the baseball game. Harold already booked the tickets. But they have just _____ _____ _____ to the stadium.
(버스를 놓쳤다)
Hana wants to wait for the next bus. However, the bus to the stadium only _____ _____. Harold thinks they'll be late for the game if they _____.
(한 시간마다 운행한다) (계속 기다린다)
Unfortunately, there is a lot of traffic on the street. They have to _____ _____ to get there in time. In this situation, what would Harold say to Hana?
(더 빠른 길을 택하다)

01 다음을 듣고, 여자가 묘사하는 아이를 고르시오.

02 대화를 듣고, 남자가 우유 배달을 중단할 기간을 고르시오.

① 2일　　　② 3일　　　③ 5일
④ 7일　　　⑤ 10일

03 다음 그림의 상황에 가장 적절한 대화를 고르시오.

① 　　② 　　③ 　　④ 　　⑤

04 대화를 듣고, 남자가 가기로 한 장소를 고르시오.

① 터미널　　　　② 사무실
③ 향초가게　　　④ 집
⑤ 소방서

05 다음을 듣고, 남자의 심정으로 가장 적절한 것을 고르시오.

① worried　　　② happy
③ sorry　　　④ curious
⑤ relieved

06 대화를 듣고, 두 사람이 대화하는 장소로 가장 적절한 곳을 고르시오.

① 경찰서　　　② 전철역　　　③ 야구장
④ 놀이터　　　⑤ 분실물 보관소

07 다음을 듣고, 두 사람의 대화가 <u>어색한</u> 것을 고르시오.

① 　　② 　　③ 　　④ 　　⑤

08 대화를 듣고, 남자가 여자에게 부탁한 일로 가장 적절한 것을 고르시오.

① 식당 예약하기
② 전화 번호 확인하기
③ 토요일 약속 취소하기
④ 의뢰인 만남 연기하기
⑤ 남자의 휴대 전화로 전화하기

09 대화를 듣고, 여자의 마지막 말에 담긴 의도로 가장 적절한 것을 고르시오.

① 위로　　　　② 비판
③ 거절　　　　④ 칭찬
⑤ 제안

10 대화를 듣고, 남자가 지불한 금액을 고르시오.

① $30　② $32　③ $36　④ $38　⑤ $40

점수

/20

11 대화를 듣고, 여자가 할 일로 가장 적절한 것을 고르시오.

① 쇼핑몰 함께가기　　② 인터넷 스토어 찾기
③ 이삿짐 포장하기　　④ 가구 고르기
⑤ 새집 구경하기

12 다음을 듣고, 내용과 일치하지 <u>않는</u> 것을 고르시오.

① 운동 장소 – 학교 체육관
② 운동 시간 – 오후 7시 ~ 10시
③ 개인 수업 – 주 3회
④ 가입비 및 월 회비 – 200,000원 / 50,000원
⑤ 셔틀콕 – 개별 구입

13 다음 전시장 배치도를 보면서 대화를 듣고, 남자가 방문할 구역을 고르시오.

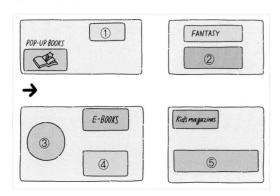

14 다음을 듣고, 무엇에 대한 설명인지 고르시오.

① 스마트폰의 기능
② 스마트폰의 장단점
③ 스마트폰의 활용 사례
④ 스마트폰 사용 시간관리
⑤ 스마트폰 사용자의 연령대

15 대화를 듣고, 오늘 여자가 할 일로 가장 적절한 것을 고르시오.

① 회의에 참석한다.
② 은행을 방문한다.
③ 백화점을 방문한다.
④ Mr. Hunter와 회의를 한다.
⑤ Mr. Barns에게 서류를 전달한다.

16 대화를 듣고, 여자의 아들의 장래 희망을 고르시오.

① 가수　　② 축구 선수　　③ 배우
④ 농구 선수　　⑤ 의사

[17~19] 대화를 듣고, 남자의 마지막 말에 대한 여자의 응답으로 가장 적절한 것을 고르시오.

17 Woman: _____

① Yes, it's Gate 40.
② No. You should go to Gate 14.
③ No, sir. You need to go to Gate 10.
④ Yes, sir. Have a nice flight.
⑤ No, sir. It's Departure Gate 40. Four- zero.

18 Woman: _____

① Can you wrap it up?
② I told you I will take it to New York.
③ Really? Then I'll give you with a lower price.
④ It's more expensive than I thought.
⑤ Thanks for your offer, but I'll stay with my parents.

19 Woman: _____

① That's okay. It wasn't your fault.
② Don't worry. I'll take good care of you.
③ It's not serious, but it will ache from time to time.
④ Why don't you join me? Mountain biking is exciting.
⑤ Oh, no. I can't live a week without mountain biking.

20 다음 상황 설명을 듣고, 판매원에게 할 말로 가장 적절한 것을 고르시오.

① Thank you. I'll come back later.
② How much is that desktop computer?
③ Can you show me the better one?
④ I'm sorry, but I didn't mean to upset you.
⑤ I should have bought the computer last month.

다시 들으면서 듣기 만점에 도전하세요!
Dictation: 스크립트의 주요 부분을 다시 들으면서!
실전 ⊕: 세부 정보가 많은 스크립트를 다른 문제로 샅샅이!

---

01 그림 정보 파악(인물)　　short-sleeved T-shirt, blue jeans, curly hair 등을 놓치지 않고 듣는다.

다음을 듣고, 여자가 묘사하는 아이를 고르시오.

① ② ③
④ ⑤

고난도

W Hello, passengers. This is an announcement from the information desk. We have a passenger here who is eagerly looking for her five-year-old boy. His name is Mark Price. He is ＿＿＿＿＿＿＿＿＿＿ ＿＿＿＿＿, ＿＿＿＿＿ ＿＿＿＿＿ and
　　　　　　짧은 소매의 티셔츠, 청바지를 입은
＿＿＿＿ ＿＿＿＿＿. He has ＿＿＿＿, ＿＿＿, ＿＿＿＿ ＿＿＿ and blue eyes. If you
　　흰색 운동화　　　　　　　　　짧은 갈색의 곱슬머리
find him, please take him to Gate 4 or the information desk. Please hurry. His plane leaves in half an hour. Thank you.

---

02 특정 정보 파악(기간)　　집을 비울 기간과 우유 배달 중단을 요청하는 기간의 일치 여부를 확인한다.

대화를 듣고, 남자가 우유 배달을 중단할 기간을 고르시오.

① 2일　　② 3일
③ 5일　　④ 7일
⑤ 10일

[Telephone rings.]

W Milk Delivery Service. How may I help you?

M Hi, I'm Joe Brown. I live in 305, DOS Apartment.

W Yes, Mr. Brown.

M I'll be traveling for a week, so I'd like to ＿＿＿＿＿ ＿＿＿＿＿ ＿＿＿＿＿.
　　　　　　　　　　　　　　　　　　　　　우유 배달을 중단하다

W I see. When do you leave and when will you be back, sir?

M I ＿＿＿＿＿＿＿＿ and I will ＿＿＿＿＿＿＿
　　9월 11일에 떠나다　　　　　　　　　　　　17일에 돌아오다
＿＿＿＿ ＿＿＿＿.

W Do you want me to hold the delivery during the period?

M ＿＿＿＿＿＿＿＿＿ ＿＿＿＿＿ ＿＿＿＿＿ ＿＿＿＿. I need it on both days.
　　9월 11일과 17일은 제외하고

W I see. Then I'll hold the delivery ＿＿＿＿＿ ＿＿＿＿＿
　　　　　　　　　　　　　　　　　9월 12일부터 16일까지
＿＿＿＿.

고난도

---

03 상황에 적절한 대화(그림)

다음 그림의 상황에 가장 적절한 대화를 고르시오.

① ② ③ ④ ⑤

① W May I see your ticket, please?
　 M Sure. Here it is.

② W ＿＿＿＿＿＿ ＿＿＿＿＿ ＿＿＿＿＿?
　　조금만 이동해 주실 수 있을까요
　 M Sure. That'll be no problem.

③ W Excuse me, but is this your Cellphone?
　 M Oh, thank you. I ＿＿＿＿＿＿＿ it.
　　　　　　　　　　잃어버릴 뻔 했다

④ W At what station do I have to get off?
　 M ＿＿＿＿＿ ＿＿＿＿＿ the next stop.
　　　~에서 내려라

⑤ W You look really tired. Why don't you sit here?
　 M That's okay. I can stand.

04 특정 정보 파악(장소)

대화를 듣고, 남자가 가기로 한 장소를 고르시오.

① 터미널　　② 사무실
③ 향초가게　　④ 집
⑤ 소방서

➕ 대화를 듣고, 남자의 심경으로 가장 적절한 것을 고르시오.

① glad　　② bored
③ annoyed　　④ curious
⑤ confused

[Cellphone rings.]

M Mandy? I'm surprised to be hearing from you during the day. Aren't you on your field trip?

W I'm at the bus terminal with my friends. The bus is leaving shortly. Where are you, Dad?

M I'm at the office, of course. I'm working on some reports.

W Dad, could you do me a favor? I'm sorry to ask this, but can you ＿＿＿＿ ＿＿＿＿ ＿＿＿＿ ?
　　_{지금 바로 집에 가다}

M Right now? Is it urgent?

W Yes, I think I ＿＿＿＿ ＿＿＿＿ ＿＿＿＿ ＿＿＿＿ ＿＿＿＿ when I
　　_{아마도 초 끄는 것을 잊다}
left the house. Would you please check for me right away?

M Well... Can't you ask your mother? She might be at home.

W I called her, but she didn't ＿＿＿＿ ＿＿＿＿ ＿＿＿＿ .
　　_{전화를 받다}

M *[Sigh]* Okay, I'll go home.

W Sorry, Dad. I'll be more careful next time.

05 심정 파악

다음을 듣고, 남자의 심정으로 가장 적절한 것을 고르시오.

① worried 걱정하는　　② happy 행복한
③ sorry 미안한　　④ curious 호기심에 찬
⑤ relieved 안도한

시상식에서 수상 소감을 말하고 있을 때의 심정을 추측해 본다.

M Well, I have no idea what to say at this moment. I wonder if I really deserve this. All I can think of is that you ＿＿＿＿ ＿＿＿＿ ＿＿＿＿ ＿＿＿＿ just to encourage
　　_{나에게 이 상을 주었다}
me to do better next time. Well, I feel like totally blank. You know, I never expected to win this award. ＿＿＿＿ ＿＿＿＿ ＿＿＿＿ ＿＿＿＿ now.
　　_{내가 얼마나 영광으로 생각하는지 말로는 표현할 수 없다}
I'll continue to do my best. ＿＿＿＿ ＿＿＿＿ ＿＿＿＿ .
　　_{나에게 이런 영광을 주어서 고맙다}

06 대화 장소 파악

대화를 듣고, 두 사람이 대화하는 장소로 가장 적절한 곳을 고르시오.

① 경찰서
② 전철역
③ 야구장
④ 놀이터
⑤ 분실물 보관소

사건의 목격자가 사건에 대해서 말하고 있는 곳이 어디인가 생각한다.

M Could you tell me ＿＿＿＿ ＿＿＿＿ ＿＿＿＿ the two people, please?
　　_{어떤 일이 일어났다}

W Okay. I think it was about 11:50 p.m.

M It was ＿＿＿＿ ＿＿＿＿ , right?
　　_{자정 쯤}

W Right. I thought the man was just passing by us.

M And then?

W Suddenly ＿＿＿＿ ＿＿＿＿ ＿＿＿＿ ＿＿＿＿ and the man ran away.
　　_{내 옆의 여자가 소리 질렀다}

M Did you see what he got from her?

W It was like her phone or her wallet. I'm not sure because it was too dark and she ran after him right away.

M OK. And you ＿＿＿＿ ＿＿＿＿ ＿＿＿＿ , either.
　　_{그들의 얼굴을 보지 못했다}

W Of course not.

07 어색한 대화 찾기

다음을 듣고, 두 사람의 대화가 <u>어색한</u> 것을 고르시오.

①　②　③　④　⑤

① **M** Why do you ＿＿＿＿ so ＿＿＿＿ ?
　　_{우울해 보이다}
　　W I had a fight with my sister. I think I hurt her feelings.

② **M** What are your plans for the vacation?
　　W I'm planning to visit my cousin in New Zealand.

③ **M** I'm going to go mountain biking on Sunday.
　　W Be sure to wear a helmet when you're riding.

④ **M** What kind of food do you eat most of the time?
　　W I ＿＿＿＿ at all.
　　　_{요리를 하지 않는다}

⑤ **M** Don't waste money. You need to be careful with it.
　　W I'll ＿＿＿＿ that ＿＿＿＿ ＿＿＿＿ .
　　　_{명심하다}

08 부탁한 일 파악

부탁은 주로 Can you ~? 또는 I wonder if ~를 이용하여 표현할 수 있음에 유의한다.

대화를 듣고, 남자가 여자에게 부탁한 일로 가장 적절한 것을 고르시오.

① 식당 예약하기
② 전화 번호 확인하기
③ 토요일 약속 취소하기
④ 의뢰인 만남 연기하기
⑤ 남자의 휴대 전화로 전화하기

That's fine with me. (나는 괜찮아.) : 상대방의 제안을 수락할 때 쓰는 표현이다.

M I just remembered I have to meet a client on Friday at 7 p.m.

W Then maybe we should meet some other time.

M How about Saturday? Are you free then?

W Yes, that's fine with me.

M Great. Let's meet at 7:00 at Dicken's restaurant.

W Okay. Oh, by the way, I have a new Cellphone number.

M Really? Wait a minute. Oh, my! I left my Cellphone at home. _____
<u>내 휴대 전화로 전화를 해 줄 수 있나</u>
_____ _____ so that I can store your number in my Cellphone?

W Sure. _____ _____ _____ _____ .
<u>당장 그렇게 하겠다</u>

M Thank you.

---

09 마지막 말 의도

대화를 듣고, 여자의 마지막 말에 담긴 의도로 가장 적절한 것을 고르시오.

① 위로   ② 비판
③ 거절   ④ 칭찬
⑤ 제안

W Hi, Robert. How are you today?

M Hi, Dr. Jin. I feel exhausted. I _____ _____ _____ do anything.
<u>~할 힘 없다</u>

W Are you eating properly these days?

M Yes. My mom always cooks for me.

W What about snacks?

M I _____ _____ _____ any junk food.
<u>먹지 않으려고 하다</u>

W I see. Do you spend a lot of time playing video games?

M Um... Yes, I guess I do play games quite often, but I don't think I'm addicted.

W I'm not saying you are. Just try to _____ more _____ _____ _____ . You will
<u>운동하는데 시간을 쓰다</u>
feel much better.

---

10 숫자 정보 파악(금액)

전체 지불 금액에서 할인된 액수를 빼는 것을 잊지 않는다.

대화를 듣고, 남자가 지불한 금액을 고르시오.

① $30
② $32
③ $36
④ $38
⑤ $40

W May I help you, sir?

M Yes. What time is the next show?

W It starts at 10:30.

M We got here _____ _____ _____ . How much is the ticket?
<u>시간에 맞게</u>

W It's $10 for an adult and $8 for a child.

M I see. Three adults and a child, please. Do you offer _____ _____ ?
<u>어르신들에 대한 할인</u>

W Yes, they get 20% off.

M Okay. Then, I need tickets for one senior, two adults and one child. _____
<u>제 신용카드입니다</u>
_____ _____ .

W All right. One senior, two adults and a child. Here you go. Have a good time.

---

11 할 일 파악

대화를 듣고, 여자가 할 일로 가장 적절한 것을 고르시오.

① 쇼핑몰 함께가기   ② 인터넷 스토어 찾기
③ 이삿짐 포장하기   ④ 가구 고르기
⑤ 새집 구경하기

W David, how's it going with your moving?

M Ugh, I didn't know there are so many things to do when you move. We are still working on it.

W Did you buy everything for your new house?

M Almost. We bought some of the furniture last week. We need to buy a new TV set soon.

W Is there anything I can help with?

M _____ _____ any online stores where we can buy a TV
<u>추천해 줄 수 있니?</u>   <u>괜찮은 가격에</u>
_____ _____ _____ ?

W Sure! I can help you with that. Just let me know the brand of TV you want. I'll _____
<u>인터넷으로 찾다</u>
_____ _____ and send you the link.

12 언급 유무 파악(담화)

다음을 듣고, 내용과 일치하지 <u>않는</u> 것을 고르시오.

① 운동 장소 – 학교 체육관
② 운동 시간 – 오후 7시 ~ 10시
③ 개인 수업 – 주 3회
④ 가입비 및 월 회비 – 200,000원 / 50,000원
⑤ 셔틀콕 – 개별 구입

W Welcome to our badminton club. I'm the court manager. As you see, we _____ _____ _____ _____. [학교 체육관을 이용하다] It is _____ _____ _____ _____ [오후 7시부터 10까지 열려 있는] from Monday through Sunday. You can _____ _____ _____ _____ [일주일에 세 번 개인 수업을 받다] : Monday, Wednesday, and Friday. The fee is 100,000 won a month. When you enter our club, you will have to pay an entrance fee. It is _____ _____, [200,000원] which includes the first month's fee. After that, you have to _____ _____ _____ _____ [매달 50,000원씩 지불하다] _____ _____ _____, [셔틀콕은 제공된다] so you don't have to bring your own.

13 지도, 위치 파악(지도) – 배치도

다음 전시장 배치도를 보면서 대화를 듣고, 남자가 방문할 구역을 고르시오.

W Welcome to the Children's Book Fair. It is the biggest event for children's books in the country.
M Thank you! Well, my kids are still _____ _____ _____ _____. [책을 읽기에 너무 어린] What do you recommend I should look at?
W I _____ you _____ _____ _____ [~을 살펴볼 것을 추천하다] the picture books and pop-up books. There are so many good ones from all over the world.
M I'd like to see the picture books. Where are they?
W Great. _____ _____ them _____ [~에서 찾을 수 있다] the Very Young Children's section.
M Where is that?
W Go down to the e-book section and turn right.
M Turn right at the e-book section?
W Yes. And they're next to the kids' magazine section.
M Thank you.

14 소재 파악(담화)

내용 설명 중 장점 뒤에 나오는 단점도 놓치지 않고 듣는다.

다음을 듣고, 무엇에 대한 설명인지 고르시오.

① 스마트폰의 기능
② 스마트폰의 장단점
③ 스마트폰의 활용 사례
④ 스마트폰 사용 시간 관리
⑤ 스마트폰 사용자의 연령대

M These days, lots of people use smart phones. As you well know, you can not only use them to make phone calls but also _____ _____ _____ [당신이 어디에 있든 인터넷을 검색하다] _____ _____ _____. You can book a hotel room and even send text messages to your friend in another country _____ _____. [무료로] However, they come with some drawbacks. For example, many kids play games for a long time which poses serious health risks. What's more, some adults spend too much time using them, which may cause _____ _____ _____. [운동 부족]

15 할 일 파악

대화를 듣고, 오늘 여자가 할 일로 가장 적절한 것을 고르시오.

① 회의에 참석한다.
② 은행을 방문한다.
③ 백화점을 방문한다.
④ Mr. Hunter와 회의를 한다.
⑤ Mr. Barns에게 서류를 전달한다.

회사를 방문한 남자에게 어떤 일을 도와 줘야하는지 알아본다.

W Good afternoon. How may I help you?

M Is Mr. Barns here? I _____ _____ _____ .
그를 만나야 하다

W Sorry, you can't. He's in a _____ _____ _____ . May I have your name,
그의 파트너와의 회의
please?

M I am Mick Hunter from ABK bank in Tokyo. Do you know when he will be available?

W I have no idea. Is there anything I can help you with?

M Well, my boss sent me here to give this sales report to him.

W Oh, that's what Mr. Barns said he would need by this evening. Would you like to leave it
with me? I'll _____ _____ _____ _____ .
그에게 건네주다

M That's very kind of you. Thank you.

16 특정 정보 파악(장래 희망)

대화를 듣고, 여자의 아들의 장래 희망을 고르시오.

① 가수   ② 축구 선수
③ 배우   ④ 농구 선수
⑤ 의사

M What happened to his ankle?

W My son had his left ankle sprained during basketball practice.

M Didn't he _____ _____ _____ last year?
그의 다리가 부러졌다

W Yes, he did. He was playing soccer at that time.

M Well, _____ _____ _____ _____ _____ enough for any
그가 신체적으로 튼튼하지 않은 것 같다
sports.

W He won't be a professional athlete. He's just learning the basics. Actually, _____
_____ _____ _____ _____ just like you.
그는 의사가 되고 싶어 한다

M Oh, I see. Let me examine his leg. I hope he has just sprained it and not broken it.

W So do I. He isn't acting as if he is in a lot of pain.

17 적절한 응답

[17~19] 대화를 듣고, 남자의 마지막 말에 대한 여자의 응답으로 가장 적절한 것을 고르시오.

Woman: _____

① Yes, it's Gate 40.
② No. You should go to Gate 14.
③ No, sir. You need to go to Gate 10.
④ Yes, sir. Have a nice flight.
⑤ No, sir. It's Departure Gate 40. Four-zero.

➕ 다음을 듣고, 대화가 일어나는 장소로 가장 적절한 것을 고르시오.

① 공항 체크인 카운터
② 공항 면세 구역
③ 비행기 내부
④ 공항 식당
⑤ 공항 안내소

탑승구 위치를 제대로 기억하지 못하는 남자에게 여자가 할 수 있는 말을 생각한다.

W Good morning. May I see your ticket?

M Here you are.

W Would you like _____ _____ _____ or an aisle seat?
창가 쪽 자리

M I'd like a window seat, please.

W Certainly. How many bags do you have?

M I have one bag to check in. And I'll _____ this one _____ _____ _____ .
비행기에 가지고 가다

W Okay. Just _____ it _____ _____ the conveyor, please.
~에 내려놓다

M All right.

W You're all checked in. Here's your boarding pass. Your seat number is 14A. Your flight is
boarding from Departure Gate 40 at 10:00.

M I'm sorry, was that Gate 14?

W _____

18 적절한 응답

팔고자 하는 가구 중 하나를 친구가 사겠다고 하는 상황에서 할 수 있는 말을 생각해 본다.

Woman: _____

① Can you wrap it up?
② I told you I will take it to New York.
③ Really? Then I'll give you with a lower price.
④ It's more expensive than I thought.
⑤ Thanks for your offer, but I'll stay with my parents.

M When are you moving to New York?
W I'm leaving next Monday.
M What's going to happen to this apartment?
W Well, I heard a new person will move in this weekend.
M Then, where will you stay this weekend?
W I don't know yet. I'll probably go to my parents' place.
M I see. What will you _____ _____ _____ ?
　　　　　　　　　　　　　　　　　가구를 처리하다
W I will sell it this week except my TV. I'm going to take it to New York.
M Hey, _____ _____ _____ _____ _____ .
　　　내가 네 소파를 사고 싶다
W _____

고난도

19 적절한 응답

2주간 발목 절대 안정이라는 의사 선생님의 소견을 듣고 여자가 할 수 있는 말을 생각해 본다.

Woman: _____

① That's okay. It wasn't your fault.
② Don't worry. I'll take good care of you.
③ It's not serious, but it will ache from time to time.
④ Why don't you join me? Mountain biking is exciting.
⑤ Oh, no. I can't live a week without mountain biking.

How long should I keep the ice on? (얼마나 오랫동안 얼음을 대고 있어야 하죠?) : How long ~?은 기간을 물어볼 때 쓰는 표현이다.

M I'd like you to _____ _____ _____ _____ when you get
　　　　　　　　발목에 얼음을 좀 대다
　home.
W Okay. How long should I keep the ice on?
M Just half an hour. It'll help to reduce the swelling.
W Half an hour, okay. Is there anything else?
M Yes. I'll give you some painkillers. _____ _____ when it hurts a lot.
　　　　　　　　　　　　　　　　　알약 두 개를 먹어라
W Thanks. Do you think I need an X-ray?
M No. Your ankle is sprained, not broken.
W That's good. Do you think I'll be able to go mountain biking again this weekend?
M No. You'll need to _____ _____ _____ _____ _____
　　　　　　　　　적어도 2주 동안은 발목을 안정시키다
　_____ _____ _____ .
W _____

---

20 상황에 적절한 말(담화)

컴퓨터를 사기에는 돈이 모자라는 상황임을 파악한다.

다음 상황 설명을 듣고, 판매원에게 할 말로 가장 적절한 것을 고르시오.

① Thank you. I'll come back later.
② How much is that desktop computer?
③ Can you show me the better one?
④ I'm sorry, but I didn't mean to upset you.
⑤ I should have bought the computer last month.

M You've wanted to buy a computer for a long time. So you _____
　　　　　　　　　　　　　　　　　　　　　　　　돈을 좀 저축해 왔다
_____ . Now you are looking around a computer shop. Then at a shop, a salesperson comes and starts showing you computers which are out of your price range. You checked the prices of many computers but _____
　　　　　　　　　　　　　　　　　　구입할 수 있는 컴퓨터를 발견하지 못했다
_____ _____ . So you can't buy a computer now. You should _____
　　　　　　　　　　　　　　　　　　　　　　　　돈을 더 저축하다
_____ . In this situation, what would you most likely say to the salesperson?

그림 정보 파악/그림 상황에 적절한 대화 찾기

무엇을 평가하는가?	일상생활이나 친숙한 일반적 주제에 관한 그림 또는 사진에 관한 말이나 대화를 듣고 세부 정보를 파악할 수 있는지를 평가한다.
어떻게 출제되는가?	• 대화를 듣고, 두 사람이 하고 있는 동작을 고르시오. • 대화를 듣고, 여자가 만든 포스터를 고르시오. • 다음 그림의 상황에 가장 적절한 대화를 고르시오.

key solution

❶ 보기의 그림을 살펴보고 그림과 관련된 어휘들에 주위해서 듣는다.

❷ 관련 어휘들이 섞인 문장이 오답으로 제시되므로 섣부르게 답을 고르지 않도록 하며, 모든 대화에 주의를 기울인다.

❸ 오답인 선택지를 하나씩 지워가며 최종 답을 고른다.

[기출로 전략 확인]

대화를 듣고, 여자가 만든 북마크를 고르시오. [2018 기출]

①   ②   ③   ④   ⑤

❶ 북마크를 보고 'heart-shaped', 'star', 'smile' 등의 어휘들을 예상해 볼 수 있다.

대화를 듣고, 여자가 만든 북마크를 고르시오.

M Emily, there's a bookmark on your desk. Did you make it?

W Yes, Dad. It's a birthday present for Rachel.

M Good job! This bookmark looks like a star. It looks nice.

W Thanks. I wanted to make it in a heart shape, but Rachel really likes stars.

M I see. You drew just a smile. Why didn't you write any words on it?

W Well, I think a smile is enough. Rachel always smiles.

M Okay. I'm sure she'll like it.

❷ 'heart shape'나 'any words'를 듣고 섣부르게 하트 모양이나 문장이 들어간 그림을 선택하지 않도록 주의한다.

❸ 별 모양에 웃는 얼굴이 그려져 있고, 어떤 문구도 쓰여져 있지 않은 북마크가 최종 답이 된다.

남 Emily, 네 책상 위에 북마크가 하나 있던데. 네가 만든 거니?

여 네, 아빠. Rachel에게 줄 생일선물이에요.

남 잘 만들었는 걸! 북마크가 별처럼 보이고. 보기에 좋구나.

여 고마워요. 하트 모양으로 만들고 싶었는데 Rachel이 별을 진짜 좋아해서요.

남 그렇구나. 웃는 얼굴도 그렸구나. 왜 문구를 쓰지 않았니?

여 음, 웃는 얼굴로 충분하다고 생각해서요. Rachel은 언제나 웃거든요.

남 그래. Rachel이 좋아하겠구나.

그림 정보 파악 / 그림 상황에 적절한 대화 찾기 유형의 발문과 보기

대화를 듣고, 두 사람이 하고 있는 동작을 고르시오.

[2015 기출]

① ② ③ ④ ⑤

만점 잡는 문장

M First, put your right hand behind your head like this.

W Okay. Now what?

M Then, hold your right elbow with your left hand. And gently pull your elbow to the left.

대화를 듣고, 여자가 찾고 있는 휴대전화의 위치로 가장 적절한 것을 고르시오.

[2015 기출]

① ② ③ ④ ⑤

만점 잡는 문장

M Which floor are you going to?

W I'm getting off on the 10th floor. Thank you.

그림 정보 파악/그림 상황에 적절한 대화 찾기에 쓰이는 어휘 및 표현

● 사물

rectangular 직사각형의   triangular 삼각형의   circular 원형의   in back of ~의 뒤에

close to ~근처에   in front of ~의 앞에   in the middle of ~의 가운데

● 동작

stretch your arms 팔을 뻗다   cross your legs 다리를 꼬다

pull your elbow 팔꿈치를 끌어 당기다   pull both your legs 두 다리를 끌어 당기다

● 상황(기계 작동법을 모르는 상황)

A Can you tell me how to use this washing machine? 이 세탁기 사용법을 알려주시겠어요?

B Okay. Let me show you how. 그럼요. 어떻게 하는지 보여드릴게요.

(자리를 양보하는 상황)

A You can have my seat. 여기 앉으세요.

B Thanks. How kind of you! 고마워요. 참 친절하군요!

01 대화를 듣고, 여자가 살 스카프를 고르시오.

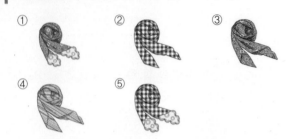

02 다음을 듣고, 여자가 남자에게 전화를 건 목적으로 가장 적절한 것을 고르시오.

① 카메라를 빌리려고
② 쓰던 카메라를 주려고
③ 카메라를 사러 같이 가려고
④ 사진 찍는 방법을 배우려고
⑤ 카메라 수리점을 알아보려고

03 다음 그림의 상황에 가장 적절한 대화를 고르시오.

① ② ③ ④ ⑤

04 대화를 듣고, 두 사람이 만나기로 한 요일을 고르시오.

① 금요일   ② 토요일
③ 일요일   ④ 목요일
⑤ 화요일

05 다음을 듣고, 자원봉사 독려와 관련해 언급되지 않은 것을 고르시오.

① 자원봉사 업무 종류   ② 자원봉사 등록 방법
③ 서비스팀 매니저 이름   ④ 커뮤니티 센터 웹사이트
⑤ 자원 봉사 지원 자격

06 대화를 듣고, 두 사람의 관계로 가장 적절한 것을 고르시오.

① hostess – guest
② teacher – student
③ policeman – citizen
④ tour guide – traveler
⑤ salesperson – customer

07 다음을 듣고, 두 사람의 대화가 어색한 것을 고르시오.

①   ②   ③   ④   ⑤

08 대화를 듣고, 남자가 여자에게 부탁한 일로 가장 적절한 것을 고르시오.

① 뮤지컬 예매하기   ② Jason 데려다 주기
③ 집으로 돌아오기   ④ 체육관 에서 물건 찾아오기
⑤ 저녁 요리하기

09 대화를 듣고, 남자의 마지막 말의 의도로 가장 적절한 것을 고르시오.

① 걱정   ② 칭찬
③ 용서   ④ 사과
⑤ 격려

10 대화를 듣고, 여자가 지불할 금액을 고르시오.

① $200   ② $240
③ $300   ④ $320
⑤ $350

점수

/20

11 대화를 듣고, 두 사람이 대화하는 장소로 가장 적절한 곳을 고르시오.

① 서점　　　　　　② 쇼핑몰
③ 등산로　　　　　④ 출판사
⑤ 결혼식장

12 다음을 듣고, Wild Water Adventures에 관해 언급되지 <u>않</u>은 것을 고르시오.

① 래프팅 할 강 이름　　② 래프팅 코스와 비용
③ 래프팅 리더 자격　　④ 래프팅 가능 연령
⑤ 래프팅 그룹 할인율

13 다음 표를 보면서 대화를 듣고, 여자가 선택할 방을 고르시오.

	Price per month	Fully furnished	Parking space	Curfew
①	$800	○	○	○
②	$700	×	×	○
③	$650	○	×	○
④	$700	○	×	×
⑤	$600	○	○	○

14 다음을 듣고, This가 가리키는 것을 고르시오.

① Plant　　　　　② Animal
③ Water　　　　　④ Air
⑤ Rain

15 대화를 듣고, 여자가 대화 직후에 할 일로 가장 적절한 것을 고르시오.

① 복사하기
② 우체국에 가기
③ 서류 준비하기
④ 책상 정리하기
⑤ 자동차 대리점에 가기

16 대화를 듣고, 남자가 선택한 음식을 고르시오.

① 햄버거　　　　　② 튀김
③ 청량음료　　　　④ 샐러드
⑤ 아이스크림

[17~19] 대화를 듣고, 여자의 마지막 말에 대한 남자의 응답으로 가장 적절한 것을 고르시오.

17 Man: _____

① Well, I don't have any cash.
② Don't forget to bring your passport.
③ That's a silly answer.
④ You'd better. Some shops don't accept credit cards—only cash.
⑤ You can keep your money in the safe at the hotel.

18 Man: _____

① Yes. I will help you out.
② Thanks. You're so helpful.
③ Do you go shopping now?
④ Right. We should learn together.
⑤ Sure. I'll let you know how to get there.

19 Man: _____

① I should have done my homework first.
② Yeah, I think I'd better rest first.
③ Wow, you're so smart to say that.
④ No, I don't want to play the game again.
⑤ Yes. Let me see how you did your homework.

20 다음 상황 설명을 듣고, 비서가 할 말로 가장 적절한 것을 고르시오.

① I'll tell him to call back.
② Sorry, he's on another line.
③ Would you leave a message?
④ Would you hold on for a second?
⑤ Do you have anything to do now?

다시 들으면서 듣기 만점에 도전하세요!
Dictation: 스크립트의 주요 부분을 다시 들으면서!
실전 ⊕: 세부 정보가 많은 스크립트를 다른 문제로 샅샅이!

---

01 그림 정보 파악(사물)   대화의 내용에서 묘사하는 표현에 유의한다.

대화를 듣고, 여자가 살 스카프를 고르시오.

① ② ③ ④ ⑤

M Good evening, ma'am. May I help you?

W Yes, I'm looking for a scarf for my friend.

M Do you have _____ _____ in mind?
   (어떤 특별한 스타일)

W Well, my friend likes flowers. Do you have one with flower pattern?

M We sure do. But floral pattern is _____ _____ _____ used to be.
   (~만큼 인기가 없는)

W Really? I didn't know that. Then how about a check scarf?

M That's a great choice. We have two different kinds. The one with trimmed lace is best seller these days.

W Looks nice, but I think _____ _____ for her.
   (그건 너무 화려하다)

M In that case, I'm sure she'll love this one.

---

02 전화한 목적   여자의 카메라가 현재 어떤 상태인지와 내일 할 일을 파악한다.

다음을 듣고, 여자가 남자에게 전화를 건 목적으로 가장 적절한 것을 고르시오.

① 카메라를 빌리려고
② 쓰던 카메라를 주려고
③ 카메라를 사러 같이 가려고
④ 사진 찍는 방법을 배우려고
⑤ 카메라 수리점을 알아보려고

[Telephone rings.]

M Hello. This is Robert. I'm not in at the moment. After the beep, please leave a message and your phone number. I'll get back to you as soon as I can.

[Beep.]

W Hi, Robert. This is Tina. Do you remember the camera I bought last week? Actually _____ _____ _____. I have to take some photos tomorrow but
   (지금 내가 곤란하다)
_____ _____ _____ _____ _____ _____. I dropped
   (내 새 카메라가 수리점에 있다)
it on the floor yesterday. It would be great _____ _____
   (내가 너의 것을 사용할 수 있다면)
_____ tomorrow. As soon as you hear this please call me at 3023-2319.

---

03 상황에 적절한 대화(그림)   그림을 그리거나 소파를 이동하는 상황이 아님에 유의한다.

다음 그림의 상황에 가장 적절한 대화를 고르시오.

① M What are you drawing?
   W I'm drawing a man _____ _____ _____.
      (개를 산책시키고 있는)
② M Have you been to this place?
   W Yes, I have. It was long ago.
③ M Where do you want to put this picture?
   W _____ _____ _____. Thank you.
      (소파 위에)
④ M This sofa looks too heavy.
   W Yeah, _____ _____ _____.
      (그것을 옮기지 맙시다)
⑤ M Where did you get the puppy?
   W It's _____ _____ _____ my brother.
      (~로부터의 선물)

① ② ③ ④ ⑤

대화를 듣고, 두 사람이 만나기로 한 요일을 고르시오.

① 금요일　　　② 토요일
③ 일요일　　　④ 목요일
⑤ 화요일

M　Sally, our last exam is on Friday. Do you have any plans for after the exam?

W　No, nothing special.

M　Then, how about playing a VR game together?

W　Sure! Let's go to that new VR game park.

M　Sounds good. ＿＿＿＿ ＿＿＿＿ ＿＿＿＿ ＿＿＿＿?
　　4시에 만나는 거 어때?

W　Oh, sorry... I've started taking violin lessons on Thursdays and Fridays. My lesson on Friday finishes at 5. How about at 6 on Friday, or ＿＿＿＿ ＿＿＿＿ ＿＿＿＿?
　　토요일 아무 때

M　I'm supposed to ＿＿＿＿ ＿＿＿＿ ＿＿＿＿ ＿＿＿＿ on the weekend.
　　할머니 댁에 가다
　　Let's meet at 6 p.m. on Friday.

W　Sounds great!

다음을 듣고, 자원봉사 독려와 관련해 언급되지 <u>않은</u> 것을 고르시오.

① 자원봉사 업무 종류
② 자원봉사 등록 방법
③ 서비스팀 매니저 이름
④ 커뮤니티 센터 웹사이트
⑤ 자원 봉사 지원 자격

W　Hello, students! We're looking for volunteers to work at the Sunshine Community Center. We need help ＿＿＿＿ ＿＿＿＿ ＿＿＿＿. Volunteers can help with various
　　일년 내내
　　duties. You can support students in 2nd to 5th grades ＿＿＿＿ ＿＿＿＿ with
　　그들을 도움으로써
　　their homework, or you can help with office duties there. The first step is to
　　＿＿＿＿ our ＿＿＿＿ ＿＿＿＿. Once you've completed our application, Ted Pedrick,
　　온라인 신청서를 작성하다
　　our Service Team Director, will contact you. You can learn more about all of our
　　volunteer opportunities on our website at www.lovecommunity.org.

남자가 여자의 집들이에 와서 이곳 저곳을 구경 하고 있다.

대화를 듣고, 두 사람의 관계로 가장 적절한 것을 고르시오.

① hostess – guest
② teacher – student
③ policeman – citizen
④ tour guide – traveler
⑤ salesperson – customer

W　Oh! Hi, Mike. Come on in.

M　Hello, Lisa. Thanks for inviting me to ＿＿＿＿ ＿＿＿＿. So this is your new place.
　　당신의 집들이

W　Yes. It's only been a week. Let me show you around.

M　I think this house is bigger than ＿＿＿＿ ＿＿＿＿ ＿＿＿＿
　　당신이 전에 살던 곳
　　＿＿＿＿.

W　Oh, yes. This is much bigger.

M　Oh, wow! The living room is very ＿＿＿＿ ＿＿＿＿ ＿＿＿＿.
　　넓고 밝은

W　Yes. What I like most is the window. It lets in a lot of light during the day.

M　It ＿＿＿＿ ＿＿＿＿ ＿＿＿＿ ＿＿＿＿, too. I envy you.
　　좋은 전망을 갖다

의문사로 시작하는 질문에 대한 답은 Yes / No로 하지 <u>않는</u>다는 점에 유의한다.

다음을 듣고, 두 사람의 대화가 <u>어색한</u> 것을 고르시오.

①　②　③　④　⑤

①　W　＿＿＿＿ ＿＿＿＿ ＿＿＿＿, Jimmy?
　　　　안색이 안 좋다
　　M　I just heard from my teacher that I won first prize in the essay contest.

②　W　You look a little excited. What's up?
　　M　I ＿＿＿＿ ＿＿＿＿ ＿＿＿＿ from one of the best companies in Seoul.
　　　　취업 제의를 받다

③　W　What are you going to do this weekend?
　　M　I've been too busy during weekdays, so I'm going to get some rest.

④　W　How was your first day of school?
　　M　Oh, it ＿＿＿＿ ＿＿＿＿ ＿＿＿＿. I made a couple of friends.
　　　　더 좋을 수 없다

⑤　W　Are you going to take biology this semester?
　　M　No. Actually ＿＿＿＿ ＿＿＿＿ math these days, not biology.
　　　　나는 ~에 흥미가 있다

08 부탁한 일 파악

대화를 듣고, 남자가 여자에게 부탁한 일로 가장 적절한 것을 고르시오.

① 뮤지컬 예매하기
② Jason 데려다 주기
③ 집으로 돌아오기
④ 체육관에서 물건 찾아오기
⑤ 저녁 요리하기

[Cellphone rings.]

M Hi, honey. Did you watch the musical with Sarah?

W Yeah. The musical you recommended was great.

M Good. I was sure you'd enjoy it. Are you busy this afternoon?

W Not really. I'm going to pick up Jason at his school and _____ 그를 도서관에 데려다가 _____ _____ .

M Then, can you do me a favor _____ 돌아오는 길에 _____ _____ _____ from the library?

W Sure. What is it?

M You know the gym I go to? I left my running shoes there. Could you get them for me? I need to wear them on the weekend.

W No problem.

M They are in locker 57 and the password is _____ 마지막 네 자리 수 _____ _____ of your Cellphone number. Thanks, honey.

09 마지막 말 의도

대화를 듣고, 남자의 마지막 말의 의도로 가장 적절한 것을 고르시오.

① 걱정   ② 칭찬
③ 용서   ④ 사과
⑤ 격려

W Guess what I got today, Johnny?

M Something good?

W I _____ 헐리우드에서 전화를 받았다 _____ _____ _____ . I'm going there to have a screen test next month.

M Wow! You mean you'll be a movie star?

W Maybe. I _____ 내 사진을 보냈다 _____ to a movie company and they called me.

M Really? So your dream is now coming true.

W Actually I'm _____ 조금 긴장되는 _____ _____ now.

M Don't worry. You'll pass the test. I'll _____ 행운을 빌다 _____ _____ for you.

10 숫자 정보 파악(금액)

구입하려는 물건과 물건의 개수 그리고 할인율을 집중해서 듣는다.

대화를 듣고, 여자가 지불할 금액을 고르시오.

① $200   ② $240
③ $300   ④ $320
⑤ $350

M Good morning, ma'am. How can I help you?

W Hi! I'm looking for a coffee table.

M How about this one? It's one of our bestselling tables.

W It looks nice. How much is it?

M _____ 정가 _____ _____ is $200, but right now there's a 30% discount.

W I'll take it. I also need two _____ ~와 어울리는 편안한 의자 _____ _____ _____ the coffee table.

M Then, I recommend these chairs. They are very comfortable, and the price is reasonable—just $50 each.

W Let me try sitting in one. Oh, it is really comfortable. Are the chairs on sale, too?

M No, ma'am, they aren't. But if you buy two of these chairs, you'll _____ 무료 쿠션을 얻다 _____ _____ , worth $10.

W All right, then. I'll take the table and two of the chairs.

11 대화 장소 파악

magazine, mountain climbing만 듣고 답을 고르지 않도록 주의한다.

대화를 듣고, 두 사람이 대화하는 장소로 가장 적절한 곳을 고르시오.

① 서점
② 쇼핑몰
③ 등산로
④ 출판사
⑤ 결혼식장

Do you have a second? : 시간 있나요?
I don't have much time. : 잠깐 시간이 있어요.

M Hello. I'm Jack Morgan from Ultimate Challenge Magazine _____ _____ . Do you have a second? *(등산에 관해 다루는)*

W Yes. But I don't have much time.

M You _____ _____ _____ _____, right? *(무언가를 사러 여기에 있다)*

W Yes. This is my first visit to _____ _____ _____ . *(이 쇼핑몰)*

M OK. I'm going to ask a question. How often do you go to the mountain?

W Well, about twice a month. I just enjoy hiking with my husband.

M OK. Thank you for your cooperation.

W You're welcome.

12 언급 유무 파악(담화)

다음을 듣고, Wild Water Adventures에 관해 언급되지 <u>않은</u> 것을 고르시오.

① 래프팅 할 강 이름
② 래프팅 코스와 비용
③ 래프팅 리더 자격
④ 래프팅 가능 연령
⑤ 래프팅 그룹 할인율

M Is your family looking for a great bonding experience this summer? _____ _____ _____ Wild Water Adventures, this is exactly what we can create for you! Bring your entire family rafting on the Hongchun River this summer and create wonderful memories together. The adventure will give your family _____ _____ _____ ! The gentle course is $80 per person, and the wild course is $140. Both courses are available for kids aged 8 and up. Discounts of 10% are available for groups of 10 or more. We _____ from K Hotel to the river for an extra $10 charge. Find out more at www.raftingparadise.com and book today! *(~의 도움으로 / 몇 년 동안 말할 이야기 / 교통을 제공하다)*

13 특정 정보 파악(도표)

여자가 원하는 방의 조건이 순서대로 언급되니 선택지를 지워가며 답을 찾는다.

다음 표를 보면서 대화를 듣고, 여자가 선택할 방을 고르시오.

	Price per month	Fully furnished	Parking space	Curfew
①	$800	○	○	○
②	$700	×	×	○
③	$650	○	×	○
④	$700	○	×	×
⑤	$600	○	○	○

➕ 다음을 듣고, 대화가 일어나는 장소를 고르시오.

① 학교
② 부동산
③ 식당
④ 버스정류소
⑤ 자전거 가게

M Come in. How can I help you?

W Hi, I was hoping to find a shared house in this neighborhood.

M Can you tell me what price range you have in mind?

W Well, I can't pay more than $700 per month. And I want to find a place that's walking distance from Korea University. I'd like to _____ _____ _____ . *(통근시간을 아끼다)*

M Okay. There are several places available.

W Oh, it needs to be furnished and _____ _____ _____, too. *(기본적인 가전제품들이 있다)*

M All right. Do you need a parking space?

W No. I walk or _____ _____ _____ _____ . *(학교에 자전거를 타고 가다)*

M That's good. Is there anything else that is important to you?

W Not really. I just hope there's no curfew at the house. I'm going to be coming back late from the library quite often, so it'd be better if there isn't a strict curfew for tenants.

M OK. This shared house looks like it'd be perfect for you.

14 소재 파악(담화)

이것의 모양과 온도에 따라 달라지는 상태 변화에 집중하여 듣는다.

다음을 듣고, This가 가리키는 것을 고르시오.

① Plant 식물
② Animal 동물
③ Water 물
④ Air 공기
⑤ Rain 비

M This is a very important thing for all forms of life. About 70 percent of your body _____ _____ _____, so you _____ _____ _____ . This _____ _____ and therefore it totally fills its container. For example, if it is in a square glass it becomes square and if it is in a flat dish it becomes flat. But this becomes _____ _____ _____ like ice when it is too cold or steam when it is too hot. *(이것으로 이루어져 있다 / 이것 없이 살 수 없다 / 형태가 없다 / 두 가지 다른 상태)*

처음에 남자가 여자에게 부탁하는 일이 무엇이었는지 놓치지 <u>않는</u>다.

대화를 듣고, 여자가 대화 직후에 할 일로 가장 적절한 것을 고르시오.

① 복사하기
② 우체국에 가기
③ 서류 준비하기
④ 책상 정리하기
⑤ 자동차 대리점에 가기

M Melisa, can you _____ _____ _____?
　　　　　　　　　　　　　　　내 부탁을 들어주다
W Sure. What is it?

M Would you _____ _____ _____ _____ _____?
　　　　　　이것을 2부 복사하다
W OK. It's your ID card, right?

M Yeah. I _____ _____ _____ to my sister who sells cars.
　　　　그것들을 보내야 한다
W Are you going to buy a new car?

M Yes. My old car is a real museum piece!

W Haha.... So she's going to do _____ _____ _____ for you?
　　　　　　　　　　　　　　　　모든 서류 작업
M That's right. After copying it, just put them on my desk. Thank you.

대화를 듣고, 남자가 선택한 음식을 고르시오.

① 햄버거　　　② 튀김
③ 청량음료　　④ 샐러드
⑤ 아이스크림

W Jake, you're not eating much today. Are you not feeling well?

M I'm fine. I'm _____ _____ _____.
　　　　　　　다이어트 중인
W Really? I don't think you need to diet. Come on, it is your favorite burger restaurant!

M I know, but I'm trying to cut down on eating junk food.

W Well, it's hard _____ _____ _____.
　　　　　　정크 푸드 먹는 것을 그만두는 것
M That's right. It's delicious, so it's not easy to cut it out completely. But it has such a bad

effect on our bodies. Most junk food is very fatty, so eating too much can cause

cardiovascular disease.

W You're right. So, you chose to have a fresh salad today. Do you want to cut out all fat

from your diet?

M Well, I'm trying to _____ _____ _____ fat _____ salt and
　　　　　　　　　　　　　　　　　　　　　　　　　～을 피하는 것뿐만 아니라 ～도 줄이다
sugar.

W I see. I think you will be able to lose weight fast and get healthier.

고난도

해외 여행을 가려는 친구가 신용카드만 쓰려고 환전을 하지 않았다는 말을 듣고 할 수 있는 말을 생각한다.

[17~19] 대화를 듣고, 여자의 마지막 말에 대한 남자의 응답으로 가장 적절한 것을 고르시오.

Man: _____

① Well, I don't have any cash.
② Don't forget to bring your passport.
③ That's a silly answer.
④ You'd better. Some shops don't accept credit cards—only cash.
⑤ You can keep your money in the safe at the hotel.

➕ 대화를 듣고, 여자의 심경으로 적합한 것을 고르시오.

① tired　　　② annoyed
③ excited　　④ sad
⑤ curious

W My family and I are going to Thailand this weekend.

M Oh, really? That's great.

W Yeah. I got all my luggage packed last night, so I'm all ready.

M Sounds good. Did you _____ _____ hotel _____?
　　　　　　　　　　　　　　　　예약하다
W Yes. My father already booked everything. The hotel has a fancy swimming pool on the

rooftop. Doesn't it sound fantastic?

M It sure does!

W Have you been to Thailand before?

M Yes, just once. You can _____ some _____ _____ _____ there. Did
　　　　　　　　　　　　　　　　　　　진짜 맛있는 길거리 음식을 즐기다
you exchange any money?

W Not yet. We'll mostly _____ our _____ _____.
　　　　　　　　　　　　　신용카드를 쓰다
M _____

18 적절한 응답

상대방이 도움이 필요하면 알려달라는 말을 했을 때 적절한 응답을 생각해 본다.

Man: _____

① Yes. I will help you out.
② Thanks. You're so helpful.
③ Do you go shopping now?
④ Right. We should learn together.
⑤ Sure. I'll let you know how to get there.

M   Hello. Do you live here?
W   Yes. Oh, you _____ _____, right?
    방금 이사 왔다
M   Yeah. I'm Carl Johnson. Nice to meet you.
W   Nice to meet you, too. I'm Lisa.
M   This place has _____ _____ _____ .
    조용하고 차분한 분위기
W   You're right. I think you'll like this town.
M   By the way, where's the nearest shopping center?
W   It's two blocks that way. _____ _____ _____
    도움이 필요하시면 알려주세요
    _____ _____ .

M   _____

19 적절한 응답

늦게까지 안 자서 졸린 사람이 할 수 있는 말을 생각해 본다.

Man: _____

① I should have done my homework first.
② Yeah, I think I'd better rest first.
③ Wow, you're so smart to say that.
④ No, I don't want to play the game again.
⑤ Yes. Let me see how you did your homework.

I should have done my homework first. : 「should have+과거분사」는 '~했어야 했는데'라는 의미로 과거에 하지 않은 일에 대한 후회나 유감을 나타낸다.

W   Ian, when did you go to sleep last night?
M   I don't know. I _____ _____ .
    아주 늦게까지 자지 않고 있었다
W   You played computer games, didn't you?
M   Yeah. It was fun to play online with my friend.
W   You _____ _____ _____ _____, right?
    인터넷 없이는 살 수 없다
M   I think so. Did you do your homework, anyway?
W   Of course I did. What about you?
M   I should start now but I'm _____ _____ _____ .
    조금 졸린
W   You must be very tired. _____ _____ _____ .
    가서 잠 좀 자라
M   _____

20 상황에 적절한 말(담화)

다음 상황 설명을 듣고, 비서가 할 말로 가장 적절한 것을 고르시오.

① I'll tell him to call back.
② Sorry, he's on another line.
③ Would you leave a message?
④ Would you hold on for a second?
⑤ Do you have anything to do now?

M   Williams calls his friend Jackson _____ _____ _____ . He needs to
    회사를 경영하는
    say something important to Jackson. But Jackson _____ _____
    점심식사를 하러 외출하다
    _____ and his secretary takes the call. When she is asked when her boss will be
    back to the office, she answers that he'll return in twenty minutes. She thinks it would
    be better to _____ _____ _____ _____ when he comes
    그녀의 상사로 하여금 Williams에게 다시 전화하도록 하다
    in. In this situation, what would the secretary say to Williams?

01 다음을 듣고, 여자가 설명하는 동작으로 가장 적절한 것을 고르시오.

02 대화를 듣고, 남자가 Janet과 통화하려고 한 목적으로 가장 적절한 것을 고르시오.

① 휴대 전화 번호를 알려주려고
② 영화관 전화번호를 알아보려고
③ 피아노 수업 시간을 알아보려고
④ 영화 초대권을 준 것에 감사하려고
⑤ 영화 구경을 같이 갈 수 있는지 알아보려고

03 다음 그림의 상황에 가장 적절한 대화를 고르시오.

①　　　　②　　　　③　　　　④　　　　⑤

04 대화를 듣고, 두 사람이 만나기로 한 장소를 고르시오.

① 대극장　　　　② 메인빌딩
③ 교실　　　　④ 카페테리아
⑤ 학교 정문

05 대화를 듣고, 두 사람이 대화하는 장소로 가장 적절한 곳을 고르시오.

① at a farm
② at a restaurant
③ at a kindergarten
④ at a grocery store
⑤ at a vegetable garden

06 대화를 듣고, 무슨 상황의 대화인지 가장 적절한 것을 고르시오.

① 구직 면접　　　　② 취업 안내
③ 경매 안내　　　　④ 직원 교육
⑤ 투자자 모집

07 다음을 듣고, 두 사람의 대화가 어색한 것을 고르시오.

①　　　　②　　　　③　　　　④　　　　⑤

08 대화를 듣고, 여자가 남자에게 부탁한 일로 가장 적절한 것을 고르시오.

① 택시를 잡아 주기
② 자동차를 고쳐 주기
③ 아이들을 돌봐 주기
④ 정비소에 연락해 주기
⑤ 이웃집에 연락해 주기

09 대화를 듣고, 여자의 마지막 말에 담긴 의도로 가장 적절한 것을 고르시오.

① 위로　　　　② 감사
③ 거절　　　　④ 칭찬
⑤ 부탁

10 대화를 듣고, 여자가 지불할 금액을 고르시오.

① $300　　　　② $330
③ $150　　　　④ $50
⑤ $45

점수

/20

11 대화를 듣고, 남자의 직업으로 가장 적절한 것을 고르시오.

① 건축가　　　　　　② 사진 작가
③ 역사학 교수　　　　④ 가구 제작자
⑤ 문화재 안내원

12 다음을 듣고, Jenny에게 일어난 일에 관해 언급되지 <u>않은</u> 것을 고르시오.

① 여행 지역　　　　　② 여행 동행자 여부
③ 여행 기간　　　　　④ 여행중 생긴 문제
⑤ 문제 해결 방법

13 다음 표를 보면서 대화를 듣고, 남자가 선택할 물통을 고르시오.

	Use	Capacity	BPA-free	Color
①	indoor	2 liters	×	blue
②	outdoor	1 liter	○	orange
③	outdoor	500 milliliters	×	black
④	outdoor	500 milliliters	○	blue
⑤	outdoor	500 milliliters	○	orange

14 다음을 듣고, 무엇에 관한 설명인지 고르시오.

① 재활용 쓰레기 문제　　② 미세먼지 문제
③ 기후변화 문제　　　　④ 동물 학대 문제
⑤ 분쟁과 난민 문제

15 대화를 듣고, 남자가 어머니날 할 일로 가장 적절한 것을 고르시오.

① 꽃 선물하기
② 용돈 드리기
③ 요리 만들어 대접하기
④ 고급 식당에서 식사 대접하기
⑤ 친구 집에서 깜짝 파티해 드리기

16 대화를 듣고, 현재 날씨를 고르시오.

① snowy　　　　　② rainy
③ sunny　　　　　④ windy
⑤ cloudy

17 대화를 듣고, 내용과 일치하지 <u>않는</u> 것을 고르시오.

① 남자는 3일 전에 의사를 만났다.
② 남자는 축구하다가 발목을 다쳤다.
③ 두 사람의 학급은 다음 주에 여행을 간다.
④ 여자는 남자에게 당분간 걷지 말라고 했다.
⑤ 남자는 이번 주에 의사에게 다시 진료 받을 예정이다.

[18~19] 대화를 듣고, 여자의 마지막 말에 대한 남자의 응답으로 가장 적절한 것을 고르시오.

18 Man: _____

① About twice a week.
② Soccer is popular in Korea.
③ Be careful when you ride a bike.
④ What do you think of playing tennis?
⑤ How about going hiking this weekend instead?

19 Man: _____

① Oh, you're mean to me.
② Thanks for cheering me up.
③ Why don't you practice more?
④ I'm glad you know how happy I am.
⑤ Sure you can borrow my fan. I don't use it much these days.

고난도
20 다음 상황 설명을 듣고, 영화배우가 여학생에게 할 말로 가장 적절한 것을 고르시오.

① Help yourself.
② Keep the change.
③ Don't be so nervous.
④ Can you show me a receipt?
⑤ Ice cream is my favorite food, too.

다시 들으면서 듣기 만점에 도전하세요!
Dictation: 스크립트의 주요 부분을 다시 들으면서!
실전 ⊕: 세부 정보가 많은 스크립트를 다른 문제로 샅샅이!

---

01 그림 정보 파악(동작)

머릿속으로 직접 지시되는 동작을 하나씩 따라해 본다.

다음을 듣고, 여자가 설명하는 동작으로 가장 적절한 것을 고르시오.

① ② ③
④ ⑤

W Having a terrible day? Then, try our kickboxing workout like this. Get into the basic position. Bend your knees and put ＿＿＿＿ ＿＿＿＿ ＿＿＿＿ ＿＿＿＿.
<u>당신의 오른발을 앞쪽에</u>
Raise your fists with ＿＿＿＿ ＿＿＿＿ ＿＿＿＿ ＿＿＿＿. Now,
<u>당신의 오른손을 앞쪽에</u>
＿＿＿＿ ＿＿＿＿ ＿＿＿＿ ＿＿＿＿. Don't stand straight as you punch. Instead, lean
<u>당신의 오른쪽 주먹으로 치다</u>
forward for more power. Bring your fist back immediately. Repeat this three times at a time.

---

02 전화한 목적

남긴 전화 메시지가 무엇인지 파악한다.

대화를 듣고, 남자가 Janet과 통화하려고 한 목적으로 가장 적절한 것을 고르시오.
① 휴대 전화 번호를 알려주려고
② 영화관 전화번호를 알아보려고
③ 피아노 수업 시간을 알아보려고
④ 영화 초대권을 준 것에 감사하려고
⑤ 영화 구경을 같이 갈 수 있는지 알아보려고

[Telephone rings.]

M Hello. Can I speak to Janet, please?

W I'm sorry. Janet is taking her piano lesson. Can you leave a message?

M Yes, please. Can you tell her Charlie called, and that a bunch of us are going ＿＿＿＿
<u>함께 영화를 보다</u>
＿＿＿＿ ＿＿＿＿ ＿＿＿＿ ＿＿＿＿ this weekend?

W Of course. Does she have ＿＿＿＿＿＿＿＿＿ ＿＿＿＿, Charlie?
<u>네 휴대 전화 번호</u>

M I think so, but it's 014-333-9898 just in case. If she wants ＿＿＿＿＿＿＿ ＿＿＿＿,
<u>우리와 함께 하기</u>
tell her to call me, please.

W 014-333-9898. I'll give her the message when she finishes her piano lesson.

M Thanks so much.

---

03 상황에 적절한 대화(그림)

다음 그림의 상황에 가장 적절한 대화를 고르시오.

① ② ③ ④ ⑤

① M Where is the nearest park?
   W It's just ＿＿＿＿＿ ＿＿＿＿.
   <u>모퉁이를 돌아서</u>

② M ＿＿＿＿＿＿＿ ＿＿＿＿＿＿＿ park here.
   <u>~해서는 안 된다</u>
   W Sorry. I didn't ＿＿＿＿＿ ＿＿＿＿. Where can I park around here?
   <u>표지판을 보다</u>

③ M How can I get to City Hall?
   W You should take bus number 145.

④ M How can we help handicapped people?
   W For example, we can give them a ride home.

⑤ M Can I ＿＿＿＿＿ this shirt?
   <u>~을 입어 보다</u>
   W Sure, go ahead. The fitting room is over there.

04 특정 정보 파악(장소)

대화를 듣고, 두 사람이 만나기로 한 장소를 고르시오.

① 대극장
② 메인빌딩
③ 교실
④ 카페테리아
⑤ 학교 정문

➕ 다음을 듣고, 남자가 여자에게 부탁한 일로 맞는 것을 고르시오.

① 학교 연극 작품선정
② 연극 연습 파트너 역할
③ 팀 프로젝트 리뷰
④ 카페테리아 청소
⑤ 방과 후 취미 활동 선택

W Hi, Max. You look upset. What's wrong?
M I'm having trouble practicing my role for the school play. I have to _____ _____ in just a few days!
<small>극장에서 공연하다</small>
W Did you memorize all the lines?
M I think so, but I'm still a bit uncertain. If I could _____ _____ _____, I think it'd make me feel more confident.
<small>파트너와 연습하다</small>
W Then let me help you.
M That would be great! How about meeting in the lobby of the main building after school?
W I have to work on a team project in the cafeteria at 3. It should only _____ _____. Can you meet me there?
<small>한 시간이 걸리다</small>
M No problem. I'll be there at 4 after school. Thanks for your offer!

05 대화 장소 파악

cheese and milk, fruits 등을 살 수 있는 곳과 관련 있는 장소를 선택한다.

대화를 듣고, 두 사람이 대화하는 장소로 가장 적절한 곳을 고르시오.

① at a farm 농장에서
② at a restaurant 식당에서
③ at a kindergarten 유치원에서
④ at a grocery store 식료품점에서
⑤ at a vegetable garden 채소밭에서

I just can't believe it. (정말 믿을 수가 없다) : 놀람을 나타낼 때 쓰는 표현이다. (=That's amazing (unbelievable).)

M I've never _____ _____ _____ so far.
<small>우유와 치즈를 맛 보았다</small>
W No kidding! I just can't believe it.
M True. You know, I live in _____ _____ _____, so there aren't foods like these.
<small>외딴 시골</small>
W Then what kinds of food do you usually have?
M I usually eat rice, _____ and fruits.
<small>유기농 채소들</small>
W Wow. Those are very healthy foods.
M _____ _____ _____ some cheese and milk for me, and some fruits for you right here?
<small>~을 사는 것이 어떠니</small>
W That's a good idea.

06 상황 파악

대화를 듣고, 무슨 상황의 대화인지 가장 적절한 것을 고르시오.

① 구직 면접
② 취업 안내
③ 경매 안내
④ 직업 교육
⑤ 투자자 모집

W Hello. I'm Tina Clark.
M Do you have any work experience _____ _____ _____?
<small>여행 안내원으로서</small>
W Yes. I've worked for a travel company for two years.
M That's great. How many countries have you visited?
W Well, around twenty. Mostly I traveled to South Asia.
M OK. So you _____ _____ _____ in the area, right?
<small>그 나라들을 잘 알고 있다</small>
W Yes. Also I can speak those languages a little.
M All right. Thank you for the interview. We'll _____ _____.
<small>이틀 후에 당신에게 전화하다</small>
W I hope to have a chance to work here.

07 어색한 대화 찾기

의견을 묻는 질문에 어떤 대답이 자연스러운지 생각해 본다.

다음을 듣고, 두 사람의 대화가 <u>어색한</u> 것을 고르시오.

①　②　③　④　⑤

① W What are you doing this Saturday?
　M Let me see. _____ _____ _____.
<small>할 일이 없다</small>
② W Are you sure you don't want a dessert?
　M Yes, I've _____ _____.
<small>충분히 먹었다</small>
③ W Do you carry shirts _____ _____ these blue jeans?
<small>~와 잘 어울리는</small>
　M Yes. How about this yellow one?
④ W What do you think of this book?
　M The book is _____ _____ now.
<small>할인 판매 중인</small>
⑤ W I want to lose weight. What sports do you suggest?
　M How about cycling or playing tennis?

08 부탁한 일 파악

대화를 듣고, 여자가 남자에게 부탁한 일로 가장 적절한 것을 고르시오.

① 택시를 잡아 주기
② 자동차를 고쳐 주기
③ 아이들을 돌봐 주기
④ 정비소에 연락해 주기
⑤ 이웃집에 연락해 주기

[Telephone rings.]

M Hello, Sarah. What's up?

W Hi, Kevin. My car's having problems again. It starts to overheat _____ _____ _____.
내가 교통 체증에 걸릴 때마다

M Didn't you have the same problem last month?

W Yes. So I took it to a mechanic then, but now _____ _____ _____.
이 일이 또 일어난다

M Sorry to hear that. I think you have to wait a while, while the engine cools down.

W I already did and I'm _____ _____ _____ to the repair shop. So, um, Kevin, could you do me a favor?
~로 가는 길에

M Sure. What is it?

W I can't get home till 8 p.m. tonight. Could you _____ _____ my kids for me?
돌보다

M Oh, Julie and Mark? Where are they now?

W They're in my neighbor harry's house. You know him, don't you?

M Of course, I do.

09 마지막 말 의도

대화를 듣고, 여자의 마지막 말에 담긴 의도로 가장 적절한 것을 고르시오.

① 위로 　　② 감사
③ 거절 　　④ 칭찬
⑤ 부탁

[Cellphone rings.]

W Hello?

M Hi, Professor Jones?

W Yes.

M Hi. It's Robert Smythe from your chemistry class.

W Hi, Robert! What can I do for you?

M I'm calling regarding the email you sent to everyone in the class. The thing is I can't open _____ _____ _____.
당신이 첨부한 파일

W Really? You're the first student I've heard from. Has anyone else had any trouble?

M Yes. Two of my classmates told me they couldn't open it either.

W I'll check and _____ _____ _____ _____.
문제가 무엇인지 알아보다

M I think the size of the file is too large. You'd better resend it as a zip file.

W Let me try. Can you check your email in 10 minutes?

M Yes. I've got my laptop open now.

W Great. I'll resend the file right away. Please let me know if you can open the file or not.

10 숫자 정보 파악(금액)

대화를 듣고, 여자가 지불할 금액을 고르시오.

① $300 　　② $330
③ $150 　　④ $50
⑤ $45

M Good evening. Can I help you?

W I'm looking for tableware to set a table.

M Do you have any particular brand in mind?

W No, I'm just looking for something that will _____ _____ my dining room.
~와 잘 어울리는

M Can you tell me about the style of your dining room?

W It's a classical style with a dark wooden dining table in the middle.

M How about this collection from Merry Porter?

W _____ _____ _____ _____ ?
얼마인가요?

M It's $300 for a full set of bone china.

W I don't need a full set.

M You can also buy a smaller set. The smaller set includes six plates and bowls. The price is only _____ _____ _____ _____ the full set.
~의 절반 가격

W Well, then, I'll take the smaller set.

11	직업 파악

고궁 안에서 허용되는 일과 금지하는 일에 대해 대화를 하고 있다.

대화를 듣고, 남자의 직업으로 가장 적절한 것을 고르시오.

① 건축가
② 사진 작가
③ 역사학 교수
④ 가구 제작자
⑤ 문화재 안내원

M Watch your step, please. Stairs are _____ _____.
_{가파르고 좁은}

W Okay. Where am I now?

M You're now in the _____ _____ _____ _____. Originally, it was just
_{궁전의 숨겨진 부분}
a small room, and three more rooms were added on its left in the 16th century.

W How many rooms were there in the palace?

M There were 33 rooms including these hidden rooms. King George added 5 rooms later and now we have 38 rooms.

W I see. Can I _____ _____ _____?
_{이 안에서 사진을 찍다}

M Yes, you can. But you're _____ _____ to in some places. There are signs to tell
_{허락되지 않은}
you. Please come this way.

W Wow, the furniture is beautiful. Is it original?

M Oh, please don't touch the furniture.

12	언급 유무 파악(담화)

다음을 듣고, Jenny에게 일어난 일에 관해 언급되지 않은 것을 고르시오.

① 여행 지역
② 여행 동행자 여부
③ 여행 기간
④ 여행중 생긴 문제
⑤ 문제 해결 방법

W While I was traveling in Canada, I rented a car and drove to the Rocky Mountains
_____ _____. On the way, my car suddenly _____ _____, so I called a
_{혼자} _{망가졌다}
24-hour service station. The service man asked me where I was, but I wasn't sure of my location. Luckily, I had an app that helps me _____ _____ _____
_{내 현재 위치를 찾다}
_____. Thanks to the app, I was able to let him know the exact latitude and longitude of my location before it got dark.

13	특정 정보 파악(도표)

남자가 원하는 물통의 사용처, 용량, 색상, 특징 등을 확인한다.

다음 표를 보면서 대화를 듣고, 남자가 선택할 물통을 고르시오.

	Use	Capacity	BPA-free	Color
①	indoor	2 liters	×	blue
②	outdoor	1 liter	○	orange
③	outdoor	500 mls	×	black
④	outdoor	500 mls	○	blue
⑤	outdoor	500 mls	○	orange

W Hi! Are you looking for a sports water bottle?

M Yes. I'm thinking of buying one.

W First you should think about what size you want. We _____ _____ —from
_{다양한 크기가 있다}
500-milliliter to two-liter bottles.

M I want one to carry with me outdoors, so a 500-milliliter bottle would be good enough.

W Then, what about this plastic bottle?

M I'm not sure. I'm looking for a product that's BPA-free. I'm _____ _____ the
_{~을 염려하는}
harmful chemicals in plastics.

W Oh, all of our products _____ _____ the finest plastics, and they're all
_{~로 만들어지다}
BPA-free.

M I see. This one looks great. Do you have it any other colors?

W We have blue, orange, and black.

M I'll take a blue one.

14	소재 파악(담화)

climate change, threat, Arctic danger 등에서 힌트를 얻는다.

다음을 듣고, 무엇에 관한 설명인지 고르시오.

① 재활용 쓰레기 문제
② 미세먼지 문제
③ 기후변화 문제
④ 동물 학대 문제
⑤ 분쟁과 난민 문제

➕ 다음을 듣고, 기후변화에 대해 알 수 없는 것을 고르시오.

① 기후변화는 동물에게 심각한 위협이 되고 있다.
② 북극곰은 위기에 처해 있다.
③ 북극곰의 움직임을 알려주는 추적장치가 있다.
④ 북극곰의 움직임을 웹에서 찾아 볼 수 있다.
⑤ 북극곰은 기후 변화에 적응이 되었다.

W Kate is concerned about climate change. She's aware that it is causing a threat to the lives of animals all over the planet. And polar bears in the Arctic _____ _____
_{위험에 빠지다}
serious _____. She often visits a website where she can see the polar bears' movements. Many researchers track polar bears using special radio collars. The collars on the bears send out signals, and researchers _____ _____ _____
_{추적할 수 있다}
their movements. This shows how polar bears are dealing with the climate change in the Arctic and, eventually, what their new life patterns will be like.

15 할 일 파악

대화를 듣고, 남자가 어머니날 할 일로 가장 적절한 것을 고르시오.

① 꽃 선물하기
② 용돈 드리기
③ 요리 만들어 대접하기
④ 고급 식당에서 식사 대접하기
⑤ 친구 집에서 깜짝 파티해 드리기

I don't know how to cook. (난 요리하는 방법을 모른다.) :「how＋to부정사」는 '~하는 방법'이라는 의미를 나타낸다.

W What are you thinking so hard about?

M This Saturday is Mother's Day. But I don't know ＿＿＿＿ ＿＿＿＿ ＿＿＿＿ ＿＿＿＿ ＿＿＿＿.
_{엄마에게 무엇을 드려야 할지}

W How about ＿＿＿＿ ＿＿＿＿ ＿＿＿＿?
_{그녀에게 꽃 드리기}

M But I don't have any money. What do you think I should do?

W Then, why don't you ＿＿＿＿ ＿＿＿＿ ＿＿＿＿ for her?
_{고급 저녁식사를 요리하다}

M A fancy dinner? But I don't know ＿＿＿＿ ＿＿＿＿.
_{요리하는 방법}

W Never mind. I'll teach you how to make an Italian dish.

M Can I learn it before Mother's Day?

W Sure. Let's go to my house and make it together now.

M Yes, let's.

16 특정 정보 파악(현재 날씨)

대화를 듣고, 현재 날씨를 고르시오.

① snowy   ② rainy
③ sunny   ④ windy
⑤ cloudy

It rains cats and dogs. : 비가 억수로 쏟아지다.

아침 날씨, 현재 날씨, 그리고 이후 날씨를 구별하여 듣는다.

W Wow, you're ＿＿＿＿ ＿＿＿＿ ＿＿＿＿ ＿＿＿＿!
_{흠뻑 젖은}

M I'm afraid I didn't hear today's weather forecast.

W The forecast said that there would be ＿＿＿＿ ＿＿＿＿ ＿＿＿＿.
_{천둥을 동반한 폭우}

M But it was fine in the morning. So I thought it wouldn't ＿＿＿＿ ＿＿＿＿ ＿＿＿＿ like this.
_{비가 억수로 쏟아지다}

W Well, take a hot shower, otherwise you'll catch a cold.

M I know. I shouldn't get sick because mid-term exams are just around the corner.

W The forecast said that the weather will be back to normal soon.

M Yeah, I heard that. I hope it will be ＿＿＿＿ ＿＿＿＿ soon.
_{화창하고 따뜻한}

W Me, too.

17 내용 일치 파악

대화를 듣고, 내용과 일치하지 <u>않는</u> 것을 고르시오.

① 남자는 3일 전에 의사를 만났다.
② 남자는 축구하다가 발목을 다쳤다.
③ 두 사람의 학급은 다음 주에 여행을 간다.
④ 여자는 남자에게 당분간 걷지 말라고 했다.
⑤ 남자는 이번 주에 의사에게 다시 진료받을 예정이다.

의사가 남자에게 어떤 조언을 했는지 생각한다.

W What happened to your leg? Why do you have a cast on?

M I ＿＿＿＿ ＿＿＿＿ when playing soccer.
_{내 발목을 삐었다}

W What a shame. As you know, our class is going on a trip next week. Do you think you can still come?

M I don't know. My doctor told me ＿＿＿＿ ＿＿＿＿ ＿＿＿＿ ＿＿＿＿.
_{당분간 걷지 말라고}

W When did you see him last?

M It was three days ago. And ＿＿＿＿ ＿＿＿＿ go see him again this Friday.
_{~하기로 되어 있다}

W Then why don't you ask him if you could go on a trip?

M I'll probably do that. I can't wait to get the cast off.

하고 싶은 운동을 묻는 질문에 적절한 응답을 생각해 본다.

[18~19] 대화를 듣고, 여자의 마지막 말에 대한 남자의 응답으로 가장 적절한 것을 고르시오.

Man: _____

① About twice a week.
② Soccer is popular in Korea.
③ Be careful when you ride a bike.
④ What do you think of playing tennis?
⑤ How about going hiking this weekend instead?

W Do you exercise a lot?
M Not really. I don't have enough time.
W You should _____ _____. Exercise is good _____ _____.
　　　　　　　　 시간을 내다　　　　　　　　　　　　　　　 당신의 건강을 위해
M I know that, but I just can't force myself to do it.
W Try to find a friend to exercise with, and then it'll be easy for you to exercise.
M Then why don't you _____ _____ with me, Serena?
　　　　　　　　　　　　　　 운동하다
W Great! _____ _____ _____ _____ _____ ?
　　　　 넌 어떤 운동을 하고 싶니
M _____

우울해 하고 있는 친구에게 용기를 주는 말을 했을 때의 반응이다.

Man: _____
① Oh, you're mean to me.
② Thanks for cheering me up.
③ Why don't you practice more?
④ I'm glad you know how happy I am.
⑤ Sure you can borrow my fan. I don't use it much these days.

W You look _____ _____ _____. What's the matter?
　　　　　　　　 좀 우울한
M Well, it's my violin techniques.
W What's wrong with them? I know you're a great violinist.
M I _____ _____ _____, but my teacher says I have to practice more.
　　 많이 연습했다
W Oh, dear. I'm sure you'll do better because you always work hard.
M I don't know. I'm _____ _____ these days.
　　　　　　　　　 정말로 스트레스 받는
W Don't _____ _____ _____. You know, I'm a big fan of yours.
　　　　 너무 심각하게 받아들이다
M _____

유명한 영화배우를 만나서 매우 당황한 사람에게 할 수 있는 말을 생각해 본다.

다음 상황 설명을 듣고, 영화배우가 여학생에게 할 말로 가장 적절한 것을 고르시오.

① Help yourself.
② Keep the change.
③ Don't be so nervous.
④ Can you show me a receipt?
⑤ Ice cream is my favorite food, too.

M A girl middle school student entered an ice cream store. She ordered an ice cream cone. While she was waiting for it there, she noticed a famous movie actor. She didn't want to _____ _____ some crazy fans. Instead, she _____ _____
　　　　　　　　　 ~처럼 행동하다　　　　　　　　　　　　　　　 침착하게 행동하는 척했다
_____. When she got out, she realized she didn't bring her ice cream cone. She went back in. And she said to the clerk that she forgot her ice cream cone. Then the clerk said, "No, you didn't. You _____ _____ _____
　　　　　　　　　　　　　　　　　　　　　 거스름돈과 함께 그것을 당신 가방에 넣었다
_____ _____." In this situation, what would the movie actor say to the girl student?

특정 정보 파악

무엇을 평가하는가?	일상생활 관련 대상이나 친숙한 일반적 주제에 관한 말이나 대화를 듣고 세부 정보를 파악할 수 있는지를 평가한다.

어떻게 출제되는가?	• 대화를 듣고, 두 사람이 만나기로 한 요일을 고르시오. • 대화를 듣고, 두 사람이 만나기로 한 장소를 고르시오. • 대화를 듣고, 여자가 냉장고를 받기로 한 날짜를 고르시오. • 대화를 듣고, 어머니가 아들을 깨울 시각을 고르시오. • 대화를 듣고, 남자가 구입할 물건을 고르시오.

key solution

❶ 지시문을 보고 어떤 정보를 찾아야 하는지 파악 한 후, 특정 정보에 주의하며 듣는다.

❷ 전체적인 상황보다는 요일, 장소, 날짜, 시간, 구입할 물건 등 특정 정보를 듣는데 집중한다.

[기출로 전략 확인]

대화를 듣고, 남자가 구입할 물건을 고르시오.　　　　　　　[2017 기출]

① gloves　　　　② helmet　　　　③ bicycle
④ backpack　　　⑤ soccer shoes

....

W Josh's birthday is coming up! He turns 15 next Wednesday.
M Yeah. What do you think about getting him soccer shoes as a birthday present?
W Actually he doesn't play soccer much these days.
M How about buying him bicycle gloves? He loves to ride his bicycle.
W He already has them. Why don't we buy him a new helmet?
M That's a good idea. I will buy it on the way home.

여 Josh의 생일이 다가오고 있어! 수요일에 15살이 되는 거야.
남 맞아. 생일선물로 축구화를 주는 거 어떻게 생각해?
여 사실 요즘 축구를 그렇게 많이 하는 거 같지 않아.
남 자전거 장갑을 사는 건 어때? 자전거 타는 거 좋아하잖아.
여 이미 갖고 있어. 새로운 헬멧을 사주는 거 어때?
남 좋은 생각이야. 집에 가는 길에 사야겠어.

❶ 남자가 구입할 물건이므로 여자가 구입할 물건과 헷갈리지 않도록 주의하면서 여자가 제안하는 물건 역시 집중하며 듣는다.

❷ 여자의 제안을 승낙하는 부분으로, 제안하는 표현과 그에 대한 답변을 듣는데 집중한다.

대화를 듣고, 여자가 무용실을 사용할 요일을 고르시오. [2018 기출]

① 월요일 ② 화요일 ③ 수요일
④ 목요일 ⑤ 금요일

만점 잡는 문장   **W** Is it available on Monday?

M No, sorry. How about next Tuesday?

W I'm afraid I can't. Is it free on Thursday?

M Yes, you can use it on Thursday.

대화를 듣고, 여자가 냉장고를 받기로 한 날짜를 고르시오. [2018 기출]

① May 7th ② May 8th ③ May 9th
④ May 10th ⑤ May 11th

만점 잡는 문장   **M** We'd like to deliver your refrigerator on May 8th. Will that be okay?

W I'm afraid not. I'll be away. Is it possible on May 9th or 10th?

M Okay. We can deliver it on May 10th.

● 요일, 장소

A Is it free on Thursday? 목요일에 사용할 수 있나요?

B Yes, you can use it on Thursday. 응. 목요일날 사용할 수 있어.

A I don't really feel like it. How about going to the shopping mall?
영화 볼 기분이 아니야. 쇼핑몰 가는 거 어때?

B Okay. You mean the one next to the bank? 그래. 은행 옆에 있는 거 말하는 거지?

● 날짜, 시간

A Is it possible on May 9th or 10th? 5월 9일이나 10일 가능한가요?

B Okay. We can deliver it on May 10th. 네. 5월 10일에 배달할 수 있어요.

A It only takes 10 minutes to go there. Please wake me up at 8.
거기 가는데 10분밖에 안 걸려. 8시에 깨워줘.

B Okay. Good night. 알겠어. 잘 자.

● 구입할 물건

A There are several holes, so you need to put in a new tube. 구멍이 여러 개 있어서 새 튜브를 넣어야 해.

B But I don't have an extra one. 하지만 여분이 없어.

A Then we need to go out and buy a new one. 그럼 나가서 새 걸 사와야지.

학년　　　반　　　번

이름

01 대화를 듣고, 남자가 선택할 포장지를 고르시오.

① 　② 　③

④ 　⑤

02 대화를 듣고, 남자가 여자에게 전화를 건 목적으로 가장 적절한 것을 고르시오.

① 저녁을 같이 먹으려고
② 농구 연습을 같이 하려고
③ 수학 학원에 같이 가려고
④ 수학 공부에 도움을 받으려고
⑤ 감기에 걸린 사실을 알리려고

03 다음 그림의 상황에 가장 적절한 대화를 고르시오.

①　　②　　③　　④　　⑤

04 대화를 듣고, 두 사람이 만나기로 한 요일을 고르시오.

① 수요일　　　　② 목요일
③ 금요일　　　　④ 토요일
⑤ 일요일

05 대화를 듣고, 남자의 직업으로 가장 적절한 것을 고르시오.

① 교사　　　　　② 회사원
③ 프로 게이머　　④ 컴퓨터 수리기사
⑤ 컴퓨터 프로그래머

06 대화를 듣고, 남자의 심정으로 가장 적절한 것을 고르시오.

① glad　　　　　② upset
③ calm　　　　　④ nervous
⑤ scared

07 다음을 듣고, 두 사람의 대화가 <u>어색한</u> 것을 고르시오.

①　　②　　③　　④　　⑤

08 대화를 듣고, 남자가 여자에게 부탁한 일로 가장 적절한 것을 고르시오.

① 공연 예매하기　　② 무대 배치 옮기기
③ 공연 연출하기　　④ 리허설 피드백하기
⑤ 무대 장치 점검하기

09 대화를 듣고, 남자의 마지막 말에 담긴 의도로 가장 적절한 것을 고르시오.

① 위로　　　　　② 비판
③ 거절　　　　　④ 반대
⑤ 격려

10 대화를 듣고, 남자가 지불해야 할 총 금액을 고르시오.

① $30　　② $50　　③ $70
④ $100　　⑤ $140

점수

/20

11 대화를 듣고, 두 사람이 대화하는 장소로 가장 적절한 곳을 고르시오.

① 병원 ② 약국
③ 정원 ④ 거실
⑤ 꽃가게

12 다음을 듣고, 언급되지 <u>않은</u> 것을 고르시오.

① 마술 쇼
② 비보이 춤
③ 교사 중창단
④ 록 밴드 연주
⑤ 오케스트라 연주

13 다음 전시장 배치도를 보면서 대화를 듣고, 여자가 방문할 구역을 고르시오.

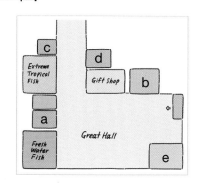

① a ② b ③ c ④ d ⑤ e

14 다음을 듣고, 무엇에 대한 설명인지 고르시오.

① paper ② can
③ vase ④ pot
⑤ wire

15 대화를 듣고, 두 사람이 대화 직후에 할 일로 가장 적절한 것을 고르시오.

① 운전 연습하기
② Rita에게 전화하기
③ 쇼핑몰에 옷 사러 가기
④ 하키 경기 보러 가기
⑤ 같이 차를 타고 나가기

16 대화를 듣고, 두 사람이 영화를 보기로 한 날짜를 고르시오.

① 10월 5일 ② 10월 15일
③ 10월 22일 ④ 10월 29일
⑤ 10월 30일

고난도
17 대화를 듣고, 여자가 아르바이트를 그만둔 이유로 가장 적절한 것을 고르시오.

① 받는 돈이 너무 적어서
② 요리가 적성에 맞지 않아서
③ 고등학생이 할 수 없는 일이라서
④ 아이 보는 일이 적성에 더 맞아서
⑤ 늦게까지 잠을 안 자는 게 어려워서

[18~19] 대화를 듣고, 여자의 마지막 말에 대한 남자의 응답으로 가장 적절한 것을 고르시오.

18 Man: _____

① You're an early bird.
② Oh, dear. It was Sunday, wasn't it?
③ You'd better start earlier next time.
④ What did your teacher tell you about?
⑤ I know some students in your school.

19 Man: _____

① I'm sure you're such a bad singer.
② Thank you for coming to my birthday.
③ Haha! Just kidding. Thank you anyway.
④ Oh, I didn't know you're a good singer.
⑤ I'll never forget how good you are at singing.

20 다음 상황 설명을 듣고, 여자가 Max에게 할 말로 가장 적절한 것을 고르시오.

① Do you like driving?
② Fill the car up, please.
③ Is your car second-hand?
④ Can you give me a ride?
⑤ Fill out this form, please.

다시 들으면서 듣기 만점에 도전하세요!
Dictation: 스크립트의 주요 부분을 다시 들으면세!
실전 ➕: 세부 정보가 많은 스크립트를 다른 문제로 살살이!

---

01 그림 정보 파악(사물)

선택지의 그림을 보면서 heart, star, flower, chocolate 등 관련된 표현을 예상해 본다.

대화를 듣고, 남자가 선택할 포장지를 고르시오.

① ② ③ ④ ⑤

W You made a great choice, sir.

M Thank you. Can you _____, please?
　　　　　　　　　　　　　그것을 선물 포장하다

W Sure. We have different kinds of wrapping paper. What type would you like?

M I don't know what to choose. How about the one with flowers?

W That's OK, but I think heart patterns are prettier.

M Is there _____ _____ _____ _____ _____, then? Only one
　　　　　　　　　　　　꽃과 하트의 혼합
pattern looks a little too simple.

W Sorry, we don't have. But we have _____ _____ _____ here, and hearts and
　　　　　　　　　　　　　　　　　　　　꽃과 별
chocolates over there.

M That's good. _____ _____ _____ _____ and she'll like this one.
　　　　　　　내 딸이 별을 좋아한다

---

02 전화한 목적

대화를 듣고, 남자가 여자에게 전화를 건 목적으로 가장 적절한 것을 고르시오.

① 저녁을 같이 먹으려고
② 농구 연습을 같이 하려고
③ 수학 학원에 같이 가려고
④ 수학 공부에 도움을 받으려고
⑤ 감기에 걸린 사실을 알리려고

[Telephone rings.]

W Hello.

M Hi, Gina. This is Paul.

W Hi, Paul. What's up?

M Do you have some time this evening?

W Yes, I'm free from 6 o'clock. Why?

M You know, I _____ _____ yesterday.
　　　　　　　　　수학 수업을 빠졌다

W Yeah. You had a cold and stayed home, didn't you?

M Right. I wonder if you could _____ _____ _____ _____.
　　　　　　　　　　　　　　　　내가 수학을 따라 잡도록 돕다

W Oh, sure. I have basketball practice until 5:30. Call me around 6 o'clock.

M OK, I will. _____ _____.
　　　　　　　　　도와줘서 고맙다

고난도

03 상황에 적절한 대화(그림)

전화로 피자를 주문하는 상황과 어울리는 대화를 생각해 본다.

다음 그림의 상황에 가장 적절한 대화를 고르시오.

① ② ③ ④ ⑤

He's on another line. : 그는 통화 중입니다.

① M What are you making?

　　W I'm cooking pizza for dinner. We _____ _____.
　　　　　　　　　　　　　　　　　　　오늘밤에 손님이 있다

② M What is your favorite food?

　　W Pizza. I love it.

③ M _____ _____ _____ _____ the pizza?
　　　~이 어땠어요
　　W It was great. I'll never forget the taste.

④ M _____ _____ _____?
　　　배달합니까
　　W Yes, we do. Your address and phone number, please.

⑤ M Can I speak to the manager, please?

　　W Sorry, but he's on another line.

04 특정 정보 파악(요일)

대화를 듣고, 두 사람이 만나기로 한 요일을 고르시오.

① 수요일　　② 목요일
③ 금요일　　④ 토요일
⑤ 일요일

➕

대화를 듣고, 두 사람의 심경으로 가장 적절한 것을 고르시오.

① confused　　② bored
③ annoyed　　④ glad
⑤ worried

[Cellphone rings.]

W Hi, Jack!

M Hi, Tracy! Did you hear that Miran ＿＿＿＿ ＿＿＿＿ ＿＿＿＿ ＿＿＿＿?
입원중이다

W Really? I saw her last week, and she didn't look well.

M I know. She has pneumonia.

W Oh, that's too bad. I find that more and more people are suffering from respiratory diseases these days.

M Right. If you are free on Friday, let's go and see her.

W I'm tied up with meetings all day on Friday. How about on Saturday?

M She said she would ＿＿＿＿ ＿＿＿＿ ＿＿＿＿ over the weekend; we'd better go and
퇴원하다
see her before the weekend.

W Then, how about going on Thursday on our lunch break?

M Okay. Let's meet on Thursday, then.

05 직업 파악

대화를 듣고, 남자의 직업으로 가장 적절한 것을 고르시오.

① 교사
② 의사
③ 프로 게이머
④ 컴퓨터 수리기사
⑤ 컴퓨터 프로그래머

It depends. : 사정에 따라 다르다.
You must be very tired. (틀림없이 아주 피곤하겠네요.) : You must be ~.는 강한 추측을 나타낼 때 쓰는 표현이다.

W Dave, how many hours do you work a day?

M It depends. I work ＿＿＿＿ ＿＿＿＿ ＿＿＿＿.
밤낮으로

W Really? You must be very tired.

M Sometimes. But I'm proud of my job.

W You must be. A lot of people can ＿＿＿＿ ＿＿＿＿ ＿＿＿＿
당신 덕분에 일을 하다
＿＿＿＿.

M Yeah. You'll never know how ＿＿＿＿ ＿＿＿＿ ＿＿＿＿ ＿＿＿＿ ＿＿＿＿.
많은 사람들이 내 프로그램을 사용하고 있다

W Do you make online games, too?

M No, I don't. I only ＿＿＿＿ ＿＿＿＿ for offices like companies, hospitals, and schools.
프로그램을 설계하다

W Don't work too much. I hope you stay fit and healthy.

M Thanks, I will.

06 심정 파악

대화를 듣고, 남자의 심정으로 가장 적절한 것을 고르시오.

① glad 기쁜　　② upset 화난
③ calm 차분한　　④ nervous 긴장된
⑤ scared 무서운

호텔에 예약이 되어 있지 않고 가장 가까운 호텔도 꽤 멀리 떨어져 있을 때의 심정을 생각해 본다.

M Hello. My name is Sam Fairbanks. I ＿＿＿＿ ＿＿＿＿ ＿＿＿＿.
예약했다

W Just a second. I'm sorry ＿＿＿＿ ＿＿＿＿ ＿＿＿＿ ＿＿＿＿
당신의 이름이 명단에 없다
＿＿＿＿.

M What are you talking about? I called last week and reserved for tonight.

W Sorry, sir. But the computer has no record.

M This is nonsense. Then, give me a room, please.

W I'm really sorry, sir. Rooms for tonight ＿＿＿＿ ＿＿＿＿.
모두 예약되었다

M My goodness! Then, is there another hotel nearby?

W I'm afraid not, sir. The nearest one is 15 km away.

M Oh, my God!

07 어색한 대화 찾기

mind가 부정적 의미로 쓰이는 것에 유의한다.

다음을 듣고, 두 사람의 대화가 <u>어색한</u> 것을 고르시오.

① ② ③ ④ ⑤

① W I'm going downtown. Can you ___ ___ ___ ___ ?
   나를 태워주다
   M No problem. Get in.

② W I'd like to use this computer ___ ___ ___ ___ .
   괜찮다면
   M Oh, I don't mind. I'll use it.

③ W Eddie is one of the funniest guys in the country.
   M You can say that again.

④ W I ___ ___ ___ ___ these days.
   체중이 너무 늘었다
   M Why don't you go on a diet?

⑤ W I have a problem. Could you ___ ___ ___ ?
   나를 도와주다
   M Sure. What is it?

08 부탁한 일

남자의 마지막 말에 주목한다.

대화를 듣고, 남자가 여자에게 부탁한 일로 가장 적절한 것을 고르시오.

① 공연 예매하기
② 무대 배치 옮기기
③ 공연 연출하기
④ 리허설 피드백하기
⑤ 무대 장치 점검하기

M Ms. White, the stage ___ ___ ___ ___ tomorrow.
   공연을 위한 준비가 되다
W Let me see. Wow, it looks great. I see you've hung white strings above the bed to make it look scarier.
M Yes. Doesn't it ___ ___ ?
   무서워 보이다
W Absolutely. Hmm... Why don't you put those chairs and the sofa next to the bed rather than in the middle?
M Why do you suggest that?
W I think it would make it easier for the actors to ___ ___ ___
   무대 위를 돌아다니다
   ___ .
M OK, that's a good idea. I'll move them. Thanks for your help. Can you stay and watch the rehearsal?
W When does the rehearsal start?
M Shortly. It'd be great if you could watch it and give us feedback.

09 마지막 말 의도

대화를 듣고, 남자의 마지막 말에 담긴 의도로 가장 적절한 것을 고르시오.

① 위로   ② 비판
③ 거절   ④ 반대
⑤ 격려

W Dad, do you have a minute?
M Sure. What's up?
W Uh... I'm thinking about ___ ___ .
   직장을 그만 두는 것
M I thought you loved working as a nurse, even though it's such hard work.
W Yes, I love helping people. I've learned so much at the hospital.
M Then, why do you want to quit?
W Well, I want to learn more about counselling. I think most patients really ___
   감정적인 지원을 필요로 하다
   ___ ___ to get over their illnesses.
M Hmm... That makes sense. So, what's your plan?
W After quitting my job at the hospital, I want to enter graduate school to get a degree in counselling.
M You're a grown-up now. It's your decision, and I will support ___
   네가 하고 싶은 게 뭐든
   ___ ___ ___ .

10 숫자 정보 파악(금액)

정가, 할인율, 구입 개수를 놓치지 않고 듣는다.

대화를 듣고, 남자가 지불해야 할 총 금액을 고르시오.

① $30   ② $50
③ $70   ④ $100
⑤ $140

It looks good on you. : 너에게 잘 어울린다.

M Why is this store so crowded?

W Maybe there's _____ _____ _____.
                    대폭 할인

M Let's see what they have in here. Oh, I like this jacket.

W It looks good on you. How much is it?

M It's $100, but it _____ _____ _____ _____.
                        지금은 50달러로 할인되어 있다

W Wow, that's a good price. Are other jackets on sale, too?

M Yes, but only this kind is 50% off. And all the other ones are only 30% off.

W So, are you going to buy this one?

M Yeah. _____ _____ _____, one for me and one for my brother.
          두 벌 살 것이다

11 대화 장소 파악

대화를 듣고, 두 사람이 대화하는 장소로 가장 적절한 곳을 고르시오.

① 병원   ② 약국
③ 정원   ④ 거실
⑤ 꽃가게

My back is killing me. : 등이 몹시 아프다.

W You don't look OK.

M My back is killing me.

W Go in and get some rest. You've been bent over too long.

M Yeah. I think I should. I had to _____ _____ _____.
                                      잡초를 뽑다

W Don't worry about them.

M I just don't want to _____ _____ _____ _____.
                          그것들이 온통 꽃 위로 자라는 것을 보다

W You're right. But I don't want to see you go to the doctor, either.

M All right. I know _____ _____, honey.
                        당신이 말하는 것

12 언급 유무 파악(담화)

다음을 듣고, 언급되지 <u>않은</u> 것을 고르시오.

① 마술 쇼 magic show
② 비보이 춤 B-boy dance
③ 교사 중창단
④ 록 밴드 연주 rock music
⑤ 오케스트라 연주
    orchestra performance

M Hello. I'm your student president. I'm going to invite all of you to the campus concert tonight. As you know, a lot of students have worked hard on the event for a long time. Let me tell you about the program. First, there will be _____ _____.
오케스트라 연주
Next, you'll see a B-boy dance by five of our fellow students. After that, a girl will _____ _____ _____ _____. Lastly, our school band will
마술 쇼를 무대에 올리다   록 음악을 연주하다
_____ _____. Don't miss the chance to enjoy the wonderful evening! Thank you.

[고난도]

13 지도, 위치 파악(지도) - 배치도

다음 전시장 배치도를 보면서 대화를 듣고, 여자가 방문할 구역을 고르시오.

① a ② b ③ c ④ d ⑤ e

W Wow! This aquarium is huge! It looks just like the ocean.

M Yeah. It is the biggest aquarium in Asia. All of the tanks _____ _____
                                                                  ~로 둘러싸이다
   a glass tunnel, so visitors can feel like they are walking under the water.

W My kids love sea turtles.

M Yes, they're _____ _____ _____. Our Sea Turtle Island exhibit is
                  아이들에게 인기가 많은
   home to two 300-pound loggerhead sea turtles, as well as reef sharks and many species of tropical fish.

W Sounds amazing. Where is it?

M _____ _____ the Great Hall and turn right at the gift shop.
    ~을 지나가다

W Turn right at the gift shop?

M Yes. Then you'll see the Extreme Tropical Fish section. Sea Turtle Island is just next to it.

W Okay. Thank you very much.

14 소재 파악(담화)

모양과 용도, 재활용 여부에 초점을 두어 듣는다.

다음을 듣고, 무엇에 대한 설명인지 고르시오.

① paper 종이 ② can 캔
③ vase 화병 ④ pot 항아리
⑤ wire 전선

W This is _____ _____ _____.
(일종의 용기)
Normally it _____ _____
(알루미늄으로 만들어진다)
_____ or other metals like tin and steel. It has
_____ _____ which are the same size, so it looks like a cylinder. This is used to
(둥근 뚜껑과 바닥)
store food or cold drinks. Anything stored in this lasts for a long time without going bad
because there's _____ _____ _____. This is one of
(그 안에 공기가 없다)
_____ _____. So you should throw this to the recycling bin after use.
(가장 많이 재활용되는 물질들)

15 할 일 파악 – 대화 직후

마지막 부분에 제안하는 것이 무엇인지 놓치지 않도록 한다.

대화를 듣고, 두 사람이 대화 직후에 할 일로 가장 적절한 것을 고르시오.

① 운전 연습하기
② Rita에게 전화하기
③ 쇼핑몰에 옷 사러 가기
④ 하키 경기 보러 가기
⑤ 같이 차를 타고 나가기

W Where are you going, Dave?
M I'm going downtown, Mom. Rita and I are going shopping together.
W Rita? She _____ _____ _____ _____. What's she like?
(너의 새 친구임이 틀림없다)
M She likes sports and she belongs to our school's hockey team.
W That's terrific! Where are you going to meet her by the way?
M In front of the Sky Mall. She _____ _____ _____.
(옷을 좀 사야 한다)
W I'm driving out to my office now. _____ _____ _____?
(태워 줄까)
M Oh, sure. Thanks, Mom.

16 특정 정보 파악(날짜)

두 사람 모두 가능한 날짜를 조정하며 여러 날짜가 등장하므로 마지막까지 집중해서 듣는다.

대화를 듣고, 두 사람이 영화를 보기로 한 날짜를 고르시오.

① 10월 5일 ② 10월 15일
③ 10월 22일 ④ 10월 29일
⑤ 10월 30일

➕
다음을 듣고, 무엇에 관한 대화인지 고르시오.

① 학교 영화관 건립 상의하기
② 영화 관람 스케줄 맞추기
③ 학교 과제 일정 나누기
④ 주말 파티 계획 세우기
⑤ 가족과의 시간에 관해 이야기하기

【고난도】

M Did you hear that we can watch movies at the school theater every weekend in October?
W Yes, I did. They're showing movies all this month, until the end of October. Can you go with me sometime?
M Well, I can't make it next weekend. I _____ _____ _____
(보고서를 끝내야 한다)
over the weekend. It's due by the 5th of October.
W As for me, I won't be free until the 15th of October because of my project.
W Then, there are only two weekends left. How about going on the third weekend— October 22 or 23?
M Sorry, I can't. I'm going to _____ it _____ _____ _____.
(가족과 함께 보낸다)
W Then, we have only one choice left—the last weekend— either October 29 or 30.
M There's a party I'm going to on October 30. Let's go to the movie on October 29.
W That will be our only chance, so let's not miss it!

17 이유 파악

대화 중 아르바이트를 하면서 힘들었던 내용에 유의한다.

대화를 듣고, 여자가 아르바이트를 그만둔 이유로 가장 적절한 것을 고르시오.

① 받는 돈이 너무 적어서
② 요리가 적성에 맞지 않아서
③ 고등학생이 할 수 없는 일이라서
④ 아이 보는 일이 적성에 더 맞아서
⑤ 늦게까지 잠을 안 자는 게 어려워서

M Susie, _____ _____ _____ a part-time job?
(가져 본 적이 있는가)
W Yes, I once had one when I was in high school.
M You did? What did you do?
W I was a server at _____ _____ but I quit after 2 months.
(멋진 레스토랑)
M Why? You were not paid well, were you?
W Hmm... Not really. I just couldn't work late every day because I had to get up early to go to school.
M I understand that. I don't think I could work like that _____ _____ _____.
(이틀 이상)
W What about you? Have you ever worked part time?
M Never. But this summer I'd like to babysit. I love babies.
W Sounds like a great idea. You will be a perfect babysitter.

18 적절한 응답

자신의 황당한 경험을 말하는 친구에게 놀라움을 표현하며 동감한다.

[18~19] 대화를 듣고, 여자의 마지막 말에 대한 남자의 응답으로 가장 적절한 것을 고르시오.

Man: _____

① You're an early bird.
② Oh, dear. It was Sunday, wasn't it?
③ You'd better start earlier next time.
④ What did your teacher tell you about?
⑤ I know some students in your school.

W Do you know what happened to me _____ _____ _____ _____?

머칠 전에
M No. What happened?
W I woke up at 7:35 in the morning.
M Oh, no. You didn't have time to get ready, did you?
W No, I didn't. So, I jumped into my clothes, _____ _____, and ran all the way to

아침을 거르다
school.
M Did you make it to school in time?
W Fortunately the school is quite close. I think I arrived there at eight. But there was one
problem _____ _____ _____.

내가 결코 생각지도 못했던
M What was that?
W No one was there. I was the only student at school!

M _____

19 적절한 응답

장난스러운 부탁을 하는 사람에게 어떻게 응답하는지 생각해 본다.

Man: _____

① I'm sure you're such a bad singer.
② Thank you for coming to my birthday.
③ Haha! Just kidding. Thank you anyway.
④ Oh, I didn't know you're a good singer.
⑤ I'll never forget how good you are at singing.

M Would you _____ _____ _____ _____ at six tomorrow morning?

아침에 전화로 깨워 주다
W No problem. But why do you want to get up so early? Tomorrow is Saturday, isn't it?
M It's my mom's birthday. I'm going to surprise her _____ _____, but I'm

아침을 준비함으로써
not sure if I can get up early.
W Don't you have an alarm clock?
M Of course I do. But it is useless because I just turn it off and _____

다시 바로 잠이 든다
_____ _____ _____.
W I understand that. Okay, I won't forget to call you tomorrow morning.
M Thank you, Nancy. Oh, one more thing. Could you _____ _____

우리 집에 오다
_____ and sing to my mom?
W Do you mean it? Are you kidding?

M _____

20 상황에 적절한 말(담화)

다음 상황 설명을 듣고, 여자가 Max에게 할 말로 가장 적절한 것을 고르시오.

① Do you like driving?
② Fill the car up, please.
③ Is your car second-hand?
④ Can you give me a ride?
⑤ Fill out this form, please.

M Max graduated from high school this month. He wants to drive a car but doesn't have
his driver's license yet. In order to drive, he _____ _____

운전시험에 합격해야 한다
_____ _____. He goes to the driving academy to learn how to drive. At the
information desk, a female clerk _____ _____ _____ _____

Max에게 종이 한 장을 준다
_____ and wants him to _____ _____ _____, such as his name, address,

정보를 적다
and phone number. In this situation, what would the woman say to Max?

01 대화를 듣고, 그림에서 Joseph을 고르시오.

02 대화를 듣고, 남자가 전화한 목적으로 가장 적절한 것을 고르시오.

① 감기에 좋은 음식을 물어보려고
② 감기약을 사다 달라고 부탁하려고
③ 재채기 멈추는 법을 물어보려고
④ 사과가 먹고 싶어서
⑤ 귀가 시간을 물어보려고

03 다음 그림의 상황에 가장 적절한 대화를 고르시오.

① ② ③ ④ ⑤

04 대화를 듣고, 주간 모임 날짜로 정한 요일을 고르시오.

① 월요일   ② 화요일
③ 수요일   ④ 목요일
⑤ 금요일

05 다음을 듣고, 행운권 추첨 행사에 관해 언급되지 <u>않은</u> 것을 고르시오.

① 행사 취지   ② 행사 일정
③ 행사 장소   ④ 행사 상품
⑤ 행사 참여 방법

06 다음 대화가 이루어지는 장소로 가장 적절한 것을 고르시오.

① 요가 스튜디오   ② 실내 체육관
③ 산 중턱   ④ 가정집
⑤ 재활 병원

고난도
07 다음을 듣고, 두 사람의 대화가 <u>어색한</u> 것을 고르시오.

① ② ③ ④ ⑤

08 대화를 듣고, 남자가 여자에게 부탁한 일로 가장 적절한 것을 고르시오.

① 아침식사 사 주기
② 외투 가져다 주기
③ 휴대 전화 빌려주기
④ 함께 친구 기다려 주기
⑤ 따뜻한 음료 사다 주기

09 다음을 듣고, 무엇에 관한 설명인지 고르시오.

① 여행지 선택과 비용   ② 여행지 문화 학습
③ 여행 위생 안전 관리   ④ 여행지 물 부족 문제
⑤ 여행지 환경 보존

10 대화를 듣고, 여자가 지불할 금액을 고르시오.

① $1   ② $2
③ $3   ④ $4
⑤ $6

점수
/20

11 대화를 듣고, 두 사람의 관계로 가장 적절한 것을 고르시오.

① 꽃가게 주인 – 손님
② 집주인 – 이삿짐 센터 직원
③ 의뢰인 – 건축 설계사
④ 세입자 – 부동산 중개인
⑤ 가구점 주인 – 배달원

12 다음을 듣고, 여행 일정에 관해 언급되지 <u>않은</u> 것을 고르시오.

① 점심 식사 장소　　② 점심 식사 메뉴
③ 점심 후 첫 일정　　④ 환영 파티 전 일정
⑤ 옵션 투어 소개

13 다음 표를 보면서 대화를 듣고, 두 사람이 지원할 일자리를 고르시오.

	Duty	Period	Camp Experience	Age Limit
①	camp counselor	overnight	○	○
②	camp counselor	day only	×	○
③	camp counselor	overnight	○	○
④	camp counselor	day only	×	×
⑤	camp counselor	overnight	○	○

14 다음을 듣고, 무엇에 관한 설명인지 고르시오.

① badges　　② uniforms
③ stamps　　④ coins
⑤ albums

15 대화를 듣고, 두 사람이 대화 직후에 있게 될 장소가 바르게 짝지어진 것을 고르시오.

	Martha	Andy
①	Cafeteria	Library
②	Library	Library
③	Cafeteria	Cafeteria
④	Library	Classroom
⑤	Classroom	Cafeteria

16 대화를 듣고, 두 사람이 가장 먼저 탈 놀이기구를 고르시오.

① Xtreme Swing
② Corkscrew
③ Hurricane Falls
④ Ferris Wheel
⑤ Antique Autos

[17~19] 대화를 듣고, 여자의 마지막 말에 대한 남자의 응답으로 가장 적절한 것을 고르시오.

17 Man: _____

① I'll keep that in mind. Thank you.
② I'll change password every month.
③ I want my card issued right away.
④ Then I'll make a deposit tomorrow.
⑤ Don't watch me enter the password.

18 Man: _____

① Give my best wishes to her.
② I will. Thanks for your advice.
③ Be careful not to catch a cold.
④ I hope you will get well soon.
⑤ Don't worry. I will be back by then.

19 Man: _____

① Go and ask for help to your teacher.
② Get your membership card again and call your parents.
③ Just go home and think about what you've done to me.
④ Don't worry about that. We're always happy with the book.
⑤ Just return the book first, and then you can borrow others.

20 다음을 듣고, 어머니에게 할 말로 가장 적절한 것을 고르시오.

① I'll prepare dinner for Dad.
② Why don't you see a doctor?
③ Go ahead. I'll go to bed early.
④ Mom, I'm still having dinner.
⑤ Go and rest. I'll wash the dishes.

다시 들으면서 듣기 만점에 도전하세요!
Dictation: 스크립트의 주요 부분을 다시 들으면서!
실전 ⊕: 세부 정보가 많은 스크립트를 다른 문제로 샅샅이!

---

01 그림 정보 파악(인물) ｜ 파티에 온 사람들의 복장과 외모 등의 특징에서 찾고 있는 사람을 알아낸다.

대화를 듣고, 그림에서 Joseph을 고르시오.

W Hey, Mark. Have you seen Joseph?

M No, I don't know who he is.

W He's my brother. He said he would _____ _____ _____ .
　　　이곳에 여섯 시까지 오다

M Hmm.... Where could he be?

W Let me look for him in the crowd. Oh, there he is. You see _____ _____
　　줄무늬 재킷을 입은 남자
_____ _____ _____ ?

M Yes. He is drinking wine, isn't he?

W No. Joseph is _____ _____ _____ . And he's eating chips.
　　　　　　　바로 옆에 있는

M Hmm, I see two men eating chips.

W He is the one _____ _____ _____ .
　　　　　　콧수염이 없다

M Okay. I got him.

---

02 전화한 목적

대화를 듣고, 남자가 전화한 목적으로 가장 적절한 것을 고르시오.

① 감기에 좋은 음식을 물어보려고
② 감기약을 사다 달라고 부탁하려고
③ 재채기 멈추는 법을 물어보려고
④ 사과가 먹고 싶어서
⑤ 귀가 시간을 물어보려고

⊕

대화를 듣고, 사야 할 물건으로 두 사람이 언급하지 **않은** 것을 고르시오.

① 꿀　　　　② 휴지
③ 기침약　　④ 녹차
⑤ 과일

[Cellphone rings.]

W Hi, James.

M Mom, where's the cold medicine? I can't find any. Ah-choo! Ugh, I can't _____ !
　　　　　　　　　　　　　　　　　　　　　　　　　재채기를 멈추다

W Did you check in the medicine cabinet?

M Yes, but there isn't any in there. Can you get some at the drugstore _____ your
　　　　　　　　　　　　　　　　　　　　　　　　　　　　　집에 오는 길에
_____ _____ ?

W Sure. Is there anything else we need?

M There are only a few boxes of tissues left. Please buy some more.

W All right, I will. Oh, do we have any honey? Please check to see if we are running out of
it. You need to _____ _____ tea when you have a cough.
　　　　　　뜨거운 꿀차를 마시다

M Let me check. *[pause]* There's plenty, so we don't need any. Uh... hey, Mom, buy some
fruit. We only have a few apples left.

W I'll get some oranges and bananas.

M Thank you, Mom.

고난도

03 상황에 적절한 대화(그림)

다음 그림의 상황에 가장 적절한 대화를 고르시오.

① ② ③ ④ ⑤

① W You didn't _____ _____ _____ , but I'll let you see the doctor right away.
　　　　　　　약속하다
　M Oh, thank you. It hurts a lot.

② W John, nail this frame on the wall.
　M Wait a moment. I'll be there.

③ W Put the hammer in the tool box.
　M I'll do that after making this wooden box.

④ W Don't point your finger at me, please.
　M Oh, I'm sorry. I didn't mean to insult you.

⑤ W _____ _____ ?
　　무슨 일이에요
　M It's my mistake. I _____ _____ _____ .
　　　　　　　　　　　　　　내 손가락을 쳤다

---

04 특정 정보 파악(요일)

각자의 사정에 의해 배제되는 요일을 지워 나가며 남아있는 요일을 확인한다.

대화를 듣고, 주간 모임 날짜로 정한 요일을 고르시오.

① 월요일　　　　② 화요일
③ 수요일　　　　④ 목요일
⑤ 금요일

M Hi, Carol.

W Hi, Knight. Welcome.

M I can't see Jane and Ben.

W They won't come.

M Really? Don't we need their opinions about what day to have a weekly conversation meeting, too?

W Sure, we do. Jane said she's free every day _____ _____ _____
_____ . And Ben _____ _____ _____.
　　　　　목요일과 일요일을 제외하고
　　　금요일에 올 수 없다

M Then we should exclude those three days. What about you?

W I have to _____ _____ _____ _____ _____ . Then we have three
　　월요일마다 여동생과 있다
days left.

M Well, I _____ _____ _____ _____ _____ .
　　화요일과 토요일에는 시간이 없다

W Well, we have only one day we all agree on. Let's make it that day.

05 언급 유무 파악(담화)

다음을 듣고, 행운권 추첨 행사에 관해 언급되지 <u>않은</u> 것을 고르시오.

① 행사 취지　　　② 행사 일정
③ 행사 장소　　　④ 행사 상품
⑤ 행사 참여 방법

W Greetings! This is Play-with-us Mall, and I'm Suzie Cox from the Customer Service Department. This _____ _____ 11 at 5 o'clock, Play-with-us Mall will open its
　　　다가오는 5월
second game store in Seoul. This is all because of _____ _____
_____ _____ _____ , and we'd like to thank you very much for that. As
　고객의 사랑과 헌신
a token of our gratitude, we are planning many great events for you! As the first event,
we will be holding a Lucky Draw event at _____ _____ _____
_____ _____ ! Everyone is welcome to join in on May 11 at 5 p.m. at the
　우리 새 가게의 개업식
new Play-with-us store. You could win one of twenty 100,000-won store gift cards. If
you need more information about the event, please call 050-777-0101 and ask for Suzie
Cox. I'll be glad to assist you in any way.

06 대화 장소 파악

hike, uphill, go back down 등의 표현으로 정답을 찾는다.

다음 대화가 이루어지는 장소로 가장 적절한 것을 고르시오.

① 요가 스튜디오　　② 실내 체육관
③ 산 중턱　　　　　④ 가정집
⑤ 재활 병원

➕ 대화를 듣고, 두 사람이 할 일로 가장 적절한 것을 고르시오.

① 산의 정상까지 등반하기
② 당이 높은 간식 먹기
③ 하산 전 스트레칭 하기
④ 옷에 방충제 뿌리기
⑤ 등산 장비 준비하기

W Jason, I'm exhausted. Can we stop walking and take a break?

M Okay. Let's stop and drink some water. Are you enjoying our hike?

W Yes. It is great, but it's so tough to walk uphill. I think I've done a lot of exercise today.

M That's great!

W Jason... [pause] Why don't we go back down now? Actually, my legs are starting to hurt.

M Sure, no problem. But, before starting back, we'd better stretch and _____
_____ _____ .
　온 몸의 긴장을 풀다

W You mean cool-down exercises? I think we've done enough exercise for today, haven't we?

M Well, cool-down exercises can _____ _____ , which can actually help
　　　　　근육 조절을 향상시키다
your body to _____ after exercising.
　　더 쉽게 회복하다

W All right. Can you show me how?

M Sure, let me show you four different cool-down exercises. First, let's start with a shoulder stretch.

도와주겠다는 호의를 받았을 때 할 수 있는 대답을 생각해 본다.

다음을 듣고, 두 사람의 대화가 <u>어색한</u> 것을 고르시오.

①   ②   ③   ④   ⑤

What's the weather like today? (오늘 날씨 어때요?) : 날씨를 물어볼 때 쓰는 표현이다. (=How's the weather today?)

① M   What's the weather like today?

   W   It's cloudy and windy.

② M   Is there anything I can help you with?

   W   Sorry, but _____ _____ _____.

어쩔 수가 없었다

③ M   Let's pull over at the next gas station.

   W   Yes, we're _____ _____ _____.

기름이 다 떨어진

④ M   How would you like to send this package?

   W   By airmail. It's the quickest way, isn't it?

⑤ M   How can you be so sure about the accident?

   W   I saw it clearly _____ _____ _____ _____.

출근길에

08 부탁한 일 파악

추위 속에서 떨며 친구를 기다리는 남자가 매점에 가는 여자에게 할 수 있는 부탁을 생각해 본다.

대화를 듣고, 남자가 여자에게 부탁한 일로 가장 적절한 것을 고르시오.

① 아침식사 사 주기
② 외투 가져다 주기
③ 휴대 전화 빌려주기
④ 함께 친구 기다려 주기
⑤ 따뜻한 음료 사다 주기

W   Randy! What are you doing here?

M   I'm waiting for Damon. I wonder what's keeping him.

W   Have you been waiting long?

M   Not that long. He was supposed to be here 20 minutes ago.

W   Why don't you call his Cellphone?

M   I've been calling it, but it's busy. By the way, where are you going?

W   I'm _____ _____ _____ _____. I missed breakfast.

학교 매점에 가고 있는

M   Then can you get me a hot drink? It's pretty cold.

W   Sure. No problem. I'll _____ _____ in a minute.

돌아오다

09 말의 내용(담화)

다음을 듣고, 무엇에 관한 설명인지 고르시오.

① 여행지 선택과 비용
② 여행지 문화 학습
③ 여행 위생 안전 관리
④ 여행지 물 부족 문제
⑤ 여행지 환경 보존

W   It is very important to reduce any chances of getting sick when you travel abroad. Try to prevent bites from mosquitoes and other bugs. Use insect repellent on uncovered skin outdoors, especially during the day. For greater protection, _____ _____ _____ _____, too. Also, be extremely careful about food and water. Only _____ _____ _____ _____. Avoid drinking tap water, and order drinks

옷 위에 뿌리다 / 병에 들었거나 끓인 물을 마시다

without ice to make sure they are safe. _____ _____ _____ _____ as often as possible, especially before eating or cooking food. Carrying an alcohol-based hand sanitizer will be helpful if water isn't available.

비누로 손을 씻다

10 숫자 정보 파악(금액)

여자가 연체한 책과 권 당 연체료를 집중해서 듣는다.

대화를 듣고, 여자가 지불할 금액을 고르시오.

① $1   ② $2
③ $3   ④ $4
⑤ $6

W   Hi. I'd like to return these two books. Sorry, they're a couple of days late.

M   Let me check. They are three days overdue, so you need to _____ _____ _____ _____.

연체료를 내다

W   How much is it?

M   Let's see. You have to pay one dollar per day for each book. So, that's three dollars for each book.

W   Here's ten dollars.

M   Hmm... It looks like there's one more book, Introduction to Economics, that's overdue under your student ID number.

W   Oh, right! I totally forgot about that. I'll _____ it _____.

내일 반납하다

M   You will have to pay a late fee when you return that book as well. Please don't _____ _____ _____ _____.

제때 책을 반납하는 것을 잊다

W   Sorry about that.

M   Here's your change.

물건을 놓을 장소를 묻고 답하는 관계를 생각해 본다.

대화를 듣고, 두 사람의 관계로 가장 적절한 것을 고르시오.

① 꽃가게 주인 – 손님
② 집주인 – 이삿짐 센터 직원
③ 의뢰인 – 건축 설계사
④ 세입자 – 부동산 중개인
⑤ 가구점 주인 – 배달원

W Be careful. _____ _____ _____.
그것은 깨지기 쉽다
M Don't worry. I'm used to this thing. Where do you want me to put it?
W Will you _____ _____ _____ _____ _____ _____ ?
냉장고 옆에 놓다
M Sure. No problem. What about this coffee table?
W _____ _____ _____ _____ _____ _____ _____. I like to drink coffee
그 테이블을 창문 옆에 두어라
with my husband, looking out the window.
M Okay. What about these vases, ma'am?
W Will you put them out on the veranda? They need fresh air and sunlight.
M All right. Oh, _____ _____ _____ _____ _____.
다른 짐이 거의 다 왔다

다음을 듣고, 여행 일정에 관해 언급되지 않은 것을 고르시오.

① 점심 식사 장소   ② 점심 식사 메뉴
③ 점심 후 첫 일정   ④ 환영 파티 전 일정
⑤ 옵션 투어 소개

W Welcome to Vietnam! I'm Miya, and I'll be your tour director during your stay in the
peaceful city of Da Nang, Vietnam. _____ _____ _____ _____ of
지연된 도착 시간 때문에
your flight, we have to make a change to the lunch reservation. Your lunch will be
served at Hoi An restaurant, not in the Farmers' restaurant. However, the main menu—
rice noodles and fried chicken—is the same. After lunch, we will
_____ _____ _____ the top of Ba Na Hill and enjoy the great view. And then,
케이블카를 타고 ~로 가다
we'll _____ _____ _____ _____ the picturesque old French
~로 보트 여행을 가다
villages. When you return from the boat trip, you will have time to relax in your hotel
rooms before our welcome reception party. If you have any questions or problems, let
me know. Thank you.

고난도

두 사람이 일하기 원하는 시기, 경력, 나이 제한 등에 집중하여 듣는다.

다음 표를 보면서 대화를 듣고, 두 사람이 지원할 일자리를 고르시오.

	Duty	Period	Camp Experience	Age Limit
①	camp counselor	overnight	○	○
②	camp counselor	day only	×	○
③	camp counselor	overnight	○	○
④	camp counselor	day only	×	×
⑤	camp counselor	overnight	○	○

W I'm looking for a summer job to do during the vacation. I'm considering
_____ _____ _____ at a summer camp.
캠프 상담사로 일하는 것
M Oh, really? I'm also looking for a summer job.
W Great, let's try to find one together.
M Okay. Well, I _____ _____ _____ _____ _____ in the evenings,
듣는 여름 수업이 하나 있다
so I can only work during the day.
W Then, let's cross the overnight ones off the list. Have you ever worked at a summer
camp before?
M No, I haven't. It'll be my first experience.
W How about choosing this one? This one is a day camp, and they don't _____ any
_____ _____ _____.
이전의 캠프 경력을 요구하다
M Sounds great. Is there an age limit? I'm going to turn 18 this winter.
W No, this one doesn't have any age limit. Let's both apply for this one.

다음을 듣고, 무엇에 관한 설명인지 고르시오.

① badges 배지
② uniforms 제복
③ stamps 우표
④ coins 동전
⑤ albums 앨범

W These are _____ _____ _____ _____ _____ _____ _____.
특정 단체에 속해 있다는 상징
People wear these on their clothes, bags, and even vehicles to show they belong to a
certain group. In most cases, people are proud of wearing these. These are also given to
people who _____ _____ _____ _____ _____ such as
대의명분을 믿거나 그것을 위해 일한다
animal rights. In some organizations such as the military, these are given to members to
_____ _____ _____. These can be made from metal, plastic, leather or
그들의 성취를 치하하다
rubber. Some people enjoy collecting these as a hobby.

15 할 일 – 대화 직후

대화를 듣고, 두 사람이 대화 직후에 있게 될 장소가 바르게 짝지어진 것을 고르시오.

	Martha	Andy
①	Cafeteria	Library
②	Library	Library
③	Cafeteria	Cafeteria
④	Library	Classroom
⑤	Classroom	Cafeteria

두 사람이 각각 어디로 이동하는지 체크하며 듣는다.

M   Martha, do you _____ _____ _____ ?
<u>잠깐 시간이 있다</u>

W   I'm afraid not, Andy. I'm going to the cafeteria.

M   Oh, are you going for a late lunch?

W   No, I'm just going to _____ _____ _____ while drinking something at
<u>내가 배운 것을 복습하다</u>
the cafeteria.

M   Really? Then I think you can help me out.

W   Well, what can I help you with?

M   I _____ _____ last week because I was sick.
<u>수업 몇 시간을 빠졌다</u>

W   Oh, I remember the day you didn't show up. Do you want to borrow my notes?

M   Yes, please. I'll photocopy them and give them back to you straight away.

W   OK. Here you go. Are you going to go to the library?

M   Yes. They have a copy machine there. Thank you, Martha.

16 특정 정보 파악(놀이 기구)

대화를 듣고, 두 사람이 가장 먼저 탈 놀이기구를 고르시오.

① Xtreme Swing
② Corkscrew
③ Hurricane Falls
④ Ferris Wheel
⑤ Antique Autos

What do you say to going on the Ferris Wheel? (Ferris Wheel을 타는 것은 어때?) : 「What do you say to -ing?」는 상대방에게 제안할 때 쓰는 표현이다.

W   We're finally here.

M   Yes. _____ _____ _____ _____ _____ .
<u>내 꿈이 실현된 것 같다</u>

W   What will we ride first?

M   What about Xtreme Swing or Corkscrew? They are going to be a thrilling experience.

W   Let's enjoy them later. Let's start with something simple. We have a lot of time.

M   Then what about Hurricane Falls?

W   I don't want to get wet at the beginning of the day.

M   Then what do you say to going on the Ferris Wheel or Antique Autos?

W   _____ _____ _____ _____ _____ . We can have an overall view
<u>Ferris Wheel을 먼저 타자</u>
of the amusement park.

M   That's a good idea. Let's get going.

17 적절한 응답

[17~19] 대화를 듣고, 여자의 마지막 말에 대한 남자의 응답으로 가장 적절한 것을 고르시오.

Man: _____

① I'll keep that in mind. Thank you.
② I'll change password every month.
③ I want my card issued right away.
④ Then I'll make a deposit tomorrow.
⑤ Don't watch me enter the password.

I opened an account. : 계좌를 개설했다.

현금인출기 사용법을 알려주고 주의 사항을 일러준 여자에게 남자가 할 수 있는 말을 생각해 본다.

M   Miss?

W   Yes. What can I do for you, sir?

M   I just opened an account and got this card, but it doesn't seem to work. Will you check
if this card works in the ATM?

W   Oh, sure, sir. Insert the card first. Yes, right there.

M   I'd like to _____ _____ _____ _____ _____ .
<u>시험으로 20달러만 인출하다</u>

W   Okay. Then choose "withdrawal" and enter your 4-digit password. Then choose the amount
and the money will come out.

M   Good. It works.

W   _____ _____ _____ , sir. Remember deposits made at an ATM may not be
<u>한 가지 더요</u>
immediately available for withdrawal.

M   _____

18 적절한 응답

Man: _____

① Give my best wishes to her.
② I will. Thanks for your advice.
③ Be careful not to catch a cold.
④ I hope you will get well soon.
⑤ Don't worry. I will be back by then.

W Good morning, Ted.

M Hi, Sue. It's beautiful today.

W Yes. You look different today.

M Really? Well, I have every reason.

W Something really good happened to you, didn't it?

M Yes. I finally became a brother. My mother _____ _____ _____ _____
　　아주 귀여운 딸을 낳았다
_____ _____ .

W Congratulations!

M Thanks. She is so cute that I can't keep my eyes off her.

W I know how you feel now. That's how I felt when I had my brother. By the way, how's your mother?

M She is fine.

W It's difficult to give birth. Make sure _____ _____ _____ _____
　　그녀를 잘 돌봐드리다
_____ .

M _____

19 적절한 응답

반납 안 된 책이 있는 상황에서 다시 책을 빌리는 상황에 유의한다.

Man: _____

① Go and ask for help to your teacher.
② Get your membership card again and call your parents.
③ Just go home and think about what you've done to me.
④ Don't worry about that. We're always happy with the book.
⑤ Just return the book first, and then you can borrow others.

W Good morning, Mr. Starr. I'd like to borrow these books.

M Good morning. Do you have _____ _____ _____ ?
　　　　회원카드

W Sorry, I forgot to bring it.

M That's okay _____ _____ _____ _____ _____ in the computer.
　　내가 네 이름을 찾는다면

W Good. I'm Jane Birkin. My last name is spelled B-I-R-K-I-N.

M OK. Umm.... Oh, you have _____ _____ _____ .
　　　　　　　　　　기한이 지난 책

W Really? I think I brought all the books back.

M No, you still have '1984' by George Orwell.

W Oh, my gosh! I _____ _____ . I'm terribly sorry. What should I do now?
　　　　완전히 잊었다

M _____

20 상황에 적절한 말(담화)

몸이 아파 힘들어 하는 어머니를 돕고자 할 때 할 말을 생각해 본다.

다음을 듣고, 어머니에게 할 말로 가장 적절한 것을 고르시오.

① I'll prepare dinner for Dad.
② Why don't you see a doctor?
③ Go ahead. I'll go to bed early.
④ Mom, I'm still having dinner.
⑤ Go and rest. I'll wash the dishes.

M Your mother _____ _____ _____ when you went to school. Now you
　　　　　　　　오늘 아침에 아파 보였다
are home and she doesn't look any better. Your dad isn't home yet. Your mother sets the table for dinner. She eats just a bit, but mostly sits at the table waiting for you to finish your meal. When you finish your dinner, she stands up to do the dishes. You think
_____ _____ _____ _____ and want to
그녀가 일찍 잠자리에 들어야 한다
_____ _____ _____ . In this situation, what will you most likely
그녀를 위해 설거지를 하다
say to your mother?

무엇을 평가하는가?	일상생활이나 친숙한 일반적 주제에 관한 말이나 대화를 듣고 화자의 의도나 목적을 추론할 수 있는지를 평가한다.
어떻게 출제되는가?	• 대화를 듣고, 여자가 남자에게 전화한 목적으로 가장 적절한 것을 고르시오. • 대화를 듣고, 남자의 마지막 말에 담긴 의도로 가장 적절한 것을 고르시오.

key solution

❶ 전화한 목적을 묻는 경우, 직접적으로 제시되는 경우와 간접적으로 제시되는 경우가 있으니 전체적인 흐름을 놓치지 않도록 주의한다.

❷ 마지막 말의 의도를 묻는 경우, 다양한 상황에 다른 표현을 숙지하는 것이 중요하다.

[기출로 전략 확인]

대화를 듣고, 여자가 남자에게 전화한 목적으로 가장 적절한 것을 고르시오.　　[2017 기출]

① 귀가가 늦을 것을 알리려고　　　　② 차를 태워달라고 부탁하려고
③ 회의 시간 변경을 요청하려고　　　④ 자동차 이상 유무를 확인하려고
⑤ 수리 기사 연락처를 물어보려고

┈┈┈┈┈┈┈┈┈┈┈┈┈┈┈┈┈┈┈┈┈┈┈┈┈┈┈

[Cellphone rings.]
M Hello, Joanne. What's up?
W Hi, Peter. I have a problem.
M What's wrong?
W My car won't start. I'm worried I'll be late.
M Really? Don't you have a meeting at 10 a.m.?
W Yes. That's why I'm calling you. Can you give me a ride?
M Sure. I'm not far from your house. Where can I pick you up?
W I'll be in the parking lot. Thanks.

❶ 차를 태워달라고 전화한 목적을 직접적으로 제시하고 있다. 차의 시동이 걸리지 않는다는 부분을 듣고 섣부르게 ④를 오답으로 선택하지 않도록 주의한다.

남 여보세요. Joanne. 무슨 일이야?
여 안녕, Peter. 나 문제가 생겼어.
남 무슨 일이야?
여 내 차 시동이 안 걸려. 지각할까 걱정이야.
남 진짜? 10시에 회의 있지 않아?
여 맞아. 그게 내가 전화한 이유야. 나 좀 태워 줄래?
남 물론이지. 네 집에서 안 머니까. 어디서 태워줄까?
여 주차장에 있을게. 고마워.

대화를 듣고, 여자가 남자에게 전화한 목적으로 가장 적절한 것을 고르시오. [2017 기출]

① 주문을 취소하려고 ② 배송 지연을 알리려고
③ 환불 방법을 알리려고 ④ 제품 이상을 문의하려고
⑤ 배송 위치를 확인하려고

만점 잡는 문장 W I'm sorry, but the T-shirts you ordered will be delayed for a few days.

대화를 듣고, 남자의 마지막 말에 담긴 의도로 가장 적절한 것을 고르시오. [2017 기출]

① 충고 ② 감사 ③ 거절
④ 요청 ⑤ 위로

만점 잡는 문장 W If you drink a glass of warm milk, you'll sleep better. (제안)
M Thank you for the tip. I'll try.

● 목적

Can you check out a Jeju guidebook for me? (부탁)
나를 위해 제주 안내서 좀 확인 해 줄래?

Please get me a cheeseburger at the Burger World next to the bakery. (부탁)
빵집 옆에 있는 Burger World에서 치즈 버거 좀 갖다 줄래?

Could you send somebody to help? (요청)
도움을 줄 수 있는 사람 좀 보내 주실 수 있나요?

Why don't we go visit him this afternoon? (제안)
오늘 오후에 그를 방문하는 거 어때?

● 의도

I love it. There couldn't be a better present for me. (감사)
좋아요. 저를 위한 더 좋은 선물을 없을 거에요.

Thank you for the tip. I'll try. (감사)
팁 고마워. 그렇게 해볼게.

I'd like to, but I have to work part-time at the school library. (거절)
그러고 싶지만 학교 도서관에서 파트타임으로 일을 해야 해요.

I'm afraid not. It would be too late. (거절)
안될 거 같아요. 그럼 너무 늦을 거에요.

You can say that again. (동의)
그 말이 맞아요.

Yeah, I can't agree with you more. (동의)
맞아요, 전적으로 동의해요.

Why don't you ask her to email it to you? (제안)
그녀한테 메일로 보내 달라고 하는 게 어때?

학년　　반　　번
이름

01 대화를 듣고, 여자가 구입하려는 벽시계를 고르시오.

① $55

② $55

③ $65

④ $65

⑤ $55

02 대화를 듣고, 여자가 남자에게 전화한 목적으로 가장 적절한 것을 고르시오.

① 뮤지컬을 예매하려고
② 오디션을 신청하려고
③ 뮤지컬 배우에 대해 이야기 하려고
④ 오디션 캐스팅을 자랑하려고
⑤ 뮤지컬 연습 일정을 잡으려고

03 다음 그림의 상황에 적절하지 않은 대화를 고르시오.

①　　②　　③　　④　　⑤

04 대화를 듣고, 두 사람이 맨 처음 가기로 한 장소를 고르시오.

① 주차장　　② 영화관
③ 신발가게　　④ 식료품점
⑤ 서점

05 대화를 듣고, Sam의 심정으로 가장 적절한 것을 고르시오.

① upset　　② frightened
③ happy　　④ excited
⑤ interested

06 대화를 듣고, 두 사람의 관계로 가장 적절한 것을 고르시오.

① doctor – nurse
② dentist – patient
③ teacher – student
④ manager – musician
⑤ customer – salesperson

07 대화를 듣고, 두 사람의 대화가 어색한 것을 고르시오.

①　　②　　③　　④　　⑤

08 대화를 듣고, 남자가 여자에게 부탁한 일로 가장 적절한 것을 고르시오.

① 자동차 딜러 소개하기　　② 자동차 구매자 소개하기
③ 중고차 검사하기　　④ 중고차 구매해주기
⑤ 자동차 현황 파악하기

09 대화를 듣고, 남자의 마지막 말에 담긴 의도로 가장 적절한 것을 고르시오.

① 위로　　② 비판
③ 거절　　④ 칭찬
⑤ 제안

10 대화를 듣고, 남자가 받을 거스름돈을 고르시오.

① $30　　② $40
③ $60　　④ $70
⑤ $90

11 대화를 듣고, 두 사람이 대화하는 장소로 가장 적절한 곳을 고르시오.

① 신발 가게
② 스케이트장
③ 눈 썰매장
④ 체조 연습장
⑤ 아이스크림 가게

12 다음을 듣고, 블루베리 축제에 관해 언급되지 <u>않은</u> 것을 고르시오.

① 축제 내용 ② 축제 기간
③ 축제 장소 ④ 축제 입장료
⑤ 축제 참석자

고난도

13 다음 표를 보면서 대화를 듣고, 남자가 선택할 여행 상품을 고르시오.

Winter Package Tour

	Destination	Rate	Period
①	Malaysia	$5,200	Jan 3 ~ Jan 8
②	Hong Kong	$5,500	Jan 4 ~ Jan 9
③	Malaysia	$3,800	Jan 2 ~ Jan 8
④	Australia	$3,900	Jan 1 ~ Jan 6
⑤	Hong Kong	$3,500	Dec 28 ~ Jan 3

14 다음을 듣고, 무엇에 관한 설명인지 고르시오.

① car
② stove
③ airplane
④ Cellphone
⑤ microwave oven

15 대화를 듣고, 남자가 대화 직후에 할 일로 가장 적절한 것을 고르시오.

① 헌혈하기
② 처방전 받기
③ 병원에 가기
④ 입원 수속 밟기
⑤ 피검사 받기

16 대화를 듣고, 남자가 할 일로 가장 적절한 것을 고르시오.

① 다른 제품 사러 가기
② 다른 제품으로 교환해 주기
③ 지퍼를 수선해 주기
④ 환불해 주기
⑤ 쿠폰 제공하기

[17~19] 대화를 듣고, 여자의 마지막 말에 대한 남자의 응답으로 가장 적절한 것을 고르시오.

17 Man: _____

① How long can I check out books?
② Thanks. I'll call the library tomorrow.
③ Really? Could you tell me where it is?
④ I'm sorry I don't have time to go there.
⑤ OK. I'll go to the bookstore and buy some.

고난도

18 Man: _____

① OK. What time do you close?
② I see. Thank you for your visit.
③ Right. I want to buy another umbrella here.
④ No, you are wrong. It didn't rain yesterday.
⑤ Maybe. Well, I should try to remember another place.

19 Man: _____

① No thanks. I already had enough.
② Thank you for saying that I'm a good cook.
③ Well, I'm afraid I am allergic to the sunlight.
④ Great. I'll go to the store to get some sandwich.
⑤ Okay. I'll read my book while you're making them.

20 다음 상황 설명을 듣고, Mark가 Sally에게 할 말로 가장 적절한 것을 고르시오.

Mark: _____

① Can you fix my car?
② Can you give me a ride?
③ What do you think of my car?
④ Can you pick me up at the cafe?
⑤ Do you know how to get to the shopping mall?

다시 들으면서 듣기 만점에 도전하세요!

Dictation: 스크립트의 주요 부분을 다시 들으면서!

실전 ⊕: 세부 정보가 많은 스크립트를 다른 문제로 샅샅이!

---

01 그림 정보 파악(사물)

square one, round one, numbers 등을 놓치지 않고 듣는다.

대화를 듣고, 여자가 구입하려는 벽시계를 고르시오.

① \$55
② \$55
③ \$65
④ \$65
⑤ \$55

W I'm looking for a simple wall clock. Would you show me one within $60?

M Sure. How about _____ _____ with numbers on it? It's $55.
　　　　　　　　　　정사각형 모양의 것

W It looks good, but _____ _____ _____ _____ _____.
　　　　　　　　　　나는 저 둥근 것이 더 좋다

M You mean the small round one without numbers?

W No, the big one looks better. And I want _____ _____ _____.
　　　　　　　　　　　　　　　　　　　　　그 위에 모든 숫자가 있는 것

M I see, but it's $65.

W Well, that's OK. I'll pay more.

---

02 전화한 목적

대화를 듣고, 여자가 남자에게 전화한 목적으로 가장 적절한 것을 고르시오.

① 뮤지컬을 예매하려고
② 오디션을 신청하려고
③ 뮤지컬 배우에 대해 이야기 하려고
④ 오디션 캐스팅을 자랑하려고
⑤ 뮤지컬 연습 일정을 잡으려고

[Cellphone rings.]

M Hi, Grace. What's up?

W Hey, I had my final audition yesterday, and guess what?

M What?

W I _____ _____ _____ a big stage musical.
　　~에서 역할을 맡다

M Really? Which one?

W Mama Mia. I am going to play one of main character's friends.

M Wow, that's amazing! Who's going to act with you?

W The cast list is unbelievable. _____ _____ _____, Suzan
　　　　　　　　　　　　　내가 가장 좋아하는 여배우 중 하나
Baker, will play the title role. I will actually practice with her in person.

M When are they going to start practicing?

W Well, they're still casting extras, so the very first meeting with other actors and staff won't be announced for a few more weeks.

M That's so exciting! _____ me _____ about how it's going!
　　　　　　　　　　　계속 알려주다

---

03 상황에 적절하지 않은 대화(그림)

다음 그림의 상황에 적절하지 **않은** 대화를 고르시오.

① ② ③ ④ ⑤

① W What's the problem with my cat?
　 M Let me check first.

② W Do you like cats?
　 M No. Actually I'm afraid of cats.

③ W Will she be OK now?
　 M Sure. She's going to be all right.

④ W Should I _____ only once a day?
　　　　　　　그녀에게 먹이를 주다
　 M Yes. For one week.

⑤ W Can I _____ _____ now?
　　　　　그녀를 집에 데리고 가다
　 M Yes. Make sure to _____ _____.
　　　　　　　　　　그녀를 따뜻하게 해 주다

---

04 특정 정보 파악(장소)

대화를 듣고, 두 사람이 맨 처음 가기로 한 장소를 고르시오.

① 주차장   ② 영화관
③ 신발가게   ④ 식료품점
⑤ 서점

➕ 대화를 듣고, 두 사람이 함께 할 일이 아닌 것을 고르시오.

① 식료품 쇼핑하기
② 쇼핑몰 가기
③ 신발 고르기
④ 차 타기
⑤ 세탁소 들르기

M Mom, I need to go to the shopping mall. Can you _____ me _____? *태워주다*

W All right. I was going to do some grocery shopping anyway.

M Thanks.

W What are you going to buy at the mall?

M I'm going to _____ some _____ _____. *새 신발을 사다*

W All right. Then I'll drop you off at the shoe store, and then I'll go to the grocery store.

M Actually, Mom, can you help me choose my shoes? Let's _____ _____ _____ you finish grocery shopping. *~후에 만나다*

W Well, then, I'll have to carry groceries all the way to the shoe store or make two trips to the car.

M Ah. Then, come with me to the shoe store first, and then we can go grocery shopping together.

W All right. let's go. Just let me grab the keys.

M Thanks. I hope the mall isn't too busy today.

05 심정 파악

대화를 듣고, Sam의 심정으로 가장 적절한 것을 고르시오.

① upset 화난   ② frightened 무서운
③ happy 행복한   ④ excited 흥분한
⑤ interested 재미있는

I'm not in the mood to talk. : 말할 기분이 아니다.

W Hi, Sam. Where are you headed?

M Don't ask me anything. _____ _____ _____ _____ _____ _____. *나는 말할 기분이 아니다*

W Come on, Sam. What happened to you? Tell me so I can help you out.

M I was at Mark's birthday party and my mom called me to come home right away.

W Oh, that's too bad. So you had to _____ _____ _____ in the middle of excitement, right? *파티장을 떠나다*

M Yeah. And my mother didn't tell me why I should hurry home.

W Hmm... I think _____ _____ _____ _____ _____ that. *틀림없이 ~에 대한 이유가 있다*

M Well, I don't care.

06 관계 파악

치아와 관련된 내용을 두 사람의 관계와 연관시키지 않도록 주의한다.

대화를 듣고, 두 사람의 관계로 가장 적절한 것을 고르시오.

① doctor – nurse 의사 – 간호사
② dentist – patient 치과 의사 – 환자
③ teacher – student 교사 – 학생
④ manager – musician 매니저 – 음악가
⑤ customer – salesperson 고객 – 영업사원

I had a toothache. : 치통을 앓았다.

W Max, _____ _____. *네가 늦었다*

M I'm sorry, Ms. Carter. I had a toothache and I went to the dentist this morning.

W Oh, you did? Are you OK, now?

M Yes. I have to see him again the day after tomorrow.

W I see. Well, let's see _____ _____ _____ _____. You know this violin competition is very important for you if you want to be a famous musician. *네가 얼마나 많이 연습했는지*

M Of course I do. And I hope my teeth won't be a problem on the stage.

W So do I. Now, why don't you _____ _____ _____? *바로 여기부터 시작하다*

대화를 듣고, 두 사람의 대화가 <u>어색한</u> 것을 고르시오.

①   ②   ③   ④   ⑤

①   M   I'd like to buy some socks for my daughter.

      W   What size does she wear?

②   M   What is _____ _____ _____?

당신의 방문 목적

      W   I'll stay at the Sunrise hotel for two weeks.

③   M   I'd like to _____ _____.

이 책들을 반납하다

      W   OK. Oh, this book _____ _____.

연체되었다

④   M   Mary, I want to _____ _____.

당신에게 부탁을 하다

      W   Oh, do you? What is it?

⑤   M   Where can I wash my hands?

      W   The bathroom is on your right.

부탁의 표현인 'Can you help me~?' 부분에 집중한다.

대화를 듣고, 남자가 여자에게 부탁한 일로 가장 적절한 것을 고르시오.

① 자동차 딜러 소개하기
② 자동차 구매자 소개하기
③ 중고차 검사하기
④ 중고차 구매해주기
⑤ 자동차 현황 파악하기

➕ 다음을 듣고, 남자의 자동차에 대해 알 수 <u>없</u>는 것을 고르시오.

① 차량 종류
② 차량 색상
③ 차량 주행거리
④ 차량 최초 구입 가격
⑤ 차량 사고 내역

[Cellphone rings.]

M   Hi, Jenny. Can I get your advice? I'd like to sell my car, but I don't know how.

W   Hmm... Why don't you contact a used car dealer?

M   I did. But they _____ me _____ _____ _____ _____. Can you help me

아주 낮은 가격을 제시하다

find someone who might buy it?

W   Well, one of my friends has been talking about buying a new car recently. I'll ask him if

      he's interested. Could you _____ _____ _____ _____ _____ you

어떤 종류의 차인지 말하다

have?

M   It's a 2013 Zet 4.

W   Okay. What color is it?

M   It's metallic silver.

W   And how many kilometers does it have on it?

M   About 20,000 kilometers.

W   The car has never been in an accident, right?

M   That's right. No accidents.

W   So, how much would you like to get for it?

M   Well, I'd like to get at least $10,000 for it. I've taken really good care of the vehicle.

대화를 듣고, 남자의 마지막 말에 담긴 의도로 가장 적절한 것을 고르시오.

① 위로   ② 비판
③ 거절   ④ 칭찬
⑤ 제안

W   Hi, Matt! Thank you for visiting my restaurant.

M   No problem. It was very nice of you to invite me.

W   Here's the menu. Please take a look and let me know when you're _____

주문할 준비가 된

_____.

M   Let me see... Shabu-shabu? What kind of food is that?

W   Oh, it's a kind of hotpot dish with thinly sliced meat and vegetables. You dip the meat

      into boiling water and then eat it.

M   Hmm... Interesting. How about dubu-tang?

W   It's _____ _____ _____ tofu and beef. Why don't you try it? It's one of

~로 만든 국

our best dishes. You'll love it.

M   Is it spicy? I can't eat anything spicy.

W   No, dubu-tang isn't spicy. I always let my customers know when they are ordering a

spicy dish.

M   All right then, I'll have that. I think it'd be really helpful for your customers if you had

_____ _____ _____ _____ _____ _____.

메뉴에 있는 음식들 사진

W   That's a good point. I'll keep that in mind.

10 숫자 정보 파악(금액)

개당 가격과 사는 수량을 말하는 부분에 집중하여 거스름돈을 계산해 본다.

대화를 듣고, 남자가 받을 거스름돈을 고르시오.

① $30   ② $40
③ $60   ④ $70
⑤ $90

W   Good evening, sir. How may I help you?

M   Hello. I'm looking for a blouse for my little daughter.

W   How old is she?

M   Nine. And she likes _____ _____ yellow, pink and orange.
<small>~같은 밝은 색들</small>

W   I see. How about the yellow ones on the rack over here? They're _____.
<small>한 벌당 30달러</small>

M   Hmm. They look great. I'll _____ _____ _____, one yellow and one
<small>그것들 두 벌을 사다</small>
orange.

W   OK. And we give a pair of gloves for free if you buy more than three blouses.

M   Oh, really? Let me think... I'm sorry _____ _____ _____. Here is
<small>세 벌 살 여유가 없다</small>
_____.
<small>100달러</small>

11 대화 장소 파악

대화를 듣고, 두 사람이 대화하는 장소로 가장 적절한 곳을 고르시오.

① 신발 가게
② 스케이트장
③ 눈 썰매장
④ 제조 연습장
⑤ 아이스크림 가게

W   Oh, Jack! Will you _____ _____ _____?
<small>내가 똑바로 서도록 도와주다</small>

M   Let's see. I think your shoes are too big.

W   Then, should I change them?

M   No, let me tighten your shoe laces.... OK.

W   Thanks. That's much better. But I still can't keep my balance.

M   Here, take my hand and get onto the ice, and you'll learn very fast.

W   Oh, my gosh! It's _____ but I feel great!
<small>너무 미끄러운</small>

M   Sure you do. Come on. Now _____ _____ _____ _____ and try to
<small>내 손을 놓아라</small>
keep your balance.

12 언급 유무 파악(담화)

다음을 듣고, 블루베리 축제에 관해 언급되지 않은 것을 고르시오.

① 축제 내용   ② 축제 기간
③ 축제 장소   ④ 축제 입장료
⑤ 축제 참석자

`고난도`

W   We invite you and all of your friends and family to our blueberry farm! Please join us to celebrate this year's blueberry harvest festival! At the festival, there is something for everyone. You can _____ _____ on our 40-acre farm, as well as
<small>블루베리 따는 것을 즐기다</small>
shopping, live music, a small petting zoo, festival rides and games, food trucks, and more. This two-day event will be held from 9 am to 5 pm on Saturday and Sunday, May 5 and 6. Our address is 532 Orchard Road. Admission and parking _____ _____.
<small>완전히 무료이다</small>
No dogs allowed. Please _____ and hats, and comfortable
<small>선크림을 바르다</small>
clothing is suggested.

13 특정 정보 파악(도표)

여행 기간, 원하는 날씨 및 가격 등에 유의하여 듣는다.

다음 표를 보면서 대화를 듣고, 남자가 선택할 여행 상품을 고르시오.

Winter Package Tour

	Destination	Rate	Period
①	Malaysia	$5,200	Jan 3 ~ Jan 8
②	Hong Kong	$5,500	Jan 4 ~ Jan 9
③	Malaysia	$3,800	Jan 2 ~ Jan 8
④	Australia	$3,900	Jan 1 ~ Jan 6
⑤	Hong Kong	$3,500	Dec 28 ~ Jan 3

[Telephone rings.]

W   FLORA TOUR COMPANY. May I help you?

M   Hello. Could you recommend a tour _____ _____ _____
<small>1월의 첫째 주쯤</small>
_____?

W   Sure. Are you going alone, sir?

M   Yes. And I want to stay in a warm place because I hate cold weather.

W   Well, how about Australia? It's summer down there now.

M   Oh, I don't like hot weather, either.

W   Then Hong Kong and Malaysia have _____ _____ _____ around that
<small>매우 따뜻한 날씨</small>
time.

M   Good. And I hope the cost will be _____ _____.
<small>4,000달러 미만</small>

W   OK, sir. No problem.

14 소재 파악(담화)

장거리 여행에 이용되고 휘발유나 디젤 같은 연료를 필요로 하는 것을 생각해 본다.

다음을 듣고, 무엇에 관한 설명인지 고르시오.

① car 자동차
② stove 난로
③ airplane 비행기
④ Cellphone 휴대 전화
⑤ microwave oven 전자레인지

M This was invented about 100 years ago. We usually use this _____ _____ _____ _____ in a short time. This is made up of a lot of parts including _____ _____ _____. This _____ _____ _____ _____ _____, but many people expect this will use electricity or solar energy in the future. Although this is _____ _____ _____ _____ in our life, we should be very careful in using this because it can be dangerous.

(장거리를 여행하기 위해 / 네 개의 바퀴 / 휘발유나 디젤과 같은 연료를 필요로 한다 / 가장 편리한 것들 중의 하나)

15 할 일 파악 – 대화 직후

병원의 여러 곳을 옮겨 다니며 검사를 받고 있는 상황임을 파악한다.

대화를 듣고, 남자가 대화 직후에 할 일로 가장 적절한 것을 고르시오.

① 헌혈하기
② 처방전 받기
③ 병원에 가기
④ 입원 수속 밟기
⑤ 피검사 받기

How have you been? (어떻게 지냈어요?) : 상대방의 안부를 물어볼 때 쓰는 표현이다.

W How have you been?

M Great. I worked out every day.

W Let's see.... You _____ _____ _____ _____.
(2킬로그램 이상 줄었다)

M I can't believe it. Two kilograms in ten days! That's why I feel much better and stronger.

W You're right. Now, why don't you _____ _____ _____ _____ for the blood test?
(3층으로 올라가다)

M Oh, I really hate needles.

W Don't worry. It only _____ _____ _____.
(약 5초간 계속된다)

16 할 일 파악

대화를 듣고, 남자가 할 일로 가장 적절한 것을 고르시오.

① 다른 제품 사러 가기
② 다른 제품으로 교환해 주기
③ 지퍼를 수선해 주기
④ 환불해 주기
⑤ 쿠폰 제공하기

M May I help you?

W Yes, I bought these pants here yesterday, but I'd like to return them.

M Oh, may I ask you why you're returning them?

W The zipper is broken. I can't _____ _____ _____. Here's the receipt.
(바지 지퍼를 내리다)

M OK, I'll change them for a new pair. Wait a minute, please.

W Okay.

M Miss? I'm terribly sorry. These pants _____ _____ _____ _____. Could you choose a different style?
(품절이 되다.)

W Oh, I really like the design and color of these pants. Would any of your other stores have a pair?

M This style is very popular, so they're all sold out. If you want, we can _____ _____ _____ _____ _____.
(고장난 지퍼를 새 것으로 교체하다)

W Do I have to pay for it?

M No, it'd be free. It'll take about 30 minutes, though.

W Okay, I'll wait.

17 적절한 응답 | 찾는 곳의 위치를 모르는 상황에서 할 수 있는 말을 생각해 본다.

[17~19] 대화를 듣고, 여자의 마지막 말에 대한 남자의 응답으로 가장 적절한 것을 고르시오.

Man: _____

① How long can I check out books?
② Thanks. I'll call the library tomorrow.
③ Really? Could you tell me where it is?
④ I'm sorry I don't have time to go there.
⑤ OK. I'll go to the bookstore and buy some.

M Excuse me, how can I _____ _____ books? (대출하다)
W Do you have a library card?
M No. This is _____ _____ _____. (이곳에 내가 처음 방문한 것)
W Then, please fill out this form and I'll make a card for you.
M OK. By the way, are there books for 3 and 4-year-old kids?
W I'm sorry. We have books only for children over 7 years old.
M Gee.... Does that mean I _____ _____ _____ for my daughter at the (책들을 사야 한다) bookstore?
W Oh, _____ _____ _____. There's a children's library near here. (당신은 그럴 필요가 없다)
M _____

18 적절한 응답

Man: _____

① OK. What time do you close?
② I see. Thank you for your visit.
③ Right. I want to buy another umbrella here.
④ No, you are wrong. It didn't rain yesterday.
⑤ Maybe. Well, I should try to remember another place.

M Excuse me. I had lunch here yesterday and I _____ _____. (내 우산을 놓고 갔다)
W Oh, there're a few umbrellas. What does it look like?
M It's big and black.
W Let's see. There are only white, yellow and red ones.
M That's strange. I think I carried an umbrella when I got here because it was raining.
W Do you remember _____ _____ _____? (당신이 떠난 시간)
M It was around 1:40. The rain cleared away then, didn't it?
W No, sir. It stopped in the evening. You probably _____ _____ _____ (당신 우산을 갖고 갔다) _____ when you left here.
M _____

19 적절한 응답 | 여자가 샌드위치를 준비하는 동안 남자가 할 수 있는 일을 생각해 본다.

Man: _____

① No thanks. I already had enough.
② Thank you for saying that I'm a good cook.
③ Well, I'm afraid I am allergic to the sunlight.
④ Great. I'll go to the store to get some sandwich.
⑤ Okay. I'll read my book while you're making them.

M It's a beautiful day, isn't it?
W It sure is. I like clear skies. _____ _____ go to the park? (우리 ~합시다)
M To the park? Why?
W We can enjoy sunbathing.
M I'd like to, but I have to finish this book by tomorrow.
W If so, I'll lay a big outdoor blanket for you on the grass. You can _____ _____ and (눕다) read your book. What do you think?
M Hmm... Sounds like a good idea. All right. Let's go.
W Wait. I think _____ _____ _____ our lunch. (나는 준비해야 한다)
M Oh, it's already 11. What will you make?
W How about cheese sandwiches? It _____ _____ much time. (걸리지 않을 것이다)
M _____

20 상황에 적절한 말(담화) | 같은 방향으로 가는 사람에게 무엇이라고 말할지 생각해 본다.

다음 상황 설명을 듣고, Mark가 Sally에게 할 말로 가장 적절한 것을 고르시오.

Mark: _____

① Can you fix my car?
② Can you give me a ride?
③ What do you think of my car?
④ Can you pick me up at the cafe?
⑤ Do you know how to get to the shopping mall?

W Mark is supposed to meet his old friend in a cafe in 20 minutes. He goes to the garage and _____ _____ _____ _____ but it won't start. He sees (그의 차에 시동을 걸려고 한다) Sally, who lives next door, come out to drive her car. Mark asks her where she is headed. She says she's going to the shopping mall. Mark _____ _____ (알게 돼서 기쁘다) _____ that she is going _____ _____ _____. In this situation, (같은 방향으로) what would Mark say to Sally?

학년 　　반 　　번
이름

01 대화를 듣고, 남자가 외출할 때 신을 신발을 고르시오.

02 대화를 듣고, 여자가 방문한 목적으로 가장 적절한 것을 고르시오.

① 머리를 자르려고
② 지갑을 구입하려고
③ 미용실에 예약하려고
④ 습득물을 돌려주려고
⑤ 분실 물건을 수령하려고

03 다음 그림의 상황에 가장 적절한 대화를 고르시오.

① 　　② 　　③ 　　④ 　　⑤

04 대화를 듣고, 여자가 집에 돌아올 요일을 고르시오.

① 금요일 　　② 토요일
③ 수요일 　　④ 월요일
⑤ 화요일

05 대화를 듣고, 두 사람의 심정으로 가장 적절한 것을 고르시오.

① funny and excited
② gloomy and calm
③ unhappy and disappointed
④ satisfied and happy
⑤ bored and tired

06 대화를 듣고, 남자가 관심을 보인 직업으로 가장 적절한 것을 고르시오.

① 체육 교사 　　② 야구 심판
③ 야구 해설가 　　④ 여행 안내원
⑤ 구장 내 관리 직원

07 다음을 듣고, 두 사람의 대화가 <u>어색한</u> 것을 고르시오.

① 　　② 　　③ 　　④ 　　⑤

08 대화를 듣고, 남자가 여자에게 부탁한 일로 가장 적절한 것을 고르시오.

① 정치학 수업 출석하기
② 미디어 수업 추천하기
③ 미디어 수업 등록해 주기
④ 주요 커리큘럼 알아보기
⑤ 학습 진로 상담하기

09 대화를 듣고, 남자의 마지막 말에 담긴 의도로 가장 적절한 것을 고르시오.

① 위로 　　② 비판
③ 거절 　　④ 제안
⑤ 격려

10 대화를 듣고, 남자가 지불해야 할 총 금액을 고르시오.

① $40 　　② $50 　　③ $70
④ $80 　　⑤ $100

점수

/20

11 대화를 듣고, 두 사람이 대화하는 장소로 가장 적절한 곳을 고르시오.

① airport ② hospital
③ restaurant ④ coffee shop
⑤ supermarket

12 다음을 듣고, 리조트 프로그램에 관해 언급되지 <u>않은</u> 것을 고르시오.

① 리조트 위치 ② 리조트 어린이 프로그램
③ 리조트 영유아 프로그램 ④ 리조트 가족 활동
⑤ 리조트 프로그램 비용

13 다음 표를 보면서 대화를 듣고, 내용과 일치하는 것을 고르시오.

	회사	가격	공사 기간	공사 개시일
①	Best Kitchen	$3,500	4 days	in a week
②	Best Kitchen	$3,000	1 week	tomorrow
③	Right Construction	$3,000	4 days	tomorrow
④	Right Construction	$3,000	1 week	tomorrow
⑤	Right Construction	$2,500	4 days	in a week

14 다음을 듣고, 무엇에 대한 설명인지 고르시오.

① 실 ② 바늘
③ 열쇠 ④ 반지
⑤ 재봉틀

15 대화를 듣고, 여자가 대화 직후에 할 일로 가장 적절한 것을 고르시오.

① 숙소 알아보기 ② 기차표 예약하기
③ 버스 노선 확인하기 ④ 기차 요금 알아보기
⑤ 렌터카 비용 알아보기

고난도
16 대화를 듣고, 오늘 날짜를 고르시오.

① August 7 ② August 16
③ August 23 ④ August 25
⑤ August 27

[17~19] 대화를 듣고, 남자의 마지막 말에 대한 여자의 응답으로 가장 적절한 것을 고르시오.

17 Woman: _____

① I think I'm ready for a change.
② Thanks for your offer, but I like it.
③ The pay is low and the hours are long.
④ I have my own office and it's spacious.
⑤ Just like you, I can travel abroad cheaply.

18 Woman: _____

① Thank you. I've been happy to work with you.
② Don't worry. I'll help you to open your shop.
③ I want to get a job in this company. What do you think?
④ Good luck to you, too. You'll be successful in running your shop.
⑤ You're welcome. I need more time to do my work in this company.

19 Woman: _____

① Great idea! Is the bus expensive to buy?
② Sounds interesting. So, where can I take the bus?
③ It sounds strange to me. I don't like tourists at all.
④ Let me tell you how much you must pay for the bus.
⑤ That sounds convenient, but I don't want to drive the bus.

20 다음 상황 설명을 듣고, Tina가 선생님께 할 말로 가장 적절한 것을 고르시오.

Tina: _____

① I want to buy a new PMP.
② I am sorry I didn't listen to you.
③ Please listen to my story this time.
④ I'm afraid that I made a big mistake.
⑤ I found my PMP on someone's desk.

다시 들으면서 듣기 만점에 도전하세요!
Dictation: 스크립트의 주요 부분을 다시 들으면서!
실전 ⊕: 세부 정보가 많은 스크립트를 다른 문제로 샅샅이!

---

01 그림 정보 파악(사물)

정장을 입고 외출을 하려다가 옷을 갈아입는 이유를 놓치지 않고 듣는다.

대화를 듣고, 남자가 외출할 때 신을 신발을 고르시오.

① ②
③ ④
⑤

W When you go out, be careful, my dear. It's slippery out there.
M Slippery? Was there a snowfall or something?
W Yeah. It snowed overnight. Look out the window.
M Oh, I should start early to make it on time.
W I think you should change your shoes.
M Don't tell me you want me to _____ _____ _____, Mom.
   등산화를 신다
W Why not? They'll _____ _____ _____ _____ _____.
   빙판 길에서 너를 안전하게 지키다
M Come on, Mom. I'm wearing a dress suit.
W Then you want to be in leather shoes and _____ _____?
   계속 넘어지다
M All right. I'll _____ _____ and _____ _____.
   내 옷을 갈아입다   당신 말대로 하다

---

02 목적 파악

대화를 듣고, 여자가 방문한 목적으로 가장 적절한 것을 고르시오.

① 머리를 자르려고
② 지갑을 구입하려고
③ 미용실에 예약하려고
④ 습득물을 돌려주려고
⑤ 분실 물건을 수령하려고

W Excuse me.
M Yes?
W I'm _____ _____ _____ Josh Hamilton. Does he work here?
   ~이라는 이름의 남자를 찾고 있는
M Yes, but we're closed now. The working hours are from 10 a.m. to 9 p.m. Besides, I guess you need to make a reservation. Josh is a very popular hairdresser.
W Oh, I see. But I'm not here to have my hair cut.
M Really? Then why are you looking for Josh?
W I _____ _____ _____ _____. A business card in it says he works here.
   길거리에서 그의 지갑을 발견했다
M Oh, I see. Let me call him and check if he can come back right now.
W Thank you.

고난도

03 상황에 적절한 대화(그림)

조수석에 탄 사람이 안전벨트를 매고 있지 않은 상황임을 파악한다.

다음 그림의 상황에 가장 적절한 대화를 고르시오.

① ② ③ ④ ⑤

Talk it easy. (진정하세요.): 긴장한 상대방을 진정시킬 때 쓰는 표현이다. (=Calm down.)

① W I wonder you can give me a ride home.
   M Sure. Get in.
② W Whew! Thank you. I _____ _____ him.
   거의 칠 뻔했다
   M Don't use your Cellphone while driving.
③ W Are you sending text messages again?
   M No. I'm editing photos I took hours ago.
④ W Are there any problems at your car? Take it easy.
   M My car won't start. I can't stand it.
⑤ W Make sure to _____ _____.
   안전벨트를 매다
   M Oh, _____ _____ _____ _____.
   나에게 상기시켜 줘서 고맙다

04 특정 정보 파악(요일)

대화를 듣고, 여자가 집에 돌아올 요일을 고르시오.

① 금요일　　② 토요일
③ 수요일　　④ 월요일
⑤ 화요일

[Cellphone rings.]

M Hi, Jenny. How are you?

W Hi, Dad. I'm fine.

M Are you having a great time there?

W Yes, I am. I miss you a lot, but it's sad that _____ _____ _____ _____ _____ _____. It's already Wednesday!
　　캠프가 끝나가다

M I'm glad to hear you miss me. When are you coming back?

W I was going to go back on Friday. But Cathy, this _____ _____ _____ _____, invited me to her place. I'd like stay with her over the weekend. Is that okay, Dad?
　　캠프에서 만난 소녀

M Hmm... Do her parents know about this?

W Yes, I met Cathy's parents when she was video chatting with them. They invited me to come over, but they wanted me to talk to you about it first.

M Okay. Can you _____ _____ _____ _____ _____?
　　그들에게 내 전화번호를 알려주다

W Of course. Then I'll see you next week.

M I'll see you on Monday, Jenny. Don't stay longer than the weekend at Cathy's. I want to see you soon.

W All right. I'll see you on Monday!

05 심정 파악

대화를 듣고, 두 사람의 심정으로 가장 적절한 것을 고르시오.

① funny and excited
② gloomy and calm
③ unhappy and disappointed
④ satisfied and happy
⑤ bored and tired

일기예보의 내용과 소풍과의 관계를 생각해 본다.

M What are you going to bring _____ _____ _____, Lisa?
　　우리의 소풍에

W I'll make some sandwiches.

M Great. Then I'll buy some _____ _____ _____.
　　과일과 음료

W Do you know who brings sausages for the barbecue?

M Jenny and Max said they would buy some.

W Now everything looks great. _____ _____ _____ I wonder what the weather will be like tomorrow.
　　그런데

M Let's check on the Internet. Oh, dear! It's going to rain all day tomorrow.

W All day? You must be kidding. It's hot and sunny outside, you see?

M Come have a look here. It looks like we're having a big storm.

W Oh, no! Then should we _____ _____ our picnic?
　　미루다

06 직업 파악

대화를 듣고, 남자가 관심을 보인 직업으로 가장 적절한 것을 고르시오.

① 체육 교사
② 야구 심판
③ 야구 해설가
④ 여행 안내원
⑤ 구장 내 관리 직원

잦은 장거리 여행, 보호 장비 착용, 파울볼 등에 의한 부상의 위험에 노출되어 있는 직업을 생각해 본다.

W What can I do for you?

M I'm interested in the job you advertised in the newspaper. I wonder what is necessary for the job.

W First, you need to pass a physical test. You have to be physically strong because _____ _____ _____ _____ _____ _____ _____ almost every three days.
　　이 일은 당신에게 장거리 여행을 요구한다

M I understand.

W After that, there will be _____ _____ _____ _____ _____. If you pass it, you'll get a three-month training course.
　　야구 규칙에 관한 필기시험

M All right. By the way, what's the hardest part of this job?

W You have to _____ _____ _____ in the middle of summer. And there is a high risk of injury. You sometimes _____ _____ _____ _____. But if you like baseball, it's worth it.
　　무거운 보호 장비를 입다　　*파울볼에 맞는다*

M Okay. Thank you.

안부를 물어보면 상대방에게도 어떻게 지냈는지 묻는 것이 자연스럽다.

다음을 듣고, 두 사람의 대화가 <u>어색한</u> 것을 고르시오.

①   ②   ③   ④   ⑤

① **W** Where did you pick up this old sofa?

   M At the antique shop downtown.

② **W** _____ _____ _____ _____ Fred?
        ~와는 어떻게 지내고 있니

   M Pretty well. We meet almost every day.

③ **W** Are you free this Saturday?

   M Yes, I am. Do you have anything in mind?

④ **W** Long time no see. _____ _____ _____?
        어떻게 지냈어

   M For five years since I graduated.

⑤ **W** I was wondering if you would like to go to a movie with me.

   M I'd love to. Which movie?

대화를 듣고, 남자가 여자에게 부탁한 일로 가장 적절한 것을 고르시오.

① 정치학 수업 출석하기
② 미디어 수업 추천하기
③ 미디어 수업 등록해 주기
④ 주요 커리큘럼 알아보기
⑤ 학습 진로 상담하기

➕ 다음을 듣고, 대화가 이루어지는 장소로 가장 적합한 것을 고르시오.

① 병원   ② 대학교 캠퍼스
③ 사무실   ④ 호텔
⑤ 버스터미널

W Hey, Jeremy. What are you doing?

M I'm trying to choose a fifth class for next semester.

W It's _____ always _____ _____.
        수업을 선택하는 것이 쉽지 않은

M Right. Have you chosen all the classes you want to take?

W Yes, I have. Three classes are related to my major, politics, and I'm also taking two media classes.

M Oh, I was thinking about _____ _____ _____. Can you recommend one?
        미디어 수업을 듣는 것

W What about Professor Jahara's class? He's really great.

M I've heard that. I should check if the class is still open.

W Great. But before you enroll, _____ _____ and course descriptions.
        자격 요건을 검토하다

M Sure. I'll review them carefully before enrolling.

W Good luck.

대화를 듣고, 남자의 마지막 말에 담긴 의도로 가장 적절한 것을 고르시오.

① 위로   ② 비판
③ 거절   ④ 제안
⑤ 격려

➕ 다음을 듣고, 두 사람에 대해 알 수 <u>없는</u> 것을 고르시오.

① 남자의 방학 계획
② 남자의 전공 분야
③ 여자의 방학 계획
④ 여자의 아프리카 방문 목적
⑤ 여자의 장래 희망

W Hi, Jason! What are your plans for this coming vacation?

M I'm going to Paris and London. I need to _____ some _____ _____ the designs of modern European architecture.
        ~에 대한 연구를 하다

W That will be _____ _____ _____.
        네 전공에 도움이 되는

M That's why I'm going there. How about you? Are you planning to take a vacation?

W I'm going to Africa.

M Wow! Are you going there for travel or work?

W I'm going to volunteer in a region struck by serious drought. I want to _____ _____ _____ _____ a lack of food or medicine.
        ~로 고통받는 아이들을 돕다

M You're going there to make a difference. It'll be a really rewarding experience for you.

10 숫자 정보 파악(금액)

정상가, 매수, 할인율을 메모하며 듣고 계산해 본다.

대화를 듣고, 남자가 지불해야 할 총 금액을 고르시오.

① $40　　② $50
③ $70　　④ $80
⑤ $100

I'd like to pay by credit card. : 신용카드로 지불하고 싶다. (cf. by check 수표로 / by cash 현금으로 / by charge 신용카드로)

[Telephone rings.]

W Hello, Global Ticket Agency. How may I help you?

M Hi. I'd like to reserve tickets to the musical *Chicago*.

W When would you like to see the musical?

M On May 9th.

W Mother's Day? It must be a present for your mother. Hold on. You're lucky. We have some tickets left.

M Great. I'd like to ＿＿＿＿＿＿ ＿＿＿ ＿＿＿. How much are they?
　　_{성인 표 두 장을 예매하다}

W They are ＿＿＿＿＿＿ ＿＿＿＿, but all shows are ＿＿＿＿＿ ＿＿＿ on that day.
　　_{평상시대로라면 한 장에 50달러}　　　_{20% 할인}

M That's great. I'd like to pay by credit card.

W All right. Wait a second.

11 대화 장소 파악

채식주의자라는 사실에 난감해하며 나가자고 제안하는 상황임을 파악한다.

대화를 듣고, 두 사람이 대화하는 장소로 가장 적절한 곳을 고르시오.

① airport 공항
② hospital 병원
③ restaurant 식당
④ coffee shop 커피숍
⑤ supermarket 슈퍼마켓

M What do you think of my choice?

W Well, it's fine except for one thing.

M Except for one thing? I wonder what it is.

W It's just that ＿＿＿＿＿ ＿＿＿＿.
　　_{나는 채식주의자이다}

M Oh, no. What an idiot I am! I'm sorry! I should have known better than to ＿＿＿
　　_{누군가를 Fred's Steak & Ribs에 데리고 오다}
＿＿＿ ＿＿＿ ＿＿＿ ＿＿＿ on a first date without asking.

W That's okay. I can drink coffee or something, instead.

M No way. I can't make someone like you ＿＿＿ ＿＿＿＿. Let's get
　　_{내가 고기를 먹는 것을 보다}
out of here.

12 언급 유무 파악(담화)

다음을 듣고, 리조트 프로그램에 관해 언급되지 **않은** 것을 고르시오.

① 리조트 위치
② 리조트 어린이 프로그램
③ 리조트 영유아 프로그램
④ 리조트 가족 활동
⑤ 리조트 프로그램 비용

W Hello, everyone. Welcome to Yatapa Resort & Spa. Our resort offers the best program for kids in the nation. The 500-acre resort ＿＿＿ ＿＿＿ part of a Native
　　　　　　　　　　　　　　　　　　　　_{~에 위치하다}
American Pueblo and offers kids ages 3 to 12 the chance to experience the art and history of this culture. Also, our childcare center ＿＿＿ ＿＿＿ ＿＿＿ for infants
　　　　　　　　　　　　　　　　　　　　　　　_{매일 문을 열다}
from six months to children three years old. With activities indoors and out, your children will be entertained with singing, arts and crafts, a ball pit, and story time. In addition to the kids' program, we ＿＿＿ other ＿＿＿ ＿＿＿ like trail riding,
　　　　　　　　　　　　　　　　　　　　　　_{가족 활동을 제공하다}
Pueblo pottery making, and Native American stories under the stars.

13 특정 정보 파악(도표)

비용, 공사 기간, 공사 개시일을 근거로 일치 여부를 파악한다.

다음 표를 보면서 대화를 듣고, 내용과 일치하는 것을 고르시오.

	회사	가격	공사 기간	공사 개시일
①	Best Kitchen	$3,500	4 days	in a week
②	Best Kitchen	$3,000	1 week	tomorrow
③	Right Construction	$3,000	4 days	tomorrow
④	Right Construction	$3,000	1 week	tomorrow
⑤	Right Construction	$2,500	4 days	in a week

W We have quotes from two companies: Best Kitchen and Right Construction.

M Let's see the details of what they said about our new kitchen. When can they start work?

W Best Kitchen said they are so busy that they cannot start work for a week. And Right Construction said that they can ＿＿＿＿＿ ＿＿＿.
　　　　　　　　　　　　　　　　　　　_{내일 일을 시작하다}

M I see. What's the price?

W Best Kitchen said it'll cost $3,500 and Right Construction said it'll ＿＿＿＿＿.
　　　　　　　　　　　　　　　　　　　　　　　　_{3,000달러의 비용이 든다}

M Then how long will it take?

W Best Kitchen said it'll take a week and Right Construction said they can ＿＿＿
　　　　　　　　　　　　　　　　　　　　　　　　　_{4일 만에 끝내다}
＿＿＿ ＿＿＿ ＿＿＿ ＿＿＿.

M Well, it's not hard to make a choice between them.

14 소재 파악(담화)

바느질할 때 사용하며, 한쪽 끝에 구멍이 있고, 다른 한쪽 끝은 뾰족한 끝이 있는 것은 무엇일지 생각해 본다.

다음을 듣고, 무엇에 대한 설명인지 고르시오.

① 실 ② 바늘
③ 열쇠 ④ 반지
⑤ 재봉틀

W This is one of the main tools you use when ＿＿＿ ＿＿＿ ＿＿＿
천 조각을 모아 바느질하다
＿＿＿ . This is ＿＿＿ ＿＿＿ ＿＿＿ ＿＿＿ ＿＿＿ ＿＿＿
한쪽 끝에 뾰족한 끝이 있는 길고 가는 도구
＿＿＿ ＿＿＿ ＿＿＿ ＿＿＿ . This also has a hole, called the eye, at the other
non-pointed end to carry thread through the fabric after the pointed end pierces it. In
the old days, mothers used this and thread to apply patches on worn-out clothes.
These days, however, they ＿＿＿ ＿＿＿ ＿＿＿ ＿＿＿ ＿＿＿
재봉틀 때문에 이것을 좀처럼 사용하지 않는다
＿＿＿ .

15 할 일 파악 – 대화 직후

남녀가 각자 할 일을 구별해서 파악한다.

대화를 듣고, 여자가 대화 직후에 할 일로 가장 적절한 것을 고르시오.

① 숙소 알아보기
② 기차표 예약하기
③ 버스 노선 확인하기
④ 기차 요금 알아보기
⑤ 렌터카 비용 알아보기

W I've heard Wellington is beautiful.
M Do you think we should go by bus?
W We don't have to. I guess we could take a train.
M We could, but it might be a good idea to rent a car.
W We could do that. The point is how much it will cost.
M I wonder ＿＿＿ ＿＿＿ ＿＿＿ ＿＿＿ to go by train.
비용이 얼마나 들지
W I'm not sure, but ＿＿＿ ＿＿＿ ＿＿＿ ＿＿＿ .
내가 알아볼 수 있다
M Why don't you do that? I'll find out about the car rental.
W Sounds good. I'll do that right away.

고난도

16 특정 정보 파악(날짜)

대화를 듣고, 오늘 날짜를 고르시오.

① August 7
② August 16
③ August 23
④ August 25
⑤ August 27

[Cellphone rings.]

W Hello, Junho. What's up?
M Hi, Soyoung. I want to tell you something. I have to change schools.
W Really? Why?
M Because of my father's job, we are going to move.
W But you're not moving right away, are you? I will see you in school, won't I?
M I'm afraid not. We're moving ＿＿＿ ＿＿＿ ＿＿＿ ＿＿＿
여름 방학이 끝나기 2일 전
＿＿＿ ＿＿＿ .
W Our vacation is ＿＿＿ ＿＿＿ ＿＿＿ , isn't it?
8월 25일에 끝나는
M Yes.
W Then we have a week to give you a good-bye party. That's a relief.

17 적절한 응답

[17~19] 대화를 듣고, 남자의 마지막 말에 대한 여자의 응답으로 가장 적절한 것을 고르시오.

Woman: _____

① I think I'm ready for a change.
② Thanks for your offer, but I like it.
③ The pay is low and the hours are long.
④ I have my own office and it's spacious.
⑤ Just like you, I can travel abroad cheaply.

W Scott, how do you like working for your new company?
M My new company? It's great! I have a nice boss and I like the people I work with.
W A nice boss and great colleagues really help. Do you get any benefits?
M Yeah. We can get great deals on trips abroad.
W Oh, cheap trips! You're so lucky.
M Yeah, I guess I'm lucky. How about you? How's your new job?
W My job _____ _____ _____ _____ .
_{당신 것만큼 좋지는 않다}
M Really? _____ _____ ?
_{왜 안 좋아}
W _____

18 적절한 응답

떠나는 사람에게 행운을 빌 때 어떤 반응을 보일지 생각한다.

Woman: _____

① Thank you. I've been happy to work with you.
② Don't worry. I'll help you to open your shop.
③ I want to get a job in this company. What do you think?
④ Good luck to you, too. You'll be successful in running your shop.
⑤ You're welcome. I need more time to do my work in this company.

W Ben, _____ _____ . I already talked with the boss.
_{나는 그만둡니다}
M Really? I can't believe you're leaving. You're _____ _____ _____ in this company.
_{가장 훌륭한 직원 중의 한 사람}
W Thank you for saying so. It was good to work with you.
M Are you leaving because of your kids?
W No, my kids are _____ _____ now. I just want to run my own business.
_{모두 다 성장한}
M Oh, I see. I know you really wanted to _____ _____ _____ . I think it's a good time to start it. Good luck to you!
_{당신 자신의 가게를 갖다}
W _____

19 적절한 응답

서울 시티 투어버스에 대해 더 알아보기 위해 할 수 있는 말을 생각한다.

Woman: _____

① Great idea! Is the bus expensive to buy?
② Sounds interesting. So, where can I take the bus?
③ It sounds strange to me. I don't like tourists at all.
④ Let me tell you how much you must pay for the bus.
⑤ That sounds convenient, but I don't want to drive the bus.

W Excuse me, but is this bus for N Seoul tower?
M Yes, you _____ _____ _____ _____ . Don't worry.
_{맞는 버스에 탔다}
W Thank you. It's hard for a tourist like me to use public transportation in a new place.
M It sure is. Which places have you been _____ _____ ?
_{지금까지}
W Well, I've been to various places like Rodeo street, Kyungbok palace, and Insa-dong.
M Did you take the Seoul City Tour Bus?
W What's that? Is it a _____ _____ ?
_{무료 버스}
M No, it's not. If you buy a one-day pass, you can easily _____ _____ _____ in Seoul.
_{여러 유명한 장소를 방문하다}
W _____

20 상황에 적절한 말(담화)

도난 사건에 대해 화가 난 선생님께 사실을 말씀드리고 오해를 풀어야 하는 상황이다.

다음 상황 설명을 듣고, Tina가 선생님께 할 말로 가장 적절한 것을 고르시오.

Tina: _____

① I want to buy a new PMP.
② I am sorry I didn't listen to you.
③ Please listen to my story this time.
④ I'm afraid that I made a big mistake.
⑤ I found my PMP on someone's desk.

M When Tina came back to her classroom _____ _____ _____ _____ , she
_{과학실로부터}
noticed her new PMP was gone. She told her homeroom teacher that someone had stolen her PMP. The teacher got angry and _____ _____ _____ . But it was not
_{그것을 찾았다}
found anywhere. Feeling depressed, Tina went home. When she got in her home, she saw her PMP on her desk. She thought she had taken it to school, but _____
_____ _____ _____ . The next day, Tina found her teacher still angry. In this
_{사실 그녀는 그러지 않았다}
situation, what would Tina most likely say to the teacher?

할 일·부탁한 일 파악

무엇을 평가하는가?	일상생활이나 친숙한 일반적 주제에 관한 말이나 대화를 듣고 일이나 사건의 순서, 전후 관계를 추론할 수 있는지를 평가한다.
어떻게 출제되는가?	• 대화를 듣고, 여자가 할 일로 가장 적절한 것을 고르시오. • 대화를 듣고, 남자가 할 일로 가장 적절한 것을 고르시오. • 대화를 듣고, 여자가 남자에게 부탁한 일로 가장 적절한 것을 고르시오. • 대화를 듣고, 남자가 여자에게 부탁한 일로 가장 적절한 것을 고르시오.

key solution

❶ 지시문을 읽고, 두 화자 중 누가 할 일인지, 누가 누구에게 부탁한 일을 묻는지 확인한다.

❷ 대화 중에 함께 제시되는 과거에 한 일 또는 상대방이 할 일과 혼동하지 않도록 한다.

❸ 부탁한 일은 'Will you ~?', 'Can you ~?' 같이 직접적인 표현을 사용하는 경우가 많다.

[기출로 전략 확인]

대화를 듣고, 여자가 남자에게 부탁한 일로 가장 적절한 것을 고르시오. [2016 기출]

① 아침 차려주기 ② 과제 도와주기 ③ 아이들 깨우기
④ 자명종 수리하기 ⑤ 차로 자녀 등교시키기

- -

M Honey, you look worried.

W Yeah, I'm going on a business trip for the next three days.

M Well, what's the matter, then?

W Our kids! They usually get up early, but mid-term exams start tomorrow.

M Right. They're really tired these days since they're staying up so late.

W I know. So, will you give them a ride to school for the next three days?

M All right, I will. Should I make them breakfast as well?

W No. They can get sandwiches near the school.

남 여보, 걱정 있어 보이는데.

여 응, 3일간 출장을 가게 됐잖아.

남 뭐가 문젠데?

여 우리 애들! 보통 일찍 일어나지만 중간고사가 내일 시작이야.

남 맞아. 요즘 굉장히 늦게 자서 피곤해 하더라.

여 알아. 그래서 3일동안 아이들을 학교에 태워 줄 수 있을까?

남 알겠어, 그렇게. 아침도 만들어주는게 좋을까?

여 아니. 애들이 학교 근처에서 샌드위치를 사 먹을거야.

❶ 지시문을 통해 '여자'가 남자에게 무언가 부탁하는 내용이 나올 것임을 인지한다.

❸ 여자가 'will you ~?' 표현을 사용한 것을 듣고, 이 문장에서 남자에게 부탁하는 내용이 나올 것임을 예상한다.

❷ 여자가 아닌 남자가 자신이 어떤 일을 해야 할 지 묻고 있는 말이고, 여자의 대답 또한 'No'임으로 정답과 혼동하지 않도록 주의한다.

대화를 듣고, 남자가 할 일로 가장 적절한 것을 고르시오. [2017 기출]

① 교실 방문   ② 콘서트 관람   ③ 팸플릿 제작
④ 공연 일정 조정   ⑤ 미술 준비물 구입

오답 찍는 문장   **M** We have to make pamphlets for our concert.
W Right, I'll do that. And how about visiting classrooms to let students know about the concert?

만점 잡는 문장   **M** Great idea. I'll visit classrooms during the break.

대화를 듣고, 남자가 여자에게 부탁한 일로 가장 적절한 것을 고르시오. [2015 기출]

① 설거지하기   ② 숙제 도와 주기   ③ 집에 바래다 주기
④ 수업 준비물 구입하기   ⑤ 학교로 영어책 가져오기

M Hi, Tiffany. I think I left my English book in your kitchen when I came over to study.

오답 찍는 문장   **W** You did. I was just about to call you. Should I bring it to your house later?

만점 잡는 문장   **M** You don't have to do that. Could you just bring it to school tomorrow?

● 할 일

Give me some of the pictures, and I'll pass them out to people.
그림을 내게 좀 주면 내가 사람들에게 나누어 줄게.

A We need to change the light bulb in the bathroom. 우리 화장실 전구를 갈아야 해.
B Okay. I'll do it right now. 알겠어. 내가 지금 할게.

A May I borrow your umbrella? 네 우산을 좀 빌려도 될까?
B Sure. It's in my locker. I'll go get it for you. 당연하지. 사물함에 있어. 내가 갖고 올게.

● 부탁한 일

Can you book tickers for us? Then, I'll buy some popcorn.
우리 티켓을 예약해 줄 수 있을까? 그러면 내가 팝콘을 살게.

Could you choose the clothes for the play? 연극을 위한 의상을 골라 주시겠어요?

A I have to return this book today, but I don't have any time.
오늘 이 책을 반납해야 하는데 내가 시간이 없어.

B No problem. I can drop it off for you. 걱정 마. 내가 대신 반납 해줄게.

학년   반   번

이름

01 다음 대화와 어울리는 표지판을 고르시오.

①

②

③

④

⑤

02 대화를 듣고, 여자가 남자에게 부탁한 일로 가장 적절한 것을 고르시오.

① 리포트 써주기
② 과제 리서치 함께 하기
③ 리서치 피드백 주기
④ 여행계획하기
⑤ 과제 준비 계획하기

03 다음 그림의 상황에 가장 적절한 대화를 고르시오.

①   ②   ③   ④   ⑤

04 대화를 듣고, 두 사람이 등산을 함께 갈 요일을 고르시오.

① 일요일
② 토요일
③ 금요일
④ 목요일
⑤ 수요일

05 대화를 듣고, 여자 또는 남자가 하는 운동으로 언급되지 않은 것을 고르시오.

① ski
② surfing
③ beach volleyball
④ beach wrestling
⑤ footvolley

06 대화를 듣고, 대화가 일어나는 장소를 고르시오.

① 거실
② 욕실
③ 지하실
④ 침실
⑤ 식당

07 다음을 듣고, 두 사람의 대화가 <u>어색한</u> 것을 고르시오.

①   ②   ③   ④   ⑤

08 대화를 듣고, 남자가 여자에게 부탁한 것을 고르시오.

① 뮤지컬 대사 외우기
② 뮤지컬 노래 배우기
③ 뮤지컬 의상 빌리기
④ 뮤지컬 무대 분장 도움 받기
⑤ 뮤지컬 공연 장소 대여하기

09 다음을 듣고, 무엇에 관한 설명인지 고르시오.

① 기억에 남는 학교 생활
② 기억에 남는 영화
③ 기억에 남는 어린시절 친구
④ 기억에 남는 가족 여행
⑤ 기억에 남는 공연

10 대화를 듣고, 여자가 받을 거스름돈을 고르시오.

① $20
② $10
③ $5
④ $50
⑤ $45

11 대화를 듣고, 여자가 할 일로 가장 적절한 것을 고르시오.

① 자신의 휴대 전화 수선하기
② 유료 어플 다운 받기
③ 자신의 휴대 전화 기능 알아보기
④ 무료 어플 찾아보기
⑤ 스팸전화 신고하기

점수 /20

12 다음을 듣고, 축제에 관해 언급되지 <u>않은</u> 것을 고르시오.

① 축제 도시   ② 축제 이름
③ 축제 기간   ④ 축제 장소
⑤ 축제 주관자

13 다음 도시의 지도를 보면서, 남자가 방문할 장소를 고르시오.

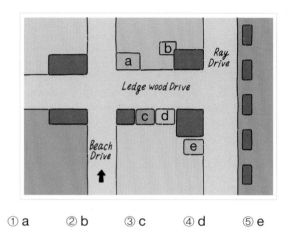

① a   ② b   ③ c   ④ d   ⑤ e

14 다음을 듣고, 무엇에 관한 설명인지 고르시오.

① 이민자 문제   ② 한국의 전통도시
③ 외국 도시 내 한인 타운   ④ 한국의 민속 축제
⑤ 한국의 전통 음식

15 대화를 듣고, 남자가 할 일로 가장 적절한 것을 고르시오.

① 자전거 수리하기   ② 자전거 구매하기
③ 자전거 시승해보기   ④ 스턴트맨 오디션 보기
⑤ 자전거 환불하기

16 대화를 듣고, 두 사람이 다운로드 받을 영화 장르를 고르시오.

① action movie
② hero movie
③ natural disaster movie
④ musical movie
⑤ romantic movie

17 대화를 듣고, 여자의 마지막 말에 대한 남자의 응답으로 가장 적절한 것을 고르시오.

Man: _____

① I'll call the clinic and see what they suggest.
② I have been throwing up whenever I eat something.
③ I just found out that you're very sick.
④ I'll wait for you here. Take your time.
⑤ You wanted me to wait for you at the hospital.

[18~19] 대화를 듣고, 남자의 마지막 말에 대한 여자의 응답으로 가장 적절한 것을 고르시오.

18 Woman: _____

① You don't keep your word.
② I've been so busy doing my homework.
③ As your friend, I'm proud of you for helping out.
④ It's worth helping others when I'm able to do it.
⑤ They ask me to do it even when I'm busy.

19 Woman: _____

① I'll bring lots of food with me.
② I've been thinking about canceling the trip.
③ I just found out that the flight is too expensive.
④ I can't wait to see your family in Okinawa.
⑤ It all sounds so exciting.

20 다음 상황 설명을 듣고, Kelly가 매니저에게 할 말로 가장 적절한 것을 고르시오

Kelly: _____

① Please stop making so much noise at night.
② I'm sorry, but I'm not responsible for what's happening here.
③ She'll leave soon. Please be patient.
④ I'm not sure what happened, but I'll figure it out and take care of it.
⑤ Don't worry. I'll tell my brother to leave the apartment as soon as possible.

다시 들으면서 듣기 만점에 도전하세요!
Dictation: 스크립트의 주요 부분을 다시 들으면세!
실전 ⊕: 세부 정보가 많은 스크립트를 다른 문제로 샅샅이!

---

01 그림 정보 파악 – 사물   'You're not allowed to ~.' 문장을 주의깊게 듣는다.

다음 대화와 어울리는 표지판을 고르시오.

① ② ③ ④ ⑤

M   Can I help you?

W   Yes, please. Is it OK to take pictures in the gallery?

M   I'm afraid not. You're not allowed to _____ any _____ _____ _____ _____ .

미술관에서 사진을 찍다

. We want to preserve our old paintings.

W   I see. One more thing, I really don't want to carry my umbrella around in the gallery, and it's wet. Is there a locker I can keep it in?

M   We do offer _____ _____ _____ _____ _____ in the main lobby.

화장실 옆에 보관함

W   Oh, great. Thanks.

---

02 부탁한 일

대화를 듣고, 여자가 남자에게 부탁한 일로 가장 적절한 것을 고르시오.

① 리포트 써주기
② 과제 리서치 함께 하기
③ 리서치 피드백 주기
④ 여행계획하기
⑤ 과제 준비 계획하기

[Cellphone rings.]

W   Hi, Jack. Did you _____ your _____ _____?

과학 보고서를 끝내다

M   Almost. I just need to check my writing to see if there are any mistakes. How about you?

W   I went on a family trip last weekend. I have to start from the very beginning with the research.

M   Well, you need to _____ _____ good _____ _____ manage your time well.

~를 위한 계획을 짜다

The deadline is less than a week away.

W   Yeah, thanks for reminding me. Could you help me do some research on the topic? It would be a great help.

M   Sure. When do you want me to help you?

W   What about tomorrow after school?

M   I'm afraid I can't. I have something important to do.

W   I see. Then, I'll do some research myself tomorrow. Are you free on Friday? If you are, maybe you could _____ me some _____ _____ _____ _____?

내 연구에 관한 피드백을 주다

M   Friday will be fine. I'll see you after school.

---

03 상황에 적절한 대화(그림)   인물들이 있는 장소와 그와 어울리는 표현을 예상하며 듣는다.

다음 그림의 상황에 가장 적절한 대화를 고르시오.

① ② ③ ④ ⑤

① W   This hamburger is so delicious.

    M   By the way, _____ _____ _____ _____ .

점심은 내가 살게

② W   I'm so tired.

    M   How about going to bed early tonight?

③ W   The movie will start soon.

    M   Let me buy some popcorn first.

④ W   Are you still watching TV?

    M   I was about to _____ it _____ .

끄다

⑤ W   How was your trip to Chicago?

    M   It was great.

두 사람 모두 합의하는 요일이 나올 때까지 집중하며 듣는다.

대화를 듣고, 두 사람이 등산을 함께 갈 요일을 고르시오.

① 일요일　　　② 토요일
③ 금요일　　　④ 목요일
⑤ 수요일

W Hi, Robert! What did you do on the weekend?

M I went to Mount Inwang with my family. We left home very early so that we could _____ _____ _____ _____ _____ . It was just amazing.
　　(꼭대기에서 일출을 보다)

W Wow, that's wonderful. I've heard that seeing the sunrise from a mountain is absolutely beautiful. I really want to try that one day.

M I can't believe you've never seen the sunrise from a mountain before! Why don't we go hiking together and see it sometime?

W Yes, I'd love to... But first I have to _____ _____ _____ _____ . Shall we go
　　　　　　　　　　　　　　　　　　　(하이킹에 익숙해지다)
to a nearby mountain next Sunday?

M Well, I am free next Sunday, but hiking on a Sunday isn't fun because it's pretty crowded. Sometimes you have to hike in a line. What about early Friday morning?

W Hmm... I have plans on Friday morning. I'm only available on the weekend.

M Then, let's meet on Saturday. It's _____ _____ _____ than on Sunday.
　　　　　　　　　　　　　　　　　　(토요일에 덜 붐비는)

W Okay, that's fine with me. I'm looking forward to hiking with you.

언급되는 운동을 차례로 지워가며 듣는다.

대화를 듣고, 여자 또는 남자가 하는 운동으로 언급되지 <u>않은</u> 것을 고르시오.

① ski
② surfing
③ beach volleyball
④ beach wrestling
⑤ footvolley

W Hi, Jack! What are you going to do this summer?

M I love playing sports and being active, so I'll _____ _____ _____ .
　　　　　　　　　　　　　　　　　　　　　　　(많은 스포츠를 하다)

W What sports do you play?

M I swim and I run, but my favorite sport is skiing.

W I ski, too. But I only ski on ski slopes that aren't too steep. I'm _____
_____ .　　　　　　　　　　　　　　　　　　　　　　　　　(다치는 것이 무서운)

M Then, do you prefer summer sports to winter sports?

W Well, yes. I like anything I can play on the beach with my friends.

M Which sport do you like best?

W I love surfing... It _____ _____ _____ _____ . I also like to play
beach volleyball.　　(나를 자유롭다고 느끼게 만들다)

M My favorite beach sport is footvolley. It's really fun to play using only your feet.

W I play it, too.

M Then, we should play together sometime.

W Okay!

대화를 듣고, 대화가 일어나는 장소를 고르시오.

① 거실　　　② 욕실
③ 지하실　　④ 침실
⑤ 식당

M Mom? I'm home!

W Did you have a good day?

M Yes, I've finally finished my science project. I'm free now!

W Don't you have homework to do?

M No. I finished everything at recess.

W Okay, but you aren't going to _____ _____ _____ just _____
_____ _____ _____ in the living room.
(저녁 시간 전부를 소파에 누워서 보내다)

M Mom, the first match of the national soccer league is this evening. I really have to watch it on the big TV.

W OK, but before it starts, please help me out with some housework.

M What do you want me to do?

W Go to your room and _____ your _____ . Your room has been
such a mess for weeks.　(책상과 책장을 정리하다)

M It'll take such a long time, Mom. Can't I eat dinner first?

W Well, then come and help me in the kitchen.

M Okay, I will.

다음을 듣고, 두 사람의 대화가 어색한 것을 고르시오.

① ② ③ ④ ⑤

① M When did the movie start?
　 W It just started about 5 minutes ago.
② M This food _____.
　　　　　　　　　　냄새가 이상하다
　 W Don't eat it. I'll make something else for you to eat.
③ M How long have you been here in Korea?
　 W I have kept my hair long.
③ M Can you do me a favor?
　 W Of course. _____ _____ _____ _____ _____?
　　　　　　무엇을 해줄까?
⑤ M Do you mind if I open the window?
　 W Not at all. Please go ahead.

여자가 도움을 주려고 하는 말에 대한 남자의 대답을 집중하며 듣는다.

대화를 듣고, 남자가 여자에게 부탁한 것을 고르시오.

① 뮤지컬 대사 외우기
② 뮤지컬 노래 배우기
③ 뮤지컬 의상 빌리기
④ 뮤지컬 무대 분장 도움 받기
⑤ 뮤지컬 공연 장소 대여하기

W How's it going with practicing for the musical?
M Pretty well. All of the members are practicing really hard.
W Has everyone _____ _____ _____ _____ _____?
　　　　　　　　모든 노래를 외웠다
M I know mine, but a few members are still struggling.
W Can I help with that?
M Thanks, but I think we can manage. We still have a couple of weeks to practice.
W Well is there anything that I can do to help?
M Yes. I can't find anyone to help with my makeup.
W I have a friend who is great at doing makeup. She used to _____ _____ _____ _____. I can ask her about it.
　　　　　　　　　　　　　　　　　　전문 메이크업 아티스트로 일하다
M Really? That would be helpful.
W Sure. I'll let you know what she says later.

our family trip, the trip, unforgettable 등으로 답을 유추한다.

다음을 듣고, 무엇에 관한 설명인지 고르시오.

① 기억에 남는 학교 생활
② 기억에 남는 영화
③ 기억에 남는 어린시절 친구
④ 기억에 남는 가족 여행
⑤ 기억에 남는 공연

W Going to Universal Studios was at the top of my wish list. So when we went there on our family trip, I was so excited. Universal Studios is located on Santosa Island in Singapore, so we took a flight there. When we entered, huge statues of the minion characters _____ _____ _____ _____. My favorite part of Universal Studios
　　　　　　　　우리를 환영하는 것처럼 보였다
was the rides. When I went on the 3-D Transformers ride, I felt like I actually met all the characters in the movie. The roller coasters there were beyond my imagination. They were _____ _____ _____. In fact, I was scared before going on the rides, but I
　　　　　빠르고 스릴 넘치는
had a lot of fun. Before we left, we watched the fireworks, and it _____
_____ even more _____. I definitely want to go there again in the future.
　　　　　　　　　　　　　　여행을 잊을 수 없게 만들었다

여자가 구입하려는 상품과 상품의 개수, 가격을 집중해서 듣는다.

대화를 듣고, 여자가 받을 거스름돈을 고르시오.

① $20　　　② $10
③ $5　　　　④ $50
⑤ $45

M Good morning. Can I help you?
W I'm looking for a T-shirt for my son. Hmm, how much are those T-shirts?
W Which ones?
M The white ones _____ _____ _____ _____.
　　　　　　　　　　파란 줄무늬가 있는
W They're $30 each.
M What sizes do you have?
W Small, medium, large, and extra large. What size are you looking for?
M Hmm.. I bought some medium-sized T-shirts last season, but he's been growing a lot. I'm not sure if a medium would still fit him.
W The shirt is 100% cotton and a bit tight, so I _____ _____ _____
_____. Besides, you can exchange it for a different size within two weeks.
　　　　　　　큰 사이즈 사는 것을 추천하다
M Okay. I'll take the large one. And how much are the sports socks over there?
W They're $15 per pair.
M Okay. I'll take one pair with my T-shirt. Here's a fifty-dollar bill.
W Thanks. Here are your receipt and your change.

11 할 일 파악

대화를 듣고, 여자가 할 일로 가장 적절한 것을 고르시오.

① 자신의 휴대 전화 수선하기
② 유료 어플 다운 받기
③ 자신의 휴대 전화 기능 알아보기
④ 무료 어플 찾아보기
⑤ 스팸전화 신고하기

M Hey, Mary. What's wrong? You look upset.

W I've been so _____ _____ _____ I get every day. I _{원하지 않는 전화로 귀찮은} don't know how to block these kinds of calls.

M First, it _____ the kind of phone you have. Do you want to block them on _{~에 달려있다} your mobile phone or on a landline phone?

W Well, I get a lot of calls on my mobile phone.

M In that case, download a call-blocking app. You can create a blacklist of numbers to block from calling your mobile phone.

W That's a good idea. Are those apps free?

M Many call-blocking apps are free or only cost a few dollars. Actually, your mobile phone may come with pre-installed functions that can _____ _____ _____ . _{특정한 번호로 오는 전화를 차단하다}

W Really? I didn't know that.

M Well, let me have a look at your phone. *[pause]* Right. See, your phone has a feature that lets you identify unwanted incoming calls.

W That's great. Before I look for an app, I will find out what built-in features my phone has to block those calls.

M Good idea.

12 언급 유무 파악(담화)

다음을 듣고, 축제에 관해 언급되지 않은 것을 고르시오.

① 축제 도시　② 축제 이름
③ 축제 기간　④ 축제 장소
⑤ 축제 주관자

축제에 대해 보기의 내용이 순서대로 언급되므로 주의깊게 듣는다.

W There are many events that _____ _____ Vancouver. Among them, the _{~로 관광객들을 끌다} Celebration of Light is one of the city's signature summer events. At this festival, the city lights up the sky over English Bay for three nights at the end of July. Every year, three countries _____ _____ _____ to amaze citizens and visitors to _{서로 경쟁하다} Vancouver. This year, an exciting music event called Heart Beat will take place at Sunset Beach. Bands will start playing festival music in the early afternoon, so _____ _____ and get ready to make a night of it! If you want to enjoy it even more, _{도시락을 가져오다} book a place in one of the official VIP viewing areas.

13 지도, 위치 파악(지도) – 배치도

다음 도시의 지도를 보면서, 남자가 방문할 장소를 고르시오.

① a　② b　③ c　④ d　⑤ e

W Welcome to the city. You're lucky to visit here during such a beautiful season.

M Thank you! It is a beautiful and peaceful city.

W That's right. We're _____ _____ _____ such a wonderful city _{~에 사는 것이 아주 자랑스러운} in Korea. Is there any place you want to visit first?

M Yes, there is. I've heard the local museum is very nice. Can you let me know how to get there?

W Sure. Are you driving or _____ _____ _____ ? _{대중교통을 이용하는}

M We're driving. We rented a car.

W That's great. So, first, follow Beach Hill Drive. Then, turn right onto Ledgewood Drive.

M Okay, so follow the road and turn right.

W Right. When you reach a T-junction at Ray Drive, turn left. Then you'll _____ _{주차할 장소를 찾다} _____ _____ _____ nearby. From the parking area, walk a short distance uphill to the entrance of the museum.

M Thank you.

14 소재 파악(담화)

다음을 듣고, 무엇에 관한 설명인지 고르시오.

① 이민자 문제
② 한국의 전통도시
③ 외국 도시 내 한인 타운
④ 한국의 민속 축제
⑤ 한국의 전통 음식

첫 문장에 소재가 등장하니 집중하여 오답을 선택하지 않도록 주의한다.

W Korea Town is the greatest single concentration of Korean people outside of Asia. They all _____ _____ _____ ; the area is also the most densely populated in the _{몇 블록 안에 살다} city. As you walk around, you'll notice the wonderful sights, sounds, aromas, and tastes of the lively community. The Main Avenue hosts the Harvest Festival Street Fair and the New Year Festival & Parade every year. The neighborhood _____ also _____ _____ _____ and other Asian dishes, including well- _{맛있는 한국 음식으로 유명하다} marinated beef and pork, fresh seafood, and a large variety of delicious noodles.

남자의 'Can I try it?'에 대한 여자의 대답을 주의깊게 듣는다.

대화를 듣고, 남자가 할 일로 가장 적절한 것을 고르시오.

① 자전거 수리하기
② 자전거 구매하기
③ 자전거 시승해보기
④ 스턴트맨 오디션 보기
⑤ 자전거 환불하기

W May I help you?

M I'm looking for a bike — a special model for bike tricks.

W What kind of tricks are you thinking of?

M I want to be able to perform aerial stunts. I don't know which one would be the best.

W Well, that all depends. But you'd better choose a bike with _____ 강하고 믿을 수 있는 뼈대 _____ to keep you safe.

M That's right. I really need to _____ 안전에 대한 확신을 느끼다 _____ when I'm on my bike.

W I'd like to recommend this one. It's a bit expensive, but the steel frame is strong but light; it's popular with riders who perform stunts.

M Can I try it?

W Sure. But _____ 그것이 손상되지 않도록 하다 _____.

대화를 듣고, 두 사람이 다운로드 받을 영화 장르를 고르시오.

① action movie
② hero movie
③ natural disaster movie
④ musical movie
⑤ romantic movie

M Miranda, what kind of movies do you like to download and watch?

W I like action movies. I can _____ 스트레스를 잊다 _____ while watching them.

M Don't you think action movies are a bit violent? They include lots of fighting and life-threatening situations.

W Well, that's why action movies feature great heroes. How about you? What kind of movies do you like?

M I like musical movies.

W Musical movies? I like to watch stage musicals, but musical movies aren't that exciting.

M Well, there are a lot of _____ 무대 뮤지컬을 각색한 영화들 _____, but I prefer original musical movies. The singing and dancing are beautiful, so many musical movies are favorites of children and adults alike.

W Okay, then let's watch one of your favorite musical movies tonight. _____ 무엇을 추천할래? _____?

M What about watching a classic? The Sound of Music!

W Good idea!

식중독에 걸려서 설사를 하느라 병원에 갈 수 없는 지인에게 할 수 있는 말을 생각한다.

대화를 듣고, 여자의 마지막 말에 대한 남자의 응답으로 가장 적절한 것을 고르시오.

① I'll call the clinic and see what they suggest.
② I have been throwing up whenever I eat something.
③ I just found out that you're very sick.
④ I'll wait for you here. Take your time.
⑤ You wanted me to wait for you at the hospital.

➕ 대화를 듣고, 남자의 심경으로 적합한 것을 고르시오.

① tired   ② annoyed
③ suprised   ④ sad
⑤ worried

[Cellphone rings]

M Hello?

W Daniel? This is Kate.

M Kate, are you on the way? I'm excited to see you.

W I can't come to see you today. I'm _____ 아파서 누워 있는 _____.

M Oh, what's the matter?

W I've got food poisoning. I feel dizzy and nauseated. And I have pretty bad diarrhea.

M That's awful. What caused it?

W I went to a seafood restaurant yesterday. There _____ 무언가 잘못됐던 게 틀림없다. _____ with the food there. I'm not sure though.

M Have you taken any medicine?

W Yes, but it doesn't seem to be working. In fact, it's getting worse.

M I think you should go and see a doctor.

W I can't go to the clinic right now because I have to _____ 계속 화장실을 가다 _____. I really can't leave the house.

M _____

18 적절한 응답

주민회관에서 봉사활동을 하는 친구에게 할 수 있는 말을 생각한다.

[18~19] 대화를 듣고, 남자의 마지막 말에 대한 여자의 응답으로 가장 적절한 것을 고르시오.

Woman: _____

① You don't keep your word.
② I've been so busy doing my homework.
③ As your friend, I'm proud of you for helping out.
④ It's worth helping others when I'm able to do it.
⑤ They ask me to do it even when I'm busy.

W Jake, I heard that the school golf club is holding tryouts for new members. They're looking for _____ _____ _____ in the national junior golf
_{~에 참가할 유망한 새로운 회원}
league. Would you like to join?
M Well... I'm afraid I can't. Sorry.
W Why not? I thought you wanted to join the club and _____
_____. Besides, you're good at all kinds of sports.
_{골프 치는 법을 배우다}
M Yes, I'd love to learn, but I'm afraid I don't have the time.
W That's disappointing. Can I ask the reason?
M Actually, I _____ _____ the community center after school.
_{~에서 봉사활동을 시작했다}
W That's interesting. What do you do there?
M I've been helping senior citizens exercise three days a week since January. Anyways, I think I can learn how to golf when I'm older.
W _____.

19 적절한 응답

여행 갈 도시에 대해 여러 가지를 추천해 주는 남자에게 할 수 있는 말을 생각한다.

Woman: _____

① I'll bring lots of food with me.
② I've been thinking about canceling the trip.
③ I just found out that the flight is too expensive.
④ I can't wait to see your family in Okinawa.
⑤ It all sounds so exciting.

＋

다음을 듣고, 남자가 언급하지 <u>않은</u> 것을 고르시오.

① 오키나와 여행 경험
② 오키나와 여행의 최적 시기
③ 오키나와의 대표 음식
④ 오키나와의 수족관
⑤ 오키나와의 거리들

M Rosie, how's it going?
W I'm so excited. I'm going on vacation this spring vacation.
M Wow, that's great. Where are you going?
W Okinawa, Japan.
M Good choice! I _____ _____ _____ _____ with my whole family.
_{2년 전에 그곳에 갔다}
W Really? Tell me about the city. What's the best time to visit?
M I think late winter or early spring is the best, and that's when you're going. When you visit, you're going to see cherry blossoms everywhere!
W Oh, good! And what should I see there?
M Well, you should visit the aquarium. It's _____ _____ _____ _____,
_{해안 바로 옆에 위치한}
so it's like you're seeing all the creatures in the ocean, not in an aquarium.
W Awesome. What else?
M Oh, you shouldn't _____ _____ _____ _____ in the city.
_{예쁜 길들을 구경하는 것을 놓치다}
There are a lot of interesting shops and great local restaurants.
W _____.

20 상황에 적절한 말(담화)

다음 상황 설명을 듣고, Kelly가 매니저에게 할 말로 가장 적절한 것을 고르시오.

Kelly: _____

① Please stop making so much noise at night.
② I'm sorry, but I'm not responsible for what's happening here.
③ She'll leave soon. Please be patient.
④ I'm not sure what happened, but I'll figure it out and take care of it.
⑤ Don't worry. I'll tell my brother to leave the apartment as soon as possible.

W Kelly lives alone in an apartment. A few weeks ago, her little sister, Rosa, came to stay with her for a month before she moves in to her dormitory. Early on Monday morning, Kelly _____ _____ _____ the apartment manager. He said he had
_{~로부터 전화를 받았다}
received several complaints about noise coming from Kelly's apartment. Kelly _____
_____ _____ at her place because she had been on a business trip and
_{소음을 낸 것을 부정했다}
hadn't been at home. And then she remembered that Rosa was preparing for her audition. She _____ _____ _____ late at night. However, Kelly knows
_{음악을 틀었을 수도 있다}
that Rosa is very considerate, so she must have realized that playing music could cause trouble with the neighbors. In this situation, what is Kelly most likely to say to the manager?

답안 체크지

실전처럼 문항별 정답을 마킹해서 확인하세요.

틀린 문제는 다시 듣고 확인하세요.

*디딤돌 홈페이지에서 다운로드 받아 교재 안에 수록된 모든 회차의 모의고사 답안 마킹에 활용하세요.

번호	답 란 .... 회
01	① ② ③ ④ ⑤
02	① ② ③ ④ ⑤
03	① ② ③ ④ ⑤
04	① ② ③ ④ ⑤
05	① ② ③ ④ ⑤
06	① ② ③ ④ ⑤
07	① ② ③ ④ ⑤
08	① ② ③ ④ ⑤
09	① ② ③ ④ ⑤
10	① ② ③ ④ ⑤
11	① ② ③ ④ ⑤
12	① ② ③ ④ ⑤
13	① ② ③ ④ ⑤
14	① ② ③ ④ ⑤
15	① ② ③ ④ ⑤
16	① ② ③ ④ ⑤
17	① ② ③ ④ ⑤
18	① ② ③ ④ ⑤
19	① ② ③ ④ ⑤
20	① ② ③ ④ ⑤
plus	① ② ③ ④ ⑤
plus	① ② ③ ④ ⑤

번호	답 란 .... 회
01	① ② ③ ④ ⑤
02	① ② ③ ④ ⑤
03	① ② ③ ④ ⑤
04	① ② ③ ④ ⑤
05	① ② ③ ④ ⑤
06	① ② ③ ④ ⑤
07	① ② ③ ④ ⑤
08	① ② ③ ④ ⑤
09	① ② ③ ④ ⑤
10	① ② ③ ④ ⑤
11	① ② ③ ④ ⑤
12	① ② ③ ④ ⑤
13	① ② ③ ④ ⑤
14	① ② ③ ④ ⑤
15	① ② ③ ④ ⑤
16	① ② ③ ④ ⑤
17	① ② ③ ④ ⑤
18	① ② ③ ④ ⑤
19	① ② ③ ④ ⑤
20	① ② ③ ④ ⑤
plus	① ② ③ ④ ⑤
plus	① ② ③ ④ ⑤

번호	답 란 .... 회
01	① ② ③ ④ ⑤
02	① ② ③ ④ ⑤
03	① ② ③ ④ ⑤
04	① ② ③ ④ ⑤
05	① ② ③ ④ ⑤
06	① ② ③ ④ ⑤
07	① ② ③ ④ ⑤
08	① ② ③ ④ ⑤
09	① ② ③ ④ ⑤
10	① ② ③ ④ ⑤
11	① ② ③ ④ ⑤
12	① ② ③ ④ ⑤
13	① ② ③ ④ ⑤
14	① ② ③ ④ ⑤
15	① ② ③ ④ ⑤
16	① ② ③ ④ ⑤
17	① ② ③ ④ ⑤
18	① ② ③ ④ ⑤
19	① ② ③ ④ ⑤
20	① ② ③ ④ ⑤
plus	① ② ③ ④ ⑤
plus	① ② ③ ④ ⑤

번호	답 란	……… 회
01	① ② ③ ④ ⑤	
02	① ② ③ ④ ⑤	
03	① ② ③ ④ ⑤	
04	① ② ③ ④ ⑤	
05	① ② ③ ④ ⑤	
06	① ② ③ ④ ⑤	
07	① ② ③ ④ ⑤	
08	① ② ③ ④ ⑤	
09	① ② ③ ④ ⑤	
10	① ② ③ ④ ⑤	
11	① ② ③ ④ ⑤	
12	① ② ③ ④ ⑤	
13	① ② ③ ④ ⑤	
14	① ② ③ ④ ⑤	
15	① ② ③ ④ ⑤	
16	① ② ③ ④ ⑤	
17	① ② ③ ④ ⑤	
18	① ② ③ ④ ⑤	
19	① ② ③ ④ ⑤	
20	① ② ③ ④ ⑤	
plus	① ② ③ ④ ⑤	
plus	① ② ③ ④ ⑤	

번호	답 란	……… 회
01	① ② ③ ④ ⑤	
02	① ② ③ ④ ⑤	
03	① ② ③ ④ ⑤	
04	① ② ③ ④ ⑤	
05	① ② ③ ④ ⑤	
06	① ② ③ ④ ⑤	
07	① ② ③ ④ ⑤	
08	① ② ③ ④ ⑤	
09	① ② ③ ④ ⑤	
10	① ② ③ ④ ⑤	
11	① ② ③ ④ ⑤	
12	① ② ③ ④ ⑤	
13	① ② ③ ④ ⑤	
14	① ② ③ ④ ⑤	
15	① ② ③ ④ ⑤	
16	① ② ③ ④ ⑤	
17	① ② ③ ④ ⑤	
18	① ② ③ ④ ⑤	
19	① ② ③ ④ ⑤	
20	① ② ③ ④ ⑤	
plus	① ② ③ ④ ⑤	
plus	① ② ③ ④ ⑤	

번호	답 란	……… 회
01	① ② ③ ④ ⑤	
02	① ② ③ ④ ⑤	
03	① ② ③ ④ ⑤	
04	① ② ③ ④ ⑤	
05	① ② ③ ④ ⑤	
06	① ② ③ ④ ⑤	
07	① ② ③ ④ ⑤	
08	① ② ③ ④ ⑤	
09	① ② ③ ④ ⑤	
10	① ② ③ ④ ⑤	
11	① ② ③ ④ ⑤	
12	① ② ③ ④ ⑤	
13	① ② ③ ④ ⑤	
14	① ② ③ ④ ⑤	
15	① ② ③ ④ ⑤	
16	① ② ③ ④ ⑤	
17	① ② ③ ④ ⑤	
18	① ② ③ ④ ⑤	
19	① ② ③ ④ ⑤	
20	① ② ③ ④ ⑤	
plus	① ② ③ ④ ⑤	
plus	① ② ③ ④ ⑤	

번호	답 란
01	① ② ③ ④ ⑤
02	① ② ③ ④ ⑤
03	① ② ③ ④ ⑤
04	① ② ③ ④ ⑤
05	① ② ③ ④ ⑤
06	① ② ③ ④ ⑤
07	① ② ③ ④ ⑤
08	① ② ③ ④ ⑤
09	① ② ③ ④ ⑤
10	① ② ③ ④ ⑤
11	① ② ③ ④ ⑤
12	① ② ③ ④ ⑤
13	① ② ③ ④ ⑤
14	① ② ③ ④ ⑤
15	① ② ③ ④ ⑤
16	① ② ③ ④ ⑤
17	① ② ③ ④ ⑤
18	① ② ③ ④ ⑤
19	① ② ③ ④ ⑤
20	① ② ③ ④ ⑤
plus	① ② ③ ④ ⑤
plus	① ② ③ ④ ⑤

_____ 회

번호	답 란
01	① ② ③ ④ ⑤
02	① ② ③ ④ ⑤
03	① ② ③ ④ ⑤
04	① ② ③ ④ ⑤
05	① ② ③ ④ ⑤
06	① ② ③ ④ ⑤
07	① ② ③ ④ ⑤
08	① ② ③ ④ ⑤
09	① ② ③ ④ ⑤
10	① ② ③ ④ ⑤
11	① ② ③ ④ ⑤
12	① ② ③ ④ ⑤
13	① ② ③ ④ ⑤
14	① ② ③ ④ ⑤
15	① ② ③ ④ ⑤
16	① ② ③ ④ ⑤
17	① ② ③ ④ ⑤
18	① ② ③ ④ ⑤
19	① ② ③ ④ ⑤
20	① ② ③ ④ ⑤
plus	① ② ③ ④ ⑤
plus	① ② ③ ④ ⑤

_____ 회

번호	답 란
01	① ② ③ ④ ⑤
02	① ② ③ ④ ⑤
03	① ② ③ ④ ⑤
04	① ② ③ ④ ⑤
05	① ② ③ ④ ⑤
06	① ② ③ ④ ⑤
07	① ② ③ ④ ⑤
08	① ② ③ ④ ⑤
09	① ② ③ ④ ⑤
10	① ② ③ ④ ⑤
11	① ② ③ ④ ⑤
12	① ② ③ ④ ⑤
13	① ② ③ ④ ⑤
14	① ② ③ ④ ⑤
15	① ② ③ ④ ⑤
16	① ② ③ ④ ⑤
17	① ② ③ ④ ⑤
18	① ② ③ ④ ⑤
19	① ② ③ ④ ⑤
20	① ② ③ ④ ⑤
plus	① ② ③ ④ ⑤
plus	① ② ③ ④ ⑤

중학영어듣기 만점 솔루션

듣기는 실전이다

중학 3

문제편

24 회

디딤돌

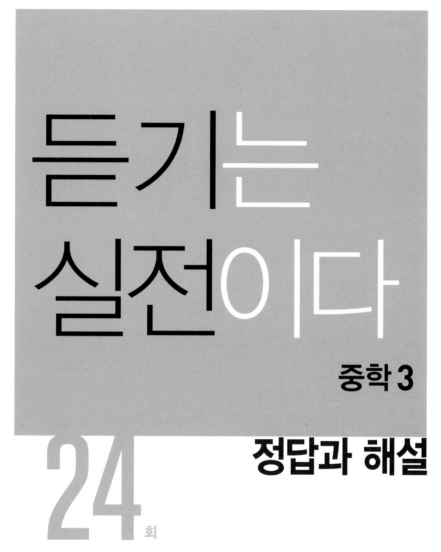

듣기는
실전이다

중학 3

정답과 해설

24회

디딤돌

영어듣기능력 진단평가 01 회

01 ④	02 ①	03 ②	04 ④	05 ③
06 ①	07 ③	08 ①	09 ③	10 ②
11 ③	12 ⑤	13 ②	14 ⑤	15 ②
16 ④	17 ⑤	18 ②	19 ⑤	20 ④

01 ④

M Emily, there's a bookmark on your desk. Did you make it?

W Yes, Dad. It's a birthday present for Rachel.

M Good job! This bookmark looks like a star. It looks nice.

W Thanks. I wanted to make it in a heart shape, but Rachel really likes stars.

M I see. You drew just a smile. Why didn't you write any words on it?

W Well, I think a smile is enough. Rachel always smiles.

M Okay. I'm sure she'll like it.

M 에밀리, 네 책상 위에 책갈피가 하나 있더라. 네가 만든 거니?

W 네, 아빠. 레이첼을 위한 생일 선물이에요.

M 잘 만들었구나! 이 책갈피는 별 같구나. 정말 좋아 보여.

W 고마워요. 하트 모양으로 만들고 싶었지만 레이첼이 별을 정말 좋아하거든요.

M 그렇구나. 웃는 얼굴을 그렸구나. 무슨 말이라도 쓰는 게 어떠니?

W 글쎄요. 웃는 얼굴로 충분한 거 같아요. 레이첼이 항상 웃고 있거든요.

M 알겠다. 그녀가 좋아할 게 분명하구나.

02 ①

W What are you doing, honey?

M I am washing shrimp. I will fry them for our dinner.

W Sounds great. Are all the ingredients ready?

M Well, let me see. I have shrimp, flour, salt, and oil.

W Wait! I don't think we have enough oil to fry all of the shrimp.

M Um..., you're right. Then, can you buy some oil from the supermarket?

W Sure, I will.

W 뭐하고 있어, 자기?

M 새우를 씻고 있어. 우리 저녁을 위해 새우를 튀길 거야.

W 맛있겠다. 모든 재료는 준비됐어?

M 음, 봐 보자. 새우, 밀가루, 소금, 그리고 기름이 있어.

W 잠깐! 모든 새우를 튀길 만큼 기름이 충분히 있는 거 같지 않아.

M 음.... 당신 말이 맞아. 그럼, 가게에서 기름 좀 사다 줄 수 있어?

W 물론, 사 올게.

03 ②

① **W** Will you pass me that sugar, please?

 M Here you are.

② **W** Can you tell me how to use this washing machine?

 M Okay. Let me show you how.

③ **W** How much is this TV?

 M It's $ 200. It's on sale.

④ **W** Can you help me move this desk?

 M Sure. I can help you.

⑤ **W** Is it okay to park my car here?

 M Sure. You can do that.

① **W** 설탕 좀 건네주실래요?

 M 여기 있습니다.

② **W** 이 세탁기를 어떻게 사용하는지 알려줄 수 있니?

 M 그래. 방법을 보여 줄게.

③ **W** 이 TV는 얼마인가요?

 M 200달러입니다, 세일 중이에요.

④ **W** 이 책상 옮기는 걸 도와줄래?

 M 물론. 도와줄게.

⑤ **W** 차를 여기에 주차해도 되나요?

 M 네. 주차해도 됩니다.

04 ④

W Hello, Mr. Thompson. I'd like to use the dancing room after school next week.

M Okay. Which day do you need the room?

W Is it available on Monday?

M No, sorry. The school band practices every Monday. How about next Tuesday?

W I'm afraid I can't. Is it free on Thursday?

M Let me see. [Pause] Yes, you can use it on Thursday.

W Great. I'll use it then. Thank you.

W 안녕하세요, Mr. Thompson. 다음 주 방과 후에 무용실을 사용하고 싶어요.

M 알겠습니다. 어느 날 사용하길 원하시나요?

W 월요일에 사용할 수 있나요?

M 아니요, 미안합니다. 학교 밴드가 매주 월요일에 연습을 하고 있어요. 다음 주 화요일은 어때요?

W 안될 거 같아요. 목요일은 괜찮나요?

M 봐 볼게요. [멈춤] 네, 목요일에 사용할 수 있겠네요.

W 잘됐네요. 그럼 그날 사용할게요. 감사합니다.

05 ③

W Excuse me. I'm looking for a guitar. Can you recommend one for me?

M Sure. How about this brand-new guitar?

W It looks heavy for me.

M Actually, it's only three kilograms. It's much lighter than other guitars.

W Wow! Is it made of plastic?

M No. It's made of wood.

W Good. What colors do you have?

M We have black and pink. And they are $300 each.

W 실례합니다. 기타를 찾고 있어요. 저를 위해 하나 추천해 주실래요?

M 물론이죠. 이 신상 기타는 어떤가요?

W 저에겐 무거울 거 같아요.

M 사실, 3킬로그램밖에 안됩니다. 다른 기타들 보다 훨씬 가벼워요.

W 와! 플라스틱으로 만들어졌나요?

M 아니요. 나무로 만들어졌어요.

W 좋네요. 색상은 어떤 것들이 있나요?

M 검정과 분홍이 있어요. 각각 300달러입니다.

06 ①

W John, we don't have much time. Did you finish buying tickets for the movie, Subway Story?

M No, I'm still trying. But it's difficult for me to use this ticketing machine.

W Why don't you go and buy tickets from the clerk?

M Look! Many people are waiting in the line over there.

W I see. But I'm worried that we might miss the first part of the movie.

M Just wait! I think I'm almost done.

W Then, let me get some popcorn and drinks quickly.

W 존, 시간이 별로 없어. 지하철 이야기 영화표 사는 거 끝났니?

M 아니, 아직 사고 있어. 하지만 이 표 판매기 사용하는 게 어려워.

W 점원한테 가서 표를 사는 게 어때?

M 봐! 많은 사람들이 저기에 줄을 서서 기다리고 있어.

W 알아. 하지만 영화의 첫 부분을 놓칠까 걱정돼.

M 기다려봐! 거의 다 된 거 같아.

W 그럼 나는 빨리 팝콘이랑 음료를 사올게.

07 ③

① **M** How did you like the pancake?

　　W I really enjoyed it. It was delicious.

② **M** I failed the singing audition again.

　　W Don't give up. You'll do better next time.

③ **M** How often do you go to the gym?

　　W It costs $ 60 a month.

④ **M** Is it possible for you to join the race?

　　W I'm not sure. My leg still hurts.

⑤ **M** What do you do in your free time?

　　W I usually enjoy cooking.

① **M** 팬케이크 어땠어?

　　W 진짜 좋았어. 정말 맛있었어.

② **W** 노래 대회에서 또 떨어졌어.

　　M 포기하지 마. 다음에 더 잘할 수 있을 거야.

③ **M** 체육관에 얼마나 자주 가니?

　　W 한 달에 40달러야.

④ **M** 경기에 참여하는 게 가능하겠니?

W 확실하지 않아. 다리가 아직 아파.

⑤ **M** 자유 시간에 무얼 하니?

　　W 보통 요리하는 것 즐겨.

08 ①

M Jenny, you look sad. What happened?

W Well, Susan got upset at me. I was an hour late for our meeting again.

M Late again? I understand how she felt. What are you going to do?

W Actually, I wrote a letter to apologize, but I don't know how to give it to her.

M Hey, I'm seeing Susan in the study group later today.

W Really? Could you pass this letter to Susan for me?

M Sure. I will.

M 제니, 슬퍼 보인다. 무슨 일이야?

W 그게, 수잔이 나에게 화가 났어. 내가 회의 시간에 또 한 시간 지각을 했어.

M 또 늦었어? 그녀가 어떤 기분일지 이해가 된다. 어떻게 할 거야?

W 사실, 사과하려고 편지를 썼는데 이걸 어떻게 그녀에게 줘야할 지 모르겠어.

M 나 오늘 늦게 공부 모임에서 수잔을 만날 거야.

W 진짜? 나를 위해 이 편지를 수잔에게 전해줄 수 있니?

M 물론, 그럴게.

09 ③

W Attention, students. I'm Linda, the school librarian. We're sorry to announce that the library will be closed next week from Monday to Wednesday. The air conditioner broke down and it'll take three days to fix it. You can't use any facilities in the library, but you can put your books in the book return box in front of the library as usual. Thank you for your patience.

W 주목해주세요, 학생분들. 저는 학교 사서인 린다입니다. 도서관이 다음 주 월요일부터 수요일까지 닫게 됨을 알려드리게 되어 유감입니다. 에어컨이 고장이 나서 고치는데 삼 일이 걸릴 예정입니다. 도서관에 있는 어떤 시설도 사용할 수 없지만 평소처럼 도서관 앞에 있는 책 반납 상자에는 여러분의 책을 넣을 수 있습니다. 여러분의 인내심에 감사드립니다.

10 ②

W Welcome to the Happy Gift Shop. How may I help you?

M Hi. I'd like to buy some gifts for my parents. Can you recommend something?

W Well, our best-sellers are coffee cups and T-shirts. The cups are $ 5 each and the T-shirts are $ 10 each.

M I'd prefer the coffee cups.

W Okay. If you buy two cups, then you can get an extra one for free.

M Oh, great! I'll take two cups.

W Good choice.

W 해피 선물 가게에 오신 것을 환영합니다. 무엇을 도와드릴까요?

M 안녕하세요. 부모님을 위한 선물을 사고 싶습니다. 무언가 추천해 주시겠어요?

W 저희 가게에서 제일 많이 팔리는 것은 커피 컵과 티셔츠입니다. 컵은 개당 5달러이고 티셔츠는 개 당 10달러입니다.

M 커피컵이 더 좋네요.

W 알겠습니다. 컵 두 개를 사시면 한 개는 무료로 가지실 수 있습니다.

M 와, 잘됐네요! 컵 두 개 주세요.

W 좋은 선택입니다.

11 ③

M It's really nice outside. How about going on a picnic in the park today?

W Okay. Let's have something like fried chicken or pizza there.

M Um..., I don't think they're good for our health. What about having something healthier?

W You're right. I think sandwiches and fruit would be better.

M Sounds good. Let me get some sandwiches.

W Then, I'll buy some apples and oranges.

M Okay. See you at the park in an hour.

M 밖에 정말 좋다. 오늘 공원에 소풍이라도 가는 게 어때?

W 좋아. 거기서 치킨이나 피자 같은 걸 먹자.

M 음... 그건 우리 건강에 안 좋을 거 같아. 더 건강한 걸 먹는 게 어때?

W 네 말이 맞아. 샌드위치와 과일이 더 좋겠다.

M 좋아. 내가 샌드위치를 살게.

W 그럼, 내가 사과랑 오렌지를 살게.

M 그래. 한 시간 후에 공원에서 보자.

12 ⑤

M Hello, students. This is your career coach, Eric Cho. I'm glad to tell you that we'll hold the Career Event again. The event will be held in the multimedia room on May 23rd. This time, we have invited a famous web designer, Paul Wilson. He's going to talk about how to design a website. If you are interested, please register through our school website. So, future web designers, hurry and sign up.

M 안녕하세요, 학생 여러분. 저는 진로 코치 에릭 조입니다. 우리가 다시 진로 행사를 열게 되었다는 걸 말씀드리게 되어 기쁩니다. 행사는 5월 23일에 멀티미디어실에서 열릴 예정입니다. 이번에, 우리는 유명한 웹 디자이너인 폴 윌슨을 초대했습니다. 그는 어떻게 웹사이트를 디자인하는지에 대해 이야기 할 것입니다. 여러분이 관심이 있다면 우리 학교 웹사이트를 통해 등록하세요. 그러니, 미래의 웹디자이너들은 서둘러 등록하세요.

13 ②

M Mary, which room is good for our meeting this Thursday?

W What about Room D?

M I heard that Robert will use it on that day.

W Hmm..., how about using one of the rooms next to the lounge? They're convenient.

M But the lounge is often crowded, so those rooms may be noisy.

W You're right. Then, we have two rooms left, Room A and Room B.

M Let's not use the room next to the restroom.

W Okay. Let's use this room.

M 마리, 이번주 목요일을 위한 우리 회의를 위해 어느 방이 좋을까요?

W D방 어때요?

M 로버트가 그날 거기를 사용한다고 들었어요.

W 흠... 라운지 옆에 있는 방들 중 하나를 사용하는 게 어떨까요? 편리하잖아요.

M 하지만 라운지는 너무 붐벼서 아마 시끄러울 거예요.

W 맞아요. 그럼, 방 두 개 남았네요, A와 B.

M 화장실 옆에 있는 방은 사용하지 말아요.

W 알겠어요. 이 방을 사용해요.

14 ⑤

W This is a team sport. Players play this on ice with skates on. For safety, players should wear a helmet and special equipment to protect their bodies. In order to score, they use a long stick to hit a small round flat object, called a *puck*, into the opposing team's net. It's one of the popular winter sports in North America.

W 이것은 팀 스포츠입니다. 선수들은 얼음 위에서 스케이트를 타고 이것을 경기합니다. 안전을 위해, 선수들은 그들의 몸을 보호하기 위한 헬멧과 특수 장비를 착용해야 합니다. 점수를 얻기 위해, 선수들은 퍽이라고 불리는 작고 둥근 납작한 물체를 긴 막대기를 사용하여 상대편 그물에 칩니다. 이것은 북아메리카에서 인기 있는 겨울 스포츠 중에 하나입니다.

15 ②

W Tom, it's raining outside. Where are you going?

M Mom, I'm going to the library. I have a science test tomorrow.

W I see. Do you want me to give you a ride there?

M Can you? Thanks.

W No problem. Let me get my coat from the room.

M Then, I'll go and get an umbrella now. I'll need it when I come back.

W Okay. I'll be with you in a minute.

W 탐, 밖에 비가 와. 어디 가니?

M 엄마, 저 도서관에 가요. 내일 과학 시험이 있어요.

W 알아. 거기까지 태워줄까?

M 그럴 수 있어요? 고마워요.

W 문제 없어. 방에서 코트를 가져올게.

M 그럼, 전 지금 가서 우산을 챙길게요. 돌아올 때 필요할 거예요.

W 그래. 곧 갈게.

16 ④

[Cellphone rings.]

W Hello?

M Hello. This is Best Electronics. Is this Ms. Smith?

W Speaking.

M We'd like to deliver your refrigerator on May 8th. Will that be okay?

W I'm afraid not. I'll be away. Is it possible on May 9th or 10th?

M Let me check the schedule. *[Pause]* Okay. We can deliver it on May 10th.

W That sounds good! Can you make it in the morning?

M Sure. We'll deliver it at 9 a.m. on May 10th.

W Thank you.

[휴대 전화가 울린다.]

W 여보세요

M 안녕하세요. 베스트 전자 제품입니다. Ms. Smith입니까?

W 저입니다.

M 고객분의 냉장고는 5월 8일에 배달해 드리려고 합니다. 괜찮으세요?

W 안될 거 같아요. 자리를 비울 겁니다. 5월 9일이나 10일 가능한가요?

M 스케줄을 확인해 보겠습니다. *[멈춤]* 네. 5월 10일에 배달할 수 있습니다.

W 잘됐네요! 오전에 가능합니까?

M 네. 5월 10일 오전 9시에 배달하겠습니다.

W 감사합니다.

17 ⑤

[Telephone rings.]

M ABC Office Supplies. How may I help you?

W Hi. I bought a printer from your shop last week, but there's a little problem with it.

M Oh, I'm sorry for your inconvenience. What's the model number?

W The model number? Where can I find it?

M It's on the back of the printer.

W Okay. Let me see. *[Pause]* It says LP-123.

M Thank you. Can you tell me what the problem is?

W The papers don't come out of the printer.

[전화벨이 울린다.]

M ABC 사무용품점입니다. 무엇을 도와드릴까요?

W 안녕하세요. 저번 주에 거기에서 프린터를 하나 샀는데요 작은 문제가 있습니다.

M 오, 불편을 드려 죄송합니다. 모델 번호가 무엇인가요?

W 모델 번호요? 어디서 볼 수 있나요?

M 프린터 뒤에 있습니다.

W 알겠습니다. 봐 볼게요. *[멈춤]* LP-123이라고 되어있습니다.

M 감사합니다. 문제가 무엇인지 말씀해 주시겠어요?

W 종이가 프린터에서 나오질 않습니다.

① 지갑을 가게에 두고 나왔어요.

② 내 컴퓨터를 빌려줄 수 없습니다.

③ 이 커피 기계가 작동하지 않습니다.

④ 등이 아파서 움직일 수 없어요.

18 ②

M Have you finished making graphs for the history presentation next Monday?

W No. I haven't even started it yet. I think I need help in making the graphs.

M I watched a useful video clip about making graphs on the Internet.

W A video clip?

M Yes. It helped me a lot. The clip was about how to make graphs for beginners like us.

W It sounds helpful. Where can I find it on the Internet?

M Let me tell you the website address.

M 다음 주 월요일 역사 발표를 위한 도표 만들기는 끝냈니?

W 아니. 아직 시작도 안했어. 도표 만드는 데 도움이 필요한 거 같아.

M 인터넷에서 도표를 만드는 것에 대한 유용한 동영상을 봤어.

W 동영상?

M 응. 도움이 많이 돼. 동영상은 우리 같은 초보자를 위해 도표를 어떻게 만드는지에 대한 거였어.

W 도움이 될 거 같네. 인터넷 어디에서 그 영상을 찾을 수 있어?

M 웹사이트 주소를 말해 줄게.

① 네 필체는 더 도움이 필요해.

③ 나는 수학 문제 푸는 것을 잘하지 않아.

④ 나는 인터넷으로 음악을 듣는 것을 즐겨.

⑤ 선생님이 우리에게 블로그 만드는 법을 보여 준다.

19 ⑤

M Julie, you were late for school today. What's up?

W I got up late and missed the bus.

M The bus? You live five minutes away from school, don't you?

W Not anymore. I moved to a new house last Saturday. And now, I need to take a bus.

M Oh, really? How long does it take to get to school then?

W At least 40 minutes by bus. I'm really worried that I might be late again.

M Then, you should do something to get up early.

W Right. I need to set the alarm for an earlier time.

M 줄리엣, 오늘 학교 지각했지. 무슨 일이야?

W 늦잠을 잤고 버스를 놓쳤어.

M 버스? 너 학교에서 5분 거리에 살잖아, 아니야?

W 더는 아니야. 지난 주 토요일에 새 집으로 이사를 했어. 그래서 지금, 버스를 타야 해.

M 아, 진짜? 그럼 등교하는데 얼마나 걸려?

W 버스로 최소 40분. 또 지각을 할까 진짜 걱정이야.

M 그럼. 일찍 일어나기 위해 무언가를 해야 해.

W 맞아. 알람을 더 이른 시간에 맞춰야겠어.

① 미안. 이번 주 토요일은 바빠.

② 문제 없어. 집에 갈 때 걸어갈게.

③ 알겠어. 방과 후에 널 만나는 거 잊지 않을게.

④ 물론이야. 넌 이번 주말에 우리 새 집에 방문할 수 있어.

20 ④

M Jiho is a new student at Daehan Middle School. On her first day, she receives a timetable from her homeroom teacher, Mr. Jung. Jiho checks it and realizes that she has to go to the music room for a music class. Later, she tries to find the room, but she can't. She sees Mr. Jung in the hallway. So, she decides to ask Mr. Jung where the music room is. In this situation, what would Jiho most likely say to Mr. Jung?

M 지호는 대한 중학교의 신입생이다. 그녀의 첫 번째 날, 그녀는 그녀의 담임 선생님인 Mr. Jung으로부터 시간표를 받았다. 지호는 그것을 확인하고 음악 수업을 위해 음악실로 가야 한다는 것을 알았다. 후에, 그녀는 음악실을 찾으려고 했지만 찾을 수 없었다. 그녀는 복도에서 Mr. Jung을 보았다. 그래서 그녀는 Mr. Jung에게 음악실이 어디 있는지 물어 보기로 결심했다. 이런 상황에서, 지호가 Mr. Jung에게 할 수 있는 말은 무엇인가?

① 음악회는 언제 시작하나요?

② 제 새 교과서를 어디에 둬야 하나요?

③ 거실에서 바이올린 연습을 할 수 있을까요?

④ 음악실이 어디인지 알려주실 수 있나요?

⑤ 이 시간표를 어떻게 복사 할 수 있나요?

영어듣기능력 진단평가 **02**회

01 ②	**02** ②	**03** ④	**04** ⑤	**05** ②
06 ④	**07** ③	**08** ①	**09** ⑤	**10** ③
11 ⑤	**12** ⑤	**13** ④	**14** ③	**15** ④
16 ②	**17** ③	**18** ①	**19** ①	**20** ②

01 ②

M How may I help you?

W I'm looking for a clock for my new house.

M Is there any kind that you like?

W I'd like to have a digital one. It's easier for my kids to read.

M Right. Do you have any design in mind? We have round ones and square ones.

W I'd like a square one.

M The one with time and date?

W Right. I'll take it.

M 무엇을 도와드릴까요?

W 제 새 집을 위한 시계를 찾고 있어요.

M 좋아하는 어떤 종류가 있나요?

W 디지털 시계를 갖고 싶어요. 아이들이 읽기 더 쉽거든요.

M 알겠습니다. 생각 중인 디자인은 있나요? 저희는 원형과 사각형이 있습니다.

W 사각형이 좋겠네요.

M 시간과 날짜가 같이 있는 거요?

W 네. 그걸로 할게요.

02 ②

[Cellphone rings.]

M Hello.

W Hello. This is Mega Home Shopping. Is this Tom Baker?

M Yes. Speaking.

W I'm sorry, but the T-shirts you ordered will be delayed for a few days.

M Really? I need them this weekend.

W Don't worry, sir. You'll get them by this Friday.

M Okay. Could you please send them as soon as possible?

W Sure. Thank you for your understanding.

[전화벨이 울린다.]

M 여보세요?

W 안녕하세요. 메가 홈 쇼핑입니다. Tom Baker씨 되시나요?

M 네. 접니다.

W 죄송합니다만 주문하신 티셔츠가 며칠 배송 지연됩니다.

M 정말요? 이번 주말에 필요한데.

W 걱정 마세요. 이번 주 금요일까지는 받아 보실 수 있습니다.

M 네. 가능하면 빨리 보내 주시겠어요?

W 물론이죠. 이해해 주셔서 감사합니다.

03 ④

① **M** Why didn't you come to the food festival?
　W I couldn't because I had to take care of my sick cat.
② **M** The food here is really good.
　W I'm glad you like it. This is my favorite place.
③ **M** Your cat looks so cute. What's his name?
　W Thanks. His name is Nabi.
④ **M** Sorry, but dogs are not allowed here.
　W Oh, I'm sorry. I didn't know that.
⑤ **M** Are you ready to order now?
　W Not yet. Can I have some more time, please?

① **M** 음식 축제에 왜 안 왔어?
　W 아픈 고양이를 돌봐야 했기 때문에 못 갔어.
② **M** 여기 음식 진짜 맛있다.
　W 좋아하니 기쁘다. 내가 제일 좋아하는 곳이야.
③ **M** 네 고양이 정말 귀엽다. 이름이 뭐야?
　W 고마워. 이름은 나비야.
④ **M** 미안하지만 개는 이곳에 들어올 수 없습니다.
　W 아, 죄송해요. 몰랐어요.
⑤ **M** 지금 주문하시겠습니까?
　W 아직요. 시간 좀 주시겠어요?

04 ⑤

[Phone rings.]
W Hello, ABC Sports Center. How can I help you?
M Hi, I'd like to register for tennis lessons.
W You can take tennis lessons once a week on Tuesdays or Thursdays.
M How much is it per month?
W It's 80,000 won.
M Can I use the court on weekends?
W No. You can only use it from Monday to Friday.
M Okay. Can I sign up for Thursday lessons now?
W Sure.

[전화벨이 울린다.]
W 안녕하세요, ABC 스포츠 센터입니다. 무엇을 도와드릴까요?
M 안녕하세요, 테니스 레슨을 등록하고 싶습니다.
W 일주일에 한 번 화요일이나 목요일에 테니스 레슨을 받으실 수 있습니다.
M 한 달에 얼마인가요?
W 8만원입니다.
M 주말에 코트를 사용할 수 있나요?
W 아니요. 월요일부터 금요일까지만 사용할 수 있습니다.
M 알겠습니다. 지금 목요일 레슨을 등록할 수 있나요?
W 네.

05 ②

W Thank you for visiting Evergreen Community Center. Let me give you a brief overview of our center. We have a variety of programs including swimming and painting. There is a cafeteria in the basement. We offer a free shuttle bus every hour. The center is open from 9 a.m. to 7 p.m., Monday through Saturday. We are closed every Sunday. We hope you'll visit us again soon. Have a nice day.

W 에버그린 주민회관에 방문해 주셔서 감사합니다. 우리 센터에 대한 간단한 개요를 말씀드리겠습니다. 우리는 수영과 그림 그리기를 포함한 다양한 프로그램을 가지고 있습니다. 지하에 카페가 하나 있습니다. 매시간 무료 셔틀 버스를 제공합니다. 센터는 월요일에서 토요일까지 9시부터 7시까지 엽니다. 우리는 일요일마다 휴관합니다. 센터를 곧 다시 방문해주시길 바랍니다. 좋은 하루 보내세요.

06 ④

M Thank you for being a guest on our show, New Books Weekly.
W Thank you for inviting me.
M Congratulations on your new book. How would you describe your book in one sentence?
W Well, it's about friendship between a boy and his dog.
M I see. And why do you think this book has become so popular among children?
W Well, maybe because dogs are children's best friends.
M You're right. Are you writing a new book now?
W Yes, I'm writing a book about a cat who lost her mother.

M 저희 New books Weekly 쇼에 손님으로 와 주셔서 감사합니다.
W 초대해 주셔서 감사합니다.
M 새로운 책을 축하 드립니다. 책을 한 문장으로 어떻게 표현할 수 있을까요?
W 글쎄요. 한 소년과 그의 개의 우정에 관한 것입니다.
M 그렇군요. 그리고 이 책이 왜 아이들 사이에서 그렇게 인기가 있게 됐다고 생각하시나요?
W 아마 개들이 아이들의 가장 친한 친구이기 때문이겠죠.
M 맞습니다. 지금 새 책을 쓰고 계신가요?
W 네, 엄마를 잃은 한 고양이에 대한 책을 쓰고 있습니다.

07 ③

① **M** Would you prefer a weekday or weekend?
　W Anytime will be fine.
② **M** What time is the library closed?
　W It's closed at 10 p.m.
③ **M** Something smells strange here.
　W I'm a stranger here, too.
④ **M** What are you going to do tomorrow?
　W I'm going to study for the midterm.
⑤ **M** Hi, may I speak to Matthew, please?
　W Sorry, he's not here.

① **M** 주중과 주말 중 뭐가 더 좋아?
　W 아무 때나 좋아.
② **M** 도서관 몇 시에 닫아?

W 오후 10시에 닫아.

③ M 여기 이상한 냄새가 나.

   W 나도 여기가 처음이야.

④ M 내일 뭐 해?

   W 중간고사 공부할 거야.

⑤ M 안녕하세요, Matthew와 통화할 수 있을까요?

   W 미안하지만 그는 여기 없어요.

08 ①

W Steve, where are you going?

M I'm going to the library to do my history homework.

W Oh, good. Could you do me a favor?

M Sure, what is it?

W I have to return this book today, but I don't have any time.

M No problem. I can drop it off for you.

W Thanks a lot.

W Steve, 어디 가니?

M 역사 숙제를 하러 도서관에 가려고요.

W 아, 잘됐다. 내 부탁 좀 들어줄래?

M 네, 뭔데요?

W 오늘 이 책을 반납해야 하는데 시간이 없어.

M 문제 없어요. 대신 반납할게요.

W 고마워.

09 ⑤

M Cathy, what's wrong? You look worried.

W Yeah, actually I forgot to bring the script for our presentation.

M Oh, no. I heard we have to submit it to Mr. Kim by today.

W I know. What should I do?

M Isn't there anyone at home?

W Yes, I think my mom is at home now.

M Then, why don't you ask her to email it to you?

M Cathy, 무슨 일이야? 걱정하는 것처럼 보여.

W 응, 사실 나 우리 발표를 위한 대본을 가져오는 것을 깜박했어.

M 이럴수가. 오늘까지 Mr. Kim께 제출 해야 한다고 들었는데.

W 알아. 어쩌지?

M 집에 아무도 없어?

W 지금 집에 엄마가 있는 거 같아.

M 그럼, 엄마한테 이메일로 보내 달라고 하는 거 어때?

10 ③

W Hello, may I help you?

M Yeah, I want to buy a swimsuit.

W This is the most popular design and it's just 20 dollars.

M Great! I'll take a medium size.

W Would you like anything else?

M Um... I also need swimming goggles. How much are they?

W The prices are from 10 dollars to 30 dollars.

M I'll take the 10 dollar one.

W Sure. Here you are.

W 안녕하세요, 무엇을 도와드릴까요?

M 네, 수영복을 사고 싶어요.

W 이게 가장 인기있는 디자인이고 20달러밖에 안해요.

M 좋네요! 중간 사이즈로 살게요.

W 다른 건 안 필요하세요?

M 음... 수경도 필요해요. 얼마인가요?

W 10달러에서 30달러까지해요.

M 10달러짜리로 주세요.

W 네. 여기 있습니다.

11 ⑤

M I'm not sure what's a good gift for Sharon's graduation.

W How about choosing her gift together, then?

M Good idea. Do you have something in mind?

W I know she really likes listening to music.

M Maybe we can buy a CD of her favorite singer.

W But we don't know who her favorite singer is.

M Then, why don't you ask her?

W Okay, I will. I'm going to see her in class this afternoon.

M Sharon의 졸업 선물로 무엇이 좋을지 모르겠어.

W 그럼 선물을 같이 고르는 거 어때?

M 좋은 생각이야. 생각하고 있는 거 있어?

W 그녀가 음악 듣는 것을 정말 좋아하는 거 알고 있어.

M 그녀가 가장 좋아하는 가수의 CD를 살 수 있겠다.

W 그런데 그녀가 가장 좋아하는 가수가 누구인지를 모르잖아.

M 그럼, 그녀한테 물어보는 거 어때?

W 좋아, 물어볼게. 오늘 오후 교실에서 그녀를 만날 거야.

12 ⑤

M Hello, Oakwood community members. This is David Kim from City Hall. I'm happy to tell you that we'll be having the Oakwood Flea Market on October 13th, 2017. You can buy and sell toys, books, and clothing at this event. There is a five-dollar registration fee for sellers. Please register at the public service center if you plan to attend. Thank you.

M 안녕하세요, 오크우드 지역 주민 여러분. 시청에서 나온 David Kim입니다. 2017년 10월 13일 오크우드 벼룩시장을 열게 되었다는 것을 알려 드리게 되어 기쁩니다. 이 행사에서 여러분은 장난감, 책, 그리고 옷을 사거나 팔 수 있습니다. 판매자는 5달러의 등록비가 있습니다. 참여할 계획이 있으시다면 공공 서비스 센터에서 등록하세요. 감사합니다.

13 ④

M Hey, Rebecca! What are you doing here?

W I'm checking the Sky Yoga website for a class.

M Really? I took a class there last year. Maybe I can help you.

W Great. Hmm... I have a dance class every Wednesday, so I can't take it then.

M Okay. I remember that Michelle and Serena were popular

instructors.

W Then I'm going to choose one of their classes.

M Good. So you should choose one of these two classes.

W Well. Then, I'll take the cheaper class.

M 야, Rebecca! 여기서 뭐해?

W 수업을 위한 스카이 요가 웹사이트를 확인하고 있었어.

M 진짜? 나 작년에 거기서 수업 하나 들었어. 내가 도와줄 수 있겠다.

W 잘됐다. 흠... 나 수요일마다 춤 수업이 있어서 그 때는 들을 수 없어.

M 좋아. Michelle과 Serena가 인기 있는 강사였다는 걸 기억해.

W 그럼 그들의 수업 중 하나를 골라야지.

M 좋아. 그럼 두 수업 중 하나 골라야겠네.

W 음. 그럼. 더 저렴한 수업을 들을래.

14 ③

W This is a very useful device for people. It's usually used in homes, hospitals, schools, and other places. The tip of this device is usually inserted into the mouth or into the ear. It's used to measure body temperature for medical purposes. The electronic type is common these days.

W 이것은 사람들에게 아주 유용한 장치입니다. 이것은 주로 집, 병원, 학교, 그리고 다른 장소들에게 사용됩니다. 이 장치의 끝부분은 보통 입이나 귀에 들어갑니다. 의료 목적으로 체온을 측정하는데 사용됩니다. 요즘에는 전자식이 흔합니다.

15 ④

[Cellphone rings.]

M Hello?

W Hi, Jack. I'm on the subway but I'm going to be late.

M Why? What happened?

W I missed my stop. I'm sorry but I'll be there in 20 minutes.

M It's all right. We still have 30 minutes before the play starts.

W Good, I'll be there as soon as I can.

M Okay. I'm at the theater now. So, I'll buy the tickets.

W That'll be great. Thanks.

[휴대 전화 벨이 울린다.]

M 여보세요?

W 안녕, Jack. 나 지하철인데 늦을 거 같아.

M 왜? 무슨 일이야?

W 나 역을 지나쳤어. 미안하지만 20분 안에 갈게/

M 괜찮아. 연극이 시작하려면 30분 남았어.

W 할 수 있는 한 빨리 갈게.

M 그래. 난 지금 극장이야. 내가 표를 살게.

W 잘됐다. 고마워.

16 ②

W Josh's birthday is coming up! He turns 15 next Wednesday.

M Yeah. What do you think about getting him soccer shoes as a birthday present?

W Actually he doesn't play soccer much these days.

M How about buying him bicycle gloves? He loves to ride his bicycle.

W He already has them. Why don't we buy him a new helmet?

M That's a good idea. I will buy it on the way home.

W Josh의 생일이 다가오고 있어! 그가 다음 주 수요일에 15살이 돼.

M 그래. 생일 선물로 축구화를 사주는 거 어떻게 생각해?

W 사실 그는 요즘에 축구를 많이 하지 않아.

M 자전거 장갑을 사주는 거 어때? 자전거 타는 거 좋아하잖아.

W 이미 갖고 있어. 새 헬멧을 사주는 거 어때?

M 좋은 생각이야. 집에 오는 길에 사야지.

17 ③

W Hi, Ben. How's your project going?

M Hi, Jessica. It's going fine. What's up?

W It's time for lunch. Why don't we go out for something?

M Sorry, I don't think I can go.

W Why? Aren't you hungry?

M Yes, I am. But I have to finish this project first.

W Okay. I'm going to get a hamburger. If you want, I can bring one for you, too.

M <u>Thank you. That would be great.</u>

W 안녕, Ben. 프로젝트는 잘 되어가니?

M 안녕, Jessica. 괜찮아. 무슨 일이야?

W 점심 시간이야. 나가서 뭐 먹는 거 어때?

M 미안, 못 갈 거 같아.

W 왜? 배가 안 고파?

M 고픈데 이 프로젝트를 우선 끝내야 해.

W 알겠어. 나 햄버거 먹을 거야. 네가 원하면 하나 사올게.

M <u>고마워. 그럼 좋겠다.</u>

① 그래. 빨리 그걸 찾길 바랄게.

② 아니, 너랑 놀고 싶어.

④ 미안. 이미 점심을 먹었어.

⑤ 진짜? 무섭지 않아?

18 ①

W Mike, are you going to join the singing contest?

M I'm thinking about it, but I'm scared to sing in front of people.

W Don't be. You're a good singer.

M At the last contest, I made a lot of mistakes during my song.

W Why don't we join the contest as a team? If you are in trouble, I can help you.

M I don't know. I don't want to look bad in front of everyone again.

W <u>Don't worry. We can be a great team.</u>

W Mike, 노래 대회에 나갈 거야?

M 생각 중인데 사람들 앞에서 노래하는 게 겁나.

W 그러지 마. 넌 훌륭한 가수야.
M 마지막 대회에서, 노래하다가 많은 실수를 했어.
W 팀으로 대회에 나가는 거 어때? 네가 문제가 생기면 내가 도울 수 있어.
M 모르겠어. 모두들 앞에서 또 안 좋은 모습 보이고 싶지 않아.
W 걱정 마. 우리는 훌륭한 팀이 될 수 있어.
② 축하해! 네가 이길 줄 알았어.
③ 아니, 난 노래에 전혀 관심이 없어.
④ 대회에 참가하는 건 생각도 안 해봤어.
⑤ 도와줘서 고마워.

19 ①

M Jane, how's our class photo book going?
W I'm collecting pictures from all of our classmates.
M Great! Will the book include pictures of all the school events this year?
W Yes, but there's a problem. There are not enough pictures of sports day.
M Oh, I have a lot of pictures of the sports day in my laptop.
W Really? I'd love to have some of those for the photo book.
M Okay. I'll send them to you by email.

M Jane, 우리 학급 포토북 어떻게 되어가고 있어?
W 우리 학급 아이들의 사진들을 모으고 있어.
M 멋져! 금년 모든 학교 행사 사진들도 있는 거야?
W 응, 하지만 문제가 있어. 운동회 사진이 충분하지 않아.
M 아, 내 노트북에 운동회 사진이 많이 있어.
W 진짜? 포토북을 위해 그 사진들 중 몇 장을 가졌으면 좋겠는데.
M 알겠어. 내가 이메일로 너에게 보낼게.
② 알겠어. 지금 네가 내 노트북을 고칠 수 있어.
③ 음. 운동회는 취소될 거야.
④ 잘됐다. 네가 알아서 그것을 마쳤다니 기뻐.
⑤ 미안. 난 운동회에 참여할 수 없어.

20 ②

M The other day, Jihoon's mother bought a pair of pants for him but they were too big. He wanted to exchange them for the right size, so he visited the store. However, the clerk told him that the size he wanted was sold out. He wants to ask if he could get his money back. In this situation, what would Jihoon most likely say to the clerk?

M 며칠 전에, Jihoon의 어머니는 그를 위해 바지를 한 벌 샀지만 너무 컸다. 그는 그것을 알맞은 크기로 교환하고 싶었다. 그래서 그는 가게에 방문했지만 점원은 그가 원하는 크기는 품절됐다고 말했다. 그는 환불을 받을 수 있는지 물어보고 싶다. 이런 상황에서, Jihoon이 점원에서 할 수 있는 말은 무엇일까?

① 그럼, 바지를 더 짧게 만들 수 있나요?
② 죄송하지만 환불 받고 싶어요.
③ 더 큰 사이즈는 언제 들어오나요?
④ 나는 이 스타일이 너무 좋아요.
⑤ 긴 바지는 제 스타일이 아닙니다.

01 ④	02 ②	03 ⑤	04 ⑤	05 ④
06 ③	07 ②	08 ⑤	09 ②	10 ③
11 ①	12 ④	13 ⑤	14 ②	15 ①
16 ③	17 ⑤	18 ③	19 ①	20 ③

01 ④

M Hey, Amy. What are you looking at?
W Balloons. Dad, I want to get one of those.
M Which balloon are you talking about? Do you want the rabbit balloon?
W No. I want the elephant balloon.
M Do you mean the elephant with a hat?
W No, not that one. I'd like the one with a ribbon on its head.
M I see which one you want. Let's get it.
W Thanks, Dad.

M Amy. 무엇을 보고 있니?
W 풍선이요. 아빠, 저 저것들 중 하나를 원해요.
M 무슨 풍선을 말하는 거니? 토끼 풍선을 원하니?
W 아니요. 코끼리 풍선이요.
M 모자를 쓴 코끼리 풍선 말하는 거니?
W 아니요, 그거 말고요. 머리에 리본이 있는 게 좋아요.
M 네가 원하는 걸 알겠구나. 사자.
W 고마워요, 아빠.

02 ②

[Cellphone rings.]
M Hello, Joanne. What's up?
W Hi, Peter. I have a problem.
M What's wrong?
W My car won't start. I'm worried I'll be late.
M Really? Don't you have a meeting at 10 a.m.?
W Yes. That's why I'm calling you. Can you give me a ride?
M Sure. I'm not far from your house. Where can I pick you up?
W I'll be in the parking lot. Thanks.

[휴대 전화 벨이 울린다.]
M 여보세요, Joanne. 무슨 일이야?
W 안녕, Peter. 나 문제가 있어.
M 무슨 일이야?
W 차가 시동이 안 걸려. 늦을까 걱정이야.
M 진짜? 오전 10시에 회의가 있지 않아?
W 그래. 그게 너에게 전화한 이유야. 나 좀 태워 줄 수 있어?
M 물론이야. 난 너네 집에서 멀지 않으니까. 어디서 태워줄까?
W 주차장에 있을게. 고마워.

03 ⑤

① **M** Would you like something to drink?
   W I'd like to have a cola.
② **M** Can you help me carry these bags, please?
   W Sure. It's my pleasure.
③ **M** Do you mind if I open the window?
   W Not at all. Go ahead.
④ **M** This bus is too noisy.
   W Right. I can't stand it anymore.
⑤ **M** You can have my seat, ma'am.
   W Thanks. How kind of you!

① **M** 뭐 마실래?
   W 콜라가 마시고 싶어.
② **M** 이 가방을 옮기는 걸 도와주시겠어요?
   W 물론이죠. 기꺼이요.
③ **M** 창문을 열어도 될까요?
   W 네. 여세요.
④ **M** 이 버스는 엄청 시끄럽네요.
   W 맞아요. 더 이상 못 견디겠어요.
⑤ **M** 여기 앉으세요.
   W 고마워요. 친절하군요!

04 ⑤

[Cellphone rings.]
W Hello, John. Do you remember our presentation will be next week?
M Yes. Why don't we meet to talk about it?
W Are you free on Tuesday?
M I'm afraid not. I promised to go to the theater with my cousin. How about Wednesday?
W Wednesday? I have a swimming lesson on Wednesday. Is Thursday good?
M Thursday is not good for me, but I'll be free on Friday.
W Friday is okay for me, too. See you then.

[휴대 전화 벨이 울린다.]
W 여보세요, John. 우리 발표가 다음 주인 거 기억하니?
M 응. 만나서 얘기하는 거 어때?
W 화요일에 괜찮아?
M 안 돼. 내 사촌과 극장에 가기로 약속했거든. 수요일 어때?
W 수요일? 수요일마다 수영 레슨이 있는데. 목요일은 괜찮니?
M 목요일은 안되는데 금요일은 괜찮아.
W 금요일은 나도 좋아. 그때 보자.

05 ④

W Thank you for visiting our booth. Let me introduce our new product, Drone-X. As you can see, the Drone-X is pocket-sized. You can control it with your smartphone. It has a control range of 100m. Also, it can fly for about 10 minutes when the battery is fully charged. This model is on sale for 50,000 won today only.

W 우리 부스를 방문해 주셔서 감사합니다. 우리의 새 제품인 Drone-X를 소개합니다. 보시다시피 Drone-X는 주머니 크기입니다. 스마트폰으로 조종할 수 있습니다. 100m의 조종 범위가 있습니다. 그리고 배터리가 가득 충전 되어있을 때 10분동안 날 수 있습니다. 이 모델은 오늘만 5만 원에 판매합니다.

06 ③

M Hello, what can I do for you?
W I need to send this package by express mail, please.
M Where do you want to send it?
W To Incheon.
M Okay, let's see how much it weighs. [pause] It's about 500 grams so it'll cost 4,000 won.
W Here's my credit card. Is it possible to deliver it by tomorrow?
M Yes, it will be delivered by tomorrow afternoon.

M 안녕하세요, 무엇을 도와드릴까요?
W 이 소포를 속달로 보내고 싶어요.
M 어디로 보내십니까?
W 인천이요.
M 알겠습니다. 무게나 얼마나 나가는지 보죠. [멈춤] 500그램이 나가니까 4천원입니다.
W 여기 신용카드요. 내일까지 배달될 수 있나요?
M 네. 내일 오후까지 배달됩니다.

07 ②

① **M** What are you going to do during your vacation?
   W I'm going to visit my grandfather.
② **M** Which bag do you prefer, the red one or the black one?
   W I'll pay by credit card.
③ **M** How often do you go to the movies?
   W Once or twice a month.
④ **M** May I take your order?
   W Yes. I'll have a cheese sandwich, please.
⑤ **M** Can I borrow your pen?
   W Sure, here you are.

① **M** 방학동안 뭐 할거야?
   W 할아버지 댁을 방문할 거야.
② **M** 어떤 가방이 더 좋아, 빨간 색 아니면 검정 색?
   W 신용카드로 결제할게요.
③ **M** 얼마나 자주 영화를 보니?
   W 한 달에 한 두 번.
④ **M** 주문하시겠습니까?
   W 네. 치즈 샌드위치 하나요.
⑤ **M** 펜을 빌릴 수 있을까요?
   W 물론이죠, 여기요.

08 ⑤

M Hi, Sunny. You look busy. What are you doing?

W Oh, Mr. Wilson. I'm preparing for the school festival play.

M That's right. Your class will perform a play. What is it about?

W It's about family. We want to tell a story about love in a family.

M Sounds good. Do you need any help?

W Yes, please. Could you choose the clothes for the play?

M Sure. That would be fun.

M 안녕, Sunny. 바빠 보인다. 뭐 하고 있어?

W 아, Mr. Wilson. 학교 축제 연극을 준비하고 있어요.

M 맞다. 너네 반은 연극을 공연하지. 무엇에 대한 거니?

W 가족에 대한 거요. 가족애에 대한 이야기를 말하고 싶어요.

M 좋구나. 도움이 필요하니?

W 네. 연극을 위한 의상을 골라 주시겠어요?

M 물론이지. 재미있겠구나.

09 ②

W You look very tired.

M Yeah. Actually, I can't get enough sleep these days.

W Why? What's the problem?

M Nothing serious. But it's difficult for me to fall asleep.

W If you drink a glass of warm milk, you'll sleep better.

M Thank you for the tip. I'll try.

W 너 매우 지쳐 보인다.

M 응. 사실, 나 요즘 잠을 충분히 못 잤어.

W 왜? 문제가 뭐야?

M 뭐 없어. 하지만 잠드는 게 어려워.

W 따뜻한 우유를 마시면 잠이 더 잘 올 거야.

M 조언 고마워. 시도해 볼게.

10 ③

M Hello. Can I take your order?

W Hi. I'd like to have a cheese burger, please.

M That will be five dollars. If you pay two dollars more, you can get a drink and fries.

W Oh, really? I'll pay two dollars more, then.

M Okay. Would you like anything else? How about dessert?

W Not for today.

M Okay. For here or to go?

W To go, please.

M 안녕하세요. 주문 하시겠어요?

W 안녕하세요. 치즈 버거 하나 부탁해요.

M 5달러입니다. 2달러를 추가하시면 음료와 감자튀김이 나옵니다.

W 아, 진짜요? 그럼 여기 2달러 더 지불하겠습니다.

M 네. 다른 건 필요 없으세요? 디저트는 어떠세요?

W 오늘은 됐어요.

M 알겠습니다. 여기서 드시겠어요 가지고 가시겠어요?

W 가지고 갈게요.

11 ①

M Finally, the exam is finished.

W Let's go out to eat and watch a movie. I really want to watch the movie, Star Ships.

M Me, too. We can also eat dinner at Farmer's Kitchen near the movie theater.

W Sounds great.

M Then, I'll check the movie schedule.

W Okay. Let's meet at 5 at the restaurant.

M See you then.

M 드디어, 시험이 끝났어.

W 나가서 먹고 영화 보자. 나 정말 영화 Star Ships이 보고 싶어.

M 나도. 우리 영화관 근처에 있는 Farmer's Kitchen에서 저녁을 먹을 수 있어.

W 잘됐다.

M 그럼, 영화 스케줄을 확인할게.

W 알겠어. 5시에 식당에서 보자.

M 그때 봐.

12 ④

M Hello, students. I'm Michael Lee, and I'm in charge of Parkway School Marathon Day. I'm happy to tell you that we'll have the annual event on May 13th, 2017. Any of our school students can join us. Also, you can run with your family members. This event includes various programs such as a food fair and a marching band. To sign up for this event, please go to the teachers' office. Thank you.

M 안녕하세요, 학생 여러분. 저는 파크웨이 학교 마라톤 날을 담당하고 있는 Michael Lee입니다. 2017년 5월 13일에 연례 행사를 진행하게 되는 것을 알리게 되어 기쁩니다. 우리 학교 학생이라면 누구나 참여할 수 있습니다. 또, 가족들과 달릴 수 있습니다. 이 행사는 음식 행사와 악단과 같은 다양한 프로그램을 포함합니다. 이 행사에 등록하려면 교무실로 가주세요. 감사합니다.

13 ⑤

M How may I help you?

W I'm looking for a printer.

M Okay. Do you want a color printer or a black and white one?

W I prefer a color printer so I can print pictures.

M Good. We have ink jet and laser.

W Ink jet is better for printing pictures, right?

M You're right. So, you have two options.

W Oh, what is the main difference?

M You can get clearer pictures with the more expensive one.

W Then, I'll take the expensive one.

M 무엇을 도와드릴까요?

W 프린터를 찾고 있어요.

M 네. 컬러 프린터를 원하시나요 흑백 프린터를 원하시나요?

W 사진을 프린트할 수 있는 컬러 프린터를 원해요.

M 네. 잉크젯과 레이저가 있습니다.

W 잉크젯이 사진을 프린트하기에 더 좋죠, 맞죠?

M 맞습니다. 그럼 두 가지 옵션이 있습니다.

W 아, 큰 차이점이 무엇인가요?

M 더 비싼 것이 더 깨끗한 사진을 뽑을 수 있습니다.

W 그럼, 더 비싼 걸 살게요.

14 ②

W This is a vehicle. It carries a lot of passengers at a time. It has restrooms that the passengers can use. Passengers can buy snacks on board and the vehicle sometimes has a snack bar. It stops at stations and people get on and get off there. It has many wheels but it can only run on rails.

W 이것은 차량입니다. 이것은 한번에 많은 승객들을 나릅니다. 이것은 승객들이 사용할 수 있는 화장실을 갖고 있습니다. 승객들은 차내에서 간식을 살 수 있고 매점을 갖고 있기도 합니다. 이것은 매 역 서고 사람들은 거기서 타고 내립니다. 이것은 많은 바퀴가 있지만 선로 위에서만 달립니다.

15 ①

W That practice was great! This will be a perfect concert.

M Yes, but we still have more work to do.

W What else do we need to do?

M We have to make pamphlets for our concert.

W Right, I'll do that. And how about visiting classrooms to let students know about the concert?

M Great idea. I'll visit classrooms during the break.

W 연습 아주 멋졌어. 완벽한 콘서트가 될 거야.

M 맞아, 하지만 우리는 아직 해야 할 일이 있어.

W 우리가 더 해야 할 게 뭐야?

M 우리 콘서트를 위한 팸플릿을 만들어야 해.

W 맞아, 내가 할게. 그리고 교실을 방문해서 학생들에게 우리 콘서트를 알리는 거 어때?

M 좋은 생각이야. 내가 쉬는 시간에 교실을 방문할게.

16 ③

M Mom, can you wake me up early tomorrow morning?

W Why? Tomorrow is Saturday. You don't need to go to school.

M Yeah, but I'm going to watch a movie with my friends.

W When does the movie begin?

M It starts at 9 a.m.

W Okay. Then, I will wake you up at 7.

M It only takes 10 minutes to go there. Please wake me up at 8.

W Okay. Good night, son.

M 엄마, 내일 아침 일찍 저 좀 깨워 주실 수 있나요?

W 왜? 내일은 토요일이잖아. 등교하지 않아도 돼.

M 네, 하지만 친구들이랑 영화 보러 갈 거예요.

W 영화가 언제 시작하는데?

M 오전 9시요.

W 그래. 그럼, 7시에 깨울게.

M 거기까지 10분밖에 안 걸려요. 8시에 깨워주세요.

W 그래. 잘 자렴, 아들.

17 ⑤

W Hey, Sean. Why were you absent from school yesterday? I was worried.

M I had a really bad cold.

W Are you all right now?

M Yes, I feel much better.

W I'm glad to hear that.

M Thanks, but I have a lot of studying to catch up on with classes.

W Poor you. Is there anything I can help you with?

M Well, can I borrow your notes from yesterday?

W <u>Sure. I'll get you my notebook this afternoon.</u>

W 야, Sean. 어제 왜 결석했어? 나 걱정했어.

M 나 진짜 심한 감기에 걸렸었어.

W 지금은 괜찮아?

M 응, 훨씬 나아졌어.

W 그렇다니 기쁘네.

M 고마워, 그런데 나 수업을 따라잡으려면 많은 공부를 해야 해.

W 불쌍해라. 내가 도와줄 만한 게 없을까?

M 어제 필기한 네 공책을 빌릴 수 있을까?

W 물론이야. 오늘 오후에 공책을 갖다 줄게.

① 나도 과학 시험에 떨어졌어.

② 난 곧 수업을 따라잡을 거야.

③ 미안. 네 파일 몇 개를 열 수 없어.

④ 맞아. 이 추운 날씨가 곧 끝났으면 해.

18 ③

M Judy, what are you going to do this weekend?

W Hmm.... Nothing special. What about you?

M I'm thinking about going to the bookstore.

W The bookstore? What are you going to buy there?

M I want to buy a new cooking magazine.

W I didn't know you're interested in cooking.

M Yes, I love to cook.

W I'd like to take a look around at the comic books. Can I join you?

M Why not? Let's go together.

M Judy, 이번 주말에 뭐 할 거야?

W 흠... 별로 없어. 너는?

M 서점에 갈까 생각 중이야.

W 서점? 거기서 뭐 사려고?

M 새로운 요리 잡지를 하나 사고 싶어.

W 네가 요리에 관심이 있는 줄 몰랐어.

M 있어. 나 요리를 좋아해.

W 나는 만화책을 한번 보고 싶은데. 같이 가도 될까?

M 당연하지. 같이 가자.

① 미안. 기억이 안 나.
② 안 됐다. 힘 내.
④ 고마워, 네 덕분이야.
⑤ 축하해. 넌 자격이 있어.

19 ①

M Hey, you look very excited today. What's up?

W Yeah, I got two tickets for the 2017 World Motor Show.

M Wow, that's great. I heard there will be a lot of nice cars.

W I heard that, too. Would you like to go with me?

M I'd love to. When is it?

W The show is from July 4th to the 11th.

M Oh, no. I already have a plan to go on a family trip at that time.

W I wish you could come to the show with me.

M 야, 오늘 엄청 흥분한 거처럼 보인다. 무슨 일이야?

W 맞아. 나 2017 세계 모터쇼 표가 두 장 있어.

M 와, 굉장하다. 멋진 차들이 많이 있다는 얘기 들었어.

W 나도 들었어. 나랑 같이 갈래?

M 응. 언제야?

W 7월 4일부터 11일까지야.

M 아, 안돼. 나 그때 이미 가족 여행에 갈 계획이 있어.

W 나랑 같이 쇼를 보러 가길 바랐는데.

② 그 영화 보는 걸 정말 즐겼어.
③ 네가 같이 가주어서 기뻐.
④ 네가 자고 여행을 못 간다니 유감이다.
⑤ 쇼가 취소됐다니 실망이야.

20 ③

M Susie found a wallet at a bus stop. She wanted to give it to the police but the police station was far away from the bus stop. So, she was thinking what to do. Suddenly, a person came to the bus stop and he seemed to be searching for something. Susie would like to ask if he was the owner of the wallet. In this situation, what would Susie most likely say to the person?

M Susie는 버스 정류장에서 지갑을 발견했다. 그녀는 그것을 경찰에게 주고 싶었지만 경찰서가 버스 정류장에서 너무 멀었다. 그래서, 그녀는 어떻게 할지 생각했다. 갑자기, 한 사람이 버스 정류장에 왔고 그는 무엇인가 찾고 있는 거처럼 보였다. Susie는 그가 지갑의 주인인지 물었다. 이 상황에서 Susie가 그 사람에게 할 수 있는 말은?

① 여기 처음이세요?
② 제가 이 지갑의 주인입니다.
③ 지갑을 찾으세요?
④ 여기서 버스를 기다려야 합니다.
⑤ 버스 정류장이 어디에 있는지 아세요?

01 ③	02 ②	03 ①	04 ③	05 ③
06 ①	07 ③	08 ④	09 ③	10 ④, ❸③
11 ②	12 ①	13 ①	14 ④	15 ③
16 ②	17 ⑤, ❸③	18 ②	19 ⑤	20 ③

01 ③

[Telephone rings.]

W Hello. This is DC Shopping Mall's service center. Can I help you?

M Yes, please.

W Can I have your name first?

M This is Peter Brown.

W What seems to be the problem, sir?

M I got the T-shirt that I <u>ordered through the Internet</u>, but there seems to <u>be a mistake</u>.

W Sorry, but can you describe it to me in detail? I wonder what it is, sir.

M I ordered a T-shirt with the letter "S" in a circle, but you sent me <u>one with the letter "T" in a square</u>.

W Okay. I'll check it out right now. Could you wait a moment?

M All right.

[전화벨이 울린다.]

W 여보세요. DC 쇼핑몰 서비스 센터입니다. 도와드릴까요?

M 네, 부탁합니다.

W 우선 이름이 뭐죠?

M Peter Brown입니다.

W 손님, 무엇이 문제인가요?

M 인터넷으로 주문한 티셔츠를 받았는데, 착오가 있는 것 같습니다.

W 죄송합니다만, 그것을 상세하게 설명해 주시겠어요? 무슨 문제인지 알고 싶네요, 손님.

M 전 동그라미 안에 'S'자가 있는 티셔츠를 주문했는데, 정사각형 안에 'T'자가 있는 것을 보내주셨습니다.

W 네. 지금 바로 확인해 보겠습니다. 잠깐 기다려 주시겠습니까?

M 알겠어요.

만점 솔루션 남자는 동그라미 안에 S자가 있는 티셔츠(a T-shirt with the letter "S" in a circle)를 주문했는데 정사각형 안에 T자가 있는 것(one with the letter "T" in a square)이 배송되었다.

02 ②

W Good afternoon. Can I help you?

M I'd like <u>to exchange</u> this MP3 player <u>for another one</u>. I bought it last Saturday.

W Okay. What seems to be the problem?

M Look at this button. It's <u>already broken</u>.

W Let me see if we have another one. Sorry, but we are <u>out of that style</u>. How about this one?

M Sorry, but I really like this style. Can you order one for me?

W Sure. Leave your number here and I'll call you when we have a new one.

M Thank you.

W You're welcome.

W 안녕하세요. 도와드릴까요?

M 이 MP3 플레이어를 다른 것으로 교환하고 싶습니다. 지난 토요일에 그것을 샀거든요.

W 알겠습니다. 무슨 문제가 있죠?

M 이 버튼 좀 보세요. 벌써 고장이 났습니다.

W 다른 것이 있나 확인해 보겠습니다. 죄송합니다만, 그 종류는 물건이 없네요. 이것은 어떻습니까?

M 미안합니다만, 이 종류가 정말 마음에 들거든요. 하나 주문해 주시겠습니까?

W 물론입니다. 여기에 전화번호를 남겨 주세요. 새것이 오면 전화드리겠습니다.

M 고맙습니다.

W 천만에요

03 ①

① **W** Why are you taking your umbrella? It is not going to rain.

   M I'm going to use it <u>for shade</u>.

② **W** Do you think this umbrella looks good on me?

   M I don't think so. It's <u>too dark</u>.

③ **W** When you go to a beach, <u>don't forget to</u> take your umbrella.

   M Don't worry. I've already packed one.

④ **W** Don't you want to go in the water when you get hot?

   M No. I don't like to swim in the ocean.

⑤ **W** What a beautiful day!

   M Yeah. I haven't seen <u>such a blue sky</u> like this before.

① **W** 왜 우산을 챙기니? 비가 오지 않을 텐데.

   M 햇빛을 차단하기 위해 그것을 사용할 거야.

② **W** 넌 이 우산이 나에게 어울린다고 생각하니?

   M 그렇게 생각하지 않아. 그것은 너무 어두워.

③ **W** 해변에 갈 때, 우산 챙기는 것 잊지 마라.

   M 걱정 마. 벌써 하나 챙겼어.

④ **W** 더울 때 물에 들어가고 싶지 않니?

   M 그래. 난 바다에서 수영하는 것을 좋아하지 않아.

⑤ **W** 정말 아름다운 날이다!

   M 그래. 전에 이처럼 푸른 하늘을 본 적이 없어.

04 ③

[Telephone rings.]

W Hello? Can I speak to Issac? This is Christine.

M Hi, Christine. It's me. What's up?

W Well, are you free this evening? If so, why don't we go to a movie?

M Sorry, but I can't go.

W Why not?

M I have an English test this Friday, and I only have two days left including today before the test.

W Only two days left? Then, let's go together some other time.

M Okay. Thanks for giving me a rain check, Christine.

[전화벨이 울린다.]

W 여보세요? Issac과 통화할 수 있나요? 저는 Christine입니다.

M 안녕, Christine. 나야. 무슨 일이니?

W 저, 오늘 저녁에 한가하니? 그렇다면, 영화 보러 가지 않을래?

M 미안하지만, 못 가.

W 왜 못 가는데?

M 이번 금요일에 영어 시험이 있거든. 시험 전에 오늘을 포함해서 이틀 밖에 남지 않았어.

W 겨우 이틀 남았다고? 그렇다면, 나중에 같이 가자.

M 좋아. 나에게 다음 기회를 줘서 고마워, Christine.

> **만점 솔루션** 영어 시험이 금요일이라고 한 상태에서, 시험일까지 오늘을 포함해서 겨우 이틀 남았다(I only have two days left including today before the test)고 했으므로 오늘은 수요일임을 알 수 있다.

05 ③

W Hi, Gilbert. Did you see Smith in class today?

M Smith? No, I didn't see him. What's the matter?

W I lent him my science textbook last Friday, and he promised to return it to me Monday.

M He might have forgotten about it.

W I guess so, but I need it for tomorrow's test. He was absent from school yesterday, too.

M Well, I heard the flu is going around these days.

W I know. By the way, do you know his Cellphone number?

M I'm afraid not. He has recently changed his Cellphone.

W Oh, what am I supposed to do now?

W 안녕, Gilbert. 오늘 수업 시간에 Smith를 봤니?

M Smith? 아니, 보지 못했는데. 무슨 일이니?

W 지난 금요일에 내 과학책을 빌려줬는데, 그가 월요일에 그것을 돌려준다고 약속했거든.

M 그가 그것에 대해 잊어버렸을지도 모르겠다.

W 나도 그렇게 생각하지만, 내일 시험을 위해 그것이 필요하거든. 그는 어제 결석도 했어.

M 음. 요즈음에 독감이 유행하고 있다고 하던데.

W 나도 알아. 그런데. 너 그의 휴대 전화 번호를 아니?

M 유감스럽게도 몰라. 그는 최근에 휴대 전화를 바꿨거든.

W 아, 이제 나 어떻게 해야지?

06 ①

W Excuse me, but you're Mr. Gerard Butler, right?

M Yes, I am.

W Wow! This is incredible! I'm so pleased to see you in this museum.

M You seem to know me well, right?

W Sure. I've seen most of all your movies. *Legends of the Fall* is one of my favorites.

M Oh, really? Thank you.

W I'm sorry to bother you, but could I have your autograph?

M Of course.

W Oh, just one more thing. Can I have a picture taken with you?

M No problem.

W 실례합니다만, Gerard Butler 씨 맞죠?

M 네, 그렇습니다.

W 왜! 믿을 수가 없네요! 이 박물관에서 당신을 만나다니 정말 기분이 좋습니다.

M 저를 잘 아시는 것 같은데, 그렇죠?

W 물론입니다. 당신의 영화 대부분을 봤습니다. '가을의 전설'은 제가 가장 좋아하는 영화들 중 하나입니다.

M 오, 그러세요? 고맙습니다.

W 귀찮게 해 드려서 죄송하지만, 당신의 사인 좀 받을 수 있나요?

M 물론입니다.

W 오, 한 가지만 더요. 같이 사진을 찍을 수 있나요?

M 물론이죠.

07 ③

① **W** What do you think of the concert?
M I think she is a nice singer. Her songs are so powerful.

② **W** I wonder if you can give me a ride home.
M No problem. Get in.

③ **W** Would you like some more cake?
M Sure. Help yourself to this cake.

④ **W** We are out of milk and bread.
M Then, let's go grocery shopping this afternoon.

⑤ **W** I want to start exercising. What sports would you recommend?
M How about swimming or cycling?

① **W** 그 음악회 어떻게 생각하니?
M 그녀는 훌륭한 가수라고 생각해. 그녀의 노래들은 정말 힘이 있어.

② **W** 나 좀 집까지 태워다 줄 수 있니?
M 물론이지. 타.

③ **W** 케이크를 좀 더 먹겠니?
M 물론이지. 이 케이크를 마음껏 먹어.

④ **W** 우유와 빵이 떨어졌네.
M 그렇다면, 오늘 오후에 식료품 쇼핑을 가자.

⑤ **W** 운동을 시작하고 싶은데. 어떤 운동을 추천해 주겠니?
M 수영이나 자전거 타기는 어때?

> **만점 솔루션** ③ '케이크를 좀 더 먹겠니?'라는 말에 '물론이지. 이 케이크를 마음껏 먹어.'라고 말하는 것은 권유를 받은 사람의 응답으로 어색하며, Thank you. I want some. 또는 No, thank you. I've had enough. 등이 알맞은 응답이다.

08 ④

W Did you hear that? What was that noise?

M That was my stomach. I didn't have time for breakfast this morning.

W James, you have to eat! It's not healthy to skip breakfast.

M I know, but I have to finish reading this book and then write a book report. The deadline is tomorrow!

W Is there anything I can do to help?

M Well, would you mind picking up some food for me?

W Not at all. What would you like to have?

M Umm… I suddenly feel very hungry. A small pizza and an orange soda, please.

W 들었어? 이 소리는 뭐지?

M 내 배에서 나는 소리야. 오전에 아침 먹을 시간이 없었어.

W 제임스, 먹어야지! 아침을 건너뛰는 건 건강하지 않아.

M 알아, 하지만 이 책을 다 읽고 독후감을 써야만 해. 마감일이 내일이야!

W 내가 도와줄 게 없을까?

M 음, 나를 위해 음식을 사다 줄 수 있어?

W 물론이야. 뭐 먹고 싶어?

M 음… 갑자기 엄청 배고파졌어. 피자 작은 사이즈 하나랑 오렌지 소다 부탁해.

09 ③

W An ecosystem is a community of plants and animals. They interact with each other and their environment. An ecosystem is balanced when the number of plants and animals stay pretty much the same. Do you know why? Well, if there are too many plant-eating animals, they will destroy the plant population by eating the plants faster than the plants can grow back. So they will starve to death.

W 생태계는 식물과 동물의 공동체이다. 그들은 서로 그리고 그들의 환경과 상호작용을 한다. 생태계는 식물과 동물의 수가 상당히 같은 수를 유지할 때 균형을 잡는다. 그 이유를 아는가? 만약 식물을 먹는 동물이 너무 많다면, 그들은 식물이 다시 자라는 것보다 빠르게 식물들을 먹어치움으로써 식물군을 파괴할 것이다. 그래서 굶어 죽을 것이다.

10 ④ | ➕ ③

M Jenny, I heard that we can get a student discount on concert tickets.

W Yes, we can. But the student discount only applies to tickets for weekday concerts.

M Really? How much are they?

W On the weekend, the tickets are $15 each. But if we go during the week, they're $12.

M Well, I don't mind paying the extra money to go on the weekend.

W Same here. Let's just go on the weekend.

M Okay. I'll buy two tickets for the concert on Saturday.

M 제니, 우리 콘서트 표를 학생 할인으로 구할 수 있다고 들었어.

W 맞아. 그런데 학생 할인은 주중 콘서트에만 적용되는 거야.

M 진짜? 얼마야?

W 주말에는 장 당 15달러야. 그런데 주중에 가면 12달러고.

M 음, 난 주말에 가서 돈을 더 내는 것도 괜찮아.

W 나도 그래. 그냥 주말에 가자.

M 그래. 토요일 콘서트 표 두 장 살게.

11 ②

M What's up? You look upset.

W Well, I think there's a problem with the computer. It isn't working.

M Oh, dear! Didn't we call the repairman and get the computer fixed several weeks ago?

W We did. What should we do now?

M I'll call the man who fixed it last time and ask him what the problem is.

W Don't you think we should just buy a new one?

M I don't think so yet. I think we can use it for at least two more years.

W I see.

M 무슨 일이니? 속상해 보이네.

W 음, 컴퓨터에 문제가 있는 것 같아. 작동이 안 돼.

M 오, 저런! 몇 주 전에 수리기사를 불러서 그 컴퓨터를 고치지 않았니?

W 그랬지. 이제 어떻게 해야 하지?

M 지난 번에 그것을 고쳤던 사람에게 전화를 해서 무엇이 문제인지 물어볼 거야.

W 그냥 새것을 사야 된다고 생각하지 않니?

M 아직은 그렇게 생각하지 않아. 내 생각에 적어도 2년은 더 그것을 사용할 수 있어.

W 알았어.

12 ①

W Attention, library users. The library will be undergoing many changes. We are going to add a new room with new shelves for more books. We will also be adding a new cafeteria, where you can enjoy drinks and snacks. All money earned from the cafeteria will be used to buy more books. Because of these changes, the library will be closed from April 20 until May 4. Any books due during that time can be returned on May 4 without penalty. Thank you for your attention.

W 주목해주세요, 도서관 이용자분들. 도서관은 많은 변화를 겪고 있습니다. 우리는 더 많은 책을 위한 새로운 선반이 있는 새로운 방을 추가할 예정입니다. 또한 여러분들이 음료를 마시거나 간식을 먹을 수 있는 카페테리아를 추가할 것입니다. 카페테리아의 모든 수익은 더 많은 책들을 사는데 쓰일 것입니다. 이런 변화들 때문에, 도서관은 4월 20일부터 5월 4일까지 휴관합니다. 그 기간 동안 반납할 책들은 5월 4일날 벌금없이 반납할 수 있습니다. 주목해 주셔서 감사합니다.

13 ①

W Excuse me, I'd like to exchange this foreign currency for Korean currency.

M Let's see... you are selling ten American dollars, right?

W Yes. I also want to exchange these Chinese bills.

M Just a minute, please. You have ten Chinese yuan, too.

W Yes, I'd like to exchange them all into Korean currency.

M Here you are. You might want to check the exchange rates on the wall and make sure that you have the correct amount.

W I had ten American dollars and ten Chinese yuan, so yes, that's all right. Thank you very much.

M My pleasure.

W 실례합니다. 이 외국 돈을 한국 돈으로 교환하고 싶습니다.

M 어디 한번 봅시다… 미국 돈 10달러를 판매하시네요, 그렇죠?

W 네. 이 중국 지폐들도 교환하고 싶습니다.

M 잠깐만요. 중국 돈 10위안도 있군요.

W 네, 그것들을 모두 한국 돈으로 바꾸고 싶습니다.

M 여기 있습니다. 벽에 걸린 환율을 보실 수 있고요 금액이 맞는지 확인해 보세요.

W 제가 미국 돈 10달러와 중국 돈 10위안이 있었으니까, 아 네, 맞습니다. 정말 감사합니다.

M 천만에요.

14 ④

M This is not a machine but an animal. This can fly, but it cannot swim. This can also say a few words. So you can understand what this is saying. Teaching this how to speak is easy and simple. You just say some words again and again to this. After a while this will repeat after you soon. But this doesn't really understand the meaning of words. Of course, there are some of these animals which can't learn to say a word. Can you guess what this is?

M 이것은 기계가 아니라 동물이다. 이것은 날 수 있지만, 수영은 할 수 없다. 이것은 또한 몇 개의 단어들도 말할 수 있다. 그래서 당신은 이것이 말하는 것을 이해할 수 있다. 이것에게 말하는 방법을 가르치기는 쉽고 간단하다. 당신은 이것에게 반복해서 몇몇 단어들을 말하기만 하면 된다. 얼마 후에 이것은 곧 당신을 따라 말할 것이다. 하지만 이것이 그 단어의 의미를 정말로 이해하는 것은 아니다. 물론, 이 동물들 중 몇몇은 말하기를 배울 수 없는 것들도 있다. 이것이 무엇인지 짐작할 수 있겠는가?

15 ②

W Hey, Nadal, do you want to play badminton this weekend?

M Sorry, but I can't play badminton well.

W Are you joking? I heard you can play badminton well. And everybody can play it.

M Well, I can't. But I can play tennis well.

W Really? I can play tennis, too. But not very well.

M Then I have an idea. Why don't we play tennis this weekend and then badminton next weekend?

W Okay. That's a good idea.

M I don't play badminton and you don't play tennis well. So we both can practice sports we're not good at.

W 어이, Nadal. 이번 주말에 배드민턴 치고 싶지 않니?

M 유감스럽게도, 나는 배드민턴을 잘 못 쳐.

W 농담하니? 배드민턴을 잘 친다고 들었는데. 그리고 누구든지 그 운동은 할 수 있어.

M 그런데, 난 못 해. 하지만 난 테니스는 잘 쳐.

W 정말? 나도 테니스 칠 수 있는데. 하지만 아주 잘 치지는 못해.

M 그렇다면 나에게 한 가지 좋은 생각이 있어. 이번 주말에 테니스를 친 다음, 다음 주말에 배드민턴 치는 게 어때?

W 그래. 좋은 생각이네.

M 난 배드민턴을 잘 못 치고, 넌 테니스를 잘 못 치니까, 우리 둘 다 잘 못하는 운동을 연습할 수 있을 거야.

16 ②

W Sorry for being late, Donald.

M That's all right. I just got here a few minutes ago.

W How much time do we have before the soccer game? Do we have to hurry up?

M No, we don't have to. It's only five fifty now.

W Then, when does the game start?

M It starts at seven. I guess it just takes twenty minutes to get to the stadium. So let's leave in thirty minutes.

W In thirty minutes? Sorry, but what time is it now again?

M I told you it's five fifty.

W Okay. Let's get started in thirty minutes.

W Donald, 어서 미안해.

M 괜찮아. 나도 몇 분 전에 이곳에 막 도착했어.

W 축구 경기 전에 시간이 얼마나 남았니? 서둘러야 하는 거 아냐?

M 아니, 그럴 필요 없어. 이제 겨우 5시 50분이야.

W 그렇다면, 언제 경기가 시작되니?

M 7시에 시작해. 내 생각에 경기장에 도착하는 데 단지 20분 걸려. 그러니까 30분 후에 출발하자.

W 30분 후에? 미안하지만, 지금 몇 시라고 했지?

M 5시 50분이라고 했잖아.

W 좋아. 30분 후에 출발하자.

> **만점 솔루션** 현재 시각이 5시 50분인 상황에서 두 사람은 30분 후에 출발하기로(Let's get stared in thirty minutes.) 했으므로 6시 20분에 출발할 것이다.

17 ⑤ | ➕③

M Hi, Karen. Can I talk to you for a minute?

W Hi, Rick! Sure!

M You know that I've always dreamed of being a musical actor, don't you?

W Yes, I know that it's your dream.

M As a matter of fact, I auditioned for a part in a musical last week. And I got the part!

W Wow, congratulations! Good for you!

M But I'm worried about what my mom will say. She doesn't want me to be a musical actor. What should I tell her?

W _____

M 안녕, 카렌. 잠깐 얘기 좀 할 수 있을까?

W 안녕, 릭! 물론이야!

M 내가 뮤지컬 배우가 되는 걸 항상 꿈꿔왔다는 걸 알고 있지?

W 응. 그게 네 꿈인 거 알고 있지.

M 사실은, 저번 주에 뮤지컬의 한 역할로 오디션을 봤어. 그리고 그 역에 붙었어!

W 와, 축하해! 잘됐다!

M 그런데 엄마가 뭐라고 말할지가 걱정이야. 엄마는 내가 뮤지컬 배우가 되길 원하지 않아. 엄마한테 뭐라고 말해야 할까?

W 네가 연기하는 걸 얼마나 좋아하는지 엄마한테 말해야 해.

① 그녀에게 말하면 안돼.

② 미래를 위해 연기를 포기해야 해.

③ 연습을 더 해야 해.

④ 그녀가 연기하도록 허락해야 해.

18 ②

W Tom, can you do me a favor?

M It depends on what it is.

W Can you lend me your MP3 player?

M I'm afraid I can't because I don't have it right now.

W Where is it?

M My dad took it away yesterday.

W How come?

M He told me to study harder instead of listening to music. It really makes me mad. As you know, music helps me study hard.

W _____

W Tom, 부탁 좀 들어 줄래?

M 어떤 부탁이냐에 달려 있지.

W 네 MP3 플레이어 좀 빌려 줄 수 있니?

M 유감스럽게도 지금 그것을 가지고 있지 않아서 빌려 줄 수가 없어.

W 어디에 있는데?

M 어제 아빠께서 빼앗아 가셨어.

W 어째서?

M 음악 감상을 하는 대신에 더 열심히 공부하라고 하셨어. 정말 미치겠어. 너도 알다시피, 음악은 내가 열심히 공부하도록 도움을 주잖아.

W 참 안됐구나.

① 내 잘못이야.

③ 네가 곧 회복되길 바라.

④ 넌 다른 MP3 플레이어를 사야 해.

⑤ 그렇다면 음악을 좀 듣는 게 어때?

19 ⑤

W Have you seen this movie before?

M No, I haven't. Have you?

W Yes, a long time ago.

M Then, what do you think of the movie?

W I don't want to complain, but I don't like the story.

M What's wrong with it?

W We know what's going to happen. It's like every other fairy tale. I mean the prince always gets married to the beautiful princess.

M Right. If you made this movie, how would you change the story?

W _____

W 전에 이 영화 봤니?

M 아니, 못 봤어. 너는?

W 봤어, 오래 전에.

M 그렇다면 그 영화를 어떻게 생각하니?

W 불평하고 싶진 않지만, 이야기가 마음에 들지 않아.

M 뭐가 잘못 됐는데?

W 무슨 일이 일어날지 알고 있어. 다른 모든 동화와 같거든. 내 말은 왕자가 항상 아름다운 공주랑 결혼하잖아.

M 맞아. 네가 영화를 만든다면, 어떻게 그 줄거리를 바꿀 건데?

W 못생긴 공주가 평범한 남자와 결혼하는 거야.

① 모든 것이 똑같아.

② 나 대신 네가 줄거리를 다시 쓸 수 있어.

③ 왕자는 부유하고 잘 생길 거야.

④ 왕자가 아름다운 공주와 함께 살 거야.

만점 솔루션 전형적인 줄거리에서 벗어난 내용이 와야 하므로, 못생긴 공주가 평범한 남자와 결혼한다는 응답이 가장 자연스럽다.

20 ③

M Bill moved to a new apartment last Saturday. He was very happy at first. He thought his apartment was a quiet place, but it wasn't. His neighbors living above made so much noise every night. So he couldn't stand it anymore and had some trouble with them last night. He went upstairs and knocked on the door. A man came out and asked what was wrong. In this situation, what would Bill say to the neighbor?

M Bill은 지난주 토요일에 새 아파트로 이사했다. 그는 처음에 아주 기분이 좋았다. 그는 그의 아파트가 조용한 장소라고 생각했지만, 그렇지 않았다. 위층에 사는 그의 이웃은 밤마다 아주 시끄러웠다. 그래서 그는 그것을 더 이상 참을 수 없었고, 지난밤에 그들과 약간의 문제가 있었다. 그는 위층으로 올라가서 문을 두드렸다. 한 남자가 나와 무슨 일인지 물었다. 이 상황에서, Bill은 그 이웃에게 무슨 말을 할까?

① 메시지 좀 전해 주시겠습니까?

② 언제 이 집으로 이사하셨죠?

③ 밤에 조용히 해 주시겠습니까?

④ 아파트에서 애완동물을 키우시는 건가요?

⑤ 당신이 제 새 이웃인지 말해 줄 수 있나요?

01 ②	**02** ②	**03** ④	**04** ②	**05** ③
06 ③	**07** ⑤	**08** ②, ➕⑤	**09** ②	**10** ⑤
11 ①	**12** ⑤, ➕⑤	**13** ①	**14** ③	**15** ②
16 ④	**17** ⑤	**18** ②	**19** ②	**20** ③

01 ②

W Chris, I think that girl is the Olympic gold medalist in tennis.

M What girl? Is she being interviewed here?

W The girl with the book in her hands. I don't think so, it looks like she's just with a friend.

M Who are you talking about? That girl on the bench is my friend's cousin.

W Not her. She's not reading a book. She's just carrying one.

M Oh, I see her. You mean the girl wearing a cap with a stack of books?

W No, not her either. She only has one book.

M I still don't know who you're talking about.

W She's standing next to the fountain and talking with another girl.

M Oh, I see her now! Yes, I've seen her on TV a few times.

W 크리스, 저 여자 올림픽에서 테니스로 금메달을 딴 여자같아.

M 어느 여자? 여기서 인터뷰하고 있는 거야?

W 손에 책을 들고 있는 여자말이야. 인터뷰하는 건 아니고 친구랑 같이 있는 거 같아.

M 누구를 말하는 거야? 벤치에 있는 여자는 내 친구의 사촌이야.

W 그녀 말고. 책을 읽고 있지는 않아. 그냥 하나 들고 있어.

M 아, 보인다. 책 한 무더기를 가지고 모자를 쓰고 있는 여자 말하는 거지?

W 아니, 그녀도 아니야. 책 한 권만 가지고 있어.

M 네가 누굴 말하는지 아직도 모르겠어.

W 분수 옆에 서있고 다른 여자애랑 말하고 있어.

M 아, 이제 보인다! 맞아, TV에서 몇 번 본적 있어.

02 ②

W Do you provide a hair-cut service for pets?

M Certainly. We not only cut their hair, but also bathe pets.

W How much is the service?

M $20 per dog regardless of its size.

W Um.... that's reasonable. All right, can you do it right now?

M Sorry, there are a lot of dogs scheduled for today. So you need to make an appointment first.

W Then, is this Friday possible?

M I think so.

W 애완동물들을 위한 이발 서비스가 있나요?

M 물론입니다. 이발뿐만이 아니라 목욕도 시킵니다.

W 그 서비스는 얼마죠?

M 사이즈와 상관없이 애완견 한 마리 당 20달러입니다.

W 음, 합리적인 가격이군요. 좋습니다, 지금 바로 그것을 해 줄 수 있나요?

M 죄송합니다만, 오늘 예정된 개들이 많습니다. 따라서 우선 예약을 하실 필요가 있습니다.

W 그렇다면, 이번 금요일이 가능한가요?

M 그렇습니다.

03 ④

① M We will be late. Let's hurry.

　 W Don't worry. We can arrive in time.

② M We'd better pull into the next gas station.

　 W Are we running out of gas?

③ M Do you need a ride home?

　 W No, thanks. My father will pick me up.

④ M Watch out! That car almost hit you!

　 W Oh, thank you! You saved my life!

⑤ M What took you so long?

　 W I got held up in traffic.

① M 늦겠어. 서두르자.

　 W 걱정하지 마. 시간에 맞게 도착할 수 있어.

② M 다음 주유소에 차를 대는 게 좋겠어.

　 W 기름이 떨어진 거야?

③ M 집까지 태워다 줄까?

　 W 아니요, 아버지가 데리러 오실 거예요.

④ M 조심해! 저 차가 하마터면 널 칠 뻔했어!

　 W 오, 고마워! 네가 내 생명을 구해 줬어!

⑤ M 왜 이렇게 오래 걸렸니?

　 W 차가 막혔어.

04 ②

W Whew! We're finally here.

M Yeah, but 30 minutes later than we expected to arrive.

W *Shotgun* has already started, so we have to wait for two hours to see it.

M I have only two and half an hour. What else have we got here?

W We have four other movies: *War in Peace*, *Bed of Flowers*, *I Have Nothing to Say*, and *Gambler*.

M I saw *I Have Nothing to Say* last week. It's worth watching.

W What about *Bed of Flowers*?

M No. Its running time is too long. How about *Gambler*?

W I don't like to know anything about gambling.

M Then we have only one choice.

W Let's see that.

W 휴! 마침내 도착했군.

M 그래, 하지만 도착하리라고 예상한 것보다 30분 늦었어.

W Shotgun은 이미 시작되었기 때문에 그것을 보려면 두 시간을 기다려야 해.

M 나는 2시간 30분밖에 시간이 없어. 다른 게 또 뭐가 있지?

W 여기 네 편의 다른 영화가 있어. War in Peace, Bed of Flowers, I Have Nothing to Say, 그리고 Gambler야.

M 지난주에 I Have Nothing to Say는 봤어. 볼 만한 영화야.

W Bed of Flowers는 어때?

M 싫어. 상영 시간이 너무 길어. Gambler는 어때?

W 나는 도박에 관한 것은 알고 싶지 않아.

M 그럼, 선택할 것이 하나밖에 없네.

W 그것을 보자.

만점 솔루션 Shotgun을 볼 수 있는 시간은 지났고, I Have Nothing to Say는 남자가 지난주에 봤으며, Bed of Flowers는 상영 시간이 너무 길어서 남자가 싫다고 했으며, Gambler는 여자가 도박에 관한 내용이 싫다고 했다. 따라서 남은 것은 War in Peace이다.

05 ③

W How can I help you?

M I'm trying to get on the three fifty train to Seoul. Am I on time?

W Not exactly. It's already three fifty-five p.m. now, but luckily that train has been delayed.

M Wow, I'm so happy about the delay.

W Okay. Can you show me your ticket?

M Here you are. Which platform does the train leave from?

W Platform six. However, you are not supposed to get on this train.

M Of course, I am. This is my train to Seoul leaving at three fifty.

W Yes, but today is Friday. Your ticket is for Saturday.

M What? Oh, I've made a terrible mistake.

W 도와드릴까요?

M 서울행 3시 50분 열차를 타려고 합니다. 제가 제 시간에 도착했나요?

W 꼭 그렇지는 않습니다. 지금 벌써 오후 3시 55분이거든요. 하지만 다행스럽게도 그 기차가 연착되었습니다.

M 와, 그 연착이 정말로 반갑군요.

W 잘 됐습니다. 승차권 좀 보여주시겠습니까?

M 여기 있습니다. 어느 승강장에서 그 기차가 출발하죠?

W 6번 승강장입니다. 그런데, 손님은 이 기차를 타셔서는 안 됩니다.

M 물론, 전 타야 합니다. 3시 50분에 출발하는 서울행 기차잖아요.

W 맞습니다만, 오늘은 금요일입니다. 손님 승차권은 토요일일 것입니다.

M 뭐라고요? 아, 제가 심각한 실수를 했군요.

06 ③

W Steve, is that you?

M Excuse me. I don't think we've.... Ah, Alice?

W That's right. I am.

M Wow! You changed a lot.

W Yeah. I lost a lot of weight. How long has it been since we met last?

M Well, maybe ten years. We learned to swim together from Mr... I can't remember his name.

W Yes. That was the year after we graduated from the same middle school.

M You're right. By the way, what do you do?

W I am a reporter. There was a big fire downtown. I'm going back to my office.

M A reporter! Your job must be exciting.

W 너 Steve 아니니?

M 죄송합니다. 뵌 적이 없는 것 같은데⋯. 아, Alice니?

W 맞아. 나야.

M 왜! 너 많이 변했구나.

W 응. 살이 많이 빠졌어. 마지막으로 만난지 몇 년이 된 거지?

M 글쎄, 10년이겠지. 어떤 선생님께 함께 수영을 배웠는데⋯ 성함이 생각이 안 나네.

W 응. 그게 우리가 같은 중학교를 졸업한 다음 해였어.

M 맞아. 그건 그렇고, 넌 무슨 일을 하니?

W 난 기자야. 시내에 대형 화재가 있었거든. 지금 사무실로 돌아가는 중이야.

M 기자라고! 일이 흥미진진하겠구나.

만점 솔루션 같은 중학교를 졸업하고 함께 수영을 배웠던 두 사람이 우연히 만난 상황이므로, 두 사람은 중학교 동창생임을 알 수 있다. 여자의 직업(기자)에 현혹되어 ① '기자 – 목격자'를 답으로 고르지 않도록 유의한다.

07 ⑤

① **W** How do you like your new school?

　 M I love it! I like the teachers.

② **W** Would you pick up a hitchhiker?

　 M That's a hard question. I guess it depends.

③ **W** Do you know where the nearest gas station is?

　 M I'm sorry, but I'm a stranger here, too.

④ **W** Can I try this on?

　 M Sure. The fitting room is over there.

⑤ **W** Long time no see. How have you been?

　 M I came here by bus, not on foot.

① **W** 새로운 학교는 어때?

　 M 마음에 들어! 선생님들이 좋으셔.

② **W** 태워달라는 사람을 차에 태울 거니?

　 M 그거 어려운 질문이네. 상황에 따라 다르겠지.

③ **W** 가장 가까운 주유소가 어디에 있는지 아세요?

　 M 미안합니다만, 저도 여기가 처음이에요.

④ **W** 이것을 입어 봐도 될까요?

　 M 물론이죠. 탈의실은 저쪽에 있어요.

⑤ **W** 오랜만이야. 어떻게 지냈니?

　 M 여기에 걸어서 온 것이 아니고 버스로 왔어.

08 ② | ➕ ⑤

[Cellphone rings.]

M *[sleepily]* Um... Hello?

W Jack? Were you sleeping?

M *[surprised]* Uh-oh! What time is it?

W It's nine thirty. The bus is leaving in fifteen minutes.

M Oh, no! My alarm didn't go off. I have the bus tickets for all of you. I should have given you the bus tickets yesterday.

W I know! I guess we'll have to buy new ones.

M Hmm... Wait! I have the ticket numbers. Can you ask someone at the ticket office to reprint the tickets?

W All right. Let me try. Give me the numbers of the tickets. I've got a pen and paper.

M Sure, I bought them on July 20, and the numbers are from AF71 to AF77.

[휴대 전화가 울린다.]

M *[졸린듯이]* 음... 누구세요?

W 잭? 자고 있었어?

M *[놀람]* 에! 지금 몇 시야?

W 9시 30분. 버스는 15분 후 떠나.

M 안돼! 알람이 울리지 않았어. 너희들 버스표 내가 갖고 있잖아. 어제 버스표를 너에게 줬어야 했는데.

W 알아! 우리가 새 버스표를 사야할 거 같네.

M 음... 기다려! 나한테 표 번호가 있어. 매표소 사람한테 버스표를 재발급해달라고 요청할 수 있을까?

W 알겠어. 한 번 해 볼게. 표 번호를 알려줘. 나한테 펜이랑 종이가 있어.

M 물론, 표는 7월 20일에 샀고 번호는 AF71부터 AF77까지야.

09 ②

M I can't understand why Christine got angry at me.

W Did you make a fool of her?

M No, I just called her by her nickname, 'Cabbage.'

W Come on. Don't you know she hates being called Cabbage?

M Really? I didn't know that.

W And in my opinion, you have to say sorry to her first.

M Yes, I will.

W And remember it's not polite to make fun of someone's appearance.

M I'll keep that in mind.

M Christine이 나에게 왜 화가 났는지 이해할 수 없어.

W 그녀를 놀렸니?

M 아니, 난 그냥 그녀를 그녀의 별명인 '양배추'라고 불렀을 뿐이야.

W 저런. 넌 그녀가 양배추라고 불리기 싫어한다는 것을 모르고 있니?

M 정말? 몰랐는데.

W 그리고 내 생각에, 넌 그녀에게 먼저 사과를 해야 해.

M 그래, 그렇게.

W 그리고 다른 사람의 외모를 가지고 놀리는 것은 예의에 어긋나는 것임을 명심해.

M 그 말을 명심할게.

10 ⑤

W Can you make two copies of this document?

M Sure. How many pages does it have?

W It's 25 pages.

M Do you want them in color, or in black and white?

W Just black and white. How much will that cost?

M We charge 50 won a page for black and white.

W Do you do binding, too?

M Of course. There's a two thousand-won extra charge.

W Please bind the two copies. I'll be back to pick them up tomorrow.

M OK. That's 50 black and white pages plus binding the two copies.

W 이 서류를 2부 복사해 주실 수 있으세요?

M 네. 쪽수가 어떻게 되죠?

W 25쪽입니다.

M 칼라 복사를 원합니까 아니면 흑백 복사를 원합니까?

W 그냥 흑백으로 해 주세요. 비용이 얼마나 되죠?

M 흑백 한 장에 50원입니다.

W 제본도 하나요?

M 물론입니다. 별도로 2,000원을 부가합니다.

W 2부를 제본해 주세요. 내일 그것들을 찾으러 오겠습니다.

M 알겠습니다. 흑백 복사 50쪽에 2부 제본이죠.

> **만점 솔루션** 25쪽을 2부 복사하므로, 총 50쪽 복사 비용이 2,500원이고, 2부를 제본하므로 4,000원이 더 부가되어 총 6,500원을 지불하면 된다.

11 ①

W Honey! We need to turn to the right here.

M Are you sure? It looks strange.

W I'm sure. It is in the B101. Don't worry. We're almost there.

M Oh, there are too many cars to count.

W I think lots of people in town are driving to this new shopping mall today.

M Yes. Wait a second. Isn't it right over there?

W Where? I don't see it.

M There. Behind that black SUV.

W Oh, you're right.

W 여보! 여기서 오른쪽으로 돌아야 해요.

M 맞는 거예요? 어쩐지 이상해 보이는데요.

W 확실해요. 차가 B101에 있어요. 걱정하지 마세요. 거의 다 왔어요.

M 오, 차가 너무 많아서 셀 수가 없군요.

W 시내에 사는 많은 사람들이 오늘 이 새로 연 쇼핑몰에 차를 몰고 오는 것 같아요.

M 그래요. 잠깐만요. 바로 저기 있는 것 아닌가요?

W 어디요? 안 보이는데요.

M 저기요. 저 검정색 레저용 차량 뒤에요.

W 오, 맞아요.

12 ⑤ | ➕ ⑤

M Most of you <u>are</u> probably <u>already aware of</u> the earthquake that hit Pohang. Many people have been left homeless and <u>are in need</u> of food and clothing. Our student council will be holding a charity event this weekend to help these people. Please join us and help us organize the event. The event will run from 9 a.m. to 5 p.m. <u>over the weekend.</u> It'll <u>be held on</u> the lawn in front of the student union building. If you're available on Saturday or Sunday, please join us. Let's work together to help the earthquake victims.

M 여러분들 대부분은 포항을 강타한 지진에 대해 이미 알고 있을 겁니다. 많은 사람들이 집을 잃었고 음식과 의류가 필요한 상황입니다. 우리 학생회는 이번 주말에 이런 사람들을 돕기 위한 자선 행사를 열 것입니다. 같이 참여하여 이 행사를 개최할 수 있도록 도와주세요. 이 행사는 주말 동안 9시부터 6시까지 운영할 것입니다. 학생회관 건물 앞에 있는 잔디밭에서 열릴 예정입니다. 토요일이나 일요일 시간이 된다면 참여해주세요. 지진 피해자를 돕기 위해 함께 일해봅시다.

13 ①

W Good morning, sir. How may I help you?

M Can I ask how to get to Seoul Museum?

W Oh, sure. Seoul Museum isn't that <u>far from here.</u> Just go out of our hotel and make a left turn. Go straight about 30 meters, and then turn right.

M So, I go out and turn left and then turn right?

W Correct. Then <u>go straight until</u> you come to a flower shop. Turn left at the flower shop, and you'll see the museum.

M Great. Thanks a lot.

W No problem. You can't miss it. The museum is huge.

W 좋은 아침입니다, 선생님. 무엇을 도와드릴까요?

M 서울 박물관에 어떻게 가는지 여쭤봐도 될까요?

W 물론입니다. 서울 박물관은 여기서 그렇게 멀지 않습니다. 호텔 밖으로 나가서 왼쪽으로 도세요. 30미터정도 쭉 간다음에 오른쪽으로 도세요.

M 그러니까, 나가서 왼쪽으로 돈 다음에 오른쪽으로 돌아라?

W 맞습니다. 그리고 꽃집이 나올 때까지 쭉 가다가 꽃집에서 왼쪽으로 돌면 박물관이 보일 겁니다.

M 알겠습니다. 감사해요.

W 아닙니다. 찾기 쉽습니다. 박물관은 아주 크거든요.

14 ③

M As a student, you can easily find this in your daily life. It is <u>long and thin.</u> There is a long piece of lead inside, which is <u>covered with wood.</u> It usually <u>has a small eraser on one end</u> so that you can erase what you wrote. As you use it, its lead is worn down, so you need to cut some wood off regularly. You can <u>use it to write something.</u> For example, you can use it to write a letter or keep a diary.

M 학생으로서 당신은 이것을 일상생활에서 쉽게 찾아볼 수 있다. 그것은 길

고 가늘다. 안쪽에는 긴 연필심이 있는데, 이 심은 목재로 둘러싸여 있다. 그것은 대개 한쪽 끝에 작은 고무 지우개가 있어서 당신이 적은 내용을 지울 수 있다. 사용하다 보면, 연필심이 닳아지므로, 당신은 목재를 규칙적으로 깎아주어야 한다. 당신은 그것을 이용해서 뭔가를 적을 수 있다. 예를 들어, 당신은 편지를 쓰거나 일기를 쓸 때 그것을 사용할 수 있다.

15 ②

M Enough is enough. You have to get up.

W What time is it, honey?

M Four o'clock in the afternoon. Wake up, sweetheart! You won't be able to sleep tonight.

W I have terrible jet lag. I can't keep my eyes open.

M I know, but I'm not going to <u>let you keep sleeping</u> in the middle of the afternoon.

W But I'm really tired and sleepy.

M Get up! I have <u>something fun for us to do together.</u>

W Don't tell me you want to walk with me in the park.

M Look what I've got. <u>Two tickets to a movie</u> at 6 o'clock.

W All right. I'll get ready.

M 잘 만큼 잤어요. 일어나야 해요.

W 몇 시예요, 여보?

M 오후 4시예요. 일어나요, 여보! 오늘 밤에 잠을 잘 수 없을 거예요.

W 시차가 끔찍해요. 눈을 뜰 수가 없어요.

M 알고는 있지만, 대낮에 당신이 잠을 자게 내버려 두지는 않을 거예요.

W 하지만 정말 피곤하고 졸려요.

M 일어나요! 우리가 함께 할 즐거운 일이 있어요.

W 설마 공원에서 산책하고 싶다는 것은 아니겠죠.

M 내가 뭘 가지고 있나 봐요. 6시에 영화를 볼 수 있는 표 두 장이에요.

W 알았어요. 준비할 게요.

16 ④

W Ticket, please.

M Sorry, but I can't remember where I put it.

W What's the license plate number of your car?

M It's 42 G 9232.

W Hold on. <u>It's $8.</u>

M Really? That much?

W Yes. We charge <u>$2 for every thirty minutes</u> after parking. And you parked your car <u>at two-thirty.</u>

M Oh, I thought it was about three.

W Look at this. You didn't park at three. It was two thirty.

M OK. I guess you're right.

W 표 주세요.

M 죄송한데요, 어디에 두었는지 기억이 안 나네요.

W 차의 등록 번호가 어떻게 되죠?

M 42 G 9232입니다.

W 잠시만요. 8달러입니다.

M 정말요? 그렇게 많이 나왔어요?

W 네. 주차한 후 30분마다 2달러씩 부과합니다. 그리고 당신은 이곳에 2시

30분에 주차를 하셨어요.

M 오, 저는 3시경이라고 생각했는데요.

W 여기 보세요. 3시에 주차하지 않으셨어요. 2시 30분이었어요.

M 알겠습니다. 아마도 당신 말이 맞겠지요.

> **만점 솔루션** 시간당 주차비는 30분마다 2달러로, 8달러를 청구하고 있으므로 주차한 지 거의 2시간이 지난 시점이다. 남자는 2시 30분에 주차를 했으므로 현재 시각은 4시 30분임을 알 수 있다.

17 ⑤

W Hi, Josh. How's it going?

M Well, I've been so tired lately.

W Yeah, actually, you do look quite tired. I've seen you studying in the library almost every day.

M Yeah, I have to study really hard because of my math class. I find that so difficult.

W I understand. Besides, the math teacher gives a lot of homework, doesn't he?

M Exactly. We're assigned twenty math questions each week.

W Oh, that's just too much.

M It takes about an hour to finish just one question. I'm totally stressed out.

W _____

W 안녕, 조쉬. 어떻게 지내?

M 그냥, 요즘 너무 지쳤어.

W 그래, 사실 너 굉장히 지쳐 보여. 거의 매일 도서관에서 공부하는 널 봤어.

M 응, 수학 수업 때문에 진짜 열심히 공부해야 해. 진짜 어렵거든.

W 이해해. 게다가, 수학선생님이 숙제도 엄청 많이 내잖아, 안 그래?

M 내 말이. 매 주 20개의 수학문제를 풀어야 해.

W 아, 진짜 너무 많다.

M 한 문제 푸는데 거의 한시간이 걸려. 진짜 스트레스 받아.

W 같이 숙제를 할 누군가를 찾아보는 거 어때?

① 과학 수업을 그만 두는 게 좋을 거라고 생각해.

② 그런 경우에는, 더 빨리 걸어야 한다고 생각해.

③ 수학은 내가 제일 좋아하는 수업이야.

④ 그럼, 시험을 통과하는 것에 정말 집중해야 해.

18 ②

W Ralph! Where are you?

M I'm in my room, Mommy.

W Oh, Ralph. Are you sending text messages again?

M Yes. I have a message to convey to my friend.

W I bet it's Ronnie.

M How do you know that?

W Why do you need to contact him so often?

M We have a lot to talk about. You know friends are supposed to share a lot.

W I know, but you need to call him more than ten times a day?

M Maybe. But how do you know how many times I talk to him over the phone?

W _____

W Ralph! 어디에 있니?

M 제 방에 있어요, 엄마.

W 오, Ralph. 또 문자 메시지를 보내는 거니?

M 네. 친구에게 보낼 메시지가 있어요.

W 틀림없이 Ronnie이겠지.

M 어떻게 그걸 아세요?

W 왜 그렇게 그와 자주 연락을 해야 하는 거니?

M 할 이야기가 많아요. 친구란 공유할 것이 많은 것을 아시잖아요.

W 알지만, 하루에 열 통화 이상을 해야 하는 거니?

M 아마도요. 그런데 얼마나 자주 그와 통화하는지를 어떻게 아세요?

W 전화 통화 기록을 보았단다.

① 그건 내 사생활이야.

③ 사람들이 항상 그렇게 말해.

④ 어제 읽은 신문을 통해 알고 있단다.

⑤ 옳지 않다는 것을 알지만, 그게 내가 할 일이야.

19 ②

M Shh! Be quiet.

W Who is it?

M If you scream, you'll get hurt. Open the door.

W All right. I'll do whatever you tell me to do. Don't hurt me, please.

M What a good girl! Turn on the light. Good. Now move to the sofa.

W Let me open my eyes. I can't see anything.

M No. Now sit down. [popping sound] Surprise!

W Tom! You scared me to death!

M I'm sorry. But this is what a surprise party is supposed to be, isn't it?

W _____

M 쉬! 조용히 해.

W 누구세요?

M 고함지르면 다치게 될 거야. 문을 열어.

W 알았어요. 시키는 대로 다 할 게요. 다치게는 마세요, 제발.

M 그래야지! 불을 켜. 잘 했어. 이제 소파로 가.

W 눈을 뜨게 해 주세요. 아무 것도 볼 수가 없어요.

M 안 돼. 이제 앉아. [펑하는 소리] 놀랐지!

W Tom! 무서워 죽는 줄 알았어!

M 미안해. 하지만 깜짝 파티가 원래 이렇잖아, 안 그래?

W 너는 도가 심했어!

① 이것은 너를 위한 것이야.

③ 친구란 것이 그런 거지.

④ 네 목소리를 못 알아들어서 미안해.

⑤ 여기서 너를 만나다니 무척 반갑네!

> **만점 솔루션** 깜짝 파티를 의도한 것이지만 여자가 상당히 두려워했으므로 투덜대는 말을 하는 것이 상황에 가장 적절한 응답이다.

20 ③

M Minho sat up late last night to finish his report and he turned it in ten minutes ago. He feels tired and sleepy. So he decides to drink coffee. He walks over to the vending machine. He happens to <u>bump into a young woman</u> holding a cup of coffee. She <u>spills her coffee all over herself</u>. In this situation, what would Minho say to the woman?

M 민호는 보고서를 마무리 짓기 위해 밤 늦게까지 잠을 자지 않았고 10분 전에 보고서를 제출했다. 그는 피곤하고 졸리다. 그래서 그는 커피를 마시기로 하고 자판기로 간다. 그는 우연히 커피 한 잔을 들고 있는 한 젊은 여성과 부딪친다. 그녀는 커피를 온 몸에 쏟는다. 이 상황에서, 민호는 여자에게 무슨 말을 할까?

① 보고서가 오늘이 마감이에요.
② 당신이 커피를 좋아하는지 궁금해요.
③ 정말 죄송합니다. 괜찮으세요?
④ 걱정하지 마세요. 시간 내에 보고서를 끝낼 거예요.
⑤ 당신을 위해 커피를 타 드릴게요. 어떻게 해 드릴까요?

영어듣기능력평가 **03** 회

01 ④, ➕③	**02** ③	**03** ②	**04** ③	**05** ⑤
06 ④	**07** ⑤	**08** ⑤	**09** ⑤	**10** ③, ➕③
11 ②	**12** ③	**13** ⑤	**14** ③	**15** ①
16 ④	**17** ②	**18** ⑤	**19** ④	**20** ①

01 ④ | ➕③

W May I help you?
B Yes! <u>I'm looking for</u> a nice T-shirt.
W What size do you wear?
B Medium, usually.
W Ah, right over here. All these T-shirts are your size.
B Hmm. I like these yellow ones. How much are they?
W This one is twelve dollars, and the other design is eighteen dollars.
B This one is <u>reasonably priced</u>, but it's too simple for me. I like the one with the stripes. May I try it on?
W Sure. The fitting room is right behind the jeans section.

W 도와드릴까요?
B 네! 괜찮은 티셔츠를 찾고 있어요.
W 무슨 사이즈를 입으세요?
B 보통 중간 사이즈요.
W 아, 여기 있네요. 이 티셔츠들이 중간 사이즈예요.
B 음. 이 노란색이 좋네요. 얼마 인가요?
W 이건 12달러이고 다른 디자인은 18달러예요.
B 이게 적당한 가격인데 저에게는 너무 단순하네요. 줄무늬가 있는 것이 마음에 드네요. 입어봐도 되나요?
W 물론이죠. 탈의실은 청바지 섹션 바로 뒤에 있어요.

02 ③

[Telephone rings.]
W Dr. Bream's office. May I help you?
M Hello. It's Tim Brown here. I'm having trouble with my left shoulder.
W I'm sorry to hear that. What day would you like to meet Dr. Bream?
M I want to see him as soon as possible. The pain is terrible.
W Let me see if I can get you in this morning. Is eleven a.m. OK?
M I have no time in the morning. How about this afternoon?
W Let's see.... There's an opening at three thirty.
M Oh, please check again. I <u>want to see him around three.</u>
W <u>How about thirty minutes earlier? There's an opening at two thirty.</u>
M That's great. Thank you.

[전화벨이 울린다.]

W Bream 박사님 병원입니다. 도와드릴까요?

M 여보세요. 전 Tim Brown입니다. 왼쪽 어깨가 아파서요.

W 저런 안 됐네요. Bream 박사님을 무슨 요일에 뵙고 싶으신가요?

M 가능한 한 빨리 뵙고 싶습니다. 통증이 심하거든요.

W 오늘 오전에 될 수 있는지 알아보겠습니다. 오전 11시에 괜찮으신가요?

M 아침에는 시간이 없습니다. 오늘 오후는 어떨까요?

W 글쎄요…. 3시 30분이 비어 있네요.

M 혹시 3시경에 뵐 수 있는지 다시 확인해 주세요.

W 30분 더 일찍은 어떤가요? 2시 30분이 비어 있어요.

M 그거 잘 됐네요. 고맙습니다.

만점 솔루션 시간에 관한 문제는 제시된 시간보다 '더 일찍(earlier)' 또는 '더 늦게(later)' 같은 말도 잘 들어야 한다. 여자가 처음에 11시를 제안했지만 남자가 오전에는 안 된다고 하며 3시경에 가능한지 묻자, 여자가 3시에서 30분 더 이른 시간을 제안하고(How about thirty minutes earlier?) 남자도 이에 동의하고 있다.

03 ②

① W I'm looking for a new Cellphone.
　M Please come in and look around. We have many choices.

② W How can I help you, sir?
　M My Cellphone stopped working this morning.

③ W Can I borrow your Cellphone for a minute?
　M Sure. Here it is.

④ W Hello, may I help you?
　M Yes, I'd like to open an account.

⑤ W You bought a new Cellphone, didn't you?
　M Yes, I did. Isn't it nice?

① W 저는 새 휴대 전화를 찾고 있어요.
　M 이리 오셔서 둘러보세요. 다양한 제품이 있습니다.

② W 손님, 뭘 도와드릴까요?
　M 제 휴대 전화가 오늘 아침에 고장 났어요.

③ W 잠깐 동안 당신의 휴대 전화를 빌릴 수 있을까요?
　M 그럼요. 여기 있습니다.

④ W 안녕하세요, 도와드릴까요?
　M 네, 계좌를 개설하고 싶은데요.

⑤ W 휴대 전화 새로 사셨네요, 그렇죠?
　M 네, 그래요. 근사하지 않아요?

04 ③

M Hi, Patricia. Are you getting ready for Saturday?

W I'm afraid not. Something's come up and I can't make it.

M What's up?

W I have to go see my grandma this afternoon. She's very sick.

M Sorry to hear that. But we still have two more days left.

W We started the project on Tuesday, right?

M Yes. And just one day has passed.

W Well, I think I can get back late tonight.

M Then we have Thursday and Friday. Give me a call early tomorrow morning, OK?

W Of course. I will.

M 안녕, Patricia. 토요일을 위한 준비가 되었어요?

W 안 된 것 같아요. 일이 생겨서 안 될 것 같아요.

M 무슨 일이에요?

W 오늘 오후에 할머니를 뵈러 가야 해요. 아주 아프세요.

M 저런 안 됐군요. 하지만 우린 이틀이나 더 남았는 걸요.

W 화요일에 그 프로젝트를 시작했죠, 맞죠?

M 네. 그리고 딱 하루 지났어요.

W 음, 전 오늘밤 늦게 돌아올 수 있을 것 같아요.

M 그러면 우리에게 목요일과 금요일이 있네요. 내일 아침 일찍 전화 주세요, 괜찮죠?

W 물론이죠. 그럴게요.

만점 솔루션 화요일에 프로젝트를 시작한지 하루가 지났다고 했으므로, 오늘은 수요일임을 알 수 있다.

05 ⑤

W I have a cute puppy. It is a white dog with black spots all over the body. I like him more because he seems to understand some words. Look at him now. If I say "sit up", he lifts the two front legs and waits for my next word. Also if I say, "Bring me a newspaper.", he goes to the front door and brings me a newspaper. He is very clever. So I call him 'Clever'.

W 저는 귀여운 강아지 한 마리를 갖고 있습니다. 몸 전체에 검은 반점이 있는 흰 강아지입니다. 그 강아지는 내 말을 잘 이해하는 것 같아서 전 그 강아지가 더욱 좋습니다. 이제 그를 보십시오. 제가 "똑바로 앉아"라고 말하면 그는 두 앞다리를 들고 내 다음 말을 기다립니다. 또한 내가 "신문을 가져와"라고 하면 그는 현관문으로 가서 신문을 내게 가져옵니다. 그는 매우 영리합니다. 그래서 나는 그를 'Clever'라고 부릅니다.

06 ④

W Good afternoon, Mr. Park. Thank you for being on Channel 9 News.

M Thanks for having me. But just call me Peter.

W Okay, Peter. Was it hard to fight the fire?

M Yes, it was very hot and the fire was moving fast! It almost reached several houses nearby.

W How long did it take to put it out?

M There were 18 fire fighters and it took about two hours.

W Do you know what caused the fire?

M Some campers might have left without putting out a fire in the forest.

W 안녕하세요, 박 선생님. 9번 채널 뉴스에 오신 것에 감사드립니다.

M 저를 초대해 주셔서 고맙습니다. 하지만 저를 그냥 Peter라고 불러 주세요.

W 알겠습니다. Peter. 그 화재와 맞서는 것이 힘들었나요?

M 그렇습니다. 매우 뜨겁고 불길이 너무 빨리 움직였어요! 거의 근처 몇몇 집들에 도달할 뻔 했습니다.

W 그것을 진화하는 데 얼마나 시간이 걸렸나요?

M 18명의 소방관들이 있었고 약 2시간 걸렸습니다.

W 화재 원인을 알고 계신가요?

M 몇몇 캠핑하는 사람들이 숲속에 모닥불을 끄지 않고 떠난 것 같습니다.

07 ⑤

① W Hey, you dropped something.
　 M Oh, it's my Cellphone. Thanks.

② W Why don't we have a pizza for lunch?
　 M That sounds like a good idea.

③ W You don't look good. What's the matter?
　 M I just have a slight fever. Don't worry.

④ W I'd like to return this MP3 player.
　 M What seems to be the problem, ma'am?

⑤ W All the rooms are booked, sir.
　 M Oh, I want to borrow this book.

① W 이봐요, 뭐 떨어뜨렸어요.
　 M 오, 제 휴대 전화네요. 감사합니다.

② W 점심으로 우리 피자 먹을래요?
　 M 그거 좋은 생각이네요.

③ W 안 좋아 보이네요. 무슨 일 있어요?
　 M 미열이 좀 있어요. 걱정 말아요.

④ W 이 MP3 플레이어를 반환하고 싶습니다.
　 M 무슨 문제이신가요, 손님?

⑤ W 모든 방이 예약되었습니다, 손님.
　 M 오, 저는 이 책을 빌리고 싶습니다.

만점 솔루션 ⑤ 여자가 하는 말의 book은 동사로 '예약하다'라는 의미로, All the rooms are booked.(모든 방이 예약되었다.)는 호텔에서 주로 사용되는 표현이다. 남자가 하는 말의 book은 명사로 '책'이라는 의미로, I want to borrow this book.(이 책을 빌리고 싶다.)은 도서관에서 주로 사용되는 표현이므로 전혀 어울리지 않는 대화이다.

08 ⑤

W Where are you going?

M I'm going to the supermarket.

W Oh, would you do me a favor while you are out?

M Sure. What's that?

W There's a laundry shop near the supermarket. So, I'd like you to check if my coat is ready.

M OK. Does the owner know your name?

W Well, I don't know. I left my phone number there so you just give it to her.

M All right. Check if your coat is ready to be picked up… that's it?

W That's it.

W 어디 가요?

M 슈퍼마켓에 가요.

W 오, 나가는 김에 부탁 좀 들어줄래요?

M 그럼요. 뭐예요?

W 슈퍼마켓 근처에 세탁소가 있어요. 내 코트가 다 되었는지 확인해 줘요.

M 알았어요. 주인이 당신 이름을 알아요?

W 글쎄요, 모르겠어요. 거기에 내 전화번호를 남겨놨으니 그 번호를 그녀에게 알려 주기만 하면 돼요.

M 알았어요. 당신의 코트가 다 되었는지 확인해 달라… 그거죠?

W 바로 그거예요.

09 ⑤

W Good morning, customers. We are glad to tell you about our store's special event. In order to celebrate Christmas, we will give out $1,000 worth of free gifts every day. When you buy things in our store, please keep your receipts. If the total amount of your receipts adds up to $100 or more, please visit our service desk and get a free gift. Again we wish you a Merry Christmas!

W 안녕하세요, 고객 여러분. 우리 가게의 특별 행사에 대해 말씀 드리게 되어 기쁩니다. 크리스마스를 축하하기 위하여, 매일 1,000달러 상당의 공짜 선물을 드리겠습니다. 만약 여러분이 우리 가게에서 물건을 사시면, 영수증을 보관해 주십시오. 영수증 총액이 100달러 이상 되면, 우리 서비스 센터를 방문하셔서 공짜 선물을 받아 가십시오. 다시 한 번 즐거운 성탄절 되시기 바랍니다!

10 ③ | ➊ ③

M Hi. I need to buy a ticket for the ferry.

W No problem. The ferry ticket is $55 per vehicle.

M All right. That is a pretty reasonable price.

W How many people are there in your car?

M Five of us: my wife, our three kids, and me.

W That price includes only four people per automobile. You'll have to pay an extra $10 for the fifth person.

M All right. My youngest son is only two years old. Do you charge the same price for him?

W Oh, children under three ride for free. They don't count toward the four person maximum.

M 안녕하세요. 여객선 표를 하나 사고 싶은데요.

W 물론이죠. 여객선 표는 차량 당 55달러입니다.

M 알겠습니다. 꽤 적당한 가격이네요.

W 차에 인원이 몇 명이나 타고 있나요?

M 다섯 명이요. 아내와 아이 셋 그리고 저요.

W 가격은 차량 당 네 사람만 포함하고 있어요. 다섯번 째 인원을 위한 추가 금액 10달러를 내야 합니다.

M 알겠습니다. 제일 어린 아들이 겨우 2살입니다. 그래도 가격은 똑같이 적용하나요?

W 아, 세 살 아래의 어린이는 무료입니다. 최대 인원인 네 사람에 포함되지 않습니다.

11 ②

M Where to, ma'am?

W The Korea Hotel, please.

M I see. Is this your first trip to Seoul?

W Yes, it is. I'm here for two weeks on business. Do you know if there is anything interesting happening in the city this weekend?

M Well, if you're interested in art, you might like a Korean traditional art exhibition at the National Museum.

W That sounds great. Are we almost at the hotel?

M Yes, here we are. That'll be eight thousand won, please.

W Here's ten thousand won. Keep the change and thanks for the information.

M 손님, 어디로 모실까요?

W 코리아 호텔입니다.

M 알겠습니다. 이번이 서울 첫 여행이신가요?

W 네, 그렇습니다. 업무상 이곳에 2주 동안 있을 것입니다. 이번 주말 도시에서 개최될 어떤 재미있는 일이 있는지 알고 계신가요?

M 음, 미술에 관심이 있으시다면, 국립박물관에서 한국 전통미술 전시회를 즐기실 수가 있습니다.

W 잘 됐군요. 거의 호텔에 왔나요?

M 네, 다 왔습니다. 8천원 되겠습니다.

W 여기 만 원이 있습니다. 거스름돈은 넣어두시고 정보를 주셔서 감사합니다.

12 ③

M Welcome to my school. My name is Ian. I'm proud of my school. Our regular classes start 8:30 a.m. and finish 3:30 p.m. After school, my school teaches music and sports. Most students attend club activities for one and a half hours. Some students are interested in music. They sing or practice playing musical instruments. Others are interested in sports. They play football, tennis, basketball, or baseball. In the evenings, they enjoy practicing their instruments and sports.

M 우리 학교에 오신 것을 환영합니다. 제 이름은 Ian입니다. 전 우리 학교가 자랑스럽습니다. 정규 수업은 오전 8시 30분에 시작해서 오후 3시 30분에 끝납니다. 방과 후, 학교에서 음악과 운동을 가르칩니다. 대부분의 학생들은 한 시간 30분 동안 클럽 활동에 참가합니다. 몇몇 학생들은 음악에 관심이 있습니다. 그들은 노래하거나 악기 연주를 연습합니다. 다른 학생들은 운동에 관심이 있습니다. 그들은 축구, 테니스, 농구, 또는 야구를 합니다. 저녁에, 그들은 악기 및 운동 연습을 즐깁니다.

만점 솔루션 클럽 활동 시간은 for one and a half hours(1시간 30분)라고 했으므로 ③이 일치하지 않는다.

13 ⑤

M Hi, it's my first day at this school. Would you mind letting me know where the teachers' office is?

W No trouble at all. When you enter the building through the front doors, there are restrooms on both sides of you. Go down the hall. The teachers room is two doors down.

M Oh, really? I heard there are only classrooms on the first floor.

W Oh, you're right. Sorry. Go upstairs. The teachers' office is on the second floor. So, after you go up to the second floor, go down the hall toward the lounge. When you're facing the lounge, the second room on your left is the teachers' office.

M Thanks a lot.

M 안녕하세요, 제가 이 학교 첫 날이에요. 교무실이 어디에 있는지 알려주실 수 있나요?

W 물론이죠. 정문을 통해 건물에 들어갔을 때 양쪽에 휴게실이 있어요. 복도를 지나가세요. 문 두개를 지나면 교무실이에요.

M 아 그래요? 일층에는 교실만 있다고 들었는데요.

W 아 맞아요. 죄송해요. 위층으로 가세요. 교무실은 이층에 있어요. 이층으로 올라가서 대합실을 향해 복도를 지나가세요. 대합실을 마주했을 때, 왼쪽에서 두 번째 방이 교무실이에요.

M 고맙습니다.

14 ②

W This was invented to help people fall safely from the sky. It has some pieces of cloths and a lot of strings. Before a person jumps out of an airplane, it is packed into a backpack. As the person is falling down, it quickly spreads out to catch the air. This slows his or her falling speed so that the person can touch the ground safely. The upper part of this usually looks like a dome, a round roof.

W 이것은 사람들이 하늘에서 안전하게 떨어지는 것을 돕기 위해 발명되었다. 그것에는 몇 개의 천 조각과 많은 줄이 있다. 사람이 비행기에서 뛰어내리기 전에, 그것은 배낭 안에 압축되어 있다. 사람이 떨어질 때, 그것은 공기를 안기 위해 재빨리 펼쳐진다. 이것은 그 사람의 떨어지는 속도를 맞춰서 안전하게 땅에 착륙하도록 해 준다. 대개 이것의 윗부분은 둥근 지붕인 돔처럼 생겼다.

만점 솔루션 fall, safely라는 말이 반복적으로 언급되므로 사람이 떨어질 때 안전하게 해 주는 물건에 대한 설명임을 알 수 있다.

15 ①

M Hi, may I help you?

W Yes, I'm looking for running shoes in size 250.

M We have a wide selection of running shoes.

W Can I try these white ones?

M Sure. Try them on. They're in size 250.

W Are these really 250? Well, they're a little tight. Can I try a larger pair in the same color?

M Sorry, but white ones are out of stock. How about these black ones? They're 255.

W Hmm… let me try them on.

M 안녕하세요. 뭘 도와드릴까요?

W 네, 사이즈 250인 운동화를 찾고 있습니다.

M 여기에 많은 종류의 운동화들이 있습니다.

W 이 흰색 것들을 신어 봐도 되겠습니까?

M 물론입니다. 신어 보세요. 그것들은 사이즈 250입니다.

W 이것들이 정말로 250입니까? 그런데, 그것들은 조금 꽉 낍니다. 똑같은 색상의 더 큰 신발을 신어 볼 수 있을까요?

M 미안합니다만, 흰색은 재고가 없습니다. 이 검정색은 어떻습니까? 그것들은 255입니다.

W 음…, 그것들을 신어 볼게요.

16 ④

W Terry, hurry up. We're late.

M Just a few seconds, Mom. I'm almost done.

W I'm afraid we'll be a little late. Let's go.

M Then are we going to take a taxi?

W No. I know it's fast but it'll cost us too much to get there. So we are going to take the subway.

M How long will it take, then?

W Well, about 30 minutes. It will be faster than the bus.

M OK, Mom.

W Terry, 서둘러라. 늦었어.

M 잠깐만요, 엄마. 거의 다 했어요.

W 아무래도 약간 늦을 것 같구나. 가자.

M 그럼 우리 택시 타고 갈 거예요?

W 아니. 택시가 빠르기는 하지만 거기까지 가려면 돈이 너무 많이 나올 거야. 그러니 지하철을 탈 거야.

M 그럼 얼마나 걸릴까요?

W 글쎄, 약 30분 정도. 버스보다 더 빠를 거야.

M 알았어요, 엄마.

17 ②

M Good afternoon. May I help you?

W Yes, please. I bought this blouse the other day. But it's too large for me.

M You can choose a smaller one. Or if you want, you can get a refund on that blouse.

W Thank you, but I'd like to choose something else. I need a skirt.

M The skirts are over here. What color would you like?

W Brown, please.

M How about this one?

W That looks nice. Let me check the size.... OK. I'll choose this one. Could you please wrap it?

M No problem. Wait a moment.

M 안녕하세요. 도와드릴까요?

W 네. 일전에 이 블라우스를 구입했습니다. 하지만 제겐 너무 크네요.

M 좀 더 작은 것으로 선택하실 수 있습니다. 원하신다면, 그 블라우스에 대해 환불을 받으실 수도 있습니다.

W 고맙습니다만, 다른 것을 고르고 싶습니다. 저는 치마가 필요하거든요.

M 치마들은 이쪽에 있습니다. 어떤 색을 원하시죠?

W 갈색으로 주세요.

M 이것은 어떻습니까?

W 멋지네요. 사이즈 확인 좀 할게요…. 좋군요. 이것으로 할게요. 포장을 해 주시겠습니까?

M 물론이죠. 잠깐만 기다리세요.

18 ⑤

W You don't look good. What happened?

M I have to print my report but my computer doesn't work.

W Oh, what seems to be the problem?

M I don't know. I pressed the power button as usual, but nothing happened.

W You can use mine if you have saved the document on your USB.

M Sorry I didn't save it on a USB memory stick.

W That's too bad. So, what will you do now?

M Well, I'll try again a couple of more times and if it still doesn't work ... I don't know.

W _____

W 안 좋아 보이네. 무슨 일 있니?

M 보고서를 인쇄해야 하는데 컴퓨터가 작동하지를 않아.

W 오, 뭐가 문제인 것 같은데?

M 모르겠어. 하던 대로 전원 버튼을 눌렀는데 작동하지 않아.

W 네 USB에 문서를 저장했으면 내 것을 써도 되는데.

M 유감이지만 USB 메모리에 저장하지 않았어.

W 저런. 그럼, 이제 어떻게 할 거니?

M 글쎄, 몇 번 더 시도해 보고 만약 여전히 작동하지 않으면… 모르겠다.

W 수리기사를 부르지 그러니?

① 좋아.

② 나쁜 생각은 아니야.

③ 내 USB를 써도 돼.

④ 그냥 조용히 있는 게 어때?

19 ④

W Hello. Can I help you?

M I'm going to a costume party on Saturday, and I'd like to rent a costume.

W What kind of costume?

M It has to be an animal costume.

W Let me see. I have a mouse costume.

M It'll be a very big mouse. Okay, I'll rent it.

W Here it is. Oh, by the way, be careful.

M Be careful? What do you mean?

W _____

W 어서 오세요. 도와드릴까요?

M 토요일에 가장 파티에 갈 거라서, 의상을 대여하고 싶어요.

W 어떤 종류의 의상 말씀이시죠?

M 동물 의상이어야 해요.

W 어디 볼까요. 쥐 복장이 있네요.

M 굉장히 큰 쥐가 되겠네요. 좋아요, 그것을 대여할게요.

W 여기 있어요. 오, 그런데, 조심하세요.

M 조심하라고요? 무슨 말씀이세요?

W <u>고양이 의상을 두 벌이나 대여해 줬거든요.</u>

① 저도 쥐가 싫어요.

② 파티에 늦지 마세요.

③ 그것이 그렇게 비싸지는 않다는 뜻이에요.

⑤ 파티가 조금 전에 취소되었어요.

만점 솔루션 가장 파티에 참석하는 남자에게 쥐 의상을 빌려주면서 주의하라고 말하자 그 의미를 묻고 있으므로, 고양이 의상이 두 벌 대여되었다는 농담식의 말이 가장 자연스럽다.

20 ①

W One of my close friends <u>had a long day</u>. First, he had a hard time going to school. The bus didn't come for twenty minutes, so he ran to the subway station. The subway <u>was crowded with</u> a lot of people. A man stepped on his foot, but he didn't say sorry. And a lady <u>kept talking</u> over her Cellphone loudly. After getting off, he ran as fast as he could. But he was ten minutes late. He had to <u>do thirty push-ups</u> before the first class. In this situation, what would you most likely say to your close friend?

W 내 절친한 친구 중 한 명은 힘든 하루를 보냈다. 우선, 그는 등교에 어려움을 겪었다. 버스가 20분 동안 오지 않아서, 그는 지하철역까지 달려가야 했다. 지하철은 많은 사람들로 붐볐다. 한 남자가 그의 발을 밟았지만, 미안하다는 말을 하지 않았다. 그리고 한 여자는 휴대 전화로 계속해서 크게 이야기를 하고 있었다. 지하철에서 내린 후, 그는 가능한 빨리 달렸다. 하지만 그는 10분 지각했다. 그는 첫 수업 전에 팔굽혀 펴기를 30번 해야 했다. 이 상황에서, 여러분은 절친한 친구에게 뭐라고 말할 것 같은가?

① 참 안됐다!

② 잘 했어.

③ 네가 해내서 기뻐!

④ 가능하면 빨리 일어나도록 해.

⑤ 다음 번에는 버스를 타는 것이 어떠니?

영어듣기능력평가 **04**회

01 ⑤	02 ④	03 ④	04 ⑤, ➊①	05 ⑤
06 ④	07 ③	08 ⑤	09 ②	10 ①
11 ④	12 ⑤	13 ②	14 ②	15 ③, ➊③
16 ②	17 ④	18 ⑤	19 ③	20 ④

01 ⑤

W Hello, shoppers. We're looking for a lost boy. His name is Marshall. He <u>was lost</u> in the sporting goods section on the third floor about twenty minutes ago. He's five years old, and he's wearing <u>a white shirt with long sleeves</u>, <u>black shorts</u>, and <u>a baseball cap with black stripes</u>. If you find him, please take him to the information desk at the main exit. Thank you.

W 쇼핑하시는 손님 여러분, 안녕하세요. 길 잃은 남자 아이를 찾고 있습니다. 이름은 Marshall입니다. 그는 약 20분 전에 3층에 있는 스포츠 용품점에서 실종됐습니다. 그는 다섯 살이고, 긴 소매의 흰 셔츠, 검정 반바지, 그리고 검정 줄무늬가 있는 야구 모자를 쓰고 있습니다. 그를 발견하시면, 정문 출구에 있는 안내 데스크로 데려 오시기 바랍니다. 감사합니다.

02 ④

[Cellphone rings.]

W Hi, Jack. I'd like to <u>talk about the plans</u> for our trip to Japan. I'm happy we're planning to visit Tokyo, Kyoto and Osaka.

M But you want to change something, right?

W Yes. <u>What about visiting</u> one more city? I want to add Kobe to the list. I really want to go there.

M Well, Sarah, that would make our trip longer and make the trip more expensive.

W I know, but I have some friends there that I'd really like to visit. We can <u>stay at their home</u> to save money.

M All right, if that's what you really want, I'm okay with it.

[휴대 전화가 울린다.]

W 안녕, 잭. 우리 일본 여행 계획에 대해 말하고 싶어. 우리가 도쿄, 교토 그리고 오사카를 방문하기로 계획한 건 마음에 들어.

M 그런데 무언가를 바꾸고 싶구나, 그렇지?

W 맞아. 도시 하나를 더 방문하는 거 어떨까? 고베를 추가하고 싶은데. 진짜 거기에 가보고 싶어.

M 글쎄, 사라야. 그건 우리 여행을 더 길고 더 많은 비용이 들게 만들 거야.

W 나도 알아 하지만 정말 방문하고 싶은 몇몇 친구들이 거기에 있어. 돈을 아끼기 위해 친구네 집에 머물 수도 있어.

M 알겠어, 네가 정말 원한다면, 난 괜찮아.

03 ④

① **W** Excuse me, is there a place near here <u>where I can buy a jacket</u>?

   M Let me see. I think there's a shop on Spring Street.

② **W** This looks much larger. Have you got something smaller?

   M Sorry, but that's <u>the last one we've got</u>.

③ **W** Have you seen my jacket anywhere?

   M I saw it on the chair yesterday.

④ **W** Excuse me. Could you <u>move your jacket</u>, please?

   M Oh, sorry. I didn't know it was bothering you.

⑤ **W** Excuse me. Can you show me that jacket?

   M Sure, but you'll have to <u>wait one minute</u>.

① **W** 실례합니다. 주변에 재킷을 살 수 있는 곳이 있나요?

   M 글쎄요. Spring가에 상점 하나가 있는 것 같아요.

② **W** 이것은 훨씬 더 커 보입니다. 더 작은 것이 있나요?

   M 죄송합니다만, 그것이 우리가 갖고 있는 마지막 것입니다.

③ **W** 어딘가에서 내 재킷을 봤나요?

   M 어제 의자 위에 있는 것을 봤습니다.

④ **W** 실례합니다. 재킷 좀 옮겨주시겠습니까?

   M 오, 미안합니다. 그것이 당신을 번거롭게 하는지 몰랐어요.

⑤ **W** 실례합니다. 그 재킷 좀 보여주시겠습니까?

   M 물론입니다. 하지만 좀 기다리셔야 할 거예요.

04 ⑤ | ➕ ①

[Cellphone rings.]

W Hey, Sam. Are you free now? Let's go to the Grand Mall together.

M Sounds good. Where do you want to meet?

W At the Grand Mall subway station. I want to <u>go to the new bookstore</u> there.

M Oh, is the new bookstore open?

W Yes, it is. I heard that it's <u>very spacious</u> with many kinds of books. They also have huge sections for music and stationery.

M Really? Then, <u>why don't we</u> just meet in front of the bookstore? Please wait for me there.

W That'll be even better. Call me when you <u>get to the bookstore</u>.

[휴대 전화가 울린다.]

W 샘, 지금 한가해? 그랜드 몰에 같이 가자.

M 좋아. 어디서 만날까?

W 그랜드 몰 지하철 역에서. 거기에 새로 생긴 서점에 가고 싶어.

M 새로운 서점이 생겼어?

W 응. 많은 책들이 있는 아주 넓은 곳이라고 들었어. 음악과 문구류를 위한 큰 공간도 있다.

M 진짜? 그럼 그냥 서점 앞에서 만나지 않을래? 거기서 기다려.

W 그럼 더 좋지. 서점에 도착하면 연락해.

05 ⑤

M Oh, you're walking <u>with the aid of crutches</u>. Is it OK if I <u>help you cross the street</u>?

W Sure, thanks. <u>It's very nice of you</u> to help me.

M You're welcome. I'm glad to help you.

W In fact, I've had a hard time crossing the street these days.

M I know <u>how it feels</u>. My friend used to have the same problem. He had his right leg in a cast, too.

W Oh, did he?

M Yes. He couldn't walk well, either. So I carried his schoolbag for him to school.

W That's nice of you!

M Oh, there are no cars passing by right now. Let's cross the street now.

M 오, 목발을 짚고 걸으시네요. 길 건너는 것을 도와드려도 괜찮겠습니까?

W 물론이죠. 고맙습니다. 저를 도와주시다니 참 친절하시군요.

M 천만에요. 도와드릴 수 있어서 기분이 좋습니다.

W 사실, 전 요즘 길 건너는 데 어려움이 있어요.

M 그 기분이 어떤 건지 알고 있습니다. 제 친구도 같은 문제가 있었거든요. 그도 오른발을 깁스했었습니다.

W 오, 그렇습니까?

M 네. 그 친구도 역시 잘 걸을 수가 없었죠. 그래서 학교까지 제가 가방을 들어줬어요.

W 정말 친절하시네요!

M 오, 지금 지나가는 차들이 없네요. 지금 길을 건너지요.

> **만점 솔루션** 발에 깁스를 하고 길을 건너야 하는 상황에서 남자의 도움을 받은 여자는 고마운 심정이었을 것이다.

06 ④

M Okay, everyone. That's all for today.

W Thank you, Mr. Jones.

M By the way, do you remember this quiz is on <u>chapters four through seven</u>?

W Chapters four through seven? I thought it was on chapters three and four.

M Nope, I'm afraid not. The second quiz was on chapters two and three.

W Oh, yeah. I forgot.

M Are there any other questions?

W Is the quiz <u>next week</u>?

M No, <u>next class</u>. Prepare for it well and see you then!

M 좋아요, 여러분. 오늘은 여기까지입니다.

W 감사합니다. Jones 선생님.

M 그런데, 이번 시험이 4장에서 7장까지라는 것 기억하고 있죠?

W 4장에서 7장까지요? 3장과 4장에 관한 것이라고 생각했거든요.

M 유감스럽지만, 아니에요. 두 번째 시험이 2장과 3장에 관한 것이었죠.

W 오, 그렇군요. 깜박했습니다.

M 다른 질문 있나요?

W 시험은 다음 주에 있나요?

M 아니요. 다음 수업 시간이에요. 잘 준비하고 그 때 봅시다!

07 ③

① M When did you arrive?

　W I just arrived about 10 minutes ago.

② M I hate history class.

　W Watch some movies about history. That'll help.

③ M How much do you pay for the swimming lessons?

　W It takes a while.

④ M Can you come to the party?

　W I'm afraid I can't. I have a lot of things to do.

⑤ M What are you going to do on the vacation?

　W I'm not sure. I'll have to think about it.

① M 언제 도착했어?

　W 10분 전에 도착했어.

② M 난 역사 수업이 싫어.

　W 역사에 관한 영화를 봐. 도움이 될 거야.

③ M 수영 수업료는 얼마니?

　W 좀 걸려.

④ M 파티에 올 수 있어?

　W 못 갈 거 같아. 해야 할 일이 많아.

⑤ M 휴가동안 뭐 할 거야?

　W 잘 모르겠어. 생각해 봐야겠다.

08 ⑤

W Sam, how many of your friends are coming over tonight?

M There'll be five of us. They want to watch the football game on TV to cheer for the Korean team.

W That sounds exciting. What kind of snacks would you like to have?

M Fried chicken and potato chips would be great.

W If I give you some money, can you go get some chicken?

M Sure, I'd be glad to.

W 샘, 오늘 밤 친구들이 몇 명이나 와?

M 다섯 명. 한국팀을 응원하려고 TV로 축구경기를 보고 싶어해.

W 재미있겠다. 먹고 싶은 간식이 뭐야?

M 치킨이랑 감자칩이 좋겠다.

W 돈을 줄 테니까 치킨 좀 사올 수 있어?

M 물론이지.

09 ②

W What's up? You look worried.

M You know, final exams are just around the corner.

W Are there any problems?

M Well, I'm confident about English and Korean, but I'm not so sure about science.

W I thought you were good at both math and science.

M Actually, I'm not.

W What do you mean?

M I don't worry about math. But the biology part in science is really difficult for me. I hope the problems are not so hard.

W Well, I'll keep my fingers crossed for you.

W 무슨 일이니? 걱정이 있는 얼굴이다.

M 알다시피, 기말고사가 얼마 남지 않았잖아.

W 무슨 문제가 있어?

M 음, 나는 영어와 국어는 자신이 있지만, 과학은 그렇게 자신 있는 게 아냐.

W 넌 수학과 과학 둘 다 잘한다고 생각했는데.

M 사실은, 그렇지 않아.

W 무슨 뜻이야?

M 수학 걱정은 안 해. 하지만 과학에서 생물 부분이 나에게 정말 어려워. 문제가 너무 어렵지 않았으면 좋겠어.

W 음, 널 위해 행운을 빌어줄게.

10 ①

W Hello! Can I get my usual morning coffee? And please make it two today. I'm getting one for my sister.

M All right. Would you like anything else with those?

W Hmm... Those plain muffins look delicious.

M They were just baked.

W Okay. I'll take three of those, then.

M All right. The coffees are $2.00 each, plus the three muffins at $1.00 each. That comes to $7.00.

W Great. Oh, I want to use my coupon card today. I've got ten stamps already.

M Well, with ten stamps, you can get one free coffee.

W 안녕하세요! 평소의 모닝 커피 부탁드려도 될까요? 그리고 오늘은 두 잔 부탁해요. 한 잔은 여동생에게 갖다 줄 거예요.

M 알겠습니다. 또 원하시는 건 없나요?

W 음... 이 플레인 머핀 맛있어 보이네요.

M 지금 막 구웠어요.

W 알겠어요. 머핀 3개도 부탁해요.

M 알겠습니다. 커피는 각각 2달러이고 각각 1달러인 머핀 3개해서 7달러입니다.

W 네. 오늘은 쿠폰을 사용하고 싶어요. 벌써 도장 10개를 모았어요.

M 도장 10개면 커피 한 잔은 무료입니다.

11 ④

M Hey, look at those kids.

W You mean the kids running on the grass? They are so cute.

M And you see their parents lying down and reading books?

W Yeah. They look so happy. Anyway, did you bring our lunch?

M Sure. You like cheese sandwiches, right?

W That's right. And where are some cold drinks?

M Gee, I totally forgot those. I'll go get some from the cafeteria.

W No. That's OK. Don't bother yourself. I have some water.

M OK then. Why don't you <u>put the big towel on the grass</u> so we can sit down?

W OK.

M 이봐요, 저 아이들 좀 봐요.

W 풀밭에서 뛰노는 아이들 말하는 거예요? 너무 귀엽네요.

M 부모들이 누워서 책 읽고 있는 거 보여요?

W 네. 너무 행복해 보이네요. 그건 그렇고, 우리 점심식사 가져왔어요?

M 물론이죠. 당신은 치즈 샌드위치를 좋아하죠, 그렇죠?

W 맞아요. 그런데 시원한 음료는 어디 있어요?

M 이런. 까맣게 잊어버렸어요. 매점에 가서 좀 사 올게요.

W 아니요. 됐어요. 그러지 말아요. 물이 좀 있어요.

M 그럼 됐네요. 앉을 수 있도록 잔디 위에 큰 수건을 까는 게 어떨까요?

W 좋아요.

12 ⑤

M Most teenagers are very sensitive about gaining weight. That's why you go on a diet. But the best way to lose weight is 'to exercise.' It's important to remember you can <u>exercise anytime anywhere</u>. You <u>don't need to go to a health club</u>. Take a walk for 20 minutes at least three times a week. Enjoy <u>riding a bike</u> during the weekend. Find a sport you like: soccer, basketball, tennis, etc. It doesn't matter whatever you choose. And <u>take the stairs</u> instead of the elevator. These things can help you lose weight and keep you in shape. Just go for it!

M 대부분의 십대들은 체중 증가에 매우 민감하다. 그것이 당신이 다이어트를 하는 이유이다. 하지만 체중을 줄이는 가장 좋은 방법은 '운동하는 것'이다. 당신은 언제 어디서나 운동할 수 있음을 기억하는 것이 중요하다. 당신은 헬스 클럽에 갈 필요가 없다. 일주일에 적어도 세 번은 20분 정도 산책을 하라. 주말에는 자전거 타기를 즐겨라. 당신이 좋아하는 운동, 즉 축구, 농구, 테니스 등을 찾아라. 무엇을 선택하든 상관없다. 그리고 승강기 대신에 계단을 이용하라. 이러한 것들이 당신으로 하여금 체중을 줄이고 건강을 유지하는 데 도움을 줄 수 있다. 자, 한 번 해 보길!

만점 솔루션 남자는 체중 감량 방법으로 take a walk(산책하기), riding a bike(자전거 타기), find a sport you like(자신이 좋아하는 운동 찾기), take the stairs(계단 이용하기)를 권하고 있으며, 헬스 클럽에 갈 필요가 없다(You don't need to go to a health club)고 직접적으로 말하고 있다.

13 ②

M Excuse me, do you know where <u>the nearest bank</u> is? I need to find an ATM.

W Well, there isn't a bank near here. But there is an ATM in the lobby of the hospital.

M Oh, where's the hospital?

W The hospital is <u>opposite the grocery store</u>. Go straight from here, and you'll see a big coffee shop on your right. Make a right turn there, and you'll see a grocery store.

M Okay, so I go straight and turn right.

W Yes, then <u>cross the road</u> at the grocery store. You can't miss the entrance of the hospital.

M Thanks a lot.

M 실례합니다. 가장 가까운 은행이 어디인지 아시나요? ATM을 찾아야 해서요.

W 여기 근처에는 은행이 없어요. 하지만 병원 로비에 ATM이 하나 있어요.

M 아, 병원이 어디인가요?

W 병원은 식료품점 건너편에 있어요. 여기서 쭉 가면 오른쪽에 큰 커피숍이 보일 거예요. 거기서 오른쪽으로 돌면 식료품점이 보여요.

M 알겠어요. 그러니까 쭉 가다가 오른쪽으로 돌아라.

W 네, 그리고 식료품점에서 길을 건너세요. 병원 입구를 찾을 수 있을 거예요.

M 감사합니다.

14 ②

W Nowadays many people enjoy bike riding in the evening. However, it may be dangerous especially in the winter months, because it is dark during those hours. We <u>have developed a bike backpack</u> to help people ride a bike safely. This backpack has little lights on it. The lights are very small, <u>bright and lightweight</u>. With this backpack, you can safely ride a bike along the road in the dark. The lights make the riders more visible to the car drivers. This can <u>reduce the risk of accidents</u> a lot.

W 요즈음 많은 사람들이 저녁에 자전거 타는 것을 즐기고 있습니다. 그러나 특히 겨울에 해당하는 달에는 그 시간 동안에 어둡기 때문에 위험할 수 있습니다. 저희는 사람들이 안전하게 자전거 타는 것을 돕기 위해 자전거 배낭을 개발했습니다. 이 배낭은 작은 조명들이 있습니다. 그 조명들은 아주 작고, 밝으며, 가볍습니다. 이 배낭이 있으면, 어둠 속에서 도로를 따라 자전거를 타면서도 훨씬 더 안전함을 느낄 수 있습니다. 그 조명들은 자전거 타는 사람들을 자동차 운전자들이 더 잘 볼 수 있게 합니다. 이것은 교통사고의 위험을 상당히 감소시켜 줍니다.

15 ③ | ➕ ③

W I'd like to send this package to Busan, please.

M Just put it on the scale. Would you like to send it <u>by express mail</u>?

W Yes. I'd like to get it there <u>as soon as possible</u>.

M Then, it will cost $30, and it will reach Busan tomorrow.

W That's <u>rather expensive</u>. But my friend needs to wear the clothes in the package at a school festival. It has to arrive before Thursday.

M It will. Do you want to send it by express mail?

W Yes.

M Fill out this form, please.

W 이 소포를 부산에 보내려고 합니다.

M 저울 위에 두세요. 속달 우편으로 보낼 건가요?

W 네. 가능하면 빨리 도착했으면 좋겠어요.

M 그럼 30달러입니다. 내일 부산에 도착할 거예요.

W 상당히 비싸네요. 하지만 친구가 학교 축제에서 이 소포안에 있는 옷을 입어야 해요. 목요일 전에 도착해야만 해요.

M 그럴 겁니다. 속달 우편으로 보내실 거죠?

W 네.

M 이 양식을 채워주세요.

만점 솔루션 남녀가 잔디에 수건을 깔고 점심식사로 샌드위치를 먹으려 하는 상황으로 보아, 공원 잔디밭에 있음을 알 수 있다.

16 ②

M Karen, long time no see.

W Daniel, it's been a long time since I saw you last time.

M How's your job going?

W Not so good. You know, I had to travel a lot for my job.

M Did you? But you enjoy travelling, don't you?

W Well, traveling all the time was really hard though. So I quit last month.

M So what are you going to do now?

W I'm interested in taking care of sick people. So I'm planning to take vocational nursing courses.

M That's wonderful! I know you always like to do volunteer work at a hospital and help others.

W Yes, I really enjoy it.

M Karen, 오랜만이다.

W Daniel, 정말 오랜만에 본다.

M 네가 하는 일은 어떠니?

W 아주 좋진 않아. 있잖아, 난 직업상 많이 여행해야 했잖아.

M 그랬니? 하지만, 넌 여행을 즐기잖아, 그렇지 않니?

W 글쎄, 늘 여행하는 것은 정말 힘들었어. 그래서 지난달에 그만뒀어.

M 그래서 이제 뭘 할 예정이니?

W 난 아픈 사람들을 돌보는 데 관심이 있어. 그래서 간호사 직업 교육을 받을 계획이야.

M 멋지다! 내가 알기에 넌 항상 병원에서 봉사활동하기를 좋아했고, 다른 사람들 돕기를 좋아하지.

W 맞아, 난 정말 그것을 즐겨.

17 ④

W Rob, did you use my computer today?

M Oh, yeah. About that... I know I shouldn't have used your computer, but I had to research something on the Internet. Why? Is anything wrong?

W Yeah. You deleted all my project files. How many times do I have to tell you not to use my computer?

M I swear I didn't do anything with your files. I just searched the web for half an hour.

W I don't care what you had to do. The thing is that my files are gone.

M I'm really sorry.

W _____

W 랍, 오늘 내 컴퓨터 썼어?

M 응. 그거 말이야... 네 컴퓨터를 쓰면 안된다는 거 알지만 인터넷으로 무언가 찾아봐야 했어. 왜? 뭐 잘못 됐어?

W 그래. 네가 내 모든 프로젝트 파일을 지웠어. 내 컴퓨터 사용하지 말라고 얼마나 말해야 하니?

M 네 파일은 건들지도 않았어. 30분 정도 인터넷에서 검색했을 뿐이야.

W 네가 뭘 했었어야 했는지는 신경 안 써. 문제는 내 파일들이 사라졌다는 거야.

M 정말 미안해.

W 다시는 내 컴퓨터 건드리지 마!

① 몸조심하세요.

② 내 컴퓨터를 너에게 팔 수 없어.

③ 넌 좋은 동생이야.

⑤ 내 컴퓨터 어디에 뒀어?

18 ⑤

W Can I help you find something?

M Yes, please. I'm looking for a men's round-necked sweater in a medium.

W How do you like this one? This style is in fashion nowadays.

M I like the style, but do you have that in many colors?

W Yes, we do. What color do you like most?

M I prefer brown sweaters. Do you have this in brown?

W Sure. Here you are.

M Looks nice, but it might be a little tight for me. Can I try it on?

W _____

W 물건 찾으시는 것을 도와드릴까요?

M 네. 중간 사이즈의 남성용 둥근 옷깃의 스웨터를 찾고 있습니다.

W 이것은 어떻습니까? 이 스타일이 요즈음에 유행입니다.

M 스타일은 마음에 듭니다만, 이 물건이 여러 색상으로 있나요?

W 네, 있습니다. 어떤 색상이 가장 마음에 드시나요?

M 전 갈색 스웨터를 더 좋아해요. 이 물건이 갈색으로 있나요?

W 물론입니다. 여기 있습니다.

M 멋지네요, 하지만 나에게 좀 꽉 끼는 것 같은데. 그것을 입어 봐도 되나요?

W 물론입니다. 탈의실은 바로 저쪽에 있습니다.

① 그것이 정말 잘 어울립니다.

② 그 물건이 빨간 색상으로도 있습니다.

③ 음, 오늘 그것을 할 필요는 없습니다.

④ 이것이 바로 당신이 찾고 있는 것입니다.

19 ③

W How do you like this song? It's one of my favorite songs.

M What a great song! I love it.

W I'm glad you like it that much.

M Do you happen to know the title of the song and the name of the musical group?

W Yes, I do. The title is 'As Long As You Love Me,' and the group is 'Backstreet Boys.'

M Is there <u>any special message</u> in the song?

W They are singing about love. The message is that they don't care about anything else as long as somebody loves them.

M It's <u>easy to sing</u>. How about singing this song with me in the school English pop song contest?

W _____

W 이 노래 마음에 드니? 그것은 내가 가장 좋아하는 노래들 중 하나거든.

M 정말 멋진 노래! 정말 마음에 들어.

W 네 마음에 그렇게 든다니 기분이 좋군.

M 혹시 노래 제목과 음악 그룹의 이름을 아니?

W 응. 알아. 제목은 'As Long As You Love Me'이고, 그룹은 'Backstreet Boys'야.

M 그 노래에 어떤 특별한 내용이 있니?

W 그들은 사랑을 노래하고 있어. 누군가 그들을 사랑하는 한 무엇이든 상관없다는 내용이야.

M 그거 노래 부르기 쉬운데. 학교 영어 팝송 대회에서 이 노래를 나와 함께 부르는 것이 어떠니?

W 그것이 바로 내가 생각하고 있었던 거야.

① 미안하지만, 난 지금 가야 해.

② 난 단기 여행을 갈 계획이야.

④ 그들의 CD를 빌려 줄 수 있는지 궁금해.

⑤ 네가 가장 좋아하는 가수의 사인을 받을 수 있니?

20 ④

W <u>No wonder</u> these days David hasn't done well in studies. He does a lot of things. Before going to school, he takes a tennis lesson. During lunch break he volunteers at the student cafeteria. After school, he practices basketball from four to five and then <u>works part-time at</u> the convenience store from six to nine. After returning home, of course, he's <u>too tired to do his homework</u>. His homeroom teacher, Mr. Scott, advises him to quit one of the activities, but David thinks <u>everything he does is important</u>. In this situation, what is David most likely to say to Mr. Scott?

W 요즈음에 David가 공부를 잘 하지 못하는 것은 당연하다. 그는 많은 것들을 하고 있다. 등교하기 전에 그는 테니스 레슨을 받는다. 점심 휴식 동안에는 학생식당에서 자원봉사활동을 한다. 방과 후에는 4시에서 5시까지 농구 연습을 한다. 그리고 편의점에서 6시에서 9시까지 아르바이트를 한다. 물론, 귀가 후에 그는 너무 피곤해서 숙제를 할 수 없다. 그의 담임인 Scott 선생님은 그에게 그 활동들 중 하나를 그만두라고 충고하신다. 그러나 David는 그가 하는 모든 것이 중요하다고 생각한다. 이 상황에서, David는 Scott 선생님께 뭐라고 말할 것 같은가?

① 선생님의 충고는 여러 면에서 유용합니다.

② 어떻게 효과적으로 공부할 수 있는지 가르쳐 주실래요?

③ 죄송합니다만, 너무 피곤해서 숙제를 할 수 없습니다.

④ 감사합니다. 하지만 그것들 중 어느 것도 포기할 수 없어요.

⑤ 조만간 그 활동들을 모두 포기할 게요.

영어듣기능력평가 **05**회

01 ③	**02** ⑤	**03** ③	**04** ②	**05** ④
06 ⑤	**07** ①	**08** ④, ➕③	**09** ④, ➕③	**10** ④
11 ①	**12** ③	**13** ③	**14** ①	**15** ②
16 ②	**17** ①	**18** ②	**19** ④	**20** ①

01 ③

M May I help you?

W I've <u>lost my luggage</u>. I think someone took it while I was using the restroom.

M Oh, that's too bad. Can you tell me what it looks like?

W It is a suitcase, so of course it's rectangular. And it's brown.

M Can you describe the suitcase in detail?

W Well, <u>one of the wheels</u> was broken, so it's not easy to pull along. Oh, and I attached a heart-shaped luggage tag on it.

M Okay. We'll look for it. Please fill out this form.

M 도와드릴까요?

W 가방을 잃어버렸어요. 제가 화장실에 있는 동안 누군가 가져간 거 같아요.

M 이런, 안됐군요. 어떻게 생겼는지 말씀해주시겠어요?

W 여행 가방인데 당연히 직사각형이고 밤색예요.

M 여행 가방을 좀 더 자세히 묘사해주시겠어요?

W 한쪽 바퀴가 망가져서 잘 안 끌려요. 아, 그리고 하트 모양의 짐 꼬리표가 달려있어요.

M 알겠습니다. 찾아볼게요. 이 양식을 작성해주세요.

02 ⑤

[Telephone rings.]

M Hello?

W Hello, Henry. This is Sara.

M Hi, Sara. What's up?

W Will you <u>do me a favor</u>?

M It <u>depends on what it is</u>.

W Can you <u>proofread my English composition</u>? It's my homework. I really need <u>a good grade</u> in this class.

M That's no problem. By the way, what time exactly is it?

W It's ten to nine.

M Then, let's meet at 11 o'clock at the library.

W Okay. See you then.

[전화벨이 울린다.]

M 여보세요?

W 안녕, Henry. 나야 Sara.

M 안녕, Sara. 무슨 일이야?

W 부탁 좀 하나 들어줄래?

M 어떤 부탁이냐에 달려 있지.

W 영어 작문 교정을 봐 줄 수 있을까? 그것은 내 숙제거든. 난 이 수업에서 점수를 정말 잘 받고 싶어.

M 그거야 쉽지. 그런데, 지금 정확히 몇 시야?

W 10분 전 9시야.

M 그렇다면, 11시에 도서관에서 만나자.

W 그래. 그 때 보자.

03 ③

① W What's wrong? You don't look well.

　M I'm not feeling well. I <u>have a</u> bad <u>headache</u>.

② W I've been waiting for his new novel to come out!

　M Same here. My friend said the novel is a great read.

③ W Jane recommended this new song.

　M Really? <u>Let me know</u> the name of the artist. I'll check it out.

④ W May I help you?

　M I'd like to <u>return this shirt</u>. It's too small for me.

⑤ W How about this one? It is very cute.

　M I don't like the color. It's too bright for me.

① W 무슨 일이야? 안 좋아 보이네.

　M 몸이 안 좋아. 두통이 있어.

② W 그의 새로운 소설이 나오길 기다렸어.

　M 나도 그래. 내 친구가 진짜 재미있다고 했어.

③ W 제인이 이 새로운 노래를 추천해줬어.

　M 진짜? 아티스트 이름 좀 알려줘. 나도 들어보게.

④ W 도와드릴까요?

　M 이 셔츠를 환불하고 싶어요. 저한테 너무 작아요.

⑤ W 이건 어때요? 아주 귀여워요.

　M 색이 마음에 안 들어요. 저한테 너무 밝아요.

04 ②

W When does the plane leave for Sydney?

M There are two planes for Sydney. Flight 351 goes via Singapore and it leaves at 3:30. Flight 488 is a nonstop flight.

W I mean the nonstop flight.

M Then, it <u>leaves at 4 o'clock</u>.

W At 4 o'clock in the afternoon?

M That's right.

W Do you think I have enough time to catch it?

M I think so. You still <u>have four hours left</u>.

W Okay. And <u>how long does it take</u> to get to Sydney?

M It <u>takes about</u> 9 hours.

W 시드니 행 비행기가 언제 떠나죠?

M 시드니 행 비행기는 두 편이 있습니다. 351 항공편은 싱가포르를 경유해서 가는데 3시 30분에 출발합니다. 488 항공편은 직항입니다.

W 전 직항을 말하는 겁니다.

M 그렇다면, 그것은 4시에 떠납니다.

W 오후 4시요?

M 그렇습니다.

W 제가 그것을 타기에 충분한 시간이 있다고 생각하나요?

M 그렇습니다. 아직도 4시간이 남아 있습니다.

W 그렇군요. 그런데 시드니에 도착하는 데 얼마나 걸리죠?

M 약 9시간 걸립니다.

만점 솔루션 4시가 되기까지 4시간이 남았다고 했으므로, 현재 시각은 12시이다.

05 ④

M Mom, I'm home. Guess what I got?

W You <u>got an A or something</u>, right?

M No, it's not that. Close your eyes.

W Come on, Jake. What is it?

M Close your eyes, please.

W All right. I am closing them.

M Now, open your eyes. <u>It's for you</u>.

W How beautiful! By the way, what's the occasion?

M Just to <u>thank you for everything</u> you do for me.

W Oh, my son!

M 다녀왔습니다. 엄마. 제가 뭘 가지고 있을까요?

W A를 받았거나 뭐 그런 것이지?

M 아니요, 그게 아니에요. 눈을 감아 보세요.

W 그러지 말고, Jake. 뭐니?

M 눈을 감아 주세요, 제발.

W 그래. 눈을 감으마.

M 이제, 눈을 떠보세요. 어머니를 위한 것이에요.

W 정말 아름답구나! 그런데, 무슨 좋은 일이라도 있니?

M 그냥 어머니가 제게 해 주신 모든 일에 대해 감사드리는 의미에요.

W 오, 우리 아들!

06 ⑤

M Are you Ms. Edward?

W Yes, I am.

M I <u>have a package for you</u>. I need your signature.

W Oh, thank you. Where should I sign?

M You should <u>sign right here at the bottom</u>.

W Oh, I see. Here it is. Will you wait for a second? I'll get you something to drink.

M That's very kind of you, but I am in a hurry.

W All right. Thank you.

M 당신이 Edward 부인이신가요?

W 네, 그런데요.

M 당신에게 온 소포가 있어요. 당신의 서명이 필요합니다.

W 오, 감사합니다. 어디에 서명해야 하나요?

M 여기 아래쪽에 서명하셔야 합니다.

W 오, 그렇군요. 여기 있습니다. 잠시만 기다리시겠어요? 제가 마실 것을 드릴게요.

M 참 친절하십니다만, 제가 좀 바빠서요.

W 알겠습니다. 감사합니다.

07 ①

① W Does this bus go to Seoul Station?

M Yes, you can take the train here.

② W Will you turn off the lights?

M Sure, no problem.

③ W Let me carry one of your bags.

M Oh, thank you very much.

④ W Thanks for giving me a ride home.

M You are welcome. It was on my way.

⑤ W How long does it take to your school?

M It takes five minutes on foot.

① W 이 버스가 서울역까지 가나요?

M 네, 여기서 기차를 탈 수 있습니다.

② W 전등을 꺼 주실래요?

M 물론이죠, 문제 없어요.

③ W 제가 가방을 하나 들어드릴게요.

M 오, 대단히 감사합니다.

④ W 집까지 태워다 줘서 고마워요.

M 천만에요. 가는 길인 걸요.

⑤ W 학교까지 얼마나 걸릴까요?

M 걸어서 5분 걸립니다.

만점 솔루션 ① 여자는 승차하고자 하는 버스가 서울역에 가는지를 묻고 있으므로 여기서 기차를 탈 수 있다는 대답은 적절하지 않다.

08 ④ | ➕ ③

W Joe, can you do me a favor? Can you mow the lawn today?

M Sure, Mom. It's been a long time since I last mowed the lawn.

W And we need to remove the dead flowers in the garden, too.

M [sigh] I know. But it's a beautiful day, Mom. I want to go out and have fun with friends.

W Come on, Joe. There are a lot of things to do around the house. You can enjoy the nice weather another day.

M OK, OK. Then, would you turn on the hose, please? I'll water the flowers first.

W Sure. Let's get to work.

W 조, 부탁 좀 해도 될까? 오늘 잔디 좀 깎아줄 수 있어?

M 물론이죠, 엄마. 마지막으로 잔디를 깎은 뒤 오랜 시간이 지났네요.

W 그리고 정원에 죽은 꽃들을 정리해야 해.

M [한숨] 알아요. 하지만 오늘 날씨가 좋아요, 엄마. 나가서 친구들이랑 놀고 싶어요.

W 이런, 조. 해야 할 집안일들이 많아. 다른 날에도 좋은 날씨는 즐길 수 있잖니.

09 ④ | ➕ ③

M Excuse me. Would you happen to be from Jeju Island?

W Um, yes, I am from there. I grew up on Jeju Island and went to elementary school there, before my family moved to Seoul.

M I thought so! Your name is Rachael, right?

W Yes, that's right! And you are... ?

M Jason. We went to Jeju Elementary School together. Don't you remember?

W Jason! Is that you? Oh my! It's been so long! We were in the same swimming club, right?

M Yes, right. I can't believe it! It's been so long to see you.

M 실례합니다. 제주 출신이신가요?

W 음, 네, 거기 출신입니다. 제주도에서 자라고 가족이 서울로 이사하기 전까지 거기서 초등학교를 다녔어요.

M 그럴 거라고 생각했어요! 이름이 레이첼 맞죠?

W 네, 맞아요! 그리고 당신은...?

M 제이슨이요. 우리 제주 초등학교를 같이 다녔는데. 기억 안 나요?

W 제이슨! 너니? 이럴 수가! 오랜만이야! 우리 같은 수영 동아리였잖아, 맞지?

M 그래, 맞아. 믿기지가 않는다! 진짜 오랜만에 본다.

10 ④

W Excuse me.

M Yes. Is there anything I can help you with?

W Yes, I need T-shirts for working out at the gym.

M Well, these shirts are nice. They don't absorb sweat. And they keep you cool when you work out.

W That's great! How much are they?

M $20 each, but they are on sale. I can give you a 30% discount.

W How lucky! Give me three of them.

W 저기요.

M 네. 제가 도와드릴 것이 있습니까?

W 네, 체육관에서 입을 운동용 티셔츠가 필요한데요.

M 그렇다면, 이 셔츠들이 좋아요. 땀을 흡수하지 않아서 운동할 때 시원하게 해 줘요.

W 좋군요! 얼마죠?

M 개당 20달러입니다만, 할인 판매 중이에요. 30% 할인해 드릴 수 있어요.

W 제가 운이 좋군요! 그 셔츠 3장 주세요.

만점 솔루션 20달러짜리 셔츠가 30% 할인 판매 중이므로 개당 14달러이며, 여자는 3장을 사고자 하므로 총 42달러를 지불해야 한다.

11 ①

M Good morning. How may I help you?

W Good morning. How long does it take to <u>develop these rolls of film</u>?

M It takes about 30 minutes.

W Wow, that's pretty quick! Last time it <u>took about a week</u> at Smith's photo shop! How much is it for each one?

M It's 30 cents each. But I can give you our special coupon. <u>With this coupon</u>, you can develop your first roll <u>for free</u>.

W That's really a good deal. I have two rolls of film.

M By the way, if you have a digital camera, you don't have to come here. You can <u>upload your digital pictures</u> directly to our website.

W Thank you.

M 안녕하세요. 뭘 도와 드릴까요?

W 네. 이 필름 한 통을 현상하는 데 얼마나 시간이 걸리나요?

M 약 30분 걸립니다.

W 와, 그거 정말 빠르네요! 지난 번 Smith 사진관에서는 약 1주일이나 걸렸는데! 한 장 당 가격은 얼마죠?

M 각각 30센트입니다. 하지만 특별 교환권을 드릴 수 있습니다. 이 교환권으로 처음 필름 한 통은 무료로 현상하실 수 있습니다.

W 그것 참 근사한 거래네요. 전 필름 두 통이 있거든요.

M 그런데, 디지털 카메라가 있다면 이곳에 오실 필요가 없습니다. 저희 웹 사이트에 직접 디지털 사진들을 전송할 수 있습니다.

W 고맙습니다.

12 ③

M What are you doing?

W I'm applying for the "Principal for a Day" contest. If I win the contest, I can be the principal for a day.

M What are you going to do if you become the principal for a day?

W First, I'll declare the day <u>"No Test, No Homework Day."</u>

M I guess students will like you a lot.

W Then, I'll allow students to <u>come to school one hour late</u>.

M That's a great idea. There'll be no students who are late.

W Finally, I'll <u>limit the day's classes to the morning</u> and <u>let the students do whatever they like</u> in the afternoon.

M Wow! It sounds like my dream school.

M 뭐 하고 있어?

W '일일교장' 대회에 응모하고 있어. 대회에서 우승하면, 하루 동안 교장이 될 수 있어.

M 하루 동안 교장이 되면 뭘 할 건데?

W 우선, '무시험, 숙제 없는 날'을 선포할 거야.

M 학생들이 널 많이 좋아하겠군.

W 그리고 학생들이 한 시간 늦게 등교하도록 할 거야.

M 그거 좋은 생각이네. 지각하는 학생이 없겠군.

W 마지막으로, 하루 수업을 오전으로 제한하고 오후에는 학생들이 좋아하는 일을 무엇이든 하게 할 거야.

M 와! 내가 꿈꾸던 학교인 것 같아.

13 ③

[Telephone rings.]

M Hello?

W Hi, Alex. I have just gotten on the train and it has just left now.

M Linda, I thought you took the 2 o'clock train.

W I was going to catch the two o'clock train, but I missed it.

M <u>If you are on the 3 o'clock train</u>, then you will arrive one hour later than scheduled.

W Yes. <u>It will take about 4 hours</u> unless there are delays. Will you pick me up at the station?

M Of course. Have a nice trip and see you then.

[전화벨이 울린다.]

M 여보세요?

W 안녕, Alex. 이제 막 기차에 탔고 지금 기차가 출발했어.

M 난 네가 2시 기차를 탔다고 생각했는데.

W 2시 기차를 타려고 했는데, 놓치고 말았어.

M 3시 기차를 탔다면, 예정된 시간보다 한 시간 늦게 도착하겠구나.

W 응. 연착되지 않으면 4시간 정도 걸릴 거야. 역에 나를 데리러 올 거지?

M 물론이지. 멋진 여행 되고 그 때 보자.

만점 솔루션 여자는 원래 오후 2시 기차를 타려고 했으나 놓쳤고 이어지는 남자의 말 If you are on the 3 o'clock train으로 보아 여자가 3시 기차를 탔음을 알 수 있다. 3시에 출발하는 기차인 ③과 ④ 중, 4시간 걸린다(It will take about 4 hours)고 했으므로 여자가 탄 기차는 ③임을 알 수 있다.

14 ①

W This is the coming in and out of air at the same time. We do this almost every day. We do this <u>when we feel bored and tired</u>. However, this helps the brain by cooling brain cells. When you do this, most people think that we are <u>sleepy</u>. We tend to do this <u>when a person next to us does this repeatedly</u>.

W 이것은 공기가 들어왔다가 동시에 나가는 것이다. 우리는 거의 매일 이것을 한다. 우리는 따분하거나 피곤할 때 이것을 한다. 하지만, 이것은 뇌세포를 시원하게 함으로써 뇌에 도움을 준다. 우리가 이것을 할 때, 대부분의 사람들은 우리가 졸린 것이라고 생각한다. 우리는 옆 사람이 반복적으로 이것을 할 때 이것을 하는 경향이 있다.

15 ②

[Mobile phone rings.]

M Hi, honey! What's up?

W I'm trying to get into our house, but the new doorlock seems to be <u>out of order</u>.

M Really? Why don't you call customer service?

W I already did. They're going to <u>send a repairman</u>.

M I see. How long is it going to take him to arrive?

W They said no more than thirty minutes.

M Then what are you going to do <u>in the meantime</u>?

W Actually, I'd like to <u>send a package to my parents</u> in America before a post office closes.

M No worries. Take your time. I'll be home within twenty minutes, and take care of the problem.

W Thanks, honey!

[휴대 전화벨이 울린다.]

M 안녕, 여보! 무슨 일이에요?

W 제가 집에 들어가려고 하는데, 새 자물쇠가 고장이 난 것 같아요.

M 정말이요? 고객서비스 센터에 전화하지 그래요?

W 벌써 했어요. 수리공을 보낸대요.

M 알았어요. 그 사람이 도착하는 데 시간이 얼마나 걸린데요?

W 30분 이내라고 했어요.

M 그러면 그 동안에 뭘 할 건데요?

W 사실, 우체국이 문을 닫기 전에 미국에 계신 부모님께 소포를 부치고 싶어요.

M 걱정 마요. 천천히 해요. 내가 20분 안에 집에 도착해서, 그 문제를 처리할게요.

W 고마워요, 여보!

16 ②

W Jake, the fine dust levels are very high today. We're running out of fine dust masks.

M Do you want me to buy some more at the drug store?

W Well, let's order them online. *[Clicking sound]* This shop has a lot of different kinds. Let's choose one.

M I saw on the news that the filter rate should be at least 90%.

W Okay, then these three models are good options. What about the price? I don't want to spend more than $30 a box.

M Then we have two options left. Shall we order the white ones?

W Yes. Let's place an order.

W 제이크, 오늘 미세 먼지 농도가 아주 높아. 미세 먼지 마스크가 얼마 안 남았어.

M 약국에서 몇 개 더 사올까?

W 음, 온라인으로 주문하자. *[클릭하는 소리]* 이 가게가 여러 종류를 파네. 하나 고르자.

M 뉴스에서 필터율이 최소 90%는 되어야 한다고 하는 걸 봤어.

W 알겠어, 그럼 이 세 모델이 좋은 선택권이네. 가격은 어때? 난 한 박스에 30달러 이상은 쓰고 싶지 않은데.

M 그럼 두 선택원이 남았네. 하얀색으로 주문할까?

W 그래. 주문하자.

17 ①

[Telephone rings.]

W Hi, Sam! Do you have any special plans for this weekend?

M Yeah, I'm going on a field trip with my history club on Saturday. We're going to Gyeongju.

W Wow! Sounds great. Actually, I've never been there, but I've heard that it's one of the best places to learn about Korean history.

M Yeah, there are a lot of old temples, towers, and of course museums. But it's always crowded with tourists.

W Well, I know that I'm not a member of your club, but can I join the trip?

M _____

[전화벨이 울린다.]

W 안녕, Sam! 이번 주말에 특별한 계획이라도 있니?

M 응, 토요일에 우리 역사 동아리랑 현장 학습에 갈 거야. 경주로 가려고.

W 와! 재미있겠다. 사실, 한 번도 가본 적 없는데 한국 역사에 대해 배울 수 있는 훌륭한 장소 중 하나라고 들었어.

M 맞아, 오래된 절과 탑 그리고 당연히 박물관도 많이 있어. 하지만 항상 여행객들로 붐비지.

W 음, 내가 너네 동아리 회원은 아닌 거 아는데 나도 그 여행에 같이 갈 수 있을까?

M 선생님한테 물어볼게.

② 비용은 잘 모르겠어.

③ 기다릴 수 없어!

④ 좋은 점수를 얻길 원해.

⑤ 전화기가 고장났어.

18 ②

W You look worried, Minwoo.

M Yes, I am worried because of Jiho.

W What's wrong with him?

M Well, he has no close friends and wants to talk to no one.

W Really? I hope it's not too serious.

M Me, too. But I can't help worrying about him.

W Then why don't you email to 'Dear Wise' to get help?

M That's a good idea! She loves to answer the questions about school life.

W Do you feel better now?

M _____.

W 민호야, 넌 걱정이 있는 것으로 보인다.

M 그래, 지호 때문에 걱정이야.

W 그에게 무슨 문제가 있는데?

M 음, 그는 친한 친구들이 없고 누구와도 이야기를 하려고 하지 않아.

W 정말? 너무 심각하지 않았으면 좋겠다.

M 나도 그래. 하지만 그에 관한 걱정을 하지 않을 수가 없네.

W 그렇다면 도움을 받기 위해 'Dear Wise'에게 전자우편을 쓰는 게 어떠니?

M 그것 참 좋은 생각이다! 그분은 학교생활에 관한 질문에 대답해 주는 것을 좋아하시니까.

W 이제 기분이 좀 나아졌니?

M 아, 그래. 조언해 줘서 고맙다.

① 나도 그 문제에 대해서 답을 할 수 있어.

③ 지금쯤 그가 기분이 좀 좋아졌으면 좋겠다.

④ 도움을 받는 데 얼마나 많은 비용이 드는지 모르겠다.

⑤ 그래, 이 약은 두통에 아주 효과가 있어.

만점 솔루션 도움을 받기 위해 'Dear Wise'에게 전자우편 쓰기를 권유하는 친구의 말에 좋은 생각이라고 맞장구친 점을 참고한다.

19 ④

M Did you enjoy your meal?

W Yes. It was nice. How much is it?

M It's $25 in total.

W Do you mind if I pay by check?

M I'm sorry, ma'am. I'm afraid that isn't possible.

W But I've always paid by check in this restaurant. What's the problem?

M We used to accept checks, but the policy has changed now. I'm sorry.

W Okay. Can I pay by credit card then?

M _____

M 음식 맛있게 드셨습니까?

W 네. 맛있었어요. 얼마죠?

M 총 25달러입니다.

W 수표로 지불해도 되나요?

M 죄송합니다, 손님. 수표는 안 될 것 같습니다.

W 그렇지만 이 식당에서 항상 수표로 지불을 했는데요. 뭐가 문제죠?

M 수표를 받았었지만, 지금은 방침이 바뀌었습니다. 죄송합니다.

W 알겠어요. 그러면 신용카드로 지불할 수 있나요?

M 물론입니다, 손님. 카드 주시겠습니까?

① 찾아주셔서 감사합니다.

② 성함이 어떻게 되시죠?

③ 저기 있는 공중전화를 사용하셔도 됩니다.

⑤ 물론이지요. 모퉁이를 돌면 은행이 있습니다.

20 ①

W Tom works for a company. He is in a meeting now. He needs a pen in order to take some notes. He finds that he forgot to bring one. Sam, his co-worker, is sitting next to Tom and he has an extra pen in his upper pocket. Tom wants to borrow the pen from him. In this situation, what would Tom say to Sam?

W Tom은 회사원이다. 그는 지금 회의에 참석하고 있다. 필기를 하기 위해서 그는 펜이 필요하다. 그는 펜을 가지고 오는 것을 깜빡 했다는 것을 알게 된다. 직장 동료인 Sam이 옆 자리에 앉아 있는데, 그의 상의 주머니에 펜이 하나 더 있다. Tom은 그에게서 그 펜을 빌리고 싶어 한다. 이 상황에서, Tom은 Sam에게 무슨 말을 할까?

① 이봐, 거기에 있는 펜을 좀 빌릴 수 있을까?

② 미안하지만, 다시 한 번 말해 줄 수 있을까?

③ 안 나오네. 다른 것을 줘 봐.

④ 필기하는 것 잊지 마. 내가 네 것을 복사할 거야.

⑤ 그것을 버리지 마. 나중에 쓸 수 있어.

---

01 ②	**02** ③	**03** ③	**04** ④, ➕④	**05** ③
06 ④	**07** ②	**08** ①, ➕⑤	**09** ②	**10** ②
11 ①	**12** ④	**13** ⑤	**14** ②	**15** ②
16 ④	**17** ③	**18** ⑤	**19** ④	**20** ①

01 ②

W Look at those Cellphone charms.

M They are cute. I want to buy one for my daughter.

W She'll be happy to get one. I think the stars look pretty.

M Sorry. She already has lots of stars in her room.

W Oh, she may be tired of stars.

M Right. So I'm going to choose one from the two heart-shaped ones.

W How about the one with some jewels? It looks beautiful to me.

M Does it? But jewels may fall out easily.

W Then you have only one choice.

W 저 휴대 전화 고리 좀 봐요.

M 귀엽군요. 딸에게 하나 사 주고 싶어요.

W 그녀가 받으면 좋아할 거예요. 별이 예쁘게 생겼네요.

M 유감이군요. 이미 그녀의 방에는 별이 많아요.

W 오, 그럼 별에 싫증이 날 수도 있겠군요.

M 맞아요. 그래서 하트 모양 두 개 중에서 고르려고요.

W 보석이 좀 박힌 것은 어떨까요? 내게는 예뻐 보이는데.

M 그래요? 하지만 보석은 쉽게 빠질 수도 있어요.

W 그럼 한 가지 선택만 있군요.

> **만점 솔루션** 딸아이가 별에 싫증이 날 수 있고(she may be tired of stars), 보석이 쉽게 빠질 수 있다(jewels may fall out easily)는 말을 종합하면, 하트 모양에 보석이 없는 ②를 살 것임을 알 수 있다.

02 ③

[Telephone rings.]

M Hello, Lara. This is Bill.

W Hi, Bill. What's up?

M You know, I couldn't come to school today.

W You're coming tomorrow?

M Yes. I'm calling you to check if I have to bring my instrument for music class.

W You mean Ms. Baker's class tomorrow?

M Yes. As I remember, I have to bring my cello.

W You're right. Gee, I almost forgot that. We're going to play our own instruments. So I have to bring my violin.

M I guess I helped you. I'll see you tomorrow. Bye.

[휴대 전화가 울린다.]

M 안녕, Lara. 나 Bill이야.

W 안녕, Bill. 무슨 일이니?

M 알다시피, 내가 오늘 학교에 못 갔잖아.

W 내일은 나와?

M 응. 음악 수업에 내 악기를 갖고 가야 하는지 알아보려고 전화했어.

W 너 내일 Baker 선생님 수업 말하는 거니?

M 응. 내가 기억하기로는, 내 첼로를 가져가야 하는데.

W 네 말이 맞아. 어휴, 하마터면 잊어버릴 뻔했어. 우리는 각자의 악기를 연주하기로 했어. 그래서 나도 내 바이올린을 가져가야 해.

M 내가 널 도운 것 같구나. 내일 만나자. 안녕.

만점 솔루션 남자의 말 I'm calling you to check if I have to bring my instrument for music class.에서 남자가 여자에게 내일 음악 수업 준비물에 대해 묻기 위해 전화를 걸었음을 알 수 있다.

03 ③

① M You cannot park here, ma'am. It's close to the bus stop.

 W Oh, I'm sorry. Is there a parking lot near here?

② M Did you fasten your seat belt?

 W Sure. I always do whenever I drive.

③ M What seems to be the problem, ma'am?

 W I hear a strange noise coming from the engine.

④ M Oh, you have a flat tire.

 W Thank you for letting me know. I'll take it to the garage.

⑤ M Are you OK now?

 W I still have a slight fever.

① M 여기에 주차하시면 안 됩니다, 손님. 버스 정류장과 가깝잖아요.

 W 오, 죄송합니다. 이 근처에 주차장이 있습니까?

② M 안전 벨트를 매셨습니까?

 W 그럼요. 운전할 때마다 항상 매는 걸요.

③ M 무슨 문제이신가요, 손님?

 W 엔진에서 이상한 소리가 들려요.

④ M 오, 타이어에 펑크가 났네요.

 W 알려줘서 감사합니다. 정비소에 가볼게요.

⑤ M 지금 괜찮으십니까?

 W 아직도 미열이 좀 있어요.

04 ④ | ➕ ④

[Cellphone rings.]

W Hi, Roy. I can't believe exams are finally over!

M Same here! What would you like to do on the first day of vacation?

W I was thinking we could go to the beach to learn how to surf.

M Well, I'd love to, but I don't want to get a sunburn on the first day of vacation. What about visiting the aquarium or going shopping?

W Come on! Let's do something new. It'll probably be more exciting.

M Okay, okay. Surfing should be at the top of our list of things to do. But first, I'm starving. Let's talk about it over lunch.

W Good idea. We can decide our plans over lunch.

M Let's meet at the Uncle Joe's Sandwich Shop in 30 minutes.

[휴대 전화가 울린다.]

W 안녕, 로이. 시험이 드디어 끝났다는 걸 믿을 수 없어!

M 나도 그래! 휴가 첫 날에 뭐 하고 싶어?

W 서핑하는 법을 배우기 위해 우리가 바닷가에 갈까 생각하고 있었어.

M 음, 좋은 생각인데 휴가 첫 날부터 햇볕에 타고 싶지는 않아. 수족관에 방문하거나 쇼핑하러 가는 건 어때?

W 그러지 말고! 뭔가 새로운 걸 해보자. 그게 아마 더 재미있을 거야.

M 알겠어. 서핑을 해야 할 일 상위 순위로 해야겠네. 그런데 우선 나 배고파. 점심 먹으면서 얘기하자.

W 좋은 생각이야. 점심 먹으면서 계획을 정하자.

M 엉클 조의 샌드위치 가게에서 30분 후에 만나자.

05 ③

M What will the weather be like during our holidays?

W It's going to be fine for the first week.

M Great. There will be no problem at the beach.

W Are we going to swim in the sea all day long?

M Of course not. I'm planning to take a walk in the nearby forest.

W Wow, that's wonderful. I like to breathe in the fresh air of the forest, too.

M And the next day we'll go to a history museum.

W That's good. I like history.

M And after that we'll enjoy dinner in a hotel near the museum.

M 휴가 동안에 날씨가 어떨 거래요?

W 첫 주에는 화창할 거예요.

M 잘됐네요. 해변에서 아무 문제 없겠어요.

W 하루 종일 바다에서 수영할 건가요?

M 물론 아니죠. 근처 숲에서 산책할 거예요.

W 와, 훌륭해요. 숲의 신선한 공기를 마시는 것도 좋아요.

M 그리고 다음 날에는 역사 박물관에 갈 거예요.

W 좋아요. 난 역사를 좋아해요.

M 그런 후 박물관 근처의 호텔에서 저녁식사를 즐길 거예요.

06 ④

M Can I help you, ma'am?

W Fill her up, please.

M Do you want me to take a look under the hood?

W Yes, please.

M You're a little low on engine oil. I'll put in some oil for free.

W Thanks.

M I'll check the battery for you, too.

W Thank you. Ah, I wonder if you can do me a favor?

M Sure. What is it?

W Well, I hate to say this, but I'm lost. Do you happen to know where the City Hall is?

M Oh, it's just up this road a bit. First, drive to the first intersection. Then you can see it on your left.

W Thanks.

M 손님, 도와드릴까요?

W 기름을 가득 채워 주세요.

M 후드 안을 좀 점검해 드릴까요?

W 네, 부탁합니다.

M 엔진 오일이 조금 부족하네요. 공짜로 조금 넣어 드리겠습니다.

W 고맙습니다.

M 배터리도 점검해 드리겠습니다.

W 고맙습니다. 그런데 부탁 좀 해도 될까요?

M 물론이죠. 뭡니까?

W 음, 말하긴 싫지만 제가 길을 잃었습니다. 혹시 시청이 어디에 있는지 아시나요?

M 아, 바로 이 도로 조금 위쪽에 있습니다. 우선, 첫 번째 교차로까지 차를 몰고 가시면 왼쪽에서 그것을 볼 수 있을 것입니다.

W 감사합니다.

07 ②

① W I don't like the color. Show me another, please.
  M How about this one? It's much brighter.

② W This meat smells strange. I'm afraid it's gone bad.
  M It's because of the cold weather. It will be OK soon.

③ W How much do I owe you?
  M It's $30 but there is a $3 delivery charge.

④ W I bought this last night and I'd like a refund.
  M What seems to be the problem, ma'am?

⑤ W Can I see your newspaper for a moment?
  M No problem. Here you are.

① W 전 그 색깔이 싫어요. 다른 색을 보여주세요.
  M 이것은 어떤가요? 훨씬 더 밝아요.

② W 이 고기는 이상한 냄새가 나요. 상한 것 같아요.
  M 추운 날씨 때문에 그래요. 곧 괜찮아질 거예요.

③ W 제가 얼마를 드려야 하죠?
  M 30달러예요. 하지만 배달비가 3달러입니다.

④ W 이것을 어젯밤에 샀는데 환불하고 싶어요.
  M 문제가 뭔가요, 손님?

⑤ W 잠깐만 신문 좀 볼 수 있을까요?
  M 그럼요. 여기 있어요.

08 ① | ➕ ⑤

W Jason, how's it going with your UCC assignment?

M I think it's going well.

W What are you doing it on?

M Well, the topic is about someone I admire. So I decided to make a UCC video about one of my family members.

W Yeah? Who did you choose?

M My grandpa—he has devoted his life to making beautiful pottery.

W Sounds wonderful!

M I'm going to film his work process to show how much effort he puts into every single piece of pottery. By the way, after I finish my UCC video, can you watch it and give me some feedback?

W 제이슨, UCC숙제 어떻게 되어가고 있어?

M 잘 되고 있는 거 같아.

W 무엇에 대해서 하고 있는데?

M 음, 주제는 내가 존경하는 누군가에 대해서야. 그래서 우리 가족 중 한 사람에 대한 UCC비디오를 만들기로 결정했어.

W 그래? 누굴 선택했어?

M 우리 할아버지. 아름다운 도자기를 만드는데 삶은 바치셨어.

W 아름다운 이야기다!

M 할아버지가 하나의 도자기를 만드는데 얼마나 많은 노력을 쏟아 붓는지 그 작업 과정을 찍을 거야. 그건 그렇고, 내 UCC비디오가 완성되면 영상을 보고서 나에게 피드백을 줄 수 있을까?

09 ②

W Where are you from?

M I am from a town near Crater Lake.

W I know Crater Lake. It's one of the most beautiful national parks in America, right?

M Yeah. I lived near the lake when I was young.

W I think you had a great time there.

M That's true only in the spring, summer and fall.

W What do you mean?

M In the winter I had to clean the snow around my house every day!

W Ha ha! Crater Lake is one of the snowiest places in the Western U.S.

W 어디 출신이죠?

M Crater Lake 근처 도시에서 왔어요.

W Crater Lake를 알아요. 미국에서 가장 아름다운 국립공원들 중 하나죠, 그렇죠?

M 맞아요. 제가 어릴 때 그 호수 근처에서 살았어요.

W 재미있었겠네요.

M 봄, 여름, 가을에만 그렇죠.

W 무슨 말이에요?

M 겨울에는 매일 집 주변의 눈을 치워야만 했어요!

W 하하! Crater Lake는 미국 서부에서 가장 눈이 많이 오는 곳들 중 하나지요.

만점 솔루션 Crater Lake 근처에서 어린 시절을 보낸 사람은 남자이므로 ②가 일치하지 않는다.

10 ②

M Good morning. How may I help you?

W I'm looking for a pair of gloves.

M Are they for you?

W No, they're for my husband.

M OK. How about these black leather ones?

W They look good. How much are they?

M $40.

W Good. I'll take them. You take credit cards, don't you?

M Sure, ma'am. But if you pay in cash, you'll get 10% off.

W Sorry I don't have enough cash now. Here's my card.

M 안녕하세요. 어떻게 도와드릴까요?

W 장갑을 고르고 있어요.

M 손님이 하실 건가요?

W 아니요, 남편 것이에요.

M 알겠습니다. 이 검정색 가죽 장갑은 어떻습니까?

W 좋아 보이는데요. 얼마인가요?

M 40달러예요.

W 좋아요. 그것으로 살게요. 신용카드 받으시죠?

M 그럼요. 손님. 그런데 만약 현금으로 지불하시면, 10% 할인 받으실 수 있습니다.

W 미안합니다만 지금 충분한 현금이 없어요. 카드 여기 있습니다.

> **만점 솔루션** 현금으로 사면 10% 할인이 되지만 여자는 현금이 없어서 할인 혜택을 받지 못하므로, 40달러를 모두 지불해야 한다.

11 ①

W This is great! There's a big TV screen.

M And the air conditioner is also very good.

W I heard from the owner that this has just opened.

M Oh, really? Look at this song book. It has a lot of the latest songs.

W It sure does. Where's the microphone?

M Right here. It's so stylish that I took it for a pen or something.

W How can I turn it on?

M Let's see. It isn't working.

W Come on. The brand-new microphone is broken!

M I'll go to the owner and ask for another one.

W 굉장하네요! TV 화면이 커요.

M 냉방기도 아주 좋아요.

W 주인에게서 이 방이 막 비었다고 들었어요.

M 오, 정말요? 이 노래책 좀 보세요. 최신 노래가 많아요.

W 정말 그렇군요. 마이크는 어디 있죠?

M 바로 여기요. 너무 세련돼서 펜이나 뭐 그런 거라고 착각했을 정도예요.

W 어떻게 켜죠?

M 어디 보자. 작동이 안 되는데요.

W 에이. 그 신형 마이크가 망가져 있네요!

M 주인한테 가서 다른 것을 부탁할게요.

12 ④

M Attention, please. The student council will be holding an information meeting called 'A talk with graduates' this Friday. We know that you have many questions about jobs in the future. I believe that this information meeting will help you know how to prepare for the job you want.

You will get some valuable information from our school's graduates. Please come to the auditorium this Friday at 4:30 to learn more about jobs you can have.

M 주목해 주십시오. 학생회에서는 이번 금요일에 '졸업생과의 대화'라는 정보 모임을 개최할 예정입니다. 여러분은 미래 직업에 대해 궁금한 것들이 많을 것입니다. 이 정보 모임이 여러분이 원하는 직업을 준비하는 방법을 알도록 도움을 줄 것이라고 믿습니다. 여러분은 학교 졸업생들로부터 유용한 정보를 얻을 수 있을 것입니다. 여러분이 가질 수 있는 직업들에 대해 더 많은 것을 배우기 위해 이번 금요일 4시 30분에 강당으로 오시기 바랍니다.

13 ⑤

M Let's buy tickets online.

W Sure. I see upper rows are much cheaper than lower rows.

M Right. I have only $30 for a ticket, but I really want to sit in the lower row.

W Then you have only one choice.

M Well, I don't want to burn my skin in the north stand. The sun is still hot in the afternoon.

W You're right. How about the middle row? All the tickets are under $30.

M That's not a bad idea. If I give up the lower row, I can enjoy the game in the south stand.

W And you won't have to worry about sunburn.

M 온라인으로 표를 삽시다.

W 좋아요. 윗줄은 아랫줄보다 훨씬 더 싸네요.

M 맞아요. 표 값으로 30달러밖에 없어요. 하지만 전 정말로 아랫줄에 앉고 싶어요.

W 그러면 선택권이 하나 밖에 없네요.

M 음, 북쪽 스탠드에서 내 피부를 태우고 싶지는 않은데. 태양이 오후에도 여전히 뜨겁거든요.

W 당신 말이 맞아요. 가운데 줄은 어때요? 표 값이 전부 30달러 미만인데요.

M 나쁘지 않네요. 만약 제가 아랫줄을 포기하면 남쪽 스탠드에서 경기를 즐길 수 있겠군요.

W 그러면 햇볕에 타는 것도 걱정할 필요가 없겠네요.

> **만점 솔루션** 남자는 Lower Row에 앉고 싶지만 30달러밖에 없으므로 North Stand를 선택해야 하는데 그곳에선 햇볕에 타서 싫다고 했다. Middle Row도 나쁘지 않다는 여자의 의견에 동의하며, 햇볕에 타지 않을 South Stand를 선택하기로 했으므로 South Stand — Middle Row가 남자가 선택할 좌석이다.

14 ②

M If you are a student, you are supposed to take this several times a semester or a year. Nobody is allowed to talk to others or make any noise during this. You will usually get a couple of sheets of paper and see a number of questions printed on them. To get a good grade, you do your best to solve as many problems as possible. Though nobody likes to take this, people think this is a necessary thing to see how hard you studied.

M 만약 당신이 학생이라면, 이것을 한 학기 혹은 일 년에 여러 번 봐야 한다. 이것 중에 아무도 다른 사람과 말하거나 소음을 내서는 안 된다. 당신은 대개 종이를 몇 장 받고 그 위에 인쇄된 많은 문제들을 보게 될 것이다. 좋은 점수를 받기 위해서, 당신은 가능한 한 많은 문제를 풀려고 최선을 다한다. 비록 아무도 이것을 좋아하지는 않지만, 사람들은 당신이 얼마나 열심히 공부했는지를 알아보기 위해 이것이 필요하다고 생각한다.

만점 솔루션 student(학생), questions, problems(문제), grade(점수) 등과 관계된 것은 '시험(exam)'이다. problem은 일반적인 문제도 되지만 시험 볼 때 풀어야 할 문제를 뜻하기도 한다.

15 ②

M What's the matter, Jessica? You don't look too well!
W I have a very bad stomachache and a high fever all afternoon.
M Did you take any medicine?
W Yes, I did. But it didn't do any good. I feel worse.
M Sorry to hear that. What did you eat for lunch?
W I just had a hamburger and French fries.
M How was the hamburger cooked?
W Rare. I always like to eat my hamburgers rare.
M Oh, Jessica, I guess you're suffering from food poisoning after eating that. Do you think you can go to the clinic?
W I can't go by myself because I've been vomiting all afternoon. Please help me.
M Okay, I will.

M Jessica 무슨 일이니? 안색이 아주 안 좋게 보이는데!
W 오후 내내 심한 복통과 고열이 있어.
M 약을 좀 먹었니?
W 응, 먹었어. 하지만 효과가 전혀 없어. 더 악화되는 느낌이야.
M 그런 말을 들으니 유감이야. 점심으로 뭘 먹었는데?
W 햄버거랑 감자튀김만 먹었어.
M 햄버거 요리 상태는 어땠니?
W 살짝 구운 것이었어. 나는 항상 살짝 구운 햄버거를 좋아하거든.
M 이런, Jessica. 내 생각에 넌 그것을 먹은 후 식중독에 걸린 것 같아. 병원에 갈 수 있겠니?
W 오후 내내 토해서 혼자서는 갈 수 없어. 도와줘.
M 알았어, 도와줄게.

16 ④

W Have you made up your mind, Paul?
M You mean after-school activities?
W Yeah. I'm thinking of taking yoga. It would be fun.
M That's a good choice, Maria. As for me, I like sports.
W I know you're into ball games like soccer, basketball, and baseball.
M You're right. Last year I really enjoyed baseball but now I'm a little tired of it.

W What will you do this year, then?
M Well, I'd like to try indoor sports like table tennis or basketball.
W There's no table tennis this year, you know.
M Really? There's only one left then.
W I'm afraid so.

W Paul, 결정했니?
M 방과 후 활동을 말하는 거지?
W 응. 난 요가를 할 생각이야. 재미있을 거야.
M 탁월한 선택인 걸, Maria. 나는 스포츠가 좋아.
W 네가 축구, 농구, 야구 같은 구기 경기를 좋아하는 걸 내가 알지.
M 맞아. 작년에 야구가 정말 좋았었는데 지금은 약간 싫증이 났어.
W 그럼 금년에는 뭘 할 거니?
M 음, 탁구나 농구 같은 실내 스포츠를 해 보고 싶어.
W 너도 알다시피 금년에는 탁구가 없어.
M 정말? 그렇다면 한 가지밖에 안 남았네.
W 유감스럽게도 그런 것 같아.

17 ③

W It's seven o'clock. I want to know what happened to Mike.
M He's just a little late.
W He's never late for dinner.
M Maybe he doesn't realize the time because he's with his friends.
W When did you see him last?
M Four thirty.
W He doesn't answer his phone. This is why I'm so worried.
M He usually keeps his phone in the pocket of his jacket. Maybe he's not wearing it now.

W 7시예요. Mike에게 무슨 일이 일어났는지 알고 싶어요.
M 그 애는 조금 늦을 뿐이에요.
W 그 앤 결코 저녁에 늦은 적이 없거든요.
M 아마도 친구들과 있어서 시간이 된 줄 모를 수도 있잖아요.
W 마지막으로 그 애를 본 게 언제죠?
M 4시 반이요.
W 전화를 받지 않아요. 그것 때문에 내가 그렇게 걱정하는 거예요.
M 그 애는 보통 재킷 주머니 안에 전화기를 넣거든요. 아마도 지금 재킷을 입고 있지 않을 거예요.

18 ⑤

W That's the latest MP3 player I really want! When did you buy it?
M Yesterday, at the Sunrise Department Store.
W Are you kidding? You and I met there and we shopped together.
M Right. But you left the store earlier.
W Yeah. I had to leave earlier because I had an appointment with the dentist.
M Right after you left, I went upstairs to see if anything was on sale.

W You mean this <u>was on sale</u>?

M It sure was. Just for one day it was 30% off!

W _____

W 그거 내가 정말 원하는 최신 MP3 플레이어잖아! 언제 샀어?

M 어제, Sunrise 백화점에서.

W 농담해? 너랑 나랑 거기에서 만나서 같이 쇼핑했잖아.

M 맞아. 하지만 네가 먼저 백화점을 떠났지.

W 그래. 치과 의사와 약속이 있어서 먼저 떠나야 했었잖아.

M 네가 떠난 뒤 바로 할인 판매 중인 것이 있는지 알아보려고 위층으로 올라갔었어.

W 너 그럼 이게 할인 판매 중이었다는 말이니?

M 그렇지. 단 하루만 30% 할인 판매 중이었어!

W <u>오, 좋은 기회를 놓친 것 같아!</u>

① 그럼 내가 네게 얼마를 줘야 하니?

② 다른 것을 살 거니?

③ 내일 그 가게에 가야 해.

④ 그것이 할인 판매 중인 것을 알고 놀랐어.

19 ④

M Cathy, have you heard about the new Italian restaurant near here?

W <u>You mean</u> the Colosseum?

M Right. I heard it serves great Italian food.

W Really? I like Italian food.

M Why don't we go there <u>someday next week</u>?

W Great idea, Mark. When are you free?

M Maybe Tuesday or Wednesday. How about you?

W I have an important meeting on Tuesday, so Wednesday will be fine.

M Good. <u>I'll treat you</u> this time.

W _____

M Cathy, 이 근처에 새로 생긴 이탈리아 식당에 대해 들어 본 적 있어요?

W Colosseum 말하는 거죠?

M 맞아요. 거기에서 아주 좋은 이탈리아 음식을 제공한다고 들었어요.

W 정말요? 전 이탈리아 음식을 좋아해요.

M 다음 주쯤 거기 가 보는 게 어때요?

W 좋죠, Mark. 언제 시간 돼요?

M 화요일이나 수요일쯤이요. 당신은요?

W 화요일에는 중요한 회의가 있으니까, 수요일이 좋겠네요.

M 좋아요. 이번에는 제가 살게요.

W <u>오, 그러실래요? Mark, 당신은 너무 친절하시네요.</u>

① 그럼 무슨 요일에 시간 되세요?

② 죄송하지만 전 이탈리아 음식을 그리 좋아하지 않아요.

③ 고맙지만 수요일에 회의가 있어요.

⑤ 탁월한 선택이네요. 이번에는 중국 음식을 먹어요.

20 ③

W People are having a party in Susan's house. At the start of the party, they eat cake, fruit, and other foods. Then they enjoy chatting for over two hours. Her father orders some Chinese food because they are hungry again. <u>A while later</u> the door bell rings. When Susan opens the door she sees a man with three pizzas. She asks him which address he has for the delivery and finds out <u>her next door neighbors ordered them</u>. In this situation, what would Susan say to him?

W 사람들이 Susan의 집에서 파티를 하고 있다. 파티가 시작할 때 그들은 케이크, 과일, 다른 음식 등을 먹는다. 그 다음 그들은 2시간 넘게 수다를 즐긴다. 사람들이 다시 배가 고파서 그녀의 아버지는 중국 음식을 시킨다. 잠시 후에 현관 벨이 울린다. Susan이 문을 열자 피자 세 판을 든 남자가 보인다. 그녀는 그에게 배달 주소지를 물어보고는 이웃 사람이 그것들을 주문했다는 것을 알게 된다. 이 상황에서, Susan은 그에게 무슨 말을 할까?

① 많이 드세요.

② 피자를 더 주문하고 싶은데요.

③ 옆집으로 가셔야 할 것 같네요.

④ 우리 집에 와 주셔서 고맙습니다.

⑤ 전화를 잘못 거셨네요.

만점 솔루션 옆집에서 주문한 피자가 Susan의 집으로 잘못 배달되어 온 상황이므로 옆집으로 가야 할 것 같다고 말하는 것이 가장 자연스럽다.

01 ②	**02** ①	**03** ③	**04** ③	**05** ④
06 ③	**07** ⑤	**08** ②	**09** ⑤, +②	**10** ②
11 ⑤	**12** ⑤	**13** ④	**14** ⑤	**15** ③
16 ④	**17** ⑤, +③	**18** ④	**19** ③	**20** ④

01 ②

M I heard you're taking a yoga class every Wednesday and Saturday.

W Yes, I am. I think it's good for the mind as well as the body.

M It's very hard, isn't it?

W No, not at all. It's easy. I'll show you one simple position.

M OK, I'll just give it a try.

W First, stand up straight with both your hands at your side. Next, breathe in deeply and bend your body backward slowly without bending your knees. Then stay still for a few seconds.

M Like this? Am I doing it right?

W Yes, you're doing it pretty well.

M 네가 매주 수요일과 토요일에 요가 수업을 받는다고 들었어.

W 그래, 맞아. 그것은 몸뿐만 아니라 정신에도 좋아.

M 아주 어렵지, 그렇지 않니?

W 아니, 전혀. 그것은 쉬워. 한 가지 간단한 자세를 보여줄게.

M 좋아, 한번 해 볼게.

W 우선, 두 손을 옆구리에 붙인 채로 똑바로 서. 다음에, 깊게 숨을 들이마시면서 무릎을 구부리지 않고 네 몸을 뒤로 천천히 구부려. 그러고 나서 잠시 가만히 있어.

M 이렇게? 내가 제대로 하고 있니?

W 그래, 너 꽤 잘 하고 있어.

02 ①

W Good afternoon. May I help you?

M Yes, please. I'd like to check these books out.

W Can I have your library card, please?

M Here it is.

W Sorry, but according to our records, you returned the book, *Harry Potter and the Sorcerer's Stone*, a day late.

M I beg your pardon. What should I do?

W You must pay a late charge before taking these books out.

M How much is it?

W It's two dollars.

W 안녕하세요. 도와드릴까요?

M 네, 부탁합니다. 이 책들을 대출하고 싶은데요.

W 도서관 카드를 보여주실래요?

M 여기 있습니다.

W 죄송합니다만, 저희 기록에 따르면, 'Harry Potter와 마법사의 돌'을 하루 늦게 반납하셨네요.

M 죄송합니다. 어떻게 해야 하죠?

W 이 책들을 대출하기 전에 연체료를 내셔야 합니다.

M 얼마죠?

W 2달러입니다.

> **만점 솔루션** 남자의 말 I'd like to check these books out.에서 남자가 도서관에 간 것은 책을 대출하기 위해서라는 것을 알 수 있다. 연체료 2달러를 내는 것은 책을 대출하기 전에 해야 하는 일이다.

03 ③

① W What would you like to order?
　M I'd like a combination pizza and a Coke.

② W This pizza looks delicious. Please tell me how to make it.
　M You can find the recipe on the Internet.

③ W Hi, I'm from Deli Pizza. Someone ordered this pizza.
　M Oh, right. Can you give it to the lady over there?

④ W I ate some pizza, and got a stomachache.
　M That's too bad. You'd better see a doctor.

⑤ W What do you think of the new teacher?
　M Well, she is friendly and helpful.

① W 무엇을 주문하시겠습니까?
　M 콤비네이션 피자와 콜라로 주세요.

② W 이 피자 맛있어 보이네요. 만드는 방법 좀 알려 주세요.
　M 인터넷에서 조리법을 찾을 수 있습니다.

③ W 안녕하세요, Deli Pizza에서 왔습니다. 어떤 분께서 이 피자를 주문하셨는데요.
　M 오, 맞습니다. 저쪽에 있는 저 여자분께 주실래요?

④ W 피자를 좀 먹었는데, 배가 아파요.
　M 안 됐군요. 진찰을 받는 것이 좋겠어요.

⑤ W 새로 오신 선생님을 어떻게 생각하세요?
　M 글쎄요, 친절하시고 도움을 많이 주세요.

04 ③

M Oh, no!

W What's the matter with you?

M Rebecca, I totally forgot your birthday. I'm so sorry.

W It doesn't really matter.

M Was it last Wednesday, the 21st? July the 21st?

W Yes, it was. But the party was three days later. It was on Saturday.

M How many friends were there at your party?

W Thirteen.

M Anyway, I'm terribly sorry again.

W That's all right.

M 아, 이런!

W 무슨 일인데?

M Rebecca, 네 생일을 완전히 잊었네. 정말 미안해.

W 정말 괜찮아.

M 생일이 지난 수요일, 21일이었지? 7월 21일 말이야?

W 그래, 맞아. 하지만 파티는 3일 후에 있었어. 토요일에.

M 파티에 얼마나 많은 친구들이 왔니?

W 13명.

M 어쨌든, 다시 한 번 정말 미안하다.

W 괜찮아.

> **만점 솔루션** Rebecca의 생일은 7월 21일이고(Wednesday / July the 21st) 실제로 그녀의 파티가 있었던 날은 3일 뒤라고(three days later / Saturday) 했으므로 생일 파티는 7월 24일에 있었음을 알 수 있다.

05 ④

W Hi, there. Was everyone all right last night?

M Well, it was raining so hard that we all ended up sleeping in the van.

W I'm glad you're all okay. But I suggest you leave here as soon as possible.

M What for? Is something wrong?

W The river is overflowing its banks due to the heavy rain. Crossing the valley can be dangerous in a few hours.

M Then we'd better get going as soon as we finish packing.

W I hope you have a safe trip home. Then I must get going to warn other campers in this site.

M Our camping experience here was just amazing! Thank you for your help.

W My pleasure! I hope to see you here again. Drive carefully down steep hills.

M I will. Have a nice day!

W 안녕하세요. 지난밤 모두 무사하셨죠?

M 음, 비가 너무 내려서 우리 모두 결국은 승합차에서 잤습니다.

W 모두 무사하다니 잘 됐군요. 하지만 이곳을 가능한 한 빨리 떠나 주시길 권합니다.

M 뭐 때문이죠? 뭔가 문제가 있나요?

W 폭우 때문에 강물이 둑에서 넘쳐 흐르고 있습니다. 몇 시간 후면 계곡을 건너는 것이 위험할 수 있습니다.

M 그렇다면 짐을 꾸리자마자 떠나는 것이 좋겠군요.

W 집까지 안전한 여행이 되시기 바랍니다. 그렇다면 이 지역에 있는 다른 야영자들에게 경고하러 가야겠네요.

M 우리 야영 경험은 정말 대단했습니다! 도와주셔서 감사합니다.

W 천만에요! 이곳에서 곧 다시 볼 수 있기 바랍니다. 가파른 언덕길을 내려가는 동안 조심해서 운전하세요.

M 그렇게 하겠습니다. 좋은 하루 되세요!

06 ③

M Isn't this a picture of you in Sokcho?

W Yes. How did you know where it was taken?

M I lived there for almost four years.

W Wow. Then, you must know a lot about Sokcho, right?

M Sure. Sokcho has a lot of beautiful beaches and great seafood restaurants.

W You can say that again! By the way, when did you live there?

M From 2002 to 2005.

W Really? I can't believe it! The last two years you were there, I was there, too.

M 이것은 속초에서 찍은 네 사진 아니니?

W 맞아. 그것을 어디에서 찍었는지 어떻게 알았니?

M 난 거의 4년 동안 그곳에서 살았거든.

W 와. 그렇다면, 넌 속초에 대해서 많이 알겠다, 그렇지?

M 물론이지. 속초에는 아름다운 해변과 좋은 해산물 식당들이 많지.

W 맞아! 그런데, 언제 그곳에 살았니?

M 2002년부터 2005년까지.

W 정말? 믿을 수가 없네! 네가 그곳에 있었던 마지막 2년 동안, 나도 역시 그곳에 있었잖아.

> **만점 솔루션** 남자는 2002년부터 2005년까지 속초에 살았고 여자는 그 기간의 마지막 두 해(The last two years)에 역시 속초에 있었다고 했다. 따라서 여자가 속초에 있었던 해는 2004년과 2005년이다.

07 ⑤

① W Our final exams are tomorrow, aren't they?
   M Yes, they are. I'm so nervous.

② W Have you seen my MP3 player, Dad?
   M Yes. I saw it on the upper shelf of the bookcase yesterday.

③ W What's the weather going to be like this weekend?
   M It's supposed to be sunny.

④ W What kind of movie would you like to see?
   M I'd like to see an adventure movie like Indiana Jones.

⑤ W If I have my laptop computer fixed, I can use it for a long time.
   M You're right. You have to buy a new one soon.

① W 우리 기말시험이 내일이야, 그렇지 않니?
   M 그래, 맞아. 난 너무 떨려.

② W 아빠, 내 MP3 플레이어 보셨어요?
   M 그래. 어제 책장 맨 위 선반에서 그것을 봤단다.

③ W 이번 주말 날씨가 어떨 거래?
   M 화창할 거야.

④ W 어떤 종류의 영화를 보고 싶니?
   M Indiana Jones 같은 모험 영화를 보고 싶어.

⑤ W 내 휴대용 컴퓨터를 수리하면, 그것을 오랫동안 쓸 수 있을 거야.
   M 맞아. 넌 곧 새것을 사야 해.

> **만점 솔루션** ⑤ 휴대용 컴퓨터를 수리하면 오래 쓸 수 있겠다는 말에 동의한 후 곧 새것을 사야 한다고 말하는 것은 어색하다.

08 ②

M Here's your order, ma'am.

W This is not what I ordered!

M The order sheet says that you ordered chicken combo A.

W Yes, but there are too many legs here.

M Sorry, ma'am, but our chicken combo A <u>comes with six drumsticks</u>.

W Really? I didn't know that. Let me check the menu. Umm... I guess you're right.

M Then would you like to <u>change your order</u>, ma'am?

W No, it's all right. It's my fault. I will take some of them home.

M Very well. Is there anything else I can do for you, ma'am?

W Yes, would you <u>give me a to-go box</u>?

M No problem, ma'am. I'll get you one right away.

M 손님, 여기 주문하신 것 나왔습니다.

W 이건 제가 주문한 게 아닌데요!

M 주문서에는 치킨 콤보 A를 주문하셨다고 쓰여 있습니다.

W 맞지만, 다리 개수가 너무 많아요.

M 손님, 죄송합니다만 저희 치킨 콤보 A에는 닭다리가 여섯 개씩 나옵니다.

W 정말요? 몰랐습니다. 메뉴판 좀 확인해 봅시다. 음... 맞는 것 같군요.

M 그렇다면 손님, 주문을 바꾸시겠어요?

W 아뇨, 괜찮아요. 제 잘못입니다. 제가 몇 개는 집에 가져가겠습니다.

M 잘 됐군요. 도와드릴 것이 더 있나요, 손님?

W 네, 포장용 상자 좀 하나 가져다 주시겠습니까?

M 알겠습니다, 손님. 즉시 하나 가져다 드리겠습니다.

09 ⑤ | ➕ ②

W Hi, Kevin. How are you today?

M *[Worried]* So so. The speech contest is next week. That means my performance is next week, too.

W You don't <u>seem to have</u> much <u>confidence</u>.

M Well, I'm practicing pretty hard every day, but I still <u>can't do well</u>.

W I'm sorry to hear that. What do you think is the problem?

M First of all, my pronunciation isn't clear enough, but I don't know how to improve it.

W Well, I think practicing while holding a pencil in your mouth could help. <u>Why don't you</u> try that?

W 안녕, 케빈. 오늘 기분 어때?

M *[걱정하며]* 그냥 그래. 웅변 대회가 다음 주야. 즉 다음주에 내가 웅변을 해야 한다는 걸 의미하지.

W 자신감이 없어 보이네.

M 그게, 매일 열심히 연습하고 있는데도 여전히 잘 할 수가 없어.

W 안타깝다. 문제가 뭐라고 생각해?

M 우선, 내 발음이 충분히 분명하지 않아. 그런데 어떻게 개선해야 할지를 모르겠어.

W 음, 입에 연필을 물고 연습하는 게 도움이 될 거라고 생각하는데. 한 번 해보는게 어때?

10 ②

M Good afternoon. May I help you?

W Yes, please. Could you help me find an easy book to read?

M Sure. What is it for, ma'am?

W I want a book for bedtime reading.

M In that case, I'd recommend this book of poems. See if you like it.

W Looks very good and the poems are easy to understand, too. How much is it?

M <u>It's $10.</u> But all poetry books are <u>20% off the regular price</u>.

W I see. Here's <u>a $10 bill</u>.

M Here's your change.

M 안녕하세요. 도와드릴까요?

W 네. 읽기 쉬운 책을 찾고 있는데 도와주실 수 있나요?

M 물론이죠. 손님, 책 용도가 뭐죠?

W 잠자기 전에 읽을 책을 원합니다.

M 그렇다면, 이 시집을 추천합니다. 그것이 마음에 드시는지 보세요.

W 아주 좋아 보이고 시들도 이해하기 쉽네요. 얼마죠?

M 10달러입니다. 하지만 모든 시집이 정가에서 20% 할인 판매합니다.

W 그렇군요. 여기 10달러 지폐가 있습니다.

M 여기 잔돈 있습니다.

> **만점 솔루션** 10달러짜리 시집을 20% 할인 받아 8달러에 사면서 10달러짜리 지폐를 냈다면, 거스름돈은 2달러이다.

11 ⑤

W Good morning. May I help you?

M Oh, yes. I'm looking for a brochure on <u>Korean cultural events</u> in Seoul.

W Is there something in particular that you're interested in?

M Well, I'm not sure, but I wonder if I can enjoy <u>Korean traditional music</u>.

W You mean you want to see <u>Korean music performances</u>, right?

M Yes, I'd love to go to a Pansori concert.

W Here's a brochure. You can find <u>the information about</u> such concerts in it.

M Thank you so much.

W 안녕하세요. 도와드릴까요?

M 오, 네. 서울에 있는 한국 문화 행사에 대한 책자를 찾고 있습니다.

W 특별히 관심 있는 어떤 것이 있습니까?

M 음, 잘은 모르지만, 한국 전통 음악을 즐길 수 있을지 궁금하군요.

W 한국 음악 공연들을 보고 싶다는 말씀이신가요?

M 네, 판소리 음악회에 가고 싶습니다.

W 여기 팸플릿이 있습니다. 그 안에서 그러한 음악회 정보를 찾으실 수 있을 겁니다.

M 정말 고맙습니다.

12 ⑤

M Welcome to <u>The Space Show</u> from Channel 17. I am <u>your host</u>, Dr. Morris, and this show will bring you <u>information on space travel</u>. <u>Today's guest speaker</u>, Professor James Hudson at the MIT University, is going to talk about space travel. He is an expert on space travel, and he believes that space travel is coming to us sooner than we think. Welcome to the show, Professor James Hudson.

M 채널 17에서 보내드리는 '우주 쇼'에 오신 것을 환영합니다. 저는 여러분의 진행자 Morris 박사입니다. 이 쇼는 여러분에게 우주 여행에 대한 정보를 제공해 드릴 것입니다. 오늘의 초청 강사로 MIT 대학에 근무하시는 James Hudson 교수께서 우주 여행에 대해 말씀해 주시겠습니다. 그분은 우주 여행에 대한 전문가로 우리가 생각하는 것보다 더 빨리 우주 여행이 우리에게 다가오고 있다고 믿고 있습니다. James Hudson 교수님께서 쇼에 오신 것을 환영합시다.

13 ④

M Excuse me. I reserved the train ticket from Seoul to Daejeon for August 20th. But I've put off my trip until 27th.
W You want to change your reservation from the 20th to the 27th, right?
M Yes, correct.
W Is that one way or round trip?
M Round trip, please.
W What time of the day would you like to go?
M In the afternoon, please.
W Let me check to see if it's available in the computer first.

M 실례합니다. 8월 20일자로 서울발 대전행 기차표를 예약했습니다. 하지만 제 여행을 27일로 연기했습니다.
W 20일에서 27일로 예약을 바꾸고 싶으신 거 맞죠?
M 네, 맞습니다.
W 편도입니까 아니면 왕복입니까?
M 왕복으로 해 주세요.
W 몇 시에 가고 싶으세요?
M 오후로 해 주세요.
W 먼저 컴퓨터에서 그것이 가능한지 확인해 보겠습니다.

14 ⑤

W As many of you already know, next Thursday, March 18, the student council will be holding a fair for the activity clubs. All the clubs can set up booths to provide information about their programs and activities. The fair will be held after school, between 5 p.m. and 8 p.m. We strongly encourage everyone—especially freshmen—to attend it and get to know about the various clubs at our school. There will be free drinks offered to all who attend. Please do not miss this great event!

W 이미 모두들 알고 있겠지만, 다음주 3월 18일인 다음 주 목요일에 학생회는 동아리활동을 위한 행사를 열 예정입니다. 모든 동아리는 프로그램과 활동에 대한 정보를 제공하는 부스를 설치할 수 있습니다. 행사는 방과 후 5시부터 8시까지 열립니다. 모두들, 특히 신입생 여러분들이 참석하여 우리 학교의 다양한 동아리에 대해 알아가기를 강하게 권장합니다. 참석하는 모두에게 무료 음료가 제공됩니다. 이 굉장한 행사를 놓치지 마세요.

15 ③

M Lisa, why don't we go to the movies?
W I don't really want to go there right now. You know, I'm starving. Let's have something to eat. It's lunchtime.
M Sounds great. Where shall we have lunch?
W How about that Italian restaurant over there?
M It looks like an expensive one.
W Yes. So I think I should get some money from the bank first.
M I think I don't have enough money, either.
W Don't worry. This is on me. I mean it's my treat.
M Thank you.

M Lisa, 영화 보러 가는 게 어때?
W 당장은 정말 가고 싶지 않아. 있잖아, 난 배가 고파 죽겠어. 뭐 좀 먹자. 점심 시간이야.
M 좋아. 어디에서 점심을 먹지?
W 저쪽에 있는 저 이탈리아 식당은 어때?
M 비싼 식당처럼 보이는데.
W 맞아. 그래서 우선 은행에서 돈을 좀 인출해야겠어.
M 나도 돈이 충분하지 않은 것 같네.
W 걱정 마. 이번에는 내가 낼게. 내가 대접한다고.
M 고마워.

16 ④

M Happy birthday, Hana.
W Thank you for coming. Come on in, Fred.
M Hana, what a pretty hat!
W My mother bought it for my birthday present. She also made this food, too.
M It looks very delicious.
W Yes, it does. It's a popular Korean fast food. Help yourself.
M I haven't tried that before. Are there noodles in it?
W Nope. It's made of white rice, ham, eggs, some vegetables, and sheets of dried seaweed.
M OK. I'll try some.

M 생일 축하해, 하나야.
W 와 줘서 고마워. 어서 들어와, Fred.
M 하나야, 정말 예쁜 모자구나!
W 엄마께서 내 생일 선물로 사 주셨어. 또한 이 음식도 만들어 주셨어.
M 정말 맛있어 보인다.
W 그래, 맞아. 그것은 인기 있는 한국식 간편 음식이야. 마음껏 먹어.
M 전에 먹어 본 적이 없는데. 그 안에 국수가 들어 있니?
W 아니. 그것은 밥, 햄, 계란, 약간의 야채, 그리고 여러 장의 김으로 만들어.
M 좋아. 좀 먹어 봐야지.

17 ⑤ | ➕ ③

[Telephone rings.]
M Hi, Gina! Do you have the novel *The Old Man and The Sea*?

W Yes, I do. That's by Hemingway, one of my favorite writers. I have a collection of his books.

M Great! Can I borrow it?

W Sure, it's worth reading. When do you need it?

M Well, actually, I have to write a book review of it by next Friday. I should start reading it as soon as possible.

W _____

[전화벨이 울린다.]

M 안녕, 지나! '노인과 바다'라는 소설책 갖고 있니?

W 응, 갖고 있어. 내가 좋아하는 작가 중 하나인 헤밍웨이의 작품이야. 헤밍웨이 도서 모음집을 갖고 있어.

M 잘됐다! 내가 빌릴 수 있을까?

W 물론이지, 읽을 가치가 있어. 언제 필요해?

M 음, 사실, 다음주 금요일까지 독후감을 써야만 해. 가능하면 빨리 읽기 시작해야 해.

W 알겠어. 내일 아침에 가져 갈게.

① 그건 계속해서 읽고 싶어.
② 나는 그가 역사상 가장 훌륭한 작가라고 생각해.
③ 널 도서관까지 태워줄 수 있어.
④ 이번주 화요일까지 그에게 그걸 돌려줘야 해.

18 ④

W Are you playing computer games again, Elvis?

M No, Mom.

W Then what are you doing now?

M I'm writing an e-mail in English to my Australian e-pal, Melina.

W You wrote an e-mail last Friday too, right?

M Yes, Mom. But I want to improve my English writing skills as fast as possible.

W Oh, I see. Then, how often do you write to your e-pal?

M _____

W Elvis, 너 또 컴퓨터 게임을 하고 있니?

M 아니에요, 엄마.

W 그럼 지금 뭐 하고 있니?

M Melina라는 호주에 사는 이메일 친구에게 영어로 이메일을 쓰고 있어요.

W 지난 금요일에도 이메일을 썼잖아, 그렇지?

M 네, 엄마. 하지만 가능한 한 빨리 영어 쓰기 기술을 개선하고 싶거든요.

W 오, 그래. 그렇다면, 요즈음에 얼마나 자주 이메일 친구에게 편지를 쓰니?

M 그녀에게 적어도 한 달에 네 번 편지를 써요.

① 그녀는 일주일에 한 번 나에게 영어를 가르쳐 줘요.
② 당신의 충고를 들어야겠어요.
③ 그녀도 나에게 금요일마다 이메일을 보내요.
⑤ 그녀는 영어로 편지 쓰는 방법을 잘 몰라요.

19 ③

W Look. Here's the 20th Century World History Quiz in the magazine.

M Oh, let me give it a try. You know, I'm a world history lover.

W All right. First question: When did the Second World War take place?

M I guess it lasted from 1939 to 1945.

W The second question: How long has the United Nations been in existence?

M Uh, since 1945 when World War II ended. So the answer is 68 years.

W Hmm. Next question: How long were the Beatles together?

M Well, they started in 1960 and broke up in 1970, so they were together for 10 years. How am I doing so far?

W _____

W 이것 좀 봐. 이 잡지에 20세기 세계 역사 퀴즈가 있어.

M 아, 내가 한 번 해 볼게. 있잖아, 난 세계사 애호가잖아.

W 좋아. 첫 번째 문제: 언제 제2차 세계대전이 일어났지?

M 내 짐작에 1939에서부터 1945년까지야.

W 두 번째 문제: UN은 얼마나 오래 동안 존재하고 있지?

M 아, 제2차 세계대전이 끝난 1945년 이후로. 그러니까 답은 68년 동안이다.

W 음, 다음 문제: 비틀즈(the Beatles) 밴드는 얼마나 오랫동안 같이 있었지?

M 음, 그들은 1960년에 시작해서 1970년에 해체됐으니까 10년 동안 같이 있었네. 내가 지금까지 어떻게 하고 있니?

W 와, 네 모든 답들이 맞았어!

① 나도 역사 애호가야.
② 넌 과거에 관심이 없구나.
④ 곧 너와 함께 도서관에 갈 것을 약속할게.
⑤ 역사가 내가 가장 좋아하는 것을 어떻게 알았어?

20 ④

M Norah was on her way home. Then she saw a nice T-shirt in a clothing store. She thought it would look good on her brother, Harry. So Norah wanted to call her brother to know about his size and his favorite color. But she forgot to take her Cellphone when she left home. There was no public phone booth around. So, Norah decided to enter the store and ask a favor of the clerk. In this situation, what would Norah say to the clerk?

M Norah는 귀가 중이었다. 그때 그녀는 옷가게에서 멋진 티셔츠를 보았다. 그녀는 그것이 그녀의 남동생 Harry에게 잘 어울릴 것이라고 생각했다. 그래서 Norah는 남동생의 사이즈와 가장 좋아하는 색상을 알기 위해 남동생에게 전화하기를 원했다. 하지만 그녀는 집을 나설 때 휴대전화 가져오는 것을 잊었다. 주변에는 공중전화 박스가 없었다. 그래서 Norah는 가게에 들어가서 점원에게 도움을 청하기로 결심했다. 이 상황에서, Norah는 점원에게 무슨 말을 할까?

① 메시지를 남겨도 될까요?
② 새 일자리가 마음에 드세요?
③ 저를 보고 싶으세요?
④ 잠깐 전화 좀 써도 되겠습니까?
⑤ 사기 전에 바로 여기서 티셔츠를 입어 봐도 됩니까?

01 ①	02 ④	03 ②	04 ②, ➕⑤	05 ⑤
06 ④	07 ①	08 ⑤	09 ④	10 ②, ➕①
11 ②	12 ⑤	13 ⑤	14 ①	15 ②
16 ②	17 ①	18 ②	19 ④	20 ②

01 ①

M I really envy my older brother. First, he has such a great sense of humor that people always laugh and smile when they are around him. Second, he is physically fit, which I envy him most. He can do many things that I can't even dream of doing. Now he is standing on his hands. He can even walk on his hands. I can't do that for a second. I can't do that even when someone holds my legs.

M 나는 형이 정말 부럽다. 우선, 형은 유머 감각이 아주 뛰어나서 그가 주변에 있으면 사람들은 웃음을 터뜨리고 미소를 짓는다. 둘째, 형은 신체적으로 튼튼한데, 난 그 점이 가장 부럽다. 그는 내가 꿈꿀 수도 없는 많은 것들을 할 수 있다. 그는 지금 물구나무서기를 하고 있다. 그는 심지어 물구나무서기를 한 채 걸을 수도 있다. 나는 그것을 단 일 초도 할 수 없다. 나는 심지어 누가 내 다리를 잡아 주더라도 할 수 없다.

02 ④

[Cellphone rings.]

W Hi, James.

M Hey, is everything ready for your trip?

W Almost. I've booked the flight tickets and guest houses. And I've almost finished packing.

M Great. How long will you stay in New Zealand?

W Ten days. Actually, James, I have a favor to ask you.

M What is it?

W The thing is, I haven't found anyone to feed my cat while I'm away. Can you help me with that?

M No problem. I'll stop by your place and take care of your cat every day. I'll give him food and empty the litter box.

W Thank you so much!

M You're welcome. You took care of my dog while I was away last month.

[휴대 전화가 울린다.]

W 안녕, 제임스.

M 여행 준비는 끝났니?

W 거의. 비행기 표랑 게스트하우스는 예약했어. 그리고 짐도 거의 다 쌌어.

M 잘됐다. 뉴질랜드에는 얼마나 머물 거야?

W 열흘간. 사실 제임스, 나 부탁할 게 있어.

M 뭔데?

W 내가 가는 동안 내 고양이 밥을 챙겨줄 사람을 구하지 못했어. 너에게 부탁해도 될까?

M 문제 없어. 너네 집에 들러서 매일 고양이를 챙겨줄게. 먹이도 주고 변기도 비워주고.

W 정말 고마워!

M 괜찮아. 저번 달 내가 없었을 때 네가 내 개도 돌봐줬잖아.

03 ②

① M How much do you want for this bike?
   W It's $150.
② M Don't be afraid and just keep on pedaling.
   W Wow, this is a lot of fun. But don't let it go.
③ M Can you wrap it up for me?
   W Sure. Hold on a second.
④ M When can I pick the bike up?
   W In two or three hours.
⑤ M How long will it take from here to your school?
   W It'll take thirty minutes by bike.

① M 이 자전거 값으로 얼마 받기를 원합니까?
   W 150달러입니다.
② M 무서워하지 말고 그냥 계속 페달을 돌려.
   W 와, 이거 굉장히 재미있는데요. 하지만 손을 놓지 마세요.
③ M 포장해 주시겠어요?
   W 물론이죠. 잠시만 기다리세요.
④ M 언제 자전거를 찾을 수 있을까요?
   W 두 시간 내지 세 시간 후에요.
⑤ M 여기서부터 학교까지는 얼마나 걸릴까요?
   W 자전거로 30분 걸려요.

04 ② | ➕⑤

M Tina, it's almost Friday. Do you have any plans for this weekend?

W Nothing special.

M Then, let's watch a movie together.

W Okay! Where do you want to watch one, at your place or at the movie theater?

M It's always more fun to go to the theater.

W I think so too. Let's watch a thriller.

M Sounds good. What about meeting at 5 on Saturday?

W Oh, sorry, but I have a tennis lesson at 4, and it finishes at 5. How about at 6 on Saturday, or anytime on Sunday?

M Then, let's meet at 6 p.m. on Saturday. See you in front of New Line Theater.

M 티나, 이제 거의 금요일이야. 이번주 주말에 무슨 계획이라도 있어?

W 특별히 없어.

M 그럼 같이 영화 보러 갈래?

W 좋아! 어디서 보길 원해, 너네 집 아니면 영화관?

M 영화관에 가는 게 항상 더 재미있지.

W 나도 그렇게 생각해. 우리 스릴러 보자.

M 좋아. 토요일 5시에 만날까?

W 아 미안하지만 나 4시에 테니스 수업이 있어서 5시에 끝나. 토요일 6시나 일요일 아무 때나 보는 건 어때?

M 그럼 토요일 6시에 보자. 뉴 라인 극장 앞에서 봐.

05 ⑤

[Telephone rings.]

W Hello.

M Hi, Jenny. It's Torres. Guess what I have?

W Torres. You know I'm working. What is it?

M All right. I've got two tickets for Jim Tommy's first concert tomorrow. Do you want to come?

W I'd like to, but I can't.

M Why? Isn't he your favorite singer?

W Yes, he is. But I've promised my co-worker that I'd work for her tomorrow night.

M Can't you reschedule it?

W Yes, but if I try, she'll be disappointed in me.

[전화벨이 울린다.]

W 여보세요.

M 안녕, Jenny. 나 Torres야. 내가 뭘 가지고 있는지 알아맞혀 볼래?

W Torres. 내가 지금 근무 중인 것을 알고 있지. 그게, 뭔데 그래?

M 알았어. 내일 있을 Jim Tommy의 첫 번째 콘서트 입장권 두 장이 있어. 가고 싶니?

W 가고는 싶지만 갈 수가 없어.

M 왜? 그는 네가 가장 좋아하는 가수 아니야?

W 맞아. 하지만 난 동료에게 내일 대신 야근을 해 주기로 약속했어.

M 재조정할 수는 없는 거야?

W 할 수는 있겠지만, 내가 그러면 그녀가 나에게 실망할 거야.

06 ④

M Jessica, come over here.

W Yes, sir.

M When you're playing defense, keep your knees bent and your body low.

W Like this?

M That's right. That way, you can keep your balance.

W Should I stand with my legs close together or far apart?

M It is best to keep them about shoulder-width apart.

W I see. I'll keep that in mind.

M Jessica, 이리 와 보렴.

W 네, 선생님.

M 방어를 할 때, 무릎을 굽히고 몸을 낮춰.

W 이렇게요?

M 그래. 그렇게 해야 균형을 잘 유지할 수 있어.

W 다리를 가까이 모으고 서 있어야 하나요, 아니면 벌리고 서 있어야 하나요?

M 어깨 넓이로 벌리는 게 가장 좋아.

W 알겠습니다. 염두에 두겠습니다.

만점 솔루션 수비할 때의 자세에 관해 설명해 주고 여자가 따라 해 보는 상황이므로 코치와 운동 선수의 관계로 볼 수 있다.

07 ①

① **M** You have the wrong number.

W Let me leave a message.

② **M** Can I speak to Damon?

W I'm sorry, but his line is busy.

③ **M** How do you come to school?

W I go to school by bicycle.

④ **M** Excuse me. What time do you have?

W It's a quarter to seven.

⑤ **M** Are you ready to order?

W Coffee will do.

① **M** 전화 잘못 거셨습니다.

W 메시지를 남길게요.

② **M** Damon과 통화할 수 있을까요?

W 죄송합니다만, 그는 통화중입니다.

③ **M** 학교에 어떻게 등교하니?

W 나는 자전거를 타고 등교해.

④ **M** 실례합니다. 몇 시입니까?

W 7시 15분 전입니다.

⑤ **M** 주문하시겠습니까?

W 커피 주세요.

만점 솔루션 ① 잘못 걸린 전화에 대해 이 사실을 알려주고 있으므로 메시지를 남기겠다는 응답은 적절하지 않다. 이런 경우 사과하고(I'm sorry.) 전화를 끊는 것이 일반적이다.

08 ⑤

W Steve, where are you going?

M I'm going to Professor Johnson's office.

W Didn't you turn in your report yet?

M Yes, I did. It was due yesterday. I'm going to ask him to write me a letter of recommendation.

W Oh, I see. Will you do me a favor?

M Sure. What is it?

W Can you check if my report was turned in? I mailed it the other day.

M No problem.

W Steve, 어디 가니?

M Johnson 교수님의 연구실에 가는 중이야.

W 보고서 아직 안 냈니?

M 냈지. 어제가 마감 기한이었잖아. 교수님께 추천서를 써 달라고 부탁드리려고.

W 오, 그렇구나. 부탁 하나 들어줄래?

M 물론이지. 뭔데?

W 내 보고서가 제출되었는지 확인해 줄래? 내가 일전에 우편으로 보냈거든.

M 그거야 쉽지.

09 ④

W Hello, riders! For your wonderful experience, I'd like to say a few things. First, make sure to hold the safety bar in front of you. Second, don't stand up during the ride. Last, don't leave your seat until the train comes to a complete stop. Now, you're ready for an exciting ride. Here we go!

W 안녕하세요, 탑승객 여러분! 멋진 경험이 될 수 있도록 몇 가지만 말씀드리고 싶습니다. 우선, 앞에 있는 안전 막대를 반드시 잡아 주세요. 그리고 탑승 동안 일어나서는 안 됩니다. 마지막으로, 기차가 완전히 멈출 때까지 좌석을 벗어나지 마세요. 이제, 여러분은 흥미진진한 탑승을 위한 준비가 되었습니다. 출발합니다!

10 ② | ➕ ①

M Good afternoon. How may I help you?

W I'd like to buy two tickets for the Dali exhibition.

M I'm sorry, but the tickets for the morning admission are sold out. We do have a few tickets left for the afternoon admission.

W Okay. I'll buy two of those.

M They're 10,000 won each. Do you have our membership card?

W Here you are.

M You have a total of 4,000 points. You can use them as 4,000 won and pay the difference, if you want.

W Yes, I'll do that. Here's 20,000 won.

M 안녕하세요. 무엇을 도와드릴까요?

W 달리 전시회 표를 두 장 사고 싶어요.

M 죄송하지만 오전 입장 표는 매진됐어요. 오후 입장 표가 약간 남아 있습니다.

W 알겠어요. 그럼 그걸로 두 장 살게요.

M 각각 만원입니다. 회원 카드를 갖고 계신가요?

W 여기요.

M 4천 포인트를 갖고 계시네요. 원하시면, 이 포인트를 4천원으로 사용해서 차액을 지불할 수도 있습니다.

W 네, 그렇게 할게요. 여기 2만원이요.

11 ②

M Hello, come on in.

W Hi. I hate to complain, but there is something wrong with this white dress.

M Really? What is it?

W Look at the dress. It turned yellow after dry-cleaned.

M Oh, no. I'm sorry about that. How can I compensate for the dress, ma'am?

W Could you dry-clean the dress again for free?

M Of course, I will do that. Also I'll give you five 50%-off coupons.

W That would be great. Thanks.

M 안녕하세요, 어서 오세요.

W 안녕하세요. 불평하긴 싫지만, 이 흰색 드레스에 뭔가 문제가 있는 것 같습니다.

M 그래요? 무슨 문제죠?

W 이 드레스를 보세요. 드라이클리닝 한 후에 노랗게 변했어요.

M 오, 이런. 죄송합니다. 손님, 그 드레스에 대한 보상을 어떻게 해 드릴까요?

W 무료로 그 드레스를 다시 드라이클리닝 해 주실 수 있죠?

M 물론, 그렇게 해 드려야죠. 또한 50% 할인 쿠폰도 5장 드리겠습니다.

W 좋습니다. 감사합니다.

12 ⑤

W Hello, everyone. I'd like to announce that there will be a jazz guitar session next Friday. We've invited the famous jazz musician Sandra Park to teach the key points of playing jazz music. While playing a popular jazz piece, she will demonstrate basic guitar skills. Those interested should register with Ms. Lee by next Wednesday. The session is free, but please bring your own guitar. Ms. Park will work one-on-one with each of the participants after her demonstration. Thank you.

W 안녕하세요, 여러분. 다음 주 금요일 재즈 기타 세션이 있다는 것을 알려드리려고 합니다. 우리는 재즈 음악 연주의 요점을 알려주기 위하여 유명한 재즈 음악가인 산드라 박을 초청하였습니다. 유명한 재즈 음악을 연주하면서 그녀는 기본적인 기타 기술을 보여줄 것입니다. 관심있으신 분들은 다음주 수요일까지 이 선생님에게 등록하세요. 이 세션은 무료지만 개인 기타를 가져오시기 바랍니다. 박 선생이 설명을 마친 뒤에 참가자 개개인과 1대 1로 연주를 봐줄 겁니다. 감사합니다.

13 ⑤

W Welcome to the Organic Mall. How may I help you?

M I want to visit the Herbal Tea Garden. Can you let me know where it is?

W Here's a map of the mall. I'll show you where it's located. We're right here next to the Green Food Restaurant.

M Oh, great! I can come back here later for lunch.

W Next to the restaurant, there's a fruit stand called True Apples. They sell apples grown without using any harmful chemicals.

M Oh, sounds great.

W If you turn left, you'll see Pies & Bakery. And next to the bakery, there's a gallery showing pictures of world organic farms. And there, across from the gallery, you'll find the Herbal Tea Garden.

W 오가닉 몰에 오신걸 환영합니다. 무엇을 도와드릴까요?

M 허브 티 가든에 가려고 하는데. 어디에 있는지 알려주실 수 있나요?

W 여기 지도가 있습니다. 위치를 보여 드릴게요. 우리가 그린 푸드 식당 바로 옆에 있습니다.

M 아 좋아요! 점심을 먹으러 나중에 여기 다시 올 수 있겠군요.

W 식당 옆에, 트루 애플스라고 불리는 과일 가게가 있습니다. 유해한 화학품을 사용하지 않고 키운 사과를 파는 곳이죠.

M 좋네요.

W 왼쪽으로 돌면 파이&베이커리가 보일 겁니다. 그리고 빵집 옆에 세계의 유기 농장 사진들을 보여주는 갤러리가 있습니다. 거기서 갤러리 건너편에서 허브 티 가든을 찾으실 수 있습니다.

14 ①

W Miranda loves animals. She has been interested in working as an animal rights activist. She has been doing volunteer work <u>at an animal shelter</u>. She takes care of abandoned or abused animals there. Last year, she adopted two cats from the shelter. She also keeps an online blog and <u>writes posts about animal rights</u>. She has been writing <u>a journal about animal testing</u>. She thinks that all experiments on animals must be stopped.

W 미란다는 동물을 좋아한다. 그녀는 동물 권리 운동가로 일하는 것에 관심이 있다. 그녀는 동물 보호소에서 봉사활동을 하고 있다. 그곳에서 버려지거나 학대 받은 동물들을 돌본다. 작년에 그녀는 보호소에서 고양이 두 마리를 입양했다. 그녀는 또한 동물 권리에 관한 온라인 블로그를 운영하며 글을 쓴다. 그녀는 동물 실험에 관한 기사를 집필하고 있다. 그녀는 동물에게 하는 모든 실험을 중단해야 한다고 생각한다.

15 ②

W I think we <u>made a right decision</u> to come out.
M Yes. At least we don't feel like being trapped in a hot cell.
W Look! There's an empty space here.
M We're lucky. Spread the mat. Wow! It's much cooler here.
W Look down the bridge. There are so many people under the bridge.
M Mary, <u>would you like to drink cold drink</u>?
W Sure.
M <u>I'll go buy some</u>. You just stay here and keep this place.

W 나오기로 결정을 잘한 것 같아요.
M 그래요. 적어도 더운 감옥에 갇혀 있다는 느낌은 안 들잖아요.
W 봐요! 여기 빈자리가 있어요.
M 우리가 운이 좋네요. 돗자리를 깔아요. 와! 이곳이 훨씬 더 시원하네요.
W 다리 밑을 봐요. 다리 밑에 많은 사람들이 있어요.
M Mary, 차가운 음료수를 마시고 싶어요?
W 물론이죠.
M 내가 가서 좀 사올게요. 여기에 있으면서 자리를 지켜요.

16 ②

M You know what? I have good news and bad news.
W What's the good news?
M I had an opportunity to <u>enter a prize-winning quiz contest</u>.
W Great! What's the bad news?
M I <u>failed to give correct answers</u> to the last two questions so I just won $100 instead of $1,000.
W You are still lucky to win $100.
M I guess you're right, but I could have won $1,000.

M 있잖아, 좋은 소식과 나쁜 소식이 하나씩 있어.
W 좋은 소식은 뭐야?
M 상금을 타는 퀴즈 대회에 참석할 수 있는 기회를 잡았어.
W 대단하군! 나쁜 소식은 뭐야?
M 마지막 두 문제의 답을 제시하지 못해서 1,000달러 대신 100달러를 받았어.
W 100달러를 받았으니 그래도 여전히 운이 좋은 거잖아.
M 네 말이 맞는 것 같아. 하지만 1,000달러를 탈 수도 있었잖아.

만점 솔루션 문제를 모두 맞힐 경우 받을 수 있는 상금이 1,000달러인데, 마지막 두 문제를 틀려서 100달러만 받았다.

17 ①

[Telephone rings.]
W Did you hear that Jenny's Big Market is closing down?
M Yeah. I'm sad to hear that <u>they're going out of business</u>.
W Me, too. Anyway, everything in the store will be 75% off.
M Seventy-five percent? That's great. I need a new Bluetooth speaker in my room. I should look for one there. Do you plan on getting anything?
W The last time I was there, I saw <u>a pair of running shoes</u> I liked. I need some because I've started jogging.
M Great! Let's go together. When does the sale begin?
W Oh, at 10 a.m. on Saturday. I think there'll be <u>long lines</u>.
M _____

[전화벨이 울린다.]
W 제니의 빅 마켓이 폐점한다는 거 알고 있었어?
M 응. 폐업하다니 슬프다.
W 나도. 아무튼, 가게의 모든 제품이 75% 세일이래.
M 75%? 굉장하다. 내 방에 새 블루투스 스피커가 필요해. 거기서 찾아야지. 넌 뭘 살 계획이야?
W 내가 마지막으로 거기 갔을 때, 마음에 드는 러닝화를 봤어. 조깅을 시작해서 그게 필요해.
M 잘됐다! 같이 가자. 세일은 언제 시작해?
W 토요일 오전10시에. 긴 줄이 있을 거 같아.
M 그럼 가능한 한 빨리 가자.

② 그럼 방을 치우자.
③ 그럼 내 자전거를 고칠게.
④ 그럼 모두에게 그것을 알릴게.
⑤ 그럼 그 프린터를 최대한 빨리 반납할게.

18 ③

M Tara, <u>have you moved into your new house</u>?
W Yes. We finally have our own place.
M So how do you feel?
W It's terrific. You know my husband and I constantly moved from one place to another. It was terrible.
M I can understand. And now are you going to <u>have a housewarming party</u>?
W _____

M Tara, 새 집으로 이사 들어갔니?
W 응. 마침내 우리 집이 생겼어.
M 그래 기분이 어때?
W 아주 좋아. 남편과 내가 이곳 저곳으로 늘 이사를 다녔잖아. 끔찍했어.

M 이해해. 그리고 지금 집들이 파티를 계획하고 있는 거지?

W 응. 다음 주 토요일이야.

① 음, 우리 집은 따뜻해.

② 물론이지. 이사 들어가는 것을 도와줄게.

④ 더 이상 이사를 다닐 필요가 없어.

⑤ 파티는 네가 도착한 이후에 시작할 거야.

19 ④

M Did you turn in our group report?

W Yes, Jack. But you should be more careful next time.

M What do you mean?

W I've taken a look at your part, found some mistakes, and corrected them.

M Oh, really? Like what?

W This is a copy of yours. Look. The year should be 2010, not 2009.

M Oh, that's right! I am sorry. And what else?

W _____

M 조별 보고서 제출했니?

W 응, Jack. 다음 번에는 좀 더 주의를 기울여 줘.

M 무슨 뜻이야?

W 네가 맡은 부분을 살펴보다가. 몇 가지 실수를 발견해서 수정했어.

M 오, 그래? 어떤 실수를 했는데?

W 이것이 네 부분의 복사본이야. 봐. 연도는 2009년이 아니라, 2010년이야.

M 오, 그렇구나! 미안해. 또 뭐가 있지?

W 여기 Eiti가 아니라 Haiti여야 해.

① 나도 실수를 했어.

② 우리가 최선을 다 했다는 것이 중요한 거야.

③ 괜찮아. 내가 할 수 있어.

⑤ 실수를 두려워하지 마.

> **만점 솔루션** 조별 보고서에서 남자가 맡은 부분에 오류가 있었다고 말하면서 그 예를 들어 주는 상황이다. 하나의 실수를 확인하고 또 뭐가 있는지를 묻고 있으므로, 또 다른 실수의 구체적인 예를 말해 주는 것이 가장 자연스럽다.

20 ②

W Mr. Park went to an English village with his students last week. There he met a native English teacher named Grey. They had a lot in common and saw eye to eye on a lot of issues. Mr. Park wanted to have an opportunity to practice his English. Mr. Grey also wanted to learn Korean. So they agreed to meet on weekends at least for three hours to practice English and Korean, and to learn about each other's cultures. In this situation, what will Mr. Park say to Mr. Grey?

W 박 선생님은 지난주 학생들과 영어마을에 갔다. 그곳에서 그분은 Gray라는 원어민 영어교사를 만났다. 그분들은 많은 공통점들이 있었고 여러 문제에 있어 의견이 완전히 똑같았다. 박 선생님은 영어를 연습할 기

회를 갖기 원했다. Grey 선생님도 또한 한국어를 배우기 원했다. 그래서 그들은 영어와 한국어, 그리고 각국의 문화에 대해 배우기 위해 주말 동안 적어도 세 시간은 만나기로 합의했다. 이 상황에서 박 선생님은 Grey 선생님께 무슨 말을 하겠는가?

① 너의 나라에 어떻게 가니?

② 우리 토요일에 만날 수 있을까 아니면 일요일에 만날 수 있을까?

③ 넌 우리 학생들에게 영어를 가르치고 싶니?

④ 너도 분명히 훌륭한 국어교사가 될 수 있을 거야.

⑤ 넌 나에게 어떤 영어사전을 추천하니?

01 ①	**02** ③	**03** ②	**04** ③, ➕④	**05** ②
06 ③	**07** ②	**08** ④, ➕③	**09** ⑤	**10** ①
11 ⑤	**12** ③	**13** ⑤	**14** ③	**15** ①
16 ②	**17** ⑤	**18** ④	**19** ③	**20** ④

01 ①

W Look at those frames. Aren't they pretty?
M Yes, they are. I want to buy one for my sister.
W Good idea. Which one would you like?
M How about the one with the moon and the stars in the corner?
W I think it's too simple. I like the one with a lot of stars.
M Well, actually a lot of things on one frame don't look good.
W Then how about this? It has only one flower.
M Hmm.... It looks simple and cute. I'll take it.

W 저 액자들 좀 봐요. 예쁘지 않아요?
M 네, 그러네요. 내 여동생을 위해 하나 사고 싶어요.
W 좋은 생각이에요. 뭐가 좋겠어요?
M 저 구석에 있는 달과 별이 있는 것은 어때요?
W 그건 너무 단순한 것 같아요. 별이 많은 것이 좋네요.
M 음, 사실 한 액자에 사물이 너무 많으면 좋아 보이지 않아요.
W 그럼 이건 어때요? 꽃 한 송이만 있네요.
M 흠…. 단순하고 귀엽네요. 그걸로 살게요.

02 ③

W Hello, School Life, Customer Service. How can I help you?
M Hi, I'd like to subscribe to your magazine.
W Sure. It's $10 a month. If you subscribe for six months, we'll give you a 5% discount of the total cost.
M What if I subscribe for one year?
W Then, you will get a 10% discount.
M Oh, that's great. Okay, I'll subscribe to your magazine for one year.
W No problem. May I have your name and address?
M My name is James Brown, and I live in 241 Paradise Apartment on Lake Street.
W That's all. Thank you very much.

W 안녕하세요. School Life 고객서비스센터입니다. 어떻게 도와드릴까요?
M 안녕하세요. 잡지 구독을 하고 싶습니다.
W 알겠습니다. 한 달에 10달러입니다. 만약 6개월 구독을 하시면 총 구독료에서 5% 할인해 드립니다.
M 일 년 구독하면 어떻게 되죠?
W 그러면 10% 할인 받을 수 있습니다.

M 아, 그거 괜찮은데요. 좋습니다, 일 년 동안 잡지 구독 신청을 하겠습니다.
W 알겠습니다. 이름과 주소를 알려 주시겠습니까?
M 제 이름은 James Brown이고, Lake Street에 있는 Paradise 아파트에 삽니다.
W 다 됐습니다. 대단히 감사합니다.

03 ②

① M Hi, Caren. Can you give me a ride?
　W Sure. Which way are you going?
② M Sorry, ma'am. We don't have any space.
　W Then, are there any other parking lots around here?
③ M Where did you park your car today?
　W I can't remember where my car is.
④ M How long will it take to go to your school?
　W Well, it'll take about 30 minutes by car.
⑤ M Ma'am. You were speeding.
　W No, I wasn't. I was driving at 80km per hour.

① M 안녕, Caren. 나 좀 태워다 줄래요?
　W 그럼요. 어느 방향인가요?
② M 실례합니다, 손님. 어떤 공간도 없네요.
　W 그렇다면, 이 주변에 다른 주차장들이 있습니까?
③ M 오늘 주차를 어디에 하셨습니까?
　W 내 차가 어디에 있는지 기억이 안 납니다.
④ M 학교까지 가는 데 얼마나 걸릴까요?
　W 음, 자동차로 대략 30분 걸릴 것입니다.
⑤ M 부인. 과속하셨습니다.
　W 아니요, 안 했어요. 시간당 80 킬로로 운전하고 있었습니다.

04 ③ | ➕④

W What's wrong, Ryan?
M Well, my mouth was a bit sore yesterday. And I have a terrible toothache this morning.
W Oh, dear. I think you should go to the dental clinic after school.
M Today? But I have to meet up with my team to talk about a group project at Ted's house. It was so difficult to arrange a time when everyone was free to meet.
W Then, why don't you go to the clinic during your lunch break?
M Can you give me a ride?
W No problem. Please get permission from your teacher to leave school.
M I will. The lunch break starts at noon.
W All right. I'll wait for you at the main gate.

W 무슨 일이야, 라이언?
M 어제 내 입이 좀 따가웠어. 그리고 오늘 아침에 끔찍한 치통에 시달렸어.
W 이런. 방과 후에 치과에 가봐.
M 오늘? 하지만 그룹 프로젝트에 대해 이야기하기 위해 테드네 집에서 팀

원들이랑 만나야 하는데. 모두들 만날 수 있는 시간을 잡기가 아주 어려웠어.

W 그러면 치과를 점심시간에 갔다 오는 거 어때?

M 나 좀 태워 줄래?

W 물론이지. 학교를 나가도 되는지 선생님한테 허락을 받아와.

M 그럴게. 점심시간은 정오에 시작해.

W 알겠어. 정문에서 기다릴게.

05 ②

W Hi, Michael. Did you say you had a party last Friday?

M Yeah. You didn't know about it? As you know, it was my birthday.

W No, I didn't know that. Did you invite me?

M Of course, I did. I sent you a Cellphone text message last week.

W Are you sure? I didn't get it. Oh, you know what? I didn't tell you something.

M What do you mean by that?

W I have a new Cellphone. I should have told you my new phone number. That's my fault.

M That's okay. But I was kind of upset that you didn't come to my party.

W Really? Let's go out for dinner today. I want to do something for your birthday.

M Thanks, but you don't have to do that.

W 안녕, Michael. 지난 금요일에 파티가 있었다고 말했니?

M 그래. 그것에 대해 모르고 있었니? 너도 알다시피, 내 생일이었어.

W 아니, 난 몰랐는데. 나를 초대했었니?

M 물론, 초대했지. 지난 주 너에게 휴대폰 문자 메시지를 보냈는데.

W 정말? 난 그것을 받지 못했는데. 아, 그런데 있잖아, 내가 너에게 말하지 않은 게 있어.

M 그게 무슨 말이야?

W 새 휴대폰을 샀거든. 내 새 전화번호를 너에게 말해 줬어야 했는데. 그것은 내 잘못이야.

M 괜찮아. 하지만 네가 내 파티에 오지 않아서 좀 당황했었어.

W 정말? 오늘 저녁식사 같이 하자. 네 생일을 위해 뭔가를 해 주고 싶네.

M 고맙지만, 그럴 필요 없어.

06 ③

W How may I help you?

M Yes. I bought this yesterday and I found this yellow stain this morning.

W Oh, I'm sorry, sir. I will exchange it for you.

M I want another one with the same design and color.

W Sorry we don't have any more now.

M That's too bad. Then can you order one for me?

W Yes. Maybe it'll take one week or so. When the new one arrives, we'll call you.

M Oh, that's too long. I would rather get my money back.

W All right, sir.

W 도와드릴까요?

M 이것을 어제 샀는데 오늘 아침에 이 노란색 얼룩을 발견했어요.

W 오, 죄송합니다, 손님. 교환해 드리겠습니다.

M 저는 똑같은 디자인과 색상의 다른 물건을 원합니다.

W 죄송합니다만 지금은 더 이상 없어요.

M 저런. 그러면 하나 주문해 줄 수 있어요?

W 네. 아마 일주일 정도 걸릴 겁니다. 새 물건이 도착하면, 전화 드리겠습니다.

M 오, 너무 오래 걸리네요. 차라리 환불 받는 게 낫겠어요.

W 좋습니다, 손님.

만점 솔루션 구입한 물건에서 얼룩을 발견한 남자가 새 물건으로 교환하고자 하나 일주일을 기다려야 하는 상황으로, 마지막에서 환불 받고 싶다(I would rather get my money back.)고 말하고 있다.

07 ②

① M Are you interested in drawing?

W Of course! I like art a lot.

② M Why don't you come skiing with us this weekend?

W Because I had too much homework to do.

③ M We'll go on a picnic this Sunday.

W I'm looking forward to it.

④ M What kind of job do you want to have in the future?

W I want to be a game developer.

⑤ M What do you usually do after school?

W I ride my bike at the park.

① M 그림 그리는 것에 관심이 있니?

W 물론이야! 난 미술을 정말 좋아해.

② M 이번 주말에 우리랑 같이 스키타는 거 어때?

W 해야 할 숙제가 너무 많았기 때문이야.

③ M 이번주 일요일에 우리 소풍 가는 거야.

W 기대하고 있어.

④ M 미래에 갖고 싶은 직업이 뭐야?

W 게임 개발자가 되고 싶어.

⑤ M 방과 후에 보통 무엇을 하니?

W 공원에서 자전거를 타.

08 ④ | ➕ ③

W I'm glad we can work together on the assignment.

M Me too, Sandy. Let's talk about the schedule.

W Sure. First, we need to choose a topic.

M Right. Let's choose one by Tuesday, after having a chance to think about it.

W All right.

M After we agree on the topic, we need to start researching and collecting materials. We should finish by June 1.

W Okay. And then, let's finish our visual aids for our presentation by [pause] June 21. Around that time, we can start practicing for the presentation.

M Great. Well, Sandy... do you think you can give the whole presentation? You're much better than I am at giving presentations.

W Oh, you want me to do it? Sure, why not? Then, can you handle making the visual aids yourself?

M Definitely. I'll do a good job.

W 우리가 같이 과제를 하게 되어서 기뻐.

M 나도야, 샌디. 스케줄에 대해 말해보자.

W 그래. 우선, 주제를 정해야 해.

M 맞아. 생각할 시간을 좀 가진 다음에, 화요일까지 하나를 고르자.

W 좋아.

M 주제를 정하고 나서, 자료 조사와 수집을 시작해야해. 6월 1일까지 끝내야 해.

W 알겠어. 그리고, 발표를 위한 시각 자료를 끝내자 [멈춤] 6월 21일까지. 그 즈음, 발표 연습을 시작할 수 있어.

M 좋아. 음, 샌디... 네가 모든 발표를 할 생각 있어? 내가 발표하는 거 보다 네가 훨씬 잘 하잖아.

W 아, 내가 다 했으면 좋겠어? 알겠어. 그러면 시각 자료 만드는 건 네가 알아서 할 수 있을까?

M 물론이지. 나 잘 할 수 있어.

09 ⑤

M When you travel to other countries, try to be prepared before you leave. If you don't know a lot about the country, you might pass by a very important place. So you must be prepared. You can read books or surf the Internet in order to learn about the history, language, culture and historical places to visit before you leave home. Then you will have a much more enjoyable trip.

M 다른 나라들을 여행할 때는 떠나기 전에 준비가 되도록 하라. 만약 그 나라에 대해 많은 것을 모른다면, 아주 중요한 장소를 그냥 지나치게 될지도 모른다. 그러므로 준비가 되어 있어야 한다. 집을 떠나기 전에 역사, 언어, 문화와 방문할 역사적 장소에 대해 배우기 위해 책을 읽거나 인터넷을 검색해 볼 수도 있다. 그러면 당신은 훨씬 더 즐거운 여행을 하게 될 것이다.

만점 솔루션 여행할 나라에 대한 책을 읽거나 인터넷을 검색해 그 나라의 역사·언어·문화 등에 대해 미리 공부해 두면 더 즐거운 여행을 할 수 있다고 말하고 있는 담화이다.

10 ①

W What can I help you with, sir?

M How much will it cost to copy this report?

W It's 10 cents per page.

M There are 40 pages. I need two copies of the whole report.

W OK, sir. They'll be ready by 2:30.

M Could you make it a little earlier? I need them by 2:00

W Well, let's see.... OK. I'll try. Please come back and pick them up then.

M Thanks. Here is $10.

W 도와드릴까요, 손님?

M 이 보고서를 복사하는데 비용이 얼마가 들죠?

W 한 쪽당 10센트입니다.

M 40쪽입니다. 보고서 전체 2부를 복사해야 합니다.

W 알겠습니다, 손님. 2시 반까지 준비될 거예요.

M 조금 더 빨리 할 수 있나요? 2시까지 필요하거든요.

W 음… 어디 보죠…. 알겠습니다. 해 보죠. 그때 오셔서 가져가십시오.

M 고맙습니다. 여기 10달러입니다.

만점 솔루션 40쪽을 한 쪽에 10센트씩 복사하면 4달러, 2부 복사하니까 모두 8달러를 지불해야 한다. 남자가 10달러를 냈으므로 거스름돈은 2달러가 된다.

11 ⑤

[Telephone rings.]

W Genesis Shipping. May I help you?

M Hello. I'm Kevin Battle of Sunny Trading. Can I speak to Julian Russell?

W Sorry. He's not in now. Would you like to leave a message?

M Thanks. Please tell him that he doesn't have to come to our company tomorrow.

W OK. Let me have him call you as soon as he gets back.

M Good. My number is 2033-1232. Hmm.... I'll call him again. What time will he be back in the office?

W He will come back in an hour. Please call back around five and you can talk to him.

M All right. Thanks. Bye.

[전화벨이 울린다.]

W Genesis 해운 회사입니다. 도와드릴까요?

M 여보세요. 전 Sunny 무역의 Kevin Battle입니다. Julian Russell과 통화할 수 있을까요?

W 죄송합니다. 지금 자리에 안 계십니다. 메시지를 남기시겠습니까?

M 고맙습니다. 내일 우리 회사에 오실 필요가 없다고 그에게 전해 주십시오.

W 알겠습니다. 그가 돌아오는 대로 전화 드리도록 하겠습니다.

M 좋습니다. 제 번호는 2033-1232입니다. 흠…. 제가 그에게 다시 전화하겠습니다. 그가 몇 시에 사무실에 돌아올까요?

W 한 시간 후에 돌아오실 거예요. 5시경 다시 전화 주시면 통화하실 수 있을 겁니다.

M 알겠습니다. 감사합니다. 안녕히 계십시오.

만점 솔루션 남자가 다시 전화를 걸겠다(I'll call him again.)고 말하고 있으므로 ⑤가 일치하지 않는 내용이다.

12 ③

M Good afternoon. Welcome to the JBS FM show and I'm your host Jerry Hoffman. Today, we have Maria Robertson in this studio. She is one of the most talented singers of our time. She was born in 1995 in Chicago and moved to New York when she was ten years old. In New York she started taking singing and dancing lessons from her uncle, Bill Smith. As you know Bill Smith was one of the world-famous entertainers during the 1990s. After six years' hard training, she became the most popular singer in the country. Please welcome Maria Robertson.

M 안녕하세요. JBS FM 쇼에 오신 것을 환영합니다. 저는 여러분의 사회자 Jerry Hoffman입니다. 오늘, 이 스튜디오에 Maria Robertson 씨를 모셨습니다. 그녀는 우리 시대의 가장 재능 있는 가수들 중의 한 분이십니다. 시카고에서 1995년에 태어났고 열 살 때 뉴욕으로 이사했습니다. 뉴욕에서 그녀의 삼촌인 Bill Smith로부터 노래와 춤 수업을 받기 시작했습니다. 여러분도 아시다시피, Bill Smith는 1990년대 세계적으로 가장 유명한 예능인들 중 한 분이십니다. 6년간의 혹독한 훈련 후, 그녀는 이 나라에서 가장 인기 있는 가수가 되었습니다. 자, Maria Robertson 씨를 환영해 주시기 바랍니다.

13 ⑤

[Cellphone rings.]

M Hi, Emma.

W Hi, Mike. I've just got off the bus at the campground. I'm right in front of the entrance. Where is your tent?

M Can you see the information center? It is across from the bus stop.

W Yes, I can see it.

M Well, walk inside the campground, passing by the information center, and you will see a small lake on your right.

W Got it.

M When you pass by the cabins around the lake, there are lots of picnic tables.

W Okay.

M You'll find a couple of tents behind them. My tent is the red one.

W Okay. I think I can find you. See you in a few minutes.

M Yup. See you!

[휴대 전화가 울린다.]

M 안녕, 엠마.

W 안녕, 마이크. 나 막 캠핑장에 버스에서 내렸어. 입구 바로 앞이야. 네 텐트는 어디에 있어?

M 정보 센터 보여? 버스 정류장 건너편이야.

W 응. 보여.

M 정보 센터를 지나서 캠핑장으로 걸어 들어와, 그럼 오른쪽에 작은 호수가 보일 거야.

W 알겠어.

M 호수 근처에 오두막들을 지나면 피크닉용 테이블이 많이 있어.

W 응.

M 그 뒤에 텐트 두 개가 보일 거야. 내 텐트는 빨간색이야.

W 알겠어. 찾을 수 있을 거 같아. 좀 있다 봐.

M 알겠어. 곧 만나.

14 ③

W We invite all of you to the Concert in the Park! It is a perfect event for the entire family to enjoy a summer night out! It's going to be held at Central Park on Saturday from 6 to 9 p.m. Bring your own picnic blanket and chairs to have a relaxing time on the lawn. Food will be available at food trucks in the park, or you can bring your own food and drinks. Please visit the park website and check out the musicians performing at the concert.

W 공원에서 열리는 콘서트에 모두를 초대합니다! 온 가족이 여름 밤을 야외에서 즐길 수 있는 완벽한 행사입니다. 콘서트는 토요일 6시부터 9시까지 센트럴 파크에서 열립니다. 잔디에서 느긋한 시간을 보낼 수 있도록 피크닉용 담요와 의자를 가져오세요. 음식은 공원에 있는 푸드 트럭을 사용할 수도 있고 본인 음식이나 음료를 가져와도 됩니다. 공원 웹사이트를 방문하여 콘서트에서 공연하는 음악가들을 확인하세요.

15 ①

M What are you reading, Susan?

W I'm reading a newspaper. Look at the pictures! I can't believe my eyes!

M What are they?

W These pictures show oil covering miles of the ocean.

M Again?

W Yes, it's near the western coast. The newspaper says it has a lot of pollution problems.

M That's true. We throw away too much and don't recycle enough.

W Yes, we're running out of places for all our garbage. Don't you think so?

M You're absolutely right. I think we should find ways to solve these environmental problems right away.

W I couldn't agree with you more.

M Susan, 뭘 읽고 있어?

W 이 신문에 사진들 좀 봐! 내 눈을 믿을 수가 없네!

M 무슨 일이 일어났는데?

W 이 사진들이 수 마일에 걸쳐 바다를 덮고 있는 기름을 보여줘.

M 또?

W 그래, 서해안 근처야. 이 신문은 또한 많은 오염 문제가 있다고 해.

M 맞아. 우리는 너무 많은 것을 버리고 흡족할 만큼 재활용하지 않아.

W 그래, 모든 쓰레기를 처리하기 위한 땅들이 고갈되고 있어. 그렇게 생각하지 않니?

M 네 말이 전적으로 맞아. 우린 당장 이러한 환경문제 해결을 위한 방안들을 찾아야 한다고 나는 생각해.

W 전적으로 동감이다.

만점 솔루션 I couldn't agree with you more.는 '더 이상 동의 할 수 없었다.'라는 의미로 부정어(not)가 있으나 강한 긍정의 의미가 있는 문장이다.

16 ②

M What are you going to do when you grow up?

W I'd like to travel to Africa and help people there.

M Sounds like a great idea. But in what way?

W I'll stay there for a while and find out how I can help sick people.

M Then how about studying medicine?

W Yes. That's what I am thinking now.

M Or you can help them by teaching them <u>how to grow more food</u>.

W You're right. Many people are starving there. But mostly I want to <u>help sick people</u>.

M 넌 커서 뭐가 될 거니?

W 난 아프리카에 가서 그곳의 사람들을 돕고 싶어.

M 훌륭한 생각인 것 같은데. 하지만 어떤 방식으로?

W 잠시 그곳에 머물면서 내가 아픈 사람들을 도울 수 있는 방법을 알아볼 거야.

M 그러면 의학을 공부하는 게 어때?

W 지금 내가 생각하는 게 바로 그거야.

M 아니면 더 많은 식량을 재배하는 방법을 가르쳐서 그들을 도울 수도 있어.

W 네 말이 맞아. 그곳의 많은 사람들이 굶주리고 있어. 하지만 주로 난 아픈 사람들을 도와주고 싶어.

17 ⑤

W Kyle, it's time you <u>got back to your homework</u>.

M Can I have 30 more minutes, Mom?

W Come on. You should finish your homework first.

M OK. But can I play games again after I finish?

W No, you can't. <u>I'm using it from now on</u>. I have <u>something to be done</u> by tomorrow.

M What about your laptop?

W It doesn't work. I <u>took it to the service center</u>.

M Again? Oh, no. When is it coming back?

W I don't know. They will call me when it's ready.

W Kyle, 다시 숙제를 할 시간이야.

M 엄마, 30분 더 하면 안 돼요?

W 얘야. 숙제를 먼저 끝내야지.

M 알았어요. 하지만 숙제 끝내고 다시 해도 돼요?

W 아니, 안 돼. 지금부터는 내가 쓸 거야. 내일까지 해야 할 일이 있단다.

M 엄마의 노트북은요?

W 작동하지를 않아. 수리점에 그것을 가져갔단다.

M 또요? 오, 이런. 언제 갖고 와요?

W 모르겠어. 다 되면 그들이 내게 전화할 거야.

> **만점 솔루션** 엄마가 컴퓨터로 일을 해야 해서 남자가 숙제를 하고 나서도 컴퓨터 게임을 할 수 없는 상황이다.

18 ④

W <u>Are you ready to order, sir</u>?

M I'll have a hamburger and a cup of cocoa, please.

W A hamburger and a cup of cocoa. Will that be all?

M Wait a second. How much is <u>an order of</u> French fries?

W It's $1.50.

M OK. I'll take that, too. <u>How much do I owe you</u> now?

W _____

W 주문하시겠습니까, 손님?

M 햄버거와 코코아 한 잔 주세요.

W 햄버거와 코코아 한 잔. 전부인가요?

M 잠깐만요. 감자튀김 1인분은 얼마죠?

W 1달러 50센트입니다.

M 좋아요. 그것도 하죠. 이제 제가 낼 돈이 얼마인가요?

W <u>모두 4달러 50센트입니다.</u>

① 고맙습니다, 손님.

② 아니요, 그렇게 생각하지 않습니다.

③ 왜 그게 그렇게 비싼가요?

⑤ 미안합니다. 전 감자튀김을 좋아하지 않습니다.

> **만점 솔루션** 남자의 마지막 말이 지불해야 할 금액이 얼마인지 묻고 있으므로, 가격을 말하는 응답이 와야 한다.

19 ③

W Quick. Get in the car. I don't want to <u>run red lights</u>.

M Hey, don't start driving yet.

W Why? The engine is running.

M It is. But it still needs to warm up first.

W What do you mean?

M When it's cold you have to <u>warm up the engine</u> before driving.

W Oh, should I wait until the car is warmed up?

M Right. That's the best way <u>not to have an engine problem</u> in the future.

W _____

W 서둘러요. 차에 타세요. 신호 위반을 하고 싶지는 않거든요.

M 이봐요, 아직 차를 운전하지 말아요.

W 왜요? 엔진이 작동하는데요.

M 그래요. 하지만 먼저 예열을 할 필요가 있어요.

W 무슨 말인가요?

M 추울 때는 운전하기 전에 엔진을 예열해 줘야 해요.

W 오, 자동차가 예열될 때까지 기다려야 하는 군요?

M 맞아요. 그게 앞으로 엔진의 문제가 없도록 하는 가장 좋은 방법이에요.

W <u>알았어요. 명심할게요.</u>

① 하지만 교통 정체가 심해요.

② 내 차가 또 고장 났어요.

④ 그럼요. 당신은 정말로 차를 좋아하네요.

⑤ 우리 지금 드라이브 가지 않을래요?

20 ④

W Paul had final exams last week. He is glad the exams <u>are all over now</u>. Christina calls Paul and tells him that she <u>wants to go bowling with him</u> at 5:00. But Paul tells her he has a piano lesson this evening. Christina <u>wants to know if he can cancel the lesson</u> and <u>take it tomorrow instead</u>. In this situation, what would Christina most likely say to Paul?

W Paul은 지난주에 기말고사를 보았다. 그는 이제 시험이 모두 끝나서 기쁘다. Christina가 Paul에게 전화를 걸어서 5시에 볼링 치러 가자고 말한다. 하지만 Paul은 오늘 저녁에 피아노 수업이 있다고 말한다. Christina는 그 수업을 취소하고 대신 내일 그 수업을 받아도 되는지 알고 싶어 한다. 이 상황에서, Christina는 Paul에게 뭐라고 말할 것 같은가?

① 나 볼링 잘 해.
② 나 대신 그 수업을 들어줄래?
③ 미안하지만 내일까지 그것을 미룰 수 없어.
④ 내일로 그 수업을 미룰 수 있니?
⑤ 오늘 너 피아노 연습을 해야 하니?

영어듣기능력평가 10회

01 ④	02 ⑤	03 ②	04 ①	05 ①
06 ②	07 ④	08 ④, ❸②	09 ③	10 ③
11 ⑤	12 ③	13 ⑤	14 ②	15 ④
16 ①	17 ②, ❸③	18 ②	19 ②	20 ⑤

01 ④

M How may I help you?
W I'm looking for an air purifier for my new house.
M These are all brand-new models.
W Oh, great. Do they make a lot of noise?
M Well, they're not that noisy—about as loud as an electronic fan.
W Then, I think I like that one that has a square base and a circle on the top. How much is it?
M It's $500. If you have our shop's membership card, we can give you a 10% discount.
W Oh, great! Then, I'll take that one.

M 무엇을 도와드릴까요?
W 새 집을 위한 공기 청정기를 찾고 있어요.
M 이것들이 다 새로 나온 모델들이에요.
W 아, 멋지네요. 소음이 많이 나요?
M 음, 그렇게 시끄럽지는 않아요. 선풍기 정도의 소음입니다.
W 그럼, 아래가 사각형이고 위가 원형인 이 제품이 마음에 드네요. 얼마인가요?
M 500달러입니다. 저희 가게 회원 카드가 있으시면 10%할인을 받으실 수 있습니다.
W 잘됐네요! 그럼 이 제품으로 할게요.

02 ⑤

[Telephone rings.]
M Hello. Who's speaking?
W Hi, Bill. It's Cindy. Can you tell me how to save images from the websites?
M No problem. Are you in front of your computer now?
W Yes, I'm ready.
M First click on the thumbnail image to see the full size version.
W I did. And then?
M Right-click on the mouse button, and select 'save as'. And select a destination on your hard drive for saving the file. Are you following me?
W Yes, I am. Now is the file available for me to use?
M Yes, it is.
W Thanks, Bill. You're always so helpful.

[전화벨이 울린다.]

M 여보세요. 누구시죠?

W 안녕, Bill. 나 Cindy야. 웹사이트에서 이미지들을 저장하는 방법 좀 알려 줄 수 있니?

M 물론이지. 지금 네 컴퓨터 앞에 있니?

W 그래, 준비됐어.

M 우선, 실물 크기 형태를 보기 위해 견본 이미지를 클릭해.

W 했어. 그 다음에?

M 마우스 버튼 오른쪽을 클릭하고 '다른 이름으로 저장하기'를 선택해. 그리고 하드 드라이브에 그 파일을 저장할 곳을 정해. 내 말 알아듣고 있니?

W 그래. 이제 그 파일을 내가 사용할 수 있는 거니?

M 응, 그래.

W 고맙다. Bill. 넌 항상 많은 도움을 주는 구나.

03 ②

① **W** May I help you?

　M Yes, I'd like to <u>exchange this shirt</u> I bought here.

② **W** *[sigh]* It was such a long trip.

　M You must be very tired. Let me take your suitcase for you.

③ **W** Excuse me. Where is Max's Kitchen?

　M I'm sorry. I'm <u>not familiar with</u> this neighborhood.

④ **W** Can you help me clean up the classroom?

　M Sure. I can help you.

⑤ **W** How are you feeling today?

　M I have a terrible headache. And I'm coughing a lot.

① **W** 도와드릴까요?

　M 네, 여기서 산 이 셔츠를 교환하고 싶습니다.

② **W** *[한숨]* 정말 긴 여행이었어.

　M 정말 지쳤겠다. 내가 네 여행 가방을 들어줄게.

③ **W** 실례합니다. 맥스의 키친이 어디인가요?

　M 죄송해요. 저도 이 동네는 잘 몰라요.

④ **W** 교실 청소하는 걸 도와줄래?

　M 물론. 내가 도와줄게.

⑤ **W** 오늘 기분이 어때?

　M 끔찍한 두통이 있어. 그리고 기침도 많이 해.

04 ①

[Telephone rings.]

W Dr. Jones's clinic. How may I help you?

M Hi, this is Kevin Clark. I <u>made an appointment</u> for Wednesday, but I'd like to see the doctor today if possible.

W I'm sorry, Mr. Clark. It's Monday today, and Monday <u>is always all booked up</u>. It's hard to schedule an appointment on such short notice.

M I <u>have a business trip</u> scheduled from Tuesday to Friday. I really need to see him before I go.

W Hmm... Let me see if I can squeeze you in. What about at 5:00 p.m. today?

M Could I see him this morning?

W Hmm... Dr. Jones has a break from 10:30. I'll <u>arrange</u> an <u>appointment</u> before then. Please arrive here by 10 at the latest.

M Okay. Thank you so much.

[전화벨이 울린다.]

W 존스 박사의 병원입니다. 무엇을 도와드릴까요?

M 안녕하세요. 저는 케빈 클락이라고 합니다. 수요일에 예약을 잡았는데 가능하면 오늘 병원에 가고 싶어서요.

W 죄송합니다. 오늘은 월요일이고, 월요일은 항상 예약이 가득 차 있습니다. 이렇게 갑작스럽게 일정을 잡는 것은 어렵습니다.

M 갑자기 목요일부터 금요일까지 출장을 가게 되었어요. 가기 전에 꼭 선생님을 뵈어야 합니다.

W 음... 비집어 넣을 수 있는지 봐야겠네요. 오늘 5시는 어떠세요?

M 오늘 오전은 안될까요?

W 음... 존스 선생님이 10시 30분부터 휴식이시니까 그 전으로 예약을 잡아 드릴게요. 적어도 10시에 오세요.

M 알겠습니다. 감사합니다.

05 ①

W Calvin, are you OK?

M Yeah, I guess. In fact, I <u>had a fight with</u> my brother and I feel bad.

W What did you fight about?

M I wanted to use the computer to play a game and he wanted to write a report. I was <u>too selfish</u>.

W Cheer up! He'll <u>get over it</u> soon.

M Thanks. I know you're right.

W Maybe you'd better call him <u>to apologize</u>.

M Good idea! Can I use your Cellphone?

W Sure! Here it is.

W Calvin, 괜찮니?

M 응, 그런 것 같아. 사실, 남동생과 싸워서 기분이 좋지 않아.

W 뭐 때문에 싸웠는데?

M 게임을 하기 위해 내가 컴퓨터를 사용하고 싶었는데, 동생이 보고서를 쓰기를 원했어. 내가 너무 이기적이었지.

W 힘 내! 동생이 곧 그것을 잊어버릴 거야.

M 고맙다. 네 말이 맞아.

W 동생에게 사과하기 위해 전화하는 게 좋겠어.

M 좋은 생각이다! 네 휴대 전화 좀 쓸 수 있니?

W 물론이지! 여기 있어.

06 ②

M OK. <u>What happened</u> next?

W The woman gave him a large box.

M A box! What did it <u>look like</u>?

W It was just square and brown. Nothing special.

M What did Mr. Smith do then?

W He took the box. And he looked very frightened.

M Why did he look frightened? What was in the box?

W I don't know. He didn't open it. He just took it and left in a hurry.

M Where did he go? And where did the woman go?

W Toward the parking lot. And the woman was still there when I heard his car drive away at top speed.

M 좋습니다. 다음에 무슨 일이 일어났죠?

W 그 여자가 그에게 큰 상자를 건넸습니다.

M 상자를요! 그것은 어떻게 생겼죠?

W 그냥 정사각형에 갈색이었습니다. 특별한 것은 없었습니다.

M 그 때 Smith 씨가 뭘 했죠?

W 그 상자를 받았습니다. 그리고 그는 매우 겁에 질린 것처럼 보였습니다.

M 왜 그가 겁에 질린 것처럼 보였죠? 그 상자에 뭐가 들었던 거죠?

W 모르겠어요. 그는 그것을 열어보지 않았습니다. 그냥 그것을 받아서 급하게 떠났습니다.

M 어디로 갔죠? 그리고 그 여자는 어디로 갔죠?

W 주차장 쪽으로요. 그리고 그의 차가 전속력으로 차를 몰고 사라지는 소리를 들었을 때, 여자는 여전히 그곳에 있었습니다.

07 ④

① **M** Do you have the time?
  W It's ten to seven.
② **M** Excuse me, but is this seat taken?
  W No, have a seat.
③ **M** I'm sorry we lost the final match.
  W Look on the bright side. You played better than before.
④ **M** Some teenagers need to work. It's unfair not to let teenagers work.
  W I cannot agree with you. They need jobs to make some money.
⑤ **M** Drinking soda is unhealthy for teenagers because their teeth can rot.
  W That's a good point.

① **M** 몇 시니?
  W 7시 10분 전이야.
② **M** 실례합니다만, 이 좌석에 사람 있나요?
  W 아니요, 앉으세요.
③ **M** 결승전에서 져서 유감이야.
  W 긍정적으로 생각해. 전보다 경기를 더 잘 했잖아.
④ **M** 어떤 십대들은 일을 할 필요가 있어. 십대들에게 일하는 것을 허락하지 않는 것은 불공평해.
  W 동의할 수 없어. 그들은 돈을 좀 벌기 위해 일이 필요할 수 있잖아.
⑤ **M** 이가 썩을 수도 있기 때문에 탄산음료를 마시는 것은 십대들의 건강에 좋지 않아.
  W 좋은 지적이야.

만점 솔루션 ④ I cannot agree with you.는 상대방 의견에 동의하지 않는 표현인데, 뒤에 십대들이 일을 할 필요가 있다는 남자의 의견에 동의하는 말을 하고 있으므로 어색하다.

08 ④ | ➕ ②

B Mom, I brought in the groceries from the car.

W Thank you, dear. I'll make dinner for you soon.

B What are you going to make?

W I'm thinking of making a spicy pork stew and salmon salad.

B Mmm... my favorites. Can I watch TV until dinner is ready?

W Of course. Oh, wait. I can't find the pork in the shopping bag.

B Well, there was nothing left in the car.

W That's strange. I remember buying it. Where did it go?

B Let me check the receipt. *[pause]* Here, you paid for the pork. See?

W Then, I must have left it at the store. Can you run back and get it?

B No problem.

B 엄마, 차에서 식료품을 갖고 왔어요.

W 고맙구나. 곧 저녁을 만들어 줄게.

B 무엇을 만들 건가요?

W 매콤한 돼지고기 스튜와 연어 샐러드를 만들까 생각 중이야.

B 음... 내가 제일 좋아하는 것들. 저녁이 될 때까지 TV를 봐도 되나요?

W 물론이지. 아, 잠깐. 쇼핑백에서 돼지고기를 찾을 수가 없네.

B 차에 남아있는 건 없어요.

W 이상하네. 돼지고기를 산 것은 기억나는데. 어디 갔지?

B 영수증을 볼게요. *[멈춤]* 여기, 돼지고기를 계산했네요. 보이죠?

W 그럼 가게에 두고 온 게 분명한데. 가서 돼지고기를 갖고 와 주겠니?

B 문제없어요.

09 ③

M Good afternoon, ladies and gentlemen. This is your purser Jinsu Kim. On behalf of Captain Park and the entire crew, welcome aboard this Korean Airlines flight from Seoul to Nagoya, Japan. It's 2:30 p.m. now. The flying time will be one hour and forty minutes. To be at your service is an honor for the captain and all his crew. Please enjoy the pleasant flight with us. Thank you.

M 승객 여러분, 안녕하세요. 전 여러분의 객실 사무장 김 진수입니다. 기장 Park과 전체 승무원을 대표하여 서울 발 일본 나고야 행 대한 항공편에 탑승하신 것을 환영합니다. 현재 시각은 오후 2시 30분입니다. 비행 시간은 1시간 40분이 될 것입니다. 여러분에게 서비스를 제공하게 된 것을 기장과 직원 모두는 영광스럽게 생각합니다. 저희와 함께 유쾌한 비행 시간 되시길 바랍니다. 감사합니다.

만점 솔루션 현재 시각이 오후 2시 30분이고 비행 시간은 1시간 40분 걸린다고 했으므로, 목적지에 오후 4시 10분에 도착할 것이다.

10 ③

M Good afternoon. May I help you?

W Yes, please. I'm looking for a digital camera. Oh, this one looks good. How much is it?

M It's $100.

W $100! I think it's a bit pricey.

M But this kind of brand-new camera usually costs $200. So, $100 is a reasonable price.

W Oh, really? But, you see, this one has some scratches on the bottom. Can I have it for half price?

M I can't do that. Listen, I can offer you a 20% discount, but that's the lowest price I can go.

W OK. I'll take it.

M 안녕하세요. 도와드릴까요?

W 네. 디지털 카메라를 찾고 있습니다. 오, 이게 멋지네요. 얼마죠?

M 100달러입니다.

W 100달러요! 좀 비싼데요.

M 하지만 이런 종류의 신상품 카메라는 대개 200달러입니다. 100달러는 합리적인 가격이에요.

W 오, 정말이세요? 하지만, 보시다시피, 아래쪽에 긁힌 자국이 좀 있는데요. 절반 가격에 살 수 있지 않나요?

M 그렇게 할 수는 없습니다. 잘 들어보세요. 20% 할인해 드릴 수 있습니다만, 그것이 제가 해 드릴 수 있는 최저 가격입니다.

W 알겠습니다. 그것을 사도록 하죠.

만점 솔루션 긁힌 자국이 있는 100달러짜리 디지털 카메라의 가격을 절반으로 할인해 줄 것을 요구했으나 20% 할인해 주기로 했으므로, 결국 지불해야 할 물건 값은 80달러이다.

11 ⑤

M I'd like to go to Incheon International Airport. Which line should I take?

W Let me see. You should take Line Number 2, and then transfer to Line Number 5 at Dongdaemun History & Culture Park.

M Is there any easy way to find the right line?

W Line Number 2 is green, and Line Number 5 is violet on all subway maps.

M Oh, I see. How much is the fare to the airport?

W It's 4,500 won.

M Two tickets, please.

W Here are your tickets and your change.

M 인천 국제 공항에 가고 싶은데요, 어느 노선을 이용해야 하나요?

W 어디 보죠. 2호선을 타고 동대문 역사 문화 공원에서 5호선으로 갈아 타셔야 합니다.

M 올바른 노선을 찾는 쉬운 방법이 있나요?

W 모든 지하철 노선도에서 2호선은 녹색이고, 5호선은 보라색입니다.

M 오, 알겠습니다. 공항까지 요금이 얼마죠?

W 4,500원입니다.

M 2장 주세요.

W 여기 승차권과 거스름돈 있습니다.

만점 솔루션 지하철로 공항에 가는 방법을 상세하게 설명해 주며 마지막에 승차권과 거스름돈을 주는 것으로 보아 지하철역에서의 대화로 볼 수 있다.

12 ③

W Jenny is a famous writer. She writes mystery novels. Her daily routine is very different from most people's. She gets up around noon. Then, she has a late breakfast. After that, she does some housework, like dusting and the laundry. At about 4 in the afternoon, she walks her dog around the neighborhood. She talks with her neighbors and buys groceries at the store. After dinner, she starts working— usually at about 9 p.m. She stays up all night and focuses on writing until the next morning.

W 제니는 유명한 작가이다. 그녀는 미스터리 소설을 쓴다. 그녀의 일과는 대부분의 사람들과 매우 다르다. 그녀는 정오 즈음에 일어난다. 그리고 늦은 아침을 먹는다. 그리고 나서 먼지 털기나 세탁 같은 약간의 집안일을 한다. 오후 4시 즈음에는 개와 함께 동네를 산책한다. 그녀는 이웃과 이야기를 나누고 가게에서 식료품을 산다. 저녁식사 후 보통 9시 즈음에 그녀는 일하기 시작한다. 그녀는 밤새 깨어 있고 다음날 아침까지 글쓰기에 집중한다.

13 ⑤

M Look! Refrigerators are on sale.

W Oh, yeah! Let's look around. We need to get a new one.

M Which color do you like better, white or silver?

W Those colors are too common. Let's get a gold one.

M I don't mind gold. What about the number of doors?

W I want one with at least three doors.

M OK. More importantly, we have to think about the capacity.

W Don't you think we need one with a capacity of 1,000 liters?

M I think that refrigerator is too big for our house. An 800-liter capacity fridge is big enough.

W If you think so, I'll follow your decision.

M 봐! 냉장고가 세일 중이야.

W 아, 그러네! 구경하자. 우리 새로운 걸 하나 사야해.

M 무슨 색이 더 좋아, 흰색 아니면 은색?

W 이 색들은 너무 흔해. 금색으로 하자.

M 금색 좋네. 문은 몇 개가 있는게 좋아?

W 최소 3개는 있는게 좋아.

M 알겠어. 더 중요하게, 우리 용량에 대해 생각해봐야해.

W 1,000리터 용량은 필요하다고 생각하지 않아?

M 그 냉장고는 우리 집에 너무 크다고 생각해. 800리터 용량인 냉장고도 충분히 커.

W 그렇게 생각한다면, 네 결정에 따를게.

14 ②

W Even though we can't remember this clearly all the time, we do this while sleeping. We are usually active in this. We are talking, moving, walking, or traveling as the other people are doing these things in this. We usually do strange and unusual things in this like flying or falling. We often have bad feelings in this like anger, fear, sadness, and tears. Can you guess what this is?

W 비록 우리가 이것을 항상 분명하게 기억할 수는 없지만, 우리는 잠을 자는 동안에 이것을 한다. 이 안에서 우리는 대개 활동적이다. 이 안에서 다른 사람들이 이러한 것들을 하고 있는 것처럼, 우리는 말하거나, 움직이거나, 걷거나 또는 여행을 한다. 우리는 대개 날아다니거나 추락하는 것과 같이 이 안에서 이상하고 별난 것들을 한다. 이 안에서 우리는 화, 두려움, 슬픔, 그리고 눈물과 같은 좋지 않은 기분들을 종종 갖는다. 이것이 무엇인지 짐작할 수 있겠는가?

15 ⑤

M Mom, can I go to A Future Science & Technology Show this Saturday?

W I'm afraid not, Jinsu. We're supposed to be at a grandma's birthday party.

M I remember. But I'm interested in future science and technology.

W I know, but we already made plans.

M Besides, it takes too much time to go to grandma's.

W Yes, it's a long trip, but let's try to look on the bright side.

M What's the bright side in visiting Grandma, Mom?

W You can enjoy beautiful sights during the bus ride and go fishing near grandma's house.

M I see, Mom.

M 엄마, 이번 토요일에 '미래 과학과 기술 쇼'에 가도 돼요?

W 유감스럽지만 안 돼, 진수야. 할머니 생신 파티에 참석하기로 되어 있어.

M 기억하고 있어요. 하지만 전 미래 과학과 기술에 대해 관심이 있잖아요.

W 알고 있지만, 벌써 계획을 했잖니.

M 게다가, 할머니 댁까지는 가는 데 시간도 너무 많이 걸리잖아요.

W 그래, 긴 여행이지만, 긍정적으로 생각하도록 하자.

M 할머니 댁을 방문하는 데 있어서 긍정적인 것이 뭔데요, 엄마?

W 버스를 타고 가는 동안에 아름다운 경치를 즐길 수 있고, 할머니 댁 근처에서 낚시를 하러 갈 수 있잖아.

M 알겠어요. 엄마.

16 ①

W Jacob, where are you off to?

M It's Saturday, so I'm going to play tennis with my friends. We're supposed to meet at our school.

W Didn't you hear the weather forecast?

M No, I didn't. What did it say?

W There's a heavy rainstorm coming soon. You shouldn't go outside.

M It's not raining now. I'm sure it'll be OK today.

W Can't you see those dark clouds coming? And the wind is getting stronger and stronger.

M But I've promised my friends to be there. Please let me go.

W The rainstorm will be here sooner than you expect.

W Jacob, 어디 가니?

M 토요일이잖아요. 그래서 친구들과 테니스 치러 가요. 우리 학교에서 만나기로 했어요.

W 일기 예보를 듣지 않았니?

M 아뇨, 듣지 못했는데요. 뭐라고 했는데요?

W 폭풍우가 곧 있단다. 밖에 나가서는 안 돼.

M 지금 비가 오고 있지 않잖아요. 오늘은 분명히 괜찮을 겁니다.

W 몰려오는 저 먹구름들이 안 보이니? 그리고 바람도 점점 거세지고 있어.

M 하지만 친구들하고 그곳에서 만나기로 약속을 했어요. 보내 주세요.

W 폭풍이 네가 예상하는 것보다 더 빨리 이곳에 올 거야.

17 ② | ➕ ③

[Telephone rings.]

M Hi, Jenny! How are you today?

W I'm so tired. I didn't get any sleep last night.

M Why not? Were you worried about the quiz today?

W No, it's because of my new upstairs neighbors.

M Oh, no. Do they make a lot of noise?

W Yes. They don't seem to sleep at night. Last night was the worst. They played loud music until almost 3 a.m.

M That's terrible.

W I think I'll have to knock on their door and talk to them about it today.

M Jenny... It might cause trouble with them.

W That's what I'm worried about.

M _____

[전화벨이 울린다.]

M 안녕, 제니! 오늘 기분 어때?

W 아주 피곤해. 어젯밤 전혀 못 잤어.

M 왜? 오늘 퀴즈 보는 거 때문에 걱정했어?

W 아니, 위층에 새로 온 이웃 때문이야.

M 이런. 이웃이 많이 시끄럽니?

W 응. 밤에 잠을 안자는 거 같아. 어젯밤은 최악이었어. 새벽3시까지 음악을 크게 틀어 놨어.

M 끔찍하다.

W 오늘 찾아가서 그 일에 대해 이야기 해야 하나 생각하고 있어.

M 제니... 그 사람들이랑 갈등이 생길 수도 있어.

W 그게 내가 걱정하는 부분이야.

M 관리 사무소에 먼저 말하는 게 좋을 거야.

18 ②

M I'm so bored. Can you play with me now?

W Sure. Any interesting games to play with me?

M Yes. I know an interesting game.

W Let me know how to play the game.

M OK. Let me explain. I'll be a baby pig, and you can be the mommy pig.

W Then, what am I supposed to do next?

M You have to give the baby pig a cookie, a sandwich, and a Coke.

W What are you going to do then?

M You know, I'm just a baby pig, so I'll just sit and eat the food.

W _____

M 너무 따분해. 지금 나랑 같이 놀 수 있니?

W 물론이지. 나랑 같이 할 재미있는 게임이라도 있니?

M 그래. 난 재미있는 게임 하나를 알고 있어.

W 그 게임하는 방법을 알려줄래?

M 좋아. 설명해 줄게. 내가 아기 돼지가 되고, 넌 엄마 돼지가 되는 거야.

W 그러고 난 다음에 내가 뭘 해야 하는 거지?

M 넌 아기 돼지에게 쿠키, 샌드위치, 그리고 콜라를 줘야 해.

W 그러면 넌 뭘 할 건데?

M 너도 알다시피 난 겨우 아기 돼지잖아. 그러니까 난 그냥 앉아서 그 음식을 먹기만 할 거야.

W 뭐라고! 그건 너무 불공평하다.

① 참 좋은 생각이다!

③ 하지만 난 동물원을 방문하고 싶어.

④ 그래, 넌 다이어트를 해야 해.

⑤ 고맙지만, 됐어. 난 배불리 먹었어.

19 ②

M What are you going to do this winter vacation, Hana?

W I'm planning to take a trip to Sydney with my family.

M How long are you going to stay there?

W Just one week.

M Where are you thinking of staying? Do you have any relatives in Sydney?

W I have no relatives there, so we're staying at a hotel.

M Did you make a reservation, then?

W _____

M 하나야, 이번 겨울 방학에 뭐 할 예정이니?

W 가족과 함께 시드니 여행을 할 계획이야.

M 그곳에 얼마나 오랫동안 머물 예정이니?

W 단 일주일이야.

M 어디서 머물 예정이니? 시드니에 친척들이 있니?

W 그곳에 친척이 없어서, 호텔에 머물 예정이야.

M 그렇다면 예약은 했니?

W 오, 거의 잊을 뻔했다.

① 신용카드로.

③ 너무 심각하게 생각하지 마.

④ 그래, 고모가 그곳에 사셔.

⑤ 아빠와 난 영어를 잘 해.

20 ⑤

W The other day, Judy asked her mom for some money to buy a drawing book. She put the money in her wallet. There was a bus card in the wallet, too. After she had a good breakfast, she started for school. She got on the bus as usual. And she looked for the wallet. Oh, no! She had left the wallet on the table. It meant she had no money, and no bus card. In this situation, what would Judy most likely say to the bus driver?

W 며칠 전에, Judy는 스케치북을 사기 위해 엄마에게 약간의 돈을 달라고 해서, 그것을 그녀의 지갑 안에 넣었다. 그 지갑에는 버스카드도 있었다. 아침식사를 배불리 먹고, 그는 등교를 했다. 그녀는 평상시처럼 버스를 탔다. 그리고 지갑을 찾았다. 오, 이런! 그녀는 지갑을 식탁에 두고 왔다. 그것은 그녀가 돈이 없고, 버스 카드도 없다는 것을 의미했다. 이 상황에서, Judy는 버스 기사에게 뭐라고 말할 것 같은가?

① 얼마죠?

② 정말 부주의한 운전사이시군요!

③ 실례합니다만, 제 지갑을 찾고 있습니다.

④ 제가 내릴 곳을 좀 알려주실 수 있나요?

⑤ 지갑을 깜박했습니다. 다음에 추가 요금을 내면 안 될까요?

01 ④	**02** ②	**03** ⑤	**04** ④	**05** ⑤
06 ④	**07** ④	**08** ①, ❸③	**09** ④	**10** ③
11 ①	**12** ②	**13** ④, ❸⑤	**14** ①	**15** ④
16 ③	**17** ④	**18** ①	**19** ②	**20** ⑤

01 ④

W Josh, let's look around the swimwear section.

M Do you want to buy a new swimsuit?

W I want to buy a rash guard instead of a swimsuit.

M What's a rash guard?

W It's tight-fitting swimwear. It's designed to be skin tight; so you can wear it like a shirt and not expose much of your skin.

M That sounds great. So, do you want a one-piece suit?

W It won't be comfortable at the beach. I'd like to buy only a rash guard shirt—a short-sleeve one.

M That sounds great. Let's have a look.

W 조쉬, 수영복 구역 좀 구경하자.

M 새 수영복을 사고 싶어?

W 수영복 대신 래쉬가드를 사고 싶어.

M 래쉬가드가 뭐야?

W 몸에 딱 붙는 수영복이야. 몸에 딱 맞게 디자인 되었기 때문에 피부를 많이 노출하지 않고 셔츠처럼 입을 수 있어.

M 굉장한데. 그럼 원피스 수트를 원하는 거야?

W 바닷가에서 편하지 않을 것 같아. 반팔로 된 래쉬가드 셔츠만 사고 싶어.

M 그게 좋겠다. 구경해 보자.

02 ②

[Telephone rings.]

W Hello, The Maestro. How may I help you?

M Hello. We have reservations for 8 o'clock tonight but I am afraid we can't make it. One of the people in our party is sick.

W Oh, I am so sorry. What's your name?

M Holland. We'd like to reschedule for next week. Is it possible?

W All right. What day do you like?

M Friday, if possible.

W We're booked up at eight. What about seven o'clock? Is it okay with you?

M That's okay. Thanks.

[전화벨이 울린다.]

W 여보세요. Maestro 식당입니다. 도와드릴까요?

M 여보세요. 오늘밤 8시에 예약이 되어 있는데, 아무래도 못 갈 것 같아요.

일행 중 한 명이 아프거든요.

W 오, 정말 안됐군요. 성함이 어떻게 되시나요?

M Holland입니다. 다음 주로 변경하고 싶은데요. 가능할까요?

W 알겠습니다. 무슨 요일이 좋으신가요?

M 가능하다면 금요일로요.

W 8시에는 예약이 되어 있습니다. 7시는 어떻습니까? 괜찮으세요?

M 괜찮습니다. 감사합니다.

03 ⑤

① W Put all those books on that shelf.

　　M Where? Right here?

② W You can't check all these books out.

　　M Really? How many books can I check out?

③ W Is there a bookstore nearby?

　　M I am afraid not.

④ W The door needs to be painted.

　　M Is that so? I'll do that right away.

⑤ W Let me open the door for you.

　　M Thank you. You are very kind.

① W 그 책들을 모두 저 선반에 놓아주세요.

　　M 어디요? 바로 여기인가요?

② W 이 책들을 모두 대출할 수는 없어요.

　　M 그래요? 몇 권까지 대출할 수 있나요?

③ W 근처에 서점이 있습니까?

　　M 없을 겁니다.

④ W 문에 페인트를 다시 칠해야 할 것 같아요.

　　M 그래요? 당장 칠할게요.

⑤ W 제가 문을 열어 드릴게요.

　　M 고맙습니다. 상당히 친절하시군요.

04 ④

M Hey, here's the schedule at the skateboarding school I go to.

W Great! I'm thinking of starting again.

M Why don't you take the same class as me? I'm taking the advanced class on Tuesdays and Thursdays.

W Hmm. I don't know. I've only taken a few skateboard lessons before.

M Then, how about the intermediate class on Friday?

W I want to take a class on the same days as you.

M Then, how about taking the beginner class on Thursdays? We can take the bus together.

W Oh, that'd be great. Let's meet on Thursdays after school.

M 여기 내가 다니는 스케이트보드 학교 스케줄이야.

W 잘됐다! 다시 시작하려고 생각 중이었어.

M 나랑 같은 수업을 듣는 거 어때? 화요일이랑 목요일 상급반을 듣고 있어.

W 음. 잘 모르겠어. 전에 스케이트보드 수업을 몇 번 들은 게 전부라.

M 그럼, 금요일에 중급반을 듣는 건 어때?

W 난 너랑 같은 날 수업을 듣고 싶어.

M 그럼 목요일에 초급반을 듣는 게 어떨까? 같이 버스를 탈 수 있어.

W 아, 그거 좋겠다. 목요일 방과 후에 보자.

05 ⑤

M Look! Doris is walking down the aisle with her uncle Johnny. She is so beautiful.

W Yes, she is. Look at the groom! He is coming down to greet her.

M Oh, what a wonderful couple! What is his name?

W Ted. He works for the same law firm as Doris works.

M Oh, I see. There are so many guests here to celebrate the day.

W Yes. There are more people than we expected.

M Maybe the groom has a lot of friends or relatives.

W Look! Ted is giving Doris a ring. What a beautiful moment!

M 보세요! Doris가 Johnny 삼촌과 결혼식 제단 쪽으로 걸어가고 있어요. 아주 아름답군요.

W 네, 정말 아름답네요. 신랑을 보세요! 그녀를 맞이하려고 내려오네요.

M 오, 정말 아름다운 커플이네요! 신랑의 이름이 뭐죠?

W Ted예요. Doris가 일하는 같은 법률 회사에서 근무하고 있어요.

M 오, 그렇군요. 이 날을 축하하러 여기에 온 하객들이 참 많군요.

W 그래요. 우리가 예상했던 것보다 더 많아요.

M 아마 신랑이 친구나 친척이 많은 모양이에요.

W 보세요! Ted가 Doris에게 반지를 주고 있어요. 참 아름다운 순간이지요!

06 ④

M What happened to your Cellphone? You didn't answer all morning.

W It doesn't work at all. I think my brother dropped it or something.

M You mean your 5-year-old brother, Joe?

W Right. He loves to play with my phone when I'm not using it.

M I think you should visit the repair shop, then.

W I know, but this is the third time he broke my phone!

M Are you sure Joe did it again?

W I am. I put it on my bed last night and this morning I found it in his toy box.

M 네 휴대폰에 무슨 일이 있어? 아침 내내 전화를 안 받더라.

W 전혀 작동하지 않아. 내 남동생이 떨어뜨리거나 했을 거야.

M 네 다섯 살짜리 동생 Joe 말이지?

W 맞아. 그 애는 내가 휴대 전화를 쓰지 않을 때 그것을 갖고 노는 걸 좋아해.

M 그렇다면 수리점을 방문해 봐야 할 것 같아.

W 알지만 동생이 내 전화기를 망가뜨린 게 이번이 세 번째야!

M Joe가 또 그랬다는 게 확실해?

W 그럼. 어젯밤에 내가 그걸 침대 위에 놓았는데 오늘 아침에 동생 장난감 통에서 발견했거든.

07 ④

① **W** I'm sorry to have kept you waiting.

　M That's okay. I just got here, too.

② **W** Is there anything to declare?

　M No. This bag is all I have.

③ **W** I was wondering if you could do me a favor.

　M Sure. What is it?

④ **W** Come in. Let me take your coat.

　M Sure. The fitting room is over there.

⑤ **W** It was nice having talked to you.

　M It was my pleasure.

① **W** 기다리게 해서 죄송합니다.

　M 괜찮아요. 저도 막 도착했어요.

② **W** 신고하실 품목이 있습니까?

　M 아니요. 이 가방이 제가 가진 모든 것입니다.

③ **W** 당신이 부탁을 들어줄 수 있을지 생각하고 있던 참이었어요.

　M 물론이죠. 뭐죠?

④ **W** 들어오세요. 제가 코트를 받아드릴 게요.

　M 물론이죠. 탈의실은 저쪽에 있어요.

⑤ **W** 당신과의 대화가 즐거웠습니다.

　M 천만에요.

08 ① | ➕ ③

M What's up? You look upset.

W I ordered a box of chocolate bars from an online store. But the chocolate bars had all melted when I got them.

M Oh, no. Did you complain to the online store?

W Sure, but they said that it wasn't their fault because the delivery service company was responsible for keeping the box cool. Anyway, they said that I can't get a refund from the store.

M What a joke!

W I know. It's not fair at all. So I'm going to write a letter to report this to a consumer rights group. Would you help me write the letter?

M Sure! I can help you with that.

M 무슨 일이야? 화나 보여.

W 온라인 가게에서 초콜릿바 한 박스를 주문했어. 그런데 내가 받았을 때 초콜릿바가 완전히 녹아 있었어.

M 이럴 수가. 온라인 가게에 항의했어?

W 물론이야, 하지만 박스를 차갑게 유지하는 건 배달 업체의 책임이기 때문에 자기네들 잘못이 아니라고 했어. 아무튼, 가게에서는 환불해 줄 수 없다고 했어.

M 장난하나!

W 내 말이. 전혀 타당하지 않잖아. 그래서 소비자 보호 단체에 이걸 보고하는 편지를 쓸 거야. 편지 쓰는 걸 도와줄래?

M 물론이지! 도와줄 수 있어.

09 ④

W I'll see you tomorrow. Bye.

M Are you going home this early?

W Yes. My mother is not well, so I have to be with her.

M Oh, I'm sorry to hear that. Can I ask what's wrong with her?

W She had a surgery last month and is still recovering.

M So you have some cooking and washing-up to do, I presume.

W Yes. After that I'm going to clean up the house.

M How nice of you. I think I should help my mom more often.

W Great idea. Then why don't you go home now and do what you said?

W 내일 봐. 안녕.

M 이렇게 일찍 집에 가?

W 응. 엄마가 몸이 안 좋으셔서 곁에 있어야 돼.

M 아, 안 됐구나. 엄마에게 무슨 문제가 있는지 물어봐도 돼?

W 지난달에 수술을 하셔서 아직도 회복 중이셔.

M 그래서 네가 음식도 하고 설거지도 해 드려야 되는구나.

W 응. 그런 다음엔 집 청소도 할 거야.

M 넌 정말 착하구나. 나도 엄마를 좀 더 자주 도와드려야겠어.

W 좋은 생각이야. 그러면 너도 지금 집에 가서 네가 말한 것을 하지 그래?

10 ③

M We're looking for a person who is good at computers.

W Don't worry. I'm good at computers.

M Great. You will work for eight hours a day from Monday to Friday. Nine to five, five days a week. Is it okay with you?

W Sure. No problem.

M You'll get paid $10 per hour. Payday is every Friday.

W I know that.

M When can you start?

W I can work from tomorrow.

M 저희는 컴퓨터를 잘하는 사람을 찾고 있어요.

W 걱정하지 마세요. 저는 컴퓨터를 잘합니다.

M 잘 됐군요. 월요일부터 금요일까지 하루 8시간 근무할 겁니다. 9시부터 5시까지, 주 5일입니다. 괜찮죠?

W 물론이죠. 문제될 것이 없습니다.

M 시간당 10달러를 받게 됩니다. 지불일은 매주 금요일이고요.

W 알고 있습니다.

M 언제부터 일을 시작할 수 있나요?

W 내일부터 일을 할 수 있습니다.

> **만점 솔루션** 시간당 10달러씩 하루 8시간 근무하게 되므로 일급은 80달러이다. 일주일에 5일 근무하므로 주급은 400달러가 된다.

11 ①

M Thank you for coming.

W Don't mention it. How did it happen?

M I have no idea. He didn't show any sign of being sick until last night.

W I can't still believe that your father passed away. He looked so healthy.

M Yes, but he was quite old, 89, you know.

W I don't know what to say. I hope he will go to heaven and be in peace.

M I guess he will. Thanks.

W Mourners are coming in. You go and greet them.

M 와 주셔서 감사합니다.

W 천만에요. 어쩌다 이런 일이 생겼어요?

M 모르겠습니다. 어젯밤까지만 해도 아픈 징후는 보이지 않으셨거든요.

W 난 아직도 당신의 아버님이 돌아가셨다는 것을 믿을 수가 없어요. 그리 건강해 보이셨는데.

M 네, 하지만 당신도 아시다시피 아버님은 89세로 꽤 연로하셨어요.

W 어떤 말씀을 드려야 할지 모르겠군요. 하늘나라로 가셔서 편안하시기를 빕니다.

M 그러시겠죠. 감사합니다.

W 조문객들이 들어오네요. 가서 맞이하세요.

> **만점 솔루션** 남자의 아버님이 돌아가셨다는 말(your father passed away), 하늘나라로 가셔서 편안하시기를 바란다는 말(he will go to heaven and be in peace), 조문객이 들어온다는 말 (Mourners are coming in.) 등을 종합해 보면, 아버님을 여읜 상주와 조문을 온 문상객 사이의 대화임을 알 수 있다.

12 ②

M It's hurricane season, isn't it? There are many things you need to get ready, aren't there? Enough bottled water, of course. You should also have canned food in case the electricity goes out. For the same reason, you need candles and matches. Finally, you need a battery-powered radio to keep yourself informed about approaching hurricanes.

M 태풍 시즌이죠, 그렇죠? 준비를 해 두어야 할 많은 것들이 있지 않겠습니까? 충분한 생수 확보, 물론이지요. 전기가 나갈 경우에 대비해서 통조림 식품을 갖추어야 합니다. 같은 이유로, 초와 성냥이 필요합니다. 마지막으로, 접근하는 태풍에 관해서도 알아야 하므로 전지용 라디오도 필요합니다.

> **만점 솔루션** 태풍에 대비하여 생수, 통조림 식품, 단전에 대비한 초와 성냥, 라디오 등을 갖출 것을 조언하고 있는 담화이다.

13 ④ | ➕ ⑤

W Okay, sir, now you have to decide which payment plan to take.

M Do you have any with three hours of free calls?

W Sure, we do. Do you make a lot of phone calls?

M Yes. I'm a sales representative, so clients call me quite often.

W I see. How about free text messages? You can choose 500, 1,000, or an unlimited number.

M I think 500 text messages should be enough for me.

W Super. Now you need to decide how much data you need.

We can offer from 1.5 GB to unlimited data.

M Well, my monthly budget for my smartphone bill is 70,000 won. Can I choose unlimited data and not go over 70,000 won?

W Yes, we can offer unlimited data for 70,000 won.

M I'll take this payment plan then.

W 알겠습니다, 손님. 이제 어떤 요금제를 선택할지 결정해야 합니다.

M 3시간 무료통화인 것이 있나요?

W 물론이죠, 있습니다. 전화 통화를 많이 하시나요?

M 네. 영업 담당자라 많은 고객들이 꽤 자주 전화합니다.

W 알겠습니다. 무료 문자는 어떠세요? 500건, 1000건 아니면 무제한 중에 고르실 수 있습니다.

M 500 문자면 충분할 거 같네요.

W 알겠습니다. 이제 데이터가 얼마나 필요한지 골라야 합니다. 1.5기가부터 무제한 데이터를 제공합니다.

M 음, 제 한달 스마트폰 요금 예산이 7만원이에요. 무제한 데이터를 고르면서 7만원이 넘지 않는 걸로 고를 수 있나요?

W 네, 저희는 7만원으로 무제한 데이터를 제공할 수 있습니다.

M 그럼 이 요금제로 하겠습니다.

14 ①

W This is a hand-held, cone-shaped device. This helps us <u>increase our voice towards a certain direction</u>. So when we speak to a large crowd in front of us, we can use this so that our voice can travel the farthest. But when a listener is to the side, it is more difficult to hear what is being said. Common uses for this are at sporting events or generally <u>when we need to address a group of people</u> in an open space.

W 이것은 손에 쥘 만한 크기의 원뿔형 모양의 도구이다. 이것은 우리의 목소리를 특정 방향으로 확대하는 데 도움을 준다. 그래서 우리는 앞에 있는 대중에게 이야기할 때, 목소리가 가장 멀리까지 전달될 수 있도록 이것을 사용할 수 있다. 그러나 듣는 사람이 측면에 있으면, 말하고 있는 내용을 듣기가 더 어려워진다. 이것은 보편적으로 스포츠 행사나 혹은 대체로 개방된 장소에서 많은 사람들에게 연설할 필요가 있을 때 사용된다.

15 ④

M What are you going to do this Saturday?

W I'm going to go to the library and get some books to read.

M What will you do after that?

W I'll read them in the afternoon.

M Well, <u>I'd like to do something with you</u> this Saturday afternoon.

W What? I don't want to go bowling again.

M My sister <u>gave me two tickets</u> to *The Moon of Seoul*. <u>Would you like to go with me?</u>

W Oh, that famous play? Sure, <u>I'd love to go.</u>

M Then, meet me at three in front of the theater.

M 이번 주 토요일에 뭐 할 거야?

W 도서관에서 가서 읽을 책을 좀 대출할 거야.

M 그 후에는 뭐 할 거야?

W 오후에 그 책들을 읽을 거야.

M 저, 이번 토요일 오후에 너와 함께 하고 싶은 일이 있어.

W 뭔데? 난 다시는 볼링을 치러 가고 싶지는 않아.

M 내 여동생이 The Moon of Seoul의 표 두 장을 줬어. 나와 함께 가고 싶니?

W 오, 그 유명한 연극 말이야? 물론, 가고 싶어.

M 그럼, 3시에 그 극장 앞에서 만나자.

16 ③

W I can't believe this!

M It was foggy when we arrived here four days ago.

W And since then, <u>it has rained for three days</u>.

M It's strange. It usually doesn't rain much around here at this time of year.

W It's <u>usually windy</u>, but not rainy like this.

M Maybe this rain will ruin our vacation.

W Not from tomorrow, I guess.

M What do you mean?

W I just heard the weather report. It'll be still cloudy this evening, but <u>we'll have sunny weather starting tomorrow</u>.

M Really? What a relief!

W 믿을 수가 없어요!

M 4일 전 이곳에 도착할 때는 안개가 끼어 있었어요.

W 그리고 그 때부터 3일 동안 비가 내리고 있어요.

M 이상해요. 일 년 중 이맘때 이 주변에는 비가 많이 내리지 않거든요.

W 대개 바람은 좀 불지만 이처럼 비가 내리지는 않죠.

M 아마도 이 비가 우리 휴가를 망쳐 놓을 것 같아요.

W 내일부터는 아닐 거예요.

M 무슨 말이에요?

W 막 일기 예보를 들었어요. 오늘밤에는 여전히 흐리지만, 내일부터는 날씨가 화창할 거예요.

M 그래요? 다행이군요!

만점 솔루션 4일 전에는 안개가 낀 날씨였고, 오늘 현재까지는 비가 내리고 있으며, 오늘밤에는 여전히 흐리겠지만 내일부터는 화창해질 것이라고(we'll have sunny weather starting tomorrow) 말하고 있다.

17 ④

W Now, have you decided which house you'll move into?

M Not yet. It's hard to choose. I need your advice.

W Gladly. First let me ask you what the most important thing in a house is.

M Well, I want a quiet place with clean air so I can take a good rest at home.

W Really? Look at this picture. This house is exactly <u>what you're looking for</u>. But it's over 20 minutes walk away from the subway station.

M That's okay to me. I love walking. By the way, is there a

fitness center near this house?
W Yes. There's one right across the street.
M Great. Can you check when the house will be available?

W 자, 어느 집으로 이사가실 건지 결정하셨나요?
M 아직요. 선택하기 어렵네요. 조언이 좀 필요해요.
W 기꺼이요. 우선 당신의 집을 결정할 때 가장 중요한 게 뭔지 물어볼게요.
M 글쎄요, 저는 집에서 충분히 휴식할 수 있도록 맑은 공기가 있는 조용한 장소를 원해요.
W 정말이요? 이 사진을 보세요. 이 집이 당신이 찾고 있는 바로 그 집이에요. 하지만 지하철에서 걸어서 20분 이상 떨어져 있죠.
M 저한테는 괜찮아요. 저는 걷는 걸 아주 좋아하죠. 그런데, 이 집 근처에 헬스장이 있나요?
W 네. 길 바로 건너편에 하나 있어요.
M 좋네요. 언제 그 집이 가능한지 확인해 주시겠어요?

18 ①
W Gary, how did the presentation go?
M It was terrible.
W Really? Didn't you say it was very important?
M Yes, but when I saw those people in front of me, I was so nervous that I had huge drops of sweat running down my face.
W I'm sorry to hear that. Don't be disappointed. Next time you make a presentation, imagine that nobody is in the room.
M _____

W Gary, 발표는 어떻게 됐어?
M 끔찍했어.
W 정말? 아주 중요한 발표라고 말하지 않았니?
M 그래, 하지만 내 앞에 있는 사람들을 보자 너무 긴장한 나머지 땀이 얼굴에 범벅이 되어 버렸어.
W 그것 참 안됐구나. 실망하지는 마. 다음번에 발표를 하게 되면 방에 아무도 없다고 상상해 봐.
M 그래 보기는 하겠지만, 해 낼 수 있을지 모르겠어.

② 괜찮아. 나도 긴장하면 땀을 흘리거든.
③ 네가 말한 대로 했는데 완벽하게 효과가 있었어.
④ 다른 사람들이 없을 때 그들을 나쁘게 말하지 마.
⑤ 내가 네 대신 그 발표를 하면 어떨까 생각 중이야.

19 ②
W You look upset. Can you tell me what's wrong?
M I was unlucky today. I got a ticket for speeding!
W Oh, that's a shame. How fast did you drive anyway?
M About 50km per hour.
W 50km per hour? I don't understand. It's not too fast.
M It is when you're within the school zone.
W Now I know why the policeman gave you a ticket. You should've been more careful near a school.

M _____
W 화가 난 것 같아. 무슨 일인지 말해 줄 수 있어?
M 오늘 운이 없었어. 과속으로 딱지를 떼였지 뭐야!
W 아, 참 안됐네. 그런데 얼마나 빨리 운전했는데?
M 약 시속 50km 정도야.
W 시속 50km라고? 이해가 안 돼. 그건 그리 빠른 게 아니잖아.
M 스쿨 존 안에 있다면 빠른 거지.
W 왜 경찰관이 네게 딱지를 발부했는지 이제 알겠다. 학교 근처에서는 좀 더 주의 해야만 했어.
M 그래. 힘든 방식으로 교훈을 얻었지.

① 좋아. 네게 지도를 보여줄게!
③ 난 그렇게 생각하지 않아. 그는 내게 무례했어
④ 맞아. 다음 번에는 학교 근처에서 운전하지 않을 거야.
⑤ 그래. 그게 바로 내가 학교를 싫어하는 이유야.

20 ⑤
W Paul goes to a bookstore to buy his favorite author's new novel. He picks it up and pays for it. When he gets home, he opens the book and finds some pages are missing. He goes back to the bookstore. He wants to let them know some pages are missing and exchange it. He walks over to the cashier at the counter. In this situation, what will Paul most likely say to the cashier?

W Paul은 자기가 가장 좋아하는 작가의 새로 나온 소설을 구입하려고 서점에 간다. 그는 그 책을 집어 들고 돈을 지불한다. 집에 도착해서 그는 책을 펼쳐보는데, 일부 페이지가 빠져 있음을 발견한다. 그는 서점으로 다시 간다. 그는 일부 페이지가 빠져 있음을 보여주고 그것을 교환하고 싶어 한다. 그는 계산대의 계산원에게로 간다. 이 상황에서, Paul은 계산원에게 뭐라고 말할 것 같은가?

① 환불해 주세요.
② 신용카드로 계산해도 되나요?
③ 책값을 부당하게 더 지불한 것 같아요.
④ 이 근처에 다른 서점이 있나요?
⑤ 죄송합니다만, 이 책을 교환하고 싶어요.

만점 솔루션 구입한 소설책의 몇 페이지가 없음을 보여주면서 교환해 달라는 말을 하는 것이 가장 적절하다.

01 ③	**02** ③	**03** ①	**04** ①	**05** ②
06 ②	**07** ③	**08** ④	**09** ③	**10** ⑤
11 ③, ➕⑤	**12** ⑤	**13** ②	**14** ⑤	**15** ①
16 ①, ➕①	**17** ③	**18** ③	**19** ④	**20** ①

01 ③

W These paintings are all impressive.

M Yes, they're all painted in a very unique style.

W Why don't you choose one to hang up in your room? It'll make your room look nice. How about this one with the skyscrapers?

M I'd prefer something a bit brighter, like this painting of sunflowers in a vase.

W Maybe that abstract painting would suit your room better— the one with circles and triangles.

M Oh, you're right. I really love it. I think it would look great hanging over my desk.

W Okay, let's get that one.

W 이 그림들 모두 인상적이다.

M 맞아, 모두 아주 독특한 스타일로 그려졌어.

W 네 방에 걸 그림으로 하나 고르는 거 어때? 방을 더 멋지게 만들어 줄 거야. 이 초고층 건물들이 있는 그림 어때?

M 꽃병에 있는 해바라기 같이 더 밝은 게 좋아.

W 저 추상화가 네 방에 더 잘 어울릴 수도 있어. 동그라미와 세모가 그려진 것 말이야.

M 아, 네 말이 맞아. 마음에 든다. 내 책상 위에 걸어 두면 아주 멋질 거 같아.

W 좋아, 저걸로 사자.

02 ③

M Hi, Mary. Where are you going?

W I'm going back to school. I forgot to do something.

M What is it? Anything important?

W Yeah. It's about joining a club. I have to sign up by today.

M That's what you forgot to do. What's the club?

W It's a kind of movie making club. You know how much I like movies.

M Wow, that's great. So you're going to be a director someday?

W Maybe. I don't know yet. I'm just interested in movies.

M 안녕, Mary. 어디 가니?

W 학교에 돌아가는 중이야. 할 일을 깜빡 했어.

M 뭔데? 중요한 거야?

W 응. 동호회에 가입하는 거야. 오늘까지 등록해야 하거든.

M 네가 잊고 안 한 게 그거구나. 어떤 동호회인데?

W 일종의 영화 만드는 동호회야. 너 내가 얼마나 영화를 좋아하는지 알잖아.

M 와, 멋지다. 그럼 너 언젠가는 감독이 되는 거야?

W 아마도. 아직은 몰라. 그냥 영화에 관심이 있을 뿐이야.

03 ①

① W What's wrong with you? You look ill.

　 M I think I'm getting seasick.

② W You don't look OK. What's the matter?

　 M My back has been aching a little since I got on board.

③ W You don't like to travel by ship, do you?

　 M Yes, I do. I really like it.

④ W What do you want to be?

　 M I'd like to be a sailor.

⑤ W Do you feel sick?

　 M No, I feel fine. Thanks.

① W 뭔가 문제가 있나요? 아파 보여요.

　 M 배 멀미를 하는 것 같아요.

② W 좋아 보이지 않네요. 무슨 일인가요?

　 M 승선한 이후로 등이 약간 아파 왔어요.

③ W 배로 여행하는 것을 좋아하지 않죠, 그렇죠?

　 M 좋아해요. 정말로 좋아하는 걸요.

④ W 뭐가 되고 싶어요?

　 M 선원이 되고 싶어요.

⑤ W 멀미 나요?

　 M 아니요, 괜찮아요. 고마워요.

04 ①

M Susan, you're really good at basketball.

W Thank you. Actually I'm not as good as I used to be.

M What do you mean?

W I was a star basketball player in high school.

M Oh, really?

W Most people don't know about me.

M Why did you become a model, not a basketball player?

W In a game I fell down and seriously twisted my ankle.

M And you quit afterwards?

W Yes.

M Susan, 정말 농구를 잘하는군요.

W 고마워요. 사실은 예전만큼 잘하지는 못해요.

M 무슨 얘기죠?

W 저는 고교 스타 농구 선수였거든요.

M 오, 정말이에요?

W 대부분의 사람들은 저에 대해 모르죠.

M 왜 농구 선수가 아닌 모델이 되었어요?

W 한 경기에서 넘어져서 발목을 심하게 접질렀어요.

M 그래서 그 후로 그만둔 거군요?

W 네.

만점 솔루션 고등학교 때는 스타 농구 선수(a star basketball player)였지만 발목 부상 후 현재 모델이 되었다(become a model)고 말하고 있다.

05 ②

W How are you feeling today?

M Much better than yesterday. <u>Thanks for coming</u>.

W What happened?

M I fell down and <u>broke my right arm</u>.

W Oh, that's too bad. When are you supposed to <u>go home</u> anyway?

M Maybe this weekend. I'll ask the doctor.

W And I also hope you <u>get the cast off</u> soon.

M So do I. Thanks again for coming.

W 오늘 어떠세요?

M 어제보다 훨씬 더 좋아요. 와 주셔서 고맙습니다.

W 어떻게 된 겁니까?

M 넘어져서 오른쪽 팔이 부러졌어요.

W 오, 참 안됐군요. 어쨌든 언제 퇴원하세요?

M 아마도 이번 주말이요. 의사 선생님께 물어봐야지요.

W 깁스도 빨리 풀기를 바랍니다.

M 저도요. 다시 한 번 와 주셔서 고맙습니다.

06 ②

W Good morning. I'm Cindy Brown. I'm new here.

M Oh, you <u>moved in yesterday</u>, right? Nice to meet you. I'm Chris, manager of this apartment.

W Nice to meet you, too. I'd like to ask you one thing. Is it okay to park my car in front of this building?

M Sure. You'll <u>see some spaces</u> there reserved for residents.

W I'm glad to hear that. And what about house pets? Is there any rules about keeping a dog?

M Sorry, pets <u>aren't allowed</u> here.

W Oh, no. I can't live without my dog. What should I do?

M Well, as long as you live here, you should follow the rules.

W Then should I throw my dog away? That's not possible.

M I'm just telling you the rules. I don't care about your dog.

W Oh, please. Could you find a way for me to <u>live with my dog</u>?

W 안녕하세요. 저는 Cindy Brown입니다. 여기에 새로 왔어요.

M 아, 어제 이사오셨군요? 만나서 반가워요. 저는 이 아파트의 관리인인 Chris입니다.

W 저도 만나서 반갑습니다. 한 가지 여쭤볼게요. 이 건물 앞에 차를 세워도 괜찮나요?

M 물론이죠. 거기에 주민을 위해 확보된 공간이 보일 겁니다.

W 그 말씀을 들으니 기쁘네요. 그리고 애완동물은 어때요? 개를 키우는 데 대한 규칙이 있어요?

M 죄송하지만 애완동물은 여기에선 금지예요.

W 아, 안돼요. 저는 개 없이 살 수 없어요. 어떻게 해야 되죠?

M 글쎄요, 여기에 사시는 한 규칙을 따르셔야죠.

W 그러면 저의 개를 내다 버려야 된다는 거예요? 그건 불가능해요.

M 저는 그저 규칙을 말씀드릴 뿐입니다. 당신의 개에 대해선 상관 안 해요.

W 아, 제발요. 제가 개와 함께 살 수 있는 방법을 좀 찾아 주실 수 있어요?

07 ③

① **W** What seems to be the problem?

M This phone <u>keeps turning off</u> when I press the "call" button.

② **W** I'd like to rent a car, please.

M What size car would you like?

③ **W** Please <u>say hello to your parents</u> for me.

M Sure. What time are you going to call them?

④ **W** I'd like to <u>ask a favor of you</u>.

M OK. What is it?

⑤ **W** I failed the driving test again.

M Oh, sorry to hear that.

① **W** 무슨 문제이신가요?

M 이 전화기가 '통화' 버튼을 누르면 계속 꺼져요.

② **W** 차를 대여하고 싶습니다.

M 어떤 크기의 차를 원하시나요?

③ **W** 저를 대신해 당신 부모님께 안부를 전해 주세요.

M 알았어요. 그들에게 몇 시에 전화하실 거예요?

④ **W** 당신에게 부탁할 게 있어요.

M 좋아요. 뭐죠?

⑤ **W** 또 운전 시험에서 떨어졌어요.

M 오, 안됐네요.

만점 솔루션 ③ say hello to는 '~에게 (대신) 안부를 전하다'는 뜻으로 이에 대한 응답은 Sure (I will). 정도가 적절하다.

08 ④

W Wow, this pizza is very tasty. Where did you get it?

M It's called Sam's Pizza. They use very good cheese and fresh vegetables.

W I'd love to order from them again. Can you let me know their phone number?

M They don't deliver. It's a very small place <u>run by the owner all by himself</u>. I can let you know the address.

W Oh, I see. Could you <u>go there with me</u> sometime?

M Sure, we can go someday after school.

W That would be great. Thanks!

W 와, 이 피자 아주 맛있다. 어디서 샀어?

M 샘스 피자라는 곳에서. 거기는 진짜 좋은 치즈랑 신선한 채소를 사용해.

W 거기서 또 주문하고 싶다. 거기 번호 좀 알려줄 수 있어?

M 거기 배달은 안 해. 주인이 혼자 운영하는 아주 작은 곳이거든. 주소는 알려줄 수 있어.

W 아, 알겠어. 나중에 나랑 같이 거기에 가 줄래?

M 물론이야, 나중에 방과 후에 가자.

W 그럼 참 좋겠다. 고마워!

09 ③

M Oh, I'm sorry for being late, Monica.

W That's all right. <u>I was browsing the books</u> at the new arrivals section.

M Did you find anything you want to buy?

W No, I don't want to buy anything. How about you? What do you want to buy?

M Nothing.

W What? Then, is there any special reason for asking me to meet you here?

M Sure. I've got surprised for you. Bernard Werber will hold a book signing here at three today to promote his new novel.

W Really? You know, I'm a big fan of him.

M I know. Why don't we go to his book signing together?

W Sounds great!

M 아, Monica, 늦어서 미안해.

W 괜찮아. 신간도서 코너에 비치된 책들을 구경하고 있었어.

M 사고 싶은 것을 찾았니?

W 아니, 사고 싶은 것이 없어. 너는 어때? 뭘 사고 싶은데?

M 없어.

W 뭐? 그렇다면, 여기에서 날 만나자고 한 특별한 이유라도 있니?

M 물론이지. 너를 놀라게 해 주려고. Bernard Werber가 그의 새 소설 판매 촉진을 위해 이곳에서 책 사인회를 3시에 해.

W 정말? 있잖아, 난 그 분의 열렬한 팬인데.

M 나도 알고 있어. 같이 그의 책 사인회에 가는 것이 어떠니?

W 좋아!

10 ⑤

M Good morning. May I help you?

W Yes. I'd like to rent a car here.

M OK. What size car do you have in mind?

W Well, any car is OK if it's not expensive.

M Good. This one is only $35 a day. But as you see, the trunk is not so spacious.

W I see. How about that one? It looks like it can carry big suitcases.

M It's $50. Would you like it?

W Yes. Does the price include tax?

M No, the tax will be 10%.

W OK. I'll rent it for two days.

M 안녕하세요. 도와드릴까요?

W 네. 여기에서 차를 빌릴까 하는데요.

M 알겠습니다. 어떤 크기의 차를 생각하고 계신가요?

W 글쎄요, 비싸지만 않으면 어떤 차든지 괜찮습니다.

M 좋습니다. 이 차는 하루에 35달러입니다. 하지만 보시다시피, 트렁크가 그리 넓지는 않습니다.

W 그렇군요. 저 차는 어떤가요? 큰 여행 가방이 들어갈 것 같은데요.

M 50달러입니다. 마음에 드십니까?

W 네. 가격에 세금이 포함되어 있습니까?

M 아니요, 세금은 10%입니다.

W 좋습니다. 그 차로 이틀 동안 빌리겠습니다.

만점 솔루션 여자가 선택한 차는 하루에 50달러로, 이틀간 빌리면 100달러이고, 세금이 10% 포함되므로 110달러를 지불해야 한다.

11 ③ | ➕ ⑤

W Daniel, I heard you're a great cook.

M Well, thanks for saying so, but I'm not that good. Cooking is just a hobby for me.

W Why don't you teach me how to cook your best dish?

M I'd love to. I can show you how to make quick and tasty dishes if you'd like. All of my recipes are pretty easy to follow.

W Really? That would be great! Just name the day so that I can go grocery shopping first.

M How about this Friday?

W Friday works for me. Text me what I need to buy.

M OK, I will soon. See you Friday!

W 다니엘, 네가 요리를 아주 잘한다고 들었어.

M 그렇게 말해줘서 고맙지만 그렇게 잘하지 않아. 요리는 그냥 취미야.

W 네가 제일 잘 만드는 음식을 어떻게 만드는지 나에게 알려주지 않겠니?

M 좋아. 네가 원하면 어떻게 빨리 맛있는 음식을 만드는 지 보여줄 수 있어. 나의 모든 요리법은 따라하기 꽤 쉽거든.

W 진짜? 그럼 참 좋겠다. 되는 날을 말해줘 식료품부터 사러 갈 수 있게.

M 이번 주 금요일 어때?

W 금요일 좋아. 무엇을 사야 하는지 문자 보내줘.

M 알겠어, 곧 보낼게. 금요일에 보자!

12 ⑤

M Bubble wrap is fifty years old. Like a lot of really cool things, it was created by accident while watching airplanes landing. Now bubble wrap is used as a packing material, protecting everything from vases to computers. Bubble wrap is also a fun toy. When you pop it, it creates a sound. When a room is full of kids and the floor is doubly covered with many pieces of bubble wrap, you don't need anything else to play with. Bubble wrap has close to a million fans on Facebook. This is Warren Robinson from the Associated Press.

M 버블 랩(발포 비닐 시트)은 50년이 되었습니다. 많은 정말로 근사한 물건들처럼, 이것도 비행기 착륙 장면을 보다가 우연히 만들어졌습니다. 지금 버블 랩은 포장 재료로 이용되며, 꽃병에서부터 컴퓨터에 이르는 모든 것들을 보호해 줍니다. 버블 랩은 또한 재미있는 장난감입니다. 버블 랩을 터뜨리면 소리가 납니다. 아이들이 가득한 방에서 마루가 몇 겹의 버블 랩으로 이중으로 덮혀 있으면, 놀 만한 다른 어떤 것이 필요하지 않습니다. 버블 랩은 페이스 북(Facebook)에 거의 100만 명에 육박하는 팬들을 가지고 있습니다. 지금까지 연합 통신의 Warren Robinson이었습니다.

만점 솔루션 버블 랩의 부작용에 대한 언급은 없다.

13 ②

M Hi. Can I help you?

W Yes, please. I'd like to buy a vacuum cleaner.

M All right, ma'am. Do you have a specific model in mind?

W　Well, as long as the suction power is over 250 air watts, it'll be OK with me.

M　About the suction power, you have three options. And what about the dust bags?

W　Let me see the brochure. It says bagless vacuums are more expensive but convenient.

M　That's right. And they consume less electricity.

W　I see. Then I'd like to buy a bagless vacuum with the lowest price tag.

M　Sure. I've got the one for you!

M　안녕하세요. 무엇을 도와드릴까요?

W　네. 진공청소기를 사고 싶어요.

M　좋습니다. 생각하고 계신 특별한 모델이 있나요?

W　글쎄요. 흡입력이 250 에어 와트 이상이라면 저한테는 좋아요.

M　흡입력에 대해서라면 세 가지 선택이 있어요. 그리고 먼지 봉투는 어떤가요?

W　안내책자를 좀 봅시다. 먼지 봉투 없는 진공청소기는 더 비싸지만 편리하다고 되어 있네요.

M　맞습니다. 그리고 그것들은 전력을 덜 소비하죠.

W　그렇군요. 그렇다면 가장 낮은 가격의 먼지 봉투 없는 진공청소기를 사는 게 좋겠어요.

M　물론이죠. 손님에게 맞는 게 하나 있습니다!

14　⑤

W　We hear about this every day, especially in the morning and at night. We want to know whether today or tomorrow will be sunny, cloudy, rainy or windy. Also we want to know how hot or how cold it will be. Some people are especially interested in this because their plans change if this is not good. Mostly we get information on this from the news but nowadays we can use the Internet.

W　우리는 매일, 특히 아침과 밤에 이것에 대해 듣는다. 우리는 오늘이나 내일 날씨가 화창할지, 흐릴지, 비가 올지, 바람이 불지 알고 싶어 한다. 우리는 얼마나 더울지 혹은 얼마나 추울지도 알고 싶어 한다. 만약 이것이 좋지 않으면 계획이 바뀌기 때문에 어떤 사람들은 이것에 대해 특히 관심이 많다. 대개 뉴스에서 이것에 대한 정보를 얻지만 요즈음에는 인터넷을 이용할 수도 있다.

15　①

W　Jack, what are you going to do this Friday evening?

M　I'm going to watch a movie with my brother.

W　Oh, you mean Tommy? Is he here now?

M　Yes. He came to see me last Sunday.

W　I want to see him soon.

M　No problem. He's going to stay here for two weeks.

W　Will you tell him to call me sometime?

M　Why don't you come with me now? We're supposed to meet at the shopping mall.

W　Oh, that's great. I really missed him.

M　You'll be surprised to see how much he's changed.

W　Jack, 이번 금요일 저녁에 뭐 할 거니?

M　형이랑 영화 보러 갈 거야.

W　오, Tommy 말하는 거니? 그가 여기 있니?

M　응. 지난 일요일에 날 만나러 왔어.

W　어서 그를 만나고 싶다.

M　문제 없어. 2주 동안 이곳에 있을 거야.

W　언제 나에게 전화하라고 그에게 말해 줄래?

M　지금 나랑 같이 가지 그래? 쇼핑몰에서 만나기로 했거든.

W　오, 그거 좋겠네. 난 정말 그가 보고 싶거든.

M　그가 얼마나 많이 변했는지 보면 너 놀랄 거야.

16　①　│　➕①

W　You need to buy a lot of things for your first year of college, right? What would you like to get first?

M　As a college student, the most important thing will be a laptop. I'll need to take notes in lectures, write essays, and make slides for presentations.

W　Right. And you'll definitely need an external hard drive so that you can store data and transfer it easily.

M　That's right. Should I also get a printer?

W　I don't think so. You can print things out at the library or the student union building. Don't bother buying one.

M　OK. Oh, I really want to get a digital camera, too. It's my dream to travel and take pictures.

W　All those gadgets are going to cost a lot.

M　Right. I guess I need a laptop before everything else. The semester starts soon!

W　네가 대학생이 된 첫 해니까 많은 걸 사야 해, 그치? 제일 먼저 뭘 갖고 싶어?

M　대학생으로서 가장 중요한 건 노트북이야. 강의 중에 필기도 해야 하고 에세이도 써야 하고 발표를 위한 자료도 만들어야 해.

W　맞아. 데이터를 저장하고 쉽게 옮길 수 있도록 외장 하드 드라이브도 꼭 필요할 거야.

M　맞아. 프린터도 사야 할까?

W　아니. 도서관이나 학생 회관 건물에서 프린트 할 수 있어. 살 필요는 없어.

M　알겠어. 아 나 디지털 카메라도 진짜 갖고 싶어. 여행가서 사진을 찍는 게 내 꿈이야.

W　이 모든 장비들이 꽤 비쌀 거야.

M　맞아. 다른 것보다 노트북이 필요한 거 같아. 학기도 곧 시작하고.

17　③

M　Hi, Cathy. Where are you going?

W　To the post office. I have something to send to my sister.

M　I'm going that way, too. What is it by the way?

W　It's my sister's book. She left it in my house when she visited me yesterday.

M　She can get it when visiting you next time.

W　You know, she is studying in the U.K. She said she needs it for a report.

M　So you're going to send it by express mail before closing time?

W Right. Let's walk faster.

M 안녕, Cathy. 어디 가요?

W 우체국에 가요. 우리 언니에게 보낼 게 있어서요.

M 나도 그쪽으로 가는데. 그런데 그건 뭐예요?

W 우리 언니 책이에요. 어제 우리 집에 왔을 때 놓고 갔거든요.

M 다음번에 방문할 때 가져가도 되잖아요.

W 알다시피, 언니는 영국에서 공부 중인데, 언니가 보고서 쓰는 데 그 책이 필요하대요.

M 그래서 마감 시간 전에 속달 우편으로 그것을 보내려는 거군요?

W 맞아요. 더 빨리 걸어가죠.

18 ③

M I'm going to the department store. Can you come with me?

W No, I have things to do by this afternoon.

M Can I buy something for you then?

W Oh, that's kind of you. Please buy some chocolate donuts.

M Again? You just had one.

W Yes. You know how I like them.

M Do you remember what the doctor said to you?

W Sure I do. But I can't help it.

M _____

M 나 백화점 가요. 나랑 같이 갈래요?

W 아니요. 오늘 오후까지 할 일들이 있어요.

M 그럼 당신을 위해 내가 뭘 좀 사다 줄까요?

W 오, 친절하시네요. 초콜릿 도넛 좀 사다 주세요.

M 또요? 방금 한 개를 먹었잖아요.

W 네. 내가 얼마나 좋아하는지 알잖아요.

M 의사 선생님께서 당신에게 했던 말 기억해요?

W 물론 기억해요. 하지만 어쩔 수가 없네요.

M 좀 줄이는 게 좋겠어요.

① 더 이상 그곳에 가지 마세요.

② 알았어요. 의사 선생님을 위해 그렇게 할게요.

④ 내 생일에 오는 게 어때요?

⑤ 우리 같이 쇼핑 갈래요?

19 ④

M You look sleepy, Jennifer. What happened?

W I worked at a restaurant last night.

M Worked at a restaurant? You mean you got a part-time job?

W Right. Yesterday was my first day.

M But you don't look good. Are you OK?

W Actually, I have a little fever.

M I don't think your new job suits you.

W Well, I'll get used to it.

M _____

M 졸려 보이네요, Jennifer. 무슨 일 있었어요?

W 어젯밤에 식당에서 일했어요.

M 식당에서 일했다고요? 시간제 일을 하고 있다는 말인가요?

W 맞아요. 어제가 첫날이었어요.

M 하지만 몸이 좋아 보이지 않는군요. 괜찮아요?

W 사실, 약간의 열이 있어요.

M 당신의 새 일이 당신과 맞지 않는 것 같네요.

W 글쎄요, 그 일에 익숙해질 거예요.

M 다른 일을 찾아보는 게 어때요?

① 더 열심히 공부하는 게 좋겠어요.

② 식당에서 일하고 싶어요.

③ 당신은 시간제 일을 가졌어야 했어요.

⑤ 휴가를 좀 내는 게 어때요?

20 ①

M Sally is a salesperson in a department store. A man comes to her and shows her a cap. He says he found that a button had fallen off when he got home. He says that he wants to exchange it for a new one. But the same one is not available. She asks the man if he would like to wait until the cap can be fixed. But he wants a new cap. In order to solve this problem, Sally wants to give his money back. In this situation, what would Sally say to him?

M Sally는 백화점의 판매원이다. 한 남자가 그녀에게 와서 모자를 보여준다. 그는 집에 갔을 때 단추가 떨어져 나가고 없는 것을 발견했다고 말한다. 그는 그녀에게 그것을 새 것으로 교환하고 싶다고 말한다. 하지만 똑같은 모자가 없다. 그녀는 그 남자에게 모자가 수선될 때까지 기다리겠는지 물어본다. 하지만 그는 새 모자를 원한다. 이 문제를 해결하기 위해, Sally는 그의 돈을 돌려주고 싶어 한다. 이 상황에서, Sally는 그 남자에게 무슨 말을 할까?

① 환불해 드릴까요, 손님?

② 얼마인가요?

③ 지금 당신의 주문을 받겠습니다.

④ 이것에 대해 얼마를 지불하시겠어요?

⑤ 우리가 당신에게 전화드릴 때까지 기다리시겠습니까?

01 ④, ➕③	02 ④	03 ①	04 ②, ➕③	05 ②
06 ⑤	07 ④	08 ③	09 ④	10 ④
11 ④	12 ④	13 ④	14 ⑤	15 ②
16 ④	17 ④	18 ⑤	19 ①	20 ③

01 ④ | ➕ ③

M May I help you?

W I'm looking for luggage for my trip.

M Are you traveling abroad?

W Yes. I'm going to South Africa.

M How about this suitcase? You can put a lot of things in it, and it's easy to pull along.

W I'm sure it'd be easy to roll it along the street in a city, but I have to travel on lots of unpaved roads in the countryside.

M I see. Then how about one of the backpacks over there?

W Those backpacks look convenient.

M Yes, they are. This backpack has a lot of pockets. It is very useful for carrying around small things. It's only $100.

W I think this one is perfect for me. I'll take it.

M 도와드릴까요?

W 여행을 위한 여행 가방을 찾고 있어요.

M 해외로 여행가시나요?

W 네. 남아프리카에 가려구요.

M 이 여행 가방은 어떠세요? 안에 많은 짐을 넣을 수 있고 끌고 다니기 쉬워요.

W 도시의 길거리에서 끌고 다니기 쉬울 거 같지만 시골의 많은 비포장도로로 여행을 해야 해요.

M 알겠습니다. 그러면 저기 있는 배낭 중 하나는 어떤가요?

W 배낭들이 편리해 보이네요.

M 네, 그렇습니다. 이 배낭은 주머니가 아주 많아요. 작은 물건들을 가지고 다니기에 아주 유용합니다. 100달러밖에 안 해요.

W 이게 저한테 딱 맞겠네요. 그걸로 주세요.

02 ④

[Telephone ring.]

M Hello, this is Kangin Insurance. How may I help you?

W Hello, this is Sarah Smith. I had a car accident this morning.

M I'm sorry to hear that. Are you Okay, ma'am?

W Fortunately, I'm, but my car got damaged.

M Can I have your license plate number and your phone number, please?

W It's 25 Na 2039 and 010-234-8778.

M Thank you for the information. Could you tell me when, where and how the accident happened?

W Yes. It was 10 a.m. I was driving slowly to find a parking spot in front of the Spring department store. Suddenly a taxi came from behind and bumped into my car.

[전화벨이 울린다]

M 여보세요, 강인 보험입니다. 뭘 도와드릴까요?

W 여보세요, 저는 Sarah Smith입니다. 오늘 아침에 자동차 사고가 있었어요.

M 안 되셨네요. 괜찮으세요?

W 다행히도, 괜찮아요. 하지만 제 차에 손상이 있어요.

M 차번호와 전화번호를 알려주시겠어요?

W 25나 2039이고 010-234-8778이에요.

M 정보 주셔서 감사합니다. 언제, 어디서, 어떻게 사고가 일어났는지 말씀해 주세요.

W 네. 오전 10시였고요. Spring 백화점 앞에서 주차장을 찾으려고 천천히 운전하고 있었죠. 갑자기 택시 한 대가 뒤에서 오더니 제 차를 받았어요.

03 ①

① **M** Do you mind if I take the last piece of cake?
  W Of course not. Help yourself.

② **M** Would you recommend a nice restaurant?
  W Sure. There's a great Korean restaurant just across from the bakery.

③ **M** What's your favorite Korean food?
  W Bulgogi is my favorite.

④ **M** Are you ready to order something for desert?
  W I'd like a piece of cake and a coffee, please.

⑤ **M** I'm getting hungry. Let's have a quick bite.
  W Why not?

① **M** 제가 마지막 케이크 조각을 먹어도 되겠습니까?
  W 물론이죠. 어서 드세요.

② **M** 좋은 레스토랑을 추천해 주시겠습니까?
  W 물론이죠. 빵집 바로 건너편에 근사한 한식당이 있습니다.

③ **M** 가장 좋아하는 한식이 뭐죠?
  W 불고기가 제가 가장 좋아하는 것입니다.

④ **M** 후식을 주문하시겠습니까?
  W 케이크 한 조각과 커피 한 잔 부탁합니다.

⑤ **M** 배가 고파요. 간단히 요기라도 해요.
  W 좋아요.

04 ② | ➕ ③

W Airline reservation center. How may I help you?

M Can I purchase a ticket to Jeju Island?

W Sure. What day would you like to travel?

M I'd like to fly this Friday.

W This Friday, May 12? Just a moment, please... *[pause]* I'm sorry, but there aren't any seats available on May 12. All flights are fully booked. There are lots of group tours these days.

M Oh, I see. Do you have any seats on Saturday morning?

W Let me see... It's not easy to <u>find a seat on short notice</u> these days. Ah-ha! How about 7 p.m. on Saturday evening? Other than that, we only have seats available on Sunday, sir.

M Okay, then. I'll take the Saturday evening flight.

W 항공 예약 센터입니다. 무엇을 도와드릴까요?

M 제주행 표를 하나 구매할 수 있을까요?

W 네. 여행가시기 원하시는 날짜가 언제 인가요?

M 이번주 금요일에 가고 싶습니다.

W 이번주 금요일이면 5월 12일이죠? 잠시만 기다려 주세요... [멈춤] 죄송합니다만 5월 12일 좌석은 다 찼습니다. 모든 항공편이 예약되었어요. 요즘에는 단체 관광객들이 많거든요.

M 아, 알겠습니다. 토요일 오전에는 좌석이 있나요?

W 잠시만요... 요즘 갑자기 좌석을 찾는 게 쉽지 않아요. 아! 토요일 저녁 7시 어떠세요? 그거 말고는 일요일에만 좌석이 있습니다.

M 알겠습니다, 그럼. 토요일 저녁 비행편으로 해주세요.

05 ②

M Now Bill is ready, <u>dressed in</u> his racing suit. He wants to win the auto race today. Though everyone in his team thinks he is the best driver, he still thinks he has to learn more. He <u>steps out of the waiting room</u> into the hallway that leads to the platform. Two other drivers, Jack and Roy, are also walking toward the platform. Bill suddenly feels his own confidence fading. There are a lot of drivers in the race, but Jack and Roy are the ones who <u>worry Bill the most</u>. They always seem to have no fear and because of this Bill couldn't sleep well last night.

M 지금 Bill은 경주복을 입고 준비된 상태다. 그는 오늘 자동차 경주에서 우승하고 싶다. 비록 그의 팀의 모든 사람이 그가 최고의 선수라고 생각하지만 그는 여전히 배울 게 많다고 생각한다. 그는 대기실 밖으로 나와 플랫폼으로 이어진 복도로 걸어간다. 다른 선수 두 명, Jack과 Roy 또한 플랫폼으로 걸어가고 있다. Bill은 갑자기 자신감이 사라지는 것을 느낀다. 경주에는 많은 선수들이 있지만 Jack과 Roy가 Bill을 가장 걱정스럽게 만드는 사람들이다. 그들은 늘 겁이 없는 듯 보이고 이것 때문에 Bill은 어젯밤에 잠을 푹 잘 수 없었다.

06 ⑤

M Good afternoon. May I help you?

W No, thanks. I'm just <u>looking around</u>.

M All right. If you need any help, please let me know.

W Sure, I will. Hmm, <u>this mattress</u> looks firm.

M You're right. It's a good brand. It comes with a lifetime warranty, so you don't need to worry about the quality.

W Do you happen to carry <u>blankets to go with</u> this mattress cover, too?

M Unfortunately, we don't. But you can get a blanket at <u>the shop across from our store</u>.

W Oh, I see. By the way, can you give me a discount?

M Sure, you can get a ten percent discount.

M 안녕하세요. 도와드릴까요?

W 고맙지만, 괜찮습니다. 그냥 둘러보고 있어요.

M 알겠습니다. 혹시 도움이 필요하시면, 말씀하세요.

W 네, 그러죠. 흠, 이 매트리스가 단단하게 보이네요.

M 맞습니다. 그것은 좋은 상품입니다. 평생 품질 보증도 해 드리므로 품질에 대해서는 걱정하실 필요가 없습니다.

W 혹시 이 매트리스 커버와 어울리는 담요들도 취급하시나요?

M 불행하게도, 없습니다. 하지만 우리 가게 건너편에 있는 가게에서 담요를 구하실 수 있습니다.

W 오, 알겠습니다. 그런데, 할인해 주실 수 있나요?

M 물론입니다, 10퍼센트 할인해 드릴 수 있습니다.

07 ④

① M Excuse me. Where's the subway station around here?
　 W It's <u>around the corner</u>, next to City Hall.

② M Excuse me, would you happen to know who that lady is over there?
　 W You mean, the one <u>with the red scarf</u>?

③ M How often do you watch movies?
　 W About <u>two times a month</u>.

④ M Can you tell me what this bag <u>is made of</u>?
　 W Sure. It's made in Korea.

⑤ M What are you planning to do next Saturday?
　 W It depends on the weather. I might play tennis unless it's too windy.

① M 실례합니다. 주변에 지하철역이 어디에 있죠?
　 W 모퉁이를 돌아서 시청 옆에 있습니다.

② M 실례합니다만, 혹시 저쪽에 있는 저 여자가 누구인지 아세요?
　 W 빨간색 스카프를 하고 있는 사람 말입니까?

③ M 얼마나 자주 영화를 관람하시나요?
　 W 한 달에 두 번 정도입니다.

④ M 이 가방이 무엇으로 만들어졌는지 아시나요?
　 W 물론이죠. 그것은 한국에서 만들어졌습니다.

⑤ M 다음 토요일에 뭘 할 계획이에요?
　 W 날씨에 달려 있습니다. 바람이 심하게 불지 않으면, 테니스를 칠 수도 있죠.

만점 솔루션 ④ '이 가방이 무엇으로 만들어졌나요?'라고 소재를 묻는 질문에 '한국에서 만들어졌어요.'라고 만들어진 장소를 말하는 것은 어색하다.

08 ③

W I'm going home now. I need to <u>get up early tomorrow</u> to catch a bus.

M Are you going somewhere?

W Yes. I'm going to Gyeongju to see my grandmother. Tomorrow is her 80th birthday.

M So, you <u>want to go to bed</u> early, don't you?

W Yes. I do. I need a good night's sleep because I feel like I'm coming down with something.

M Alright then. I'll see you next Monday.

W Do me a favor. Will you <u>give me a wake up call</u> early in the morning?

M Don't you have an alarm clock?

W I do, but I'm afraid I might turn off the alarm and fall back to sleep again.

W 난 지금 집에 가요. 버스를 잡으려면 내일 아침 일찍 일어나야 해요.

M 어디 가나요?

W 네. 할머니를 뵈러 경주에 가요. 내일이 80회 생신이거든요.

M 그래서 일찍 잠자리에 들려 하는군요, 그렇죠?

W 네. 그리고 지금 좀 피곤해서 잠을 잘 자야 해요.

M 좋아요. 그럼 다음 월요일에 봅시다.

W 부탁 하나만 들어줘요. 아침 일찍 전화로 저를 좀 깨워 줄래요?

M 알람시계 갖고 있지 않아요?

W 갖고 있지요. 하지만 알람을 끄고 다시 잠들까봐 걱정돼서요.

09 ④

M How did you like the movie, Amy?

W I was <u>very disappointed.</u>

M Me, too. Maybe we expected too much.

W Yeah. I <u>fell asleep</u> a few times, too.

M But I think the lead character's acting wasn't that bad.

W I agree. His acting was just great, but <u>the plot was too boring</u>.

M You're right. I <u>couldn't understand</u> what the story was about at all.

W Yeah. Me, neither.

M Amy, 영화 어땠니?

W 아주 실망했어.

M 나도, 그래. 아마도 우리 기대가 너무 컸던 모양이야.

W 그래. 난 몇 차례 졸기도 했어.

M 하지만 주연 배우의 연기는 그렇게 나쁘지 않았어.

W 그래. 그의 연기는 아주 대단했어. 하지만 줄거리가 너무 지루했어.

M 맞아. 이야기가 무엇에 대한 것인지 난 이해할 수 없었어.

W 그래. 나도 마찬가지야.

10 ④

W Look at these goose down jackets! I'd better get one.

M Me too! They start at $150.

W I think $150 is reasonable. I like this blue one. Oh. It's $250.

M That's quite expensive. Why do you prefer that one?

W It's made of 100% goose down, and it's <u>long enough to cover</u> my thighs. I think it'll keep me much warmer.

M Hmm. I need to get a cheaper one. This red one will be good for me. It's $150, and that's <u>within my budget</u>.

W Okay! Hey! If we buy two, they'll give us a 10% discount.

M Really? Then, I'll pay for both of them. You can pay me back later.

W Sounds good.

W 이 거위털 재킷 좀 봐! 하나 사야겠어.

M 나도! 150달러부터 시작하네.

W 150달러면 적정한 가격이라고 생각해. 난 이 파란색이 좋아. 아. 이건 250달러네.

M 꽤 비싸네. 그게 왜 더 좋은 거야?

W 100% 거위털이고 내 허벅지를 충분히 가릴 수 있는 길이야. 이거 훨씬 따뜻할 거 같아.

M 흠. 난 더 저렴한 걸로 할래. 이 빨간 색이 나에게 어울릴 거 같아. 150 달러이고 내 예산이랑 맞아.

W 알겠어! 야! 두 벌을 사면 10% 할인해준대.

M 진짜? 그럼, 내가 두 벌 다 계산할게. 나중에 돈 줘.

W 좋은 생각이야.

11 ④

M Long time no see, Judy.

W What a nice surprise, Paul!

M By the way, where are you going?

W I'm going to the exhibition to write a report about Korean art.

M That's cool. But, Judy, it's two o'clock already. I think the exhibition is <u>closed</u> <u>at 2 o'clock on weekends</u>.

W Don't worry. I already <u>checked the time on</u> the Internet. It says it <u>closes at 5 o'clock</u> today.

M Really? I didn't know that. Then, have a good time!

W Thanks.

M 오랜만이다, Judy.

W Paul, 웬일이야!

M 그런데, 어디 가고 있니?

W 한국 예술에 대한 보고서를 쓰기 위해 전람회에 가는 중이야.

M 멋지다. 그런데, Judy, 벌써 2시야. 내 생각에 전람회는 주말에는 2시에 문을 닫아.

W 걱정 마. 벌써 인터넷에서 시간을 확인했어. 오늘은 5시에 문을 닫는데.

M 정말이니? 몰랐네. 그렇다면, 좋은 시간 보내!

W 고맙다.

만점 솔루션 5시에 문을 닫는다고 했으므로 오늘은 토요일이다.

12 ④

W Hello, students. This September, we will be celebrating the 50th anniversary of our school's foundation and the very first K-pop Dance Festival. The festival will <u>run for three days</u> starting on August 7. Two hundred alumni members are expected to come and enjoy this festival. We'll <u>offer</u> K-pop <u>dance lessons</u> every afternoon. Admission to the festival <u>is free of charge</u>. The highlight of the festival will be a stage dance performance on the last day. Come and enjoy! You'll have a great time!

W 안녕하세요, 학생 여러분들. 이번 9월, 50주년 개교기념일과 첫 번째 케이팝 댄스 페스티벌을 기념할 것입니다. 축제는 8월 7일부터 3일간 열릴 예정입니다. 200명의 졸업생들이 방문하여 이 축제를 즐길 것입니

다. 매일 오후 케이팝 춤 강의를 제공할 것입니다. 축제의 입장료는 무료입니다. 축제의 가장 중요한 부분은 마지막 날 무대 춤 공연이 될 것입니다. 오셔서 즐기세요! 굉장한 시간을 보내게 될 것입니다!

13 ④

W Kevin, I can't find my tablet anywhere.
M I think I put it in the drawer in the hall cabinet. You usually keep it there.
W I've already checked, but it's not there. [sigh] Kevin, I have a very important meeting with my client. I really have to leave now.
M I'm sorry, Mom. Let me think... Did you check the coffee table in the living room?
W I did. But it's not there, either. There's only a pile of books on the coffee table!
M Calm down, Mom. Oh! It might be in my backpack on the couch.
W I'll check. Yes, it was in your backpack. Next time, please put it back in the right place after using it.
M Okay. Sorry.

W Kevin, 내 태블릿을 찾을 수가 없어.
B 제가 복도 캐비닛 서랍에 둔 거 같은데요. 보통 거기에 보관하잖아요.
W 이미 확인해 봤는데, 거기에도 없어. [한숨] Kevin, 나 고객과 아주 중요한 회의가 있어. 진짜 당장 출발해야 해.
B 미안해요, 엄마. 생각해볼게요... 거실에 있는 탁자 확인해 봤어요?
W 했지. 하지만 거기에도 없었어. 탁자위에는 책 한 무더기만 있었어!
B 진정해요, 엄마. 아! 소파 위에 있는 제 책가방 안에 있을 수도 있어요.
W 확인해볼게. 그래, 네 책가방 안에 있었네. 다음에는 사용한 후에 올바른 장소에 놓으렴.
B 알겠어요. 죄송해요.

14 ⑤

W If you have a fever, you have to check yourself by using this.
First, take the cover off the tip.
Second, push the button to turn the unit on.
Third, place the sensor tip well into your ear.
Fourth, keep still for about 5 seconds.
Fifth, when the maximum temperature is reached, the unit will beep.
Finally, read and record the temperature.
You'd better see a doctor if you have too high a temperature.

W 만약 열이 있다면, 이것을 이용해서 스스로 확인해 봐야 한다.
첫 번째, 끝부분에서 뚜껑을 제거하라.
두 번째, 그 장치의 전원을 켜기 위해 버튼을 눌러라.
세 번째, 귀 속으로 감지기 끝을 잘 넣어라.
네 번째, 약 5초 정도 가만히 있어라.
다섯 번째, 최고 온도에 도달하면, 그 장치가 삐 소리를 낼 것이다.

마지막으로, 온도를 읽고 기록하라.
만약 온도가 너무 높으면 의사의 진찰을 받는 것이 좋다.

15 ②

M Good afternoon, ma'am. Can I help you?
W Yes, I'm looking for a couple of traditional Korean dolls.
M Sorry, we don't carry dolls. We sell only pottery here.
W I'm sorry. What did you say you sell?
M Korean traditional pottery, you know, like bowls or plates.
W Oh, I see. Then where can I buy dolls near here?
M I have no idea, but you could try the tourist information center. They might be able to help you there.
W Where is it? Is it far from here?
M No, just one block that way and it's on you right.
W Oh, thank you. Bye.

M 안녕하세요? 뭘 도와드릴까요?
W 네. 전통 한국 인형을 몇 개 찾고 있어요.
M 죄송하지만 인형은 취급하지 않아요. 여기선 도자기만 팔지요.
W 실례지만 뭘 파신다고 말씀하셨어요?
M 한국 전통 도자기요, 아시다시피 사발과 접시 같은 거죠.
W 아, 알겠어요. 그러면 이 근처 어디에서 인형을 살 수 있나요?
M 모르겠어요. 관광 정보 센터에 가셔야 할 것 같아요. 거기에서 도움을 좀 받으실 거예요.
W 그게 어디죠? 여기에서 먼가요?
M 아뇨. 이쪽으로 한 블록만 가시면 오른쪽에 있어요.
W 아, 고마워요. 안녕히 계세요.

16 ④

W Hi, Jack! Our holiday starts next week.
M That's right.
W Are you going to travel somewhere?
M Yes, I'm going on a trip to Asia with my family.
W Oh? Where are you going?
M We're flying to Taiwan on June 24 and then taking a connecting flight to Korea. We're going to spend a week in Korea, until June 30.
W Wow, that's great!
M Then we're going to visit Japan for a week. On July 7, we're flying back to Taiwan again to spend a week there. We're going to leave Taiwan to return home on July 14.
W That's so exciting! I went to Taiwan last year, and I loved it. I can't wait to hear about your trip.

W 안녕, Jack! 우리 휴가가 다음 주부터 시작해.
M 맞아.
W 어딘가로 여행 가니?
M 응, 가족들이랑 아시아로 여행을 갈 거야.
W 어디로 가는데?
M 6월 24일에 대만으로 갔다가 연결편을 타고 한국에 가. 한국에서 6월 30일까지 일주일을 머물 거야.
W 와, 굉장하다!

M 그리고 일주일동안 일본을 방문할 거야. 7월 7일에 다시 대만으로 가서 거기서 일주일을 머물 거야. 7월 14일에 대만에서 집으로 돌아올 예정이야.

W 진짜 재미있겠다! 작년에 대만에 갔었는데 좋았어. 빨리 네 여행 이야기를 듣고 싶다.

17 ④

W Ted, who are these people in this picture?

M Here are my parents and down here are my older sisters, Eva and Lisa. I don't have any brothers.

W Are you the youngest in your family?

M Yes, I am. Both of my sisters are older than me. And both of them are married.

W Then these are their husbands, right?

M Yes. Eva got married to Paul and this is their daughter, Judy.

W What about Lisa?

M She got married, but she doesn't have any children yet.

W Ted, 이 사진에 있는 이 사람들은 누구니?

M 이쪽은 우리 부모님이시고, 여기 아래쪽은 누나들인 Eva와 Lisa야. 남자형제들은 없어.

W 네 가족 중에 네가 가장 나이가 어리니?

M 응, 그래. 여자형제 둘 다 모두 나보다 나이가 더 많아. 둘 다 결혼했고.

W 그러면 이분들은 누나의 남편들이시지, 맞지?

M 그래. Eva는 Paul과 결혼했고, 이 애가 그분들의 딸 Judy야.

W Lisa는?

M 결혼했지만, 아직 자녀는 없어.

만점 솔루션 누나의 딸은 사촌(cousin)이 아니라, 조카(niece)이다.

18 ⑤

M You look down. Do you have any problems?

W Yes, I do.

M What is that bothering you?

W Thanks for asking, but leave me alone.

M Come on, Laura. I'm your best friend. Maybe I can help.

W Actually, I'm planning to take part in the English speech contest next week.

M Wow, that sounds cool. Then, what's the problem?

W I'm so nervous whenever I'm on stage. Any advice?

M _____

M 너 우울해 보인다. 무슨 문제가 있니?

W 응, 그래.

M 너를 괴롭히는 게 뭔데?

W 고맙기는 한데, 나 좀 혼자 있게 둬.

M 그러지만, Laura. 난 너의 가장 친한 친구잖아. 내가 도와줄 수도 있어.

W 사실은, 다음 주에 영어 말하기 대회에 참가할 계획이거든.

M 와, 멋지다. 그런데, 뭐가 문제야?

W 난 무대에 설 때마다 너무 긴장돼. 조언해 줄 거라도 있니?

M 그냥 힘 내! 기억해. 넌 영어를 잘 하잖아.

① 바로 그게 내가 생각하고 있던 거야.

② 네가 내 부탁을 들어줄 수 있는지 궁금해.

③ 네 영어 교과서를 빌릴 수 있니?

④ 대신에 음악 경연대회에 참가하는 것이 어떠니?

19 ①

W How may I help you?

M I'd like to buy an electronic dictionary for my son.

W Do you have anything special in mind?

M No, I don't.

W Then, how about this PowerDic 2000? It contains four languages: Korean, English, Japanese, and Chinese.

M Can I play MP3 files with it?

W Sure.

M That's the one I've been looking for. I'll take it.

W Your son will like it. How do you want to pay for this?

M _____

W 어떻게 도와드릴까요?

M 아들에게 줄 전자사전을 구입하고 싶은데요.

W 생각하고 계신 특별한 것이 있나요?

M 아니, 없습니다.

W 그렇다면, 이 PowerDic 2000은 어떻습니까? 그것은 한국어, 영어, 일본어, 중국어 같은 4개의 언어를 포함하고 있습니다.

M 그것으로 MP3 파일도 재생할 수 있습니까?

W 물론이죠.

M 그것이 바로 제가 찾는 것이네요. 그것으로 구입하겠습니다.

W 그것이 아드님 마음에 들 거예요. 어떻게 지불하시겠습니까?

M 현금으로요.

② 하지만 디자인이 마음에 들지 않습니다.

③ 그것이 너무 비싸지 않으면 합니다.

④ 이것을 선물 포장할 수 있나요?

⑤ 그것에 주목하실 필요는 없습니다.

20 ③

M Harold and his sister Hana are going to watch the baseball game. Harold already booked the tickets. But they have just missed the bus to the stadium. Hana wants to wait for the next bus. However, the bus to the stadium only runs every hour. Harold thinks they'll be late for the game if they keep waiting. Unfortunately, there is a lot of traffic on the street. They have to take a faster way to get there in time. In this situation, what would Harold say to Hana?

M Harold와 그의 여동생 Hana는 야구 경기를 볼 예정이다. Harold는 이미 표를 예약했다. 하지만 그들은 경기장으로 가는 버스를 방금 놓쳤다. Hana는 다음 버스를 기다리기를 원한다. 하지만, 경기장으로 가는 그 버스는 한 시간마다 운행한다. Harold는 만약 그들이 계속 기다린다면, 경기에 늦을 것이라고 생각한다. 불행하게도, 도로는 교통 혼잡이 심하다. 그들은 시간 안에 그곳에 도착하기 위해 더 빠른 길을 택해야만 한다. 이 상황에서, Harold는 Hana에게 무슨 말을 할까?

① Hana야, 유감스럽게도 T–money가 충분하지 않아.
② Hana야, 여기서 다음 버스를 기다리는 것이 어떠니?
③ Hana야, 경기장까지 지하철을 타는 것이 좋겠다.
④ Hana야, 오늘 야구 경기를 어떻게 생각하니?
⑤ Hana야, 오늘은 대신에 영화 보러 가는 것이 어떠니?

만점 솔루션 교통 혼잡이 심한 상황에서 경기장에 늦지 않게 도착하는 방법을 제안해야 하므로, 지하철을 타자는 말이 가장 알맞다.

영어듣기능력평가 **14**회

01 ②	**02** ③	**03** ②	**04** ④, ➊③	**05** ②
06 ①	**07** ④	**08** ⑤	**09** ⑤	**10** ③
11 ②	**12** ⑤	**13** ⑤	**14** ②	**15** ⑤
16 ⑤	**17** ⑤, ➊①	**18** ③	**19** ⑤	**20** ①

01 ②

W Hello, passengers. This is an announcement from the information desk. We have a passenger here who is eagerly looking for her five-year-old boy. His name is Mark Price. He is wearing a short-sleeved T-shirt, blue jeans and white running shoes. He has short, brown, curly hair and blue eyes. If you find him, please take him to Gate 4 or the information desk. Please hurry. His plane leaves in half an hour. Thank you.

W 안녕하세요, 탑승객 여러분. 안내 데스크에서 드리는 안내 방송입니다. 이곳에 다섯 살 된 남자아이를 애타게 찾고 계시는 승객이 한 분 계십니다. 남자아이의 이름은 Mark Price입니다. 그는 반팔 티셔츠와 청바지를 입고 있고 하얀색 운동화를 신고 있습니다. 짧은 갈색의 곱슬머리로, 파란 눈을 가진 아이입니다. 그 아이를 보시면 4번 탑승구나 안내 데스크로 데려와 주시기 바랍니다. 서둘러 주시기 바랍니다. 아이의 비행기가 30분 후에 출발합니다. 감사합니다.

02 ③

[Telephone rings.]

W Milk Delivery Service. How may I help you?
M Hi, I'm Joe Brown. I live in 305, DOS Apartment.
W Yes, Mr. Brown.
M I'll be traveling for a week, so I'd like to hold the milk delivery.
W I see. When do you leave and when will you be back, sir?
M I leave on September 11th and I will be back on the 17th.
W Do you want me to hold the delivery during the period?
M Except September 11th and 17th. I need it on both days.
W I see. Then I'll hold the delivery from September 12th to the 16th.

[전화벨이 울린다.]

W 우유 배달 서비스입니다. 뭘 도와드릴까요?
M 안녕하세요, 저는 Joe Brown입니다. DOS 아파트 305호에 살고 있습니다.
W 네, Brown 씨.
M 제가 일주일 동안 여행을 하게 되어서 우유 배달을 잠시 중단하고 싶습니다.
W 알겠습니다. 고객님, 언제 떠나시고 언제 돌아오시죠?
M 9월 11일에 떠나서 17일에 돌아올 겁니다.
W 그 기간 동안 우유 배달을 중단해 주기를 원하시나요?

M 9월 11일과 17일은 제외하고요. 그 이틀 동안은 우유가 필요합니다.

W 알겠습니다. 그러면 9월 12일부터 16일까지 배달을 중단하겠습니다.

만점 솔루션 남자는 집을 비우는 7일 중, 실제 2일은 우유가 필요하고 5일 동안(9월 12일부터 16일까지)만 중단하려고 하고 있다.

03 ②

① W May I see your ticket, please?
　 M Sure. Here it is.

② W Could you move over there?
　 M Sure. That'll be no problem.

③ W Excuse me, but is this your Cellphone?
　 M Oh, thank you. I almost lost it.

④ W At what station do I have to get off?
　 M Get off at the next stop.

⑤ W You look really tired. Why don't you sit here?
　 M That's okay. I can stand.

① W 표 좀 보여주시겠어요?
　 M 물론이죠. 여기 있어요.

② W 조금만 이동해 주실 수 있을까요?
　 M 물론이죠. 문제 없어요.

③ W 실례합니다만, 이것이 당신 휴대 전화 아닌가요?
　 M 오, 감사합니다. 하마터면 잃어버릴 뻔 했네요.

④ W 어느 역에서 제가 내려야 하나요?
　 M 다음 역에서 내리세요.

⑤ W 정말 피곤해 보이네요. 여기 앉으시지 그러세요?
　 M 괜찮습니다. 서 있을 만합니다.

만점 솔루션 두 여자가 함께 앉을 수 있도록 옆의 남자에게 조금 이동해 달라는 상황이므로, 이동해 달라고 양해를 구하자 기꺼이 그렇게 해 주겠고 대답하는 대화가 가장 적절하다.

04 ④ | ➕ ③

[Cellphone rings.]

M Mandy? I'm surprised to be hearing from you during the day. Aren't you on your field trip?

W I'm at the bus terminal with my friends. The bus is leaving shortly. Where are you, Dad?

M I'm at the office, of course. I'm working on some reports.

W Dad, could you do me a favor? I'm sorry to ask this, but can you go home right now?

M Right now? Is it urgent?

W Yes, I think I forgot to put out the aroma candle when I left the house. Would you please check for me right away?

M Well... Can't you ask your mother? She might be at home.

W I called her, but she didn't answer the phone.

M *[Sigh]* Okay, I'll go home.

W Sorry, Dad. I'll be more careful next time.

[휴대 전화가 울린다.]

M 맨디? 낮에 전화를 하다니 놀랐구나. 현장 학습 간 거 아니었니?

W 친구들이랑 버스터미널에 있어요. 버스가 곧 출발해요. 아빠, 어디세요?

M 난 물론 사무실이지. 보고서를 작성 중이란다.

W 아빠, 부탁 좀 해도 될까요? 죄송하지만 지금 바로 집에 갈 수 있어요?

M 지금 당장? 급한 일이니?

W 네, 제가 집을 나갈 때 아로마 초 끄는 것을 잊었어요. 얼른 확인 좀 해 줄 수 있어요?

M 음... 엄마한테 부탁하면 안될까? 집에 있을 텐데.

W 엄마한테 전화했었는데 전화를 안 받아요.

M *[한숨]* 알겠다. 집에 가볼게.

W 미안해요, 아빠. 다음에는 더 조심할게요.

05 ②

M Well, I have no idea what to say at this moment. I wonder if I really deserve this. All I can think of is that you gave this award to me just to encourage me to do better next time. Well, I feel like totally blank. You know, I never expected to win this award. Words can't express how honored I feel now. I'll continue to do my best. Thank you for honoring me.

M 음, 지금 이 순간 무슨 말을 해야 할지 모르겠습니다. 제가 정말 이것을 받을 자격이 있는 것일까 하는 생각이 듭니다. 제가 생각할 수 있는 것이라고는 단지 다음에 더 잘 하라고 격려하기 위해서 저에게 이 상을 주셨을 거라는 것뿐입니다. 뭐랄까, 머리가 텅 빈 느낌입니다. 여러분도 아시다시피, 저는 이 상을 타리라고는 예측도 못 했어요. 지금 제가 얼마나 영광으로 생각하는지 말로는 표현할 수 없습니다. 계속해서 최선을 다하겠습니다. 저에게 이런 영광을 주셔서 감사합니다.

06 ①

M Could you tell me what happened to the two people, please?

W Okay. I think it was about 11:50 p.m.

M It was around midnight, right?

W Right. I thought the man was just passing by us.

M And then?

W Suddenly the girl beside me screamed and the man ran away.

M Did you see what he got from her?

W It was like her phone or her wallet. I'm not sure because it was too dark and she ran after him right away.

M OK. And you didn't see their faces, either.

W Of course not.

M 두 사람 사이에 무슨 일이 있었는지 말씀해 주시겠어요?

W 좋아요. 제 생각엔 오후 11시 50분이었어요.

M 자정 쯤 되었네요?

W 맞아요. 저는 그 남자가 그냥 우리를 지나가고 있다고 생각했죠.

M 그리고는요?

W 갑자기 제 옆의 여자가 소리를 지르더니 그 남자가 뛰어 달아났어요.

M 그가 여자에게서 무얼 갖고 갔는지 봤어요?

W 전화 아니면 지갑이었던 것 같아요. 너무 어두웠고 그 여자가 남자를 뒤쫓아 뛰었기 때문에 잘 모르겠네요.

M 좋습니다. 그리고 그 사람들 얼굴도 역시 못 봤지요?

W 물론 못 봤어요.

07 ④

① **M** Why do you look so down?
　W I had a fight with my sister. I think I hurt her feelings.
② **M** What are your plans for the vacation?
　W I'm planning to visit my cousin in New Zealand.
③ **M** I'm going to go mountain biking on Sunday.
　W Be sure to wear a helmet when you're riding.
④ **M** What kind of food do you eat most of the time?
　W I don't cook at all.
⑤ **M** Don't waste money. You need to be careful with it.
　W I'll keep that in mind.

① **M** 왜 그렇게 우울해 보여?
　W 여동생이랑 싸웠어. 내가 그녀의 기분을 상하게 한 것 같아.
② **M** 네 휴가 계획이 뭐야?
　W 뉴질랜드에 있는 사촌을 방문하려고 해.
③ **M** 나 일요일에 산악자전거를 타러 갈 거야.
　W 자전거를 탈 때 헬멧 꼭 쓰도록 해.
④ **M** 보통 어떤 종류의 음식을 먹어?
　W 난 요리를 전혀 안 해.
⑤ **M** 돈을 낭비하지 마. 조심해야 해.
　W 명심 할게.

08 ⑤

M I just remembered I have to meet a client on Friday at 7 p.m.
W Then maybe we should meet some other time.
M How about Saturday? Are you free then?
W Yes, that's fine with me.
M Great. Let's meet at 7:00 at Dicken's restaurant.
W Okay. Oh, by the way, I have a new Cellphone number.
M Really? Wait a minute. Oh, my! I left my Cellphone at home. Can you call my Cellphone so that I can store your number in my Cellphone?
W Sure. I'll do that right away.
M Thank you.

M 이제 막 기억이 났는데, 일요일 저녁 7시에 고객을 만나 봐야 해.
W 그러면 다음에 만나야겠네.
M 토요일은 어때? 그 때 시간 돼?
W 응, 나는 괜찮아.
M 잘 됐다. Dicken's 레스토랑에서 7시에 만나자.
W 좋아. 오, 그건 그렇고, 내 휴대 전화 번호가 바뀌었어.
M 그래? 잠시만. 오, 이런! 내 휴대 전화를 집에 두고 왔네. 내가 내 휴대 전화에 네 번호를 저장할 수 있도록 내 휴대 전화로 전화를 해 줄 수 있니?
W 물론이지. 당장 그렇게 할게.
M 고마워.

09 ⑤

W Hi, Robert. How are you today?
M Hi, Dr. Jin. I feel exhausted. I have no energy to do anything.
W Are you eating properly these days?

M Yes. My mom always cooks for me.
W What about snacks?
M I try not to eat any junk food.
W I see. Do you spend a lot of time playing video games?
M Um... Yes, I guess I do play games quite often, but I don't think I'm addicted.
W I'm not saying you are. Just try to spend more time getting exercise. You will feel much better.

W 안녕하세요, 로버트. 오늘 기분 어때요?
M 안녕하세요, 진 선생님. 지쳤어요. 힘이 하나도 없어요.
W 요즘 제대로 먹고 있나요?
M 네. 엄마가 항상 절 위해 요리해주세요.
W 간식은요?
M 정크 푸드는 안 먹으려고 하고 있어요.
W 알겠어요. 비디오 게임을 하는데 많은 시간을 쓰나요?
M 음... 네, 게임을 꽤 자주 하긴 해요 그래도 중독됐다고 생각하지는 않아요.
W 중독됐다고 말하는 게 아니에요. 운동하는데 시간을 더 쓰도록 노력하라는 거예요. 기분이 훨씬 나아질 거예요.

10 ③

W May I help you, sir?
M Yes. What time is the next show?
W It starts at 10:30.
M We got here right on time. How much is the ticket?
W It's $10 for an adult and $8 for a child.
M I see. Three adults and a child, please. Do you offer a senior discount?
W Yes, they get 20% off.
M Okay. Then, I need tickets for one senior, two adults and one child. Here's my credit card.
W All right. One senior, two adults and a child. Here you go. Have a good time.

W 무엇을 도와드릴까요, 손님?
M 네. 다음 번 공연이 몇 시지요?
W 10시 30분에 시작해요.
M 시간에 맞게 왔군요. 표 값은 얼마예요?
W 성인은 10달러고 아동은 8달러입니다.
M 알겠습니다. 어른 세 명에 아이 한 명 부탁해요. 어르신은 할인해 주나요?
W 네. 성인 표에서 20% 할인이에요.
M 좋아요. 그럼 어르신 한 분, 성인 두 명, 그리고 아이 한 명 표가 필요해요. 여기 신용카드 받으세요.
W 좋습니다. 어르신 한 분, 성인 두 명, 그리고 아이 하나요. 여기 있습니다. 즐거운 시간 보내세요.

만점 솔루션 성인 표 값은 10달러인데 경로우대로 20% 할인하면 8달러이므로, 총 36달러를 지불하였다.

11 ②

W David, how's it going with your moving?

M Ugh, I didn't know there are so many things to do when you move. We are still working on it.

W Did you buy everything for your new house?

M Almost. We bought some of the furniture last week. We need to buy a new TV set soon.

W Is there anything I can help with?

M Can you recommend any online stores where we can buy a TV for a good price?

W Sure! I can help you with that. Just let me know the brand of TV you want. I'll search the Internet and send you the link.

W 데이빗, 이사 가는 거 어떻게 되어가고 있어?

M 아, 나는 네가 이사할 때 이렇게 많은 것을 해야 하는지 몰랐어.

W 새 집을 위한 물건들은 다 샀어?

M 거의. 저번 주에 가구 몇 점을 샀어. 곧 새 TV수상기를 사야해.

W 내가 도울 수 있는 일이 없을까?

M 괜찮은 가격에 TV를 살 수 있는 온라인 가게를 추천해 줄 수 있을까?

W 물론이야! 그건 도와줄 수 있어. 네가 원하는 TV 브랜드만 알려줘. 인터넷으로 찾아보고 링크를 보내줄게.

12 ⑤

W Welcome to our badminton club. I'm the court manager. As you see, we use the school gymnasium. It is open from 7 p.m. to 10 p.m. from Monday through Sunday. You can take individual lessons three times a week: Monday, Wednesday, and Friday. The fee is 100,000 won a month. When you enter our club, you will have to pay an entrance fee. It is 200,000 won, which includes the first month's fee. After that, you have to pay 50,000 won every month. Shuttle cocks are provided, so you don't have to bring your own.

W 저희 배드민턴 클럽에 오신 것을 환영합니다. 저는 코트 운영위원장입니다. 보시다시피, 저희는 학교 체육관을 이용하고 있습니다. 체육관은 월요일부터 일요일까지 오후 7시부터 10까지 열려 있습니다. 일주일에 세 번인 월요일, 수요일, 금요일에 개인 수업을 받을 수 있습니다. 강습비는 한 달에 100,000원입니다. 저희 클럽에 가입하시게 되면 가입비를 지불하셔야 합니다. 첫 달 회비를 포함하여 200,000입니다. 그 이후에는 매달 50,000원씩 지불하셔야 합니다. 셔틀콕은 제공되므로 개별적으로 가져오실 필요는 없습니다.

13 ⑤

W Welcome to the Children's Book Fair. It is the biggest event for children's books in the country.

M Thank you! Well, my kids are still too young to read books. What do you recommend I should look at?

W I recommend you take a look at the picture books and pop-up books. There are so many good ones from all over the world.

M I'd like to see the picture books. Where are they?

W Great. You can find them in the Very Young Children's section.

M Where is that?

W Go down to the e-book section and turn right.

M Turn right at the e-book section?

W Yes. And they're next to the kids' magazine section.

M Thank you.

W 어린이 책 박람회에 오신 걸 환영합니다. 어린이 책을 위한 국내에서 가장 큰 행사입니다.

M 감사합니다. 우리 아이들은 책을 읽기에는 아직 너무 어립니다. 제가 무엇을 봐야 하는지 추천해 주시겠어요?

W 그림책과 팝업북을 살펴보실 것을 추천해요. 전세계의 많은 좋은 책들이 있어요.

M 그림책이 보고싶군요. 어디에 있나요?

W 잘됐네요. 그림책은 아주 어린 어린이 구역에서 찾으실 수 있어요.

M 그게 어디에 있나요?

W 전자책 구역으로 내려가다가 오른쪽으로 도세요.

M 전자책 구역에서 오른쪽으로 돌아라?

W 네. 어린이 잡지 구역 옆에 있어요.

M 고맙습니다.

14 ②

M These days, lots of people use smart phones. As you well know, you can not only use them to make phone calls but also surf the Internet no matter where you are. You can book a hotel room and even send text messages to your friend in another country for free. However, they come with some drawbacks. For example, many kids play games for a long time which poses serious health risks. What's more, some adults spend too much time using them, which may cause lack of exercise.

M 요즘에는 많은 사람들이 스마트폰을 사용한다. 당신도 잘 알다시피 전화를 거는 것뿐만 아니라 당신이 어디에 있건 인터넷 검색도 할 수 있다. 호텔 방을 예약할 수도 있고 다른 나라에 있는 친구에게 무료로 문자를 보낼 수도 있다. 하지만 이것들은 문제 또한 일으킬 수 있다. 예를 들어, 많은 아이들은 너무 오랜 시간 동안 게임을 하기 때문에 결국엔 건강에 심각한 위협이 될 수 있다. 게다가, 몇몇 어른들 역시 이것들을 사용하는 데 너무 오랜 시간을 소비하는데, 이는 운동 부족을 일으킬 수 있다.

15 ⑤

W Good afternoon. How may I help you?

M Is Mr. Barns here? I need to see him.

W Sorry, you can't. He's in a meeting with his partner. May I have your name, please?

M I am Mick Hunter from ABK bank in Tokyo. Do you know when he will be available?

W I have no idea. Is there anything I can help you with?

M Well, my boss sent me here to give this sales report to him.

W Oh, that's what Mr. Barns said he would need by this evening. Would you like to leave it with me? I'll hand it over

W to him.

M That's very kind of you. Thank you.

W 안녕하세요? 뭘 도와드릴까요?

M Barns 씨가 여기에 계신가요? 그 분을 뵈어야 하는데요.

W 죄송하지만 안 되시겠네요. 파트너와 지금 회의 중이세요. 성함을 말씀해 주시겠어요?

M 저는 도쿄의 ABK 은행에서 온 Mick Hunter라고 합니다. 언제 가능하실지 아시나요?

W 모르겠어요. 제가 뭐 도와드릴 일이 있나요?

M 음, 저의 사장님이 그분에게 이 판매보고서를 갖다 드리라고 저를 보내셨어요.

W 아, 오늘 저녁까지 필요하다고 Barns 씨가 말했던 거군요. 여기에 놓으실래요? 제가 그에게 전해드리겠습니다.

M 정말 친절하시네요. 감사합니다.

16 ⑤

M What happened to his ankle?

W My son had his left ankle sprained during basketball practice.

M Didn't he have his leg broken last year?

W Yes, he did. He was playing soccer at that time.

M Well, I don't think he is physically fit enough for any sports.

W He won't be a professional athlete. He's just learning the basics. Actually, he wants to be a doctor just like you.

M Oh, I see. Let me examine his leg. I hope he has just sprained it and not broken it.

W So do I. He isn't acting as if he is in a lot of pain.

M 그의 발목이 어떻게 된 거죠?

W 아들이 농구 연습 도중에 왼쪽 발목을 삐었어요.

M 그가 작년에는 다리가 부러지지 않았나요?

W 네, 그랬죠. 그 때는 축구를 하고 있었어요.

M 음, 그가 스포츠를 하기에는 신체적으로 튼튼하지 않은 것 같아요.

W 프로 선수가 되지는 않을 겁니다. 그는 단지 기본기를 배우고 있는 중이에요. 사실, 그는 선생님처럼 의사가 되고 싶어 해요.

M 오, 그렇군요. 아드님의 다리를 검사해 볼게요. 아드님의 다리가 부러진 것이 아니고 단순히 삔 것이기를 바랍니다.

W 저도 그래요. 그가 대단한 고통에 시달리는 것처럼 행동하지는 않네요.

만점 솔루션 여자의 말에서 남자의 장래 희망에 대한 언급이 나오고 있다. 의사인 남자에게 당신처럼 의사가 되고 싶어 한다(he wants to be a doctor just like you)고 말하고 있으므로 여자 아들의 장래 희망은 의사임을 알 수 있다.

17 ⑤ | ➕ ①

W Good morning. May I see your ticket?

M Here you are.

W Would you like a window seat or an aisle seat?

M I'd like a window seat, please.

W Certainly. How many bags do you have?

M I have one bag to check in. And I'll carry this one on the plane.

W Okay. Just put it down on the conveyor, please.

M All right.

W You're all checked in. Here's your boarding pass. Your seat number is 14A. Your flight is boarding from Departure Gate 40 at 10:00.

M I'm sorry, was that Gate 14?

W _____

W 안녕하세요. 표를 볼 수 있을까요?

M 여기 있습니다.

W 창가 쪽과 통로 쪽 중 어느 좌석이 좋으세요?

M 창가 쪽으로 부탁드립니다.

W 알겠습니다. 가방은 몇 개 갖고 계세요?

M 부칠 가방 하나가 있습니다. 이 가방은 비행기에 가지고 갈 겁니다.

W 알겠습니다. 가방을 운반대 위에 올려주세요.

M 알겠습니다.

W 탑승 수속이 다 끝났습니다. 여기 탑승권입니다. 좌석 번호는 14A입니다. 10시에 40번 출발 탑승구에서 탑승하시면 됩니다.

M 죄송합니다. 14번 탑승구요?

W 아니요. 40번 출발 탑승구요. 4-0이요.

18 ③

M When are you moving to New York?

W I'm leaving next Monday.

M What's going to happen to this apartment?

W Well, I heard a new person will move in this weekend.

M Then, where will you stay this weekend?

W I don't know yet. I'll probably go to my parents' place.

M I see. What will you do with your furniture?

W I will sell it this week except my TV. I'm going to take it to New York.

M Hey, I'd like to buy your sofa.

W _____

M 언제 뉴욕으로 이사를 갈 거니?

W 다음 주 월요일에 떠날 거야.

M 이 아파트는 어떻게 되는 거야?

W 글쎄, 새로운 사람이 이번 주말에 이사 들어온다고 들었어.

M 그럼, 넌 이번 주말에 어디에서 머무를 거야?

W 아직 몰라. 아마도 부모님 댁으로 갈 것 같아.

M 그렇구나. 가구는 어떻게 처리할 거니?

W TV를 제외하고 이번 주에 팔려고. TV는 뉴욕에 가지고 갈 거야.

M 이봐, 내가 네 소파를 사고 싶어.

W 그래? 그러면 내가 싼 값으로 줄게.

① 그것을 포장해 줄래?

② 내가 뉴욕에 가져가겠다고 말했잖아.

④ 그것이 내가 생각했던 것보다 더 비싸네.

⑤ 제의는 고맙지만 부모님 댁에서 머물게.

19 ⑤

M I'd like you to put some ice on your ankle when you get home.

W Okay. How long should I keep the ice on?

M Just half an hour. It'll help to reduce the swelling.

W Half an hour, okay. Is there anything else?

M Yes. I'll give you some painkillers. Take two pills when it hurts a lot.

W Thanks. Do you think I need an X-ray?

M No. Your ankle is sprained, not broken.

W That's good. Do you think I'll be able to go mountain biking again this weekend?

M No. You'll need to rest your ankle for at least a couple of weeks.

W _____

M 집에 도착해서 발목에 얼음을 좀 대도록 하세요.

W 알겠습니다. 얼마나 오랫동안 얼음을 대고 있어야 하죠?

M 30분만 대고 계세요. 부기를 가라앉히는 데 도움이 될 겁니다.

W 30분이요. 알겠습니다. 달리 또 필요한 것이 있을까요?

M 네. 진통제를 좀 드릴게요. 많이 아플 때 알약 두 개를 드세요.

W 감사합니다. 엑스레이가 필요하지는 않을까요?

M 아니요. 발목이 삐었을 뿐, 부러진 것은 아니에요.

W 다행이군요. 이번 주말에 다시 산악자전거를 타러 갈 수 있을까요?

M 안돼요. 적어도 2주 동안은 발목을 안정시켜야 합니다.

W 오, 안돼요. 산악자전거를 타지 않고는 일주일도 살 수가 없어요.

① 괜찮아요. 당신 잘못이 아니었어요.

② 걱정하지 말아요. 내가 당신을 잘 돌볼게요.

③ 그렇게 심각하지는 않지만, 가끔씩 쑤실 거예요.

④ 함께 가시죠? 산악자전거는 재미있어요.

20 ①

M You've wanted to buy a computer for a long time. So you have saved some money. Now you are looking around a computer shop. Then at a shop, a salesperson comes and starts showing you computers which are out of your price range. You checked the prices of many computers but didn't find one you could afford. So you can't buy a computer now. You should save more money. In this situation, what would you most likely say to the salesperson?

M 당신은 오랫동안 컴퓨터를 사고 싶어 했다. 그래서 돈을 좀 저축해 왔다. 지금 당신은 컴퓨터 매장을 둘러보고 있다. 그 때 어느 한 매장의 판매원이 와서 당신의 가격 범위를 벗어난 컴퓨터를 보여주기 시작한다. 당신은 많은 컴퓨터의 가격을 확인해 보았지만 구입할 수 있는 컴퓨터를 발견하지 못했다. 따라서 당신은 지금 컴퓨터를 살 수가 없다. 당신은 돈을 더 저축해야 한다. 이 상황에서, 당신은 판매원에게 뭐라고 말할 것 같은가?

① 감사합니다. 나중에 다시 올게요.

② 저 데스크탑 컴퓨터는 얼마죠?

③ 더 좋은 것을 보여주시겠습니까?

④ 죄송합니다만 제가 당신을 화나게 할 의도는 없었습니다.

⑤ 지난달에 그 컴퓨터를 샀어야 했어요.

01 ②	**02** ①	**03** ③	**04** ①	**05** ⑤
06 ①	**07** ①	**08** ④	**09** ⑤	**10** ②
11 ②	**12** ③	**13** ④, ➕②	**14** ③	**15** ①
16 ④	**17** ④, ➕③	**18** ②	**19** ②	**20** ①

01 ②

M Good evening, ma'am. May I help you?

W Yes, I'm looking for a scarf for my friend.

M Do you have any particular style in mind?

W Well, my friend likes flowers. Do you have one with flower pattern?

M We sure do. But floral pattern is not as popular as used to be.

W Really? I didn't know that. Then how about a check scarf?

M That's a great choice. We have two different kinds. The one with trimmed lace is best seller these days.

W Looks nice, but I think it's too showy for her.

M In that case, I am sure she'll love this one.

M 안녕하세요. 뭘 도와드릴까요?

W 네, 친구의 생일 선물로 줄 스카프를 찾고 있어요.

M 생각하고 계시는 특별한 스타일이 있나요?

W 글쎄요, 친구가 꽃을 좋아해요. 꽃무늬 있는 것 있어요?

M 물론 있지요. 하지만 꽃무늬는 예전만큼 인기가 없어요.

W 정말이요? 몰랐어요. 그러면 체크무늬 스카프는 어때요?

M 좋은 선택이죠. 두 가지 종류가 있어요. 장식된 레이스가 있는 게 요즘 잘 팔리죠.

W 좋아 보이네요, 하지만 그건 친구에게는 너무 화려한 것 같아요.

M 그런 경우라면 이것을 좋아하실 겁니다.

02 ①

[Telephone rings.]

M Hello. This is Robert. I'm not in at the moment. After the beep, please leave a message and your phone number. I'll get back to you as soon as I can.

[Beep.]

W Hi, Robert. This is Tina. Do you remember the camera I bought last week? Actually I'm in trouble now. I have to take some photos tomorrow but my new camera is in the service center. I dropped it on the floor yesterday. It would be great if I can use yours tomorrow. As soon as you hear this please call me at 3023-2319.

[전화벨이 울린다.]

M 여보세요. 저는 Robert입니다. 저는 외출 중입니다. 삐 소리 후에 메모와 전화번호를 남겨주세요. 가능한 한 곧 연락드리겠습니다.

[삐.]

W 안녕, Robert. 난 Tina야. 너 내가 지난주에 산 카메라 기억해? 사실 지금 내가 곤란해. 내일 사진 몇 장을 찍어야 하는데 내 새 카메라가 수리점에 있어. 어제 바닥에 떨어뜨렸거든. 만약 내가 너의 것을 내일 사용할 수 있다면 정말 좋을 것 같아. 이 말을 듣자마자 바로 내게 3023–2319로 전화 좀 해 줘.

03 ③

① M What are you drawing?
　W I'm drawing a man walking his dog.
② M Have you been to this place?
　W Yes, I have. It was long ago.
③ M Where do you want to put this picture?
　W Above the sofa. Thank you.
④ M This sofa looks too heavy.
　W Yeah, let's not move it.
⑤ M Where did you get the puppy?
　W It's a present from my brother.

① M 뭘 그리고 있어요?
　W 개를 산책시키는 남자를 그리고 있어요.
② M 이곳에 와 본 적이 있어요?
　W 네, 오래 전에요.
③ M 이 그림을 어디에 걸까요?
　W 소파 위에요. 감사합니다.
④ M 이 소파 너무 무거워 보이는데요.
　W 그래요, 옮기지 맙시다.
⑤ M 강아지 어디서 얻었어요?
　W 오빠의 선물이에요.

04 ①

M Sally, our last exam is on Friday. Do you have any plans for after the exam?
W No, nothing special.
M Then, how about playing a VR game together?
W Sure! Let's go to that new VR game park.
M Sounds good. What about meeting at 4?
W Oh, sorry... I've started taking violin lessons on Thursdays and Fridays. My lesson on Friday finishes at 5. How about at 6 on Friday, or anytime on Saturday?
M I'm supposed to go to my grandma's house on the weekend. Let's meet at 6 p.m. on Friday.
W Sounds great!

M 샐리, 우리 마지막 시험이 금요일이야. 시험 끝나고 뭐 계획이라고 있어?
W 아니, 특별히 없어.
M 그럼, 같이 VR게임하는 거 어때?
W 좋아! VR게임 파크에 가자.
M 좋아. 4시에 만나는 거 어때?
W 아, 미안... 나 4시에 치과 검진을 예약했어. 금요일 5시나 토요일 아무 때나 어때?

M 주말에는 할머니 댁에 가기로 되어있어. 금요일 5시에 만나자.
W 좋아!

05 ⑤

W Hello, students! We're looking for volunteers to work at the Sunshine Community Center. We need help all year round. Volunteers can help with various duties. You can support students in 2nd to 5th grades by helping them with their homework, or you can help with office duties there. The first step is to fill out our online application. Once you've completed our application, Ted Pedrick, our Service Team Director, will contact you. You can learn more about all of our volunteer opportunities on our website at www.lovecommunity.org.

W 안녕하세요, 학생 여러분들! 선샤인 커뮤니티 센터에서 자원봉사자를 찾고 있습니다. 우리는 일년 내내 도움이 필요합니다. 자원봉사자는 여러가지 일을 도울 수 있습니다. 2학년에서 5학년까지의 학생들의 숙제를 도와줌으로써 지원할 수 있고 그곳에서 사무적인 일을 도울 수도 있습니다. 첫 번째 단계는 온라인 신청서를 작성하는 것입니다. 지원서를 작성하면, 우리 서비스 팀 책임자인 팀 패드릭이 당신에게 연락할 것입니다. 웹사이트 www.lovecommunity.org에서 우리의 모든 자원봉사 기회에 대해 더 배울 수 있습니다.

06 ①

W Oh! Hi, Mike. Come on in.
M Hello, Lisa. Thanks for inviting me to your housewarming. So this is your new place.
W Yes. It's only been a week. Let me show you around.
M I think this house is bigger than the one you lived in before.
W Oh, yes. This is much bigger.
M Oh, Wow! The living room is very spacious and bright.
W Yes. What I like most is the window. It lets in a lot of light during the day.
M It has a nice view, too. I envy you.

W 아! 안녕하세요, Mike. 들어오세요.
M 안녕하세요, Lisa. 집들이에 초대해 줘서 감사합니다. 이곳이 당신의 새 집이네요.
W 네. 일주일밖에 안 되었어요. 제가 보여 드리죠.
M 전에 사시던 집보다 더 큰 것 같네요.
W 아, 예. 훨씬 크죠.
M 와! 거실이 아주 넓고 밝은데요.
W 네. 제가 제일 좋아하는 건 창문이에요. 낮엔 많은 빛이 들어오게 하죠.
M 전망도 역시 좋군요. 부럽습니다.

07 ①

① W Why the long face, Jimmy?
　M I just heard from my teacher that I won first prize in the essay contest.
② W You look a little excited. What's up?

M I got a job offer from one of the best companies in Seoul.

③ W What are you going to do this weekend?

M I've been too busy during weekdays, so I'm going to get some rest.

④ W How was your first day of school?

M Oh, it couldn't be better. I made a couple of friends.

⑤ W Are you going to take biology this semester?

M No. Actually I'm interested in math these days, not biology.

① W 왜 안색이 안 좋아, Jimmy?

M 논술 대회에서 내가 1등 했다고 선생님이 방금 말씀하시는 걸 들었어.

② W 좀 들뜬 표정이야. 무슨 일이지?

M 서울에서 제일 좋은 회사 중 한 곳으로부터 취업 제의를 받았거든.

③ W 이번 주말에 뭐 할 거야?

M 주중에 너무 바빠서 휴식을 좀 취하려고 해.

④ W 학교 첫날 어땠어?

M 아, 너무 좋았어. 친구도 몇 명 사귀었지.

⑤ W 이번 학기에 생물 수업 들을 거야?

M 아니. 사실 요즘 난 생물이 아니고 수학에 관심이 있어.

08 ④

[Cellphone rings.]

M Hi, honey. Did you watch the musical with Sarah?

W Yeah. The musical you recommended was great.

M Good. I was sure you'd enjoy it. Are you busy this afternoon?

W Not really. I'm going to pick up Jason at his school and take him to the library.

M Then, can you do me a favor on the way back from the library?

W Sure. What is it?

M You know the gym I go to? I left my running shoes there. Could you get them for me? I need to wear them on the weekend.

W No problem.

M They are in locker 57 and the password is the last four digits of your Cellphone number. Thanks, honey.

[휴대 전화가 울린다.]

M 안녕, 여보. 사라랑 같이 뮤지컬 봤어?

W 응. 당신이 추천한 뮤지컬 정말 좋았어.

M 잘됐다. 당신이 좋아할 거라 확신했어. 오늘 오후에 바빠?

W 아니. 학교에서 Jason을 태우고 도서관에 데려다줄 거야.

M 그럼, 도서관에서 돌아오는 길에 부탁 하나만 해도 될까?

W 물론. 뭔데?

M 내가 가는 체육관 알지? 거기에 러닝화를 두고 왔어. 그것 좀 가져다 줄 수 있어? 주말에 신어야 해.

W 문제 없어.

M 신발은 57번 보관함에 있고 비밀번호는 당신 휴대번호 번호 마지막 네 자리 수야. 고마워, 여보.

09 ⑤

W Guess what I got today, Johnny?

M Something good?

W I got a call from Hollywood. I'm going there to have a screen test next month.

M Wow! You mean you'll be a movie star?

W Maybe. I sent my photos to a movie company and they called me.

M Really? So your dream is now coming true.

W Actually I'm a little nervous now.

M Don't worry. You'll pass the test. I'll cross my fingers for you.

W Johnny, 오늘 내가 뭘 받았는지 알아 맞혀 봐요.

M 좋은 거예요?

W 할리우드에서 전화를 받았어요. 다음 달에 스크린 테스트를 받으러 그곳에 갈 거예요.

M 와! 당신이 영화 스타가 된다는 말이에요?

W 아마도요. 영화 회사에 제 사진들을 보냈는데 그들이 제게 전화를 한 거예요.

M 정말이요? 당신의 꿈이 이제 현실로 이루어지는 거네요.

W 사실 저 지금 조금 긴장되요.

M 걱정하지 마요. 테스트에 통과할 거예요. 행운을 빌어줄게요.

만점 솔루션 cross one's fingers는 검지와 중지를 포개서 열십자(+)를 만드는 행동으로, 행운을 빌어줄 때 쓰는 표현이다.

10 ②

M Good morning, ma'am. How can I help you?

W Hi! I'm looking for a coffee table.

M How about this one? It's one of our bestselling tables.

W It looks nice. How much is it?

M The original price is $200, but right now there's a 30% discount.

W I'll take it. I also need two comfortable chairs to go with the coffee table.

M Then, I recommend these chairs. They are very comfortable, and the price is reasonable—just $50 each.

W Let me try sitting in one. Oh, it is really comfortable. Are the chairs on sale, too?

M No, ma'am, they aren't. But if you buy two of these chairs, you'll get a free cushion, worth $10.

W All right, then. I'll take the table and two of the chairs.

M 안녕하세요. 무엇을 도와드릴까요?

W 안녕하세요. 탁자를 찾고 있습니다.

M 이건 어떠세요? 가장 잘 나가는 탁자 중 하나입니다.

W 괜찮네요. 얼마인가요?

M 정가는 200달러이지만 지금 30% 세일 중입니다.

W 그걸로 할게요. 탁자와 어울리는 편안한 의자 두 개도 필요해요.

M 그럼, 이 의사를 추천할게요. 아주 편안하고 가격도 합리적입니다. 개 당 50달러밖에 안 합니다.

W 하나에 앉아볼게요. 와, 정말 편하네요. 의자들도 세일 중인가요?

M 아니요, 의자는 아닙니다. 하지만 의자 두 개를 사시면 10달러짜리 쿠션을 하나 드립니다.

W 알겠습니다. 그럼, 탁자와 의자 두 개 주세요.

11 ②

M Hello. I'm Jack Morgan from Ultimate Challenge Magazine dealing with mountain climbing. Do you have a second?

W Yes. But I don't have much time.

M You are here to buy something, right?

W Yes. This is my first visit to this shopping mall.

M OK. I'm going to ask a question. How often do you go to the mountain?

W Well, about twice a month. I just enjoy hiking with my husband.

M OK. Thank you for your cooperation.

W You're welcome.

M 안녕하세요, 전 등산에 관해 다루는 Ultimate Challenge 잡지에서 나온 Jack Morgan입니다. 시간 있으신가요?

W 네. 하지만 시간이 많지는 않습니다.

M 무언가를 사러 여기 오셨죠?

W 네. 이 쇼핑몰에 처음 왔습니다.

M 좋습니다. 질문을 하나 드릴게요. 산에 얼마나 자주 가십니까?

W 음, 한 달에 두 번이요. 남편과 그저 가벼운 등산을 즐깁니다.

M 알겠습니다. 협조해 주셔서 감사합니다.

W 천만에요.

12 ③

M Is your family looking for a great bonding experience this summer? With the help of Wild Water Adventures, this is exactly what we can create for you! Bring your entire family rafting on the Hongchun River this summer and create wonderful memories together. The adventure will give your family stories to tell for years! The gentle course is $80 per person, and the wild course is $140. Both courses are available for kids aged 8 and up. Discounts of 10% are available for groups of 10 or more. We provide transportation from K Hotel to the river for an extra $10 charge. Find out more at www.raftingparadise.com and book today!

M 이번 여름 가족들이 큰 유대감을 형성하는 경험을 찾고 있나요? 와일드 워터 어드벤쳐스의 도움으로, 그게 바로 당신을 위해 우리가 만들어 낼 수 있는 것입니다! 이번 여름 가족 전체를 데리고 홍천강에 래프팅을 하러 오세요 그리고 같이 멋진 추억을 만드세요. 모험은 가족들에게 몇 년 동안이나 이야기할 거리를 만들어 줄 겁니다! 순한 과정은 인 당 80 달러이고 격렬한 과정은 140달러입니다. 두 과정 다 8살의 어린이과 그 이상만 이용할 수 있습니다. 10명이나 그 이상일 경우 10%의 할인이 적

용됩니다. 우리는 K호텔에서 강까지 추가 10달러로 교통편을 제공합니다. www.raftingparadise.com에서 더 많이 알아보시고 오늘 예약하세요!

13 ④ | ➕ ②

M Come in. How can I help you?

W Hi, I was hoping to find a shared house in this neighborhood.

M Can you tell me what price range you have in mind?

W Well, I can't pay more than $700 per month. And I want to find a place that's walking distance from Korea University. I'd like to save on commuting time.

M Okay. There are several places available.

W Oh, it needs to be furnished and have all the basic appliances, too.

M All right. Do you need a parking space?

W No. I walk or ride my bike to school.

M That's good. Is there anything else that is important to you?

W Not really. I just hope there's no curfew at the house. I'm going to be coming back late from the library quite often, so it'd be better if there isn't a strict curfew for tenants.

M OK. This shared house looks like it'd be perfect for you.

M 들어오세요. 무엇을 도와드릴까요?

W 안녕하세요, 이 주변에 셰어하우스를 찾길 희망하는데요.

M 생각 중인 가격대를 알려주실 수 있나요?

W 음, 한 달에 700달러 이상은 지불할 수 없어요. 그리고 고대에서 걸어서 갈 수 있는 곳을 찾고 싶어요. 통근 시간을 아끼고 싶거든요.

M 알겠습니다. 이용 가능한 곳이 여러 곳 있습니다.

W 아, 가구가 비치되어있고 모든 기본적인 가전제품들이 있어야 해요

M 알겠습니다. 주차장이 필요한가요?

W 아니요. 학교에 걸어가거나 자전거를 타고 갈 거예요.

M 잘됐네요. 다른 중요한 거 더 없나요?

W 없어요. 그냥 통금 시간이 없었으면 좋겠어요. 도서관에서 꽤 자주 늦게 돌아올 거라서 세입자에게 엄격한 통금 시간이 없으면 좋겠네요.

M 알겠습니다. 이 셰어하우스가 당신에게 완벽해 보이네요.

14 ③

M This is a very important thing for all forms of life. About 70 percent of your body is made up of this, so you cannot live without this. This has no shape and therefore it totally fills its container. For example, if it is in a square glass it becomes square and if it is in a flat dish it becomes flat. But this becomes two different states like ice when it is too cold or steam when it is too hot.

M 이것은 모든 형태의 생물에게 아주 중요한 것 중의 하나이다. 당신 몸의 약 70퍼센트가 이것으로 이루어져 있어서 당신은 이것 없이는 살 수 없다. 이것은 형태가 없어서 이것이 담겨 있는 용기를 완전히 채울 수 있다. 예를 들어, 만약 이것이 네모난 유리컵 안에 있으면 사각형이 되고, 만약 이것이 평평한 접시에 있으면 평평해진다. 하지만 이것은 너무 추

우면 얼음으로 또는 너무 더우면 증기로 되는 것처럼 두 가지 다른 상태가 된다.

만점 솔루션 사람의 몸의 70퍼센트가 이것으로 이루어져 있다는 사실과 온도에 따라 얼음과 증기로 존재한다는 사실에서 '물(water)'임을 알 수 있다.

15 ①

M Melisa, can you do me a favor?

W Sure. What is it?

M Would you make two copies of this?

W OK. It's your ID card, right?

M Yeah. I need to send them to my sister who sells cars.

W Are you going to buy a new car?

M Yes. My old car is a real museum piece!

W Haha.... So she's going to do all the document work for you?

M That's right. After copying it, just put them on my desk. Thank you.

M Melisa, 부탁 좀 들어줄래요?

W 물론이죠. 뭐죠?

M 이것을 2부 복사해 줄래요?

W 알았어요. 신분증이죠?

M 네. 그것들을 자동차를 파는 제 여동생에게 보내야 해요.

W 새 자동차를 사려는 거예요?

M 네. 내 옛날 자동차는 진짜 박물관 전시감이에요!

W 하하…. 그러니까 그녀가 당신을 위해 모든 서류 작업을 해 줄 거군요?

M 맞아요. 복사 후에 그냥 그것들을 제 책상 위에 놓아 주세요. 고마워요.

16 ④

W Jake, you're not eating much today. Are you not feeling well?

M I'm fine. I'm on a diet.

W Really? I don't think you need to diet. Come on, it is your favorite burger restaurant!

M I know, but I'm trying to cut down on eating junk food.

W Well, it's hard to stop eating junk food.

M That's right. It's delicious, so it's not easy to cut it out completely. But it has such a bad effect on our bodies. Most junk food is very fatty, so eating too much can cause cardiovascular disease.

W You're right. So, you chose to have a fresh salad today. Do you want to cut out all fat from your diet?

M Well, I'm trying to not only avoid fat but also reduce salt and sugar.

W I see. I think you will be able to lose weight fast and get healthier.

W 제이크, 오늘 잘 못 먹는데. 어디 안 좋아?

M 난 괜찮아. 다이어트 중이야.

W 진짜? 너 다이어트 할 필요가 없다고 생각하는데. 그러지 말고, 여기 네가 제일 좋아하는 버거 레스토랑이잖아.

M 알지만 정크 푸드를 줄이려고 노력 중이야.

W 음. 정크 푸드를 안 먹는 건 힘들지.

M 맞아. 맛있어서 완전히 끊기 쉽지 않아. 하지만 그게 몸에 나쁜 영향을 끼치잖아. 대부분의 정크 푸드는 지방이 아주 많으니까 너무 많이 먹으면 심혈관질환을 일으킬 수도 있어.

W 네가 옳아. 그래서 네가 오늘 신선한 샐러드를 먹기로 정했구나. 식단에서 지방을 아예 빼길 원하는 거야?

M 음, 지방을 피하는 것뿐만 아니라 소금이랑 설탕도 줄이려고 노력 중이야.

W 알겠어. 나는 네가 금방 살을 빼고 건강해질 수 있을 거라 생각해.

17 ④ | ➕ ③

W My family and I are going to Thailand this weekend.

M Oh, really? That's great.

W Yeah. I got all my luggage packed last night, so I'm all ready.

M Sounds good. Did you make a hotel reservation?

W Yes. My father already booked everything. The hotel has a fancy swimming pool on the rooftop. Doesn't it sound fantastic?

M It sure does!

W Have you been to Thailand before?

M Yes, just once. You can enjoy some really delicious street food there. Did you exchange any money?

W Not yet. We'll mostly use our credit cards.

M _____

W 우리 가족이랑 나는 이번 주말에 태국에 갈 거야.

M 아 진짜? 좋겠다.

W 응. 어젯밤에 짐도 다 쌌어. 준비가 끝났어.

M 잘됐네. 호텔 예약은 했어?

W 응. 아빠가 이미 모든 걸 예약했어. 호텔 옥상에는 멋진 수영장도 있어. 진짜 멋지지 않아?

M 진짜 멋지다!

W 너 전에 태국 가봤어?

M 응. 딱 한번. 거기서 진짜 맛있는 길거리 음식을 즐길 수 있을 거야. 환전 했어?

W 아니 아직. 거의 신용 카드만 쓸 거야.

M 환전하는 게 좋아. 몇몇 가게들은 신용 카드를 안 받고 현금만 받거든.

① 글쎄, 나 현금이 없는데.

② 여권 챙기는 거 잊지 마.

③ 그거 참 바보 같은 대답이다.

⑤ 호텔 금고에 돈을 보관할 수 있어.

18 ②

M Hello. Do you live here?

W Yes. Oh, you just moved in, right?

M Yeah. I'm Carl Johnson. Nice to meet you.

W Nice to meet you, too. I'm Lisa.

M This place has a quiet and calm atmosphere.

W You're right. I think you'll like this town.

M By the way, where's the nearest shopping center?

W It's two blocks that way. Let me know if you need any help.

M _____

M 안녕하세요. 여기 사시나요?

W 네. 오, 방금 이사 오셨죠, 맞죠?

M 네. 전 Carl Johnson이라고 해요. 만나서 반갑습니다.

W 저도 만나서 반갑습니다. 전 Lisa예요.

M 이곳은 조용하고 차분한 분위기네요.

W 당신 말이 맞아요. 이 마을을 좋아하게 될 거예요.

M 그런데, 가장 가까운 쇼핑 센터는 어디 있나요?

W 저쪽으로 두 블록 떨어져 있어요. 도움이 필요하시면 알려주세요.

M 고맙습니다. 정말 도움이 되어 주시네요.

① 네. 당신을 도와드릴게요.

③ 지금 쇼핑 가세요?

④ 맞아요. 우린 함께 배워야 해요.

⑤ 물론이죠. 거기 어떻게 가는지 알려드릴게요.

19 ②

W Ian, when did you go to sleep last night?

M I don't know. I stayed up very late.

W You played computer games, didn't you?

M Yeah. It was fun to play online with my friend.

W You can't live without the Internet, right?

M I think so. Did you do your homework, anyway?

W Of course I did. What about you?

M I should start now but I'm a little bit sleepy.

W You must be very tired. Go get some sleep.

M _____

W Ian, 어젯밤에 언제 잤니?

M 몰라. 아주 늦게까지 자지 않고 있었어.

W 너 컴퓨터 게임했지, 그렇지?

M 응. 친구와 온라인으로 게임하는 게 재미있거든.

W 넌 인터넷 없이는 못 살겠네, 그렇지?

M 그럴 것 같아. 그나저나, 너 숙제했니?

W 물론 했지. 너는?

M 지금 시작해야 하는데 조금 졸려.

W 당연히 아주 피곤할 거야. 가서 잠 좀 자라.

M 그래, 먼저 쉬는 게 나을 거 같다.

① 난 숙제를 먼저 해야 했어.

③ 와, 그렇게 말하다니 너 정말 똑똑하구나.

④ 아니, 다시는 게임하고 싶지 않아.

⑤ 응. 네가 숙제를 어떻게 했는지 보자.

20 ①

M Williams calls his friend Jackson who runs a company.

He needs to say something important to Jackson. But Jackson is out for lunch and his secretary takes the call. When she is asked when her boss will be back to the office, she answers that he'll return in twenty minutes. She thinks it would be better to have her boss call Williams back when he comes in. In this situation, what would the secretary say to Williams?

M Williams는 회사를 경영하는 친구인 Jackson에게 전화를 건다. 그는 Jackson에게 중요한 뭔가를 말해야 한다. 하지만 Jackson은 점심식사를 하러 외출하고 그의 비서가 전화를 받는다. 그녀는 자신의 상사가 사무실에 언제 돌아오는지 질문을 받자 20분 안에 돌아올 것이라고 대답한다. 그녀는 상사가 들어오면 그로 하여금 Williams에게 다시 전화하도록 하는 게 좋겠다고 생각한다. 이 상황에서, 그 비서는 Williams에게 무슨 말을 할까?

① 그에게 전화하라고 말씀드릴게요.

② 죄송합니다만, 다른 전화를 받고 계세요.

③ 메시지를 남겨 주실래요?

④ 잠깐만 기다려 주실래요?

⑤ 지금 할 일이 있으신가요?

만점 솔루션 자리를 비운 상사가 돌아오면 전화를 드리라고 말하겠다고 하는 상황이므로, '나중에 다시 ~에게 전화하다'라는 의미의 call back이라는 표현을 사용해 말을 하는 것이 적절하다.

01 ②	**02** ⑤	**03** ②	**04** ④, ➕②	**05** ④
06 ①	**07** ④	**08** ③	**09** ⑤	**10** ③
11 ⑤	**12** ③	**13** ④	**14** ③, ➕⑤	**15** ③
16 ②	**17** ④	**18** ④	**19** ②	**20** ③

01 ②

W Having a terrible day? Then, try our kickboxing workout like this. Get into the basic position. Bend your knees and put your right foot in front. Raise your fists with your right hand in front. Now, punch with your right fist. Don't stand straight as you punch. Instead, lean forward for more power. Bring your fist back immediately. Repeat this three times at a time.

W 힘든 하루를 보내시나요? 그렇다면, 다음과 같은 저희 킥복싱 운동을 해 보세요. 기본 자세를 취하세요. 무릎을 구부리고 오른발을 앞쪽에 놓으세요. 오른손을 앞에 두고 두 주먹을 올리세요. 이제, 오른쪽 주먹으로 치세요. 칠 때 똑바로 서 있지 마세요. 그 대신에, 더 많은 힘을 얻기 위해 앞으로 숙이세요. 즉시 주먹을 뒤로 빼세요. 한 번에 이 동작을 세 번 반복하세요.

02 ⑤

[Telephone rings.]
M Hello. Can I speak to Janet, please?
W I'm sorry. Janet is taking her piano lesson. Can you leave a message?
M Yes, please. Can you tell her Charlie called, and that a bunch of us are going to see a movie together this weekend?
W Of course. Does she have your Cellphone number, Charlie?
M I think so, but it's 014-333-9898 just in case. If she wants to join us, tell her to call me, please.
W 014-333-9898. I'll give her the message when she finishes her piano lesson.
M Thanks so much.

[전화벨이 울린다.]
M 안녕하세요. Janet과 통화할 수 있나요?
W 미안하구나. Janet은 피아노 수업을 받고 있거든. 전할 말이 있니?
M 네. Charlie가 전화했다고 전해 주세요. 그리고 우리 몇 명이 모여서 이번 주말에 함께 영화를 볼 거라고 전해 주실 수 있죠?
W 물론이다. Charlie, Janet이 네 휴대 전화 번호를 가지고 있니?
M 그럴 걸요. 하지만 혹시 모를 경우를 대비해서 014-333-9898입니다. 우리와 함께 하기를 원하면, 저에게 전화하라고 전해 주세요.
W 014-333-9898이지. 피아노 수업이 끝나면 메시지를 전해 주마.
M 정말 고맙습니다.

03 ②

① M Where is the nearest park?
  W It's just around the corner.
② M You're not supposed to park here.
  W Sorry. I didn't see the sign. Where can I park around here?
③ M How can I get to City Hall?
  W You should take bus number 145.
④ M How can we help handicapped people?
  W For example, we can give them a ride home.
⑤ M Can I try on this shirt?
  W Sure, go ahead. The fitting room is over there.

① M 가장 가까운 공원이 어디에 있죠?
  W 바로 모퉁이를 돌아서 있습니다.
② M 이곳에 주차하시면 안 됩니다.
  W 미안합니다. 표지판을 보지 못했습니다. 이 주변 어디에 주차하면 되죠?
③ M 시청에 어떻게 가죠?
  W 145번 버스를 타셔야 합니다.
④ M 장애가 있는 사람들을 어떻게 도울 수 있죠?
  W 예를 들어, 집까지 차를 태워 줄 수 있습니다.
⑤ M 이 셔츠를 입어 봐도 됩니까?
  W 물론입니다. 어서 입어 보세요. 탈의실은 저쪽에 있습니다.

04 ④ | ➕②

W Hi, Max. You look upset. What's wrong?
M I'm having trouble practicing my role for the school play. I have to perform at the theater in just a few days!
W Did you memorize all the lines?
M I think so, but I'm still a bit uncertain. If I could practice with a partner, I think it'd make me feel more confident.
W Then let me help you.
M That would be great! How about meeting in the lobby of the main building after school?
W I have to work on a team project in the cafeteria at 3. It should only take an hour. Can you meet me there?
W No problem. I'll be there at 4 after school. Thanks for your offer!

W 안녕, 맥스. 화 나 보여. 무슨 일이야?
M 학교 연극에서 맡은 역할을 연습하는 거에 어려움을 겪고 있어. 며칠 후에 극장에서 공연해야 하는데!
W 대사는 다 외웠어?
M 외운 거 같은데 확실하지 않아. 파트너와 연습할 수 있다면 더 자신감 있게 할 수 있을 텐데.
W 그러면 내가 도와줄게.
M 그럼 좋겠다! 방과 후에 본채 로비에서 만나는 거 어때?
W 3시에 카페테리아에서 팀 프로젝트를 해야 해. 딱 한 시간 정도 걸릴 거야. 거기서 볼 수 있을까?
M 문제 없어. 방과 후 4시에 거기 갈게. 도와줘서 고마워.

05 ④

M I've never tasted cheese and milk so far.

W No kidding! I just can't believe it.

M True. You know, I live in a remote country, so there aren't foods like these.

W Then what kinds of food do you usually have?

M I usually eat rice, organic vegetables and fruits.

W Wow. Those are very healthy foods.

M Why don't we buy some cheese and milk for me, and some fruits for you right here?

W That's a good idea.

M 난 지금까지 치즈와 우유를 맛 본 적이 없어.

W 설마! 정말 믿을 수가 없는데.

M 사실이야. 있잖아, 난 외딴 시골에 살거든, 그래서 그곳에는 이런 음식들이 없어.

W 그렇다면 넌 대개 어떤 종류의 음식을 먹니?

M 난 대개 밥, 유기농 채소, 그리고 과일을 먹어.

W 와. 그것들은 정말 건강에 좋은 식품들이잖아.

M 여기서 날 위해 치즈와 우유를 좀 사고, 널 위해 과일을 좀 사는 것이 어떠니?

W 그것 참 좋은 생각이네.

만점 솔루션 치즈, 우유, 과일 등을 살 수 있는 장소는 식료품점이다. cheese and milk만 듣고 '목장(a farm)'을 답으로 고르거나, organic vegetables만 듣고 '채소밭(a vegetable garden)'을 답으로 고르지 않도록 유의한다.

06 ①

W Hello. I'm Tina Clark.

M Do you have any work experience as a tour guide?

W Yes. I've worked for a travel company for two years.

M That's great. How many countries have you visited?

W Well, around twenty. Mostly I traveled to South Asia.

M OK. So you are familiar with the countries in the area, right?

W Yes. Also I can speak those languages a little.

M All right. Thank you for the interview. We'll call you in two days.

W I hope to have a chance to work here.

W 안녕하세요? 전 Tina Clark입니다.

M 관광 안내원으로서 일한 경험이 있나요?

W 네. 2년 동안 여행 회사에서 일했습니다.

M 잘 됐네요. 몇 나라를 다녀봤나요?

W 글쎄요, 약 20개 나라요. 대부분 남아시아로 다녀왔습니다.

M 좋네요. 그럼 그 지역의 나라들을 잘 아시겠군요?

W 네. 또한 그 나라의 언어들도 조금 할 수 있죠.

M 알겠습니다. 인터뷰 감사합니다. 이틀 후에 전화드리겠습니다.

W 여기에서 일할 기회가 주어지길 바랍니다.

07 ④

① **W** What are you doing this Saturday?

M Let me see. Nothing much to do.

② **W** Are you sure you don't want a dessert?

M Yes, I've had enough.

③ **W** Do you carry shirts to go with these blue jeans?

M Yes. How about this yellow one?

④ **W** What do you think of this book?

M The book is on sale now.

⑤ **W** I want to lose weight. What sports do you suggest?

M How about cycling or playing tennis?

① **W** 이번 토요일에 뭐 할 거예요?

M 글쎄요. 할 일이 없는데요.

② **W** 정말 후식을 원하지 않으십니까?

M 네. 충분히 먹었습니다.

③ **W** 이 청바지와 어울리는 셔츠를 취급하시나요?

M 네. 이 노란색 셔츠는 어떻습니까?

④ **W** 이 책을 어떻게 생각하세요?

M 그 책은 지금 할인 판매 중이에요.

⑤ **W** 체중 감량을 원하는데, 어떤 운동을 제안해 주시겠습니까?

M 자전거를 타거나 테니스를 치는 것은 어떻습니까?

만점 솔루션 ④ '이 책을 어떻게 생각하세요?'라고 상대방의 의견을 묻는 질문에, '그 책은 지금 할인 판매 중이에요.'라고 사실을 말하는 것은 어색하다.

08 ③

[Telephone rings.]

M Hello, Sarah. What's up?

W Hi, Kevin. My car's having problems again. It starts to overheat whenever I'm in heavy traffic.

M Didn't you have the same problem last month?

W Yes. So I took it to a mechanic then, but now it's happening again.

M Sorry to hear that. I think you have to wait a while, while the engine cools down.

W I already did and I'm on my way to the repair shop. So, um, Kevin, could you do me a favor?

M Sure. What is it?

W I can't get home till 8 p.m. tonight. Could you look after my kids for me?

M Oh, Julie and Mark? Where are they now?

W They're in my neighbor Harry's house, You know him, don't you?

M Of course, I do.

[전화벨이 울린다.]

M 안녕, Sarah. 무슨 일이야?

W 안녕, Kevin. 내 차에 문제가 또 생겼어. 교통 체증에 걸릴 때마다 과열되기 시작해.

M 지난달에도 같은 문제가 있지 않았어?

W 응. 그래서 그때 정비사에게 갖고 갔었는데 지금 또 그 일이 생기네.

M 그것 참 안됐구나. 내 생각엔 엔진이 식을 때까지 잠시 동안 기다려야 할 것 같아.

W 이미 그렇게 했고 정비소로 가는 중이야. 그래서, 음, Kevin, 부탁 하나만 들어 줄 수 있어?

M 물론. 뭔데?

W 오늘 밤 8시까지 내가 집에 갈 수 없어. 나 대신 아이들을 돌봐줄 수 있어?

M 아, Julie와 Mark 말이지? 아이들이 지금 어디 있지?

W 이웃 Harry의 집에 있어. 그 사람 알지. 그렇지?

M 물론이지.

09 ⑤

[Cellphone rings.]

W Hello?

M Hi, Professor Jones?

W Yes.

M Hi. It's Robert Smythe from your chemistry class.

W Hi, Robert! What can I do for you?

M I'm calling regarding the email you sent to everyone in the class. The thing is I can't open the file you attached.

W Really? You're the first student I've heard from. Has anyone else had any trouble?

M Yes. Two of my classmates told me they couldn't open it either.

W I'll check and figure out what the problem is.

M I think the size of the file is too large. You'd better resend it as a zip file.

W Let me try. Can you check your email in 10 minutes?

M Yes. I've got my laptop open now.

W Great. I'll resend the file right away. Please let me know if you can open the file or not.

[휴대 전화가 울린다.]

W 여보세요?

M 안녕하세요, 존스 교수님?

W 네.

M 안녕하세요. 교수님의 화학 수업을 듣는 로버트 스미스라고 합니다.

W 안녕하세요, 로버트! 무슨 용건인가요?

M 수업을 듣는 모두에게 보내신 이메일을 보고 전화 드렸어요. 사실 교수님께서 첨부한 파일을 열 수가 없어요.

W 정말요? 그런 말을 한 학생은 당신이 처음이네요. 문제가 있는 다른 학생들이 또 있나요?

M 네. 학급에서 두 명이 파일을 열 수 없다고 저에게 말했어요.

W 확인하고 문제가 무엇인지 알아볼게요.

M 파일 크기가 너무 큰 거 같아요. 압축 파일로 다시 보내주시면 좋겠어요.

W 한번 해볼게요. 10분 후에 이메일을 확인해볼 수 있나요?

M 네. 지금 노트북을 켰어요.

W 잘됐네요. 지금 바로 파일을 다시 보낼게요. 파일이 열리거나 열리지 않거나 나에게 알려줘요.

10 ③

M Good evening. Can I help you?

W I'm looking for tableware to set a table.

M Do you have any particular brand in mind?

W No, I'm just looking for something that will go well with my dining room.

M Can you tell me about the style of your dining room?

W It's a classical style with a dark wooden dining table in the middle.

M How about this collection from Merry Porter?

W How much does it cost?

M It's $300 for a full set of bone china.

W I don't need a full set.

M You can also buy a smaller set. The smaller set includes six plates and bowls. The price is only 50% of the cost of the full set.

W Well, then, I'll take the smaller set.

M 안녕하세요. 무엇을 도와드릴까요?

W 식탁을 차릴 때 쓸 식기를 찾고 있어요.

M 생각하고 계신 특별한 브랜드가 있나요?

W 아니요, 그냥 제 식당과 잘 어울릴 무언가 찾고 있어요.

M 손님 식당이 어떤 스타일인지 말씀해 주시겠어요?

W 중간에 어두운 목조 식탁이 있는 고전적인 스타일예요.

M 메리 포터의 이 컬렉션 어떤가요?

W 얼마인가요?

M 본차이나제 전체 구성으로 300달러입니다.

W 전체 구성은 필요하지 않아요.

M 더 작은 구성으로 구매하실 수 있습니다. 여섯 개의 접시와 그릇이 포함되는 구성입니다. 가격은 전체 구성의 50%밖에 안됩니다.

W 그렇다면 작은 구성으로 구매할게요.

11 ⑤

M Watch your step, please. Stairs are steep and narrow.

W Okay. Where am I now?

M You're now in the hidden part of the palace. Originally, it was just a small room, and three more rooms were added on its left in the 16th century.

W How many rooms were there in the palace?

M There were 33 rooms including these hidden rooms. King George added 5 rooms later and now we have 38 rooms.

W I see. Can I take pictures in here?

M Yes, you can. But you're not allowed to in some places. There are signs to tell you. Please come this way.

W Wow, the furniture is beautiful. Is it original?

M Oh, please don't touch the furniture.

M 발 조심하세요. 계단이 가파르고 좁습니다.

W 네, 알겠어요. 지금 여긴 어디죠?

M 지금 계신 곳은 궁전의 숨겨진 부분입니다. 원래는 그냥 작은 방이었는데, 16세기에 왼쪽으로 방 세 개가 추가되었어요.

W 궁전에 방이 몇 개였죠?

M 이 숨겨진 방들을 포함해서 33개가 있었어요. George 왕이 후에 다섯 개를 추가해서 지금은 38개가 되었죠.

W 그렇군요. 이 안에서 사진 찍어도 돼요?

M 네, 됩니다. 하지만 어떤 곳에서는 금지되었어요. 이를 말해주는 표시가 있습니다. 이쪽으로 오세요.

W 와, 가구가 아름답군요. 진품인가요?

M 아, 가구에 손대지 마세요.

12 ③

W While I was traveling in Canada, I rented a car and drove to the Rocky Mountains by myself. On the way, my car suddenly broke down, so I called a 24-hour service station. The service man asked me where I was, but I wasn't sure of my location. Luckily, I had an app that helps me find out my current location. Thanks to the app, I was able to let him know the exact latitude and longitude of my location before it got dark.

W 캐나다를 여행 중일 때, 나는 차를 빌려서 혼자서 록키 산맥으로 운전했다. 가는 길에, 차가 갑자기 망가져서 24시간 정비소에 전화했다. 직원이 내가 어디인지 물어봤지만 나는 내 위치를 확신할 수 없었다. 다행히, 내 현재 위치를 찾도록 도움을 줄 수 있는 앱을 갖고 있었다. 그 앱 덕분에 나는 어두워 지기 전에 그에게 내 위치의 정확한 위도와 경도를 알려줄 수 있었다.

13 ④

W Hi! Are you looking for a sports water bottle?

M Yes. I'm thinking of buying one.

W First you should think about what size you want. We have several sizes—from 500-milliliter to two-liter bottles.

M I want one to carry with me outdoors, so a 500-milliliter bottle would be good enough.

W Then, what about this plastic bottle?

M I'm not sure. I'm looking for a product that's BPA-free. I'm concerned about the harmful chemicals in plastics.

W Oh, all of our products are made of the finest plastics, and they're all BPA-free.

M I see. This one looks great. Do you have it any other colors?

W We have blue, orange, and black.

M I'll take a blue one.

W 안녕하세요! 스포츠 물병을 찾고 계신가요?

M 네. 하나 살까 생각 중입니다.

W 우선 원하시는 크기를 생각하셔야 합니다. 저희는 500밀리리터부터 2리터 병까지 다양한 크기가 있습니다.

M 밖에서 들고 다닐 수 있는 걸 원하기 때문에 500밀리리터 병이 괜찮을 거 같아요.

W 그럼, 이 플라스틱 병은 어떠세요?

M 잘 모르겠네요. BPA가 없는 물건을 찾고 있어요. 플라스틱에 있는 유해한 화학 약품이 걱정되어서요.

W 아, 저희 모든 제품은 최고급의 플라스틱으로 만들어졌고 모두 BPA가 없습니다.

M 알겠습니다. 이거 괜찮네요. 다른 색상도 있나요?

W 파란색, 주황색, 그리고 검은색이 있습니다.

M 파란색으로 할게요.

14 ③ | ➕ ⑤

W Kate is concerned about climate change. She's aware that it is causing a threat to the lives of animals all over the planet. And polar bears in the Arctic are in serious danger. She often visits a website where she can see the polar bears' movements. Many researchers track polar bears using special radio collars. The collars on the bears send out signals, and researchers are able to track their movements. This shows how polar bears are dealing with the climate change in the Arctic and, eventually, what their new life patterns will be like.

W 케이트는 기후 변화에 대해 걱정하고 있다. 그녀는 기후 변화가 지구에 사는 모든 동물들의 삶을 위협하게 될 것이라는 것을 알고 있다. 그리고 북극에 사는 북극곰들도 심각한 위험에 처해있다. 그녀는 종종 북극곰의 움직임을 볼 수 있는 웹사이트에 방문한다. 많은 연구자들이 특수한 무선 송신기를 이용하여 북극곰을 추적한다. 곰에게 달린 송신기는 신호를 내보내고 연구자들은 그들의 움직임을 추적할 수 있다. 이것은 북극곰들이 북극에서의 기후변화를 어떻게 견디고 있는지, 그리고 결과적으로 그들의 새로운 생활 양식이 어떠한지 보여준다.

15 ③

W What are you thinking so hard about?

M This Saturday is Mother's Day. But I don't know what to give to my mom.

W How about giving her some flowers?

M But I don't have any money. What do you think I should do?

W Then, why don't you cook a fancy dinner for her?

M A fancy dinner? But I don't know how to cook.

W Never mind. I'll teach you how to make an Italian dish.

M Can I learn it before Mother's Day?

W Sure. Let's go to my house and make it together now.

M Yes, let's.

W 뭘 그렇게 열심히 생각하고 있니?

M 이번 토요일이 어머니날이잖아. 엄마께 무엇을 드려야 할지 모르겠어.

W 꽃을 드리는 게 어때?

M 하지만 난 돈이 전혀 없거든. 어떻게 해야 되지?

W 그렇다면, 엄마를 위해 고급 저녁식사를 요리하는 것이 어떠니?

M 고급 저녁식사? 하지만 난 요리하는 방법을 모르는데.

W 걱정 마. 내가 이탈리아 음식 만드는 법을 가르쳐 줄게.

M 내가 어머니날 전에 그것을 배울 수 있을까?

W 물론이지. 지금 우리 집에 가서 같이 만들어 보자.

M 그래, 가자.

16 ②

W Wow, you're wet to the skin!

M I'm afraid I didn't hear today's weather forecast.

W The forecast said that there would be a rainstorm with thunder.

M But it was fine in the morning. So I thought it wouldn't rain cats and dogs like this.

W Well, take a hot shower, otherwise you'll catch a cold.

M I know. I shouldn't get sick because mid-term exams are just around the corner.

W The forecast said that the weather will be back to normal soon.

M Yeah, I heard that. I hope it will be sunny and warm soon.

W Me, too.

W 와, 넌 흠뻑 젖었구나!

M 유감스럽게도 오늘 일기 예보를 듣지 못했어.

W 일기 예보에 따르면 천둥을 동반한 폭우가 내릴 거라고 했어.

M 하지만 오전에는 화창했잖아. 그래서 비가 억수로 쏟아지지는 않을 거라고 생각했지.

W 음, 뜨거운 샤워를 해, 그렇지 않으면 감기에 걸릴 거야.

M 알아. 중간고사가 얼마 남지 않아서 아프면 안 돼.

W 일기 예보에 따르면 날씨가 곧 평상시로 돌아갈 거래.

M 그래, 나도 들었어. 곧 화창하고 따뜻해졌으면 좋겠다.

W 나도 그래.

17 ④

W What happened to your leg? Why do you have a cast on?

M I sprained my ankle when playing soccer.

W What a shame. As you know, our class is going on a trip next week. Do you think you can still come?

M I don't know. My doctor told me not to walk for a while.

W When did you see him last?

M It was three days ago. And I'm supposed to go see him again this Friday.

W Then why don't you ask him if you could go on a trip?

M I'll probably do that. I can't wait to get the cast off.

W 다리가 어떻게 된 거야? 깁스를 하고 있네.

M 축구하다가 발목을 삐었어.

W 안됐구나. 너도 알겠지만 우리 반이 다음 주에 여행을 가잖아. 너도 갈 수 있을 것 같아?

M 모르겠어. 의사선생님이 당분간 걷지 말라고 하셨어.

W 그 분을 마지막으로 본 게 언젠데?

M 3일 전이야. 그리고 이번 금요일에 가서 다시 뵈어야 해.

W 그럼 여행갈 수 있겠냐고 여쭤보지 그래?

M 물론 그래야지. 가능한 한 빨리 깁스를 풀고 싶어.

18 ④

W Do you exercise a lot?

M Not really. I don't have enough time.

W You should make time. Exercise is good for your health.

M I know that, but I just can't force myself to do it.

W Try to find a friend to exercise with, and then it'll be easy for you to exercise.

M Then why don't you work out with me, Serena?

W Great! What exercise would you like to do?

M _____

W 넌 운동을 많이 하니?

M 꼭 그렇지는 않아. 시간이 충분하지 않거든.

W 시간을 내야 해. 운동은 건강에 유익하잖아.

M 나도 알고 있지만, 억지로 그것을 할 수가 없어.

W 함께 운동할 친구를 찾아 봐. 그러면 넌 운동하기가 수월해질 거야.

M 그렇다면 Serena, 네가 나랑 함께 운동하는 것이 어떠니?

W 좋지! 넌 어떤 운동을 하고 싶니?

M 테니스 치는 것을 어떻게 생각하니?

① 일주일에 두 번 정도.

② 한국에서 축구가 인기 있어.

③ 자전거를 탈 때 조심해.

⑤ 대신에 이번 주말에 하이킹 가는 것이 어떠니?

19 ②

W You look a little down. What's the matter?

M Well, it's my violin techniques.

W What's wrong with them? I know you're a great violinist.

M I practiced a lot, but my teacher says I have to practice more.

W Oh, dear. I'm sure you'll do better because you always work hard.

M I don't know. I'm really stressed out these days.

W Don't take it so hard. You know, I'm a big fan of yours.

M _____

W 좀 울적해 보여. 무슨 일 있어?

M 글쎄, 내 바이올린 테크닉 때문이야.

W 뭐가 문제인데? 네가 훌륭한 바이올린 연주자라는 걸 아는데.

M 연습을 많이 했지만 선생님은 내가 더 연습을 해야 한다고 말씀하셔.

W 아, 이런. 네가 항상 열심히 하니까 넌 분명히 더 잘할 거야.

M 모르겠어. 요즘엔 스트레스가 정말 많이 쌓여.

W 너무 심각하게 생각하지 마. 난 너의 왕팬인 거 알잖아.

M 기운 북돋아 줘서 고마워.

① 아, 농담하고 있네.

③ 더 연습하지 그래?

④ 내가 얼마나 행복한지 알아줘서 기뻐.

⑤ 물론 내 부채를 빌려가도 돼. 요즘엔 많이 쓰지 않아.

20 ③

M A girl middle school student entered an ice cream store.

She ordered an ice cream cone. While she was waiting for it there, she noticed a famous movie actor! She didn't want to <u>act like</u> some crazy fans. Instead, she <u>pretended to act cool</u>. When she got out, she realized she didn't bring her ice cream cone. She went back in. And she said to the clerk that she forgot her ice cream cone. Then the clerk said, "No, you didn't. You <u>put it in your bag with your change</u>." In this situation, what would the movie actor say to the girl student?

M 한 중학교 여학생이 아이스크림 가게에 들어갔다. 그녀는 아이스크림콘을 주문했다. 그곳에서 그것을 기다리는 동안, 그녀는 한 유명한 영화배우를 보았다! 그녀는 일부 열성팬들처럼 행동하고 싶지 않았다. 그 대신에, 그녀는 침착하게 행동하는 척했다. 그녀가 밖으로 나왔을 때, 그녀는 아이스크림콘을 가져오지 않은 것을 알았다. 그녀는 다시 들어갔다. 그리고 점원에게 아이스크림 챙기는 것을 잊었다고 말했다. 그러자 점원은 "아니요, 그렇지 않습니다. 거스름돈과 함께 당신 가방에 그것을 넣었습니다."라고 말했다. 이 상황에서, 그 영화배우는 여학생에게 무슨 말을 할까?

① 마음껏 드세요.
② 거스름돈은 가지세요.
③ 너무 긴장하지 마세요.
④ 영수증을 보여주시겠습니까?
⑤ 아이스크림도 내가 제일 좋아하는 음식입니다.

만점 솔루션 아이스크림콘을 가방에 넣었다는 것은 유명한 영화배우를 보고 당황했다는 의미이므로 긴장하지 말라는 말을 해 주는 것이 가장 적절하다.

01 ④

W You made a great choice, sir.

M Thank you. Can you <u>gift-wrap it</u>, please?

W Sure. We have different kinds of wrapping paper. What type would you like?

M I don't know what to choose. How about the one with flowers?

W That's OK, but I think heart patterns are prettier.

M Is there <u>a mix of flowers and hearts</u>, then? Only one pattern looks a little too simple.

W Sorry, we don't have. But we have <u>flowers and stars</u> here, and hearts and chocolates over there.

M That's good. <u>My daughter likes stars</u> and she'll like this one.

W 정말 훌륭한 선택을 하셨네요.

M 고맙습니다. 그것을 선물 포장해 주실 수 있나요?

W 물론이죠. 여러 종류의 포장지들이 있는데요. 어떤 종류가 마음에 드세요?

M 무엇을 골라야 할지 모르겠네요. 꽃이 있는 것은 어때요?

W 좋습니다, 하지만 제 생각에는 하트 무늬가 더 예쁜데요.

M 그러면 꽃과 하트가 섞인 것이 있나요? 한 가지 무늬는 좀 단순해 보이네요.

W 죄송합니다만, 그것은 없어요. 하지만 여기 꽃과 별이 섞인 것이 있고요, 그리고 하트와 초콜릿이 섞인 것이 저쪽에 있어요.

M 좋습니다. 제 딸이 별을 좋아하니까 이것을 좋아할 거예요.

02 ④

[Telephone rings.]

W Hello.

M Hi, Gina. This is Paul.

W Hi, Paul. What's up?

M Do you have some time this evening?

W Yes, I'm free from 6 o'clock. Why?

M You know, I <u>missed math class</u> yesterday.

W Yeah. You had a cold and stayed home, didn't you?

M Right. I wonder if you could <u>help me catch up on math</u>.

W Oh, sure. I have basketball practice until 5:30. Call me around 6 o'clock.

M OK, I will. <u>Thanks for helping</u>.

[전화벨이 울린다.]

W 여보세요.

M 안녕, Gina. 나 Paul이야.

W 안녕. Paul. 무슨 일이야?

M 오늘 저녁에 시간 좀 있어?

W 응. 6시부터 한가해. 왜?

M 너도 알겠지만, 내가 어제 수학 수업을 빠졌잖아.

W 그래. 너 감기 걸려서 집에 있었잖아?

M 맞아. 내가 수학을 따라 잡는 데 네가 도움을 줄 수 있을까 해서.

W 오, 물론이지. 내가 5시 30분까지 농구 연습이 있거든. 6시쯤 전화해.

M 좋아, 그럴게. 도와줘서 고마워.

만점 솔루션 I wonder if you help me catch up on math.에 남자가 전화를 건 목적이 나타나 있다. 즉, 남자는 수학 수업을 못 들은 것에 대한 도움을 받고 싶어 여자에게 전화를 했다.

03 ④

① M What are you making?
   W I'm cooking pizza for dinner. We have guests tonight.
② M What is your favorite food?
   W Pizza. I love it.
③ M How did you like the pizza?
   W It was great. I'll never forget the taste.
④ M Do you deliver?
   W Yes, we do. Your address and phone number, please.
⑤ M Can I speak to the manager, please?
   W Sorry, but he's on another line.

① M 무엇을 만들고 있어요?
   W 저녁으로 피자를 만들고 있어요. 오늘밤에 손님들이 오거든요.
② M 가장 좋아하는 음식이 뭐죠?
   W 피자예요. 정말 좋아하죠.
③ M 피자 어땠어요?
   W 훌륭했어요. 그 맛을 잊지 못할 거예요.
④ M 배달합니까?
   W 네. 주소와 전화번호를 알려주세요.
⑤ M 지배인과 이야기를 할 수 있을까요?
   W 죄송합니다만, 통화 중이세요.

04 ② | ➕ ⑤

[Cellphone rings.]

W Hi, Jack!

M Hi, Tracy! Did you hear that Miran is in the hospital?

W Really? I saw her last week, and she didn't look well.

M I know. She has pneumonia.

W Oh, that's too bad. I find that more and more people are suffering from respiratory diseases these days.

M Right. If you are free on Friday, let's go and see her.

W I'm tied up with meetings all day on Friday. How about on Saturday?

M She said she would leave the hospital over the weekend;

we'd better go and see her before the weekend.

W Then, how about going on Thursday on our lunch break?

M Okay. Let's meet on Thursday, then.

[휴대 전화가 울린다.]

W 안녕, 잭!

M 안녕, 트레이시! 너 미란이가 입원했다는 소식 들었어?

W 진짜? 저번 주에 만났었는데, 좋아 보이지 않더라.

M 알아. 폐렴에 걸렸대.

W 이런, 정말 안됐다. 요즘에 호흡기 질환으로 고통받는 사람들이 점점 많아진다고 하더라.

M 맞아. 금요일에 시간 괜찮으면 같이 병문안 가자.

W 금요일은 하루 종일 회의가 잡혀 있어. 토요일은 어때?

M 미란이가 주말에 퇴원한다고 했어. 주말 전에 보는 게 좋을 거 같아.

W 그럼, 목요일 점심시간에 가는 거 어때?

M 그래. 그럼 목요일에 보자.

05 ⑤

W Dave, how many hours do you work a day?

M It depends. I work day and night.

W Really? You must be very tired.

M Sometimes. But I'm proud of my job.

W You must be. A lot of people can do their work thanks to you.

M Yeah. You'll never know how many people are using my programs.

W Do you make online games, too?

M No, I don't. I only design programs for offices like companies, hospitals, and schools.

W Don't work too much. I hope you stay fit and healthy.

M Thanks, I will.

W Dave, 하루에 몇 시간 일하죠?

M 사정에 따라 달라요. 밤낮으로 일하죠.

W 정말이요? 틀림없이 아주 피곤하겠네요.

M 종종 그렇죠. 하지만 저는 제 일이 자랑스러워요.

W 분명 그럴 거예요. 많은 사람들이 당신 덕분에 일을 할 수 있지요.

M 그래요. 얼마나 많은 사람들이 제 프로그램을 사용하고 있는지 모를 거예요.

W 온라인 게임도 만드나요?

M 아니요. 회사, 병원, 학교 같은 사무실에서 사용되는 프로그램만 설계해요.

W 너무 일을 많이 하지 말아요. 당신이 건강하게 지내면 좋겠어요.

M 고마워요. 그렇게 할게요.

06 ②

M Hello. My name is Sam Fairbanks. I had a reservation.

W Just a second. I'm sorry your name is not on the list.

M What are you talking about? I called last week and reserved for tonight.

W Sorry, sir. But the computer has no record.

M This is nonsense. Then, give me a room, please.

W I'm really sorry, sir. Rooms for tonight <u>are all booked</u>.

M My goodness! Then, is there another hotel nearby?

W I'm afraid not, sir. The nearest one is 15 km away.

M Oh, my God!

M 안녕하세요. 제 이름은 Sam Fairbanks입니다. 예약한 것이 있어요.

W 잠시만요. 죄송하지만 성함이 명단에 없는데요.

M 무슨 말씀하시는 거예요? 지난주에 전화해서 오늘밤 예약을 했는데요.

W 죄송합니다, 손님. 하지만 컴퓨터에 기록이 없네요.

M 말도 안 돼요. 그럼, 방을 하나 주세요.

W 정말 죄송한데요, 손님. 오늘밤에는 방이 모두 예약되었어요.

M 이런! 그러면 근처에 다른 호텔이 있나요?

W 없어요, 손님. 가장 가까운 것이 15킬로미터 떨어져 있어요.

M 오, 이런!

07 ②

① **W** I'm going downtown. Can you <u>give me a ride</u>?
   M No problem. Get in.

② **W** I'd like to use this computer <u>if you don't mind</u>.
   M Oh, I don't mind. I'll use it.

③ **W** Eddie is one of the funniest guys in the country.
   M You can say that again.

④ **W** I <u>gained too much weight</u> these days.
   M Why don't you go on a diet?

⑤ **W** I have a problem. Could you <u>give me a hand</u>?
   M Sure. What is it?

① **W** 나 시내에 가는데, 좀 태워 줄 수 있어?
   M 물론. 어서 타.

② **W** 괜찮다면 이 컴퓨터를 쓰고 싶은데.
   M 아, 괜찮아. 내가 그걸 쓸 거야.

③ **W** Eddie는 우리나라에서 제일 재미있는 사람 중 하나지.
   M 나도 동감이야.

④ **W** 요즘 체중이 너무 늘었어.
   M 다이어트를 좀 하지 그래?

⑤ **W** 문제가 생겼어. 날 좀 도와줄래?
   M 물론. 문제가 뭔데?

08 ④

M Ms. White, the stage <u>is ready for the play</u> tomorrow.

W Let me see. Wow, it looks great. I see you've hung white strings above the bed to make it <u>look scarier</u>.

M Yes. Doesn't it look scary?

W Absolutely. Hmm... Why don't you put those chairs and the sofa next to the bed rather than in the middle?

M Why do you suggest that?

W I think it would make it easier for the actors to <u>move around on the stage</u>.

M OK, that's a good idea. I'll move them. Thanks for your help. Can you stay and watch the rehearsal?

W When does the rehearsal start?

M Shortly. It'd be great if you could watch it and give us feedback.

M 화이트씨, 내일 공연을 위한 무대가 준비됐어요.

W 한번 봅시다. 와, 멋지네요. 침대 위에 무서워 보이도록 하얀 끈들을 매달아 놓았네요.

M 네. 무서워 보이나요?

W 물론이죠. 흠... 저기 의자와 소파를 중앙이 아니라 침대 옆에 두는 게 어떨까요?

M 왜 그렇게 생각하시나요?

W 그래야 배우들이 무대 위를 돌아다니기 더 쉬울 거 같아요.

M 알겠습니다. 좋은 생각이네요. 옮기겠습니다. 도와 주셔서 감사해요. 계속 있다가 리허설도 봐주실 수 있나요?

W 리허설이 언제 시작하죠?

M 곧 시작해요. 리허설을 보고 저희에게 피드백을 주시면 좋겠어요.

09 ⑤

W Dad, do you have a minute?

M Sure. What's up?

W Uh... I'm thinking about <u>quitting my job</u>.

M I thought you loved working as a nurse, even though it's such hard work.

W Yes, I love helping people. I've learned so much at the hospital.

M Then, why do you want to quit?

W Well, I want to learn more about counselling. I think most patients really <u>need emotional support</u> to get over their illnesses.

M Hmm... That makes sense. So, what's your plan?

W After quitting my job at the hospital, I want to enter graduate school to get a degree in counselling.

M You're a grown-up now. It's your decision, and I will support <u>whatever you want to do</u>.

W 아빠, 잠깐 시간 있어요?

M 그럼. 무슨 일이니?

W 어... 저 직장을 그만 두려고요.

M 간호사로 일하는 걸 좋아한다고 생각했는데, 아주 힘든 일이긴 해도 말이다.

W 네, 사람들을 돕는 건 좋아요. 병원에서 아주 많은 걸 배웠어요.

M 그럼, 왜 그만두려고 하는 거니?

W 상담하는 걸 더 배우고 싶어요. 대부분의 환자들이 병을 극복하는데 감정적인 지원을 정말 필요로 하고 있어요.

M 흠... 말이 되는 구나. 그럼, 네 계획은 뭐니?

W 병원 일을 그만 두고, 상담 학위를 얻기 위해 대학원에 입학하고 싶어요.

M 넌 이제 성인이야. 그게 네 결정이라면 아빠는 네가 하려는 게 무엇이든 지지할게.

10 ④

M Why is this store so crowded?

W Maybe there's <u>a big sale</u>.

M Let's see what they have in here. Oh, I like this jacket.

W It looks good on you. How much is it?

M It's $100, but it is now discounted to $50.

W Wow, that's a good price. Are other jackets on sale, too?

M Yes, but only this kind is 50% off. And all the other ones are only 30% off.

W So, are you going to buy this one?

M Yeah. I'll buy two, one for me and one for my brother.

M 왜 이 가게가 이렇게 붐비지?

W 아마 여기서 대폭 할인 행사가 있는 것 같아.

M 이 안에 뭐가 있는지 보자. 오, 이 재킷 맘에 든다.

W 너한테 잘 어울려. 얼마야?

M 100달러인데, 지금 50달러로 할인되었어.

W 와, 좋은 가격인데. 다른 재킷들도 할인 판매 중이야?

M 응, 하지만 이 종류만 50% 할인이야. 그리고 다른 것들은 모두 30%만 할인이야.

W 그러면, 너 이거 살 거야?

M 응. 두 벌 살 거야. 하나는 내 것이고 하나는 내 동생 것으로.

만점 솔루션 50달러로 할인 판매 중인 재킷을 두 벌 사기로 했으므로 100달러를 지불해야 한다.

11 ③

W You don't look OK.

M My back is killing me.

W Go in and get some rest. You've been bent over too long.

M Yeah. I think I should. I had to pull out the weeds.

W Don't worry about them.

M I just don't want to see them grow all over the flowers.

W You're right. But I don't want to see you go to the doctor, either.

M All right. I know what you mean, honey.

W 안색이 안 좋아 보여요.

M 등이 아파 죽겠어요.

W 들어가서 좀 쉬세요. 당신은 너무 오래 몸을 구부리고 있었어요.

M 맞아요. 그런 것 같아요. 잡초를 뽑아야 했죠.

W 잡초는 너무 걱정 마세요.

M 난 그냥 그것들이 온통 꽃 위로 자라는 것을 보고 싶지 않아서 그래요.

W 맞아요. 하지만 나도 당신이 의사에게 가는 것을 보고 싶지 않아요.

M 좋아요. 당신이 말하는 것을 알겠어요.

만점 솔루션 남자가 정원에서 잡초를 뽑고 있던 상황으로, 등이 아프다는 말만 듣고 병원을 답으로 선택하지 않도록 주의한다.

12 ③

M Hello. I'm your student president. I'm going to invite all of you to the campus concert tonight. As you know, a lot of students have worked hard on the event for a long time. Let me tell you about the program. First, there will be an orchestra performance. Next, you'll see a B-boy dance by five of our fellow students. After that, a girl will put on a magic show. Lastly, our school band will play some rock music. Don't miss the chance to enjoy the wonderful evening! Thank you.

M 안녕하세요? 저는 학생 회장입니다. 여러분 모두를 오늘밤 교내 음악회에 초대하고자 합니다. 아시다시피, 많은 학생들이 오랫동안 이번 행사를 위해 열심히 해 왔습니다. 프로그램에 대해 말씀드릴게요. 우선, 오케스트라 공연이 있을 거예요. 다음으로, 5명의 학생 친구들이 하는 비보이 춤을 보게 될 겁니다. 그 뒤에는, 한 여학생이 마술 쇼를 무대에 올릴 거예요. 마지막으로, 학교 밴드가 록 음악을 연주할 거예요. 훌륭한 저녁을 즐길 기회를 놓치지 마세요! 감사합니다.

13 ③

W Wow! This aquarium is huge! It looks just like the ocean.

M Yeah. It is the biggest aquarium in Asia. All of the tanks are surrounded by a glass tunnel, so visitors can feel like they are walking under the water.

W My kids love sea turtles.

M Yes, they're really popular with children. Our Sea Turtle Island exhibit is home to two 300-pound loggerhead sea turtles, as well as reef sharks and many species of tropical fish.

W Sounds amazing. Where is it?

M Go through the Great Hall and turn right at the gift shop.

W Turn right at the gift shop?

M Yes. Then you'll see the Extreme Tropical Fish section. Sea Turtle Island is just next to it.

W Okay. Thank you very much.

W 와! 이 수족관 엄청 크네요! 마치 바다같아요.

M 네. 아시아에서 가장 큰 수족관입니다. 탱크들이 유리 터널로 둘러싸여 있어서 방문객들이 물 속을 걷는 거 같은 기분을 느낄 수 있죠.

W 우리 아이들이 바다 거북이를 좋아해요.

M 네, 바다 거북이는 아이들에게 정말 인기가 많습니다. 저희 바다 거북이 아일랜드 전시장은 흑기흉상어와 많은 종류의 열대어 뿐만 아니라, 300파운드 나가는 붉은 바다 거북이 두 마리의 집입니다.

W 엄청나군요. 그게 어디인가요?

M 그레이트 홀을 지나서 가다가 기념품 가게에서 오른쪽으로 도세요.

W 기념품 가게에서 오른쪽으로 돌아라?

M 네. 그러면 익스트림 열대어 구역이 보이실 거예요. 바다 거북이 아일랜드는 바로 그 옆입니다.

W 알겠어요. 감사해요.

14 ②

W This is a kind of container. Normally it is made of aluminum or other metals like tin and steel. It has a round top and a bottom which are the same size, so it looks like a cylinder. This is used to store food or cold drinks. Anything stored in this lasts for a long time without going bad because there's no air in it. This is one of the most recycled materials. So you should throw this to the recycling bin after use.

W 이것은 용기(그릇)의 일종이다. 보통 이것은 알루미늄 또는 주석과 철

같은 다른 금속으로 만들어진다. 이것은 같은 크기의 둥근 뚜껑과 바닥이 있어서 원기둥처럼 보인다. 이것은 음식이나 찬 음료들을 저장하는 데 사용된다. 이것 안에는 공기가 없기 때문에 이것 안에 저장된 어떤 것이라도 상하지 않고 오래 간다. 이것은 가장 많이 재활용되는 물질들 중 하나이다. 그러므로 사용 뒤에 이것을 재활용 통에 버려야 한다.

> **만점 솔루션** 금속 재질로 둥근 뚜껑과 바닥이 같은 크기로 되어 있고 진공 상태로 오랫동안 음식을 저장하는 특징을 갖고 있는 용기는 '캔 (can)'이다.

15 ⑤

W Where are you going, Dave?

M I'm going downtown, Mom. Rita and I are going shopping together.

W Rita? She must be your new friend. What's she like?

M She likes sports and she belongs to our school's hockey team.

W That's terrific! Where are you going to meet her by the way?

M In front of the Sky Mall. She needs to buy some clothes.

W I'm driving out to my office now. Do you need a ride?

M Oh, sure. Thanks, Mom.

W Dave, 어디 가니?

M 시내에 가요, 엄마. Rita와 전 같이 쇼핑 가기로 했어요.

W Rita라고? 새 친구로구나. 어떤 아이니?

M 그 애는 운동을 좋아해요. 그리고 우리 학교 하키 팀 소속이에요.

W 굉장한데! 그런데 어디서 만나기로 했어?

M Sky Mall 앞에서요. 그 애가 옷을 좀 사야 하거든요.

W 내가 지금 사무실에 차를 갖고 갈 건데. 태워 줄까?

M 오, 물론이죠. 고마워요, 엄마.

16 ④ | ➕②

M Did you hear that we can watch movies at the school theater every weekend in October?

W Yes, I did. They're showing movies all this month, until the end of October. Can you go with me sometime?

M Well, I can't make it next weekend. I have to finish a paper over the weekend. It's due by the 5th of October.

W As for me, I won't be free until the 15th of October because of my project.

W Then, there are only two weekends left. How about going on the third weekend—October 22 or 23?

M Sorry, I can't. I'm going to spend it with my family.

W Then, we have only one choice left—the last weekend— either October 29 or 30.

M There's a party I'm going to on October 30. Let's go to the movie on October 29.

W That will be our only chance, so let's not miss it!

M 10월 매주 주말 학교 극장에서 영화를 볼 수 있다는 거 들었어?

W 응, 들었어. 10월이 끝날 때까지 이번 달 내내 영화를 보여준대. 언제 나

랑 같이 갈래?

M 음, 다음 주는 안돼. 주말 동안 끝내야 할 보고서가 있거든. 10월 5일까지 해야 해.

W 나는 프로젝트 때문에 10월 15일까지 바빠.

M 그럼 두 주 밖에 안 남네. 3번째 주말인 10월 22일이나 23일은 어때?

W 미안, 안돼. 가족들과 보내야 해.

M 그럼, 한 가지 선택밖에 없네. 마지막 주인 10월 29일과 30일.

W 10월 30일에는 가야하는 파티가 있어. 10월 29일에 영화 보러 가자.

M 그게 우리의 하나뿐인 기회니까 놓치지 말자.

17 ⑤

M Susie, have you ever had a part-time job?

W Yes, I once had one when I was in high school.

M You did? What did you do?

W I was a server at a fancy restaurant but I quit after 2 months.

M Why? You were not paid well, were you?

W Hmm... Not really. I just couldn't work late every day because I had to get up early to go to school.

M I understand that. I don't think I could work like that more than two days.

W What about you? Have you ever worked part time?

M Never. But this summer I'd like to babysit. I love babies.

W Sounds like a great idea. You will be a perfect baby sitter.

M Susie, 아르바이트를 해 본 적 있어?

W 응, 고등학생 때 한 번 해 봤지.

M 그래? 뭘 했는데?

W 멋진 레스토랑에서 종업원으로 일했는데 두 달 뒤에 그만뒀어.

M 왜? 급여가 좋지 않았구나. 그렇지?

W 흠… 꼭 그렇진 않아. 다음 날 아침 일찍 학교에 가야 해서 매일 늦게까지 일할 수가 없었던 것뿐이야.

M 이해가 간다. 난 이틀 이상 그 일을 할 수 없을 것 같아.

W 너는 어때? 아르바이트 해 봤어?

M 한 번도 안 해 봤어. 하지만 이번 여름엔 아이 보는 일을 하고 싶어. 난 아기가 좋아.

W 좋은 생각 같아. 넌 완벽한 베이비시터가 될 거야.

18 ②

W Do you know what happened to me a few days ago?

M No. What happened?

W I woke up at 7:35 in the morning.

M Oh, no. You didn't have time to get ready, did you?

W No, I didn't. So, I jumped into my clothes, skipped breakfast, and ran all the way to school.

M Did you make it to school in time?

W Fortunately the school is quite close. I think I arrived there at eight. But there was one problem I'd never thought of.

M What was that?

W No one was there. I was the only student at school!

M _____

W 며칠 전에 나한테 무슨 일이 있었는지 알아?

M 아니, 무슨 일이 일어났는데

W 7시 35분에 일어났어.

M 오, 이런. 준비할 시간이 없었네, 그렇지?

W 물론이지. 옷을 허겁지겁 입고, 아침은 거르고, 학교까지 내내 뛰었어.

M 제시간에 학교에 들어갈 수 있었어?

W 다행히도 학교가 무척 가까워. 8시에 학교에 도착했다고 생각했어. 하지만 내가 생각지도 못했던 문제가 하나 있었던 거야.

M 그게 뭐였는데?

W 아무도 없었다는 거지. 학교에서 학생은 나 혼자였지.

M 아, 이런. 일요일이었구나?

① 넌 일찍 일어나는구나.
③ 다음번엔 더 일찍 출발하는 게 좋겠다.
④ 선생님이 너에게 뭐라고 하시든?
⑤ 네 학교 학생 몇 명을 내가 알아.

19 ③

M Would you give me a wake-up call at six tomorrow morning?

W No problem. But why do you want to get up so early? Tomorrow is Saturday, isn't it?

M It's my mom's birthday. I'm going to surprise her by preparing breakfast, but I'm not sure if I can get up early.

W Don't you have an alarm clock?

M Of course I do. But it is useless because I just turn it off and fall right back to sleep.

W I understand that. Okay, I won't forget to call you tomorrow morning.

M Thank you, Nancy. Oh, one more thing. Could you come to my place and sing to my mom?

W Do you mean it? Are you kidding?

M _____

M 내일 아침 여섯 시에 전화해서 깨워 줄 수 있어?

W 물론이지. 하지만 무엇 때문에 그렇게 일찍 일어나고 싶은데? 내일은 토요일이잖아.

M 엄마 생신이야. 아침을 준비해서 엄마를 놀라게 하려고 하는데 내가 일찍 일어날 수 있을 것 같지 않아.

W 알람시계 있지 않아?

M 당연히 있지. 하지만 사실 그건 내가 곧바로 다시 잠들기 때문에 소용이 없어.

W 이해가 된다. 좋아. 내일 아침 전화하는 것 잊지 않을게.

M 고마워, Nancy. 아, 하나 더. 우리 집에 와서 엄마를 위해 노래 불러 줄 수 있어?

W 진심으로 하는 얘기야? 내가 얼마나 노래를 못하는지 알잖아?

M 하하! 농담이야. 어쨌든 고마워.

① 네가 노래를 못하는 거 난 확신해.
② 내 생일에 와 줘서 고마워.
④ 아, 나는 네가 노래를 잘 하는지 몰랐어.
⑤ 네가 얼마나 노래를 잘 하는지 결코 잊지 못할 거야.

20 ⑤

M Max graduated from high school this month. He wants to drive a car but doesn't have his driver's license yet. In order to drive, he has to pass the driving test. He goes to the driving academy to learn how to drive. At the information desk, a female clerk gives Max a sheet of paper and wants him to write down information, such as his name, address, and phone number. In this situation, what would the woman say to Max?

M Max는 이번 달에 고등학교를 졸업했다. 그는 차를 운전하고 싶지만 아직 운전 면허가 없다. 운전을 하기 위해, 그는 운전시험에 합격해야 한다. 그는 운전을 배우러 운전 학원에 간다. 안내 데스크에서 여자 사무원은 Max에게 종이 한 장을 주고 그가 이름, 주소, 전화번호 같은 그에 관한 정보를 적기를 원한다. 이 상황에서, 여자는 Max에게 무슨 말을 할까?

① 운전 하는 것을 좋아하세요?
② 차에 기름을 가득 채워 주세요.
③ 당신 차는 중고차인가요?
④ 태워 주실래요?
⑤ 이 양식을 작성해 주세요.

01 ④	**02** ②, ➕④	**03** ⑤	**04** ③	**05** ⑤
06 ③, ➕③	**07** ②	**08** ⑤	**09** ③	**10** ⑤
11 ②	**12** ⑤	**13** ④	**14** ①	**15** ①
16 ④	**17** ①	**18** ②	**19** ⑤	**20** ⑤

01 ④

W Hey, Mark. Have you seen Joseph?
M No, I don't know who he is.
W He's my brother. He said he would <u>be here by six</u>.
M Hmm.... Where could he be?
W Let me look for him in the crowd. Oh, there he is. You see <u>the man in a striped jacket</u>?
M Yes. He is drinking wine, isn't he?
W No. Joseph is <u>right beside him</u>. And he's eating chips.
M Hmm, I see two men eating chips.
W He is the one <u>without a moustache</u>.
M Okay. I got him.

W 이봐, Mark. Joseph 봤어?
M 아니. 나는 그 사람이 누군지 모르는데.
W 우리 오빠야. 이곳에 여섯 시까지 온다고 했거든.
M 음…. 어디 있는 거지?
W 사람들 속에서 찾아볼게. 아, 저기 있다. 줄무늬 재킷을 입고 있는 남자 보여?
M 응. 와인을 마시고 있구나, 그렇지 않니?
W 아냐. Joseph은 바로 그 사람 옆에 있어. 그리고 과자를 먹고 있지.
M 음, 과자를 먹는 사람이 두 명 보이는데.
W 그는 콧수염이 없어.
M 알겠어. 그를 찾았어.

02 ② | ➕④

[Cellphone rings.]
W Hi, James.
M Mom, where's the cold medicine? I can't find any. Ah-choo! Ugh, I can't <u>stop sneezing</u>!
W Did you check in the medicine cabinet?
M Yes, but there isn't any in there. Can you get some at the drugstore <u>on your way home</u>?
W Sure. Is there anything else we need?
M There are only a few boxes of tissues left. Please buy some more.
W All right, I will. Oh, do we have any honey? Please check to see if we are running out of it. You need to <u>drink hot honey tea</u> when you have a cough.
M Let me check. *[pause]* There's plenty, so we don't need any. Uh... hey, Mom, buy some fruit. We only have a few apples left.
W I'll get some oranges and bananas.
M Thank you, Mom.

[휴대 전화가 울린다.]
W 여보세요, 제임스.
M 엄마, 감기약 어디 있어요? 찾을 수가 없어요. 에취! 아, 재채기가 멈추질 않아요!
W 약장은 찾아봤니?
M 네, 하지만 거기 없었어요. 엄마가 집에 오는 길에 약국에서 좀 사다주면 안될까요?
W 물론이지. 또 필요한 건 없니?
M 화장지가 몇 상자 안 남았어요. 더 사다 주세요.
W 알겠다. 아, 우리 꿀 있니? 다 떨어졌는지 한번 확인해 보렴. 감기에 걸렸을 때는 뜨거운 꿀차를 마셔야 해.
M 한번 봐 볼게요. *[멈춤]* 많이 있어서 살 필요 없어요. 아... 엄마, 과일 좀 사다 주세요. 사과가 조금밖에 안 남았어요.
W 오렌지랑 바나나를 사갈게.
M 고마워요, 엄마.

03 ⑤

① W You didn't <u>make an appointment</u>, but I'll let you see the doctor right away.
　 M Oh, thank you. It hurts a lot.
② W John, nail this frame on the wall.
　 M Wait a moment. I'll be there.
③ W Put the hammer in the tool box.
　 M I'll do that after making this wooden box.
④ W Don't point your finger at me, please.
　 M Oh, I'm sorry. I didn't mean to insult you.
⑤ W <u>What happened</u>?
　 M It's my mistake. I <u>hit my finger</u>.

① W 약속은 하지 않으셨지만, 당장 의사 선생님의 진찰을 받도록 해 드릴게요.
　 M 오, 감사합니다. 많이 아프네요.
② W John, 이 액자를 벽에 못으로 박아 주세요.
　 M 잠시만 기다려요. 곧 갈게요.
③ W 망치를 도구함에 넣으세요.
　 M 이 나무 상자를 만든 후에 그렇게 할게요.
④ W 손가락으로 저를 가리키지 마세요.
　 M 오, 죄송합니다. 모욕을 주려는 의도는 아니었습니다.
⑤ W 무슨 일이에요?
　 M 제 실수에요. 제 손가락을 치고 말았어요.

04 ③

M Hi, Carol.
W Hi, Knight. Welcome.
M I can't see Jane and Ben.
W They won't come.
M Really? Don't we need their opinions about what day to have a weekly conversation meeting, too?

W Sure, we do. Jane said she's free every day <u>except for Thursdays and Sundays</u>. And Ben <u>cannot come on Fridays</u>.

M Then we should exclude those three days. What about you?

W I have to <u>be with my sister on Mondays</u>. Then we have three days left.

M Well, I <u>don't have any time on Tuesdays and Saturdays</u>.

W Well, we have only one day we all agree on. Let's make it that day.

M 안녕, Carol.

W 안녕, Knight. 어서 와.

M Jane하고 Ben이 안 보이네.

W 그들은 안 올 거야.

M 그래? 주간 회화 모임을 어느 요일에 가질지에 대해 그들의 의견도 중요하지 않아?

W 물론, 중요하지. Jane은 목요일과 일요일을 제외하고는 어느 요일이든 한가하다고 했어. 그리고 Ben은 금요일에 올 수 없고.

M 그럼 그 세 요일은 제외해야겠군. 넌 어때?

W 나는 월요일마다 여동생과 있어야 해. 그럼 세 요일만 남았네.

M 그런데, 나는 화요일과 토요일에는 시간이 없어.

W 그러면, 우리가 모두 동의하는 요일이 단 하나네. 그 날로 정하자.

만점 솔루션 Jane은 목요일과 일요일이 안 되고 Ben은 금요일이 안 된다고 했으며, Carol은 월요일, Knight는 화요일과 토요일이 안 된다고 했으므로, 남은 하나의 요일은 수요일이 된다.

05 ⑤

W Greetings! This is Play-with-us Mall, and I'm Suzie Cox from the Customer Service Department. This <u>coming May 11 at 5 o'clock</u>, Play-with-us Mall will open its second game store in Seoul. This is all because of <u>the love and dedication of our customers</u>, and we'd like to thank you very much for that. As a token of our gratitude, we are planning many great events for you! As the first event, we will be holding a Lucky Draw event at <u>our opening ceremony of the new store</u>! Everyone is welcome to join in on May 11 at 5 p.m. at the new Play-with-us store. You could win one of twenty 100,000-won store gift cards. If you need more information about the event, please call 050-777-0101 and ask for Suzie Cox. I'll be glad to assist you in any way.

W 안녕하세요! 플레이 위드 어스 몰입니다. 저는 고객 서비스 부서의 수지 콕스입니다. 다가오는 5월 11일 5시에, 플레이 위드 어스 몰은 서울에 두 번째 게임 가게를 엽니다. 이 모든 것은 고객 여러분의 사랑과 헌신 덕분이고 저희는 그것에 매우 감사드리고 싶습니다. 감사의 표시로 저희는 여러분들을 위한 많은 엄청난 행사를 계획하고 있습니다! 첫 행사로, 저희는 새 가게의 개업식에서 행운권 추첨 행사를 열 것입니다! 5월 11일 5시에 새로운 플레이 위드 어스 가게에 오시는 모든 분을 환영합니다. 여러분은 20개 중 하나인 10만원짜리 가게 상품권을 타게 될 수도 있습니다. 행사에 대한 더 많은 정보를 원하시면, 050-777-0101로 전화

하셔서 수지 콕스를 찾아주세요. 할 수 있는 일이라면 무엇이든 기꺼이 돕겠습니다.

06 ③ | ➕ ③

W Jason, I'm exhausted. Can we stop walking and take a break?

M Okay. Let's stop and drink some water. Are you enjoying our hike?

W Yes. It is great, but it's so tough to walk uphill. I think I've done a lot of exercise today.

M That's great!

W Jason... *[pause]* Why don't we go back down now? Actually, my legs are starting to hurt.

M Sure, no problem. But, before starting back, we'd better stretch and <u>relax our entire bodies</u>.

W You mean cool-down exercises? I think we've done enough exercise for today, haven't we?

M Well, cool-down exercises can <u>increase muscle control</u>, which can actually help your body <u>to recover more easily</u> after exercising.

W All right. Can you show me how?

M Sure, let me show you four different cool-down exercises. First, let's start with a shoulder stretch.

W 제이슨, 나 지쳤어. 걷는 거 잠깐 멈추고 쉬면 안될까?

M 알겠어. 멈추고 물을 좀 마시자. 하이킹 즐기고 있니?

W 응. 아주 좋아. 그런데 오르막길이 걷기 너무 힘들다. 오늘 운동을 엄청 많이 한 거 같아.

M 잘됐네!

W 제이슨... *[멈춤]* 지금 내려가면 안될까? 사실, 나 다리가 아프기 시작했어.

M 물론, 문제 없어. 그런데, 내려가기 전에, 스트레칭을 해서 온 몸의 긴장을 푸는 게 좋을 거야.

W 마무리 운동 말하는 거지? 오늘은 충분히 운동을 한 거 같은데, 그렇지 않아?

M 마무리 운동은 근육 조절을 향상시킬 수 있고, 그게 운동 후에 네 몸이 더 쉽게 회복하는 데 도움을 줄 수 있어.

W 알겠어. 어떻게 하는지 보여줄래?

M 물론, 네 가지 다른 마무리 운동을 보여줄게. 우선, 어깨 스트레칭을 시작하자.

07 ②

① M What's the weather like today?
　 W It's cloudy and windy.

② M Is there anything I can help you with?
　 W Sorry, but <u>I couldn't help it</u>.

③ M Let's pull over at the next gas station.
　 W Yes, we're <u>running out of gas</u>.

④ M How would you like to send this package?
　 W By airmail. It's the quickest way, isn't it?

⑤ M How can you be so sure about the accident?

W I saw it clearly on my way to work.

① **M** 오늘 날씨 어때요?

　W 흐리고 바람이 부네요.

② **M** 제가 도와드릴 일이 있을까요?

　W 죄송합니다만, 어쩔 수가 없었어요.

③ **M** 다음 주유소에서 차를 세우죠.

　W 좋아요, 기름도 떨어지고 있어요.

④ **M** 이 소포를 어떻게 보내시겠어요?

　W 항공 우편으로요. 그것이 가장 빠른 방법이죠, 그렇죠?

⑤ **M** 그 사고에 대해 어떻게 그렇게 확신하시죠?

　W 출근길에 제가 분명히 봤어요.

만점 솔루션 ② 남자는 도울 일이 있으면 알려달라는 의미로 말했지만, 대답의 help는 '피하다'의 의미로 '피할 수가(어쩔 수가) 없었다'는 의미가 되어 어색한 대화가 된다.

08 ⑤

W Randy! What are you doing here?

M I'm waiting for Damon. I wonder what's keeping him.

W Have you been waiting long?

M Not that long. He was supposed to be here 20 minutes ago.

W Why don't you call his Cellphone?

M I've been calling it, but it's busy. By the way, where are you going?

W I'm going to the school store. I missed breakfast.

M Then can you get me a hot drink? It's pretty cold.

W Sure. No problem. I'll be back in a minute.

W Randy! 여기서 뭐 하고 있어?

M Damon을 기다리고 있어. 무슨 일로 이렇게 늦는지 모르겠네.

W 오래 기다렸어?

M 그렇게 오래는 아니야. 20분 전에 오기로 되어 있었는데.

W 그의 휴대 전화로 전화를 해 보지 그래?

M 계속 전화를 하고 있는데, 통화 중이야. 그건 그렇고, 넌 어디 가니?

W 학교 매점에 가고 있는 중이야. 아침을 걸렀거든.

M 그러면 따뜻한 음료를 사다 줄 수 있을까? 몹시 추워서.

W 물론이지. 문제 없어. 곧 올게.

09 ③

W It is very important to reduce any chances of getting sick when you travel abroad. Try to prevent bites from mosquitoes and other bugs. Use insect repellent on uncovered skin outdoors, especially during the day. For greater protection, spray it on your clothing, too. Also, be extremely careful about food and water. Only drink bottled or boiled water. Avoid drinking tap water, and order drinks without ice to make sure they are safe. Wash your hands with soap as often as possible, especially before eating or cooking food. Carrying an alcohol-based hand sanitizer will be helpful if water isn't available.

W 해외여행 중일 때 아플 수 있는 모든 가능성을 줄이는 것은 매우 중요합니다. 모기나 다른 벌레들에게 물리는 것을 예방하도록 하세요. 특히 낮 동안에는, 실외에서 방충제를 드러난 피부에 뿌리세요. 더 향상된 보호를 위해서는 옷 위에도 뿌리도록 하세요. 또 음식이나 물에 굉장히 주의하세요. 병에 들어있거나 끓인 물만 마시세요. 수돗물을 마시는 것을 피하고 음료가 안전한지 확실하게 하기 위해 얼음이 없는 음료를 주문하세요. 특히 음식을 먹기 전과 요리하기 전에, 가능하면 자주 비누로 손을 씻으세요. 물을 사용할 수 없다면 알코올이 들어간 손 세정제를 들고 다니는 것이 도움이 될 것입니다.

10 ⑤

W Hi. I'd like to return these two books. Sorry, they're a couple of days late.

M Let me check. They are three days overdue, so you need to pay a late fee.

W How much is it?

M Let's see. You have to pay one dollar per day for each book. So, that's three dollars for each book.

W Here's ten dollars.

M Hmm... It looks like there's one more book, Introduction to Economics, that's overdue under your student ID number.

W Oh, right! I totally forgot about that. I'll return it tomorrow.

M You will have to pay a late fee when you return that book as well. Please don't forget to return your books on time.

W Sorry about that.

M Here's your change.

W 안녕하세요. 책 두 권을 반납하고 싶습니다. 죄송해요, 이틀 연체되었어요.

M 확인해 보겠습니다. 삼일 연체되었기 때문에 연체료를 내야 합니다.

W 얼마인가요?

M 어디 한번 볼까요. 권 당 하루에 1달러씩 내야합니다. 그러니까, 권 당 3달러가 되겠네요.

W 여기 10달러입니다.

M 흠... 한 권이 더 있는 거 같은데요. 경제학책이 당신의 학생증 번호로 연체되어 있습니다.

W 아, 맞다! 완전히 잊고 있었어요. 내일 반납하겠습니다.

M 그 책을 반납할 때 역시 연체료를 내야할 겁니다. 책을 제때 반납해야 하는 것을 잊지 마세요.

W 죄송해요.

M 여기 잔돈입니다.

11 ②

W Be careful. It's easy to break.

M Don't worry. I'm used to this thing. Where do you want me to put it?

W Will you put it next to the refrigerator?

M Sure. No problem. What about this coffee table?

W Put the table next to the window. I like to drink coffee with my husband, looking out the window.

M Okay. What about these vases, ma'am?

W Will you put them out on the veranda? They need fresh air and sunlight.

M All right. Oh, <u>another load is almost here.</u>

W 조심하세요. 그것은 깨지기 쉬워요.

M 걱정하지 마세요. 이런 일에 익숙해요. 어디다 놓을까요?

W 냉장고 옆에 놓아 주시겠어요?

M 물론이죠. 간단하네요. 이 커피 테이블은 어디다 둘까요?

W 그 테이블은 창문 옆에 두세요. 남편과 창 밖을 내다보면서 커피를 마시고 싶거든요.

M 됐습니다. 이 꽃병들은 어떻게 하죠, 사모님?

W 그것들을 베란다로 내 주시겠어요? 신선한 공기와 햇빛이 필요해요.

M 알겠습니다. 오, 다른 짐이 거의 다 왔네요.

12 ⑤

W Welcome to Vietnam! I'm Miya, and I'll be your tour director during your stay in the peaceful city of Da Nang, Vietnam. <u>Due to the delayed arrival</u> of your flight, we have to make a change to the lunch reservation. Your lunch will be served at Hoi An restaurant, not in the Farmers' restaurant. However, the main menu—rice noodles and fried chicken—is the same. After lunch, we will <u>take the cable car to</u> the top of Ba Na Hill and enjoy the great view. And then, we'll <u>take a boat trip to</u> the picturesque old French villages. When you return from the boat trip, you will have time to relax in your hotel rooms before our welcome reception party. If you have any questions or problems, let me know. Thank you.

W 베트남에 어서 오세요! 저는 미야이고 당신이 베트남의 평화로운 도시 다낭에서 머물동안 당신의 여행 책임자가 될 것입니다. 비행 도착시간 지연으로 점심 예약을 변명해야 했습니다. 점심은 파머스 레스토랑이 아닌 호이안 레스토랑에서 먹게 될 것입니다. 하지만 주메뉴는 쌀국수와 닭튀김으로 같습니다. 점심식사 후, 케이블카를 타고 바나힐의 정상으로 가서 아름다운 경치를 즐길 것입니다. 그리고나서, 그림 같은 옛 프랑스 마을로 보트여행을 갈 것입니다. 보트여행에서 돌아오면 환영 축하 파티 전까지 호텔 방에서 편하게 쉴 시간을 갖게 됩니다. 어떤 문의사항이나 질문이 있다면 알려주세요. 감사합니다.

13 ④

W I'm looking for a summer job to do during the vacation. I'm considering <u>working as a camp counselor</u> at a summer camp.

M Oh, really? I'm also looking for a summer job.

W Great, let's try to find one together.

M Okay. Well, <u>I have a summer class to take</u> in the evenings, so I can only work during the day.

W Then, let's cross the overnight ones off the list. Have you

ever worked at a summer camp before?

M No, I haven't. It'll be my first experience.

W How about choosing this one? This one is a day camp, and they don't <u>require</u> any <u>previous camp experience</u>.

M Sounds great. Is there an age limit? I'm going to turn 18 this winter.

W No, this one doesn't have any age limit. Let's both apply for this one.

W 방학동안 할 여름 직업을 찾고 있어. 여름 캠프에서 캠프 상담사로 일해 볼까 생각 중이야.

M 아, 진짜? 나도 여름 직업을 찾는 중인데.

W 잘됐다, 같이 찾아보자.

M 그래. 나 저녁시간에는 여름 수업을 하나 듣고 있어서 낮에만 일할 수 있어.

W 그럼, 목록에서 밤사이에 일하는 건 지우자. 전에 여름 캠프에서 일한 적 있어?

M 아니, 없어. 이게 내 첫 경험이 될 거야.

W 이걸 선택하는 거 어때? 낮 캠프이고 어떤 캠프 경력도 필요하지 않아.

M 좋아. 나이 제한은 없어? 나 이번 겨울에 18이 되는데.

W 아니, 이건 나이 제한이 없어. 우리 둘 다 이 일에 지원하자.

14 ①

W These are <u>a symbol of belonging to a certain group</u>. People wear these on their clothes, bags, and even vehicles to show they belong to a certain group. In most cases, people are proud of wearing these. These are also given to people who <u>believe in and work for a cause</u> such as animal rights. In some organizations such as the military, these are given to members to <u>praise their accomplishments</u>. These can be made from metal, plastic, leather or rubber. Some people enjoy collecting these as a hobby.

W 이것은 특정 단체에 속해 있다는 상징이다. 사람들은 특정 단체에 속한다는 것을 보여주기 위해 이것을 옷, 가방, 그리고 심지어 차량에까지 달기도 한다. 대부분의 경우, 사람들은 이것을 달고 있는 것을 자랑스러워 한다. 이것은 동물의 권리와 같이 대의명분을 믿거나 그것을 위해 일하는 사람들에게 주기도 한다. 군대와 같은 몇몇 조직에서는 구성원들의 성취를 치하하기 위해 이것을 주기도 한다. 이것은 금속, 플라스틱, 가죽 혹은 고무로 만들어질 수 있다. 취미로 이것을 모으는 것을 좋아하는 사람들도 있다.

15 ①

M Martha, do you <u>have a minute</u>?

W I'm afraid not, Andy. I'm going to the cafeteria.

M Oh, are you going for a late lunch?

W No, I'm just going to <u>review what I learned</u> while drinking something at the cafeteria.

M Really? Then I think you can help me out.

W Well, what can I help you with?

M I missed some classes last week because I was sick.

W Oh, I remember the day you didn't show up. Do you want to borrow my notes?

M Yes, please. I'll photocopy them and give them back to you straight away.

W OK. Here you go. Are you going to go to the library?

M Yes. They have a copy machine there. Thank you, Martha.

M Martha, 잠깐 시간 좀 있어?

W 안 될 것 같은데. 식당에 가는 중이거든.

M 아, 거기에서 늦은 점심을 먹으려고 가니?

W 아니, 그냥 식당에서 뭔가를 마시면서 배운 것을 복습하러 가려고.

M 그래? 그러면 날 도와줄 수 있겠구나.

W 글쎄, 내가 뭘 도와줄 수 있을까?

M 지난주에 내가 아파서 수업을 빠졌거든.

W 아, 네가 출석 안 한 날이 기억난다. 그래서, 내 공책을 빌리고 싶구나?

M 그래. 부탁해. 금방 복사하고 바로 돌려줄게.

W 좋아. 여기 있어. 도서관으로 갈 거니?

M 그래. 거기에 복사기가 있잖아. 고마워, Martha.

16 ④

W We're finally here.

M Yes. It's like my dream came true.

W What will we ride first?

M What about Xtreme Swing or Corkscrew? They are going to be a thrilling experience.

W Let's enjoy them later. Let's start with something simple. We have a lot of time.

M Then what about Hurricane Falls?

W I don't want to get wet at the beginning of the day.

M Then what do you say to going on the Ferris Wheel or Antique Autos?

W Let's ride the Ferris Wheel first. We can have an overall view of the amusement park.

M That's a good idea. Let's get going.

W 마침내 도착했어.

M 응. 내 꿈이 실현된 것 같아.

W 뭘 먼저 탈까?

M Xtreme Swing이나 Corkscrew는 어때? 긴장감 넘치는 체험이 될 거야.

W 그것들은 나중에 즐기자. 간단한 것으로 시작하자고. 우린 시간이 많잖아.

M 그럼 Hurricane Falls는 어때?

W 하루의 시작부터 물에 젖고 싶지는 않아.

M 그럼 Ferris Wheel이나 Antique Autos를 타는 것은 어때?

W Ferris Wheel을 먼저 타자. 이 놀이공원을 전반적으로 살펴볼 수 있잖아.

M 좋은 생각이야. 가자.

17 ①

M Miss?

W Yes. What can I do for you, sir?

M I just opened an account and got this card, but it doesn't seem to work. Will you check if this card works in the ATM?

W Oh, sure, sir. Insert the card first. Yes, right there.

M I'd like to withdraw $20 just as a test.

W Okay. Then choose "withdrawal!" and enter your 4-digit password. Then choose the amount and the money will come out.

M Good. It works.

W One more thing, sir. Remember deposits made at an ATM may not be immediately available for withdrawal.

M _____

M 아가씨?

W 네. 뭘 도와드릴까요, 손님?

M 막 계좌를 개설하고 이 카드를 받았는데, 안 되는 것 같아요. 현금인출기에 이 카드가 되는지 확인해 줄래요?

W 오, 물론이죠, 손님. 먼저 카드를 넣으세요. 네, 바로 거기에요.

M 시험으로 20달러만 인출하고 싶어요.

W 알겠습니다. 그런 다음 '인출'을 선택하시고 4자리 비밀번호를 입력하세요. 그리고 나서 금액을 선택하시면 돈이 나올 거예요.

M 좋아요. 되는군요.

W 한 가지 더요. 손님. 현금인출기에서 입금한 예금은 인출이 바로 안 될 수도 있다는 것을 기억해 두세요.

M 명심하겠습니다. 감사합니다.

② 매달 비밀번호를 바꿀게요.

③ 즉시 카드를 발급해 주세요.

④ 그럼 내일 입금할게요.

⑤ 제가 비밀번호를 입력하는 것을 지켜보지 마세요.

> **만점 솔루션** 여자의 도움을 받아 현금인출기 사용법을 배웠고 참고 사항도 들었으므로, '명심하겠다.'는 말과 함께 감사를 표하는 말이 응답으로 가장 적절하다.

18 ②

W Good morning, Ted.

M Hi, Sue. It's beautiful today.

W Yes. You look different today.

M Really? Well, I have every reason.

W Something really good happened to you, didn't it?

M Yes. I finally became a brother. My mother gave birth to a very cute daughter.

W Congratulations!

M Thanks. She is so cute that I can't keep my eyes off her.

W I know how you feel now. That's how I felt when I had my brother. By the way, how's your mother?

M She is fine.

W It's difficult to give birth. Make sure you take good care of her.

M _____

W 안녕, Ted.

M 안녕, Sue. 오늘 날씨 좋네.

W 그래. 너 오늘 뭔가 달라 보인다.

M 정말? 사실, 그럴 만한 이유가 있어.

W 뭔가 아주 좋은 일이 생긴 거로구나, 그렇지?

M 응. 내가 마침내 오빠가 됐어. 어머니께서 아주 귀여운 딸을 낳으셨거든.

W 축하해!

M 고마워. 너무 귀여워서 눈을 뗄 수가 없었어.

W 지금 네 심정 내가 알지. 남동생이 생겼을 때 나도 그랬거든. 그건 그렇고, 어머니는 어떠셔?

M 괜찮으셔.

W 출산은 아주 힘든 일이야. 어머니를 반드시 잘 돌봐드리도록 해.

M <u>그럴게. 조언 고마워.</u>

① 어머니에게 안부를 전해 줘.

③ 감기에 걸리지 않게 조심해.

④ 네가 곧 회복되기를 바라.

⑤ 걱정하지 마. 그 때쯤이면 내가 돌아올 거야.

19 ⑤

W Good morning, Mr. Starr. I'd like to borrow these books.

M Good morning. Do you have <u>a membership card</u>?

W Sorry, I forgot to bring it.

M That's okay <u>if I can find your name</u> in the computer.

W Good. I'm Jane Birkin. My last name is spelled B-I-R-K-I-N.

M OK. Umm.... Oh, you have <u>an overdue book</u>.

W Really? I think I brought all the books back.

M No, you still have '1984' by George Orwell.

W Oh, my gosh! I <u>totally forgot</u>. I'm terribly sorry. What should I do now?

M _____

W 안녕하세요, Starr 선생님. 이 책들을 빌리고 싶어요.

M 안녕. 회원 카드 있어?

W 죄송하지만 갖고 오는 것을 잊었어요.

M 내가 컴퓨터에서 네 이름을 찾을 수 있다면 괜찮아.

W 좋아요. 저는 Jane Birkin이에요. 제 성의 철자는 B–I–R–K–I–N이죠.

M 좋아. 음···. 아, 너 기한이 지난 책이 있구나.

W 정말이요? 책을 다 반납한 것으로 생각하는데요.

M 아냐. George Orwell이 쓴 '1984'를 아직도 갖고 있어.

W 아, 이런! 까맣게 잊었어요. 정말 죄송해요. 이젠 어떻게 해야 하죠?

M <u>그 책을 먼저 반납해. 그러고 나면 다른 책을 빌릴 수 있어.</u>

① 가서 선생님께 도움을 청해.

② 회원 카드를 다시 갖고 와서 부모님께 전화해.

③ 집에 가서 네가 나에게 한 일에 대해 생각해 봐

④ 걱정하지 마. 우리는 그 책 때문에 항상 즐거워.

20 ⑤

M Your mother <u>looked sick this morning</u> when you went to school. Now you are home and she doesn't look any better. Your dad isn't home yet. Your mother sets the table for dinner. She eats just a bit, but mostly sits at the table waiting for you to finish your meal. When you finish your dinner, she stands up to do the dishes. You think <u>she needs to go to bed early</u> and want to <u>do the dishes for her</u>. In this situation, what will you most likely say to your mother?

M 당신이 아침에 등교할 때 어머니가 아파 보이셨다. 지금 당신은 집에 와 있는데 어머니가 전혀 좋아지신 것 같지가 않다. 아버지는 아직 퇴근을 안 하셨다. 어머니는 저녁식사를 차리신다. 어머니는 약간만 드시고, 대부분의 시간을 식탁에 앉아서 당신이 식사를 마치기를 기다리신다. 당신이 저녁식사를 마치자, 어머니는 설거지를 하려고 일어나신다. 당신은 어머니가 일찍 잠자리에 들어야 한다고 생각하고, 당신이 어머니를 위해 설거지를 하기를 원한다. 이 상황에서, 당신은 어머니에게 뭐라고 말할 것 같은가?

① 아버지 저녁은 제가 준비할게요.

② 의사 선생님의 진찰을 받아보지 그래요?

③ 마저 하세요. 전 일찍 잘게요.

④ 어머니, 저 아직 저녁식사 중이에요.

⑤ 가서 쉬세요. 설거지는 제가 할게요.

만점 솔루션 몸이 아픈 어머니가 일찍 잠자리에 드시도록 어머니 대신 설거지를 하고자 하는 상황이다.

01 ③	**02** ④	**03** ②	**04** ③, ➕⑤	**05** ①
06 ③	**07** ②	**08** ②, ➕④	**09** ⑤	**10** ②
11 ②	**12** ⑤	**13** ③	**14** ①	**15** ⑤
16 ③	**17** ③	**18** ⑤	**19** ⑤	**20** ②

01 ③

W I'm looking for a simple wall clock. Would you show me one within $60?

M Sure. How about the square one with numbers on it? It's $55.

W It looks good, but I like that round one better.

M You mean the small round one without numbers?

W No, the big one looks better. And I want all the numbers on it.

M I see, but it's $65.

W Well, that's OK. I'll pay more.

W 단순한 벽시계를 찾고 있는데요. 60달러 이내에서 좀 보여주실래요?

M 그럼요. 숫자가 있는 저 정사각형 모양의 벽시계는 어떤가요? 55달러입니다.

W 좋아 보이네요. 그런데 전 저 둥근 것이 더 좋아요.

M 숫자가 없는 저 작은 둥근 것을 말씀하시는 건가요?

W 아니요, 저 큰 것이 더 좋아 보이네요. 그리고 전 모든 숫자가 있는 것을 원해요.

M 알겠습니다, 하지만 저것은 65달러입니다.

W 음, 괜찮습니다. 더 지불하죠.

02 ④

[Cellphone rings.]

M Hi, Grace. What's up?

W Hey, I had my final audition yesterday, and guess what?

M What?

W I got a role in a big stage musical.

M Really? Which one?

W Mama Mia. I am going to play one of main character's friends.

M Wow, that's amazing! Who's going to act with you?

W The cast list is unbelievable. One of my favorite actresses, Suzan Baker, will play the title role. I will actually practice with her in person.

M When are they going to start practicing?

W Well, they're still casting extras, so the very first meeting with other actors and staff won't be announced for a few more weeks.

M That's so exciting! Keep me posted about how it's going!

[휴대 전화가 울린다.]

M 안녕, 그레이스. 무슨 일이야?

W 안녕, 나 어제 마지막 오디션을 봤는데, 어떻게 됐는지 알아?

M 어떻게 됐는데?

W 큰 무대의 뮤지컬에서 역할을 맡게 됐어.

M 진짜? 어떤 거?

W 맘마미아. 주인공의 친구 중 한 명을 맡게 됐어.

M 와, 굉장하다! 누구랑 같이 연기 해?

W 출연진들이 믿을 수 없을 정도야. 내가 가장 좋아하는 배우 중 하나인, 수잔 베이커가 주인공 역할이야. 그녀랑 직접 만나서 연습을 할 거야.

M 연습은 언제 시작하는데?

W 음, 엑스트라들을 아직 뽑고 있어서 다른 배우들이랑 직원들이랑 하는 첫 미팅은 앞으로 몇 주동안은 발표되지 않을 거야.

M 진짜 재미있겠다! 어떻게 되어가고 있는지 계속 소식 전해줘!

03 ②

① W What's the problem with my cat?
  M Let me check first.

② W Do you like cats?
  M No. Actually I'm afraid of cats.

③ W Will she be OK now?
  M Sure. She's going to be all right.

④ W Should I feed her only once a day?
  M Yes. For one week.

⑤ W Can I take her home now?
  M Yes. Make sure to keep her warm.

① W 제 고양이의 문제가 뭔가요?
  M 먼저 검사해 보겠습니다.

② W 고양이 좋아해요?
  M 아니요. 사실 전 고양이가 무서워요.

③ W 이제 그녀가 괜찮을까요?
  M 그럼요. 괜찮을 겁니다.

④ W 하루에 겨우 한 번 먹이를 줘야 하나요?
  M 네. 일주일 동안은요.

⑤ W 이제 그녀를 집에 데리고 가도 되나요?
  M 네. 꼭 따뜻하게 해 주셔야 합니다.

04 ③ | ➕⑤

M Mom, I need to go to the shopping mall. Can you give me a ride?

W All right. I was going to do some grocery shopping anyway.

M Thanks.

W What are you going to buy at the mall?

M I'm going to get some new shoes.

W All right. Then I'll drop you off at the shoe store, and then I'll go to the grocery store.

M Actually, Mom, can you help me choose my shoes? Let's meet up after you finish grocery shopping.

W Well, then, I'll have to carry groceries all the way to the shoe store or make two trips to the car.

M Ah. Then, come with me to the shoe store first, and then we can go grocery shopping together.

W All right. let's go. Just let me grab the keys.

M Thanks. I hope the mall isn't too busy today.

M 엄마, 저 쇼핑몰에 가야해요. 좀 태워주시겠어요?

W 그래. 어차피 식료품을 사러 가려고 했으니까.

M 고마워요.

W 몰에서는 무엇을 사려고 하니?

M 새 신발을 사려고요.

W 그래. 그럼 신발 가게에서 내려주고 나는 식료품점에 가야겠다.

M 사실, 엄마, 제가 신발 고르는 걸 도와주실 수 있나요? 식료품을 다 사고 나서 만나요.

W 그럼 내가 식료품들을 들고 신발가게에 가거나 차까지 두 번 왔다 갔다 해야 해.

M 아, 그럼. 우선 저랑 같이 신발가게를 갔다가 같이 식료품을 사러 가요.

W 그래. 그렇게 하자. 우선 키를 가지고 올게.

M 고마워요. 오늘 몰이 많이 붐비지 않았으면 좋겠어요.

05 ①

W Hi, Sam. Where are you headed?

M Don't ask me anything. I'm not in the mood to talk.

W Come on, Sam. What happened to you? Tell me so I can help you out.

M I was at Mark's birthday party and my mom called me to come home right away.

W Oh, that's too bad. So you had to leave the party in the middle of excitement, right?

M Yeah. And my mother didn't tell me why I should hurry home.

W Hmm... I think there must be a reason for that.

M Well, I don't care.

W 안녕, Sam. 어디 가?

M 묻지 마. 말할 기분이 아니야.

W 이봐, Sam. 무슨 일이 있었는데? 내게 말해 봐, 그래야 내가 돕지.

M Mark의 생일 파티에 갔었는데, 엄마가 당장 집으로 오라고 전화를 하신 거야.

W 오, 안됐다. 그래서 한창 재미있을 때 파티장을 떠나야 했구나, 그렇지?

M 맞아. 그런데 우리 엄마는 왜 내가 서둘러 집에 와야 했는지 말씀해 주지를 않으셨어.

W 흠… 틀림없이 이유가 있을 거야.

M 글쎄, 알게 뭐야.

06 ③

W Max, you're late.

M I'm sorry, Ms. Carter. I had a toothache and I went to the dentist this morning.

W Oh, you did? Are you OK, now?

M Yes. I have to see him again the day after tomorrow.

W I see. Well, let's see how much you practiced. You know this violin competition is very important for you if you want

to be a famous musician.

M Of course I do. And I hope my teeth won't be a problem on the stage.

W So do I. Now, why don't you start from right here?

W Max, 늦었구나.

M 죄송합니다. Carter 선생님. 치통이 있어서 오늘 아침에 치과에 다녀왔습니다.

W 오, 그랬니? 지금은 괜찮니?

M 네. 모레 다시 그 선생님께 다녀와야 해요.

W 알겠다. 음, 네가 얼마나 많이 연습했는지 보자. 알다시피 네가 유명한 음악가가 되고 싶다면 이 바이올린 대회가 아주 중요하단다.

M 물론이죠, 알고 있습니다. 그런데 제 치아가 무대에서 문제가 되지 않았으면 좋겠어요.

W 나도 그렇단다. 그럼, 바로 여기부터 시작해 볼까?

만점 솔루션 바이올린 대회를 언급하고 수업을 시작하자고 하는 것에서 교사와 학생의 대화임을 알 수 있다. 치통과 치과 의사에 대한 내용만 듣고 치과 의사와 환자의 관계로 오해하면 안 된다.

07 ②

① **M** I'd like to buy some socks for my daughter.
  W What size does she wear?

② **M** What is the purpose of your visit?
  W I'll stay at the Sunrise hotel for two weeks.

③ **M** I'd like to return these books.
  W OK. Oh, this book is overdue.

④ **M** Mary, I want to ask you a favor.
  W Oh, do you? What is it?

⑤ **M** Where can I wash my hands?
  W The bathroom is on your right.

① **M** 제 딸에게 줄 양말 몇 켤레를 사고 싶은데요.
  W 몇 사이즈를 신나요?

② **M** 방문 목적이 무엇인가요?
  W 2주 동안 Sunrise 호텔에 머물 겁니다.

③ **M** 이 책들을 반납하고 싶은데요.
  W 알겠습니다. 오, 이 책은 연체되었네요.

④ **M** Mary, 부탁 하나 하고 싶은데요.
  W 오, 그래요? 뭐죠?

⑤ **M** 어디에서 손을 씻나요?
  W 화장실은 당신의 오른편에 있습니다.

08 ② | ➕ ④

[Cellphone rings.]

M Hi, Jenny. Can I get your advice? I'd like to sell my car, but I don't know how.

W Hmm... Why don't you contact a used car dealer?

M I did. But they offered me a very low price. Can you help me find someone who might buy it?

W Well, one of my friends has been talking about buying a new car recently. I'll ask him if he's interested. Could you tell me what kind of car you have?

M It's a 2013 Zet 4.

W Okay. What color is it?

M It's metallic silver.

W And how many kilometers does it have on it?

M About 20,000 kilometers.

W The car has never been in an accident, right?

M That's right. No accidents.

W So, how much would you like to get for it?

M Well, I'd like to get at least $10,000 for it. I've taken really good care of the vehicle.

[휴대 전화가 울린다.]

M 안녕, 제니. 나 조언 좀 구할 수 있을까? 내 차를 팔고 싶은데 어떻게 해야 할지 잘 모르겠어.

W 흠… 중고차 딜러에게 연락해보는 거 어때?

M 했어. 그런데 너무 낮은 가격을 부르더라. 차를 살 수도 있는 누군가를 찾는 걸 도와줄 수 있을까?

W 내 친구 중에 한명이 최근에 새 차를 사는 거에 대해 이야기 한 적이 있어. 관심이 있는지 물어볼게. 차가 무슨 종류인지 말해줄래?

M 2013년에 나온 제트4야.

W 알겠어. 무슨 색이야?

M 금속 느낌이 나는 은색이야.

W 몇 킬로미터를 달렸어?

M 대략 2만 킬로미터.

W 차가 사고가 났던 적은 없지, 맞지?

M 응. 그런 적 없어.

W 그럼, 가격은 얼마를 받고 싶어?

M 음, 적어도 만달러는 받았으면 해. 차를 진짜 소중히 다뤘거든.

09 ⑤

W Hi, Matt! Thank you for visiting my restaurant.

M No problem. It was very nice of you to invite me.

W Here's the menu. Please take a look and let me know when you're ready to order.

M Let me see… Shabu-shabu? What kind of food is that?

W Oh, it's a kind of hotpot dish with thinly sliced meat and vegetables. You dip the meat into boiling water and then eat it.

M Hmm… Interesting. How about dubu-tang?

W It's a soup made with tofu and beef. Why don't you try it? It's one of our best dishes. You'll love it.

M Is it spicy? I can't eat anything spicy.

W No, dubu-tang isn't spicy. I always let my customers know when they are ordering a spicy dish.

M All right then, I'll have that. I think it'd be really helpful for your customers if you had images of the dishes on the menu.

W That's a good point. I'll keep that in mind.

W 안녕, 맷! 우리 레스토랑을 방문해줘서 고마워.

M 아니야. 초대해줘서 고마워.

W 여기 메뉴야. 한 번 보고 주문할 준비가 되면 알려줘.

M 어디 보자… 샤브샤브? 이건 어떤 음식이야?

W 아, 얇게 썬 고기와 채소가 들어간 핫팟 요리의 한 종류야. 끓고 있는 물에 고기를 담갔다가 먹는 거야.

M 흠… 흥미로운데. 두부탕은 뭐야?

W 두부랑 소고기가 들어간 국이야. 한번 먹어보는게 어때? 가장 잘 나가는 음식 중 하나야. 너도 좋아할 거야.

M 매워? 난 매운 건 전혀 못 먹는데.

W 아니, 두부탕은 맵지 않아. 난 고객들이 매운 음식을 시킬 때면 맵다고 말해.

M 알겠어 그럼. 그걸로 할게. 메뉴에 있는 음식들 사진이 있으면 고객들에게 정말 도움이 될 거 같아.

W 좋은 지적이네. 명심할게.

10 ②

W Good evening, sir. How may I help you?

M Hello. I'm looking for a blouse for my little daughter.

W How old is she?

M Nine. And she likes bright colors like yellow, pink and orange.

W I see. How about the yellow ones on the rack over here? They're $30 each.

M Hmm. They look great. I'll take two of them, one yellow and one orange.

W OK. And we give a pair of gloves for free if you buy more than three blouses.

M Oh, really? Let me think… I'm sorry I can't afford three. Here is $100.

W 안녕하세요, 손님. 어떻게 도와드릴까요?

M 안녕하세요. 딸에게 줄 블라우스를 고르고 있어요.

W 딸이 몇 살인가요?

M 아홉 살입니다. 딸은 노란색, 핑크색, 오렌지색 같은 밝은 색들을 좋아해요.

W 그렇군요. 여기 선반에 있는 노란색 블라우스는 어떨까요? 한 벌당 30달러인데요.

M 흠. 좋네요. 두 벌 살게요. 노란색과 오렌지색으로요.

W 좋아요. 그리고 세 벌 이상의 블라우스를 사시면 장갑 한 켤레를 공짜로 드립니다.

M 오, 정말요? 글쎄요… 세 벌 살 여유가 없네요. 여기 100달러입니다.

11 ②

W Oh, Jack! Will you help me stand straight?

M Let's see. I think your shoes are too big.

W Then, should I change them?

M No, let me tighten your shoe laces…. OK.

W Thanks. That's much better. But I still can't keep my balance.

M Here, take my hand and get onto the ice, and you'll learn very fast.

W Oh, my gosh! It's so slippery but I feel great!

M Sure you do. Come on. Now <u>let go of my hand</u> and try to keep your balance.

W 어이, Jack! 내가 똑바로 서도록 좀 도와줄래?

M 어디 보자. 네 신발이 너무 큰 것 같다.

W 그럼, 교환해야 할까?

M 아니, 네 신발 끈을 조여 줄게…. 됐어.

W 고마워. 훨씬 낫네. 하지만 여전히 균형을 잡을 수가 없어.

M 자, 내 손 잡고 얼음판으로 나와 봐. 그러면 아주 빨리 배울 거야.

W 아이고, 맙소사! 너무 미끄러워. 하지만 굉장하네!

M 그래 넌 할 수 있어. 자. 내 손을 놓고 균형을 잡아 봐.

12 ⑤

W We invite you and all of your friends and family to our blueberry farm! Please join us to celebrate this year's blueberry harvest festival! At the festival, there is something for everyone. You can <u>enjoy picking blueberries</u> on our 40-acre farm, as well as shopping, live music, a small petting zoo, festival rides and games, food trucks, and more. This two-day event will be held from 9 am to 5 pm on Saturday and Sunday, May 5 and 6. Our address is 532 Orchard Road. Admission and parking <u>are completely free</u>. No dogs allowed. Please <u>wear sunscreen</u> and hats, and comfortable clothing is suggested.

W 당신과 당신의 친구 그리고 가족들을 우리 블루베리 농장에 초대합니다. 금년 블루베리 수확 축제에 참여하세요! 축제에서는 모두를 위한 무언가 있습니다. 40에이커 농장에서 블루베리 따기에 더하여 쇼핑과 라이브 음악, 작은 동물원, 축제 놀이기구 그리고 게임, 푸드 트럭 등을 즐길 수 있습니다. 이틀간 열리는 행사는 5월 4일과 6일, 토요일과 일요일 9시부터 5시까지 열립니다. 우리 주소는 과수원길 532입니다. 입장료와 주차는 완전히 무료입니다. 개는 허용되지 않습니다. 선크림을 바르고 모자를 쓰고 편한 옷을 입기를 권장합니다.

13 ③

[Telephone rings.]

W FLORA TOUR COMPANY. May I help you?

M Hello. Could you recommend a tour <u>around the first week of January</u>?

W Sure. Are you going alone, sir?

M Yes. And I want to stay in a warm place because I hate cold weather.

W Well, how about Australia? It's summer down there now.

M Oh, I don't like hot weather, either.

W Then Hong Kong and Malaysia have <u>nice and warm weather</u> around that time.

M Good. And I hope the cost will be <u>under $4,000</u>.

W OK, sir. No problem.

[전화벨이 울린다.]

W FLORA TOUR COMPANY입니다. 도와드릴까요?

M 안녕하세요. 1월 첫째 주쯤에 다녀올 여행지 좀 추천해 주실래요?

W 물론이죠. 혼자 가실 건가요, 손님?

M 네. 그리고 제가 추운 날씨를 싫어하기 때문에 따뜻한 곳에서 있고 싶어요.

W 음. 호주는 어떻습니까? 거기는 지금 여름인데요.

M 오, 전 더운 날씨도 싫어해요.

W 그러면 홍콩과 말레이시아가 그 때쯤이면 매우 따뜻한 날씨예요.

M 좋아요. 그런데 비용이 4,000달러 미만이면 좋겠어요.

W 좋습니다. 손님. 문제 없습니다.

> **만점 솔루션** 홍콩과 말레이시아 중 4,000달러 미만이면서 1월 첫째 주에 가능한 것은 ③이다.

14 ①

M This was invented about 100 years ago. We usually use this <u>to travel a long distance</u> in a short time. This is made up of a lot of parts including <u>four wheels</u>. This <u>needs fuels like gasoline or diesel</u>, but many people expect this will use electricity or solar energy in the future. Although this is <u>one of the most convenient things</u> in our life, we should be very careful in using this because it can be dangerous.

M 이것은 대략 100년 전에 발명되었다. 우리는 보통 짧은 시간에 장거리를 여행하기 위해 이것을 사용한다. 이것은 네 개의 바퀴를 포함하여 많은 부품으로 이루어져 있다. 이것은 휘발유나 디젤과 같은 연료를 필요로 한다. 하지만 많은 사람들은 미래에 이것이 전기나 태양 에너지를 사용할 것이라고 기대한다. 비록 이것이 우리 생활에서 가장 편리한 것들 중의 하나이기는 하지만, 위험할 수 있기 때문에 이것을 사용하는 데 상당한 주의를 기울여야 한다.

> **만점 솔루션** 네 개의 바퀴(four wheels)를 갖고 있고 연료(fuels)를 필요로 하며 자칫하면 위험할 수도 있는 인간의 발명품은 '자동차(car)'이다.

15 ⑤

W How have you been?

M Great. I worked out every day.

W Let's see.... You <u>lost over 2 kilograms</u>.

M I can't believe it. Two kilograms in ten days! That's why I feel much better and stronger.

W You're right. Now, why don't you <u>go up to the third floor</u> for the blood test?

M Oh, I really hate needles.

W Don't worry. It only <u>lasts about 5 seconds</u>.

W 어떻게 지냈어요?

M 잘 지냈죠. 매일 운동했어요.

W 어디 봐…. 2킬로그램 이상 줄었네요.

M 믿을 수가 없어요. 10일에 2킬로그램이라니! 그래서 제가 몸이 더 좋아지고 더 튼튼해졌다는 기분이 들었군요.

W 맞아요. 이제, 피검사를 위해 3층으로 올라가실래요?

M 오, 난 정말 주사 바늘이 싫은데.

W 걱정 마세요. 겨우 5초 걸려요.

16 ③

M May I help you?

W Yes, I bought these pants here yesterday, but I'd like to return them.

M Oh, may I ask you why you're returning them?

W The zipper is broken. I can't unzip the pants. Here's the receipt.

M OK, I'll change them for a new pair. Wait a minute, please.

W Okay.

M Miss? I'm terribly sorry. These pants are out of stock. Could you choose a different style?

W Oh, I really like the design and color of these pants. Would any of your other stores have a pair?

M This style is very popular, so they're all sold out. If you want, we can replace the broken zipper with a new one.

W Do I have to pay for it?

M No, it'd be free. It'll take about 30 minutes, though.

W Okay, I'll wait.

M 도와드릴까요?

W 네, 이 바지를 어제 여기서 샀는데 반품하고 싶어요.

M 아, 왜 반품하려고 하는지 물어봐도 될까요?

W 지퍼가 고장났어요. 바지 지퍼를 내릴 수가 없어요. 여기 영수증이요.

M 알겠습니다. 내 바지로 교환해 드릴게요. 잠시만 기다려주세요.

W 네.

M 정말 죄송합니다. 이 바지는 재고가 없어요. 다른 스타일을 고르실 수 있을까요?

W 아, 이 바지의 디자인과 색상이 정말 마음에 들었는데. 다른 가게에도 없나요?

M 이 스타일은 인기가 많아서 다 품절입니다. 원하시면 망가진 지퍼를 새 것으로 교체해 드릴 수 있어요.

W 돈을 지불해야 하나요?

M 아니요, 무료입니다. 하지만 30분 정도 걸려요.

W 알겠어요. 기다릴게요.

17 ③

M Excuse me, how can I check out books?

W Do you have a library card?

M No. This is my first visit here.

W Then, please fill out this form and I'll make a card for you.

M OK. By the way, are there books for 3 and 4-year-old kids?

W I'm sorry. We have books only for children over 7 years old.

M Gee.... Does that mean I have to buy books for my daughter at the bookstore?

W Oh, you don't have to. There's a children's library near here.

M _____

M 실례합니다. 책을 어떻게 대출하나요?

W 도서 카드 있나요?

M 아니요. 여기 처음 오는데요.

W 그러면, 이 양식을 작성해 주시면 카드를 만들어 드리겠습니다.

M 알겠습니다. 그런데, 서너 살 된 아이들을 위한 책이 있나요?

W 죄송합니다. 일곱 살 이상의 아이들을 위한 책들만 있습니다.

M 이런…. 그렇다면 제 딸 책은 서점에서 사야 된다는 말씀이신가요?

W 오, 그러실 필요는 없습니다. 이 근처에 어린이 도서관이 있습니다.

M 정말요? 어디 있는지 좀 알려 주실래요?

① 얼마 동안 책을 빌릴 수 있나요?

② 고맙습니다. 제가 내일 도서관에 전화해 보겠습니다.

④ 미안합니다. 거기 갈 시간이 없습니다.

⑤ 알겠습니다. 서점에 가서 책을 사겠습니다.

18 ⑤

M Excuse me. I had lunch here yesterday and I left my umbrella.

W Oh, there're a few umbrellas. What does it look like?

M It's big and black.

W Let's see. There are only white, yellow and red ones.

M That's strange. I think I carried an umbrella when I got here because it was raining.

W Do you remember the time you left?

M It was around 1:40. The rain cleared away then, didn't it?

W No, sir. It stopped in the evening. You probably carried your umbrella with you when you left here.

M _____

M 실례합니다. 어제 여기에서 점심을 먹었는데 제 우산을 놓고 갔어요.

W 오, 우산 몇 개가 있어요. 어떻게 생긴 건가요?

M 크고 검은색입니다.

W 어디 보죠. 흰색, 노란색, 그리고 빨간색만 있습니다.

M 이상하네요. 비가 오고 있어서 여기에 올 때 우산을 갖고 온 것 같은데.

W 떠나신 시간을 기억하시나요?

M 대략 1시 40분이었어요. 그 때 비가 그쳤었잖아요, 그렇죠?

W 아니요, 손님. 저녁에 비가 그쳤습니다. 아마 손님이 여기를 떠나실 때 우산을 갖고 가셨을 거예요.

M 그럴 수도 있겠네요. 음, 다른 곳을 기억해 봐야겠는걸요.

① 알겠습니다. 몇 시에 문을 닫으시나요?

② 알겠습니다. 방문해 주셔서 감사합니다.

③ 맞습니다. 여기 다른 우산을 사고 싶습니다.

④ 아니요, 당신이 틀리셨어요. 어제는 비가 오지 않았습니다.

19 ⑤

M It's a beautiful day, isn't it?

W It sure is. I like clear skies. Why don't we go to the park?

M To the park? Why?

W We can enjoy sunbathing.

M I'd like to, but I have to finish this book by tomorrow.

W If so, I'll lay a big outdoor blanket for you on the grass. You can lie down and read your book. What do you think?

M Hmm... Sounds like a good idea. All right. Let's go.

W Wait. I think I should prepare our lunch.

M Oh, it's already 11. What will you make?

W How about cheese sandwiches? It <u>won't take</u> much time.

M _____

M 오늘 아름다운 날이지?

W 정말 그렇네. 난 맑은 하늘이 좋아. 우리 공원에 갈까?

M 공원에? 왜?

W 일광욕을 즐길 수 있지.

M 그렇게 하고 싶지만 내일까지 이 책을 끝내야 해.

W 그렇다면, 내가 널 위해 잔디 위에 큰 야외용 돗자리를 펼게. 넌 누워서 책을 읽으면 돼. 어떻게 생각해?

M 음… 좋은 생각인 것 같아. 좋아. 가자.

W 잠깐. 점심을 준비해야 할 것 같아.

M 아, 벌써 11시네. 뭘 만들 건데?

W 치즈 샌드위치 어때? 시간이 별로 안 걸릴 거야.

M 좋아. 네가 샌드위치 만드는 동안 난 책을 읽을게.

① 아니, 됐어. 이미 많이 먹었어.

② 내가 요리를 잘 한다고 말해줘서 고마워.

③ 글쎄, 난 햇빛 알러지가 있는데.

④ 좋아. 내가 가게에 가서 샌드위치를 좀 사올게.

20 ②

W Mark is supposed to meet his old friend in a cafe in 20 minutes. He goes to the garage and <u>tries to start his car</u> but it won't start. He sees Sally, who lives next door, come out to drive her car. Mark asks her where she is headed. She says she's going to the shopping mall. Mark is <u>happy to know</u> that she is going <u>in the same direction</u>. In this situation, what would Mark say to Sally?

W Mark는 카페에서 20분 후 옛 친구를 만나기로 되어 있다. 그는 차고로 가서 자동차에 시동을 걸려고 하지만 차가 시동이 걸리지 않는다. 그는 옆집에 사는 Sally가 그녀의 차를 몰기 위해 나오는 것을 보게 된다. Mark는 그녀에게 어디로 가는지 묻는다. 그녀는 쇼핑몰에 갈 거라고 말한다. Mark는 그녀가 같은 방향으로 간다는 것을 알게 돼서 기쁘다. 이 상황에서, Mark는 Sally에게 무슨 말을 할까?

① 제 자동차 좀 고쳐 주실래요?

② 저 좀 태워 주실래요?

③ 제 차에 대해 어떻게 생각하세요?

④ 카페에서 저 좀 태워 주실래요?

⑤ 쇼핑몰에 가는 방법을 아시나요?

01 ⑤	**02** ④	**03** ⑤	**04** ④	**05** ③
06 ②	**07** ④	**08** ②, +②	**09** ⑤, +⑤	**10** ④
11 ③	**12** ⑤	**13** ③	**14** ②	**15** ④
16 ②	**17** ③	**18** ①	**19** ②	**20** ④

01 ⑤

W When you go out, be careful, my dear. It's slippery out there.

M Slippery? Was there a snowfall or something?

W Yeah. It snowed overnight. Look out the window.

M Oh, I should start early to make it on time.

W I think you should change your shoes.

M Don't tell me you want me to <u>wear climbing boots</u>, Mom.

W Why not? They'll <u>keep you safe on the icy road</u>.

M Come on, Mom. I'm wearing a dress suit.

W Then you want to be in leather shoes and <u>keep falling down</u>?

M All right. I'll <u>change my clothes</u> and <u>do what you say</u>.

W 외출할 때는 조심해라, 얘야. 밖은 미끄럽단다.

M 미끄럽다고요? 눈 같은 거라도 왔어요?

W 그래. 밤새 눈이 왔어. 창 밖을 봐.

M 오, 시간에 맞춰 가려면 일찍 출발해야겠어요.

W 내 생각에는 네가 신발을 바꿔 신어야겠구나.

M 설마 제가 등산화 신기를 원하는 건 아니시겠죠, 엄마.

W 왜 아니겠니? 등산화가 빙판길에서 너를 안전하게 지켜 줄 거야.

M 아 참, 엄마. 제가 양복을 입고 있거든요.

W 그럼 넌 가죽 구두를 신고 계속 넘어지기를 원하는 거니?

M 좋아요. 옷을 갈아입고 엄마 말씀대로 할게요.

> **만점 솔루션** 눈이 온 사실을 모르고 정장을 입고 나가려던 남자는 빙판길 안전을 위해 등산화를 신으라는 엄마의 말에 결국 옷을 갈아입고 엄마 말대로 하기로 했으므로 등산화를 신을 것이다.

02 ④

W Excuse me.

M Yes?

W I'm <u>looking for a man named</u> Josh Hamilton. Does he work here?

M Yes, but we're closed now. The working hours are from 10 a.m. to 9 p.m. Besides, I guess you need to make a reservation. Josh is a very popular hairdresser.

W Oh, I see. But I'm not here to have my hair cut.

M Really? Then why are you looking for Josh?

W I <u>found his wallet on the street</u>. A business card in it says he works here.

M Oh, I see. Let me call him and check if he can come back right now.

W Thank you.

W 실례합니다.

M 네?

W Josh Hamilton이라는 이름의 남자를 찾고 있는데요. 여기서 일을 하나요?

M 그렇습니다만, 지금 영업이 끝났습니다. 영업시간은 오전 10시부터 오후 9시까지입니다. 게다가, 당신은 예약을 하셔야 할 겁니다. Josh는 아주 유명한 미용사거든요.

W 오, 그렇군요. 그렇지만 제가 이곳에 머리를 자르려고 온 것은 아니에요.

M 그래요? 그럼 왜 Josh를 찾고 있는 거죠?

W 길거리에서 그의 지갑을 발견했어요. 안쪽에 있는 명함에 그가 여기서 일을 한다고 적혀 있었어요.

M 오, 그렇군요. 그에게 전화를 해서 당장 들어올 수 있는지 알아볼게요.

W 감사합니다.

만점 솔루션 여자의 말 I found his wallet on the street.에서 길에서 주운 지갑의 주인을 찾아주려고 미용실에 들른 것임을 확인할 수 있다.

03 ⑤

① **W** I wonder you can give me a ride home.
　M Sure. Get in.
② **W** Whew! Thank you. I almost hit him.
　M Don't use your Cellphone while driving.
③ **W** Are you sending text messages again?
　M No. I'm editing photos I took hours ago.
④ **W** Are there any problems at your car? Take it easy.
　M My car won't start. I can't stand it.
⑤ **W** Make sure to fasten your seat belt.
　M Oh, thank you for reminding me.

① **W** 저를 집까지 태워주실 수 있나요?
　M 물론이죠. 타세요.
② **W** 휘! 고마워요. 하마터면 그를 칠 뻔 했어요.
　M 운전 중에는 휴대 전화를 사용하지 마세요.
③ **W** 또 문자 메시지를 보내고 있나요?
　M 아니요. 몇 시간 전에 찍은 사진들을 편집하고 있어요.
④ **W** 차에 무슨 문제가 있나요? 진정하세요.
　M 시동이 걸리지 않아요. 참을 수가 없네요.
⑤ **W** 반드시 안전벨트를 매세요.
　M 오, 상기시켜 주셔서 감사합니다.

04 ④

[Cellphone rings.]

M Hi, Jenny. How are you?

W Hi, Dad. I'm fine.

M Are you having a great time there?

W Yes, I am. I miss you a lot, but it's sad that the camp is coming to an end. It's already Wednesday!

M I'm glad to hear you miss me. When are you coming back?

W I was going to go back on Friday. But Cathy, this girl I met at camp, invited me to her place. I'd like stay with her over the weekend. Is that okay, Dad?

M Hmm... Do her parents know about this?

W Yes, I met Cathy's parents when she was video chatting with them. They invited me to come over, but they wanted me to talk to you about it first.

M Okay. Can you let them know my phone number?

W Of course. Then I'll see you next week.

M I'll see you on Monday, Jenny. Don't stay longer than the weekend at Cathy's. I want to see you soon.

W All right. I'll see you on Monday!

[휴대 전화가 울린다.]

M 안녕, 제니. 잘 지내고 있니?

W 안녕하세요, 아빠. 전 잘 있어요.

M 거기서 좋은 시간 보내고 있니?

W 네, 아빠가 많이 보고 싶지만 캠프가 끝나가는 것이 슬퍼요. 벌써 수요일이네요!

M 내가 그립다니 기쁘구나. 언제 돌아오니?

W 금요일이요. 하지만 캠프에서 만난 캐시가 자기 집으로 절 초대했어요. 주말 동안 캐시네 집에서 머물고 싶어요. 괜찮죠, 아빠?

M 흠... 캐시 부모님들도 이걸 알고 계시니?

W 네, 캐시 부모님들은 캐시가 비디오 채팅을 할 때 만났어요. 저를 초대해 주셨는데 우선 아빠한테 말하길 원하셨어요.

M 그래. 캐시 부모님에게 내 전화번호를 전해주겠니?

W 물론이죠. 그럼 다음 주에 봐요.

M 월요일에 보자꾸나, 제니. 주말보다 길게 머무는 건 안된다. 빨리 보고싶구나.

W 알겠어요. 월요일에 봐요!

05 ③

M What are you going to bring to our picnic, Lisa?

W I'll make some sandwiches.

M Great. Then I'll buy some fruits and drinks.

W Do you know who brings sausages for the barbecue?

M Jenny and Max said they would buy some.

W Now everything looks great. By the way I wonder what the weather will be like tomorrow.

M Let's check on the Internet. Oh, dear! It's going to rain all day tomorrow.

W All day? You must be kidding. It's hot and sunny outside, you see?

M Come have a look here. It looks like we're having a big storm.

W Oh, no! Then should we put off our picnic?

M Lisa, 우리 소풍에 뭘 갖고 갈 거야?

W 샌드위치를 좀 만들까 해.

M 좋아. 그러면 내가 과일과 마실 것을 살게.

W 바베큐할 소시지를 누가 갖고 오는지 알아?

M Jenny와 Max가 좀 살 거라고 말했어.

W 이제 모든 게 잘 된 것 같아. 그런데 내일 날씨가 어떨지 궁금한데.

M 인터넷에서 확인해 보자. 아, 이런! 내일 종일 비가 올거래.

W 하루 종일? 농담하는 거지? 바깥은 덥고 해가 났잖아.

M 여기 와서 봐. 큰 폭풍이 올 것 같아.

W 아니, 안 돼! 그러면 소풍을 연기해야 하나?

만점 솔루션 소풍을 가려고 하는데 큰 폭풍이 온다는 일기 예보를 듣고 실망하고 있다.

06 ②

W What can I do for you?

M I'm interested in the job you advertised in the newspaper. I wonder what is necessary for the job.

W First, you need to pass a physical test. You have to be physically strong because this job requires you to travel long distances almost every three days.

M I understand.

W After that, there will be a written test about baseball rules. If you pass it, you'll get a three-month training course.

M All right. By the way, what's the hardest part of this job?

W You have to wear heavy protective gears in the middle of summer. And there is a high risk of injury. You sometimes get hit by foul balls. But if you like baseball, it's worth it.

M Okay. Thank you.

W 뭘 도와드릴까요?

M 당신이 신문에 광고한 일자리에 관심이 있습니다. 그 일자리에 필요한 것이 무엇인지 궁금합니다.

W 우선, 체력 테스트에 합격해야 합니다. 이 일은 거의 3일마다 장거리 여행을 요구하기 때문에 체력적으로 강해야 합니다.

M 그렇군요.

W 그런 다음, 야구 규칙에 관한 필기시험이 있을 겁니다. 그것에 합격하면, 3개월간의 훈련 과정이 있습니다.

M 알겠습니다. 그건 그렇고, 이 일의 가장 힘든 점은 무엇입니까?

W 한 여름에도 무거운 보호 장비를 입어야 한다는 점입니다. 그리고 부상의 위험성이 높습니다. 가끔 파울볼에 맞는 경우가 있어요. 그러나 야구를 좋아하면 그럴 만한 가치는 있습니다.

M 알겠습니다. 감사합니다.

07 ④

① W Where did you pick up this old sofa?
   M At the antique shop downtown.
② W How are you getting along with Fred?
   M Pretty well. We meet almost every day.
③ W Are you free this Saturday?
   M Yes, I am. Do you have anything in mind?
④ W Long time no see. How have you been?
   M For five years since I graduated.
⑤ W I was wondering if you would like to go to a movie with me.

M I'd love to. Which movie?

① W 어디서 이 낡은 소파를 구입했니?
   M 시내에 있는 골동품 가게에서.
② W Fred와는 어떻게 지내고 있니?
   M 아주 잘 지내. 우리는 거의 매일 만나.
③ W 이번 토요일에 시간이 있니?
   M 응, 있어. 생각하고 있는 일이라도 있니?
④ W 오랜만이야. 어떻게 지냈어?
   M 졸업하고 5년만이야.
⑤ W 나와 영화 한 편 보러 가고 싶은지 궁금해서.
   M 가고 싶어. 어떤 영화야?

08 ② | ➕ ②

W Hey, Jeremy. What are you doing?

M I'm trying to choose a fifth class for next semester.

W It's not always easy to choose classes.

M Right. Have you chosen all the classes you want to take?

W Yes, I have. Three classes are related to my major, politics, and I'm also taking two media classes.

M Oh, I was thinking about taking a media class. Can you recommend one?

W What about Professor Jahara's class? He's really great.

M I've heard that. I should check if the class is still open.

W Great. But before you enroll, review the requirements and course descriptions.

M Sure. I'll review them carefully before enrolling.

W Good luck.

W 안녕, 제레미. 뭐라고 있어?

M 다음 학기 다섯 번째 수업을 고르고 있어.

W 수업을 고르는 건 항상 쉽지 않지.

M 맞아. 넌 들을 수업을 다 선택했어?

W 응. 수업 3개는 전공인 정치학과 관련이 있고 미디어 수업도 두 개 들을 거야.

M 아, 미디어 수업 듣는 걸 생각하고 있었어. 하나 추천해줄래?

W 자하라 교수님 수업 어때? 진짜 좋아.

M 들어본 적 있어. 수업이 아직도 열려 있는지 봐야겠다.

W 좋아. 하지만 등록하기 전에 자격 요건이랑 강좌 설명서를 검토해봐.

M 물론이야. 등록하기 전에 자세히 봐 볼 거야.

W 행운을 빌어.

09 ⑤ | ➕ ⑤

W Hi, Jason! What are your plans for this coming vacation?

M I'm going to Paris and London. I need to do some research on the designs of modern European architecture.

W That will be helpful for your major.

M That's why I'm going there. How about you? Are you planning to take a vacation?

W I'm going to Africa.

M Wow! Are you going there for travel or work?

W I'm going to volunteer in a region struck by serious

W drought. I want to help children suffering from a lack of food or medicine.

M You're going there to make a difference. It'll be a really rewarding experience for you.

W 안녕, 제이슨! 다가오는 휴가를 위한 너의 계획은 뭐니?

M 파리와 런던을 갈 거야. 근대 유럽 건축 디자인에 대한 연구를 할 필요가 있거든.

W 네 전공에 도움이 되겠다.

M 그게 내가 거기 가는 이유야. 너는 어때? 휴가 계획 중이야?

W 난 아프리카에 갈 거야.

M 와! 여행이나 일때문에 거기에 가는 거야?

W 심각한 가뭄으로 타격을 받은 지역으로 봉사활동 가는 거야. 음식이나 약이 부족해서 고통받는 아이들을 돕고 싶어.

M 차이를 만들기 위해 그곳에 가는 구나. 너에게 정말 가치 있는 경험이 될 거야.

10 ④

[Telephone rings.]

W Hello, Global Ticket Agency. How may I help you?

M Hi. I'd like to reserve tickets to the musical Chicago.

W When would you like to see the musical?

M On May 9th.

W Mother's Day? It must be a present for your mother. Hold on. You're lucky. We have some tickets left.

M Great. I'd like to reserve two adults tickets. How much are they?

W They are normally $50 each, but all shows are 20% off on that day.

M That's great. I'd like to pay by credit card.

W All right. Wait a second.

[전화벨이 울린다.]

W 안녕하세요, Global Ticket Agency입니다. 어떻게 도와드릴까요?

M 안녕하세요. 뮤지컬 '시카고'의 표를 예매하고 싶은데요.

W 언제 그 뮤지컬을 보고 싶으세요?

M 5월 9일이에요.

W 어머니날이군요? 어머니께 드릴 선물이겠군요. 잠시만 기다리세요. 운이 좋으시네요. 몇 장의 표가 남아 있습니다.

M 잘 됐군요. 성인 표 두 장을 예매하고 싶은데요. 얼마죠?

W 평상시대로라면 입장료가 한 장에 50달러이지만, 그 날은 모든 쇼를 20% 할인해 드립니다.

M 그것 좋군요. 신용카드로 지불하고 싶습니다.

W 알겠습니다. 잠시만 기다리세요.

만점 솔루션 어머니날에는 뮤지컬 표가 평상시 가격인 50달러에서 20% 할인되어 예매되고 있다. 따라서 표의 가격은 40달러이며 남자는 두 장을 예매하고자 하므로 남자가 지불할 총 금액은 80달러가 된다.

11 ③

M What do you think of my choice?

W Well, it's fine except for one thing.

M Except for one thing? I wonder what it is.

W It's just that I'm a vegetarian.

M Oh, no. What an idiot I am! I'm sorry! I should have known better than to take someone to Fred's Steak & Ribs on a first date without asking.

W That's okay. I can drink coffee or something, instead.

M No way. I can't make someone like you watch me eat meat. Let's get out of here.

M 저의 선택에 대해 어떻게 생각하십니까?

W 글쎄요, 한 가지를 제외하고는 좋아요.

M 한 가지를 제외하고요? 그게 뭐일지 궁금하네요.

W 그저 제가 채식주의자라는 점이에요.

M 오, 이런. 제가 바보 같은 짓을 했군요! 첫 번째 데이트에서 상대방에게 물어보지도 않고 Fred's Steak & Ribs에 데리고 오는 것보다는 더 현명했어야만 했는데.

W 괜찮아요. 대신, 제가 커피를 마시거나 그럴 수 있거든요.

M 절대 안 됩니다. 당신과 같은 분께 제가 고기를 먹는 것을 보고 있게 할 수는 없어요. 나갑시다.

만점 솔루션 남자가 첫 데이트에서 여자를 근사한 스테이크 식당으로 안내했으나, 여자가 채식주의자라는 사실을 알고 식당을 나가려고 하는 상황이다.

12 ⑤

W Hello, everyone. Welcome to Yatapa Resort & Spa. Our resort offers the best program for kids in the nation. The 500-acre resort is located on part of a Native American Pueblo and offers kids ages 3 to 12 the chance to experience the art and history of this culture. Also, our childcare center is open daily for infants from six months to children three years old. With activities indoors and out, your children will be entertained with singing, arts and crafts, a ball pit, and story time. In addition to the kids' program, we offer other family activities like trail riding, Pueblo pottery making, and Native American stories under the stars.

W 안녕하세요, 여러분. 야타파 리조트 앤 스파에 오신 것을 환영합니다. 저희 리조트는 전국의 아이들을 위한 최고의 프로그램을 제공합니다. 500에이커의 리조트는 아메리카 원주민 푸에블로의 일부에 위치해 있으며 3세에서 12세의 아이들에게 이 문화의 예술과 역사를 경험할 수 있는 기회를 제공합니다. 또한, 6개월부터 3살 사이의 아기들을 위한 보육원도 매일 문을 엽니다. 실내와 실외 활동을 하면서, 아이들은 노래, 미술, 공예, 볼풀 그리고 이야기 시간으로 즐거워할 것입니다. 어린이 프로그램뿐만 아니라, 저희는 시골길 승마, 푸에블로 도자기 만들기, 그리고 별 아래에서 아메리카 원주민 이야기 같은 다른 가족 활동들을 제공합니다.

13 ③

W We have quotes from two companies: Best Kitchen and Right Construction.

M Let's see the details of what they said about our new kitchen. When can they start work?

W Best Kitchen said they are so busy that they cannot start work for a week. And Right Construction said that they can begin work tomorrow.

M I see. What's the price?

W Best Kitchen said it'll cost $3,500 and Right Construction said it'll cost $3,000.

M Then how long will it take?

W Best Kitchen said it'll take a week and Right Construction said they can finish it in four days.

M Well, it's not hard to make a choice between them.

W Best Kitchen과 Right Construction 두 개 회사로부터 두 개의 견적서를 받았어요.

M 우리의 새로운 부엌에 관해 그들이 말하고 있는 내용을 자세히 살펴봅시다. 그들이 언제 일을 시작할 수 있죠?

W Best Kitchen은 너무 바빠서 일주일 동안은 일을 시작할 수 없다고 하네요. 그리고 Right Construction은 내일 일을 시작할 수 있다고 했어요.

M 그렇군요. 가격은 어때요?

W Best Kitchen은 3,500달러가 들 것이라고 말하고, Right Construction은 3,000달러가 들거라고 말하네요.

M 그렇다면 기간은 얼마나 걸리죠?

W Best Kitchen은 일주일 걸릴 것이라고 말하고, Right Construction은 4일 만에 끝낼 수 있다고 하네요.

M 그렇다면, 두 회사 중에서 고르기가 어렵지 않네요.

만점 솔루션 Best Kitchen은 공사를 일주일 후에나 시작할 수 있으며 공사 비용 3,500달러에 공사 기간이 일주일이 걸린다고 한 반면, Right Construction은 내일 공사를 시작할 수 있고 공사 비용은 3,000달러이며 공사 기간은 4일이 걸린다고 했다.

14 ②

W This is one of the main tools you use when you sew pieces of cloth together. This is a long slender tool with a pointed tip at one end. This also has a hole, called the eye, at the other non-pointed end to carry thread through the fabric after the pointed end pierces it. In the old days, mothers used this and thread to apply patches on worn-out clothes. These days, however, they rarely use this because of sewing machines.

W 이것은 천 조각을 모아 바느질할 때 사용하는 주요 도구 중의 하나이다. 이것은 한쪽 끝에 뾰족한 끝이 있는 길고 가는 도구이다. 이것의 뾰족하지 않은 다른 한쪽 끝에는 눈이라고 불리는 구멍이 있어서 뾰족한 끝이 직물을 뚫고 간 후에 실이 직물을 통과하도록 운반해 준다. 옛날에, 어머님들은 이것과 실을 이용해 헤어진 옷에 천 조각을 대기도 했다. 그러나 요즈음, 그들은 재봉틀 때문에 이것을 좀처럼 사용하지 않는다.

15 ④

W I've heard Wellington is beautiful.

M Do you think we should go by bus?

W We don't have to. I guess we could take a train.

M We could, but it might be a good idea to rent a car.

W We could do that. The point is how much it will cost.

M I wonder how much it will cost to go by train.

W I'm not sure, but I could find out.

M Why don't you do that? I'll find out about the car rental.

W Sounds good. I'll do that right away.

W Wellington이 아름답다고 들었어.

M 버스를 타고 가야 할까?

W 그럴 필요는 없어. 기차를 타고 갈 수 있을 거야.

M 그럴 수도 있겠지만, 차를 빌리는 것도 좋은 생각일 거야.

W 그렇게 할 수도 있지. 문제는 비용이 얼마나 드는가야.

M 기차로 가는 것은 얼마나 들지 궁금하네.

W 잘은 모르지만, 알아볼 수는 있어.

M 네가 알아보지 그래? 나는 차 임대료에 관해 알아볼게.

W 그거 좋겠네. 당장 알아볼게.

만점 솔루션 Wellington으로의 여행을 계획하고 있는 두 사람이 여행 방법에 관해 대화를 나누고 있다. 남자가 기차를 이용하는 비용이 얼마일지 궁금해 하자 여자가 알아볼 수 있다고 답하며 당장 알아보겠다(I'll do that right away.)고 말하고 있다.

16 ②

[Cellphone rings.]

W Hello, Junho. What's up?

M Hi, Soyoung. I want to tell you something. I have to change schools.

W Really? Why?

M Because of my father's job, we are going to move.

W But you're not moving right away, are you? I will see you in school, won't I?

M I'm afraid not. We're moving two days before the summer vacation is over.

W Our vacation is over on August 25th, isn't it?

M Yes.

W Then we have a week to give you a good-bye party. That's a relief.

[휴대 전화가 울린다.]

W 안녕, 준호야. 무슨 일이야?

M 안녕, 소영아. 내가 너에게 하고 싶은 말이 있어. 나 학교를 옮겨.

W 정말? 왜?

M 아빠 직장 때문에, 우리는 이사를 갈 거야.

W 하지만 지금 당장 이사를 가는 것은 아니지, 그렇지? 학교에서 보게 되는 거지, 아니야?

M 안 될 것 같아. 여름 방학이 끝나기 2일 전에 이사를 갈 거야.

W 우리 방학이 8월 25일에 끝나지, 그렇지?

M 응.

W 그럼 너에게 이별 파티를 해 주기에 일주일이 있구나. 그나마 다행이다.

만점 솔루션 남자가 이사 가는 날은 방학이 끝나기 2일 전이고, 방학은 8월 25

일에 끝나므로 남자가 이사 가는 날은 8월 23일이다. 그 때까지 일주일의 시간이 남아 있다고 했으므로 오늘은 8월 16일이다.

17 ③

W Scott, how do you like working for your new company?

M My new company? It's great! I have a nice boss and I like the people I work with.

W A nice boss and great colleagues really help. Do you get any benefits?

M Yeah. We can get great deals on trips abroad.

W Oh, cheap trips! You're so lucky.

M Yeah, I guess I'm lucky. How about you? How's your new job?

W My job isn't as good as yours.

M Really? Why not?

W _____

W Scott, 새로운 회사에서 일하는 것이 어때?

M 새로운 회사가 어떠냐고? 아주 좋아! 상사가 멋지고 함께 일하는 사람들도 마음에 들어.

W 멋진 상사와 대단한 동료들은 정말 도움이 돼. 어떤 혜택이 있니?

M 응. 좋은 가격으로 해외 여행을 갈 수 있어.

W 오, 싼 여행이라! 너는 운이 아주 좋구나.

M 그래, 운이 좋은 것 같아. 너는 어때? 새로 시작한 일은 어떤데?

W 내 직장은 네 것만큼 좋지는 않아.

M 정말? 왜 안 좋아?

W 봉급은 낮고 근무 시간은 길어.

① 기분전환을 할 준비가 된 것 같아.
② 너의 제안에 감사하지만, 난 그것을 좋아해.
④ 내 사무실이 있는데 넓어.
⑤ 너처럼 난 싸게 해외 여행을 할 수 있어.

만점 솔루션 여자의 직장에 관해 묻는 남자의 말에 여자가 별로 좋지 않다고 대답하자 남자는 왜 좋지 않은지를 묻고 있으므로 부정적인 내용의 대답이 오는 것이 적절하다.

18 ①

W Ben, I'm quitting. I already talked with the boss.

M Really? I can't believe you're leaving. You're one of the best employees in this company.

W Thank you for saying so. It was good to work with you.

M Are you leaving because of your kids?

W No, my kids are all grown up now. I just want to run my own business.

M Oh, I see. I know you really wanted to have your own shop. I think it's a good time to start it. Good luck to you!

W _____

W Ben, 저 그만둬요. 이미 사장님과 얘기했어요.

M 정말요? 당신이 떠난다니 믿을 수 없어요. 이 회사에서 가장 훌륭한 직원 중 한 사람인데요.

W 그렇게 말씀하시니 감사해요. 당신과 함께 일해서 좋았어요.

M 아이들 때문에 그만 두시나요?

W 아뇨, 아이들은 이제 다 컸어요. 그냥 제 사업을 운영하고 싶은 거죠.

M 아, 그렇군요. 당신이 자신만의 가게를 정말로 갖고 싶어 했다는 거 알죠. 시작하기에 좋은 때인 것 같아요. 행운을 빌어요!

W 고마워요. 당신과 함께 일해서 행복했어요.

② 걱정 마세요. 제가 당신의 가게 여는 것을 도와드릴게요.
③ 저는 이 회사에서 일자리를 얻고 싶지 않아요. 어떻게 생각해요?
④ 당신에게도 행운을 빌어요. 당신의 가게 운영에 성공할 거예요.
⑤ 천만에요. 이 회사에서 일할 시간이 더 필요해요.

19 ②

W Excuse me, but is this bus for N Seoul tower?

M Yes, you got on the right bus. Don't worry.

W Thank you. It's hard for a tourist like me to use public transportation in a new place.

M It sure is. Which places have you been so far?

W Well, I've been to various places like Rodeo street, Kyungbok palace, and Insa-dong.

M Did you take the Seoul City Tour Bus?

W What's that? Is it a free bus?

M No, it's not. If you buy a one-day pass, you can easily visit several famous places in Seoul.

W _____

W 실례합니다만, 이 버스가 N 서울 타워로 가나요?

M 네, 버스를 제대로 타셨어요. 걱정하지 마세요.

W 감사합니다. 저 같은 여행자가 새로운 장소에서 대중교통을 이용하기란 어렵군요.

M 정말 그렇죠. 지금까지 어떤 곳들을 가 보셨나요?

W 글쎄요, 다양한 곳에 갔었죠. 이를 테면 로데오 거리, 경복궁, 그리고 인사동이요.

M Seoul City Tour Bus를 타셨나요?

W 그게 뭐죠? 무료 버스인가요?

M 아뇨. 1일 패스를 사면 서울의 여러 유명한 장소를 쉽게 방문할 수 있어요.

W 흥미로운 것 같아요. 그러면, 어디에서 그 버스를 탈 수 있죠?

① 훌륭한 생각이에요! 그 버스는 사려면 비싼가요?
③ 저에겐 낯설게 들려요. 저는 관광객을 전혀 안 좋아 해요.
④ 버스 요금을 얼마 내야 하는지 알려드릴게요.
⑤ 편리하게 보이지만 저는 그 버스를 운전하고 싶지 않아요.

20 ④

M When Tina came back to her classroom from the science lab, she noticed her new PMP was gone. She told her homeroom teacher that someone had stolen her PMP. The teacher got angry and searched for it. But it was not found anywhere. Feeling depressed, Tina went home. When she got in her home, she saw her PMP on her desk. She thought she had taken it to school, but in fact she hadn't.

The next day, Tina found her teacher still angry. In this situation, what would Tina most likely say to the teacher?

M 과학실로부터 그녀의 교실에 돌아왔을 때, Tina는 그녀의 새 PMP가 없어진 것을 알았다. 그녀는 담임선생님께 누군가 자신의 PMP를 훔쳐 갔다고 말씀드렸다. 선생님은 화가 나서 그것을 찾았다. 하지만 그건 어디에도 없었다. 우울해져서 Tina는 집에 갔다. 자기 방에 들어섰을 때 그녀는 자기의 책상 위에 있는 PMP를 보았다. 그녀는 그것을 학교에 갖고 갔다고 생각했는데 사실은 그러지 않은 것이었다. 다음 날, Tina는 선생님이 여전히 화가 나 있는 것을 알았다. 이 상황에서, Tina가 선생님께 뭐라고 말할 것 같은가?

① 저는 새 PMP를 사고 싶어요.
② 제가 말을 안 들어서 죄송해요.
③ 이번에는 제 말을 좀 들어 주세요.
④ 제가 큰 실수를 저지른 것 같아요.
⑤ 누군가의 책상 위에서 제 PMP를 찾았어요.

---

01 ③	02 ③	03 ③	04 ②	05 ④
06 ①	07 ③	08 ④	09 ④	10 ③
11 ③	12 ⑤	13 ②	14 ④	15 ③
16 ④	17 ①, ➊⑤	18 ③	19 ⑤, ➊③	20 ④

01 ③

M Can I help you?
W Yes, please. Is it OK to take pictures in the gallery?
M I'm afraid not. You're not allowed to take any photos in the gallery. We want to preserve our old paintings.
W I see. One more thing, I really don't want to carry my umbrella around in the gallery, and it's wet. Is there a locker I can keep it in?
M We do offer lockers next to the restrooms in the main lobby.
W Oh, great. Thanks.

M 도와드릴까요?
W 네, 부탁합니다. 미술관에서 사진을 찍어도 되나요?
M 안됩니다. 미술관에서는 어떤 사진도 찍을 수 없습니다. 오래된 그림들을 보존해야 하거든요.
W 알겠습니다. 한가지 더요, 미술관 안에서 우산을 들고 다니고 싶지 않거든요, 우산이 젖었어요. 우산을 넣어둘 만한 보관함이 있나요?
M 메인 로비에 있는 화장실 옆에 보관함이 있습니다.
W 아, 잘됐네요. 감사합니다.

02 ③

[Cellphone rings.]
W Hi, Jack. Did you finish your science report?
M Almost. I just need to check my writing to see if there are any mistakes. How about you?
W I went on a family trip last weekend. I have to start from the very beginning with the research.
M Well, you need to make a good plan to manage your time well. The deadline is less than a week away.
W Yeah, thanks for reminding me. Could you help me do some research on the topic? It would be a great help.
M Sure. When do you want me to help you?
W What about tomorrow after school?
M I'm afraid I can't. I have something important to do.
W I see. Then, I'll do some research myself tomorrow. Are you free on Friday? If you are, maybe you could give me some feedback on my research?
M Friday will be fine. I'll see you after school.

[휴대 전화가 울린다.]

W 안녕, 잭. 과학 보고서 쓰는 거 끝냈니?

M 거의. 실수 한 게 없는지 확인하기만 하면 돼. 너는 어때?

W 저번 주말에 가족 여행을 갔거든. 연구에 대한 조사를 맨 처음부터 시작해야해.

M 시간 분배를 잘 하도록 계획을 짜야 할 거야. 마감일이 일주일도 안 남았어.

W 응, 알려줘서 고마워. 주제에 대해 조사하는 걸 도와줄 수 있어? 큰 도움이 될 거야.

M 물론이야. 언제 도와줄까?

W 내일 방과 후 어때?

M 안될 거 같아. 해야 하는 중요한 일이 있거든.

W 알겠어. 그럼 내일 혼자서 조사해야겠다. 금요일은 괜찮아? 그렇다면 내 연구에 대해 피드백을 줄 수 있을까?

M 금요일은 괜찮아. 방과 후에 보자.

03 ③

① W This hamburger is so delicious.
  M By the way, lunch is on me.
② W I'm so tired.
  M How about going to bed early tonight?
③ W The movie will start soon.
  M Let me buy some popcorn first.
④ W Are you still watching TV?
  M I was about to turn it off.
⑤ W How was your trip to Chicago?
  M It was great.

① W 이 햄버거 진짜 맛있다.
  M 그건 그렇고, 점심은 내가 살게.
② W 너무 지쳤어.
  M 오늘밤은 일찍 자는 게 어때?
③ W 영화가 곧 시작할 거야.
  M 우선 팝콘을 사자.
④ W 아직도 TV보고 있어?
  M 지금 막 끄려고 했어.
⑤ W 시카고 여행은 어땠어?
  M 좋았어.

04 ②

W Hi, Robert! What did you do on the weekend?

M I went to Mount Inwang with my family. We left home very early so that we could see the sunrise from the peak. It was just amazing.

W Wow, that's wonderful. I've heard that seeing the sunrise from a mountain is absolutely beautiful. I really want to try that one day.

M I can't believe you've never seen the sunrise from a mountain before! Why don't we go hiking together and see it sometime?

W Yes, I'd love to... But first I have to get used to hiking. Shall we go to a nearby mountain next Sunday?

M Well, I am free next Sunday, but hiking on a Sunday isn't fun because it's pretty crowded. Sometimes you have to hike in a line. What about early Friday morning?

W Hmm... I have plans on Friday morning. I'm only available on the weekend.

M Then, let's meet on Saturday. It's less crowded on Saturday than on Sunday.

W Okay, that's fine with me. I'm looking forward to hiking with you.

W 안녕, 로버트! 주말에 뭐 했어?

M 가족들이랑 인왕산에 갔어. 꼭대기에서 일출을 보려고 아주 일찍 집에서 나왔어. 진짜 멋있었어.

W 와, 멋지다. 산에서 일출을 보는 건 정말 아름답다고 들었어. 나도 언젠가 일출을 보고 싶어.

M 네가 한 번도 산에서 일출을 본 적 없다니 믿을 수 없어! 나중에 같이 하이킹하고 일출을 보는 거 어때?

W 좋아. 그런데 우선 하이킹에 익숙해져야겠지. 다음주 일요일에 근처에 있는 산에 가지 않을래?

M 음. 다음 주 일요일 괜찮긴 한데 꽤 붐비기 때문에 일요일에 하이킹하는 건 재미있지 않아. 가끔은 줄을 서서 하이킹해야 할 수도 있어. 금요일 아침 일찍은 어때?

W 흠... 금요일 아침에는 선약이 있어서 주말에만 시간이 되는데.

M 그럼, 토요일에 만나자. 토요일이 일요일보다는 덜 붐벼.

W 그래. 그건 괜찮아. 너와 하이킹 가는 거 기대된다.

05 ④

W Hi, Jack! What are you going to do this summer?

M I love playing sports and being active, so I'll play a lot of sports.

W What sports do you play?

M I swim and I run, but my favorite sport is skiing.

W I ski, too. But I only ski on ski slopes that aren't too steep. I'm afraid of getting injured.

M Then, do you prefer summer sports to winter sports?

W Well, yes. I like anything I can play on the beach with my friends.

M Which sport do you like best?

W I love surfing... It makes me feel so free. I also like to play beach volleyball.

M My favorite beach sport is footvolley. It's really fun to play using only your feet.

W I play it, too.

M Then, we should play together sometime.

W Okay!

W 안녕, 잭! 이번 여름 뭐 할 거니?

M 스포츠와 활동적인 걸 좋아해서 많은 스포츠를 할 거야.

W 무슨 스포츠를 하는데?

M 수영이랑 달리기. 하지만 가장 좋아하는 스포츠는 스키야.

W 나도 스키 타. 하지만 너무 가파르지 않은 스키장에서만 스키를 타. 다치는 게 무서워.

M 그럼 겨울 스포츠보다 여름 스포츠를 더 좋아해?

W 응. 친구들과 바닷가에서 할 수 있는 스포츠는 다 좋아.

M 제일 좋아하는 스포츠가 뭐야?

W 서핑을 좋아해... 내가 자유롭다고 느끼게 해주거든. 비치 발리볼도 좋아해.

M 내가 제일 좋아하는 해변 스포츠는 풋발리야. 발만 이용해서 하는 게 정말 재미있어.

W 나도 풋발리 해.

M 그럼. 나중에 같이 하자.

W 좋아!

06 ①

M Mom? I'm home!

W Did you have a good day?

M Yes, I've finally finished my science project. I'm free now!

W Don't you have homework to do?

M No. I finished everything at recess.

W Okay, but you aren't going to spend the whole evening just lying on this couch in the living room.

M Mom, the first match of the national soccer league is this evening. I really have to watch it on the big TV.

W OK, but before it starts, please help me out with some housework.

M What do you want me to do?

W Go to your room and organize your desk and bookshelf. Your room has been such a mess for weeks.

M It'll take such a long time, Mom. Can't I eat dinner first?

W Well, then come and help me in the kitchen.

M Okay, I will.

M 엄마? 저 집에 왔어요!

W 좋은 하루 보냈니?

M 네, 드디어 과학 프로젝트를 끝냈어요. 이제 자유예요!

W 해야 할 숙제가 있지 않니?

M 아니요. 휴식 시간에 모든 걸 끝냈어요.

W 그래. 하지만 저녁 시간 전부를 거실 소파에 누워서 보내지는 않겠지.

M 엄마, 국내 축구리그 첫 번째 경기가 오늘 저녁에 해요. 큰 TV로 봐야만 해요.

W 알겠다, 하지만 그 전에, 집안일을 도와주렴.

M 제가 뭘 하길 원하세요?

W 네 방에 가서 책상과 책장을 정리하렴. 네 방이 몇 주 동안 아주 엉망이다.

M 그건 너무 오랜 시간이 걸려요, 엄마. 저녁부터 먹으면 안될까요?

W 그럼 먹고 부엌에 와서 나를 도와주렴.

M 알겠어요.

만점 솔루션 'Go to your room'이나 'help me in the kitchen'에서 대화가 남자의 방이나 식당에서 일어나는 것이 아님을 알 수 있다. 'you aren't going to spend the whole evening ~ in the living room.'이라고 말하는 여자의 말에서 대화가 거실에서 일어나고 있음을 짐작할 수 있다.

07 ③

① M When did the movie start?

　W It just started about 5 minutes ago.

② M This food smells bad.

　W Don't eat it. I'll make something else for you to eat.

③ M How long have you been here in Korea?

　W I have kept my hair long.

④ M Can you do me a favor?

　W Of course. What can I do for you?

⑤ M Do you mind if I open the window?

　W Not at all. Please go ahead.

① M 영화 언제 시작했어?

　W 5분 전에 막 시작했어.

② M 이 음식 냄새가 이상해.

　W 먹지 마. 네가 먹을 음식 다른 거 만들어 줄게.

③ M 한국에는 얼마나 있었나요?

　W 머리를 길게 기르고 있어.

④ M 부탁 좀 해도 될까?

　W 물론이야. 뭘 해줄까?

⑤ M 창문을 열어도 될까요?

　W 네. 여세요.

08 ④

W How's it going with practicing for the musical?

M Pretty well. All of the members are practicing really hard.

W Has everyone memorized all of the songs?

M I know mine, but a few members are still struggling.

W Can I help with that?

M Thanks, but I think we can manage. We still have a couple of weeks to practice.

W Well, is there anything that I can do to help?

M Yes. I can't find anyone to help with my makeup.

W I have a friend who is great at doing makeup. She used to work as a professional makeup artist. I can ask her about it.

M Really? That would be helpful.

W Sure. I'll let you know what she says later.

W 뮤지컬 연습하는 건 어떻게 되어가?

M 잘 되고 있어. 모든 사람들이 정말 열심히 연습하고 있어.

W 다들 모든 노래를 외운 거야?

M 난 내 노래는 아는데 몇몇 사람들은 아직 고생 중이야.

W 도와줄까?

M 고맙지만 우리가 할 수 있을 거 같아. 아직 2주 동안 연습할 기간이 있거든.

W 내가 뭐 도와줄 만한 거 없을까?

M 있어. 내 메이크업을 도와줄 사람을 찾지 못했어.

W 메이크업을 잘 하는 친구가 하나 있어. 전문 메이크업 아티스트로 일했던 친구야. 그녀에게 물어볼게.

M 진짜? 도움이 될 거야

W 물론. 친구가 나중에 뭐라고 말했는지 알려줄게.

09 ④

W Going to Universal Studios was at the top of my wish list. So when we went there on our family trip, I was so excited. Universal Studios is located on Santosa Island in Singapore, so we took a flight there. When we entered, huge statues of the minion characters seemed to welcome us. My favorite part of Universal Studios was the rides. When I went on the 3-D Transformers ride, I felt like I actually met all the characters in the movie. The roller coasters there were beyond my imagination. They were fast and thrilling. In fact, I was scared before going on the rides, but I had a lot of fun. Before we left, we watched the fireworks, and it made the trip even more unforgettable. I definitely want to go there again in the future.

W 유니버설 스튜디오에 가는 것은 나의 가장 큰 꿈이었다. 그래서 가족여행에서 그 곳에 가게 되었을 때 나는 굉장히 흥분했다. 유니버설 스튜디오는 싱가포르에 있는 산토사 섬에 위치해 있기 때문에 우리는 그곳까지 비행기를 타고 갔다. 우리가 들어갔을 때, 엄청나게 큰 미니언 캐릭터 동상들이 우리를 환영해주는 거처럼 보였다. 유니버설 스튜디오에서 내가 가장 좋아했던 부분은 놀이기구였다. 3D 트랜스포머 놀이기구를 탔을 때, 나는 내가 영화 속 모든 캐릭터들을 직접 만난 것처럼 느꼈다. 그곳의 롤러코스터는 내 상상 이상이었다. 빠르고 스릴 넘쳤다. 사실, 놀이기구를 타기 전에는 무서웠지만 아주 재미있었다. 우리가 떠나기 전에 불꽃놀이를 봤는데 그것은 여행을 더욱 더 잊을 수 없도록 만들었다. 나중에 그곳에 다시 한번 꼭 가고 싶다.

10 ③

M Good morning. Can I help you?

W I'm looking for a T-shirt for my son. Hmm, how much are those T-shirts?

W Which ones?

M The white ones with the blue stripes.

W They're $30 each.

M What sizes do you have?

W Small, medium, large, and extra large. What size are you looking for?

M Hmm.. I bought some medium-sized T-shirts last season, but he's been growing a lot. I'm not sure if a medium would still fit him.

W The shirt is 100% cotton and a bit tight, so I recommend buying a large size. Besides, you can exchange it for a different size within two weeks.

M Okay. I'll take the large one. And how much are the sports socks over there?

W They're $15 per pair.

M Okay. I'll take one pair with my T-shirt. Here's a fifty-dollar bill.

W Thanks. Here are your receipt and your change.

M 안녕하세요. 도와드릴까요?

W 아들을 위한 티셔츠를 찾고 있어요. 흠, 이 티셔츠들은 얼마인가요?

W 어느 거요?

M 하얀 바탕에 파란 줄무늬가 있는 거요.

W 30달러입니다.

M 사이즈는 어떻게 있나요?

W S, M, L 그리고 XL가 있습니다. 어떤 사이즈를 찾으세요?

M 흠... 지난 계절에 M사이즈 티셔츠를 샀는데 많이 자랐어요. M사이즈가 맞을지 잘 모르겠네요.

W 셔츠가 100% 면이라 조금 딱 맞기 때문에 L사이즈를 추천합니다. 게다가, 2주 안에 다른 사이즈로 교환할 수도 있어요.

M 알겠습니다. L로 하지요. 저기 있는 스포츠 양말은 얼마인가요?

W 15달러입니다.

M 좋아요. 티셔츠랑 양말 한 켤레주세요. 여기 50달러입니다.

W 고맙습니다. 여기 영수증과 잔돈입니다.

> **만점 솔루션** 여자는 30달러짜리 티셔츠 하나와 15달러짜리 스포츠 양말을 한 켤레사고 50달러를 냈다. 50−(30+15)=5이므로 여자가 받을 거스름돈은 5달러이다.

11 ③

M Hey, Mary. What's wrong? You look upset.

W I've been so bothered by all the unwanted calls I get every day. I don't know how to block these kinds of calls.

M First, it depends on the kind of phone you have. Do you want to block them on your mobile phone or on a landline phone?

W Well, I get a lot of calls on my mobile phone.

M In that case, download a call-blocking app. You can create a blacklist of numbers to block from calling your mobile phone.

W That's a good idea. Are those apps free?

M Many call-blocking apps are free or only cost a few dollars. Actually, your mobile phone may come with pre-installed functions that can block calls from specific numbers.

W Really? I didn't know that.

M Well, let me have a look at your phone. *[pause]* Right. See, your phone has a feature that lets you identify unwanted incoming calls.

W That's great. Before I look for an app, I will find out what built-in features my phone has to block those calls.

M Good idea.

M 메리, 무슨 일이야? 화나 보여.

W 매일 원하지도 않는 전화 때문에 엄청 귀찮아. 이런 종류의 전화들을 어떻게 막는지 모르겠어.

M 우선, 네가 어떤 종류의 전화를 가지고 있느냐에 달려있어. 휴대 전화에서 차단하길 원해, 유선 전화에서 차단하길 원해?

W 휴대 전화로 많은 전화가 와.

M 그런 경우에는 전화차단 앱을 다운받아. 전화번호 블랙리스트를 만들어서 차단할 수 있어.

W 좋은 생각이다. 그런 앱들은 무료야?

M 많은 전화차단 앱은 무료거나 몇 달러만 내면 돼. 사실, 네 휴대 전화에 특정 번호를 차단할 수 있는 기능이 이미 설치되어 있을 수도 있어.

W 진짜? 그건 몰랐어.

M 내가 한번 봐 볼게. *[멈춤]* 됐다. 봐, 네 전화에 원하지 않는 전화를 식별할 수 있는 기능이 있어.

W 잘됐다. 앱을 찾기 전에, 이런 전화들을 차단하는 내제된 기능이 내 전화에 있는지 알아봐야지.

M 좋은 생각이야.

만점 솔루션 전화차단 무료 어플이나 유료 어플이 대화 중 언급되긴 하였으나, 남자가 여자의 휴대 전화에 번호 차단 기능이 있다는 것을 알려주었고 여자가 'I will find out what built–in features my phone has ~.'라고 말했으니 여자가 할 일은 '자신의 휴대 전화 기능 알아보기'이다.

12 ⑤

W There are many events that <u>draw tourists to</u> Vancouver. Among them, the Celebration of Light is one of the city's signature summer events. At this festival, the city lights up the sky over English Bay for three nights at the end of July. Every year, three countries <u>compete against each other</u> to amaze citizens and visitors to Vancouver. This year, an exciting music event called Heart Beat will take place at Sunset Beach. Bands will start playing festival music in the early afternoon, so <u>bring a picnic</u> and get ready to make a night of it! If you want to enjoy it even more, book a place in one of the official VIP viewing areas.

W 관광객들을 벤쿠버로 끌어들이는 많은 축제들이 있습니다. 그 중에서, 빛의 축제는 도시의 특징적인 여름 축제들 중 하나입니다. 이 축제에서는 7월 말 삼일동안 도시는 잉글리시 베이 위 하늘로 조명을 밝힙니다. 매년, 3개 국이 벤쿠버의 시민들과 관광객들을 놀라게 하는 것으로 경쟁합니다. 금년, 하트 비트라고 불리우는 흥미로운 음악 축제가 선셋 바닷가에서 열립니다. 이른 오후부터 밴드들이 축제 음악을 연주하기 시작할 테니 도시락을 가져오고 밤을 즐길 준비를 하세요! 더 즐기고 싶다면 공식 VIP관전 구역 중 하나를 예약하세요.

13 ②

W Welcome to the city. You're lucky to visit here during such a beautiful season.

M Thank you! It is a beautiful and peaceful city.

W That's right. We're <u>so proud to live in</u> such a wonderful city in Korea. Is there any place you want to visit first?

M Yes, there is. I've heard the local museum is very nice. Can you let me know how to get there?

W Sure. Are you driving or <u>using public transportation</u>?

M We're driving. We rented a car.

W That's great. So, first, follow Beach Hill Drive. Then, turn right onto Ledgewood Drive.

M Okay, so follow the road and turn right.

W Right. When you reach a T-junction at Ray Drive, turn left.

Then you'll <u>find a place to park</u> nearby. From the parking area, walk a short distance uphill to the entrance of the museum.

M Thank you.

W 도시에 오신 걸 환영합니다. 이렇게 아름다운 계절에 이곳을 방문하다니 행운이십니다.

M 고마워요! 아름답고 평온한 도시네요.

W 맞습니다. 한국에 이렇게 멋진 도시에 산다는 것을 자랑스럽게 여기고 있습니다. 우선 방문하고 싶은 곳이 있나요?

M 네, 있습니다. 지역 박물관이 아주 좋다고 들었습니다. 어떻게 가는지 알려주실 수 있나요?

W 물론이죠. 운전하시나요 아니면 대중교통을 이용하시나요?

M 운전할 겁니다. 차를 빌렸어요.

W 잘됐네요. 그럼, 우선, 비치 힐 드라이브를 따라가세요. 그리고, 레지우드 드라이브에서 오른쪽으로 도세요.

M 알겠습니다. 길을 따라가다가 오른쪽으로 돌라는 거죠.

W 네. 레이 드라이브에서 T자형 삼거리가 나오면 왼쪽으로 도세요. 그러면 근처에 주차할 곳을 찾을 수 있어요. 주차장에서 박물관 입구까지 짧은 비탈길을 걸으세요.

M 고마워요.

14 ③

W Korea Town is the greatest single concentration of Korean people outside of Asia. They all <u>live within several blocks</u>; the area is also the most densely populated in the city. As you walk around, you'll notice the wonderful sights, sounds, aromas, and tastes of the lively community. The Main Avenue hosts the Harvest Festival Street Fair and the New Year Festival & Parade every year. The neighborhood is also <u>known for its delicious Korean food</u> and other Asian dishes, including well-marinated beef and pork, fresh seafood, and a large variety of delicious noodles.

W 한인 타운은 아시아밖 한국 사람들의 최대 단일 집단입니다. 그들은 모두 몇 블록 안에 살고 있습니다. 그 지역은 또한 도시에서 가장 인구 밀도가 높습니다. 당신이 걸어 다닐 때, 생기 넘치는 공동체의 아름다운 장면, 소리, 아로마 그리고 맛을 알아차릴 수 있을 겁니다. 주 도로는 매년 추수 감사제 거리 축제와 새해 축제와 퍼레이드를 주최합니다. 이웃들은 또한 맛있는 한국 음식과 잘 양념된 소고기와 돼지고기, 신선한 해산물, 그리고 다양한 종류의 맛있는 국수들을 포함하는 다른 아시아 음식들로 명성이 높습니다.

15 ③

W May I help you?

M I'm looking for a bike—a special model for bike tricks.

W What kind of tricks are you thinking of?

M I want to be able to perform aerial stunts. I don't know which one would be the best.

W Well, that all depends. But you'd better choose a bike with <u>a strong and reliable frame</u> to keep you safe.

M That's right. I really need to <u>feel confident about my safety</u> when I'm on my bike.

W I'd like to recommend this one. It's a bit expensive, but the steel frame is strong but light; it's popular with riders who perform stunts.

M Can I try it?

W Sure. But <u>make sure not to damage it</u>.

W 도와드릴까요?

M 자전거 묘기를 위한 특별한 자전거 모델을 찾고 있어요.

W 어떤 묘기를 생각하고 계세요?

M 공중 묘기를 공연할 수 있었으면 해요. 무엇이 제일 좋은 건지 모르겠네요.

W 그건 상황에 따라 달라요. 하지만 당신을 안전하게 지켜줄 강하고 믿을 수 있는 뼈대를 가진 자전거를 고르는 게 좋겠죠.

M 맞아요. 제가 자전거를 탈 때, 안전에 대해 확신을 느낄 필요가 있어요.

W 이 제품을 추천하고 싶네요. 조금 비싸긴 하지만 강철 뼈대가 아주 강하지만 가벼워요. 묘기를 하는 사람들에게 인기가 있죠.

M 타봐도 되나요?

W 물론이죠. 하지만 자전거가 손상되지 않게 조심하세요.

16 ④

M Miranda, what kind of movies do you like to download and watch?

W I like action movies. I can <u>forget about all my stress</u> while watching them.

M Don't you think action movies are a bit violent? They include lots of fighting and life-threatening situations.

W Well, that's why action movies feature great heroes. How about you? What kind of movies do you like?

M I like musical movies.

W Musical movies? I like to watch stage musicals, but musical movies aren't that exciting.

M Well, there are a lot of <u>movies adapted from stage musicals</u>, but I prefer original musical movies. The singing and dancing are beautiful, so many musical movies are favorites of children and adults alike.

W Okay, then let's watch one of your favorite musical movies tonight. <u>What do you recommend</u>?

M What about watching a classic? The Sound of Music!

W Good idea!

M 미란다, 어떤 영화를 다운로드해서 보고싶어?

W 난 액션 영화를 좋아해. 그걸 보면서 내 스트레스를 잊을 수 있어.

M 액션 영화는 조금 폭력적이지 않아? 싸우고 생명을 위협하는 장면들이 많이 포함되어 있잖아.

W 글쎄. 그래서 액션 영화들이 굉장한 히어로들을 특징으로 하지. 넌 어때? 넌 어떤 영화를 좋아해?

M 난 뮤지컬 영화를 좋아해.

W 뮤지컬 영화? 난 무대 뮤지컬 보는 건 좋아하는데 뮤지컬 영화는 그렇게 흥미롭지 않더라.

M 무대 뮤지컬을 각색한 영화들이 많이 있지만 난 오리지널 뮤지컬 영화를 더 좋아해. 노래와 춤이 아름다워서 많은 뮤지컬 영화가 아이들과 어른들이 가장 좋아하는 영화이기도 해.

W 알겠어. 그럼 오늘 밤 네가 좋아하는 뮤지컬 영화 중 하나를 보자. 무엇을 추천할래?

M 고전을 보는 건 어때? 사운드 오브 뮤직!

W 좋은 생각이야!

17 ① | ➕ ⑤

[Cellphone rings.]

M Hello?

W Daniel? This is Kate.

M Kate, are you on the way? I'm excited to see you.

W I can't come to see you today. I'm <u>sick in bed</u>.

M Oh, what's the matter?

W I've got food poisoning. I feel dizzy and nauseated. And I have pretty bad diarrhea.

M That's awful. What caused it?

W I went to a seafood restaurant yesterday. There <u>must have been something wrong</u> with the food there. I'm not sure though.

M Have you taken any medicine?

W Yes, but it doesn't seem to be working. In fact, it's getting worse.

M I think you should go and see a doctor.

W I can't go to the clinic right now because I have to <u>keep going to the restroom</u>. I really can't leave the house.

M _____

[휴대 전화가 울린다.]

M 여보세요?

W 다니엘? 나 케이트야.

M 케이트, 오고 있는 중이야? 널 볼 생각에 설렌다.

W 오늘 널 보러 못 가. 나 아파서 누워있어.

M 무슨 일이야?

W 식중독에 걸렸어. 어지럽고 메스꺼워. 그리고 설사도 하고.

M 끔찍하네. 왜 그렇게 된 거야?

W 어제 해산물 레스토랑에 갔거든. 거기 음식이 무언가 잘못됐던 게 틀림없어. 확실하지는 않아.

M 약은 먹었어?

W 응, 하지만 듣질 않네. 사실, 더 나빠지고 있어.

M 병원에 가는게 좋을 거 같아.

W 계속 화장실을 가야 해서 지금 당장은 병원에 갈 수 없어. 집 밖을 나갈 수가 없어.

M 내가 병원에 전화해서 어떻게 해야 할지 알아볼게.

② 난 뭘 먹을 때마다 토를 했어.

③ 네가 아주 아픈 걸 이제 막 알았어.

④ 여기서 널 기다릴게. 천천히 해.

⑤ 내가 병원에서 널 기다리길 원했잖아.

18 ③

W Jake, I heard that the school golf club is holding tryouts for new members. They're looking for <u>potential new members to participate</u> in the national junior golf league. Would you like to join?

M Well... I'm afraid I can't. Sorry.

W Why not? I thought you wanted to join the club and <u>learn how to golf</u>. Besides, you're good at all kinds of sports.

M Yes, I'd love to learn, but I'm afraid I don't have the time.

W That's disappointing. Can I ask the reason?

M Actually, I <u>started volunteering at</u> the community center after school.

W That's interesting. What do you do there?

M I've been helping senior citizens exercise three days a week since January. Anyways, I think I can learn how to golf when I'm older.

W _____.

W 제이크, 나 학교 골프 클럽에서 새로운 회원을 뽑기 위한 평가전을 연다고 들었어. 국내 주니어 골프 리그에 참가할 유망한 새로운 회원을 찾고 있다고 해. 가입하지 않을래?

M 음... 안될 거 같아. 미안.

W 왜? 난 네가 클럽에 가입해서 골프치는 법을 배우길 원한다고 생각했는데. 게다가, 넌 모든 스포츠를 다 잘하잖아.

M 그래, 배우고 싶지만 시간이 없을 거 같아.

W 실망스럽네. 이유를 물어봐도 될까?

M 사실, 나 방과 후에 주민회관에서 봉사활동을 시작했어.

W 흥미로운데. 거기서 뭐 해?

M 1월부터 주 3일 노인분들의 운동을 돕고 있어. 아무튼, 골프는 내가 더 나이가 들어서 배울 수 있다고 생각해.

W <u>네 친구로서, 남을 돕는 네가 자랑스러워.</u>

① 넌 약속을 지키지 않아.
② 숙제를 하느라 내가 너무 바빴어.
④ 내가 할 수 있을 때 남을 돕는 건 가치 있지.
⑤ 내가 바쁠 때도 하라고 그들이 요구했어.

19 ⑤ | ➕ ③

M Rosie, how's it going?

W I'm so excited. I'm going on vacation this spring vacation.

M Wow, that's great. Where are you going?

W Okinawa, Japan.

M Good choice! I <u>went there two years ago</u> with my whole family.

W Really? Tell me about the city. What's the best time to visit?

M I think late winter or early spring is the best, and that's when you're going. When you visit, you're going to see cherry blossoms everywhere!

W Oh, good! And what should I see there?

M Well, you should visit the aquarium. It's <u>located right by the</u> seashore, so it's like you're seeing all the creatures in the ocean, not in an aquarium.

W Awesome. What else?

M Oh, you shouldn't <u>miss looking around the pretty streets</u> in the city. There are a lot of interesting shops and great local restaurants.

W _____

M 로지, 요즘 어때?

W 아주 설레. 이번 봄 방학 때 여행을 갈 거야.

M 와, 잘됐다. 어디로 가?

W 일본 오키나와.

M 좋은 선택이다! 난 이년 전에 가족들이랑 갔었어.

W 진짜? 도시에 대해 말해줘. 방문하기 제일 좋은 때가 언제야?

M 늦겨울이나 초봄이 제일 좋다고 생각하는데 바로 네가 가는 때야. 거기 가면 벚꽃을 모든 곳에서 볼 수 있을 거야.

W 아, 잘됐다! 거기서 무엇을 봐야해?

M 수족관을 방문해야 해. 해안 바로 옆에 있어서 수족관이 아니라 바다 속에서 생명체들을 보는 느낌이야.

W 멋지다. 다른 거는?

M 도시의 예쁜 길들을 구경하는 걸 놓치지 마. 흥미로운 가게들이랑 멋진 지역 식당들이 많이 있어.

W <u>진짜 재미있겠다.</u>

① 많은 음식을 가져갈 거야.
② 여행을 취소할까 생각 중이야.
③ 비행기가 너무 비싸다는 걸 방금 알았어.
④ 오키나와에 있는 너의 가족들을 빨리 보고 싶어.

20 ④

W Kelly lives alone in an apartment. A few weeks ago, her little sister, Rosa, came to stay with her for a month before she moves in to her dormitory. Early on Monday morning, Kelly <u>got a call from</u> the apartment manager. He said he had received several complaints about noise coming from Kelly's apartment. Kelly <u>denied making any noise</u> at her place because she had been on a business trip and hadn't been at home. And then she remembered that Rosa was preparing for her audition. She <u>might have played music</u> late at night. However, Kelly knows that Rosa is very considerate, so she must have realized that playing music could cause trouble with the neighbors. In this situation, what is Kelly most likely to say to the manager?

W 켈리는 아파트에 혼자 산다. 몇 주 전, 그녀의 여동생 로사가 기숙사에 들어가기 전 한달동안 켈리와 머물기 위해 왔다. 이른 월요일 아침, 켈리는 아파트 관리인에게 전화를 한 통 받았다. 그는 켈리 아파트에서 나는 소음으로 불평사항들을 받았다고 말했다. 켈리는 출장 때문에 집에 없었기 때문에 그녀의 집에서 소음이 난 것을 부정했다. 그리고 그녀는 로사가 오디션을 연습했던 것을 기억했다. 그녀가 늦은 밤 음악을 틀었을 수도 있다. 하지만 켈리는 로사가 아주 배려 깊은 성격이라 음악을 트는 것이 이웃에 문제를 유발할 수도 있다는 것을 알았음에 틀림없다

는 것을 안다. 이런 상황에서, 켈리는 관리인에게 할 말로 가장 적절한
것은?

① 밤에 너무 많은 소음을 만들지 마세요.
② 죄송하지만 여기서 일어난 일에 저는 책임이 없어요.
③ 그녀는 곧 떠날 겁니다. 인내심을 가지세요.
④ 무슨 일이 일어났는지 잘 모르겠지만 알아보고 처리할게요.
⑤ 걱정 마세요. 남동생에게 가능하면 빨리 아파트를 떠나라고 말할 겁니다.

자신 있는 영어 실력! 디딤돌 영어 시리즈

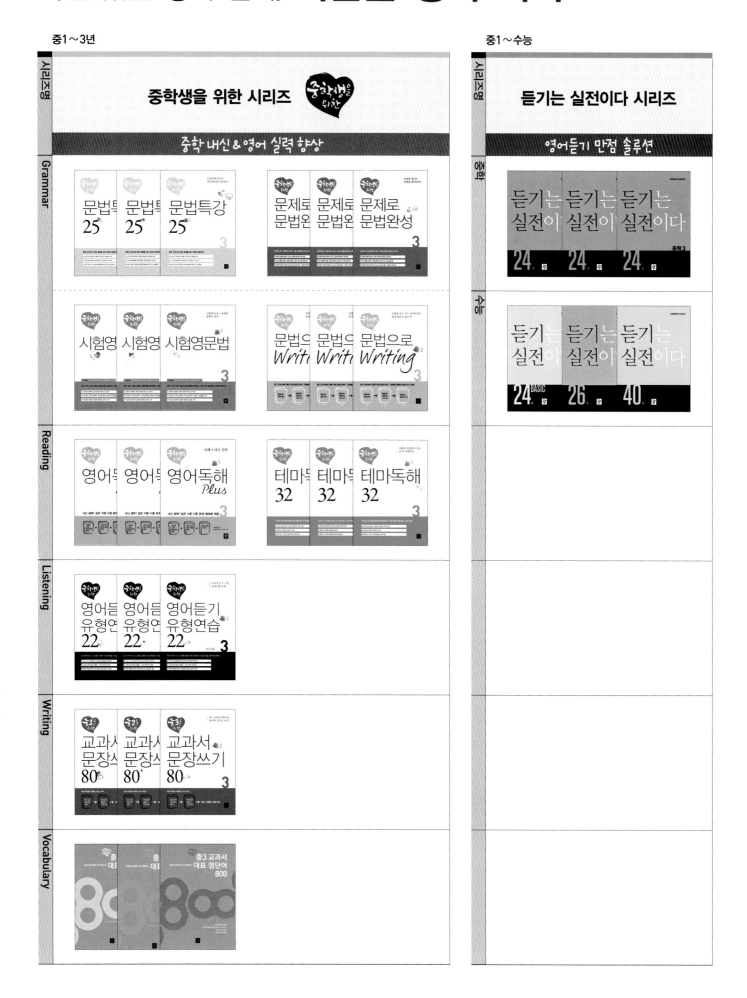

듣기 만점에 도전한다!

중학 영어듣기능력평가에 딱 맞춘 실전모의고사로!
(실제 시험처럼 영국식 발음, 미국식 발음을 동시에)
Dictation & 다른 문제로 한 번 더(실전 Plus)!
만점 듣기 표현 2단계 리스닝 & 주요 어휘 및 표현 암기로!

- 듣기 MP3 파일 및 해설편 PDF 파일 무료 다운로드 www.didimdol.co.kr
- 회별 QR 코드를 인식하여 언제 어디서나 듣기 MP3 파일 재생

중학영어듣기 만점 솔루션

듣기는
실전이다

중학 3
Plus Book

24
회

듣기는
실전이다

중학 3

Plus Book

24회

디딤돌

Step 1 우리말 보면서 영어 듣기

		1회	2회	3회
1	그것을 상세하게 설명해 주시겠어요?	☐	☐	☐
2	새것이 오면 전화드리겠습니다.	☐	☐	☐
3	난 바다에서 수영하는 것을 좋아하지 않아.	☐	☐	☐
4	영화 보러 가지 않을래?	☐	☐	☐
5	너 그의 휴대 전화 번호를 아니?	☐	☐	☐
6	이 박물관에서 당신을 만나다니 정말 기분이 좋습니다.	☐	☐	☐
7	케이크를 좀 더 먹겠니?	☐	☐	☐
8	뭐 먹고 싶어?	☐	☐	☐
9	생태계는 식물과 동물의 공동체이다.	☐	☐	☐
10	토요일 콘서트 표 두 장 살게.	☐	☐	☐
11	컴퓨터에 문제가 있는 것 같아.	☐	☐	☐
12	도서관은 4월 20일부터 5월 4일까지 휴관합니다.	☐	☐	☐
13	그것들을 모두 한국 돈으로 바꾸고 싶습니다.	☐	☐	☐
14	얼마 후에 이것은 곧 당신을 따라 말할 것이다.	☐	☐	☐
15	배드민턴을 잘 친다고 들었는데.	☐	☐	☐
16	축구 경기 전에 시간이 얼마나 남았니?	☐	☐	☐
17	잠깐 얘기 좀 할 수 있을까?	☐	☐	☐
18	유감스럽게도 지금 그것을 가지고 있지 않아서 빌려 줄 수가 없어.	☐	☐	☐
19	그 영화를 어떻게 생각하니?	☐	☐	☐
20	한 남자가 나와 무슨 일인지 물었다.	☐	☐	☐

Step 2 듣고 따라 말하기

		1회	2회	3회
1	Can you describe it to me in detail?	☐	☐	☐
2	I'll call you when we have a new one.	☐	☐	☐
3	I don't like to swim in the ocean	☐	☐	☐
4	Why don't we go to a movie?	☐	☐	☐
5	Do you know his Cellphone number?	☐	☐	☐
6	I'm so pleased to see you in this museum.	☐	☐	☐
7	Would you like some more cake?	☐	☐	☐
8	What would you like to have?	☐	☐	☐
9	An ecosystem is a community of plants and animals.	☐	☐	☐
10	I'll buy two tickets for the concert on Saturday.	☐	☐	☐
11	I think there's a problem with the computer.	☐	☐	☐
12	The library will be closed from April 20 until May 4.	☐	☐	☐
13	I'd like to exchange them all into Korean currency.	☐	☐	☐
14	After a while this will repeat after you soon.	☐	☐	☐
15	I heard you can play badminton well.	☐	☐	☐
16	How much time do we have before the soccer game?	☐	☐	☐
17	Can I talk to you for a minute?	☐	☐	☐
18	I'm afraid I can't because I don't have it right now.	☐	☐	☐
19	What do you think of the movie?	☐	☐	☐
20	A man came out and asked what was wrong.	☐	☐	☐

Step 1 우리말 보면서 영어 듣기

		1회	2회	3회
1	벤치에 있는 여자는 내 친구의 사촌이야.	☐	☐	☐
2	그 서비스는 얼마죠?	☐	☐	☐
3	왜 이렇게 오래 걸렸니?	☐	☐	☐
4	그것을 보려면 두 시간을 기다려야 해.	☐	☐	☐
5	승차권 좀 보여주시겠습니까?	☐	☐	☐
6	그건 그렇고, 넌 무슨 일을 하니?	☐	☐	☐
7	미안합니다만, 저도 여기가 처음이에요.	☐	☐	☐
8	버스는 15분 후 떠나.	☐	☐	☐
9	넌 그녀에게 먼저 사과를 해야 해.	☐	☐	☐
10	내일 그것들을 찾으러 오겠습니다.	☐	☐	☐
11	차가 너무 많아서 셀 수가 없군요.	☐	☐	☐
12	지진 피해자를 돕기 위해 함께 일해봅시다.	☐	☐	☐
13	꽃집에서 왼쪽으로 돌면 박물관이 보일 겁니다.	☐	☐	☐
14	당신은 편지를 쓰거나 일기를 쓸 때 그것을 사용할 수 있다.	☐	☐	☐
15	우리가 함께 할 즐거운 일이 있어요.	☐	☐	☐
16	어디에 두었는지 기억이 안 나네요.	☐	☐	☐
17	수학 수업 때문에 진짜 열심히 공부해야 해.	☐	☐	☐
18	또 문자 메시지를 보내는 거니?	☐	☐	☐
19	시키는 대로 다 할 게요.	☐	☐	☐
20	그녀는 커피를 온 몸에 쏟는다.	☐	☐	☐

Step 2 듣고 따라 말하기

		1회	2회	3회
1	That girl on the bench is my friend's cousin.	☐	☐	☐
2	How much is the service?	☐	☐	☐
3	What took you so long?	☐	☐	☐
4	We have to wait for two hours to see it.	☐	☐	☐
5	Can you show me your ticket?	☐	☐	☐
6	By the way, what do you do?	☐	☐	☐
7	I'm sorry, but I'm a stranger here, too.	☐	☐	☐
8	The bus is leaving in fifteen minutes.	☐	☐	☐
9	You have to say sorry to her first.	☐	☐	☐
10	I'll be back to pick them up tomorrow.	☐	☐	☐
11	There are too many cars to count.	☐	☐	☐
12	Let's work together to help the earthquake victims.	☐	☐	☐
13	Turn left at the flower shop, and you'll see the museum.	☐	☐	☐
14	You can use it to write a letter or keep a diary.	☐	☐	☐
15	I have something fun for us to do together.	☐	☐	☐
16	I can't remember where I put it.	☐	☐	☐
17	I have to study really hard because of my math class.	☐	☐	☐
18	Are you sending text messages again?	☐	☐	☐
19	I'll do whatever you tell me to do.	☐	☐	☐
20	She spills her coffee all over herself.	☐	☐	☐

Step 1 우리말 보면서 영어 듣기

		1회	2회	3회
1	무슨 사이즈를 입으세요?	☐	☐	☐
2	아침에는 시간이 없습니다.	☐	☐	☐
3	계좌를 개설하고 싶은데요.	☐	☐	☐
4	일이 생겨서 안 될 것 같아요.	☐	☐	☐
5	그는 현관문으로 가서 신문을 내게 가져옵니다.	☐	☐	☐
6	저를 초대해 주셔서 고맙습니다.	☐	☐	☐
7	점심으로 우리 피자 먹을래요?	☐	☐	☐
8	슈퍼마켓 근처에 세탁소가 있어요.	☐	☐	☐
9	만약 여러분이 우리 가게에서 물건을 사시면, 영수증을 보관해 주십시오.	☐	☐	☐
10	세 살 아래의 어린이는 무료로 탑니다.	☐	☐	☐
11	거스름돈은 넣어두시고 정보를 주셔서 감사합니다.	☐	☐	☐
12	대부분의 학생들은 한 시간 30분 동안 클럽 활동에 참가합니다.	☐	☐	☐
13	일층에는 교실만 있다고 들었는데요.	☐	☐	☐
14	그것에는 몇 개의 천 조각과 많은 줄이 있다.	☐	☐	☐
15	이 검정색은 어떻습니까?	☐	☐	☐
16	버스보다 더 빠를 거야.	☐	☐	☐
17	어떤 색을 원하시죠?	☐	☐	☐
18	보고서를 인쇄해야 하는데 컴퓨터가 작동하지를 않아.	☐	☐	☐
19	의상을 대여하고 싶어요.	☐	☐	☐
20	지하철은 많은 사람들로 붐볐다.	☐	☐	☐

Step 2 듣고 따라 말하기

		1회	2회	3회
1	What size do you wear?	☐	☐	☐
2	I have no time in the morning.	☐	☐	☐
3	I'd like to open an account.	☐	☐	☐
4	Something's come up and I can't make it.	☐	☐	☐
5	He goes to the front door and brings me a newspaper.	☐	☐	☐
6	Thanks for having me.	☐	☐	☐
7	Why don't we have a pizza for lunch?	☐	☐	☐
8	There's a laundry shop near the supermarket.	☐	☐	☐
9	When you buy things in our store, please keep your receipts.	☐	☐	☐
10	Children under three ride for free.	☐	☐	☐
11	Keep the change and thanks for the information.	☐	☐	☐
12	Most students attend club activities for one and a half hours.	☐	☐	☐
13	I heard there are only classrooms on the first floor.	☐	☐	☐
14	It has some pieces of cloths and a lot of strings.	☐	☐	☐
15	How about these black ones	☐	☐	☐
16	It will be faster than the bus.	☐	☐	☐
17	What color would you like?	☐	☐	☐
18	I have to print my report but my computer doesn't work.	☐	☐	☐
19	I'd like to rent a costume.	☐	☐	☐
20	The subway was crowded with a lot of people.	☐	☐	☐

영어듣기능력평가 04회
만점 듣기 표현

Step 1 우리말 보면서 영어 듣기

		1회	2회	3회
1	길 잃은 남자 아이를 찾고 있습니다.	☐	☐	☐
2	우리 일본 여행 계획에 대해 말하고 싶어	☐	☐	☐
3	어딘가에서 내 재킷을 봤나요?	☐	☐	☐
4	서점에 도착하면 연락해.	☐	☐	☐
5	저를 도와주시다니 참 친절하시군요.	☐	☐	☐
6	잘 준비하고 그 때 봅시다!	☐	☐	☐
7	휴가동안 뭐 할 거야?	☐	☐	☐
8	오늘 밤 친구들이 몇 명이나 와?	☐	☐	☐
9	넌 수학과 과학 둘 다 잘한다고 생각했는데.	☐	☐	☐
10	오늘은 쿠폰을 사용하고 싶어요.	☐	☐	☐
11	매점에 가서 좀 사 올게요.	☐	☐	☐
12	주말에는 자전거 타기를 즐겨라.	☐	☐	☐
13	병원은 식료품점 건너편에 있어요.	☐	☐	☐
14	요즈음 많은 사람들이 저녁에 자전거 타는 것을 즐기고 있습니다.	☐	☐	☐
15	이 양식을 채워주세요.	☐	☐	☐
16	난 아픈 사람들을 돌보는 데 관심이 있어.	☐	☐	☐
17	내 컴퓨터 사용하지 말라고 얼마나 말해야 하니?	☐	☐	☐
18	이 물건이 여러 색상으로 있나요?	☐	☐	☐
19	그 노래에 어떤 특별한 내용이 있니?	☐	☐	☐
20	등교하기 전에 그는 테니스 레슨을 받는다.	☐	☐	☐

Step 2 듣고 따라 말하기

		1회	2회	3회
1	We're looking for a lost boy.	☐	☐	☐
2	I'd like to talk about the plans for our trip to Japan.	☐	☐	☐
3	Have you seen my jacket anywhere?	☐	☐	☐
4	Call me when you get to the bookstore.	☐	☐	☐
5	It's very nice of you to help me.	☐	☐	☐
6	Prepare for it well and see you then!	☐	☐	☐
7	What are you going to do on the vacation?	☐	☐	☐
8	How many of your friends are coming over tonight?	☐	☐	☐
9	I thought you were good at both math and science.	☐	☐	☐
10	I want to use my coupon card today.	☐	☐	☐
11	I'll go get some from the cafeteria.	☐	☐	☐
12	Enjoy riding a bike during the weekend.	☐	☐	☐
13	The hospital is opposite the grocery store.	☐	☐	☐
14	Nowadays many people enjoy bike riding in the evening.	☐	☐	☐
15	Fill out this form, please.	☐	☐	☐
16	I'm interested in taking care of sick people.	☐	☐	☐
17	How many times do I have to tell you not to use my computer?	☐	☐	☐
18	Do you have that in many colors?	☐	☐	☐
19	Is there any special message in the song?	☐	☐	☐
20	Before going to school, he takes a tennis lesson.	☐	☐	☐

Step 1 우리말 보면서 영어 듣기

		1회	2회	3회
1	어떻게 생겼는지 말씀해주시겠어요?	☐	☐	☐
2	11시에 도서관에서 만나자.	☐	☐	☐
3	그의 새로운 소설이 나오길 기다렸어.	☐	☐	☐
4	제가 그것을 타기에 충분한 시간이 있다고 생각하나요?	☐	☐	☐
5	눈을 감아 주세요, 제발.	☐	☐	☐
6	여기 아래쪽에 서명하셔야 합니다.	☐	☐	☐
7	집까지 태워다 줘서 고마워요.	☐	☐	☐
8	나가서 친구들이랑 놀고 싶어요.	☐	☐	☐
9	진짜 오랜만에 본다.	☐	☐	☐
10	제가 도와드릴 것이 있습니까?	☐	☐	☐
11	처음 필름 한 통은 무료로 현상하실 수 있습니다.	☐	☐	☐
12	내가 꿈꾸던 학교인 것 같아.	☐	☐	☐
13	멋진 여행 되고 그 때 보자.	☐	☐	☐
14	우리가 이것을 할 때, 대부분의 사람들은 우리가 졸린 것이라고 생각한다.	☐	☐	☐
15	새 자물쇠가 고장이 난 것 같아요.	☐	☐	☐
16	미세 먼지 마스크가 얼마 안 남았어.	☐	☐	☐
17	이번 주말에 특별한 계획이라도 있니?	☐	☐	☐
18	그는 친한 친구들이 없고 누구와도 이야기를 하려고 하지 않아.	☐	☐	☐
19	수표로 지불해도 되나요?	☐	☐	☐
20	필기를 하기 위해서 그는 펜이 필요하다.	☐	☐	☐

Step 2 듣고 따라 말하기

		1회	2회	3회
1	Can you tell me what it looks like?	☐	☐	☐
2	Let's meet at 11 o'clock at the library.	☐	☐	☐
3	I've been waiting for his new novel to come out!	☐	☐	☐
4	Do you think I have enough time to catch it?	☐	☐	☐
5	Close your eyes, please.	☐	☐	☐
6	You should sign right here at the bottom.	☐	☐	☐
7	Thanks for giving me a ride home.	☐	☐	☐
8	I want to go out and have fun with friends.	☐	☐	☐
9	It's been so long to see you.	☐	☐	☐
10	Is there anything I can help you with?	☐	☐	☐
11	You can develop your first roll for free.	☐	☐	☐
12	It sounds like my dream school.	☐	☐	☐
13	Have a nice trip and see you then.	☐	☐	☐
14	When you do this, most people think that we are sleepy.	☐	☐	☐
15	The new doorlock seems to be out of order.	☐	☐	☐
16	We're running out of fine dust masks.	☐	☐	☐
17	Do you have any special plans for this weekend?	☐	☐	☐
18	He has no close friends and wants to talk to no one.	☐	☐	☐
19	Do you mind if I pay by check?	☐	☐	☐
20	He needs a pen in order to take some notes.	☐	☐	☐

Step 1 우리말 보면서 영어 듣기

		1회	2회	3회
1	딸에게 하나 사 주고 싶어요.	☐	☐	☐
2	우리는 각자의 악기를 연주하기로 했어.	☐	☐	☐
3	알려줘서 감사합니다.	☐	☐	☐
4	수족관에 방문하거나 쇼핑하러 가는 건 어때?	☐	☐	☐
5	박물관 근처의 호텔에서 저녁식사를 즐길 거예요.	☐	☐	☐
6	혹시 시청이 어디에 있는지 아시나요?	☐	☐	☐
7	잠깐만 신문 좀 볼 수 있을까요?	☐	☐	☐
8	주제는 내가 존경하는 누군가에 대해서야.	☐	☐	☐
9	제가 어릴 때 그 호수 근처에서 살았어요.	☐	☐	☐
10	지금 충분한 현금이 없어요.	☐	☐	☐
11	주인한테 가서 다른 것을 부탁할게요.	☐	☐	☐
12	여러분은 미래 직업에 대해 궁금한 것들이 많을 것입니다.	☐	☐	☐
13	전 정말로 아랫줄에 앉고 싶어요.	☐	☐	☐
14	당신은 가능한 한 많은 문제를 풀려고 최선을 다한다.	☐	☐	☐
15	병원에 갈 수 있겠니?	☐	☐	☐
16	탁구나 농구 같은 실내 스포츠를 해 보고 싶어.	☐	☐	☐
17	마지막으로 그 애를 본 게 언제죠?	☐	☐	☐
18	너 그럼 이게 할인 판매 중이었다는 말이니?	☐	☐	☐
19	다음 주쯤 거기 가 보는 게 어때요?	☐	☐	☐
20	그들은 2시간 넘게 수다를 즐긴다.	☐	☐	☐

Step 2 듣고 따라 말하기

		1회	2회	3회
1	I want to buy one for my daughter.	☐	☐	☐
2	We're going to play our own instruments.	☐	☐	☐
3	Thank you for letting me know.	☐	☐	☐
4	What about visiting the aquarium or going shopping?	☐	☐	☐
5	We'll enjoy dinner in a hotel near the museum.	☐	☐	☐
6	Do you happen to know where the City Hall is?	☐	☐	☐
7	Can I see your newspaper for a moment?	☐	☐	☐
8	The topic is about someone I admire.	☐	☐	☐
9	I lived near the lake when I was young.	☐	☐	☐
10	I don't have enough cash now.	☐	☐	☐
11	I'll go to the owner and ask for another one.	☐	☐	☐
12	We know that you have many questions about jobs in the future.	☐	☐	☐
13	I really want to sit in the lower row.	☐	☐	☐
14	You do your best to solve as many problems as possible.	☐	☐	☐
15	Do you think you can go to the clinic?	☐	☐	☐
16	I'd like to try indoor sports like table tennis or basketball.	☐	☐	☐
17	When did you see him last?	☐	☐	☐
18	You mean this was on sale?	☐	☐	☐
19	Why don't we go there someday next week?	☐	☐	☐
20	They enjoy chatting for over two hours.	☐	☐	☐

Step 1 우리말 보면서 영어 듣기

		1회	2회	3회
1	그것은 몸뿐만 아니라 정신에도 좋아.	☐	☐	☐
2	이 책들을 대출하고 싶은데요.	☐	☐	☐
3	만드는 방법 좀 알려 주세요.	☐	☐	☐
4	파티에 얼마나 많은 친구들이 왔니?	☐	☐	☐
5	이곳을 가능한 한 빨리 떠나 주시길 권합니다.	☐	☐	☐
6	그것을 어디에서 찍었는지 어떻게 알았니?	☐	☐	☐
7	이번 주말 날씨가 어떨 거래?	☐	☐	☐
8	도와드릴 것이 더 있나요, 손님?	☐	☐	☐
9	문제가 뭐라고 생각해?	☐	☐	☐
10	읽기 쉬운 책을 찾고 있는데 도와주실 수 있나요?	☐	☐	☐
11	그 안에서 그러한 음악회 정보를 찾으실 수 있을 겁니다.	☐	☐	☐
12	이 쇼는 여러분에게 우주 여행에 대한 정보를 제공해 드릴 것입니다.	☐	☐	☐
13	몇 시에 가고 싶으세요?	☐	☐	☐
14	참석하는 모두에게 무료 음료가 제공됩니다.	☐	☐	☐
15	뭐 좀 먹자.	☐	☐	☐
16	엄마께서 내 생일 선물로 사 주셨어.	☐	☐	☐
17	가능하면 빨리 읽기 시작해야 해	☐	☐	☐
18	가능한 한 빨리 영어 쓰기 기술을 개선하고 싶거든요.	☐	☐	☐
19	언제 제2차 세계대전이 일어났지?	☐	☐	☐
20	주변에는 공중전화 박스가 없었다.	☐	☐	☐

Step 2 듣고 따라 말하기

		1회	2회	3회
1	I think it's good for the mind as well as the body.	☐	☐	☐
2	I'd like to check these books out.	☐	☐	☐
3	Please tell me how to make it.	☐	☐	☐
4	How many friends were there at your party?	☐	☐	☐
5	I suggest you leave here as soon as possible.	☐	☐	☐
6	How did you know where it was taken?	☐	☐	☐
7	What's the weather going to be like this weekend?	☐	☐	☐
8	Is there anything else I can do for you, ma'am?	☐	☐	☐
9	What do you think is the problem?	☐	☐	☐
10	Could you help me find an easy book to read?	☐	☐	☐
11	You can find the information about such concerts in it.	☐	☐	☐
12	This show will bring you information on space travel.	☐	☐	☐
13	What time of the day would you like to go?	☐	☐	☐
14	There will be free drinks offered to all who attend.	☐	☐	☐
15	Let's have something to eat.	☐	☐	☐
16	My mother bought it for my birthday present.	☐	☐	☐
17	I should start reading it as soon as possible.	☐	☐	☐
18	I want to improve my English writing skills as fast as possible.	☐	☐	☐
19	When did the Second World War take place?	☐	☐	☐
20	There was no public phone booth around.	☐	☐	☐

Step 1 우리말 보면서 영어 듣기

		1회	2회	3회
1	그는 내가 꿈꿀 수도 없는 많은 것들을 할 수 있다.	☐	☐	☐
2	너네 집에 들러서 매일 고양이를 챙겨줄게.	☐	☐	☐
3	포장해 주시겠어요?	☐	☐	☐
4	이번주 주말에 무슨 계획이라도 있어?	☐	☐	☐
5	재조정할 수는 없는 거야?	☐	☐	☐
6	염두에 두겠습니다.	☐	☐	☐
7	나는 자전거를 타고 등교해.	☐	☐	☐
8	보고서 아직 안 냈니?	☐	☐	☐
9	기차가 완전히 멈출 때까지 좌석을 벗어나지 마세요.	☐	☐	☐
10	회원 카드를 갖고 계신가요?	☐	☐	☐
11	이 흰색 드레스에 뭔가 문제가 있는 것 같습니다.	☐	☐	☐
12	관심있으신 분들은 다음주 수요일까지 이 선생님에게 등록하세요.	☐	☐	☐
13	점심을 먹으러 나중에 여기 다시 올 수 있겠군요.	☐	☐	☐
14	그녀는 동물 보호소에서 봉사활동을 하고 있다.	☐	☐	☐
15	차가운 음료수를 마시고 싶어요?	☐	☐	☐
16	좋은 소식과 나쁜 소식이 하나씩 있어.	☐	☐	☐
17	폐업하다니 슬프다.	☐	☐	☐
18	마침내 우리 집이 생겼어.	☐	☐	☐
19	다음 번에는 좀 더 주의를 기울여 줘.	☐	☐	☐
20	그분들은 많은 공통점들이 있었고 여러 문제에 있어 의견이 완전히 똑같았다.	☐	☐	☐

Step 2 듣고 따라 말하기

		1회	2회	3회
1	He can do many things that I can't even dream of doing.	☐	☐	☐
2	I'll stop by your place and take care of your cat everyday.	☐	☐	☐
3	Can you wrap it up for me?	☐	☐	☐
4	Do you have any plans for this weekend?	☐	☐	☐
5	Can't you reschedule it?	☐	☐	☐
6	I'll keep that in mind.	☐	☐	☐
7	I go to school by bicycle.	☐	☐	☐
8	Didn't you turn in your report yet?	☐	☐	☐
9	Don't leave your seat until the train comes to a complete stop.	☐	☐	☐
10	Do you have our membership card?	☐	☐	☐
11	There is something wrong with this white dress.	☐	☐	☐
12	Those interested should register with Ms. Lee by next Wednesday.	☐	☐	☐
13	I can come back here later for lunch.	☐	☐	☐
14	She has been doing volunteer work at an animal shelter.	☐	☐	☐
15	Would you like to drink cold drink?	☐	☐	☐
16	I have good news and bad news.	☐	☐	☐
17	I'm sad to hear that they're going out of business.	☐	☐	☐
18	We finally have our own place.	☐	☐	☐
19	You should be more careful next time.	☐	☐	☐
20	They had a lot in common and saw eye to eye on a lot of issues.	☐	☐	☐

Step 1 우리말 보면서 영어 듣기

		1회	2회	3회
1	내 여동생을 위해 하나 사고 싶어요.	☐	☐	☐
2	이름과 주소를 알려 주시겠습니까?	☐	☐	☐
3	이 주변에 다른 주차장들이 있습니까?	☐	☐	☐
4	오늘 아침에 끔찍한 치통에 시달렸어.	☐	☐	☐
5	내 새 전화번호를 너에게 말해 줬어야 했는데.	☐	☐	☐
6	차라리 환불 받는 게 낫겠어요.	☐	☐	☐
7	방과 후에 보통 무엇을 하니?	☐	☐	☐
8	주제를 정해야 해.	☐	☐	☐
9	떠나기 전에 준비가 되도록 하라.	☐	☐	☐
10	조금 더 빨리 할 수 있나요?	☐	☐	☐
11	메시지를 남기시겠습니까?	☐	☐	☐
12	그녀는 우리 시대의 가장 재능 있는 가수들 중의 한 분이십니다.	☐	☐	☐
13	나 막 캠핑장에 버스에서 내렸어.	☐	☐	☐
14	본인 음식이나 음료를 가져와도 됩니다.	☐	☐	☐
15	이 사진들이 수 마일에 걸쳐 바다를 덮고 있는 기름을 보여줘.	☐	☐	☐
16	넌 커서 뭐가 될 거니?	☐	☐	☐
17	숙제를 먼저 끝내야지.	☐	☐	☐
18	이제 제가 낼 돈이 얼마인가요?	☐	☐	☐
19	운전하기 전에 엔진을 예열해 줘야 해요.	☐	☐	☐
20	그는 이제 시험이 모두 끝나서 기쁘다.	☐	☐	☐

Step 2 듣고 따라 말하기

		1회	2회	3회
1	I want to buy one for my sister.	☐	☐	☐
2	May I have your name and address?	☐	☐	☐
3	Are there any other parking lots around here?	☐	☐	☐
4	I have a terrible toothache this morning.	☐	☐	☐
5	I should have told you my new phone number.	☐	☐	☐
6	I would rather get my money back.	☐	☐	☐
7	What do you usually do after school?	☐	☐	☐
8	We need to choose a topic.	☐	☐	☐
9	Try to be prepared before you leave.	☐	☐	☐
10	Could you make it a little earlier?	☐	☐	☐
11	Would you like to leave a message?	☐	☐	☐
12	She is one of the most talented singers of our time.	☐	☐	☐
13	I've just got off the bus at the campground.	☐	☐	☐
14	You can bring your own food and drinks.	☐	☐	☐
15	These pictures show oil covering miles of the ocean.	☐	☐	☐
16	What are you going to do when you grow up?	☐	☐	☐
17	You should finish your homework first.	☐	☐	☐
18	How much do I owe you now?	☐	☐	☐
19	You have to warm up the engine before driving.	☐	☐	☐
20	He is glad the exams are all over now.	☐	☐	☐

Step 1 우리말 보면서 영어 듣기

		1회	2회	3회
1	소음이 많이 나나요?	☐	☐	☐
2	지금 네 컴퓨터 앞에 있니?	☐	☐	☐
3	교실 청소하는 걸 도와줄래?	☐	☐	☐
4	월요일은 항상 예약이 가득 차 있습니다.	☐	☐	☐
5	남동생과 싸워서 기분이 좋지 않아.	☐	☐	☐
6	그냥 정사각형에 갈색이었습니다.	☐	☐	☐
7	이 좌석에 사람 있나요?	☐	☐	☐
8	쇼핑백에서 돼지고기를 찾을 수가 없네.	☐	☐	☐
9	비행 시간은 1시간 40분이 될 것입니다.	☐	☐	☐
10	절반 가격에 살 수 있지 않나요?	☐	☐	☐
11	올바른 노선을 찾는 쉬운 방법이 있나요?	☐	☐	☐
12	그녀는 이웃과 이야기를 나누고 가게에서 식료품을 산다.	☐	☐	☐
13	우리 용량에 대해 생각해봐야해.	☐	☐	☐
14	이 안에서 우리는 대개 활동적이다.	☐	☐	☐
15	긍정적으로 생각하도록 하자.	☐	☐	☐
16	폭풍우가 곧 있단다.	☐	☐	☐
17	오늘 퀴즈 보는 거 때문에 걱정했어?	☐	☐	☐
18	그 게임하는 방법을 알려줄래?	☐	☐	☐
19	그곳에 얼마나 오랫동안 머물 예정이니?	☐	☐	☐
20	그녀는 지갑을 식탁에 두고 왔다.	☐	☐	☐

Step 2 듣고 따라 말하기

		1회	2회	3회
1	Do they make a lot of noise?	☐	☐	☐
2	Are you in front of your computer now?	☐	☐	☐
3	Can you help me clean up the classroom?	☐	☐	☐
4	Monday is always all booked up.	☐	☐	☐
5	I had a fight with my brother and I feel bad.	☐	☐	☐
6	It was just square and brown.	☐	☐	☐
7	Is this seat taken?	☐	☐	☐
8	I can't find the pork in the shopping bag.	☐	☐	☐
9	The flying time will be one hour and forty minutes.	☐	☐	☐
10	Can I have it for half price?	☐	☐	☐
11	Is there any easy way to find the right line	☐	☐	☐
12	She talks with her neighbors and buys groceries at the store.	☐	☐	☐
13	We have to think about the capacity.	☐	☐	☐
14	We are usually active in this.	☐	☐	☐
15	Let's try to look on the bright side.	☐	☐	☐
16	There's a heavy rainstorm coming soon.	☐	☐	☐
17	Were you worried about the quiz today?	☐	☐	☐
18	Let me know how to play the game.	☐	☐	☐
19	How long are you going to stay there?	☐	☐	☐
20	She had left the wallet on the table.	☐	☐	☐

영어듣기능력평가 11 회

만점 듣기 표현

Step 1 우리말 보면서 영어 듣기

		1회	2회	3회
1	새 수영복을 사고 싶어?	☐	☐	☐
2	무슨 요일이 좋으신가요?	☐	☐	☐
3	제가 문을 열어 드릴게요.	☐	☐	☐
4	나랑 같은 수업을 듣는 거 어때?	☐	☐	☐
5	이 날을 축하하러 여기에 온 하객들이 참 많군요.	☐	☐	☐
6	내 남동생이 떨어뜨리거나 했을 거야.	☐	☐	☐
7	당신과의 대화가 즐거웠습니다.	☐	☐	☐
8	편지 쓰는 걸 도와줄래?	☐	☐	☐
9	엄마를 좀 더 자주 도와드려야겠어.	☐	☐	☐
10	내일부터 일을 할 수 있습니다.	☐	☐	☐
11	어떤 말씀을 드려야 할지 모르겠군요.	☐	☐	☐
12	초와 성냥이 필요합니다.	☐	☐	☐
13	전화 통화를 많이 하시나요?	☐	☐	☐
14	이것은 우리의 목소리를 특정 방향으로 확대하는 데 도움을 준다.	☐	☐	☐
15	나와 함께 가고 싶니?	☐	☐	☐
16	3일 동안 비가 내리고 있어요.	☐	☐	☐
17	이 집이 당신이 찾고 있는 바로 그 집이에요.	☐	☐	☐
18	아주 중요한 발표라고 말하지 않았니?	☐	☐	☐
19	과속으로 딱지를 떼였지 뭐야!	☐	☐	☐
20	그는 책을 펼쳐보는데, 일부 페이지가 빠져 있음을 발견한다.	☐	☐	☐

Step 2 듣고 따라 말하기

		1회	2회	3회
1	Do you want to buy a new swimsuit?	☐	☐	☐
2	What day do you like?	☐	☐	☐
3	Let me open the door for you.	☐	☐	☐
4	Why don't you take the same class as me?	☐	☐	☐
5	There are so many guests here to celebrate the day.	☐	☐	☐
6	I think my brother dropped it or something.	☐	☐	☐
7	It was nice having talked to you.	☐	☐	☐
8	Would you help me write the letter?	☐	☐	☐
9	I think I should help my mom more often.	☐	☐	☐
10	I can work from tomorrow.	☐	☐	☐
11	I don't know what to say.	☐	☐	☐
12	You need candles and matches.	☐	☐	☐
13	Do you make a lot of phone calls?	☐	☐	☐
14	This helps us increase our voice towards a certain direction.	☐	☐	☐
15	Would you like to go with me?	☐	☐	☐
16	It has rained for three days.	☐	☐	☐
17	This house is exactly what you're looking for.	☐	☐	☐
18	Didn't you say it was very important?	☐	☐	☐
19	I got a ticket for speeding!	☐	☐	☐
20	He opens the book and finds some pages are missing.	☐	☐	☐

Step 1 우리말 보면서 영어 듣기

		1회	2회	3회
1	내 책상 위에 걸어 두면 아주 멋질 거 같아.	☐	☐	☐
2	너 내가 얼마나 영화를 좋아하는지 알잖아.	☐	☐	☐
3	배 멀미를 하는 것 같아요.	☐	☐	☐
4	대부분의 사람들은 저에 대해 모르죠.	☐	☐	☐
5	넘어져서 오른쪽 팔이 부러졌어요.	☐	☐	☐
6	개를 키우는 데 대한 규칙이 있어요?	☐	☐	☐
7	저를 대신해 당신 부모님께 안부를 전해 주세요.	☐	☐	☐
8	거기는 진짜 좋은 치즈랑 신선한 채소를 사용해.	☐	☐	☐
9	여기에서 날 만나자고 한 특별한 이유라도 있니?	☐	☐	☐
10	어떤 크기의 차를 생각하고 계신가요?	☐	☐	☐
11	네가 요리를 아주 잘한다고 들었어.	☐	☐	☐
12	이것도 비행기 착륙 장면을 보다가 우연히 만들어졌습니다.	☐	☐	☐
13	생각하고 계신 특별한 모델이 있나요	☐	☐	☐
14	우리는 오늘이나 내일 날씨가 화창할지, 흐릴지, 비가 올지, 바람이 불지 알고 싶어 한다.	☐	☐	☐
15	형이랑 영화 보러 갈 거야.	☐	☐	☐
16	다른 것보다 노트북이 필요한 거 같아.	☐	☐	☐
17	마감 시간 전에 속달 우편으로 그것을 보내려는 거군요?	☐	☐	☐
18	오늘 오후까지 할 일들이 있어요.	☐	☐	☐
19	어젯밤에 식당에서 일했어요.	☐	☐	☐
20	한 남자가 그녀에게 와서 모자를 보여준다.	☐	☐	☐

Step 2 듣고 따라 말하기

		1회	2회	3회
1	I think it would look great hanging over my desk.	☐	☐	☐
2	You know how much I like movies.	☐	☐	☐
3	I think I'm getting seasick.	☐	☐	☐
4	Most people don't know about me.	☐	☐	☐
5	I fell down and broke my right arm.	☐	☐	☐
6	Is there any rules about keeping a dog?	☐	☐	☐
7	Please say hello to your parents for me.	☐	☐	☐
8	They use very good cheese and fresh vegetables.	☐	☐	☐
9	Is there any special reason for asking me to meet you here?	☐	☐	☐
10	What size car do you have in mind?	☐	☐	☐
11	I heard you're a great cook.	☐	☐	☐
12	It was created by accident while watching airplanes landing.	☐	☐	☐
13	Do you have a specific model in mind?	☐	☐	☐
14	We want to know whether today or tomorrow will be sunny, cloudy, rainy or windy.	☐	☐	☐
15	I'm going to watch a movie with my brother.	☐	☐	☐
16	I guess I need a laptop before everything else.	☐	☐	☐
17	You're going to send it by express mail before closing time?	☐	☐	☐
18	I have things to do by this afternoon.	☐	☐	☐
19	I worked at a restaurant last night.	☐	☐	☐
20	A man comes to her and shows her a cap.	☐	☐	☐

Step 1 우리말 보면서 영어 듣기

		1회	2회	3회
1	해외로 여행가시나요?	☐	☐	☐
2	갑자가 택시 한 대가 뒤에서 오더니 제 차를 받았어요.	☐	☐	☐
3	좋은 레스토랑을 추천해 주시겠습니까?	☐	☐	☐
4	요즘에는 단체 관광객들이 많거든요.	☐	☐	☐
5	그는 오늘 자동차 경주에서 우승하고 싶다.	☐	☐	☐
6	10퍼센트 할인해 드릴 수 있습니다.	☐	☐	☐
7	바람이 심하게 불지 않으면, 테니스를 칠 수도 있죠.	☐	☐	☐
8	버스를 잡으려면 내일 아침 일찍 일어나야 해요.	☐	☐	☐
9	이야기가 무엇에 대한 것인지 난 이해할 수 없었어.	☐	☐	☐
10	나중에 돈 줘.	☐	☐	☐
11	벌써 인터넷에서 시간을 확인했어.	☐	☐	☐
12	매일 오후 케이팝 춤 강의를 제공할 것입니다.	☐	☐	☐
13	진짜 당장 출발해야 해.	☐	☐	☐
14	만약 열이 있다면, 이것을 이용해서 스스로 확인해 봐야 한다.	☐	☐	☐
15	뭘 파신다고 말씀하셨어요?	☐	☐	☐
16	가족들이랑 아시아로 여행을 갈 거야.	☐	☐	☐
17	이 사진에 있는 이 사람들은 누구니?	☐	☐	☐
18	고맙기는 한데, 나 좀 혼자 있게 둬.	☐	☐	☐
19	그것이 바로 제가 찾는 것이네요.	☐	☐	☐
20	그들은 경기장으로 가는 버스를 방금 놓쳤다.	☐	☐	☐

Step 2 듣고 따라 말하기

		1회	2회	3회
1	Are you traveling abroad?	☐	☐	☐
2	Suddenly a taxi came from behind and bumped into my car.	☐	☐	☐
3	Would you recommend a nice restaurant?	☐	☐	☐
4	There are lots of group tours these days.	☐	☐	☐
5	He wants to win the auto race today.	☐	☐	☐
6	You can get a ten percent discount.	☐	☐	☐
7	I might play tennis unless it's too windy.	☐	☐	☐
8	I need to get up early tomorrow to catch a bus.	☐	☐	☐
9	I couldn't understand what the story was about at all.	☐	☐	☐
10	You can pay me back later.	☐	☐	☐
11	I already checked the time on the Internet.	☐	☐	☐
12	We'll offer K-pop dance lessons every afternoon.	☐	☐	☐
13	I really have to leave now.	☐	☐	☐
14	If you have a fever, you have to check yourself by using this.	☐	☐	☐
15	What did you say you sell?	☐	☐	☐
16	I'm going on a trip to Asia with my family.	☐	☐	☐
17	Who are these people in this picture?	☐	☐	☐
18	Thanks for asking, but leave me alone.	☐	☐	☐
19	That's the one I've been looking for.	☐	☐	☐
20	They have just missed the bus to the stadium.	☐	☐	☐

Step 1 우리말 보면서 영어 듣기

		1회	2회	3회
1	안내 데스크에서 드리는 안내 방송입니다.	☐	☐	☐
2	우유 배달을 잠시 중단하고 싶습니다.	☐	☐	☐
3	어느 역에서 제가 내려야 하나요?	☐	☐	☐
4	친구들이랑 버스터미널에 있어요.	☐	☐	☐
5	저는 이 상을 타리라고는 예측도 못 했어요.	☐	☐	☐
6	저는 그 남자가 그냥 우리를 지나가고 있다고 생각했죠.	☐	☐	☐
7	나 일요일에 산악자전거를 타러 갈 거야.	☐	☐	☐
8	그러면 다음에 만나야겠네.	☐	☐	☐
9	비디오 게임을 하는데 많은 시간을 쓰나요?	☐	☐	☐
10	다음 번 공연이 몇 시지요?	☐	☐	☐
11	저번 주에 가구 몇 점을 샀어.	☐	☐	☐
12	저희 클럽에 가입하시게 되면 가입비를 지불하셔야 합니다.	☐	☐	☐
13	제가 무엇을 봐야 하는지 추천해 주시겠어요?	☐	☐	☐
14	요즘에는 많은 사람들이 스마트폰을 사용한다.	☐	☐	☐
15	제가 그에게 전해드리겠습니다.	☐	☐	☐
16	그가 대단한 고통에 시달리는 것처럼 행동하지는 않네요.	☐	☐	☐
17	가방은 몇 개 갖고 계세요?	☐	☐	☐
18	새로운 사람이 이번 주말에 이사 들어온다고 들었어.	☐	☐	☐
19	많이 아플 때 알약 두 개를 드세요.	☐	☐	☐
20	당신은 컴퓨터 매장을 둘러보고 있다.	☐	☐	☐

Step 2 듣고 따라 말하기

		1회	2회	3회
1	This is an announcement from the information desk.	☐	☐	☐
2	I'd like to hold the milk delivery.	☐	☐	☐
3	At what station do I have to get off?	☐	☐	☐
4	I'm at the bus terminal with my friends.	☐	☐	☐
5	I never expected to win this award.	☐	☐	☐
6	I thought the man was just passing by us.	☐	☐	☐
7	I'm going to go mountain biking on Sunday.	☐	☐	☐
8	Then maybe we should meet some other time.	☐	☐	☐
9	Do you spend a lot of time playing video games?	☐	☐	☐
10	What time is the next show?	☐	☐	☐
11	We bought some of the furniture last week.	☐	☐	☐
12	When you enter our club, you will have to pay an entrance fee.	☐	☐	☐
13	What do you recommend I should look at?	☐	☐	☐
14	These days, lots of people use smart phones.	☐	☐	☐
15	I'll hand it over to him.	☐	☐	☐
16	He isn't acting as if he is in a lot of pain.	☐	☐	☐
17	How many bags do you have?	☐	☐	☐
18	I heard a new person will move in this weekend.	☐	☐	☐
19	Take two pills when it hurts a lot.	☐	☐	☐
20	You are looking around a computer shop.	☐	☐	☐

영어듣기능력평가 **15**회

만점 듣기 표현

Step 1 우리말 보면서 영어 듣기

		1회	2회	3회
1	꽃무늬 있는 것 있어요?	☐	☐	☐
2	너 내가 지난주에 산 카메라 기억해?	☐	☐	☐
3	이곳에 와 본 적이 있어요?	☐	☐	☐
4	주말에는 할머니 댁에 가기로 되어있어.	☐	☐	☐
5	자원봉사자는 여러가지 일을 도울 수 있습니다.	☐	☐	☐
6	집들이에 초대해 줘서 감사합니다.	☐	☐	☐
7	학교 첫날 어땠어?	☐	☐	☐
8	거기에 러닝화를 두고 왔어.	☐	☐	☐
9	행운을 빌어줄게요.	☐	☐	☐
10	가장 잘 나가는 탁자 중 하나입니다.	☐	☐	☐
11	이 쇼핑몰에 처음 왔습니다.	☐	☐	☐
12	이번 여름 가족들이 큰 유대감을 형성하는 경험을 찾고 있나요?	☐	☐	☐
13	생각 중인 가격대를 알려주실 수 있나요?	☐	☐	☐
14	이것은 모든 형태의 생물에게 아주 중요한 것 중의 하나이다.	☐	☐	☐
15	새 자동차를 사려는 거예요?	☐	☐	☐
16	지방을 피하는 것뿐만 아니라 소금이랑 설탕도 줄이려고 노력 중이야	☐	☐	☐
17	어젯밤에 짐도 다 쌌어.	☐	☐	☐
18	가장 가까운 쇼핑 센터는 어디 있나요?	☐	☐	☐
19	어젯밤에 언제 잤니?	☐	☐	☐
20	그의 비서가 전화를 받는다.	☐	☐	☐

Step 2 듣고 따라 말하기

		1회	2회	3회
1	Do you have one with flower pattern?	☐	☐	☐
2	Do you remember the camera I bought last week?	☐	☐	☐
3	Have you been to this place?	☐	☐	☐
4	I'm supposed to go to my grandma's house on the weekend.	☐	☐	☐
5	Volunteers can help with various duties.	☐	☐	☐
6	Thanks for inviting me to your housewarming.	☐	☐	☐
7	How was your first day of school?	☐	☐	☐
8	I left my running shoes there.	☐	☐	☐
9	I'll cross my fingers for you.	☐	☐	☐
10	It's one of our bestselling tables.	☐	☐	☐
11	This is my first visit to this shopping mall.	☐	☐	☐
12	Is your family looking for a great bonding experience this summer?	☐	☐	☐
13	Can you tell me what price range you have in mind?	☐	☐	☐
14	This is a very important thing for all forms of life.	☐	☐	☐
15	Are you going to buy a new car?	☐	☐	☐
16	I'm trying to not only avoid fat but also reduce salt and sugar.	☐	☐	☐
17	I got all my luggage packed last night.	☐	☐	☐
18	Where's the nearest shopping center?	☐	☐	☐
19	When did you go to sleep last night?	☐	☐	☐
20	His secretary takes the call.	☐	☐	☐

Step 1 우리말 보면서 영어 듣기

		1회	2회	3회
1	힘든 하루를 보내시나요?	☐	☐	☐
2	전할 말이 있니?	☐	☐	☐
3	이곳에 주차하시면 안 됩니다.	☐	☐	☐
4	대사는 다 외웠어?	☐	☐	☐
5	난 지금까지 치즈와 우유를 맛 본 적이 없어.	☐	☐	☐
6	2년 동안 여행 회사에서 일했습니다.	☐	☐	☐
7	이 책을 어떻게 생각하세요?	☐	☐	☐
8	정비소로 가는 중이야.	☐	☐	☐
9	파일 크기가 너무 큰 거 같아요.	☐	☐	☐
10	식탁을 차릴 때 쓸 식기를 찾고 있어요.	☐	☐	☐
11	가구에 손대지 마세요.	☐	☐	☐
12	직원이 내가 어디인지 물어봤지만 나는 내 위치를 확신할 수 없었다.	☐	☐	☐
13	하나 살까 생각 중입니다.	☐	☐	☐
14	북극에 사는 북극곰들도 심각한 위험에 처해있다.	☐	☐	☐
15	내가 이탈리아 음식 만드는 법을 가르쳐 줄게.	☐	☐	☐
16	일기 예보에 따르면 천둥을 동반한 폭우가 내릴 거라고 했어.	☐	☐	☐
17	축구하다가 발목을 삐었어.	☐	☐	☐
18	넌 어떤 운동을 하고 싶니?	☐	☐	☐
19	선생님은 내가 더 연습을 해야 한다고 말씀하셔.	☐	☐	☐
20	그녀는 침착하게 행동하는 척했다.	☐	☐	☐

Step 2 듣고 따라 말하기

		1회	2회	3회
1	Having a terrible day?	☐	☐	☐
2	Can you leave a message?	☐	☐	☐
3	You're not supposed to park here.	☐	☐	☐
4	Did you memorize all the lines?	☐	☐	☐
5	I've never tasted cheese and milk so far.	☐	☐	☐
6	I've worked for a travel company for two years.	☐	☐	☐
7	What do you think of this book?	☐	☐	☐
8	I'm on my way to the repair shop.	☐	☐	☐
9	I think the size of the file is too large.	☐	☐	☐
10	I'm looking for tableware to set a table.	☐	☐	☐
11	Please don't touch the furniture.	☐	☐	☐
12	The service man asked me where I was, but I wasn't sure of my location.	☐	☐	☐
13	I'm thinking of buying one.	☐	☐	☐
14	Polar bears in the Arctic are in serious danger.	☐	☐	☐
15	I'll teach you how to make an Italian dish.	☐	☐	☐
16	The forecast said that there would be a rainstorm with thunder.	☐	☐	☐
17	I sprained my ankle when playing soccer.	☐	☐	☐
18	What exercise would you like to do?	☐	☐	☐
19	My teacher says I have to practice more.	☐	☐	☐
20	She pretended to act cool.	☐	☐	☐

Step 1 우리말 보면서 영어 듣기

		1회	2회	3회
1	무엇을 골라야 할지 모르겠네요.	☐	☐	☐
2	내가 어제 수학 수업을 빠졌잖아.	☐	☐	☐
3	그 맛을 잊지 못할 거예요.	☐	☐	☐
4	금요일은 하루 종일 회의가 잡혀 있어.	☐	☐	☐
5	당신이 건강하게 지내면 좋겠어요.	☐	☐	☐
6	근처에 다른 호텔이 있나요?	☐	☐	☐
7	날 좀 도와줄래?	☐	☐	☐
8	리허설이 언제 시작하죠?	☐	☐	☐
9	상담 학위를 얻기 위해 대학원에 입학하고 싶어요.	☐	☐	☐
10	너 이거 살 거야?	☐	☐	☐
11	등이 아파 죽겠어요.	☐	☐	☐
12	많은 학생들이 오랫동안 이번 행사를 위해 열심히 해 왔습니다.	☐	☐	☐
13	아시아에서 가장 큰 수족관입니다.	☐	☐	☐
14	이것은 음식이나 찬 음료들을 저장하는 데 사용된다.	☐	☐	☐
15	태워 줄까?	☐	☐	☐
16	한 가지 선택밖에 없네.	☐	☐	☐
17	아르바이트 해 봤어?	☐	☐	☐
18	내가 생각지도 못했던 문제가 하나 있었던 거야.	☐	☐	☐
19	내일 아침 전화하는 것 잊지 않을게.	☐	☐	☐
20	그는 운전을 배우러 운전 학원에 간다.	☐	☐	☐

Step 2 듣고 따라 말하기

		1회	2회	3회
1	I don't know what to choose.	☐	☐	☐
2	I missed math class yesterday.	☐	☐	☐
3	I'll never forget the taste.	☐	☐	☐
4	I'm tied up with meetings all day on Friday.	☐	☐	☐
5	I hope you stay fit and healthy.	☐	☐	☐
6	Is there another hotel nearby?	☐	☐	☐
7	Could you give me a hand?	☐	☐	☐
8	When does the rehearsal start?	☐	☐	☐
9	I want to enter graduate school to get a degree in counselling.	☐	☐	☐
10	Are you going to buy this one?	☐	☐	☐
11	My back is killing me.	☐	☐	☐
12	A lot of students have worked hard on the event for a long time.	☐	☐	☐
13	It is the biggest aquarium in Asia.	☐	☐	☐
14	This is used to store food or cold drinks.	☐	☐	☐
15	Do you need a ride?	☐	☐	☐
16	We have only one choice left.	☐	☐	☐
17	Have you ever worked part time?	☐	☐	☐
18	There was one problem I'd never thought of.	☐	☐	☐
19	I won't forget to call you tomorrow morning.	☐	☐	☐
20	He goes to the driving academy to learn how to drive.	☐	☐	☐

만점 듣기 표현

Step 1 우리말 보면서 영어 듣기

		1회	2회	3회
1	줄무늬 재킷을 입고 있는 남자 보여?	☐	☐	☐
2	감기에 걸렸을 때는 뜨거운 꿀차를 마셔야 해.	☐	☐	☐
3	모욕을 주려는 의도는 아니었습니다.	☐	☐	☐
4	나는 월요일마다 여동생과 있어야 해.	☐	☐	☐
5	여러분들을 위한 많은 엄청난 행사를 계획하고 있습니다.	☐	☐	☐
6	지금 내려가면 안될까	☐	☐	☐
7	제가 도와드릴 일이 있을까요?	☐	☐	☐
8	따뜻한 음료를 사다 줄 수 있을까?	☐	☐	☐
9	음식이나 물에 굉장히 주의하세요.	☐	☐	☐
10	그 책을 반납할 때 역시 연체료를 내야할 겁니다.	☐	☐	☐
11	어디다 놓을까요?	☐	☐	☐
12	어떤 문의사항이나 질문이 있다면 알려주세요.	☐	☐	☐
13	우리 둘 다 이 일에 지원하자.	☐	☐	☐
14	취미로 이것을 모으는 것을 좋아하는 사람들도 있다.	☐	☐	☐
15	잠깐 시간 좀 있어?	☐	☐	☐
16	하루의 시작부터 물에 젖고 싶지는 않아.	☐	☐	☐
17	금액을 선택하시면 돈이 나올 거예요.	☐	☐	☐
18	어머니께서 아주 귀여운 딸을 낳으셨거든.	☐	☐	☐
19	이 책들을 빌리고 싶어요.	☐	☐	☐
20	당신이 아침에 등교할 때 어머니가 아파 보이셨다.	☐	☐	☐

Step 2 듣고 따라 말하기

		1회	2회	3회
1	You see the man in a striped jacket?	☐	☐	☐
2	You need to drink hot honey tea when you have a cough.	☐	☐	☐
3	I didn't mean to insult you.	☐	☐	☐
4	I have to be with my sister on Mondays.	☐	☐	☐
5	We are planning many great events for you!	☐	☐	☐
6	Why don't we go back down now?	☐	☐	☐
7	Is there anything I can help you with?	☐	☐	☐
8	Can you get me a hot drink?	☐	☐	☐
9	Be extremely careful about food and water.	☐	☐	☐
10	You will have to pay a late fee when you return that book as well.	☐	☐	☐
11	Where do you want me to put it?	☐	☐	☐
12	If you have any questions or problems, let me know.	☐	☐	☐
13	Let's both apply for this one.	☐	☐	☐
14	Some people enjoy collecting these as a hobby.	☐	☐	☐
15	Do you have a minute?	☐	☐	☐
16	I don't want to get wet at the beginning of the day.	☐	☐	☐
17	Choose the amount and the money will come out.	☐	☐	☐
18	My mother gave birth to a very cute daughter.	☐	☐	☐
19	I'd like to borrow these books.	☐	☐	☐
20	Your mother looked sick this morning when you went to school.	☐	☐	☐

영어듣기능력평가 **19**회

만점 듣기 표현

Step 1 우리말 보면서 영어 듣기

		1회	2회	3회
1	단순한 벽시계를 찾고 있는데요.	☐	☐	☐
2	큰 무대의 뮤지컬에서 역할을 맡게 됐어.	☐	☐	☐
3	제 고양이의 문제가 뭔가요?	☐	☐	☐
4	오늘 몰이 많이 붐비지 않았으면 좋겠어요.	☐	☐	☐
5	말할 기분이 아니야.	☐	☐	☐
6	네가 얼마나 많이 연습했는지 보자.	☐	☐	☐
7	이 책들을 반납하고 싶은데요.	☐	☐	☐
8	중고차 딜러에게 연락해보는 거 어때?	☐	☐	☐
9	좋은 지적이네.	☐	☐	☐
10	세 벌 이상의 블라우스를 사시면 장갑 한 켤레를 공짜로 드립니다.	☐	☐	☐
11	네 신발이 너무 큰 것 같다.	☐	☐	☐
12	입장료와 주차는 완전히 무료입니다.	☐	☐	☐
13	제가 추운 날씨를 싫어하기 때문에 따뜻한 곳에서 있고 싶어요.	☐	☐	☐
14	우리는 보통 짧은 시간에 장거리를 여행하기 위해 이것을 사용한다	☐	☐	☐
15	피검사를 위해 3층으로 올라가실래요?	☐	☐	☐
16	이 바지는 재고가 없어요.	☐	☐	☐
17	책을 어떻게 대출하나요?	☐	☐	☐
18	어떻게 생긴 건가요?	☐	☐	☐
19	내일까지 이 책을 끝내야 해.	☐	☐	☐
20	그는 차고로 가서 자동차에 시동을 걸려고 하지만 차가 시동이 걸리지 않는다.	☐	☐	☐

Step 2 듣고 따라 말하기

		1회	2회	3회
1	I'm looking for a simple wall clock.	☐	☐	☐
2	I got a role in a big stage musical.	☐	☐	☐
3	What's the problem with my cat?	☐	☐	☐
4	I hope the mall isn't too busy today.	☐	☐	☐
5	I'm not in the mood to talk.	☐	☐	☐
6	Let's see how much you practiced.	☐	☐	☐
7	I'd like to return these books.	☐	☐	☐
8	Why don't you contact a used car dealer?	☐	☐	☐
9	That's a good point.	☐	☐	☐
10	We give a pair of gloves for free if you buy more than three blouses.	☐	☐	☐
11	I think your shoes are too big.	☐	☐	☐
12	Admission and parking are completely free.	☐	☐	☐
13	I want to stay in a warm place because I hate cold weather.	☐	☐	☐
14	We usually use this to travel a long distance in a short time.	☐	☐	☐
15	Why don't you go up to the third floor for the blood test?	☐	☐	☐
16	These pants are out of stock.	☐	☐	☐
17	How can I check out books?	☐	☐	☐
18	What does it look like?	☐	☐	☐
19	I have to finish this book by tomorrow.	☐	☐	☐
20	He goes to the garage and tries to start his car but it won't start.	☐	☐	☐

Step 1 우리말 보면서 영어 듣기

		1회	2회	3회
1	밤새 눈이 왔어.	☐	☐	☐
2	당신은 예약을 하셔야 할 겁니다.	☐	☐	☐
3	또 문자 메시지를 보내고 있나요?	☐	☐	☐
4	언제 돌아오니?	☐	☐	☐
5	내일 날씨가 어떨지 궁금한데.	☐	☐	☐
6	야구 규칙에 관한 필기시험이 있을 겁니다.	☐	☐	☐
7	어떻게 지냈어?	☐	☐	☐
8	수업이 아직도 열려 있는지 봐야겠다.	☐	☐	☐
9	음식이나 약이 부족해서 고통받는 아이들을 돕고 싶어.	☐	☐	☐
10	신용카드로 지불하고 싶습니다.	☐	☐	☐
11	제가 바보 같은 짓을 했군요!	☐	☐	☐
12	저희 리조트는 전국의 아이들을 위한 최고의 프로그램을 제공합니다.	☐	☐	☐
13	그들이 언제 일을 시작할 수 있죠?	☐	☐	☐
14	그들은 재봉틀 때문에 이것을 좀처럼 사용하지 않는다.	☐	☐	☐
15	문제는 비용이 얼마나 드는가야.	☐	☐	☐
16	여름 방학이 끝나기 2일 전에 이사를 갈 거야.	☐	☐	☐
17	상사가 멋지고 함께 일하는 사람들도 마음에 들어.	☐	☐	☐
18	당신이 떠난다니 믿을 수 없어요.	☐	☐	☐
19	버스를 제대로 타셨어요.	☐	☐	☐
20	선생님은 화가 나서 그것을 찾았다.	☐	☐	☐

Step 2 듣고 따라 말하기

		1회	2회	3회
1	It snowed overnight.	☐	☐	☐
2	I guess you need to make a reservation.	☐	☐	☐
3	Are you sending text messages again?	☐	☐	☐
4	When are you coming back?	☐	☐	☐
5	I wonder what the weather will be like tomorrow.	☐	☐	☐
6	There will be a written test about baseball rules.	☐	☐	☐
7	How have you been?	☐	☐	☐
8	I should check if the class is still open.	☐	☐	☐
9	I want to help children suffering from a lack of food or medicine.	☐	☐	☐
10	I'd like to pay by credit card.	☐	☐	☐
11	What an idiot I am!	☐	☐	☐
12	Our resort offers the best program for kids in the nation.	☐	☐	☐
13	When can they start work?	☐	☐	☐
14	They rarely use this because of sewing machines.	☐	☐	☐
15	The point is how much it will cost.	☐	☐	☐
16	We're moving two days before the summer vacation is over.	☐	☐	☐
17	I have a nice boss and I like the people I work with.	☐	☐	☐
18	I can't believe you're leaving.	☐	☐	☐
19	You got on the right bus.	☐	☐	☐
20	The teacher got angry and searched for it.	☐	☐	☐

Step 1 우리말 보면서 영어 듣기

		1회	2회	3회
1	미술관에서는 어떤 사진도 찍을 수 없습니다.	☐	☐	☐
2	시간 분배를 잘 하도록 계획을 짜야 할 거야.	☐	☐	☐
3	오늘밤은 일찍 자는 게 어때?	☐	☐	☐
4	너와 하이킹 가는 거 기대된다.	☐	☐	☐
5	겨울 스포츠보다 여름 스포츠를 더 좋아해?	☐	☐	☐
6	집안일을 도와주렴.	☐	☐	☐
7	머리를 길게 기르고 있어.	☐	☐	☐
8	모든 사람들이 정말 열심히 연습하고 있어.	☐	☐	☐
9	그곳의 롤러코스터는 내 상상 이상이었다.	☐	☐	☐
10	사이즈는 어떻게 있나요?	☐	☐	☐
11	이런 종류의 전화들을 어떻게 막는지 모르겠어.	☐	☐	☐
12	도시락을 가져오고 밤을 즐길 준비를 하세요!	☐	☐	☐
13	지역 박물관이 아주 좋다고 들었습니다.	☐	☐	☐
14	그 지역은 또한 도시에서 가장 인구 밀도가 높습니다.	☐	☐	☐
15	이 제품을 추천하고 싶네요.	☐	☐	☐
16	그걸 보면서 내 스트레스를 잊을 수 있어.	☐	☐	☐
17	어지럽고 메스꺼워.	☐	☐	☐
18	넌 모든 스포츠를 다 잘하잖아.	☐	☐	☐
19	흥미로운 가게들이랑 멋진 지역 식당들이 많이 있어.	☐	☐	☐
20	그녀가 늦은 밤 음악을 틀었을 수도 있다.	☐	☐	☐

Step 2 듣고 따라 말하기

		1회	2회	3회
1	You're not allowed to take any photos in the gallery.	☐	☐	☐
2	You need to make a good plan to manage your time well.	☐	☐	☐
3	How about going to bed early tonight?	☐	☐	☐
4	I'm looking forward to hiking with you.	☐	☐	☐
5	Do you prefer summer sports to winter sports?	☐	☐	☐
6	Please help me out with some housework.	☐	☐	☐
7	I have kept my hair long.	☐	☐	☐
8	All of the members are practicing really hard.	☐	☐	☐
9	The roller coasters there were beyond my imagination.	☐	☐	☐
10	What sizes do you have?	☐	☐	☐
11	I don't know how to block these kinds of calls.	☐	☐	☐
12	Bring a picnic and get ready to make a night of it!	☐	☐	☐
13	I've heard the local museum is very nice.	☐	☐	☐
14	The area is also the most densely populated in the city.	☐	☐	☐
15	I'd like to recommend this one.	☐	☐	☐
16	I can forget about all my stress while watching them.	☐	☐	☐
17	I feel dizzy and nauseated.	☐	☐	☐
18	You're good at all kinds of sports.	☐	☐	☐
19	There are a lot of interesting shops and great local restaurants.	☐	☐	☐
20	She might have played music late at night.	☐	☐	☐

듣기는
실전이다

중학 3

24회

Plus Book

디딤돌

01

Can I have your name first?	먼저 성함을 알 수 있을까요?
order	주문하다
describe	묘사하다
through the Internet	인터넷을 통해
in detail	상세하게

02

exchange A for B	A를 B로 교환하다
broken	고장이 난
out of	~이 품절된
order	주문하다

03

be going to	~할 예정이다(= will)
for shade	햇빛을 가리기 위해
look good on	~에 어울리다
don't forget to	~ 꼭 ~해라
pack	(짐 등을) 싸다
such a blue sky	그렇게 푸른 하늘

04

Are you free?	시간 있니?
Why don't we ~?	우리 ~하지 않을래? (제안)
including	~을 포함해서
some other time	언젠가 다음에
give a rain check	다음 기회를 주다

05

in class	수업시간에
promise to	~하기로 약속하다
might have+과거분사	~했을지도 모른다(과거에 대한 막연한 추측)
be absent from	~에 빠지다
go around	(독감 등이) 유행하다
be suppose to	~해야 하다

06

seem to	~인 것 같다
favorite	가장 좋아하는 것
bother	귀찮게 하다
autograph	(유명 인사의) 사인
have a picture taken	사진을 찍다

07

What do you think of ~?	~을 어떻게 생각하니?
give a ride	차를 태워 주다
help oneself to	~을 마음껏 먹다
out of	~이 떨어진
go -ing	~하러 가다
recommend	추천하다
How about -ing?	~하는 게 어떠니?(제안)

08

skip breakfast	아침을 건너뛰다
deadline	마감일
pick up	~을 사다

09

ecosystem	생태계
community	공동체
interact with	~와 상호작용하다
environment	환경
be balanced	균형을 유지하는
plant-eating animal	초식동물
destroy	파괴하다
plant population	식물군
by -ing	~함으로써
starve to death	굶어 죽다

10

get a student discount	학생 할인을 받다
apply to	~에 적용되다
pay extra money	별도로 돈을 지불하다

11

upset	화가 난
fix	수리하다
work	작동하다
several	몇몇의
at least	적어도

12	
□ undergo changes	변화를 겪다
□ add	추가하다
□ earn	(돈을) 벌다
□ penalty	벌금
13	
□ exchange A for B	A를 B로 교환하다
□ foreign currency	외국 통화
□ bill	지폐
□ change A into B	A를 B로 바꾸다
14	
□ not A but B	A가 아니라 B인
□ how to speak	말하는 방법
□ after a while	얼마 후에, 잠시 후에
□ repeat after	~을 따라서 말하다
15	
□ practice	연습하다
□ be good at	~에 능숙하다 (↔ be poor at)
16	
□ a few minutes ago	몇 분 전에
□ hurry up	서두르다
□ take	(시간 등이) 걸리다
□ get to	~에 도착하다 (= reach)
□ get started	출발하다 (= start)
□ in thirty minutes	30분 후에
17	
□ dream of	~을 꿈꾸다
□ audition for	~을 위해 오디션을 하다
□ Good for you!	잘됐다!
18	
□ do a favor	부탁을 들어 주다
□ depend on	~에 달려 있다
□ lend	빌려주다 (↔ borrow)
□ take away	빼앗다
□ instead of	~하는 대신에
□ mad	미칠 듯이 화가 난

□ as you know	너도 알다시피
□ all the time	항상 (= always)
□ How come?	어째서? (= Why?)
19	
□ a long time ago	오래 전에
□ think of	~에 대해 생각하다
□ complain	불평하다
□ fairy tale	동화
□ get married to	~와 결혼하다 (= marry)
□ ordinary	평범한
□ change	바꾸다
20	
□ move	이사하다
□ at first	처음에
□ have some trouble with	~와 문제가 있다
□ neighbor	이웃
□ make a noise	소란을 피우다
□ stand	참다
□ knock on	~을 두드리다
□ keep a pet	애완동물을 기르다

영어듣기능력평가 02회

01
☐ carry	들고 있다
☐ a stack of	~ 한 무더기
☐ fountain	분수

02
☐ pet	애완동물
☐ not only A but also B	A 뿐만이 아니라 B도 역시
☐ bathe	목욕시키다
☐ regardless of	~와 상관없이
☐ reasonable	합리적인
☐ make an appointment	예약하다

03
☐ in time	제시간에
☐ pull into	~에 차를 대다
☐ run out of gas	기름이 떨어지다
☐ ride	태워 주기
☐ pick up	데리러 오다[가다]
☐ get held up in traffic	교통에 막히다, 차가 막히다

04
☐ finally	마침내
☐ expect	기대하다
☐ worth	~할 가치가 있는
☐ running time	상영 시간
☐ gambling	도박
☐ choice	선택

05
☐ on time	정각에
☐ be delayed	연착되다
☐ be supposed to	~하기로 되어 있다
☐ terrible	심각한, 끔찍한

06
☐ lose weight	체중이 줄다 (↔ gain weight)
☐ maybe	아마도
☐ graduate	졸업하다
☐ must be	~임에 틀림없다

07
☐ hitchhiker	자동차 편승 여행자
☐ depend	의지하다, 달려 있다
☐ gas station	주유소
☐ stranger	낯선 사람
☐ try ~ on	입어 보다
☐ fitting room	탈의실
☐ by bus	버스로
☐ Long time no see.	오랜만이야.
☐ on foot	걸어서

08
☐ go off	(경보기 등이) 울리다
☐ ask	요청하다
☐ reprint	다시 인쇄하다

09
☐ get angry at	~에 화 나다
☐ make a fool of	~를 놀리다
☐ call one by one's nickname	~를 별명으로 부르다
☐ make fun of	~를 놀리다
☐ appearance	외모

10
☐ make two copies	2부 복사를 하다
☐ document	서류
☐ charge	(비용을) 청구하다
☐ bind	묶다, 제본하다
☐ extra charge	추가 비용
☐ pick up	(물건 등을) 챙기다

11
☐ turn to the right	우측으로 돌다
☐ strange	이상한
☐ too ~ to ...	너무나 ~해서 …할 수 없는
☐ count	세다
☐ Wait a second.	잠깐만요.

□ SUV	레저용 차량 (= sports utility vehicle)	□ totally	완전히
12		□ stress out	스트레스를 받다
□ be aware of	~을 알다	**18**	
□ earthquake	지진	□ text message	문자 메시지
□ in need	어려움에 처한	□ convey	전달하다
□ charity event	자선 행사	□ I bet ~	틀림없이 ~이다
□ organize	(어떤 일을) 준비하다	□ contact	연락하다
□ available	시간 [여유]이 있는	□ be supposed to	~해야 한다
13		□ share	공유하다
□ get to	~에 도착하다	□ talk ~ over the phone	전화 통화를 하다
□ make a left turn	좌회전하다	□ private	개인적인
□ huge	거대한	**19**	
14		□ quiet	조용한
□ lead	연필심	□ scream	고함을 지르다
□ erase	지우다	□ hurt	다치게 하다
□ wear down	닳다	□ scare ~ to death	아주 두렵게 하다
□ regularly	규칙적으로	□ go too far	지나치다
□ keep a diary	일기를 쓰다	□ recognize	알아보다
15		□ voice	목소리
□ enough	충분한	**20**	
□ sweetheart	(부르는 말) 당신, 자기	□ sit up late	늦게까지 자지 않다
□ jet leg	시차에 따른 피로	□ vending machine	자판기
□ keep one's eyes open	눈을 뜨고 있다	□ happen to	우연히 ~하다
□ in the middle of	~의 한가운데	□ bump into	부딪히다
□ get ready	준비하다	□ due	마감시한이 된
16		□ wonder	궁금히 여기다
□ license plate number	차량 번호		
□ Hold on.	잠시만요.		
□ charge	부과하다		
□ every thirty minutes	30분마다		
□ park	주차하다		
17			
□ lately	최근에		
□ quite	꽤		
□ assign	(일 등을) 맡기다[부과하다]		

01
☐ reasonably priced	적정하게 가격이 매겨진
☐ stripes	줄무늬
☐ try on	~을 입어보다

02
☐ trouble	병, 고생
☐ as soon as possible	가능한 한 빨리
☐ pain	통증
☐ opening	빈 자리
☐ around	대략

03
☐ choice	선택
☐ borrow	빌리다
☐ for a minute	잠깐
☐ open an account	(은행에) 계좌를 개설하다

04
☐ get ready for	준비를 갖추다
☐ come up	일어나다, 생기다
☐ make it	(순조롭게) 시간에 대다, 성공하다
☐ pass	지나다
☐ get back	돌아오다
☐ give ~ a call	~에게 전화하다

05
☐ cute	귀여운
☐ puppy	강아지
☐ spot	반점, 얼룩
☐ all over the body	몸 전체에
☐ sit up	똑바로 앉다
☐ lift	들다
☐ front leg	앞다리
☐ wait for	기다리다
☐ bring	가져오다
☐ clever	영리한

06
☐ fight the fire	화재와 맞서다
☐ reach	~에 이르다 (= arrive at)

(06 계속)
☐ put out	진화하다 (= extinguish)
☐ cause	유발시키다
☐ without –ing	~하는 것 없이
☐ forest	숲

07
☐ drop	떨어뜨리다
☐ slight	약간의
☐ fever	열
☐ return	반환하다
☐ book	예약하다
☐ borrow	빌리다

08
☐ Would you do me a favor?	내 부탁 좀 들어 줄래요?
☐ laundry shop	세탁소
☐ owner	주인
☐ leave	남기다 (left –left)
☐ pick up	찾아오다

09
☐ customer	고객
☐ special	특별한
☐ in order to	~하기 위해서
☐ celebrate	경축하다, 기념하다
☐ give out	배포하다, 나누어 주다
☐ free gift	공짜 선물
☐ receipt	영수증
☐ total	총계의
☐ amount	양, 액
☐ add up to	총계가 ~에 이르다

10
☐ ferry	연락선, 여객선
☐ reasonable	적당한
☐ automobile	자동차
☐ charge	(요금값을) 청구하다
☐ for free	무료로
☐ count	계산에 넣다, 포함시키다

11

Where to?	어디로 모실까요?
on business	업무상
be interested in	~에 관심이 있다
traditional	전통적인
keep the change	거스름돈을 가지다

12

welcome	환영하다
be proud of	~을 자랑스러워하다
regular class	정규 수업
attend	참가하다
practice	연습하다
play a musical instrument	악기를 연주하다

13

front door	정문
upstairs	위층으로
lounge	휴게실
face	~을 마주보다[향하다]

14

invent	발명하다
safely	안전하게
cloth	천, 옷감
string	줄, 끈
jump out of	~로부터 뛰어내리다
backpack	등짐
spread out	펴다, 벌리다
catch the air	바람을 안다
slow	속력을 늦추다
ground	땅
so that	~하도록

15

running shoes	운동화
selection	모음
try on	~을 착용해 보다
tight	꽉 끼는
out of stock	재고가 없는

16

cost	~의 비용이 들다
get	(장소)에 도달하다
How long will it take?	얼마나 걸릴까요?

17

get a refund on	~에 대해 환불을 받다
wrap	포장하다

18

happen	일어나다, 발생하다
print	인쇄하다
work	작동하다
press	누르다
as usual	평소처럼
save	저장하다
document	문서
a couple of	두 개의, 몇몇의
memory	[컴퓨터]기억 장치

19

costume party	가장 파티
rent	대여하다
careful	조심하는

20

close	절친한
have a long day	힘든 하루를 보내다
have a hard time -ing	~하는 데 어려움을 겪다
be crowded with	~로 붐비다
step on one's foot	발을 밟다
get off	(차 등에서) 내리다

01

☐ look for	~을 찾다
☐ lost	길 잃은
☐ goods	상품, 물품
☐ section	코너
☐ sleeve	(옷의) 소매
☐ shorts	반바지
☐ stripe	줄무늬
☐ information desk	안내 데스크
☐ main exit	정문 출구

02

☐ expensive	비싼
☐ stay	머물다[묵다]

03

☐ much	(비교급 앞) 훨씬
☐ bother	귀찮게 하다
☐ wait one minute	잠깐 기다리다

04

☐ subway station	지하철 역
☐ spacious	넓은
☐ stationery	문구류

05

☐ with the aid of	~의 도움으로
☐ crutch	목발
☐ cross the street	길을 건너다
☐ in fact	사실 (= as a matter of fact)
☐ I know how it feels.	그 기분이 어떤지 알고 있다.
☐ used to	~하곤 했다
☐ have a leg in a cast	한쪽 다리를 깁스하다
☐ carry	나르다
☐ pass by	옆으로 지나가다

06

☐ That's all for today.	오늘은 여기까지입니다.
☐ chapter	장(章)
☐ through	~의 끝에서 끝까지
☐ prepare for	~을 준비하다

07

☐ arrive	도착하다
☐ pay for	(돈 등을) 치르다

08

☐ come over	(~의 집에) 들르다
☐ cheer	응원하다
☐ snack	간단한 간식

09

☐ be just around the corner	(거리·시간) 바로 다가와 있다
☐ be confident about	~에 대해 자신 있다
☐ both A and B A와 B	둘 다
☐ biology	생물
☐ keep one's fingers crossed	행운을 빌다

10

☐ usual	평상시의, 보통의
☐ plain	(음식이) 담백한, 양념을 치지 않은.

11

☐ mean	뜻하다, 의미하다
☐ grass	풀밭
☐ anyway	어쨌든, 하여튼
☐ totally	완전히, 모조리, 전혀
☐ forget	잊다 (forgot – forgotten)
☐ cafeteria	카페테리아, 매점
☐ bother oneself	~에 대해 걱정하다

12

☐ be sensitive about	~에 대해 민감하다
☐ That's why ~.	그것이 ~하는 이유이다.
☐ go on a diet	다이어트를 하다
☐ don't need to	~할 필요가 없다
☐ at least	적어도
☐ instead of	~ 대신에
☐ keep in shape	몸매를 유지하다
☐ go for	~을 목표로 하다

13

☐ opposite	다른 쪽의[건너편의]
☐ make a right turn	우회전하다

□ grocery store	식료품점	
□ entrance	입구	

14

□ especially	특히
□ develop	개발하다
□ lightweight	가벼운
□ visible	눈에 보이는
□ reduce	감소시키다
□ risk	위험

15

□ package	소포
□ scale	저울
□ express mail	속달 우편
□ rather	꽤, 상당히
□ fill out	(양식을) 작성하다

16

□ Long time no see.	오랜만이다.(= It's been a long time since I saw you last time.)
□ enjoy -ing	~하기를 즐기다
□ quit	그만두다
□ take care of	~를 돌보다(= care for, look after)
□ be planning to	~할 예정이다
□ take a vocational course	직업 교육을 받다
□ do volunteer work	자원봉사활동을 하다

17

□ research	연구[조사]하다
□ delete	삭제하다
□ half an hour	30분
□ be gone	없어지다

18

□ round-necked	목이 둥근
□ medium	중간 크기의
□ be in fashion	유행하다
□ nowadays	요즈음에
□ prefer	더 좋아하다
□ tight	꽉 끼는

19

□ How do you like ~?	~이 마음에 드니?
□ title	제목
□ as long as	~하는 한

20

□ no wonder	~은 당연하다
□ work part-time at	~에서 아르바이트를 하다
□ convenience store	편의점
□ too ~ to ...	...하기에 너무 ~한
□ advise	충고하다
□ quit	그만두다
□ situation	상황

01	
☐ restroom	화장실
☐ rectangular	직사각형의
☐ in detail	상세하게
☐ attach	붙이다
☐ luggage tag	수하물 꼬리표, 짐표
02	
☐ do ~ a favor	부탁을 들어주다
☐ proofread	교정하다
☐ composition	작문
03	
☐ look well	건강해 보이다
☐ have a headache	두통이 있다
☐ recommend	추천하다
04	
☐ leave	떠나다
☐ via	~를 경유하여
☐ nonstop flight	직항편
☐ catch	~를 타다
☐ have one hour left	한 시간이 남다
☐ get to	~에 도착하다
05	
☐ guess	추측하다
☐ occasion	경사스러운 일
06	
☐ package	소포
☐ signature	서명
☐ sign	서명하다
☐ in a hurry	서두르는
07	
☐ turn off	끄다 (↔ turn on)
☐ give ~ a ride	태워주다
☐ on one's way	도중에
☐ on foot	걸어서
08	
☐ mow the lawn	잔디를 깎다

☐ have fun	재미있게 놀다
☐ turn on	(전기 · 수도 등을) 켜다
☐ water	(화초 등에) 물을 주다
09	
☐ grow up	성장하다
☐ It's been so long!	정말 오랜만이다!
10	
☐ work out	운동하다
☐ gym	체육관
☐ absorb	흡수하다
☐ sweat	땀
☐ on sale	할인 판매 중인
☐ discount	할인
☐ lucky	운 좋은
11	
☐ develop	(필름을) 현상하다
☐ take about a week	약 1주일이 걸리다
☐ coupon	교환권
☐ for free	공짜로 (= for nothing)
☐ a good deal	양호한 거래
☐ upload	전송하다
☐ directly	직접적으로
12	
☐ come to school	등교하다
☐ heart attack	심장발작
☐ I'm sorry to hear that.	그것 참 안됐구나.
☐ Not yet.	아직은 아니에요.
13	
☐ take the train	기차를 타다
☐ miss	놓치다
☐ later than	~보다 늦게
☐ schedule	~을 예정하다
☐ delay	지연
14	
☐ at the same time	동시에
☐ bored	지루한

□ cell	세포		**20**		
□ tend to	~하는 경향이 있다		□ company	회사	
□ next to	~ 옆에		□ in order to	~하기 위해서	
□ repeatedly	반복해서		□ take notes	필기하다	
15			□ forget to	~할 것을 잊다	
□ out of order	고장 난		□ co-worker	직장 동료	
□ customer service	고객서비스 센터		□ extra	여분의	
□ repairman	수리공		□ upper	위의	
□ in the meantime	그 동안에		□ borrow	빌리다	
□ send a package	소포를 보내다				
□ within twenty minutes	20분 이내에				
□ take care of the problem	그 문제를 처리하다				
16					
□ fine dust	미세 먼지				
□ run out of	~을 다 써버리다				
□ drug store	약국				
□ place an order	주문하다				
17					
□ field trip	현장 학습				
□ temple	절				
□ crowded with	~로 복잡한[붐비는]				
□ join	함께 하다[합류하다]				
18					
□ have no close friends	친한 친구들이 없다				
□ can't help -ing	~하지 않을 수 없다				
□ questions about school life	학교생활에 관한 질문들				
□ feel better	기분이 나아지다				
19					
□ meal	식사, 한 끼 식사				
□ in total	모두 합해서				
□ Do you mind if ~?	~하면 꺼려하시겠습니까?				
□ pay by check	수표로 지불하다				
□ used to	~하곤 했다				
□ accept	받아들이다, 수납하다				
□ policy	방침				
□ by credit card	신용 카드로				

01

□ charm	작은 장식물[품]
□ may	~일 수도 있다, ~일지도 모른다
□ be tired of ~	~에 싫증 나다
□ jewel	보석
□ fall out	빠져[떨어져] 나가다
□ choice	선택(권)

02

□ if	~인지 아닌지
□ bring	가져오다
□ instrument	악기
□ almost	하마터면
□ own	자신의

03

□ close	가까운
□ parking lot	주차장
□ fasten	묶다
□ whenever	~할 때마다
□ strange	이상한
□ flat tire	펑크 난 타이어
□ garage	자동차 정비 공장
□ still	아직도, 여전히
□ slight	약간의
□ fever	열

04

□ get a sunburn	햇볕에 타다
□ aquarium	수족관

05

□ during	~ 동안에
□ holiday	휴가, 휴일
□ beach	해변
□ all day long	하루 종일
□ plan	계획하다
□ forest	숲
□ breathe in	숨을 들이쉬다
□ museum	박물관

06

□ fill up	(차에) 기름을 가득 채우다
□ take a look	~을 보다
□ a little low on	~이 약간 부족하다
□ put in	넣다
□ for free	공짜로
□ intersection	교차로

07

□ bright	밝은
□ meat	고기
□ go bad	상하다
□ owe	빚지고 있다
□ delivery	배달
□ charge	요금
□ refund	환불

08

□ go well	잘 되어가다
□ admire	존경하다
□ devote	(노력 · 시간 · 돈을) 바치다, 쏟다
□ pottery	도자기
□ effort	수고, 노력

09

□ national park	국립공원
□ have a great time	즐겁게 지내다

10

□ leather	가죽
□ take	사다, 받다
□ pay in cash	현금으로 지불하다
□ get off	~을 할인 받다

11

□ air conditioner	냉방기, 에어컨
□ open	비어 있는
□ latest	최신의
□ microphone	마이크
□ stylish	현대식의, 유행의
□ take A for B	A를 B로 잘못 알다

turn on	켜다	vomit	토하다
brand-new	신형의	**16**	
broken	망가진	make up one's mind	결정하다 (= decide)
ask for	부탁하다, 요구하다	after-school activity	방과 후 활동
12		choice	선택
student council	학생회	as for me	나에 대해 말하자면
hold	개최하다	indoor sports	실내 운동
graduate	졸업생	table tennis	탁구
future	미래	be into	~에 열중하다
valuable	유용한	**17**	
information	정보	happen	(사건 따위가 우연히) 일어나다
prepare for	~을 준비하다	late for	~에 늦은
auditorium	강당	realize	깨닫다, 알아차리다
13		wear	입다
lower	맨 아래	**18**	
row	줄, 열	department store	백화점
burn	태우다, 햇볕에 타다	appointment	약속
give up	포기하다	upstairs	2층에[으로]
don't have to	~할 필요 없다 (= need not)	on sale	할인 판매 중인
sunburn	화상	surprise	놀라게 하다
14		miss	놓치다
be supposed to	~하기로 되어 있다, ~해야 한다	chance	기회
be allowed to	~하도록 허락되다	**19**	
make a noise	소란피우다	near here	이 근처에
usually	대개, 보통	serve	(음식을) 차려내다
grade	점수	free	한가한, 선약 없는
do one's best	최선을 다하다	treat	대접하다, 한턱 내다
solve	문제를 풀다	**20**	
necessary	필요한	address	주소
15		delivery	배달
stomachache	복통	find out	알아내다
do good	효과가 있다		
rare	(고기 등을) 살짝 익힌		
suffer from	~로 고생하다		
food poisoning	식중독		
clinic	진료소		

01

☐ take a yoga class	요가 수업을 받다
☐ A as well as B	B뿐만 아니라 A도 역시
☐ position	자세
☐ give it a try	한번 해 보다
☐ breathe in	숨을 들이 마시다
☐ deeply	깊게

02

☐ check out	(책을) 대출하다
☐ according to	~에 따르면
☐ return	반납하다
☐ I beg your pardon.	죄송합니다.
☐ pay a late charge	연체료를 내다

03

☐ order	주문하다
☐ recipe	조리법
☐ had better	~하는 편이 좋다
☐ see a doctor	의사의 진찰을 받다

04

☐ last	지난
☐ terribly	몹시, 굉장히
☐ What's the matter with you?	무슨 일인데?
☐ That's all right.	괜찮아.

05

☐ end up -ing	~하는 것으로 끝나다
☐ van	승합차
☐ suggest	제안하다
☐ as soon as possible	가능하면 빨리
☐ What for?	왜? (= Why?)
☐ overflow	넘쳐흐르다
☐ bank	둑
☐ valley	계곡
☐ get going	떠나다
☐ warn	경고하다
☐ experience	경험
☐ steep hill	가파른 언덕

06

☐ seafood	해산물
☐ You can say that again!	(동의) 맞아! (= I agree with you.)
☐ I can't believe it!	믿을 수가 없어!

07

☐ final exam	기말시험
☐ nervous	신경이 쓰이는
☐ shelf	선반
☐ bookcase	책장
☐ adventure movie	모험 영화
☐ laptop computer	휴대용 컴퓨터
☐ fix	수리하다

08

☐ order sheet	주문서
☐ come with	(상품 등이) ~한 상태로 나오다
☐ drumstick	(닭 · 오리 등의) 다리
☐ to-go box	포장용 상자

09

☐ speech contest	웅변 대회
☐ confidence	자신감
☐ pronunciation	발음
☐ clear	분명한
☐ improve	개선하다, 향상시키다

10

☐ bedtime	잠잘 시간, 취침 전의
☐ recommend	추천하다
☐ understand	이해하다
☐ bill	지폐
☐ change	거스름돈

11

☐ look for	~을 찾다
☐ brochure	브로슈어, 홍보용 책자
☐ cultural	문화의
☐ in particular	특별히
☐ wonder	궁금하다
☐ traditional	전통의

□ performance	공연	□ e-pal	이메일 친구 (= an electronic pal)
□ information	정보	□ improve	개선하다
12		□ skill	기술
□ host	(프로그램의) 진행자	**19**	
□ space travel	우주여행	□ magazine	잡지
□ guest speaker	초청 강사	□ give it a try	한번 해 보다
□ expert	전문가	□ take place	발생하다 (= happen)
13		□ be in existence	존재하다
□ put off	연기하다 (= postpone)	□ break up	해체하다
□ until	~때까지	□ so far	지금까지
□ change one's reservation	예약을 변경하다	□ be interested in	~에 관심이 있다
□ one way	편도권(↔ round trip)	**20**	
14		□ be on one's way home	귀가 길에 있다
□ fair	축제, 행사	□ clothing store	옷가게
□ set up	설치하다	□ look good on	~에게 어울리다 (= suit)
□ provide	제공하다	□ favorite	가장 좋아하는
□ encourage	권장하다	□ public phone booth	공중전화 박스
□ attend	참석하다	□ decide	결심하다
15		□ enter	들어가다
□ starve	굶주리다		
□ look like	~처럼 보이다		
□ enough	충분한		
□ This is on me.	이것은 내가 낼게.		
□ treat	대접		
16			
□ popular	인기 있는		
□ try	(음식 등을) 맛보다		
□ noodle	국수		
□ be made of	~으로 만들어지다		
□ vegetable	채소		
□ dried seaweed	김		
17			
□ be worth -ing	할 가치가 있다		
□ book review	서평		
18			
□ write	쓰다 (wrote – written)		

01	
□ envy	부러워하다
□ physically	신체적으로
□ fit	튼튼한
□ dream of	꿈꾸다
□ stand on one's hands	물구나무 서다
□ for a second	잠시 동안
□ hold	잡다

02	
□ be ready for	~할 준비가 되다
□ book	예약하다
□ feed	밥을 먹이다
□ stop by	(~에) 잠시 들르다
□ empty	비우다
□ litter box	애완 동물 변기

03	
□ be afraid	두려워하다
□ keep on -ing	계속하여 ~하다
□ let it go	~을 놓다
□ wrap up	포장하다
□ Hold on a second.	잠시만 기다리세요.
□ by bike	자전거로

04	
□ Nothing special.	특별한 계획 없어요.
□ tennis lesson	테니스 수업
□ anytime	언제든지

05	
□ I'd like to, but I just can't.	그러고 싶지만 할 수가 없어.
□ promise	약속하다
□ co-worker	직장 동료
□ reschedule	일정을 재조정하다
□ disappoint	실망하다

06	
□ defense	수비
□ bent	굽힌
□ keep one's balance	몸의 균형을 유지하다

□ shoulder-width	어깨 넓이 폭의
□ apart	떨어진, 벌린
□ keep ~ in mind	~을 염두에 두다

07	
□ have the wrong number	전화를 잘못 걸다
□ leave a message	메시지를 남기다
□ by bicycle	자전거를 타고
□ His line is busy.	그는 통화 중이다.
□ do	충분하다 (= be enough)
□ Are you ready to order?	주문하시겠어요?

08	
□ turn in	제출하다
□ due	제출기일이 된
□ letter of recommendation	추천서
□ do ~ a favor	~의 부탁을 들어주다
□ mail	우편으로 보내다

09	
□ rider	탑승객
□ safety bar	안전 막대
□ ride	탑승
□ come to a complete stop	완전히 멈추다
□ Here you go!	출발합니다!

10	
□ exhibition	전시회
□ admission	입장
□ be sold out	매진되다
□ difference	(수·양의) 차, 차액

11	
□ complain	불평하다
□ dry-clean	드라이클리닝 하다
□ compensate for	~에 대한 보상을 하다
□ for free	무료로

12	
□ announce	알리다
□ demonstrate	보여주다
□ register	등록하다

□ one-on-one	1대 1로		**18**	
□ participant	참가자		□ finally	마침내
□ demonstration	설명		□ terrific	아주 좋은
13			□ constantly	계속해서
□ be located	위치해 있다		□ terrible	끔찍한
□ harmful	유해한		□ housewarming party	집들이
□ chemicals	화학 약품		□ not ~ until ...	… 하고 나서야 비로소 ～하다
14			**19**	
□ right	권리		□ turn in	제출하다
□ shelter	(학대 받는 동물들의) 보호소		□ take a look at	～을 살펴보다
□ abandoned	버려진, 유기된		□ part	부분
□ abused	학대 받은		□ mistake	실수
□ adopt	입양하다		□ correct	수정하다
□ journal	신문[잡지]		□ copy	사본, 복사본
□ experiment	실험		□ do one's best	최선을 다하다
15			□ manage	가까스로 ～하다
□ make a decision	결정하다		**20**	
□ at least	적어도		□ a native English teacher	원어민 영어교사
□ feel like -ing	～하고 싶은 기분이다		□ have a lot in common	공통점이 많다
□ trap	가두다		□ see eye to eye on	～에 대해 의견이 완전히 일치하다
□ cell	감옥		□ opportunity	기회
□ empty	텅 빈		□ agree	합의하다
□ spread	펼치다		□ at least	적어도
□ too ~ to ...	너무나 ～해서 …할 수 없는		□ culture	문화
□ drink	음료수			
16				
□ You know what?	있잖아.			
□ opportunity	기회			
□ prize-winning	상금을 타는			
□ earn	(돈 등을) 벌다			
□ correct	옳은			
17				
□ close down	폐점하다			
□ go out of business	폐업하다			
□ lineup	(사람의) 줄			

01
□ frame	액자
□ moon	달
□ corner	구석
□ a lot of	많은 ~
□ actually	사실은, 실제로
□ I'll take it.	그걸로 살게요, 그걸로 하죠.

02
□ customer service	고객서비스센터
□ subscribe to	~를 구독신청하다
□ discount	깎아주다

03
□ give me a ride	나를 태워주다
□ then	그러면
□ parking lot	주차장
□ park	주차하다
□ speed	속도위반을 하다

04
□ sore	아픈[따가운]
□ have a toothache	이가 아프다
□ dental clinic	치과
□ meet up	~와 만나다
□ arrange	조정하다
□ get permission	허가를 얻다

05
□ invite	초대하다
□ mean	의미하다
□ fault	잘못
□ kind of	약간 (= sort of)
□ upset	당황한
□ don't have to	~할 필요가 없다 (= need not)

06
□ stain	얼룩
□ order	주문하다
□ arrive	도착하다
□ would rather	차라리 ~하는 편이 낫다

□ get one's money back	돈을 돌려받다

07
□ developer	개발자
□ ride my bike	내 자전거를 타다

08
□ assignment	과제
□ topic	주제
□ research	조사하다
□ material	자료
□ visual aids	시각 자료
□ presentation	발표
□ practice	연습하다

09
□ travel	여행하다
□ prepare	준비하다
□ pass by	지나치다
□ history	역사
□ language	언어
□ culture	문화
□ historical	역사적인
□ enjoyable	즐거운
□ trip	여행

10
□ cost	~의 비용이 들다
□ copy	복사하다
□ be ready	준비되다
□ pick up	가지고 가다

11
□ shipping	해운업, 선박회사
□ trading	무역(회사)
□ Can I speak to ~?	~와 통화할 수 있을까요?
□ Would you like to leave a message?	메시지를 남기시겠어요?
□ company	회사
□ as soon as	~하자마자
□ get back	돌아오다
□ call back	다시 전화 걸다

12	
□ welcome	환영하다
□ host	사회자
□ talented	재주 있는
□ be born	태어나다
□ move	이사하다
□ take	(수업을) 받다
□ world-famous	세계적으로 유명한
□ entertainer	예능인
□ popular	인기 있는
13	
□ get off	내리다
□ campground	야영지
□ pass by	지나치다
14	
□ entire	전체의, 온
□ available	이용할 수 있는
□ check out	~을 확인하다
15	
□ cover	뒤덮다
□ ocean	바다, 대양
□ near	근처에
□ the western coast	서해안
□ pollution problem	오염 문제
□ run out of	~이 고갈되다
□ garbage	쓰레기
□ absolutely	절대적으로
□ way	방안
□ environmental problem	환경 문제
16	
□ grow up	자라다, 성장하다
□ stay	머물다
□ for a while	잠시 동안
□ medicine	의학
□ grow	재배하다
□ starve	굶주리다

□ mostly	주로, 대개는
□ sick	아픈
17	
□ get back to one's homework	다시 숙제하다
□ from now on	지금부터 계속
□ be done	끝내다
□ service center	수리점
□ ready	준비가 된
18	
□ order	주문하다
□ Will that be all?	전부인가요?
□ owe	(금액을) 내야 하다
□ come to	(가격이) ~가 되다
□ expensive	비싼(↔ cheap)
19	
□ (Be) Quick!	빨리!
□ get in	~에 타다
□ run red lights	빨간 신호를 무시하고 달리다
□ warm up the engine	엔진을 예열하다
□ until	~까지
□ in the future	앞으로, 장래에
20	
□ be all over	모두 끝나다
□ cancel	취소하다
□ instead	그 대신
□ put off	미루다
□ be supposed to	~해야 하다

01

□ air purifier	공기 청정기
□ brand-new	아주 새로운, 신품의
□ electronic fan	선풍기

02

□ Who's speaking?	누구세요?
□ save	저장하다
□ thumbnail image	견본 이미지
□ select	선택하다
□ destination	목적지, 보낼 곳
□ follow	따라가다, 이해하다
□ helpful	도움이 되는

03

□ exchange	교환하다
□ familiar with	~에 친숙한, 익숙한

04

□ make an appointment	예약하다
□ on short notice	갑자기, 충분한 예고없이
□ business trip	출장
□ squeeze	밀어[집어]넣다

05

□ have a fight with~	~와 싸우다
□ selfish	이기적인
□ get over	극복하다(= overcome)
□ apologize	사과하다

06

□ square	정사각형
□ Nothing special.	특별한 것이 없다.
□ frightened	겁에 질린
□ leave in a hurry	급하게 떠나다
□ toward	~ 쪽으로
□ drive away	차로 가버리다
□ at top speed	전속력으로

07

□ Do you have the time?	몇 시니?
□ Have a seat.	앉아.

□ unfair	부당한
□ let	허락하다
□ be unhealthy for	~의 건강에 좋지 않다
□ rot	썩다
□ That's a good point.	좋은 지적이다.

08

□ make dinner	저녁식사를 준비하다
□ check the receipt	영수증을 확인하다

09

□ purser	객실 사무장
□ on behalf of	~을 대신하여
□ captain	기장, 선장
□ entire	전체의
□ crew	승무원
□ Welcome aboard.	저희 비행기에 승선하신 것을 환영합니다.
□ flight time	비행 시간
□ be at one's service	~을 서비스하다
□ honor	영광, 자랑
□ pleasant	유쾌한

10

□ a bit	약간
□ pricey	비싼
□ brand-new	신상품의
□ reasonable	합리적인
□ scratch	긁힌 자국
□ for half price	절반 가격에

11

□ transfer to	~로 갈아타다
□ violet	보라색
□ subway map	지하철 노선도
□ fare	교통비
□ change	거스름돈

12

□ routine	일상
□ different from	~와 다른
□ dust	먼지를 털다[닦다]

13	
☐ common	흔한
☐ capacity	용량
☐ follow one's decision	결정에 따르다

14	
☐ even though	비록 ∼이지만
☐ remember	기억하다 (↔ forget)
☐ all the time	항상 (= always)
☐ while	∼하는 동안에
☐ usually	대개
☐ active	활동적인
☐ unusual	평범하지 않은 (↔ usual)
☐ fear	두려움
☐ sadness	슬픔
☐ tear	눈물

15	
☐ technology	기술
☐ be interested in	∼에 관심이 있다
☐ make a plan	계획을 세우다
☐ besides	게다가 (cf. beside ∼옆에)
☐ look on the bright side	긍정적인 면을 보다
☐ sight	풍경
☐ go -ing	∼하러 가다

16	
☐ be off to	∼로 향하다
☐ weather forecast	일기예보
☐ get stronger and stronger	점점 더 세지다
☐ promise	약속하다

17	
☐ get sleep	수면을 취하다
☐ play music	음악을 틀다
☐ cause trouble	문제를 일으키다

18	
☐ bored	지루한
☐ finish	∼하기를 마치다
☐ explain	설명하다 (n. explanation)

19	
☐ be planning to	∼할 계획이다(= be going to / will)
☐ relative	친척
☐ stay	∼에 머물다
☐ take it so hard	너무 심각하게 생각하다

20	
☐ drawing book	스케치북
☐ put A in B	A를 B에 넣다
☐ wallet	지갑
☐ start for	∼로 출발하다
☐ get on	∼을 타다
☐ as usual	평상시대로
☐ leave A on B	A를 B 위에 두다

01
□ look around	둘러보다
□ instead of	~대신에
□ tight-fitting	몸에 딱 붙는
□ expose	드러내다
□ comfortable	편안한
□ have a look	보다

02
□ reservation	예약
□ make it	도착하다, 성공하다
□ party	일행
□ reschedule	일정을 재조정하다
□ Is it okay with you?	괜찮으세요?

03
□ shelf	선반
□ check out	대출하다
□ nearby	근처에
□ right away	즉시

04
□ take	듣다[수강하다]
□ advanced class	상급반
□ intermediate class	중급반
□ beginner class	초급반

05
□ aisle	통로, 복도
□ groom	신랑
□ law firm	법률 회사
□ guest	손님
□ celebrate	축하하다
□ relative	친척

06
□ happen to	~에 일이 생기다
□ or something	~ 같은 것
□ used to	~하곤 했다
□ repair shop	수리점

07
□ declare	신고하다
□ wonder	궁금해 하다
□ do ~ a favor	~의 부탁을 들어주다
□ fitting room	탈의실
□ pleasure	즐거움, 기쁨

08
□ melt	녹다[녹이다]
□ complain	불평[항의]하다
□ fault	잘못, 책임
□ responsible for	~에 책임이 있는
□ get a refund	환불받다
□ consumer rights group	소비자 보호 단체

09
□ surgery	외과수술
□ recover	회복하다
□ presume	추측하다

10
□ be good at	~을 잘하다 (↔ be poor at)
□ nine to five	9시 출근 5시 퇴근
□ per	~마다, ~당
□ payday	지불일

11
□ pass away	돌아가시다
□ healthy	건강한
□ in peace	평안히
□ mourner	조문객, 문상객
□ greet	맞이하다

12
□ hurricane	태풍, 허리케인
□ get ~ ready ~	을 갖추다, 준비시키다
□ canned food	통조림 식량
□ in case	~의 경우에 대비해서
□ electricity	전기
□ match	성냥
□ keep ~ informed about	~에게 …에 대해 알리다

12

□ celebrate	기념하다, 축하하다
□ anniversary	기념일
□ foundation	설립, 창립
□ run	운영[제공]하다
□ alumni	졸업생들
□ free of charge	무료로

13

□ drawer	서랍
□ a pile of	한 더미

14

□ by -ing	～함으로써
□ take off	벗기다
□ tip	끝부분
□ turn on	(전원 등을) 켜다 (↔ turn off)
□ sensor	감지기
□ keep still	가만히 있다
□ maximum	최고의
□ temperature	온도
□ record	기록하다

15

□ a couple of	두어 개의
□ traditional	전통적인
□ carry	취급하다, 팔다
□ doll	인형
□ pottery	도자기
□ bowl	그릇
□ plate	접시
□ tourist information center	관광정보센터

16

□ connecting flight	연결 비행기
□ return	돌아오다

17

□ both	양쪽, 두 사람 다
□ get married to	～와 결혼하다

18

□ bother	괴롭히다
□ leave alone	혼자 두다
□ take part in	～에 참가하다
□ nervous	긴장한
□ whenever	～할 때마다
□ be on stage	무대에 서다
□ advice	충고, 조언

19

□ electronic dictionary	전자사전
□ have ~ in mind	～을 염두에 두다
□ contain	포함하다
□ language	언어
□ pay for	～에 대한 대금을 지불하다
□ pay attention to	～에 주의를 집중하다

20

□ book	예약하다 (= reserve)
□ miss	놓치다
□ however	그러나
□ run every hour	매 시간마다 운행하다
□ in time	제 시간에 (cf. on time 정각에)

01
□ passenger	탑승객
□ announcement	안내방송
□ eagerly	간절하게, 애타게
□ short-sleeved	짧은 소매의
□ gate	문, 탑승구
□ plane	비행기

02
□ hold	중단하다
□ delivery	배달
□ during	~ 동안
□ period	기간

03
□ move over	옮기다
□ almost	하마터면
□ get off	내리다

04
□ field trip	현장 학습
□ shortly	곧
□ forget to	(~할 것을) 잊다
□ put out	

05
□ deserve	~의 자격이 있다
□ award	상
□ encourage	격려하다
□ blank	텅 빈
□ express	표현하다
□ honored	명예로운

06
□ around midnight	자정 쯤
□ pass by	~를 지나가다
□ scream	소리 지르다
□ run away	도망치다
□ wallet	지갑

07
□ down	우울한
□ wear a helmet	헬멧을 쓰다
□ most of the time	대부분의 시간

08
□ remember	기억하다
□ client	고객, 의뢰인
□ That's fine with me.	(동의) 좋아.
□ store	저장하다

09
□ properly	적절히
□ addicted	중독된
□ get exercise	운동하다

10
□ adult	성인
□ senior discount	경로 우대 할인
□ get ~ off	~를 할인하다
□ credit card	신용카드
□ Here you go.	여기 있습니다.(= Here you are.)

11
□ moving	이사
□ furniture	가구
□ search	찾다

12
□ gymnasium	체육관 (= gym)
□ take lessons	수업을 받다
□ enter	가입하다
□ entrance fee	가입비
□ include	포함하다
□ provide	제공하다

13
□ recommend	추천하다
□ picture book	그림책

14
□ these days	요즘
□ as you well know	당신도 잘 알듯이
□ normal	보통의, 정상의
□ surf the Internet	인터넷 검색을 하다

□ no matter	~에 관계 없이	□ sprain	삐다
□ for free	무료로	□ rest	쉬게 하다
□ drawback	단점, 결점	□ fault	잘못, 실수
□ lack of exercise	운동 부족, 운동 결핍	□ ache	쑤시다
15		**20**	
□ need to	~할 필요가 있다, ~해야 한다	□ for a long time	오랫동안
□ have no idea	모른다	□ save	저축하다
□ sales report	판매 보고서	□ salesperson	점원
□ leave	놓아두다	□ out of price range	가격 범위를 벗어난
□ hand ~ over	~를 전해주다	□ afford	~할 여유가 있다
16			
□ ankle	발목		
□ sprain	삐다		
□ physically	신체적으로		
□ fit	적합한, 건강한		
□ basic	기초		
□ act	행동하다		
□ as if	마치 ~처럼		
17			
□ aisle seat	통로 쪽 좌석		
□ boarding pass	탑승권		
□ departure gate	출발 탑승구		
18			
□ happen to	~에게 생기다		
□ stay	머무르다		
□ yet	아직		
□ do with	처리하다		
□ furniture	가구		
□ except	~을 제외하고		
□ wrap up	포장하다		
□ offer	제의, 제안		
19			
□ ankle	발목		
□ reduce	가라앉히다		
□ swelling	부풀어 오름		
□ painkiller	진통제		

01	
□ look for	~를 찾다
□ have ~ in mind	~를 마음에 두고 있다
□ flower pattern	꽃 무늬
□ popular	인기 있는
□ not as A as B	B만큼 A하지 않은
□ check	체크 (무늬)
□ trimmed lace	장식 레이스가 있는
□ showy	화려한, 야한

02	
□ beep	삐 소리
□ leave	남기다
□ in trouble	곤경에 빠진
□ take photos	사진을 찍다
□ drop	떨어뜨리다

03	
□ draw	그림을 그리다
□ walk	산책시키다
□ let's not ~	~하지 말자
□ puppy	강아지
□ present	선물

04	
□ exam	시험
□ be supposed to	~하기로 되어 있다

05	
□ volunteer	자원봉사자
□ duties	업무
□ support	지원하다
□ application	신청서
□ opportunity	기회

06	
□ invite	
□ housewarming	집들이
□ show ~ around	~에게 구경시켜 주다
□ spacious	넓은
□ view	전망

□ envy	부러워하다

07	
□ long face	안색이 안 좋은, 우울해 보이는
□ essay contest	논술 대회
□ job offer	일자리 제의
□ couldn't be better	더 나을 수 없다, 최고다
□ biology	생물학
□ semester	학기

08	
□ pick up	~를 태우러 가다
□ digit	숫자

09	
□ guess	추측하다
□ come true	실현되다
□ worry	걱정하다
□ pass	합격하다
□ cross one's fingers for	~에게 행운을 빌다

10	
□ bestselling	가장 많이 팔리는
□ go with	어울리다
□ reasonable	합리적인

11	
□ ultimate	최후의
□ challenge	도전
□ magazine	잡지
□ deal with	다루다, 관계하다
□ mountain climbing	산악 등반
□ visit	방문
□ twice	두 번
□ cooperation	협력, 협조

12	
□ bonding	유대(감)
□ provide	제공하다
□ transportation	차편

13	
□ appliance	가전제품

curfew	통금 시간	help ~ out	~을 도와주다
strict	엄격한	**19**	
14		stay up late	늦게까지 자지 않고 있다
forms of life	생명체	sleepy	졸린
be made up of	~로 구성되어 있다	must be	틀림없이 ~이다
therefore	그러므로	get some sleep	잠을 좀 자다
totally	완전히, 모조리	**20**	
fill	채우다	run a company	회사를 경영하다
container	그릇, 용기	secretary	비서
square	사각형	take the call	전화를 받다
flat	편평한	return	돌아오다
state	상태	call back	다시 ~에게 전화하다
steam	증기, 수증기	be on another line	다른 전화를 받고 있다
15		hold on	(전화를) 끊지 않고 기다리다
make copies	복사하다		
ID card	신분증 (= Identification card)		
document	문서, 서류		
put on	~위에 놓다		
16			
cut down	줄이다		
completely	완전히		
effect	영향		
cardiovascular	심혈관의		
disease	질병		
avoid	피하다		
reduce	줄이다		
17			
make a reservation	예약하다		
fancy	고급의; 화려한		
exchange	환전하다		
credit card	신용 카드		
18			
move in	이사해 오다		
quiet	조용한		
calm	고요한, 조용한, 평온한		
atmosphere	대기, 공기, 분위기		

01
□ workout	운동
□ basic	기본의
□ position	자세
□ bend	구부리다
□ raise	올리다
□ fist	주먹
□ punch	때리다
□ lean	숙이다
□ forward	앞으로
□ immediately	즉시 (= at once)
□ repeat	반복하다
□ at a time	한 번에

02
□ a bunch of	한 무리의
□ just in case	만일을 대비해서

03
□ handicapped	장애가 있는
□ for example	예를 들어
□ try on	(옷 등을) 입어 보다
□ Go ahead.	어서하세요.

04
□ perform	공연하다
□ memorize	암기하다
□ confident	자신감 있는

05
□ taste	~을 맛보다
□ so far	지금까지
□ No kidding!	설마!
□ remote	외딴
□ organic vegetable	유기농 채소

06
□ experience	경험
□ tour guide	여행 안내원
□ work for	~에 근무하다
□ travel company	여행 회사

□ be familiar with ~	~을 잘 알고 있다, ~에 익숙하다

07
□ Nothing much to do.	할 일이 많지 않다.
□ I've had enough.	배불리 먹었다.
□ carry	(물건 등을) 취급하다
□ go with	~와 어울리다
□ be on sale	할인 판매 중인

08
□ overheat	과열되다
□ be in heavy traffic	교통체증에 걸려 있다
□ mechanic	정비사, 수리공
□ cool down	식다, 냉각되다
□ on one's way to	~로 가는 길인
□ repair shop	정비소
□ do ~ a favor	~의 부탁을 들어주다
□ look after	돌보다

09
□ chemistry	화학
□ regarding	~에 관하여[대하여]
□ attach	첨부하다
□ figure out	알아내다

10
□ tableware	식기
□ particular	특정한

11
□ watch one's step	발을 조심하다
□ steep and narrow	가파르고 좁은
□ hidden	숨겨진
□ palace	궁전
□ century	세기
□ including	~를 포함하여
□ take pictures	사진을 찍다
□ be allowed to	~하는 게 허락되다
□ sign	표시, 안내판
□ furniture	가구

12	
□ rent	빌리다
□ by oneself	혼자서
□ break down	고장 나다
□ location	위치
□ current	현재의
□ latitude	위도
□ longitude	경도

13	
□ several	다양한
□ product	상품, 제품

14	
□ be concerned about	~을 걱정하다
□ climate change	기후 변화
□ be in danger	위기에 처하다
□ movement	이동
□ researcher	연구자
□ track	추적하다
□ deal with	대처하다
□ Arctic	북극

15	
□ Mother's Day	어머니날
□ fancy	고급의, 일류의

16	
□ be wet to the skin	흠뻑 젖다
□ rainstorm	폭풍우
□ thunder	천둥
□ rain cats and dogs	비가 억수로 내리다
□ otherwise	그렇지 않으면
□ catch a cold	감기에 걸리다
□ get sick	병에 걸리다
□ be just around the corner	(거리 · 시간적으로) 바로 임박하다
□ normal	정상

17	
□ cast	깁스
□ sprain	삐다

□ ankle	발목
□ What a shame.	안 됐구나.
□ go on a trip	여행을 가다
□ for a while	당분간
□ be supposed to	~하기로 되어 있다
□ get the cast off	깁스를 풀다

18	
□ exercise	운동하다 (= work up)
□ a lot	많이 (= much)
□ make time	시간을 만들다
□ be good for	~에 유익하다
□ force oneself	강요하다

19	
□ a little down	좀 우울한, 약간 의기소침한
□ practice	연습하다
□ stressed out	스트레스를 받는
□ take ~ so hard	심각하게 여기다

20	
□ enter	들어가다
□ notice	알아보다
□ famous	유명한
□ act like	~처럼 행동하다
□ crazy fan	열성팬
□ pretend	~인 체하다
□ act cool	침착하게 행동하다
□ realize	깨닫다
□ go back in	~에 다시 들어가다

01
- gift-wrap　선물 포장하다
- different　다양한
- wrapping paper　포장지
- pattern　모양
- mix　혼합(물)

02
- miss　(수업에) 결석하다
- wonder　~인가 하고 생각하다
- catch up on　(뒤진 일 등을) 되찾다
- practice　연습
- until　~까지

03
- guest　손님
- never　결코 ~하지 않다
- deliver　배달하다
- address　주소
- be on another line　다른 전화를 받고 있다

04
- pneumonia　폐렴
- suffer from　~로 고통받다
- respiratory　호흡 기관의
- lunch break　점심시간

05
- It depends.　사정에 따라 다르다.
- be proud of　~을 자랑스러워하다
- thanks to　~ 덕분에
- fit　적합한, 건강한

06
- reservation　예약 (v. reserve)
- nonsense　터무니없는 것
- book　예약하다
- nearby　가까이에

07
- go downtown　시내에 가다
- give ~ a ride　~를 태워주다

- if you don't mind　당신이 괜찮다면
- You can say that again.　동감이야.
- gain weight　체중이 늘다
- give ~ a hand　~를 도와주다

08
- string　끈, 줄
- scary　무서운

09
- quit　그만두다
- emotional　정서의, 감정의
- get over　회복[극복]하다
- illness　병
- make sense　이해가 되다
- graduate school　대학원

10
- crowded　붐비는
- go on　(어떤 일이) 진행되다
- look good on　~에게 어울리다

11
- back　등
- get rest　휴식을 취하다
- bend　구부리다 (– bent–bent)
- pull out　뽑아내다
- weed　잡초

12
- invite　초대하다
- performance　공연, 연주
- fellow　동료
- put on　무대에 올리다, 공연하다
- magic　마술
- lastly　마지막으로

13
- be surrounded by　~에 둘러싸이다
- popular with　~에게 인기있는
- exhibit　전시장
- species　종(생물 분류의 기초 단위)

☐ amazing	놀라운	**19**	
14		☐ wake-up call	깨워 주는 전화
☐ container	용기, 담는 그릇	☐ prepare	준비하다
☐ normally	보통	☐ useless	쓸모 없는
☐ aluminum	알루미늄	☐ fall back to sleep	다시 잠이 들다
☐ metal	금속	☐ kidding	농담하는
☐ tin	주석	☐ Do you mean it?	진심이야?
☐ steel	강철	**20**	
☐ bottom	바닥	☐ driver's license	운전면허증
☐ cylinder	원통	☐ yet	아직
☐ store	저장하다	☐ academy	학원, 학교
☐ go bad	상하다	☐ female	여성의 (↔ male)
☐ recycled material	재활용되는 물질	☐ clerk	사무원, 점원
☐ recycling bin	재활용 통	☐ a sheet of paper	종이 한 장
15			
☐ downtown	시내에, 도심지에		
☐ belong to	~에 소속되다		
☐ terrific	멋진, 훌륭한		
☐ drive out	차를 몰고 나가다		
☐ ride	(차를) 태워 주기		
16			
☐ paper	보고서		
☐ miss	놓치다		
17			
☐ part-time job	시간제 일, 아르바이트		
☐ fancy restaurant	멋진 식당		
☐ quit	그만두다		
☐ paid well	좋은 급여를 받은		
☐ babysit	아기를 보다		
18			
☐ get ready	준비가 되다		
☐ jump into one's clothes	허겁지겁 옷을 입다		
☐ skip	빠뜨리다, 건너 뛰다		
☐ all the way to	~까지 가는 내내		
☐ early bird	일찍 일어나는 사람		

01	
□ by six	여섯 시까지
□ in the crowd	사람들[군중] 속에서
□ striped jacket	줄무늬 재킷
□ right beside	바로 옆에
□ moustache	콧수염

02	
□ cold medicine	감기약
□ sneeze	재채기하다
□ run out of	~을 다 써버리다.

03	
□ nail	못으로 박다
□ frame	액자
□ hammer	망치
□ tool box	도구함

04	
□ opinion	의견
□ weekly	매주의, 주 1회의
□ conversation	대화
□ on Fridays	금요일마다
□ exclude	제외하다 (↔ include)
□ agree on	~에 동의하다

05	
□ Greetings!	안녕하세요!
□ dedication	헌신
□ gratitude	고마움, 감사
□ opening ceremony	개업식

06	
□ take a break	쉬다
□ uphill	오르막길로
□ increase	향상시키다
□ recover	회복하다

07	
□ What's the weather like?	날씨가 어때?
□ I can't help it.	어쩔 수 없다.
□ pull over	차를 세우다

□ gas station	주유소
□ run out of	~이 바닥나다, 떨어지다
□ by airmail	항공 우편으로
□ on one's way	도중에

08	
□ I wonder what's keeping him.	무슨 일로 이렇게 늦는지 모르겠다.
□ school store	학교 매점
□ in a minute	곧, 잠시 후에

09	
□ reduce	줄이다
□ prevent from	~을 막다, 예방하다
□ repellent	방충제
□ tap water	수돗물
□ sanitizer	세정제

10	
□ overdue	기한이 지난
□ late fee	연체료
□ on time	시간을 어기지 않고
□ change	거스름돈

11	
□ be used to	~에 익숙하다
□ refrigerator	냉장고
□ load	짐

12	
□ tour director	여행 책임자
□ due to	~때문에
□ picturesque	그림 같은
□ welcome reception	환영회

13	
□ cross	가로줄을 긋다
□ overnight	밤을 새는
□ require	요구하다
□ previous	이전의

14	
□ vehicle	차
□ believe in	~을 믿다

cause	명분	can't keep eyes off	눈을 뗄 수가 없다
such as	~와 같은 (= like)	give one's best wishes to	~에게 안부를 전해주다
right	권리	**19**	
organization	조직	membership card	회원 카드
military	군대	overdue	기한이 지난
praise	치하하다, 칭찬하다	get ~ back	반납하다
accomplishment	성취	totally	완전히
be made from	~로 만들어지다	terribly	정말로
leather	가죽	**20**	
rubber	고무	set the table	식탁을 차리다
hobby	취미	meal	식사
15		do the dishes	설거지를 하다
review	복습하다	be headed	~로 향하다
while	~하면서	direction	방향
show up	나타나다, 출석하다	situation	상황
photocopy	복사하다		
straight away	즉시, 당장		
16			
come true	실현되다		
thrilling	긴장감이 넘치는		
get wet	물에 젖다		
overall	전체적인		
amusement park	놀이공원		
17			
open an account	계좌를 개설하다		
work	작동하다		
ATM	현금자동인출기 (= Automatic Teller Machine)		
insert	삽입하다		
withdraw	인출하다 (n. withdrawal)		
4-digit password	4자리 비밀번호		
deposit	예금		
immediately	즉시 (= at once)		
18			
different	다른		
have every reason to	~하는 것도 당연하다		
give birth to	~을 낳다		

01
□ within	~이내에
□ square	정사각형
□ mean	의미하다
□ pay	지불하다

02
□ role	역할
□ main character	주인공
□ unbelievable	믿기 어려울 정도인

03
□ check	검사하다
□ be afraid of	~을 두려워하다
□ feed	먹이를 주다
□ once	한 번
□ take	데리고 가다
□ make sure to	틀림없이 ~하다
□ keep ~ warm	~을 따뜻하게 해 주다

04
| □ drop off | (차에서) 내려주다 |
| □ grab | 급히 ~하다 |

05
□ be headed	~로 향하다, 나아가다
□ I'm not in the mood to talk.	말할 기분이 아니다.
□ in the middle of	~의 중간에
□ excitement	흥분, 자극
□ hurry	서두르다
□ care	신경 쓰다, 상관하다

06
□ toothache	치통
□ dentist	치과의사
□ practice	연습하다
□ competition	대회, 경기
□ musician	음악가
□ on the stage	무대 위에서

07
□ purpose	목적
□ visit	방문
□ return	반납하다
□ overdue	기한이 지난
□ wash	씻다
□ bathroom	화장실

08
□ contact	연락하다
□ recently	최근에
□ take good care of	~을 매우 소중히 여기다

09
| □ try | 먹어보다 |
| □ keep in mind | 명심하다 |

10
□ rack	선반
□ a pair of	한 켤레의
□ can't afford	~할 여유가 없다

11
□ straight	똑바로
□ change	교환하다, 바꾸다
□ tighten	(바짝) 죄다
□ shoe lace	신발 끈
□ keep balance	균형을 잡다
□ get onto the ice	얼음판으로 나오다
□ slippery	미끄러운
□ let go of	(쥐고 있던 것을) 놓다

12
□ pick	(과일 등을) 따다
□ admission	입장료
□ sunscreen	자외선 차단제

13
□ recommend	추천하다
□ tour	여행
□ around	약, ~쯤
□ cost	비용
□ destination	목적지

14	
☐ invent	발명하다
☐ usually	보통, 대체로
☐ distance	거리
☐ be made up of	~로 이루어져 있다
☐ wheel	바퀴
☐ fuel	연료
☐ expect	기대하다
☐ electricity	전기
☐ solar energy	태양 에너지
☐ convenient	편리한
☐ dangerous	위험한
15	
☐ work out	운동하다
☐ lose	잃다 (– lost–lost)
☐ blood test	피검사
☐ needle	주사(의 한 대)
☐ last	지속되다
16	
☐ return	반품하다
☐ unzip	지퍼를 열다
☐ terribly	대단히, 몹시
☐ be out of stock	품절[매진]이 되어
☐ replace	교체하다
17	
☐ library card	도서 카드
☐ visit	방문
☐ fill out	(서식·문서 등의) 빈 곳을 채우다
☐ form	양식
☐ bookstore	서점
☐ don't have to	~할 필요가 없다
18	
☐ That's strange.	그것 이상하네.
☐ carry	가지고 있다
☐ clear away	(비가) 개다
☐ probably	아마도

☐ try to	~하려고 노력하다
☐ remember	기억하다
19	
☐ Why don't we ~?	우리 ~ 하는 게 어때?
☐ sunbathing	일광욕
☐ lay	놓다
☐ outdoor blanket	야외용 담요, 돗자리
☐ lie down	눕다
☐ prepare	준비하다
20	
☐ garage	차고
☐ won't start	시동이 안 걸리다
☐ next door	옆집
☐ be headed	~로 향하다
☐ direction	방향
☐ situation	상황
☐ form	양식
☐ bookstore	서점
☐ don't have to	~할 필요가 없다

01

□ go out	외출하다
□ slippery	미끄러운
□ snowfall	강설, 눈이 옴
□ overnight	밤새껏, 밤새도록
□ make it	시간에 대다
□ on time	제 시간에
□ climbing boots	등산화
□ icy road	빙판길
□ dress suit	(남자의) 야외복, 정장
□ leather shoes	가죽 구두

02

□ besides	게다가
□ hairdresser	미용사
□ wallet	지갑
□ come back	돌아오다

03

□ give ~ a ride	~을 태워주다
□ drive	운전하다
□ edit	편집하다
□ park	주차하다
□ Take it easy.	진정하세요.
□ fasten one's seat belt	안전벨트를 매다
□ remind	상기시키다

04

□ come to an end	끝나다
□ come over	(~의 집에) 들르다

05

□ what ~ will be like	~가 어떨지
□ Oh, dear!	아니, 이런!
□ storm	폭풍
□ put off	연기하다

06

□ necessary	필요한
□ physical	신체의

□ require	요구하다, 필요로 하다
□ distance	거리
□ protective gear	보호 장비
□ in the middle of	~의 중앙에
□ risk	위험
□ worth	~할 만한 가치가 있는

07

□ pick up	구하다, 구입하다
□ antique	골동품
□ get along with	~와 지내다
□ have ~ in mind	~을 염두에 두다

08

□ semester	학기
□ major	전공
□ politics	정치학
□ enroll	등록하다
□ requirement	자격 요건
□ description	설명서

09

□ coming	다가오는
□ architecture	건축
□ region	지역
□ strike	(재난 등이 갑자기) 발생하다[덮치다]
□ lack	부족, 결핍
□ rewarding	보람 있는

10

□ reserve	예약하다
□ adult	성인
□ normally	평상시에는
□ off	감하여

11

□ except for	~을 제외하고
□ vegetarian	채식주의자
□ What an idiot I am!	내가 얼마나 바보 같은지!
□ know better than to ~	~할 만큼 어리석지 않다

□ instead	대신		□ colleague	직장 동료
12			□ benefit	이득
□ be located	위치해 있다		□ abroad	해외로
□ childcare center	보육원		□ as good as	~만큼 좋은
□ infant	유아, 아기		□ spacious	넓은
□ entertain	즐겁게 해 주다		**18**	
□ pottery	도자기		□ quit	그만두다
13			□ one of the best	가장 ~한 사람들 중의 하나
□ quote	명세서		□ employee	고용인, 직원
□ detail	자세한 사항		□ because of	~ 때문에
□ so ~ that ...	너무 ~해서 …하다		□ grown up	성장한
□ cost	비용이 들다		□ run one's own business	자신의 사업을 하다
□ make a choice	선택을 하다		□ Good luck to you.	행운을 빌어.
14			**19**	
□ sew	바느질하다		□ get on	~에 타다
□ slender	가느다란		□ tourist	관광객
□ tip	끝부분		□ public transportation	대중 교통
□ thread	실		□ so far	지금까지
□ pierce	꿰뚫다, 관통하다		□ various	다양한
□ apply	붙이다		□ one-day pass	1일 정기권
□ patch	헝겊 조각		□ several	여러 가지
□ sewing machine	재봉틀		□ convenient	편리한
15			**20**	
□ don't have to	~할 필요가 없다		□ science lab	과학 (실험)실
□ take a train	기차를 타다		□ notice	알아차리다
□ find out	알아보다		□ search for	~를 찾다, 탐색하다
□ rental	임대[임차]료		□ feel depressed	우울함을 느끼다
16			□ in fact	사실은
□ move	이사 가다[오다]		□ several	여러 가지
□ I'm afraid not.	아닐 거야.		□ convenient	편리한
□ be over	끝나다			
□ give ~ a good-bye party	~에게 이별 파티를 열어주다			
□ That's a relief.	다행이다.			
17				
□ company	회사			

01

☐ take pictures	사진을 찍다
☐ allow	허락하다, 허가하다
☐ preserve	보존하다
☐ carry around	들고 다니다

02

☐ family trip	가족 여행
☐ manage time	간을 관리하다
☐ deadline	마감일

03

☐ be on	(돈이) ~에 걸려 있다
☐ turn off	(전기·수도 등을) 끄다

04

☐ sunrise	일출
☐ peak	(산의) 정상
☐ nearby	인근의
☐ in a line	줄을 지어

05

☐ ski slope	스키 연습장
☐ steep	가파른
☐ get injured	부상을 당하다

06

☐ at recess	휴식 시간에
☐ match	경기, 시합
☐ help out	~를 도와주다
☐ organize	정리하다
☐ take time	시간이 걸리다

07

☐ Do you mind if ~?	~해도 될까요?
☐ Please go ahead.	하세요.

08

☐ practice	연습하다
☐ memorize	암기하다
☐ struggle	분투[고투]하다
☐ be great at	~에 능숙한

09

☐ take a flight	비행기를 타다
☐ statue	조각상
☐ beyond one's imagination	상상 이상으로
☐ firework	불꽃놀이

10

☐ I'm not sure if ~.	~인지 잘 모르겠다.
☐ fit	(의복 등이) 맞다
☐ exchange	교환하다

11

☐ bother	신경 쓰이게 하다, 괴롭히다
☐ block	막다, 차단하다
☐ landline phone	(지상 통신선으로 연결되는) 일반 전화
☐ function	기능
☐ specific	특정한
☐ identify	확인하다[알아보다]

12

☐ draw	끌어당기다

□ signature	특징
□ compete	경쟁하다
□ amaze	놀라게 하다
13	
□ public transportation	대중교통
□ T-junction	T자형 삼거리
□ uphill	오르막길
14	
□ concentration	집단
□ densely populated	인구가 조밀한
□ lively	활기[생기] 넘치는
15	
□ trick	묘기
□ aerial stunt	공중 묘기
□ reliable	믿을[신뢰할] 수 있는
□ damage	손상을 주다, 훼손하다
16	
□ violent	폭력적인
□ life-threatening	생명을 위협하는
□ adapt from	~로 각색하다
17	
□ food poisoning	식중독
□ dizzy	어지러운
□ feel nauseated	구역질이 나다
□ diarrhea	설사
□ awful	끔찍한, 지독한
□ get worse	악화되다

18	
□ tryout	실력[적격] 시험
□ potential	가능성이 있는
□ participate in	~에 참가하다
□ Would you like to ~?	~할래?
19	
□ How's it going?	요즘 어때?
□ by	~옆[가]에
□ seashore	해안
□ look around	둘러보다
20	
□ dormitory	기숙자
□ manager	관리자
□ complaint	불평[항의]
□ deny	부인[부정]하다
□ business trip	출장
□ prepare	준비하다
□ considerate	사려 깊은

중학영어듣기 만점 솔루션

듣기는
실전이다

중학3

24회

디딤돌